SOCIAL STUDIES

MACMILLAN

Macmillan Social Studies

THE UNITED STATES AND THE OTHER AMERICAS

SENIOR AUTHOR
John Jarolimek

Allen Y. King
Ida Dennis
Florence Potter

GEOGRAPHY CONSULTANT
Loyal Durand, Jr.

Macmillan Publishing Company
New York
Collier Macmillan Publishers
London

Macmillan Publishing Company
866 Third Avenue, New York, New York 10022
Collier Macmillan Canada, Inc.

Printed in the United States of America
ISBN 0-02-147380-3
9 8 7 6 5 4 3 2

Acknowledgments

The publisher gratefully acknowledges permission to reprint the following
copyrighted material:

Excerpt from article on Jane Addams and excerpt from article on John
Cabot: Reprinted with permission of the *New Book of Knowledge,*
copyright © 1983, Grolier Inc.
Excerpt from *A Child's Geography of the World* by V. M. Hillyer and
E. G. Huey. Copyright 1929 by the Century Company; copyright 1951
by Appleton-Century-Crofts, Inc.; copyright 1957 by Mercantile Safe
Deposit and Trust Co. Reprinted by permission of E.P. Dutton, Inc.

Cover:
Illustration by Robert LoGrippo

Maps:
Joe LeMonnier and Bielat Studios, Chris Ellithorpe, Robert Forget, Yvette
Heyden, Liska and Associates, Cathy Meindl, Jeff Mellander, Jay Songero,
Lowell Stumpf, George Suyeoka, John Walter & Associates. Map Skills
developed and produced by Educational Challenges, Inc., Alexandria, VA.

Illustrations:
Dev Appleyard, Yoshi Miyake, Tak Murakami, Alexis Oussenko,
Hima Pamoedjo

Photographs:
Abbot Hall, Marblehead, Ma.: Original of this painting hangs in the
Selectmen's Room, 69
Courtesy of American Heritage Pub. Co., Inc.:
Collection of Christopher Reed, 88; Nebraska State Historical Society,
Soloman D. Butcher Collection, 181
American Museum of Natural History, courtesy of the Library Services
Department: 25 center left, top and bottom right, 37, 39 detail, 50, 326
Art Resource: Scala, 44, 477, Joseph Martin, National Portrait Gallery,
Washington, D.C., 579 bottom right, Historical Society of Pennsylvania,
170; Snark International, 215 center right, The Library of Congress, 191;
© Peter Vadnai, 218 bottom
Atoz/Van Cleve: © Betty Crowell, 346
The Bettmann Archive, Inc.: 31, 43, 62 top, 74, 77 top right, 107, 117 left
center, 178, 195, 200, 202, 207, 231, 302, 303, 384, 415, 419, 549, 571,
Photograph by Lewis Hine, 193
Black Star Publishing Co., Inc.: © Brad Hess, 556; © Ernest R. Manewal,
403; © Bill Ray, 215 top left; © Fred Ward, 489; © Doug Wilson, 13
© Lee Boltin: 40
Brown Bros: 267, 347, 350
California State Library, Sacramento: Photograph Collection, 411, 551
© Cameramann Int., Inc.: 288 top, 296, 322, 330, 332, 335, 336, 343, 349
right, 367 bottom, 369, 394, 439, 440, 442 bottom left and right, 443,
482, 497
Courtesy CBS, Inc.: 77 center right
Chicago Historical Society: 166 bottom
Cities Service: 363 left
Colour Library International: 63 center right and bottom
The Connecticut Historical Society: 540
© J. Dan Coop: 354 bottom
© Martha Cooper: 533
In the Collection of the Corcoran Gallery of Art: J.P. Newell; *Lazell, Perkins
& Co. Bridgewater, Mass.; Manufacturers of all Descriptions of Forgings
for Steam-Ships and Rail-Roads, Castings and all Kinds of Machinery*;
Museum Purchase, Mary E. Maxwell Fund, 166 top
Culver Pictures, Inc.: 146, 163, 210, 233, 268, 422
The Department of the Treasury: 232
© Greg Dorata: 24 bottom
Eastern National Park & Monument Association, 106
Courtesy Fraunces Tavern Museum, New York City, 96
© Freeport Sulphur: 363 right
Gamma Liaison: © Charlon, 214 center; © Dirck Halstead, 214 top and
bottom

Continued on page 600

CONTENTS

Maps

Diagrams, Charts, and Graphs

THE WORLD
POLITICAL

ARCTIC OCEAN

Chukchi Sea

Beaufort Sea

Baffin Bay

Greenland (Den.)

Jan Mayen (Nor.)

Arctic Circle

Alaska (U.S.)

ICELAND

Faeroe Is. (Den.)

Bering Sea

Hudson Bay

UNITED KINGDOM

CANADA

IRELAND EUROPE

NORTH AMERICA

ATLANTIC OCEAN

FRANC

St. Pierre and Miquelon (Fr.)

SPAI

UNITED STATES

PORTUGAL

Azores Is. (Port.)

Bermuda (U.K.)

MOROCCO

PACIFIC OCEAN

Madeira Is. (Port.)

Gulf of Mexico

Canary Is. (Sp.)

Tropic of Cancer

MEXICO

BAHAMAS

WESTERN SAHARA

Hawaii (U.S.)

CUBA

DOMINICAN REPUBLIC

MAURITANIA

Puerto Rico (U.S.)

HAITI

ST. CHRISTOPHER AND NEVIS

BURKINA FASO

JAMAICA

ANTIGUA AND BARBUDA

CAPE VERDE

BELIZE

Guadeloupe (Fr.)

DOMINICA

SENEGAL

GUATEMALA

HONDURAS

Martinique (Fr.)

GAMBIA

Caribbean Sea

Netherlands Antilles (Neth.)

BARBADOS

GUINEA

EL SALVADOR

NICARAGUA

SAINT LUCIA

ST. VINCENT AND THE GRENADINES

BISSAU GUINEA

COSTA RICA

GRENADA

SIERRA LEONE

TRINIDAD AND TOBAGO

PANAMA

VENEZUELA

GUYANA

LIBERIA

SURINAME

IVORY COAST

COLOMBIA

French Guiana (Fr.)

GHANA

Christmas I. (Gilbert I.)

Equator

Galápagos Is. (Ec.)

ECUADOR

Ascension (St. Helena)

SOUTH AMERICA

WESTERN SAMOA

PERU

BRAZIL

TONGA

French Polynesia (Fr.)

BOLIVIA

St. Helena (U.K.)

Cook Is. (N.Z.)

PARAGUAY

Tropic of Capricorn

Pitcairn Is. (U.K.)

CHILE

ATLANTIC OCEAN

Easter I. (Chile)

Juan Fernández Is. (Chile)

URUGUAY

Tristan da Cunha (St. Helena)

ARGENTINA

PACIFIC OCEAN

Falkland Is. (U.K.)

South Georgia (Falkl. Is.)

Antarctic Circle

ANTARCTICA

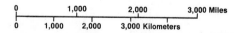

| 0 | 1,000 | 2,000 | 3,000 Miles |
| 0 | 1,000 | 2,000 | 3,000 Kilometers |

ALB.	= ALBANIA	LIECH.	= LIECHTENSTEIN
AND.	= ANDORRA	LUX.	= LUXEMBOURG
AUS.	= AUSTRIA	MON.	= MONACO
BEL.	= BELGIUM	NETH.	= NETHERLANDS
BUL.	= BULGARIA	S.M.	= SAN MARINO
CZECH.	= CZECHOSLOVAKIA	SWITZ.	= SWITZERLAND
E.GER.	= EAST GERMANY	W.GER.	= WEST GERMANY
HUNG.	= HUNGARY	YUGO.	= YUGOSLAVIA

A-3

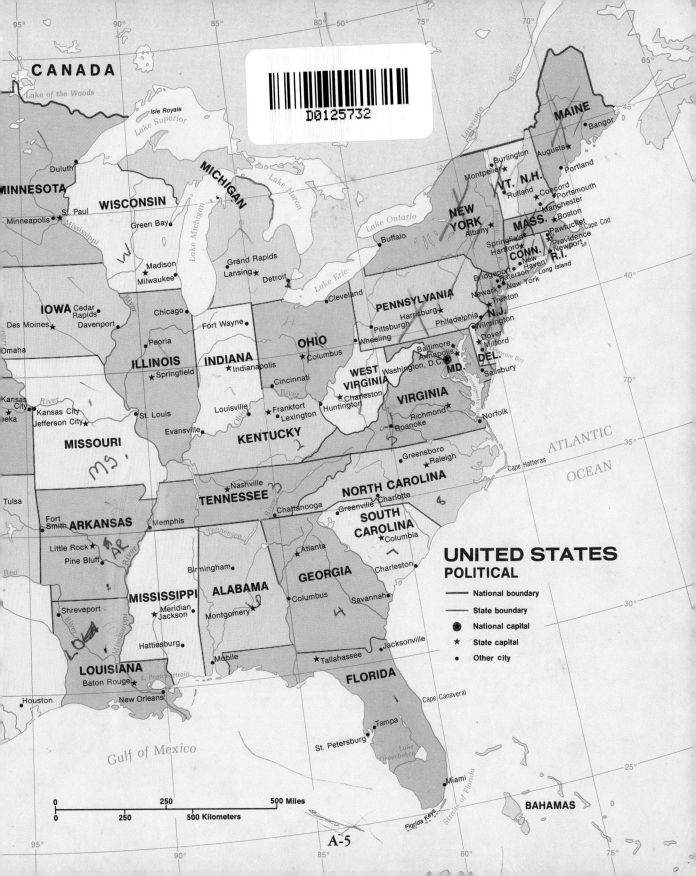

UNITED STATES
POLITICAL

National boundary
State boundary
National capital
State capital
Other city

NORTH AMERICA

| 0 | 100 | 200 | 400 | 600 Miles |
| 0 | 161 | 322 | 644 | 966 Kilometers |

⊗ National Capitals   • Other Cities

Mountains   Hills

Plateaus   Plains

A-9

© Rand McNally & Co.

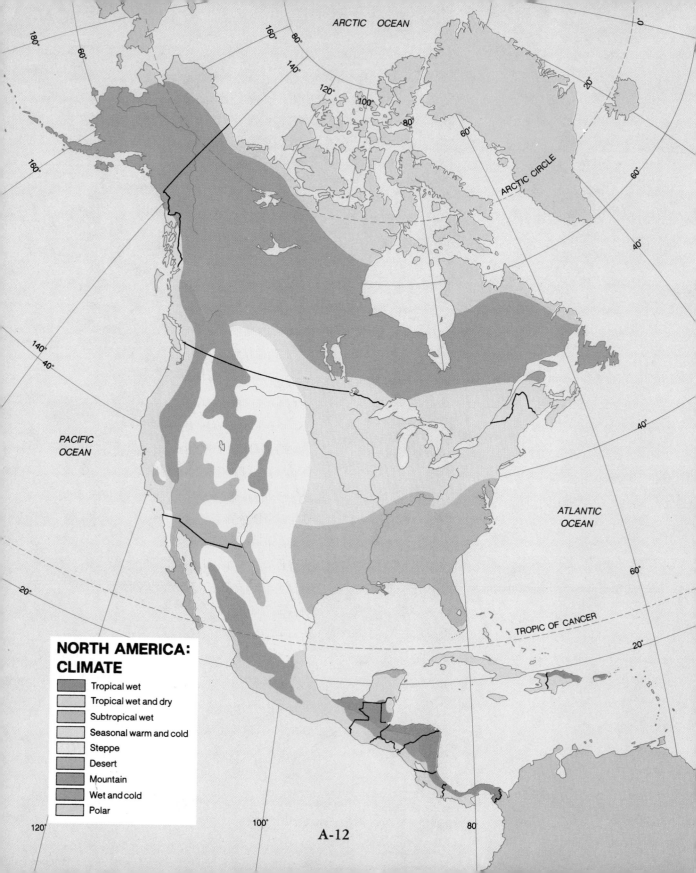

ARCTIC OCEAN

ARCTIC CIRCLE

PACIFIC
OCEAN

ATLANTIC
OCEAN

TROPIC OF CANCER

NORTH AMERICA:
CLIMATE

- Tropical wet
- Tropical wet and dry
- Subtropical wet
- Seasonal warm and cold
- Steppe
- Desert
- Mountain
- Wet and cold
- Polar

A-12

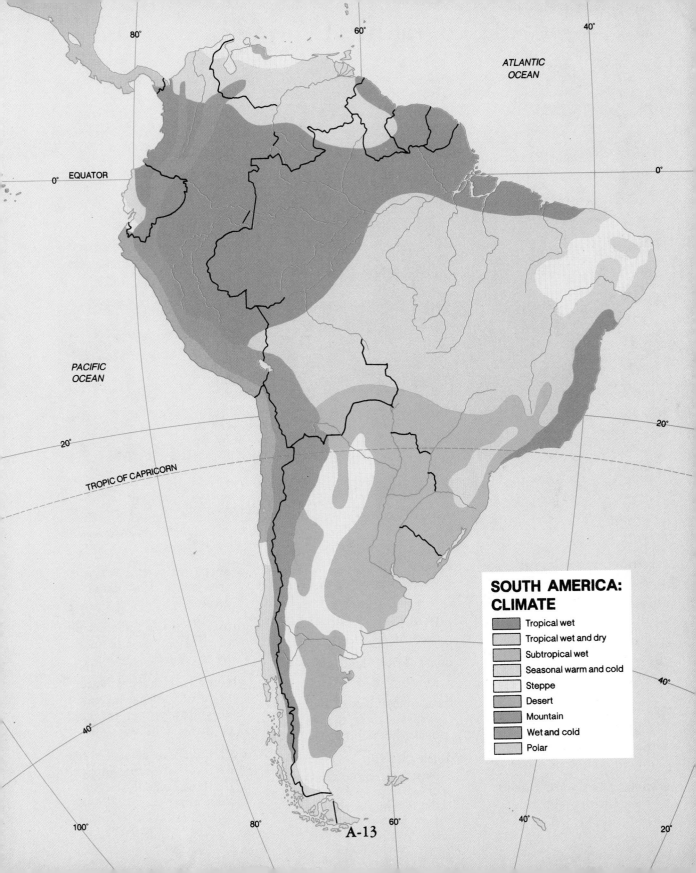

80°

60°

40°

ATLANTIC
OCEAN

EQUATOR

0°

0°

PACIFIC
OCEAN

20°

20°

TROPIC OF CAPRICORN

40°

40°

SOUTH AMERICA:
CLIMATE

Tropical wet
Tropical wet and dry
Subtropical wet
Seasonal warm and cold
Steppe
Desert
Mountain
Wet and cold
Polar

100°

80°

60°

40°

20°

A-13

Dictionary of Geographical Terms

archipelago (ar′kə pel′ ə gō′): a large group of islands

basin (bā′sin): all the land drained by a river and its tributaries

bay (bā): an arm of a sea or lake, extending into the land, usually smaller than a gulf

canal (kə nal′): a waterway built to connect two other bodies of water

canyon (kan′yən): a deep valley with steep sides

cape (kāp): a point of land extending from the coastline into the sea or a lake

cliff (klif): a high, steep face of rock or earth

coast (kōst): land along a sea or ocean

dam (dam): a wall built across a river to hold back the water

delta (del′tə): land at the mouth of a river, made of sand and silt, usually shaped like a triangle

desert (dez′ərt): a very dry area where few plants grow

dune (dōōn): a hill, mound, or ridge of sand formed by the wind

glacier (glā′shər): a large body of ice that moves very slowly over the land or down a valley

gulf (gulf): an arm of a sea or lake extending into the land, usually larger than a bay

A-14

harbor (här′bər): a protected place on an ocean, sea, lake, or river where ships can anchor safely

hill (hil): a rounded and raised landform, not as high as a mountain

icecap (īs′kap′): a dome-shaped glacier covering a land area and moving out from the center in all directions

island (ī′lənd): a body of land entirely surrounded by water, smaller than a continent

isthmus (is′məs): a strip of land bordered by water that connects two larger bodies of land

lake (lāk): a body of water entirely surrounded by land

mountain (mount′ən): a high rounded or pointed landform with steep sides, higher than a hill

mountain pass (mount′ən pas′): a narrow gap in the mountains

mouth (mouth): the place where a river flows into the ocean or into another body of water

oasis (ō ā′sis): a place in the desert that is fertile because it has a water supply

ocean (ō′shən): the body of salt water covering nearly three fourths of the earth's surface

peninsula (pə nin′sə lə): land extending from a larger body of land, nearly surrounded by water

plain (plān): an area of flat or almost flat land

plateau (pla tō′): flat land with steep sides, raised above the surrounding land

port (pôrt): a place where ships load and unload goods

reservoir (rez′ər vwär′): a body of water formed behind a dam

ridge (rij): a long and narrow chain of hills or mountains

river (riv′ər): a large stream of water that flows across the land and usually empties into a lake, ocean, or another river

sea (sē): a large body of water partly or entirely enclosed by land; another term for the ocean

sound (sound): a long inlet or arm of the sea

tributary (trib′yə ter′ē): a river or stream that flows into a larger river or stream

valley (val′ē): an area of low land between hills or mountains

waterfall (wô′tər fôl′): a flow of water falling from a high place

Map Symbols

Map symbols vary from map to map. Some maps use the same or similar symbols. Other maps use different symbols. You will see some of the commonly used symbols shown below on the maps in this book.

international boundary

state or other boundary

national capital

state or other capital

town or city

interstate highway   28   28

railroad

airport

bridge

hills

mountains

mountain peak

1 The United States— Its Land and People

Unit Preview

Two large continents are in the Western Hemisphere. They are North America and South America. The United States is in the continent of North America. It also is in the part of the world where climates are mild.

The United States is a large country with many kinds of land. It has lowlands along the coasts and in the central part of the country. The major mountains are the Appalachians in the East, the Alaska Range, and the Rocky Mountains in the West. The West has several other mountains. Among the western mountains are high, flat places.

The land of the United States is rich in natural resources. It has forests, many minerals, and good soil for farming. The country's many bays, long rivers, and large lakes give Americans ways to travel. Waterways also are used for fishing and sport.

The United States was settled by people from all over the world. Many of them became naturalized citizens. Most immigrants settled on the East Coast, a crowded part of the country. In the 1970s, Americans began moving to the Sun Belt.

Historians and archeologists help Americans learn about their heritage. Historians study old records and talk to people about the past. Archeologists study the things left by people long ago.

Things to Discover

If you look carefully at the picture, map, and time line, you can answer these questions.
1. The boundary lines on the map show where in North America the United States is found. Where in North America is the United States? In what part of the Americas is South America?
2. The picture shows the north Atlantic shore, near where the English settlers landed over 300 years ago. Why would this be a good place for ships to land?
3. When did most Americans make their living by farming?
4. When did the United States begin to have many more cities?

Words to Learn

You will meet these words in this unit. As you read, you will learn what they mean and how to pronounce them. The Word List will help you.

altitude	immigrant
archeologists	latitude
artifacts	naturalized citizens
citizens	oral history
climate	precipitation
culture	slaves
density	tundra
historian	

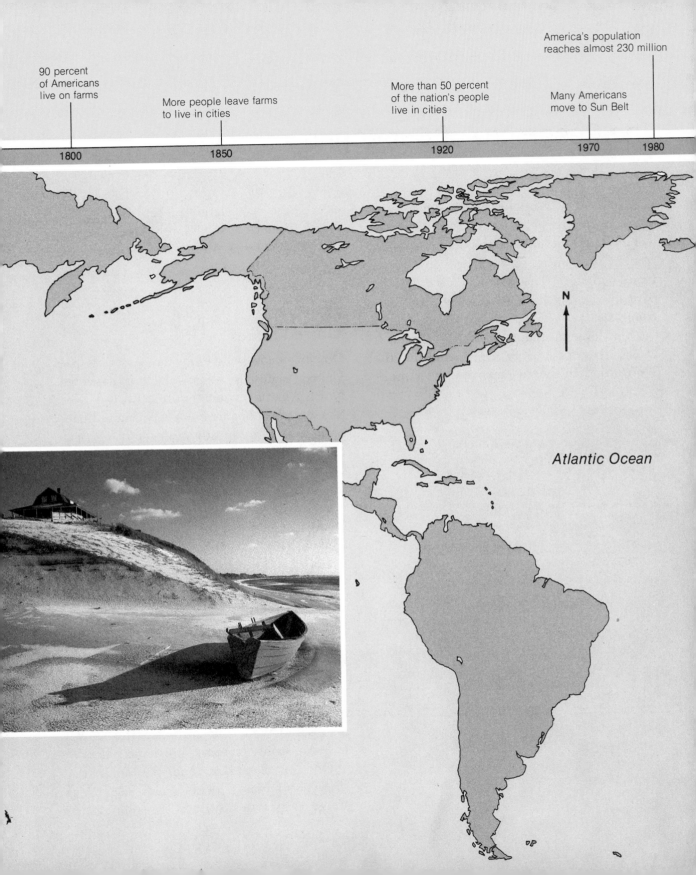

90 percent
of Americans
live on farms

1800

More people leave farms
to live in cities

1850

More than 50 percent
of the nation's people
live in cities

1920

America's population
reaches almost 230 million

Many Americans
move to Sun Belt

1970   1980

N

Atlantic Ocean

1

The Geography of Our Country

Look at the title of this book. What is it? What two places on earth does the title name? The first place that is named is the country, or nation, in which you live—the United States. The second place is the part of the earth in which you live—the Americas.

Now look at the map on this page. It shows that two large continents in the Western Hemisphere make up the Ameri-cas. These two large pieces of land are North America and South America. Be-tween these two places are the islands in the Caribbean Sea.

Physical Features of The United States

Do you know where in the Americas the United States is found? If you answered North America, you are correct. It is easy to pick out the boundaries of the United States because they are mostly made up of physical, or land, features. As an example, find the Great Lakes on the map on pages 6 and 7. These large lakes make up part of the north-ern boundary of the country. What gulf is found just south of the United States? Note that most of the United States stretches be-tween the Atlantic Ocean and the Pacific Ocean.

Landforms

The map on pages A-6 and A-7 is a physi-cal map. It shows land of the United States —shape, coastlines, and bodies of water. This map also shows what kinds of land make up the surface of America. As the map shows you, the United States mostly has mountains, plateaus, hills, and plains.

On the map key, find the color that shows mountains. This land rises high above the earth's surface. Mountains may

This map shows the Western Hemisphere. Is Hawaii part of the Western Hemisphere? Where is Central America found?

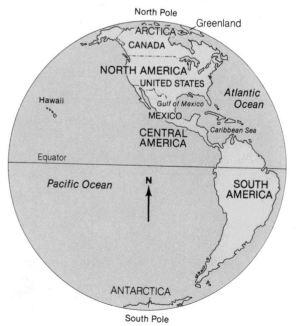

4

The Piedmont has many large farms. Here, in Pennsylvania, a large highway runs through the rolling hills of the Piedmont.

have sharp peaks or they may be gently rounded at top. As you can see, mountains cover much of the western part of North America. What is the name of the largest group of mountains in the west?

Now find the color for plateaus (pla tōz') on the map key. This land also rises above the earth's surface, but plateaus usually are flat on top. They also often are found among mountains. Find examples of plateaus in the western part of the country.

What color does the map use to show hills? Hills also are highland. However, they are lower than mountains. Where are the major hilly areas in the United States?

Plains are another kind of land shown on the map. These landforms are low, flat areas of the earth's surface. The plains usually do not rise much above the level of the sea and are often found along the seacoast. Plains also appear far inland, where they may be higher above sea level.

Physical Regions

The map on pages 6 and 7 shows you where to find the mountains and other landforms of the United States. Suppose you are taking a trip across the United States to see its land and its physical regions. You might start out from Delaware on the Atlantic Coast. There you will be near sea level.

Eastern Regions

The first part of your trip west will take you across the Atlantic Coastal Plain. This wide plain curves along the Atlantic Coast all the way from New Jersey in the northeast to Texas in the southwest. The plain is called the Gulf Coastal Plain along the Gulf of Mexico.

As you travel farther west across the plain, you will come to higher country—the Piedmont (pēd'mont). The Piedmont is an area of rolling hills that stretches from southern New York south to Alabama.

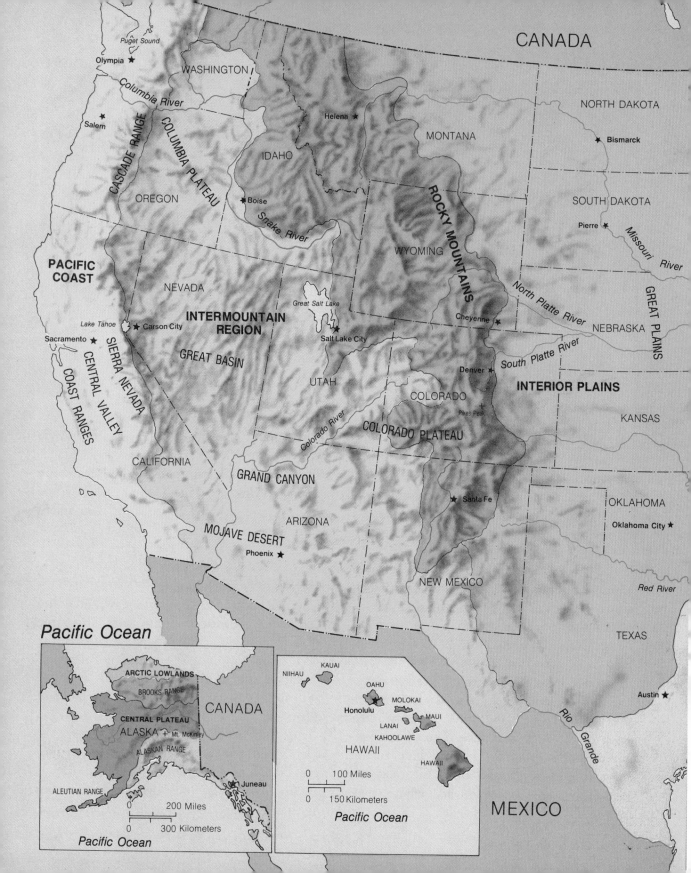

Geographical Regions of the United States

N

MINNESOTA

Lake Superior

WISCONSIN

★ St. Paul

IOWA

Des Moines ★

Lincoln ●

Topeka ●

Jefferson City ★
MISSOURI

OZARK HIGHLANDS

OZARK PLATEAU

ARKANSAS

Little Rock ★

Lake Michigan

Madison ★

MICHIGAN

Lansing ★

Lake Huron

ILLINOIS

INDIANA

Indianapolis ★

Springfield ★

Lake Michigan

OHIO

Columbus ★

Ohio   River

Frankfort ★

KENTUCKY

Nashville ●

TENNESSEE

Tennessee   River

ALABAMA

Atlanta ★

GEORGIA

Lake Erie

Lake Ontario

St. Lawrence River

MAINE

Augusta ★

VT.   N.H.

Montpelier ★   Concord ★

NEW YORK

Albany ★   MASS.   Boston ★

Hartford ★   CONN.   Providence ★
R.I.

ALLEGHENY PLATEAU

ALLEGHENY MOUNTAINS

PENN.

Harrisburg ★   Trenton ★
N.J.

MD.   Dover ★
DEL.
Annapolis ★

Washington, D.C. ☆

W. VA.

Charleston ●

CUMBERLAND PLATEAU

Richmond ★

VIRGINIA

APPALACHIAN MOUNTAINS

NORTH CAROLINA

Raleigh ★

PIEDMONT

FALL LINE

S.C.

Columbia ★

ATLANTIC COASTAL PLAIN

Chesapeake Bay

Mississippi   River

Jackson ★

L.A.

MISSISSIPPI

Montgomery ★

COASTAL LOWLANDS

GULF COASTAL PLAIN

Tallahassee ★

FLORIDA

Lake Okeechobee

Baton Rouge ★

Atlantic Ocean

Gulf of Mexico

0   300 Miles

0   450 Kilometers

The drier, western part of the Plains has many grasslands. The green plants in the back are desert plants called yucca.

Piedmont is a French word that means "at the foot of a mountain." Rivers rush across the Piedmont to fall onto the Atlantic Coastal Plain. The line along which the waters fall to the lowlands is called the Fall Line.

After crossing the Piedmont you reach the Appalachian (ap'ə lā'chē ən) Mountains. These mountains are low and rounded and in many places are more like high hills. Wind and rain have smoothed down the peaks of the Appalachians over the ages. There are many valleys among the mountains. Rivers flow through many of the valleys.

West of the Allegheny Mountains you will cross a plateau. This high flat area is called the Allegheny (al'ə gā'nē) Plateau in the north. In the south it is called the Cumberland Plateau.

America's Interior

On the west, the plateau land slopes down into gently rolling plains. These Interior Plains make up much of the central part of the country. In a few places plateaus rise above the plains. One such place is the Ozark Plateau to the south. The western part of the Interior Plains is called the Great Plains. It is drier than the rest of the area. In the past tall grass covered all of the Interior Plains.

Western Regions

Once you have crossed the Plains, you will see tall, sharp mountains rising before you. They are the Rocky Mountains, which often reach higher than 14,000 feet (4,264 m) above sea level. The Rocky Mountains stretch along the entire western part of the country from Canada in the north almost to Mexico in the south. As you travel through

The Rocky Mountains have many pine forests and clear lakes. On the tallest mountain peaks, the snow never melts.

the Rockies you will see some of the most beautiful sights in the United States.

To the west of the Rocky Mountains is a lower, flatter area called the Intermountain Region. It lies between the Rocky Mountains and two mountain ranges on the west, the Cascade Range and the Sierra (sē er′ə) Nevada. Although the Intermountain Region is lower than the mountains around it, its land is still high. In some places rivers have made deep cuts through the earth. Plateaus often rise high above the rivers.

Next you cross the Sierra Nevada, which are not as rugged as the Rockies. The Sierras slope down into wide, flat valleys on the west. These valleys end at the Coast Ranges, running all the way from northern Washington to southern California. Your journey comes to an end when you reach the beach along the Pacific Coast.

Alaska and Hawaii

You have to travel still farther to see the rest of the land of the United States. Alaska is far to the north, along the Pacific Coast. Alaska has mountains in the north and south. To the north of the Brooks Range is a *tundra* (tun′drə), a large treeless plain. The tundra is so cold that the soil below the surface is always frozen. Central Alaska has plateaus.

Now find Hawaii on the map on pages 6 and 7. What kinds of land does Hawaii have? The mountains that you see are the tops of old volcanoes. Thousands of years ago these volcanoes rose out of the ocean, pouring forth lava, hot gases, ashes, and pieces of rock. The lava and ashes that settled around the mountains turned into rich soil in which grass and other plants grew. Although the volcanoes of Hawaii are old, some of them are especially active.

9

Waterways

In addition to showing landforms, the map on pages 6–7 shows river systems. A river system is a river and all of its branches, or tributaries (trib'yə ter'ēz). From high above the earth a river system would look like a tree trunk with many branches.

The Mississippi River system is the longest river system in North America. Its waters run through much of the center of the United States. Another large river system is the St. Lawrence River system, which runs all the way from the Great Lakes east to the Atlantic Ocean. Find these river systems on the map on pages 6 and 7.

Study the nation's coastline along the Atlantic and Pacific oceans. Notice that neither coast is smooth. A coastline that curves in and out usually has many bays along it. A bay is a good place for ships to dock because its water is not as rough as open ocean water. The fact that the United States has many bays means that the country has many places where ships can land. Seaports have grown on many of these bays.

Its coastlines have helped the United States to become an important trading country. These coastlines made it possible for Americans to build a wonderful transportation system. People and goods can be sent here by ship from anywhere in the world. Ships can travel from one place along the coast to another.

Americans also can travel inland for long ways by water. Look again at the map on pages 6–7 and find the major rivers and lakes of the United States. You can see why the Mississippi River and the Great Lakes are used for travel by so many Americans. What states can you travel to by sailing along the Great Lakes?

In the north, the Mississippi River flows along western Wisconsin. What do you think the green areas in the river are?

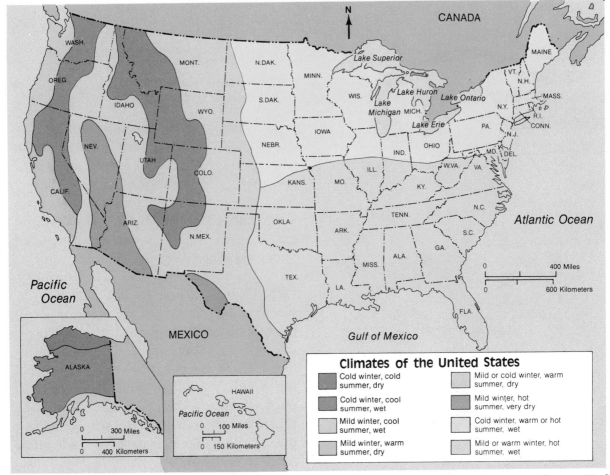

Climates of the United States

- Cold winter, cold summer, dry
- Cold winter, cool summer, wet
- Mild winter, cool summer, wet
- Mild winter, warm summer, dry
- Mild or cold winter, warm summer, dry
- Mild winter, hot summer, very dry
- Cold winter, warm or hot summer, wet
- Mild or warm winter, hot summer, wet

The United States has many *climates*. Find where you live on the map. What kinds of winters and summers does your state have? Is the climate wet or dry?

Water transportation was the most important means of moving about before railroads, automobiles, and airplanes were made. It was quicker and cheaper to travel by water than by horse. Sometimes travel by water was the only way to get from one place to another.

Waterways have many uses besides transportation. Many of the waterways in the United States, for example, have been used as a source of energy. Americans have used rushing rivers to power machines in early factories. More recently, rushing or falling waters have been harnessed to create electric power. In addition, rivers, lakes, and ocean shores offer swimming, fishing, boating, water skiing and other water sports.

Climate

The United States has several kinds of *climates* (klī′mitz). Climate is the weather that an area has over a long period of time. Several conditions make up a place's climate.

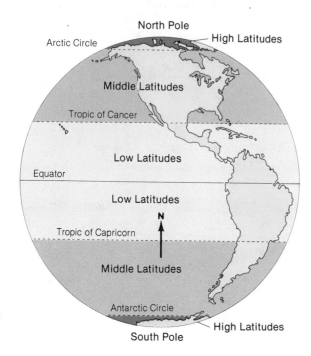

North Pole
Arctic Circle
High Latitudes
Middle Latitudes
Tropic of Cancer
Low Latitudes
Equator
Low Latitudes
N
Tropic of Capricorn
Middle Latitudes
Antarctic Circle
High Latitudes
South Pole

This map shows the *latitudes* of North and South America. How does the map show the difference between the low and middle latitudes? Where on the map are the high latitudes found?

The amount of rainfall and snowfall—called *precipitation* (pri sip′ə tā′shən)—in a year is one of the things that help to make up climate. The temperature, that is, how cold or warm a place is during the year, is another thing that forms climate. The length of its summers and winters also is part of an area's climate.

How do all of these conditions work together to form a climate? Suppose that you lived in the southeastern part of the United States. You would have a great deal of rainfall during the year. It also would be warm or hot all year round. Therefore, your climate would be described as wet and warm or hot all year round.

The climate of the northeastern part of the United States is very different. The winters are cold, the summers are warm, and there is precipitation all year. Therefore, this area is said to have a seasonal warm and cold wet climate. Look at the map on page 11. What part of the United States has a hot, very dry climate?

Latitude

Note the line that runs east and west across the middle of the map on this page. This is the equator. The equator is an imaginary line halfway between the North Pole and the South Pole. The equator also is the place where the sun's rays hit the earth directly and, therefore, most strongly. Most places along the equator have the hottest climates on earth.

Note the other lines that are drawn on this map. The equator and all the lines that run east-west show *latitude* (lat′ə tōod). Latitude is distance north and south of the equator. Places closest to the equator are said to be in the low latitudes. Places a little farther away from the equator are said to be in the middle latitudes. The latitudes farthest away are the high latitudes. The places closest to the North Pole and the South Pole are in the high latitudes.

Lands in the middle latitudes have cool or cold climates and lands in the high latitudes have very cold climates. Look once again at the map on this page. Does North America or South America have more places with hot climates?

Altitude

As you have learned, places in the middle latitudes usually have cooler climates than places closer to the equator. Not all climates in the middle latitudes are the same, though. Many things can make the climate of one place different from that of a place not far away. For example, *altitude* (al'tə tōod') helps to form climate. Altitude is the height of the land above the earth's surface, or above sea level. Places above sea level generally are cooler than places nearer sea level. The higher you go, the cooler the temperature becomes. This means that mountains can be cool even in low latitudes.

Oceans

The nearness of a place to the ocean also helps to form its climate. The ocean helps to make the weather milder. Therefore, places near the ocean generally are colder in summer and warmer in winter than places inland. In some places ocean currents make the water even warmer. Currents are like rivers of water that flow in the oceans. Some currents carry warm water along with them. One such current flows along the Pacific Coast and helps to give places along that coast a warmer climate. A warm current that flows part way along the Atlantic Coast helps to give the southeastern part of the United States a warm climate.

Climate and Ways of Life

Think about all the conditions that help to make up a place's climate. Then look at the southeastern states on the climate map. You learned that this area has a warm and wet cli-

The Pacific Ocean often hits the coast of Washington State with great force. Why do you think this happens?

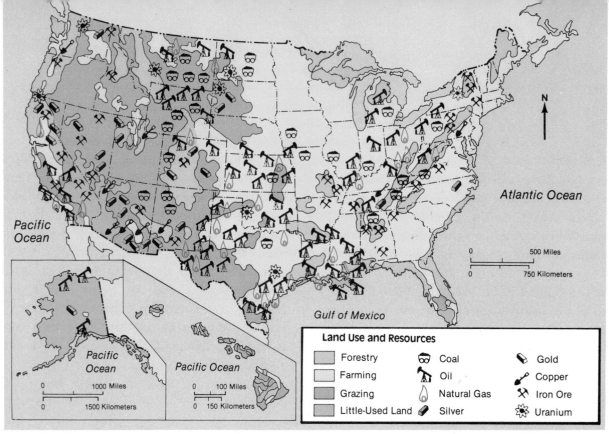

This map shows where some of America's most important resources can be found. What resources does your state have?

mate. What does this mean to the people who live there? It means that these states have hot or warm summers and mild winters. Areas in warm climates have long growing seasons. Thus crops can be grown for a long part of each year.

Now look at the northeastern part of the nation. The climate there is moist, but it is colder than the areas to the south. Northeastern winters are longer, and the summers are shorter. The growing season is shorter too.

Farther to the west—west of the Mississippi River—the climate is drier. The eastern part of this area receives enough precipitation to help grasses to grow. In other parts, however, the land is almost desert.

Such dry lands do not get enough precipitation to allow many plants to grow. Parts of this region have long cold winters.

Along the Pacific Coast the climate is very pleasant. It never gets very cold, and growing seasons are long. In the southern part of the Pacific Coast area, the summers are warm and dry and the winters are warm and wet. Places along the northern Pacific Coast are always wet.

Having so many different climates has made it possible for people in the United States to grow different kinds of foods and to have many different ways to make a living. For example, fruits such as oranges need a warm climate in which to grow, and they do well in states like California and

Florida. Apples grow well in cooler climates. Cattle and sheep graze on the drier grasslands.

The many regions and climates of the United States allow Americans to follow many sports. Snow skiing is a favorite sport in the cold areas where there are snow-capped mountains. Water skiing is popular all year in warm southern climates. What other sports can you think of that depend on certain climate conditions?

Natural Resources

Having different kinds of land and climates also means that the United States has many natural resources. Natural resources are the materials found in and on the earth that people need and use. Water, good soil, and forests are natural resources. Coal mined from the ground is a natural resource also.

Good soil is one of the most important natural resources of the United States. Because of this soil Americans grow large amounts of food—fruits, vegetables, and grains such as wheat and corn. Farmers also grow crops such as cotton, tobacco, and plants used to make dye. Trees and bushes are also natural resources. In the past, forests covered the eastern and northwestern parts of the United States. These forests were home for many kinds of animals. Wood cut from the forests has been used to build homes, ships, furniture, and tools. There are fewer forests now, but Americans still have many uses for wood.

Coal and oil are used as sources of energy, for heating homes, running cars, and operating machines. Another important mineral, iron ore, is needed to make steel. Gold, silver, and other precious metals are used in jewelry.

Water is necessary to life. People need water to drink. Rivers, lakes, and oceans give us fish for food. You have already seen how the many waterways of the country are used for transportation, energy, and sports.

All of these blessings—good land and plenty of water, many kinds of climates, and abundant minerals—have helped the United States to improve and grow. By using its resources carefully now and in the future the United States can continue to grow and to make life comfortable for its people.

Do You Know?

1. Is the United States located in the Western or the Eastern Hemisphere?
2. What physical region covers the southeastern part of the United States?
3. How is the tundra different from the Interior Plains?
4. How many major climate regions does the United States have? What are they?
5. Name four natural resources found in the United States.

Before You Go On

Using New Words

altitude	precipitation
climate	tundra
latitude	

The phrases below explain the words or terms listed above. Number a paper from 1 through 5. After each number write the word or term that matches the definition.

1. A large treeless plain that is so cold its soil remains frozen
2. The weather in an area over a long period of time
3. Height of the land above sea level
4. Rain and snow
5. Distance north or south of the equator

Finding the Facts

1. Where in the Americas is the United States located?
2. What two oceans are located east and west of the United States?
3. What is the difference between a mountain and a plateau?
4. What are plains?
5. How are the Appalachian Mountains different from the Rocky Mountains?
6. Name a physical region in the southern part of the United States.
7. Where is Alaska located?
8. How were the Hawaiian Islands formed?
9. What is a river system? What is the longest river system in North America?
10. Why was the United States able to develop so many seaports?
11. From what point is altitude measured?
12. Mountain A is 5,200 feet (1,560 meters) above sea level. Mountain B is 10,000 feet (3,000 meters) high. On which mountaintop would the temperature be lower? Why?
13. What does being near the ocean do to a place's climate?
14. What are natural resources? Give two examples.
15. Why is it important for a nation to have abundant natural resources?

2

We Are All Americans

The United States is the fourth-largest country in the world in size. Only the Soviet Union, Canada, and China have more land. The United States also has the fourth largest population in the world. China, India, and the Soviet Union are the only nations that have more people than the United States.

The United States has more than 230 million people spread out over thousands of miles. In spite of the nation's size, Americans all have many important things in common. For example, they believe in freedom and trust that their government will protect this freedom.

The American Belief in Freedom

The American people have always shared a belief in freedom. Americans believe that all people should be free to do all that they are able to do. However, many freedoms make up the freedom to act. One American President, President Franklin Roosevelt, believed that the following four freedoms were the most important of all!

1. All people must be free to speak out for what they believe to be right. That means that people also must be free to speak out against what they believe to be wrong.
2. People must be free to choose and follow their own religious beliefs.

3. Everyone must have freedom from want. People must be able to take care of their most important needs—to feed, clothe, and house themselves.
4. People must not fear cruel government action. They must have a government in which all citizens are free to take part and whose laws treat everyone equally. People also must have a government that protects them against attacks from others, inside and outside the nation.

What other freedoms do people need to live full and satisfying lives? They need freedom and equality of opportunity. They need an equal chance to gain a good education. They also need to be able to make their own choices in life. As one famous writer has said, "No one can be perfectly free until all are free." What do you suppose is meant by these words?

A Nation of Immigrants

Americans share something else besides a belief in freedom. Americans are all *immigrants* (im′ə grənts) to this country or family members of people who were immigrants. An immigrant is a person who moves from one country to settle in another country.

The first immigrants to come here were the ancestors of the American Indians. They came thousands of years ago. In the last few hundred years, millions more immigrants have come from all parts of the world.

Why Did People Come?

The United States is a nation of immigrants. Men, women, and children came to this nation from nearly every place on earth. Look at the world map on pages A-2 and A-3. You will find it hard to name any country or part of the world that immigrants did not leave to come to America.

Thousands of years after the American Indians settled here, the first immigrants from Europe arrived. People who wanted to farm in Europe often could not find land. Many others could not find jobs in the towns and cities of Europe. Many Europeans decided to leave their homelands and to make a new start in the open lands of America.

Immigrants from Europe also had other reasons for coming here. Some nations did not allow their people to follow their religions as they wished. Many Europeans believed they would find that freedom in America. Other Europeans did not like the way their governments treated them. Therefore they came to be free of such governments.

From Where Did People Come?

Most of the first immigrants from Europe came from England, Scotland, and Wales. Immigrants from all of these areas settled along the Atlantic Coast. Immigrants from Spain had settled in the Americas earlier, but mostly in the lands to the south of the United States. In the United States the Spaniards settled mainly in Florida and in southwestern areas such as New Mexico and California.

Immigrants came from several places in Northern and Western Europe. They came from France, the Netherlands, Germany, and Sweden, for example. Later they came from Southern and Eastern Europe. Most of these later immigrants were from Italy, Austria-Hungary, Poland, Russia, and Greece. They came from Ireland, too.

Many people came to America from Africa. However, most of these Americans did not come as willing immigrants. Instead, they were brought over as *slaves* (slāvz). Slaves are people who are owned by other people and who are made to work for their owners. Before the law ended the slave trade, almost 10 million black Africans were shipped to the Americas.

Immigrants to the United States have also come from Asia. In the 1800s large numbers of people from China and Japan

Immigrants to the United States 1820 to 1979	
Europe	36 million
Asia	3 million
Other parts of the Americas	9 million
Other parts of the world	573,000

These students are preparing for the citizenship exams they must take and pass in order to become *citizens*.

came to the United States in search of jobs. Today the United States has immigrants from all parts of Asia—from Korea, the Philippines, India, Vietnam, Laos, and many areas of the Middle East.

Millions of immigrants have come to the United States from other parts of the Americas. They have come from places to our south—from Mexico, from Central and South America, and from the islands in the Caribbean Sea. Immigrants have also come from America's neighbor to the north—Canada. Today more immigrants from other parts of the Americas come to the United States than from anywhere else. These newcomers leave their homes to find jobs and freedom in the United States.

Becoming a Citizen

Most immigrants want to become *citizens* (sit′ə zənz) of the United States. A citizen is a person who is a member of a country and who is protected by its laws. In return for this protection, citizens owe their country loyalty and help.

There are two ways that a person can become a citizen of the United States. One way is to be born here. Most persons who are born on American soil have American citizenship. Such people are called native-born citizens.

The other way to become a citizen of the United States is to be given citizenship by government. The first step in becoming a citizen is to enter the country legally. This means that a person must be allowed by the United States government to enter and live in the country. A person must live in the United States for five years before he or she can ask the government for citizenship.

Those who ask for citizenship must prove that they are good and trustworthy people. They must take a test to show they are able to read, write, and speak English and that they know important facts about American history and government. Those who pass this test then become *naturalized* (nach'ər ə līzd') *citizens.*

Naturalized citizens have the same citizenship rights as native-born citizens. There is one exception though. A naturalized citizen cannot become President or Vice-President of the United States.

How Are We Alike and Different?

As you have seen, the United States was built by immigrants from all over the world. One American poet called the United States "a nation of nations." By this the poet meant that the United States has joined together people from many countries to make one country.

People who come from different parts of the world have different *cultures* (kul'chərz). Culture is the way of life of a people. It includes the ways that people make a living, the language they speak, and the rules they live under. Culture also includes religious beliefs, the arts, the kinds of food that are eaten, and customs. As you can see, a people's culture is made up of all that people do to live their lives.

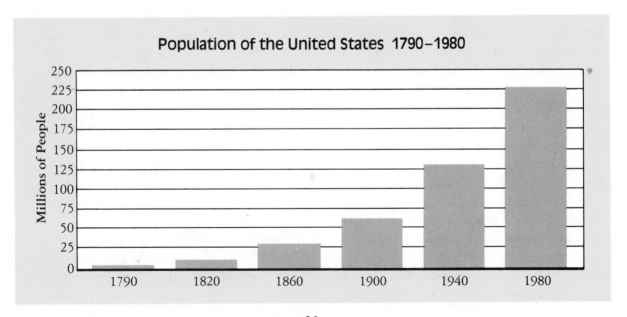

All the different people who came to the United States brought their cultures with them. Italian immigrants, for example, brought pizza, pasta, and other foods. Words from many different languages have been added to English. Just think of: moccasin (American Indian), bravo (Italian), prairie (French), rodeo (Spanish), frankfurter (German), judo (Japanese), sauna (Finnish), wok (Chinese), and guru (Indian). These are just a few of the many hundreds of words in English that come from different cultures.

The British culture became important in the United States because so many early immigrants were from Great Britain. Later immigrants, however, had ways that were very different from those of the British and from each other.

What happened when different cultures came together in the same place? Sometimes they clashed. People with one set of religious beliefs sometimes disliked people with a different set of beliefs. People with one skin color sometimes disliked people with another skin color. Yet over the years the many cultures made life in the United States richer and more interesting. Each culture has added something to the American way of life. Moreover, people from every culture have made contributions in science, the arts, education, government, and many walks of life.

Today Americans share a culture. Most people in the United States speak English, but with many foreign words added to it.

They live under the same rules of government. They follow many of the same customs—shaking hands and celebrating birthdays, for example. Many Americans also have their own special holidays, such as Passover, Chinese New Year, and Greek Easter. Another holiday, Día de la raza, means Day of the Race in Spanish and is also called Columbus Day. The American culture continues to accept ways from other cultures.

Where We Live

During the early years of the United States most of its people made their living by farming. The country's few cities were small. Nine tenths of Americans lived on farms or in small towns in rural areas.

By the middle of the 1800s this pattern of settlement had changed greatly. There were many cities, and they were growing rapidly. By 1920 more than half of all Americans were living in urban, or city areas.

Today more than two thirds of all Americans live in urban areas. An urban area includes a city and its suburbs, or smaller communities that are around the city. That means the United States is now a nation of cities.

Population and Density

Look at the chart on page 20. It shows how the population of the United States has grown over the years. About how many people lived in the United States in 1790? About how many people lived here in 1900? What was the population in 1980?

People who study population use the term *density* (den'sə tē) to describe how closely together people live in a place. If a great many people live closely together in a place, the place is said to have a high population density. A place with only a few people, living far apart, has a low population density.

In the early years of our country, areas along the Atlantic Coast were the most crowded places in the nation. Lands farther west had many fewer people. Today many areas of the United States have high population densities. Most people like to live in places that have good soil, plenty of water, and a pleasant climate. People must also choose places where they can find jobs or make a living. The northeastern area that runs from Boston, Massachusetts, south to Washington, D.C., is one of the most crowded areas in the nation. Other areas with dense populations are along the Pacific Coast, around the Great Lakes, and along the Mississippi River Valley.

Population Movement

In recent years Americans have changed where they choose to live in the United States. Large numbers of people have left the Northeast and the Midwest to move to the South and the Southwest. The states of the South and the Southwest are called the "Sun Belt" because they usually have sunny and warm weather. In only 10 years, from 1970 to 1980, the number of people in Florida nearly doubled. The number of people in Arizona more than doubled. The population of Texas grew larger by one fourth.

Americans are moving to the Sun Belt for many reasons. Some are going there to retire. After they stop working, many citizens want to leave the cold winters of the northern states. Some Americans are moving to the Sun Belt to find jobs. Many companies have set up factories and offices in the Sun Belt, where the pleasant weather draws workers. Also, areas in the Sun Belt often are less crowded than places in the East and Midwest that have been settled longer. However, if people keep moving to the Sun Belt in large numbers, many places there also will have high population densities.

Do You Know?

1. Why is the United States called a nation of immigrants?
2. How were the early immigrants different from the newer immigrants?
3. What is a naturalized citizen?
4. Why does the United States have many areas of high population density?
5. What is the Sun Belt?

3

Studying American History

During the next few months, you are going to be studying American history. Do you know what history is? The answer lies in the word itself. History is the story of the things that have happened in the past. American history is the story of the things that have happened in and to the United States.

American history tells about the people who helped to form the American way of life—their actions, their beliefs, their hopes. It tells about great events in the country's past. American history also explains how people have changed and the causes for the changes.

Why We Study History

What is the reason for studying history? Of what use is history to us? The answer is that history helps us to understand what is happening today. Knowing what happened in the past helps us to understand what is happening in the present.

Think about your own life. Suppose you woke up tomorrow and remembered nothing about your own past. Suppose you had no idea of when you were born. You did not know whether you had any family or friends. You did not even know your name or where you were. If this happened to you, you would feel upset and confused. You would not understand what was happening to you.

Learning about American history helps us in the same way that knowing our own life history does. American history tells us where our country came from and how it changed. It helps us understand why things happen in our country in the way they do. Knowing about American history also helps us to feel at home in our country.

Studying American history helps us for yet another reason. It helps to answer some of our desire to know. Many people want to know about those who came before them. How did people of the past live? What did they do? Why did the cultures of some people not last? What lessons can we learn from the past that may help us to deal with the future?

How We Learn About the Past

The people who study the past are called *historians* (his tôr′ē ənz). It is not always easy for historians to learn about the people and events of the past. Often people do not write about their lives. Also, some of what is written is lost or destroyed. Historians, therefore, must use many different sources to find out about the past.

Primary and Secondary Sources

One kind of source is called a primary source. This source often is a record that comes from the time that is being studied.

A

Digging Up The Past

Every year we find out more about the rich heritage of the
North American Indians. Things that the Indians used
hundreds of years ago have been found in all parts of our
country. These items often are in the ground, and archeologists
must dig ditches, or trenches, to find them (A). Working on
such a "dig" can be exciting. The woman cleaning the basket
(B), for example, is learning about her own past. The basket
was made long ago in Washington State by a member of her
Makah tribe.

   Sometimes an artifact such as this round brick house (D) is
found above ground. It was built in Arizona over 700 years
ago by the Cohonina Indians.

   Archeologists often find dishes and pieces of pottery (C and
F). They are important because they tell about a people's skills.
This religious banner, or flag, of the Arapaho Indians tells us
something about their religious beliefs (E). The "Winter
Count" painted on buffalo skin by the Sioux of South Dakota
shows a Sioux camp during one winter (G). ▪

D

B

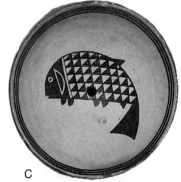

C

E

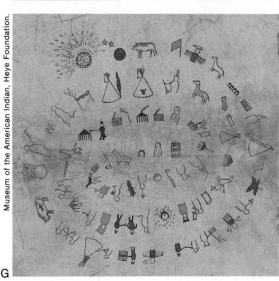

G

F

25

Primary sources include written laws and other legal documents, or official papers. Historians often study birth certificates, for example, because they tell when people were born. A picture also can be a primary source. A photograph might show how people dressed at the time the photograph was taken. Letters, diaries, and other first-person accounts are still other important primary sources. A first-person account is a record made by a person who actually saw and heard what happened.

Historians also use secondary sources. A story of an event written by someone who did not live at the time it happened is a secondary source. The reporter used facts that he or she had learned from someone else to write the story.

Oral History

Now that there are motion picture cameras and tape recorders people can record history as it happens. Tape recorders also are used in interviewing, or questioning people about events. Interviews in which people talk about their past are called *oral* (or'əl) *history.* Today historians often ask older people about their lives and about events in their neighborhood. What is said is then used to write the history of the community. In the past, this oral, or spoken, history was the only kind of history that some people had. Parents told stories of the past to their children, who passed it on. Oral history. was the only way to remember the past.

Digging for Evidence

Historians sometimes use the findings of *archeologists* (är kē ol'ə jistz) to help learn about the past. An archeologist is a person who actually "digs up" facts about the past. That is, archeologists dig in the ground to find things that earlier people left behind—buildings, tools, food, clothing, statues, and anything else they made and used.

Suppose that archeologists found the remains of a village where Indians lived 400 years ago. By digging at that site, or the place where the village stood, the archeologists found old arrowheads, bits of pottery bowls, and stone tools. These human-made remains are called *artifacts* (är'tə faktz). By studying artifacts, archeologists and historians can learn much about how the Indians of the village they found lived and worked long ago.

After historians gather their facts, they put all they have learned together in a history book such as this one. The book is then given to students to add to their knowledge of the past—their own and their country's history.

Do You Know?

1. What is history?
2. How is a primary source different from a secondary source?
3. What is oral history?
4. Why do archaeologists study artifacts?

To Help You Learn

Using New Words

archeologist   historian
artifacts   immigrant
citizens   naturalized citizen
culture   oral history
density   slaves

The phrases below explain the words or terms listed above. Number a paper from 1 through 10. After each number write the word or term that matches the definition.

1. Story of the past told in interviews by people who were living at the time being studied
2. A person who becomes a member of a country by going through the steps set by the government
3. A person who studies the past
4. A scientist who digs in the ground to find evidence of the past
5. People who are owned by other people
6. The closeness with which people in an area live to one another
7. Human-made remains of the past, such as tools or arrowheads
8. A person who moves to a new country to live
9. The way of life of a people
10. People who are members of a country and who are protected by its laws

Finding the Facts

1. How can knowing the latitude of a place help you to figure out its climate?
2. Name three of the physical regions of the United States. Where is each region located?
3. Name three mountain ranges in the United States.
4. What are three important uses for water and waterways?
5. How can climate help to form a people's way of life?
6. What are two freedoms in which Americans believe?
7. Name some of the reasons that immigrants came to the United States.
8. What is the difference between a native-born citizen and a naturalized citizen?
9. Why are many people moving to the Sun Belt?
10. Why is it important to study American history?
11. Give two examples of primary sources.

Learning from Maps

1. Turn to the map on page 14. This map uses many signs, or symbols, to stand for natural

resources. They are listed in the box at the bottom and are part of the legend, or map key. What symbol on the map stands for gold? For uranium? The map also uses color as a symbol. What color on the map stands for forest? For water? What other symbols and colors are listed in the map key?

2. Turn to the map on pages 6 and 7. It shows the different natural regions of the United States.

- Name the regions shown on the map.
- In which region is your state located?
- Notice the way the word "Intermountain" is written on the map. The words "Great Basin" are not written the same way. Using larger letters or all capital letters helps you see that a region such as the Intermountain Region is larger than the Great Basin. Locate the Coastal Lowlands. Name two smaller regions that are part of the Coastal Lowlands.

Using Study Skills

1. **Bar Graph:** The bar graph on this page shows the amount of precipitation—rainfall and snowfall—that falls in five cities during a year. Look at the graph carefully. Then answer these questions.

- Which city has the most precipitation?
- Which city has the least precipitation?
- Which cities have less than 40 inches (100 cm) of precipitation a year?
- Which cities have between 30 inches and 50 inches (75 and 125 cm) of precipitation a year?

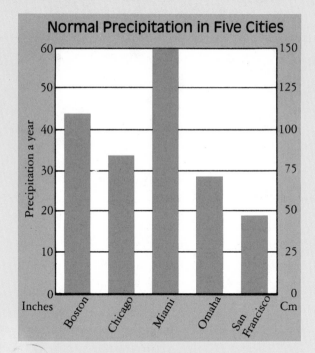

Normal Precipitation in Five Cities

2. **Pictures:** Did you know that you can "read" pictures to learn things? Instead of looking at words, you look at what is in the picture. You may study the people shown in the picture, their actions, or the way they are dressed. You may look at any buildings in the picture and read any signs that are on them. By studying the pictures in this book in this way, you can learn much about the United States and its history.

Turn to the pictures on pages 24 and 25. Study each picture carefully. Who are the people shown here? What are they doing? How can you learn about the past by doing this kind of work?

3. **Time Line:** Mary Sanchez interviewed her grandmother, Rosa Sanchez, to learn more about the past as her grandmother remembered it. Rosa Sanchez remembered many events from her life. After the interview Mary arranged some of the events she learned in a time line. Look carefully at the time line that Mary made. Then answer these questions.

28

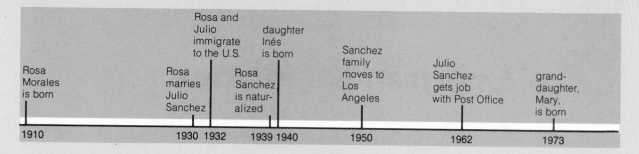

Timeline:
- Rosa Morales is born — 1910
- Rosa marries Julio Sanchez — 1930
- Rosa and Julio immigrate to the U.S. — 1932
- Rosa Sanchez is naturalized — 1939
- daughter Inés is born — 1940
- Sanchez family moves to Los Angeles — 1950
- Julio Sanchez gets job with Post Office — 1962
- granddaughter, Mary, is born — 1973

- When was Rosa Sanchez born?
- What happened in 1939?
- Which came first—Rosa's move to the United States or her marriage?
- Did Julio Sanchez start to work at the Post Office before or after the family moved to Los Angeles?
- When was Mary Sanchez born?

Thinking It Through

1. How does climate help you to choose your clothing? The sports you take part in? The kind of work you may do?
2. Is oral history an example of a primary source or a secondary source? Explain your answer.
3. Give three examples of the ways in which immigrants have made the culture of your state richer.

Projects

1. Archeologists learn about the past by digging up artifacts. Suppose you were to bury six things you use today for future archeologists to find. What things would you choose to bury that would tell people far in the future what your life is like today? Explain your choices.
2. Your class might like to have a social studies club. If so, hold a class meeting to talk about setting it up.

Every club has committees to do its work. A committee is made up of a group of people who do one kind of work or project. Each committee should have a leader or chairperson for a project.

One group of students might like to belong to the Explorers' Committee. The members of this committee will find out more about faraway places.

The Explorers' Committee might find out more about the places from which immigrants came to the United States. What was life like in those places? Why did people choose to leave there to come to this country?

Some students might like to start a Research Committee. They will learn more about people and events in the past.

The Research Committee might want to learn about the ways in which immigrants have made American culture richer. How did the United States gain from the work of individual immigrants? How have immigrant cultures added new things to American culture?

Other students might form a Reading Committee. They will find interesting books to read and share with the class.

The Reading Committee might look for information about the work of archeologists in the United States. Where were the earliest American artifacts found? What do these finds tell about the early people of America?

2 American Beginnings

Unit Preview

Thousands of years ago there were no people living in North and South America. The northwestern tip of North America was separated from Asia by a narrow channel of ocean. When glaciers caused the oceans to lower, land appeared between Asia and North America. People and animals then walked between the two continents.

The people who made the crossing to the Americas were later called Indians by the Europeans. Indians settled in all parts of the continents. They learned to use the resources of the land. They began to build civilizations.

The Vikings were the first Europeans to reach North America. However, they did not stay. Almost 500 years later the explorer Christopher Columbus came upon the Americas while trying to sail west to Asia. Many Europeans came to the Americas after Columbus. They soon found out that these lands were not Asia but a new land.

Columbus and other explorers claimed much land in the Americas for Spain. They started colonies in South America and North America. The English, French, and Dutch also gained land in North America. France settled what is now Canada. New Netherland was started by the Dutch along the Hudson River. The English started settlements at Jamestown and Plymouth.

Things to Discover

If you look carefully at the picture, map, and time line, you can answer these questions.

1. The arrows on the map show the routes taken by people who came to North America. To what parts of the continent did most people come? What ocean did they cross?
2. The picture shows what Christopher Columbus did when he first landed in the Americas. What did Columbus do?
3. Did Columbus sail to America before or after the city of Tenochtitlán was built?
4. Did Ponce de León reach Florida before or after Cortés conquered Mexico?
5. How long after Jamestown was Quebec founded?

Words to Learn

You will meet these words in this unit. As you read, you will learn what they mean and how to pronounce them. The Word List will help you.

adobe	missions
charter	nomads
civilization	potlatch
colonies	sagas
empire	totem poles
expedition	Vikings
glaciers	

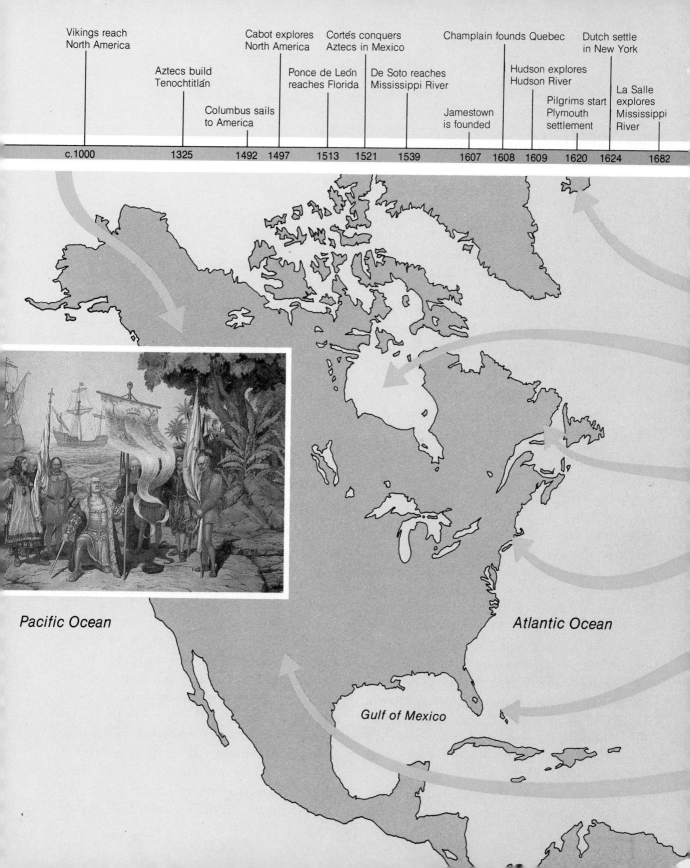

Vikings reach
North America

Aztecs build
Tenochtitlán

Columbus sails
to America

Cabot explores
North America

Ponce de León
reaches Florida

Cortés conquers
Aztecs in Mexico

De Soto reaches
Mississippi River

Jamestown
is founded

Champlain founds Quebec

Hudson explores
Hudson River

Pilgrims start
Plymouth
settlement

Dutch settle
in New York

La Salle
explores
Mississippi
River

| c.1000 | 1325 | 1492 | 1497 | 1513 | 1521 | 1539 | 1607 | 1608 | 1609 | 1620 | 1624 | 1682 |

Pacific Ocean

Atlantic Ocean

Gulf of Mexico

1

The First Americans

Who were the first Americans? Where did these early people come from? How did they come? When did they come, and why?

The people that we today call Indians or Native Americans were the first American people. Today scientists know that these people came to North and South America from Asia. They came in several groups over thousands of years. But how and why did they come?

The Coming of the Indians

About 50,000 years ago the earth was a much colder place than it is now. Huge sheets of ice, called *glaciers* (glā'shərz), covered much of the earth. This time is called the Ice Age. During the Ice Age much of the earth's water was frozen into glaciers. This caused the level of the sea to lower. As a result, areas of land that had been under water were sometimes above the water.

One such area was the Bering Strait (bēr'ing strāt), between northeastern Asia and northwestern North America. A strait is a narrow body of water that connects two larger bodies of water. During the Ice Age the Bering Strait often was above water. It formed a kind of land bridge between the two continents.

When the land bridge appeared, animals began to cross it. Groups of hunters fol-lowed the animals from Asia to what is now Alaska.

Moving Through North and South America

In time the earth grew warmer and the glaciers melted. Ocean water again covered the land bridge between Asia and North America. Animals and hunters had no way to return to Asia. Many of them moved south and east through North America and South America. Within a few thousand years, small groups of Indians lived throughout the two continents.

Life Among the Indians

The Indians lived as *nomads* (nō'madz), or wandering hunters, for a long time. They used spears with sharp stone points as weapons. Over the years, however, the Indians made new tools and discovered new ways of doing things. For example, they learned how to make the bow and arrow. With this weapon, hunters did not have to get as close to the animals as when using a spear. The bow and arrow made hunting easier and less dangerous.

One of the most important Indian dis-coveries was made in what is now Mexico. About 5,000 years ago the Indians there learned that they could plant seeds and grow their own food. In time they settled

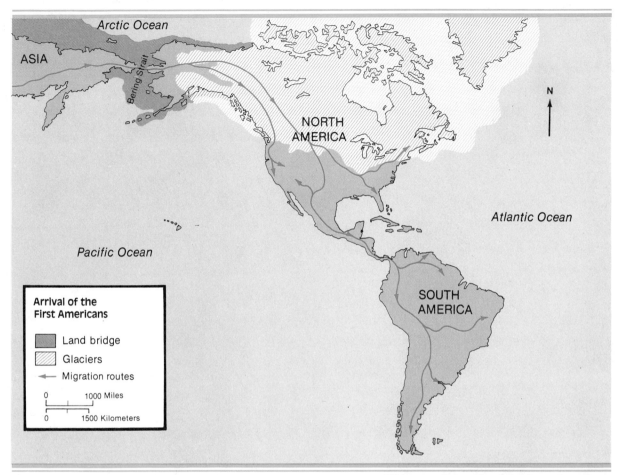

This map shows the Americas when the Indians began arriving from Asia. In what part of the Americas were the *glaciers*?

down in communities. They grew fields of maize (corn), pumpkins and other squashes, potatoes, peppers, beans, and tomatoes. They also grew tobacco and cotton.

Once the Indians settled down as farmers, they needed new skills. Many groups became skilled at weaving baskets, for example. Some of the baskets were woven so tightly that they could hold water.

Indians in each area worked out their own way of doing things. Such differences led the Indians to form many cultures. See the map on page 34.

Hunters and Gatherers

The Indians along the West Coast lived comfortably without farming. The land along the west coast of what is now the United States is very rich in natural resources. As a result, Indians who settled there were able to live by hunting and gathering.

The Pacific Northwest

Nature gave the Indians of the Pacific Northwest almost all of the resources they needed. The climate there was wet but

Indian Groups of the Americas

0   1,000 Miles

0   1,500 Kilometers

N

Bering Strait

Eskimo

Aleut

Eskimo

Eskimo

PACIFIC
NORTHWEST

FAR NORTH

Hudson Bay

Pacific Ocean

Nootka

Blackfoot

Cree

Chippewa

Huron

Ottawa

Iroquois

Nez Perce

Mohawk

INTERMOUNTAIN

Mandan

Fox

Pequot

Tillamook

Modoc

Potawatomi

Sauk

Shoshone

Delaware

PLAINS

EASTERN
WOODLANDS

Pomo

Ute

Illinois

Sioux

CALIFORNIA

SOUTHWEST

Shawnee

Navajo

Cheyenne

Cherokee

Chumash

Hopi

Creek

Pueblo

Catawba

Apache

Comanche

Atlantic Ocean

Natchez

Seminole

Gulf of Mexico

Caribe

MEXICO

Caribbean Sea

SOUTH
AMERICA

Inca

Aztec

Maya

CENTRAL
AMERICA
AND THE
CARIBBEAN

0   500 Miles

0   750 Kilometers

mild. Wild berries and other plants grew thickly. Salmon and other fish filled the many rivers of the area. In the Pacific Ocean were many fish and sea animals such as seals and otters.

Along the Pacific Coast were many thick forests. The Indians used trees from the forests to build strong plank houses. Tree trunks also were carved into *totem poles* (tō′təm pōlz). These wooden carvings of people and of animals important to a family were placed in front of the houses. Tree trunks were also used to make large wooden canoes.

With their needs easily taken care of, the Indians of the Pacific Northwest were able to enjoy life. With so many resources at hand, many of the Pacific Northwest Indians also grew wealthy. They liked to show off their wealth in a special feast called a *potlatch* (pot′lӓch). At the feast, a host and hostess gave their guests hundreds of gifts, based on the importance of the guests. Among the gifts were canoes, blankets, fur robes, and decorated sheets of copper. The guests usually repaid their hosts and hostesses by holding their own potlatches.

California

To the south of the Pacific Northwest is the area we call California. Most of California enjoyed a mild climate. Southern California, however, was much warmer and drier.

Food was plentiful in California. Fish and small game were caught. The Indians also gathered wild berries, seeds, roots, and nuts to eat. They made flour from the acorns they gathered. To hold the flour, the Indians wove beautiful baskets.

The Indians of California lived in small villages along the coast and in deep, green valleys. Because of the pleasant climate and large amounts of food, many Indians settled there. In fact, California had more people than most other areas.

Intermountain Region

Between the Sierra Nevada and Rocky Mountains is the high, flat Intermountain Region. Life was not so pleasant for the people who lived there—the Intermountain Indians. The climate in this area was very dry. The winters in the mountain heights were icy cold, snowy, and stormy.

Few Indians lived in the Intermountain Region. Those who did traveled about in small groups, always in search of wild berries and nuts, rabbits, lizards, and birds. They had to find enough food to keep them alive all year long. That meant they had to store enough to get them through the hard snowy winters.

Hunters and Farmers

Scientists think that the idea of farming spread from Mexico to the north. Farming then began in the Southwest and along the Gulf Coast. Later, it spread even farther north. In some places, though, the land was too dry for the Indians to farm.

The Southwest

The hot and dry valleys of present-day Arizona, New Mexico, southern Colorado, and Utah were home for the Indians of the Southwest. In the northern part of the area, there are many cliffs and canyons. Land in the south is flat and desert-like.

The Southwest had few trees and few rivers and streams, but the Indians found a way to live there. They discovered they could grow crops in the dry soil if they could get enough water. They dug channels from rivers and streams to irrigate, or bring water to, their fields.

Some of the early Indian groups of the Southwest made their homes in the cliffs. They hollowed out rooms in the cliff walls. In some places there were several levels, or stories, of rooms. This made the cliff look like an apartment building. The Indians used ladders to go from one level to another. Other Indians of the Southwest built their own "apartment buildings." These Indians put up buildings of *adobe* (ə dō′bē). Adobe is brick made of sun-dried clay.

When the Spaniards came to the Southwest they called the Indians who lived in these apartment buildings the Pueblo (pweb′lō) Indians. Pueblo is the Spanish word for village.

The Indians of the Southwest made many beautiful items, including pottery bowls and jars. They wove warm blankets of wool. The Indians also hammered silver into jewelry. Today groups such as the Navajos (nav′ə hōz′) continue to make these items.

The Plains

The land to the east of the Rocky Mountains is flat and low and covered by tall, tough grasses. Most of the region forms the Great Plains. The Plains stretch from Canada south to Mexico, from the Rocky Mountains to east of the Mississippi River.

Many groups of Indians lived in the Plains. The Cheyenne (shī′en′) and other Indians of the drier western areas met their needs by hunting. However, the groups who lived nearer the Great Lakes and Mississippi River were both hunters and farmers. These farmers lived in villages along rivers or streams for most of the year. Since there were few trees in the Plains, each farming family lived in an earthen lodge. This house was made of a few logs and large chunks of earth.

In summer, groups such as the Iowas left their villages to hunt buffalo, or bison. Huge herds of buffalo roamed the Plains. A hunting party usually was made up of about 20 families. Everyone had a job to do. Woman cooked and were in charge of moving. They tied their belongings, including animals skins, to long poles. When it was time to set up camp, the women used the poles and animal skins to make tepees (tē′pēz′) for their families to live in.

The Eastern Woodlands

The Eastern Woodlands was another area that was rich in resources. Stretching from Canada to the Gulf of Mexico, from the Mississippi River to the Atlantic Ocean,

36

The Iroquois of the Eastern Woodlands used the resources of the forests. The women in the picture are collecting sap from maple trees to make maple sugar.

this land was green and covered with forests. Animals filled these woodlands.

The Indians of the Eastern Woodlands lived as farmers and hunters. To clear the land for farming, the Indians used the "slash-and-burn" way of working. First they cut down the trees. Then the Indians set fire to the bushes and plants growing there. When that was burned off, the Indians planted corn and other vegetables.

In the northern part of the Woodlands, some of the Indians lived in wigwams (wig'womz). Wigwams are round houses made of sheets of bark stretched over a wooden frame. Other groups, such as the Iroquois (ir'ə kwoi'), lived in longhouses, which also are wooden frames covered with bark. Each longhouse was divided into three parts. One family lived in each part.

Far North and Very Far West

The lands of Alaska and Hawaii are separated from the rest of the United States. Because Alaska is part of North America, however, it was settled much like the rest of the Americas. Hawaii, though, has a very different history from the other parts of the nation.

Eskimos

The Eskimos who settled in Alaska were the last people to cross over from Asia. This land of the Far North is a hard place to live in. It is almost always cold. In some areas the land never thaws.

The Eskimos made their living in the Far North by hunting and by fishing. They hunted the caribou (kar'ə boo'), which is an animal like a moose. Among the sea ani-

The Maya painted plates, vases, and other items with beautiful pictures. Maya writing is shown around the people.

mals they hunted were seals, otters, walruses, and whales. Salmon was their chief fish.

Hunting kept the Eskimos on the move. In the winter the Eskimos lived in log houses covered with earth. When they traveled in winter, the Eskimos built igloos, houses made of blocks of ice and snow. Tents of animal skin were used in summer.

Polynesians

Thousands of miles to the west of North America are the Hawaiian Islands. The people who first settled in Hawaii were not Indians. They were Polynesians (pol'i nē'zhənz). The Polynesians had sailed to the Hawaiian Islands in about 750 A.D. from a group of islands much farther south. In the Hawaiian Islands the Polynesians enjoyed a warm, pleasant climate. Tropical fruits grew wild everywhere. Both the Pacific Ocean and inland bodies of water were filled with fish.

Because the islands were warm all year long, the Polynesians needed only light clothing. Houses were made of wooden frames covered with woven grass. This allowed air to blow through and keep the inside cool. Cloth was made from pounded tree bark.

Indians of Mexico and Central America

Mexico, Central America, and northwestern South America were rich in many kinds of natural resources. As you read, the Indians of Mexico were the first American group to farm. They also became skilled craftsworkers and builders, priests and priestesses, and scholars. They began arranging governments for themselves. They also studied the skies and nature. They figured out how to measure. All of these things are part of creating a *civilization* (siv'ə li zā'shən), a way of life that has reached a high level.

The skills of the early Mexicans spread to nearby areas—to Central America and to South America.

The Maya

The Maya (mä′yə) Indians lived in what is now part of southern Mexico and Guatemala. They may have settled there about 4,500 years ago. Over hundreds of years the Maya formed a rich culture.

One of the important things that the Maya formed was a written language. They used pictures to stand for their words. For example, the picture of an eye stood for the word "eye". The Maya made up special drawings to stand for numbers. By studying what the Maya wrote, we know that they measured time by changes in the position of the stars at different times of year. This understanding of the stars led the Maya to make a calendar and a system of arithmetic.

Religion was very important in the lives of the Maya. They believed in many gods and goddesses. The main Mayan gods and goddesses included a god of corn, a god of rain, and a god of the sun. Feasts were held often to honor the gods. The great temples where these ceremonies were held had many beautiful carvings and paintings.

The Maya culture was greatest from about 300 A.D. to 900 A.D. Cities began to grow up around the great temples. Then the Maya culture mysteriously grew weaker. The Maya began to leave the cities they had built. Before long, jungles covered over the Maya cities.

This page from an old Spanish book explains the Aztec way of life. Among the drawings are an Aztec house, animals, and plants.

The Aztecs

In the 1200s a new civilization appeared in the valley of central Mexico. It was formed by the Aztecs. These Indians had been a hunting people in northern Mexico. They suddenly began to move south, attacking other Indian groups as they went. Soon the Aztecs had power over much of Mexico.

In about the year 1325 the Aztecs built their capital city of Tenochtitlán (tä nōch tē tlän′) on a marshy island in a lake. Several bridges connected the island to the mainland. At the time Tenochtitlán was one of the largest and most beautiful cities in the world. A great temple of the war god rose high above the city. Temples, parks, markets, and roads were everywhere. Later, Tenochtitlán was destroyed and Mexico City was built where it had stood.

This small carving in tin was made by the Indians of Peru. From it, we know that the Incas wore hats and jewelry. We also know that the Incas loved music.

The Incas of Peru

Another great early Indian culture formed in South America. In the high Andes Mountains along the Pacific Coast lived an Indian group called the Incas. They found a way to farm and to put up huge buildings of stone. The Incas made flat areas called terraces on the mountainsides. The terraces were like steps. Each one was bordered by a stone wall. The walls kept the soil from washing away in heavy rain. On these terraces the Incas grew potatoes, peppers, squash, corn, and many other crops.

In about the 1100s the Incas began attacking other Indian groups in western South America. By the 1500s the Incan civilization stretched from what is now Colombia to present-day Chile. The Incas called themselves the Kingdom of the Sun.

They prayed to a god of the sun, as well as many other gods and goddesses. The most powerful person in the Incan society was the ruler, who was believed to be a descendant of the sun god.

The Inca ruler lived in a grand palace in the capital city of Cuzco (koo'skō). It was high in the mountains, in present-day Peru. Cuzco had buildings made of huge blocks of stone. Roads lined with stone connected all of the Inca lands. Messengers were stationed along the roads, often every two miles (3.2 km).

The land of the Incas was rich in gold and silver. Craftsworkers turned these precious metals into beautiful pieces of jewelry. Such objects added to the richness of the Incan civilization.

Do You Know?

1. How did the first Americans come to North America?
2. Why did the Pacific Northwest Indians hold potlatches?
3. What kind of homes did the Indians of the Southwest build?
4. What kind of homes did the Plains Indians live in when they hunted buffalo?
5. Why was life so hard for the Eskimos?
6. Which groups of Indians lived in Mexico, Central America, and South America? What were some of their accomplishments?

2
Europeans Reach the Americas

For thousands of years the Indians lived in North and South America, forming rich cultures. They never became great sailors, though. Therefore the Indians did not learn that other peoples lived on other continents far away.

However, people from Europe began to sail into the oceans farther and farther away from shore. One day the journeys of these seafarers would taken them all the way to the Americas.

Voyages of the Vikings

The first Europeans to reach the Americas probably were the *Vikings* (vī′kingz). These seafaring people came from what are now the countries of Norway, Sweden, and Denmark in northern Europe. The Vikings sailed in long, narrow ships, which moved by sail and by oar.

One of the first places reached by the Vikings who sailed west was Iceland. Some Vikings settled in Iceland and formed communities. From there the Vikings sailed farther west, looked for other lands. They found Greenland and settled there, too. Their leader was Eric the Red, who was known for his bushy red beard.

Old Viking stories called *sagas* (sä′gəz) tell what happened then. Eric had a son named Leif (lēf) Ericson. In about 1000 A.D. Leif decided to sail west from Green-

land to look for a wooded land that another sailor had seen from afar while he was lost at sea. After many days "Leif the Lucky" and his crew found this land. They landed on the northeastern coast of North America.

No one knows exactly where the Vikings landed. However, the sagas say that the Vikings found many grape vines growing there. Leif therefore named the area Vinland. The Vikings also explored other areas of North American before they sailed back to Greenland.

The *Vikings* with Leif Ericson landed somewhere on the northeastern coast of North America. Why do you think the Vikings in the picture are excited?

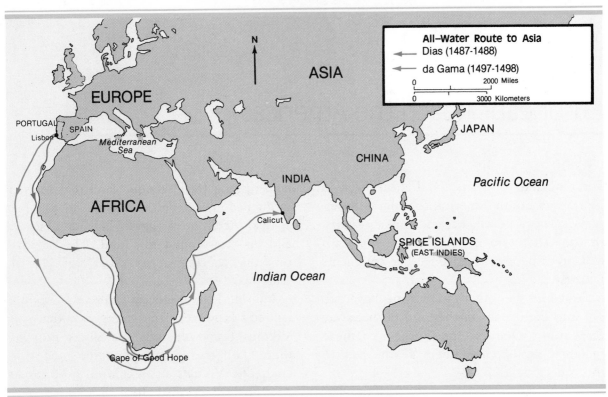

It was not until the late 1400s that the Portuguese sailed around the southern tip of Africa. According to the map, which navigator explored the east coast of Africa?

Soon other Vikings came to North America to settle, but the Vikings did not stay long. Troubles arose with the Indians, and the Viking settlers gave up and returned to Greenland. It would be nearly 500 years before the Americas were "discovered" again by Europeans.

Search for New Trade Routes

The Europeans did not come again to the Americas until they started to look for trade routes to Asia. Europeans had begun to visit India, China, Japan, and the Spice Islands off the Asian shore in the 1200s. Europeans called these lands the East. They were rich in goods the Europeans wanted— gold, jewels, silks, rugs, perfumes, fine pottery, polished steel, and spices to flavor food and keep it from spoiling.

Overland travel to and from the East was hard and slow. Much of the land that had to be crossed was very dry or very mountainous. There also were dangers from thieves along the way. Known water routes were easier, but they were controlled by non-Europeans. All these problems made the goods from the East very costly in Europe. Therefore, many Europeans decided to try to find new water routes to Asia.

Prince Henry the Navigator

The first European country to find a new water route to the East was Portugal.

Prince Henry, the son of King John I of Portugal, was interested in sea travel. Therefore, he began a school for sailors. There he gathered the best mapmakers and ship designers he could find. He also brought in the best navigators, or sailors who guide ships on their voyages.

Prince Henry's careful study of seagoing earned him the name "Henry the Navigator." At his school the Prince tried to get faster ships. New sailing instruments helped sailors find their way across oceans.

Prince Henry decided that Portuguese sailors should try to reach the East by sailing south along the west coast of Africa. He hoped they could sail round the tip of Africa, go north along the east coast, and continue east into the Indian Ocean. No European had ever sailed so far south or so far away from the coast. Sailors feared the dangers that might be there. Sea stories said that the southern ocean waters were so hot that they boiled.

King John II of Portugal gave the sailors an order. "Sail as far south as you dare. Then build a tower on the shore to show where you turned back." Year by year towers were put up farther south on the coast.

This picture shows some of the sea monsters the Europeans thought they would find if they sailed far from the coast.

A Water Route is Found

Finally in 1488 Captain Bartholomeu Dias (bär'too loo mā'oo dē'əs) reached the southern tip of Africa. There he ran into a

In this painting, Christopher Columbus seems to be a thoughtful but determined person. Why do you think that Columbus is often shown that way?

terrible storm at sea. When the storm ended, Dias was happy to report, "We are east of Africa and sailing north! On to India!" But his fearful crew refused to sail on. Dias had to return to Portugal. The king decided to name the southern tip of Africa the Cape of Good Hope.

Ten years later Prince Henry's wish at last came true. Captain Vasco da Gama (väs'kō də gä'mə) sailed around Africa and reached India. His ship returned loaded with spices, silks, and other valuable goods. Portugal had found its all-water route to the East!

Columbus Plans to Sail West

Portugal's neighbor Spain also wanted to find an all-water route to the East. A navigator named Christopher Columbus believed he could find a route for Spain. He asked the Spanish king and queen, Ferdinand and Isabella, to pay for his trip. He wanted to sail not south but west. Since he believed the earth is round, he thought Asia could be reached by sailing west. Columbus believed that the distance to Asia this way would be about 3,500 miles (5,600 km). Others did not agree with him. They believed that the distance was much greater.

Christopher Columbus was born in Genoa, Italy, which was a great seaport. At 19 years of age Columbus became a sailor. A few years later he worked as a mapmaker in Portugal. After talking to ships' captains

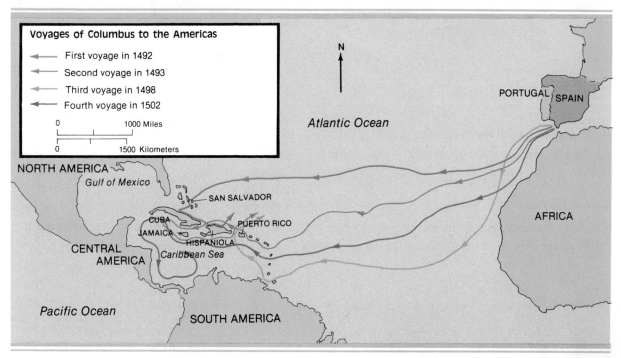

This map traces the four voyages that Columbus made while searching for a western route to Asia. Where did Columbus land on his first trip? On which trip did he see Central America?

and navigators about their trips at sea, Columbus decided to try to sail west to Asia. The king of Portugal would not pay for such a trip. Columbus then went to Spain. Ferdinand and Isabella finally agreed to back his plans.

First Voyage of Columbus

On Friday, August 3, 1492, Columbus and a crew of 90 sailors set off from Palos, Spain. They sailed three ships—the *Niña,* the *Pinta,* and the *Santa Maria.* For more than two months they sailed on, ever westward. Day by day the crew grew more afraid. Would they ever see land again? Many wanted to turn back.

Luckily, signs of land soon appeared. Land birds flew overhead. Two days passed.

Then on October 12 the lookout shouted, "Tierra! (tyer′ə) Tierra!" Land! Land! It was land at last!

Columbus thought he had reached the Indian Ocean and the Indies. Therefore he called the people he found living on the islands "Indians." He named the first island he reached San Salvador, which means Holy Savior in Spanish. Columbus claimed all the lands he touched for Spain. But Columbus had not reached the Indian Ocean. He had sailed into the Caribbean Sea. San Salvador was not an island off the Indies. It was one of the Bahama Islands.

Neither Columbus nor his crew knew that they had not reached India. They sailed back to Spain sure that they had. Columbus took with them six Indians and a

45

little bit of gold the explorers had found. In Spain the members of the crew were honored by Ferdinand and Isabella.

Later Voyages

Columbus made three more voyages west. Each time he found more islands. Once he touched the coast of South America. Another time he traveled along the coast of Central America. But he never found the rich silk and spices that Asia promised.

Columbus believed that if he just kept searching he would finally reach China and Japan. However, that dream never came

The Spaniards sailed to many parts of the world in their search for an all-water route to Asia. Which explorer reached the Mississippi River? Which explorers reached the Pacific Ocean?

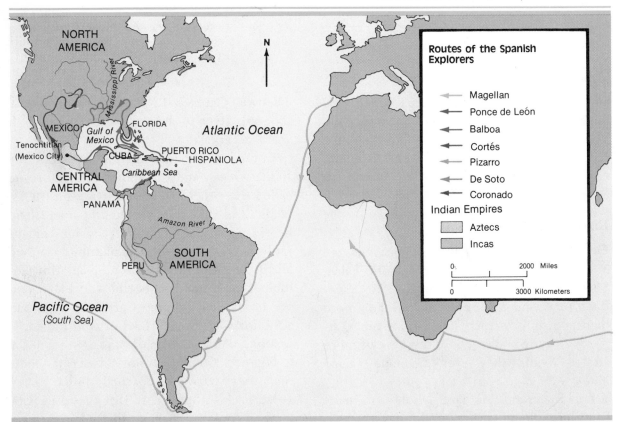

Routes of the Spanish Explorers

- Magellan
- Ponce de León
- Balboa
- Cortés
- Pizarro
- De Soto
- Coronado

Indian Empires
- Aztecs
- Incas

0   2000 Miles
0   3000 Kilometers

NORTH AMERICA
Mississippi River
MEXICO
FLORIDA
Gulf of Mexico
Tenochtitlán (Mexico City)
CUBA
PUERTO RICO
HISPANIOLA
CENTRAL AMERICA
Caribbean Sea
PANAMA
Amazon River
PERU
SOUTH AMERICA
Atlantic Ocean
Pacific Ocean (South Sea)
N

true for him. He died a disappointed and bitter man. Columbus never realized that he had found a "New World" that had been unknown to Europe.

Naming "America"

The first person to understand what Columbus had found was an Italian named Amerigo Vespucci (ve spoo'chē). In 1501 Vespucci sailed south along the east coast of South America. Seeing so much land led Vespucci to believe that Columbus had found an entire continent, not just a few islands.

A German geographer later learned of Vespucci's discovery. He put Vespucci's continent on his map of the world and named it America. This was a form of the name Amerigo.

A Portuguese Accident

In 1500 a ship that was sailing down the coast of Africa was blown off course. The winds took the ship all the way across the Atlantic Ocean. It reached the coast of South America, in what is now Brazil. The ship's captain was Pedro Cabral (kə bräl'). He claimed the land he saw for Portugal.

Other Spaniards Explore the Americas

The voyages of Columbus caused many Spaniards to become interested in the lands he had reached. Adventurers wanted to search for gold there. Other Spaniards were eager to find new lands for their country. Another group, the Spanish priests, wanted to teach the Christian religion to the "Indians."

Ponce de León Explores Florida

Juan Ponce de León (hwän pōns' dā lā on') was the first Spaniard to reach what is now the United States. He had led several trips in search of gold. During Ponce de León's travels in the Caribbean, Indians told him of a magical "fountain of youth." They said that anyone who drank its waters would never grow old.

In the spring of 1513 Ponce de León reached a land north of Cuba. It was full of flowers, so he called it Florida. His crew then went ashore and claimed the land for Spain. They searched for the magical fountain, but never found it. They also did not find any gold.

Balboa Finds the Pacific

Also in 1513, Vasco Núñez de Balboa (väs'kō noo'nyəz dā bal bō'ə) made a startling discovery. He was in charge of an *expedition* (eks'pə dish'ən), or exploring party, to Panama in Central America. Indians told him to travel 50 miles (80 km) west. There he would find "great waters, very great waters," they said.

Balboa and a few followers set off across the Isthmus (is'məs) of Panama. An isthmus is a narrow neck of land connecting two larger bodies of land. The Spaniards made their way over mountains and through steaming jungles. Near the top of the last mountain, Balboa ordered the others to stop. He continued the climb alone.

From the mountain top Balboa looked out on a vast sea. Its waters were quiet and blue. As the first European to look on these waters, Balboa claimed them for Spain. He named the sea the "South Sea." Today we call it the Pacific, or peaceful, Ocean.

Magellan Circles the World

Balboa's discovery proved that the lands the Spaniards had reached were not part of Asia. An ocean lay between the Americas and the Indies. To reach Asia ships would have to sail still farther west.

Ferdinand Magellan (mə jel'ən) was a Portuguese navigator who wanted to sail southwest from Europe. He thought he would find a water route through South America. The Portuguese king was not interested in such a trip. But the king of Spain agreed to pay for the voyage. Sailing for Spain, Magellan set out with five ships in September 1519.

Magellan's ships searched for a water route through South America for a year. Many members of the crew wanted to turn back to Spain. One ship did slip away and escape home. Another was shipwrecked. Finally, in October 1520, Magellan's ships found a water passage near the southern tip of South America. Three ships sailed 320 miles (512 km) through icy and stormy waters before they reached the Pacific Ocean. This passage is now called the Strait of Magellan in honor of the explorer.

The worst was far from over, though. For months Magellan's ships sailed northwest, without ever seeing land. Many of the crew grew ill and died of hunger and disease. In March 1521 the ships at last came upon a group of islands. Magellan named the islands the Philippines, after Prince Philip, the son of the king of Spain. While in the Philippines Magellan took part in a local fight and was killed.

Three years after Magellan's expedition left Spain, one ship, the *Victoria,* returned home. It was the first ship ever to sail completely around the earth. However, the losses had been great. Of the 265 members who had begun the voyage, only 18 people returned.

Do You Know?

1. Who were the Vikings? What did they accomplish?
2. Why was Prince Henry of Portugal known as "Henry the Navigator"?
3. Why did Europeans want to find a new trade route to Asia?
4. Where in the Americas did Columbus land on his first voyage?
5. How did America get its name?

Before You Go On

Using New Words

glaciers	adobe	sagas
nomads	civilization	expedition
totem poles	Vikings	potlatch

The phrases below explain the words or terms listed above. Number a paper from 1 through 9. After each number write the word or term that matches each definition.

1. The first Europeans to reach North America
2. An advanced way of life that includes governments, many kinds of skilled workers, the study of nature, and often a way of writing
3. Huge sheets of ice
4. A type of brick made of sun-dried clay
5. A group of people sent to explore an area
6. A feast given by Pacific Northwest Indians to show off the wealth of the host and hostess
7. Wandering hunters
8. Old stories that tell the history of the Vikings
9. Sculptures made from tree trunks by the Pacific Northwest Indians

Finding the Facts

1. Who were the first people to live in the Americas? Where did they come from? How did these people get to the Americas?
2. Why was life fairly easy for the Pacific Northwest Indians?
3. Why did few Indians live in the Intermountain Region?
4. How were houses of the Southwest Indians different from houses of the Eastern Woodland Indians?
5. Name two parts of the Maya culture that helped make the life of its people richer.
6. Describe the city of Tenochtitlán in the 1300s.
7. How do we know about the voyages of the Vikings?
8. Why did Europeans want to trade with Asia?
9. How did Prince Henry of Portugal help Europeans learn more about the world?
10. What was Columbus hoping to find when he sailed west from Spain?
11. Why did Columbus call the people of the Caribbean Islands "Indians"?

3

The Search for Riches Continues

Europeans were sure they would find riches in the Americas if they kept on looking for them. The Spaniards searched the warmer lands. Explorers from other nations, however, decided to keep looking for a route to Asia.

Cortés Conquers the Aztecs

Just a few months before Magellan set sail, a Spanish adventurer set out on a different kind of trip. While in Cuba, Hernando Cortés (er nän′dō kôr tes′) heard tales of a land called Mexico. The tales said that the Aztecs who lived there owned great amounts of gold and jewels.

Cortés decided to conquer the Aztecs and to take their gold. Therefore, he formed a small army and sailed for Mexico. After a long march inland and upland, Cortés and his army reached the Aztec capital of Tenochtitlán. The Spaniards were stunned at what they saw. Few cities in Europe were as beautiful as Tenochtitlán.

Montezuma (mon′tə zoo′mə) was the Aztec ruler at the time. He offered Cortés gifts of gold, silver, and fine cloth. Montezuma hoped the Spaniards would take the

The Aztecs of Mexico thought Cortés was a god. Therefore, they gave him many gifts when he arrived there in the 1500s.

50

gifts and leave. But Cortés wanted all the treasures of the Aztecs. He took Montezuma prisoner, and fighting broke out. The wooden and stone Aztec weapons were no match for the iron guns and swords of the Europeans. By 1521 Cortés had conquered the Aztec people.

Pizarro Conquers the Incas

In 1532 Francisco Pizarro (fran sis′kō pi zär′ō) conquered the Incas of Peru, in much the same way that Cortés had taken Mexico. Pizarro had heard about the golden treasures of the Incas while he was in Panama with Balboa. As soon as he could, Pizarro gathered an army and sailed for Peru.

Once again guns defeated an Indian people. Pizarro killed the Inca ruler. Then Pizarro's army captured the Incas' cities and their gold. Spain had won another rich prize.

Spaniards Explore Inland

In the early 1500s several groups of Spanish explorers traveled through the central part of what is now the United States. They did not find gold, but they saw wonders such as the Mississippi River and the Grand Canyon.

De Soto Finds the Mississippi River

One of the men with Pizarro in Peru was Hernando De Soto (də sō′tō). De Soto had heard tales of another golden treasure. Indians told him that "Seven Cities of Cibola

(sē′bə lə)" were far north of Mexico. These cities were said to be rich in gold and other treasures.

In 1539 De Soto set out from Florida and traveled north and west in search of the seven cities. His group never found the cities, but they did reach the river that the Indians called the "Father of Waters." It was the great Mississippi River.

The Travels of Coronado

Interest in the "Seven Cities" did not die. Another expedition soon went to search for them. It was led by Francisco Vasquez de Coronado (kôr′ə nä′dō). The guide of the group was Estevanico (es′tā vä nē′kō). He was a North African who had been on other trips in the Americas.

In 1540 Coronado's expedition traveled north from Mexico to search for the fabled cities. He failed to find them. On the journey, though, the group saw the Grand Canyon, in present-day Arizona. The explorers claimed much of what is now the southwestern part of the United States for Spain.

Looking for a Northwest Passage

England, France, the Netherlands, and other European nations also were interested in the Americas. Like Magellan, their explorers wanted to find a water passage through the Americas to Asia. They decided to explore North America for this passage, which they called the Northwest Passage.

This old map tells us what the Europeans with Cartier thought they would find in North America. How is Canada shown here?

Cabot Sails for the English

England had sent its first explorer to sail west to find Asia in 1497. At that time Europeans did not yet know that there was a North America. The lands the Europeans had reached were thought to be islands.

John Cabot was an Italian navigator hired by the English king. In 1497 Cabot sailed west from England with only one ship and a crew of 18. A few weeks later he reached shore. He called it a "new-found land." Like Columbus, Cabot thought he had reached Asia. However, the place he had reached was an island off the coast of Canada. He called it Newfoundland.

The next year, 1498, Cabot again sailed west from England. This time he only sailed near the North American mainland. England later claimed much of North America because of the explorations of Cabot.

French Explorers Reach the Atlantic Coast

France began its search for a Northwest Passage in 1524. The French king hired an Italian navigator named Giovanni da Verrazano (jē ō vän′ē dä ver′ə zän′ō) to find it. Verrazano explored much of the eastern coast of the present-day United States.

The Frenchman Jacques Cartier (zhäk kär tē ā′) set out to look for the Northwest Passage 10 years later. Cartier thought he had found it when he sailed into the Gulf of St. Lawrence and up the St. Lawrence River. But he soon reached a point where his ship could go no farther because of the rapids. He was near the place where the present-day city of Montreal (mon′trē ôl′) is built. Disappointed, Cartier turned the ship around and sailed back.

The French Journey Inland

The French did not give up on their search for the Northwest Passage. In 1603 Samuel de Champlain (sham plān′) sailed farther up the St. Lawrence River to search for the Northwest Passage. In 1615 he also set out to find the large lakes that he heard were to the west. He made it as far as Lake Huron and Lake Ontario.

Marquette and Joliet

In 1673, two more French explorers reached the Great Lakes. There Father Jacques Marquette (zhäk mär ket′) and Louis Joliet (l ōō′ē jō′lē et′) heard the Indians talking about the "mitchee seepee." These Indian words mean "great flowing water." Marquette and Joliet thought that perhaps this water was the Northwest Passage.

From Lake Michigan the two explorers made their way south by canoe. They followed two small rivers and then came upon the "mitchee seepee." The explorers began paddling down it. After a while, Marquette and Joliet realized that the "great flowing water," the Mississippi River, flowed only south. It did not turn west. The explorers decided to turn back.

Robert de La Salle

In 1682 the French explorer Robert Cavelier, sieur de La Salle (sur də lə sal′) finished the journey that Marquette and Joliet had begun. La Salle and 54 French and Indian explorers made it all the way down the Mississippi River. They then sailed into the Gulf of Mexico. La Salle claimed the Mississippi River and all the land around it for France. In honor of King Louis XIV of France, La Salle named the whole area Louisiana.

Hudson—for the Netherlands and England

In the early 1600s the Netherlands joined the search for the Northwest Passage to Asia. In 1609 the Dutch East India company hired Henry Hudson, who was English, to find a Northwest Passage.

In his search for the Northwest Passage, Hudson in his ship the *Half Moon* sailed across the Atlantic Ocean. Hudson explored several bays with no success. Then Hudson reached New York Bay and began sailing up a great river. But 150 miles (240 km) up the river, he decided that the river did not lead westward. Disappointed, Hud-

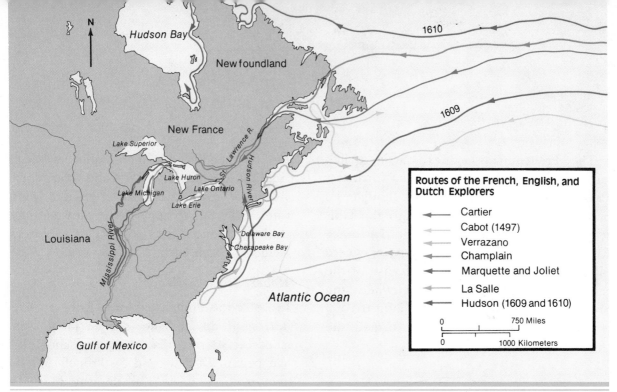

Cabot's voyage gave England a claim to North America. Which French explorers are on the map? Trace Hudson's routes.

son returned to the Netherlands. As a result of Hudson's voyage, the Netherlands claimed the area around the great river. This river is now called the Hudson River.

In 1610 a group of English traders hired Hudson to try once more to find a Northwest Passage. This time Hudson sailed farther north along Canada's coastline. There he made his way into a great bay. Today this body of water is called Hudson Bay. Hudson spent several weeks exploring the huge bay. Then winter set in. Ice froze Hudson's ship, the *Discovery,* and he and his crew had to stay in the bay for months.

By spring the starving, sick crew angrily put Hudson, his son, and seven other men into a small boat with no food or water. Then the crew cast the boat adrift. None of

the castaways was ever heard of again. Hudson's explorations, however, made it possible for England to claim another large part of North America.

Do You Know?

1. Why were the conquests of Cortés and Pizarro important to Spain?
2. Which Spanish explorer first saw the Mississippi River?
3. What part of North America did Jacques Cartier explore?
4. Who claimed Louisiana for France?
5. Why were Henry Hudson's voyages important?

4

The First American Colonies

By the 1600s several European nations claimed lands in the Americas. To hold onto the lands they claimed, the Europeans decided to send people overseas to settle in America. They would start *colonies* (kol'ə nēz). A colony is a settlement that lies far away from the country that governs it. Spain was the first country to set up colonies in the Americas.

Colonies for Spain

Spain claimed a large part of the land in the Americas. These lands included most of South America, Central America, Mexico, the islands of the Caribbean, Florida, and what is now the southwestern part of the United States. Spain's land in North America was called New Spain.

Spain had great hopes for its American *empire* (em'pīr). An empire is a group of lands and people under the control of one country. The Spaniards wanted the colonies of their empire to provide wealth for Spain. They looked forward to gold and silver from mines in Mexico and Peru. The Spaniards also started farms and ranches that would supply food, leather, and wool.

St. Augustine in Florida

The first lasting Spanish settlement in the present-day United States was made in Florida. The spot chosen for it was near the place where Ponce de León first had landed on North American soil. The settlement was named St. Augustine.

St. Augustine was built in 1565 as a fort. Its purpose was to drive away the French and any others who might try to take land in Florida. The fort also was given the job of protecting the "treasure fleets" that sailed from Mexico to Spain. In time a lovely city grew up around the fort. Today St. Augustine is the oldest city in the United States.

The Development of the Missions

Many Spanish settlements began as *missions* (mish'ənz). Missions were places, started by priests called missionaries, where they could stay while teaching the Indians about Christianity. The mission was built around a church. There were many buildings, including barns for animals, tool sheds, and storage rooms.

A fort almost always was built near a mission. Soldiers at the fort guarded the mission and nearby ranches and farms. Once the mission and fort were finished, Spanish settlers followed. A new community was founded.

Missions in California

In 1769 missionaries and Spanish soldiers moved into what is now California. Span-

This drawing is of a California *mission*. The square in front of the church was a busy place. Near the church are storehouses and other places for living and working.

iards led by Father Junipero Serra (hoō nē′pə rō ser′ə) set up a mission near present-day San Diego. This was the first of 21 missions he founded in California. Many of California's important cities today grew up around or near these missions. San Francisco, Monterey, Santa Barbara, and Santa Clara are a few of these cities.

French Colonies

While Spain's empire grew larger, other European nations began to start their own settlements. The French, the Dutch, and the Swedes hoped that they, too, would gain wealth from the lands they claimed in North America. Like Spain, France was able to build a large empire.

France Profits from Fish and Fur

The land claimed by France's explorers was very large. New France was made up of all the land around the St. Lawrence River, the Great Lakes, and the entire Mississippi River. New France was important to France because it had two very important natural resources—fish and furs. Both resources were in great demand in Europe.

Many French fishing boats came to the Grand Banks near Newfoundland, which had huge schools of fish. Fishing stations were opened along the Atlantic Coast. French hunters and traders came to New France to take part in the fur trade. They set up trading posts along the St. Lawrence and Mississippi rivers. Most of these traders were single and kept on the move.

The French king sent Samuel de Champlain to set up permanent settlements in New France. In 1608 Champlain came upon an Indian village high on top of a cliff along the St. Lawrence River. Here he founded Quebec, France's first permanent settlement in America. In 1608 Champlain also founded a trading post called Montreal farther up the river. Both settlements grew into important centers for the fur trade.

Champlain wanted French families to come to New France and start farms. Within a few years, there were many farms along the banks of the St. Lawrence and the Mississippi rivers. In honor of what he had done, Champlain is called "the Father of New France."

The Dutch in New Netherland

In 1624, fifteen years after Henry Hudson sailed up the Hudson River, Dutch fur traders arrived in America. They set up fur-trading posts along the river. The Dutch West India Company also began to settle the land along the Hudson River. The colony that developed was called New Netherland.

The Dutch West India Company chose Peter Minuit (min′ə wit) to be the governor of New Netherland. In 1624 Minuit arranged for the Indians of Manhattan Island to sell the island to him for about 24 dollars worth of beads and other small items. Manhattan was then named New Amsterdam. Minuit made New Amsterdam

the capital of the colony of New Netherland. New Amsterdam soon grew into a busy trade center. Later its name was changed to New York.

Some members of the Dutch West India Company bought large pieces of land along the Hudson River from the company. The landowners divided each piece of land into many small farms. These farms made their owners rich.

The Dutch and Swedes had a few small *colonies* in North America. Where along the Atlantic Coast was the Swedish colony? The Dutch colony?

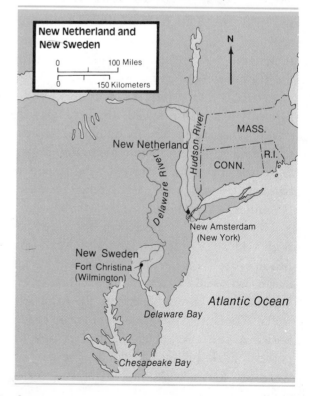

New Netherland and New Sweden

0   100 Miles

0   150 Kilometers

N

New Netherland

Hudson River

Delaware River

MASS.

CONN.

R.I.

New Amsterdam (New York)

New Sweden
Fort Christina (Wilmington)

Atlantic Ocean

Delaware Bay

Chesapeake Bay

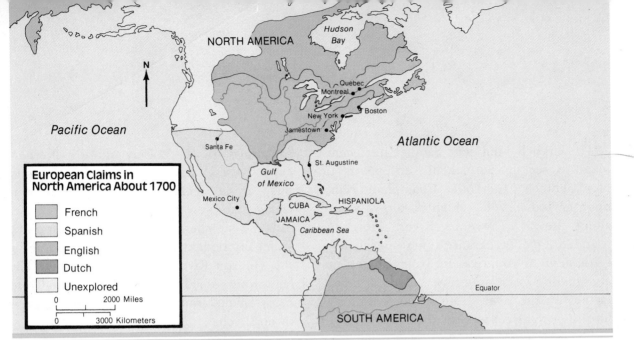

By 1700 the Spaniards, French, and English had claimed large parts of North America. Which place was not explored?

New Sweden on the Delaware

In 1631 the Dutch West India Company replaced Peter Minuit as governor. Minuit then went to Sweden and helped to form the New Sweden Company.

In 1638 two ships of colonists under Minuit's leadership sailed up the Delaware River. Once again Minuit bought land from the Indians. On this land he founded Fort Christina, named in honor of the queen of Sweden. Today, this settlement is called Wilmington, Delaware.

The colonists cleared land for farms on both sides of the Delaware River. The Swedes used logs from the trees they cut down to make cabins. The logs were stacked one above another to form the walls. Then mud was placed in the spaces between the logs. This held the logs together and kept out the wind. The Swedes were the first settlers in North America to build log cabins. Other settlers soon copied this type of house because it was quick and easy to build.

The Swedish farms did well because of the fertile soil along the Delaware river. The colony of New Sweden spread into parts of what are now Delaware, New Jersey, and Pennsylvania.

Do You Know?

1. What is a colony?
2. Why did the Spanish missionaries come to the Americas?
3. Who started the first permanent French settlements in North America?
4. What was the name of the Dutch colony in North America?

5

The English Colonies

The English started colonies in the Americas soon after the Spaniards. However, it took time for the English to succeed. The land and climate along the northeastern coast of North America caused many problems at first.

Queen Elizabeth Looks to North America

In 1558 a young woman came to the throne of England. She was Queen Elizabeth I. The new queen had great hopes for her country. She had watched Spain grow wealthy from the gold, silver, and other riches sent from America. Now she wanted her country to gain profits from America, too.

Queen Elizabeth secretly encouraged English pirates, called "sea dogs," to attack the treasure fleets. After the sea dogs captured a ship, they carried their booty back to England.

Drake Sails Around the World

Queen Elizabeth was a great admirer of the sailor Francis Drake. Therefore she gladly backed his plan to sail to the west coast of South America and rob one of Spain's greatest treasure ships. Drake succeeded. However, to escape the Spaniards he had to sail back to England by way of the Pacific Ocean, the Indian Ocean, and the Cape of Good Hope. This voyage made him the first Englishman to sail around the world.

When Drake arrived back in England, Queen Elizabeth came aboard his ship, the *Golden Hind*. There she showed her thanks by making him a knight—Sir Francis Drake.

Queen Elizabeth of England welcomed Francis Drake as soon as he returned from his trip around the world. She visited him aboard his ship, the *Golden Hind*.

The First English Colony

Queen Elizabeth also wanted English colonies to be started in the Americas. Therefore, she offered a *charter* (char'tər), or written permission to a person or group, to make a settlement. A charter gave its holders a large piece of land. It also gave them the right to govern that land and to trade.

The Lost Colony—Roanoke

Sir Walter Raleigh (rô'lē) was one of the first people to ask the Queen for a charter. Elizabeth gladly granted Raleigh the right to colonize an area he named Virginia. The place Raleigh chose for the first settlement was Roanoke Island, off the coast of present-day North Carolina. In 1585 Raleigh sent a group to colonize Roanoke Island. But the colonists did not like living there. When an English ship came by the next year, the colonists happily boarded it.

Two years later Raleigh tried again. This time he sent over 100 men, women, and children to Roanoke. They sailed under the leadership of Governor John White.

It soon became clear that the colony would need help to get through the coming winter. Governor White set sail for England, promising to return soon. White left behind his family, including his granddaughter, Virginia Dare. She was the first English child born in North America.

It was three years before Governor White returned to Roanoke Island. In the meantime, war had broken out between England and Spain. No English ships sailed to America at this time. When White's ship finally returned to Roanoke, no settlers ran out to meet it. The ship's sailors entered the town. Forts and houses stood empty.

The only clue was the word CROATOAN carved on a doorpost. There was an island named Croatoan nearby, but there were no colonists there either. What had happened to them? No one has ever solved the mystery of the "Lost Colony."

The Founding of Jamestown

Raleigh's lack of success did not stop others from trying to start colonies for England. In 1606 English merchants formed the London Company and the Plymouth Company. Both of these companies received charters for land in Virginia from the English king, James I.

In December 1606 the London Company sent three ships and 144 men across the stormy Atlantic Ocean. It was spring of 1607 before the worn-out travelers sailed into Chesapeake Bay and up the James River. They named the river for their king. On land that stuck out into the river they built their settlement of Jamestown.

The Jamestown colonists faced many problems. The place they had chosen to settle was low and swampy. There were many mosquitoes and other insects. Then, too, few of the men had the skills needed to live in the wilderness. They did not know how to put up buildings or how to farm. The colonists only wanted to search

Virginia tobacco sold well in London. What does the ad tell you about the tobacco grown in the Virginia *colony*?

for gold. The result was that when winter came, the colony was not prepared. The food the settlers had brought with them from England ran out. Many of the men starved. By spring, only 40 of the colonists were alive.

At this time a strong leader, Captain John Smith, took charge of the colony. The captain was able to get some food from the Indians. He then made a rule for the survivors: "He who will not work shall not eat."

Then Captain Smith was badly injured in a gunpowder explosion. He returned to England to be cared for and never came back to America. Without Smith's leadership, many of the settlers again refused to work. Some of them also angered the neighboring Indians, bringing on Indian attacks. During the very cold winter of 1609–1610 many colonists died. This period was so difficult it came to be called "the starving time." By the spring only a few settlers were alive.

Jamestown Succeeds

Three more ships of settlers were sent to Jamestown. Among the new colonists were many skilled workers and farmers. This was the turning point for the colony. More people wanted to settle in Jamestown after the London Company decided to give the settlers their own land to work. Then in 1619 about 90 women arrived in Jamestown to marry the male settlers. Until then most of the settlers had been men. In that same year the first blacks arrived in Jamestown.

John Rolfe, one of the colonists, found a way to bring wealth to Jamestown. He began to grow tobacco, which Europeans had begun to smoke. King James disliked the habit and called smoking "hateful to the nose, harmful to the brain, dangerous to the lungs." Nonetheless, the Jamestown settlers grew all the tobacco they could. Many grew wealthy.

The Founding of Plymouth

The Plymouth Company also found a group that was willing to go to America. The group was called the Pilgrims. The Pilgrims were people who left England to search for religious freedom. England had one chief religion—the Church of England. According to English law, all citizens had to pay to support this religion. But the Pilgrims did not want to belong to the Church of England. They wanted to separate themselves from it.

The Pilgrims decided to go to the Netherlands. There they could worship as they wished. But within a few years, the Pilgrims wanted to leave the Netherlands.

A

Early Settlements

The people who settled America long ago built many kinds of houses. The only ones that lasted, however, were those made out of stone and brick. In the Navajo National Monument in Arizona, we still can see houses that were built into the cliffs (E). Many families lived there in apartments. Parts of early European forts also remain. This fort was built by the Spaniards in St. Augustine, Florida (F).

We also know what early settlements look like from old pictures. This French fort on Parris Island, South Carolina, for example, was left to fall apart (A). The Dutch town of Albany once looked like this picture (C). Its old buildings were torn down to put up skyscrapers.

To save America's heritage, some places decided to rebuild their old buildings. As a result, we can visit Jamestown, Virginia, to see what the first permanent English settlement in the country looked like (B). Old Sturbridge Village in Massachusetts also has many old homes and shops (D). The people who work in these places wear clothing like that of the settlers.

E

B

C

D

F

63

They missed the English way of life. The Pilgrims also feared that their children were becoming more Dutch than English.

The Pilgrims decided to settle in America. The Plymouth Company and the English king gave them permission to start a colony in Virginia. In August 1620, two small ships set sail for America from England. They were the *Speedwell* and the *Mayflower*. The *Speedwell* soon proved too leaky for the voyage. Its passengers went aboard the *Mayflower*. The tiny ship set off alone, crowded with 101 settlers and its crew.

The *Mayflower* headed for Virginia, but it went off course. In November sailors finally saw land. It was the coast of present-day Massachusetts, much farther north than Virginia. The Pilgrims decided they would settle where they were rather than sail south to Virginia. They would have more religious freedom in their own colony. Before going ashore, however, the Pilgrims drew up a plan of government. They promised to live together peacefully. They also agreed to make only "just and equal laws . . . for the general good of everyone." Their plan came to be called the Mayflower Compact.

The Pilgrims called their settlement Plymouth. They started to work immediately, but winter soon set in. Without enough food and good shelter, half the Pilgrims died. In spring the survivors could have gone back to England. Instead, they stayed on, planting crops and building sturdy homes.

Indians and Pilgrims

Luckily, the Pilgrims had the help of the Indians. One of these Indians was named Squanto (skwän′tō). He had once been kidnapped by an English sea captain and had learned to speak English. Squanto taught the Pilgrims how to hunt and how to plant seeds of corn wrapped in a herring. The herring fertilized the soil, or made it richer.

By the fall of 1621 the Pilgrims were able to harvest their own crops. They knew how to hunt the game around them—turkey, geese, ducks, and deer. To give thanks the Pilgrims held a grand feast. They invited Squanto and other Indian friends to join them. At this first Thanksgiving, the meal included roast deer and duck, clams, cornbread, and wine made from wild grapes. There were still hard times ahead for the Pilgrims. But they had succeeded in founding the second permanent English settlement in America.

Do You Know?

1. Where was Sir Walter Raleigh's colony located?
2. What was the first permanent English colony in America?
3. Why did Jamestown finally succeed?
4. Who settled the colony of Plymouth?
5. What was the Mayflower Compact?

To Help You Learn

Using New Words

colonies   missions
empire   charter

The phrases below explain the words listed
above. Number a paper from 1 through 4.
After each number write the word that matches
each definition.

1. Settlements built around a church and run
   by missionaries to teach the people of the
   area about Christianity
2. Written permission given by the
   government to set up a settlement
3. Groups of settlers living far away from the
   country that governs them
4. Lands and people under the power of one
   country

Finding the Facts

1. Why did early peoples cross northern Asia
   into North America?
2. Why did Europeans want an all-water trade
   route to Asia?
3. What did Magellan's voyage prove about
   the Americas?
4. What part of what is now the United
   States did Ponce de León, De Soto, and
   Coronado each explore for Spain?
5. Which explorer first claimed land in the
   Americas for England? How did England
   try to hold its claim?

6. What explorer claimed land in North
   America for the Netherlands?
7. What part of North America did each of
   the following Frenchmen explore: Cartier,
   Champlain, Joliet and Marquette, and
   La Salle?
8. How did Swedish settlers build their log
   cabins? Why did other settlers soon copy
   this type of house?
9. What was England's first permanent
   settlement in America? When was it
   founded?
10. Why did the Pilgrims come to North
    America?

Learning from Maps

1. Look at the map of major Indian groups on
   page 34. Name the major Indian groups.
   Which group lived farthest west? To which
   group did the Seminole belong? To which
   group did the Sioux belong? How does the
   map show the boundaries between each
   group?
2. Turn to the map of Columbus's voyages on
   page 45. During what years did Columbus
   make his voyages? Use the scales of
   distance to measure the distance from Spain
   to San Salvador.
3. Look at the map showing routes of major
   Spanish explorers in the Americas on page
   46. How does the map help you tell one

explorer's route from another? How does the map show Coronado's route? Which explorer traveled from Hispaniola to Panama? Which river did De Soto cross? From which island did Ponce de León begin his travels?

4. Turn to the map showing the routes of French, English, and Dutch explorers on page 54. Where did Verrazano explore? To what part of North America did Hudson sail in 1609? What place did Hudson reach in 1610? Who sailed up the St. Lawrence River? Which explorers made their way to the Mississippi River? Which explorer sailed all the way down the river to the Gulf of Mexico?

5. Study the map of North America in 1700 on page 58. Which country claimed the largest part of North America? Who had charge of the land where Jamestown was built? Which country had charge of the lands where Santa Fe and St. Augustine were started?

Using Study Skills

1. **Pictures.** Look again at the pictures on pages 37 and 39. They show Indian life before Europeans came to the Americas. Does anything about the Indian ways of life shown in these pictures seem to be alike? In what ways are the Indians shown to be different from one another?

2. **Chart.** One way to organize information is to put it into chart form. Below is an incomplete chart about early settlements in the Americas. The first row has been completed for you. Copy the chart onto a sheet of paper. Then complete the chart.

Name of Settlement	Year Founded	Where Founded	Founding Country
St. Augustine	1565	Florida	Spain
	1607	Virginia	
Quebec			
	1620	Massachusetts	
New Amsterdam		New York	
	1769	California	

Thinking It Through

1. There were no European journeys to the Americas for almost 500 years after the Vikings left North America. Why do you think so many Europeans came to the Americas after the voyages of Columbus?
2. Someone once said that Columbus's landing in America was "a lucky accident." Do you agree with this statement? Explain.
3. How did each of these things help Jamestown to succeed: (a) Captain John Smith's leadership, (b) the growing of tobacco, (c) the arrival of women in 1619?
4. Today American spaceships reach planets that are far from the earth as they explore the universe. How is space exploration today like the journeys to the Americas in the 1400s and 1500s? How is it different?

Projects

1. The Explorers' Committee might find out more about Henry Hudson's last voyage. As you know, Hudson, his son, and seven sailors were put aboard a small boat and left to themselves. They were never heard from again. Why did this happen? What do people think became of Hudson?
2. The Research Committee might study American Indian names. More than half of the 50 states in the United States have Indian names. Does your state have an Indian name? What Indian groups lived in your state before the Europeans arrived? Use an encyclopedia to find out how these early Indians lived.
3. The Reading Committee might look for books with stories the Aztecs believed in and told their children. Members of the committee might, for example, tell the class stories of the Plumed Serpent and the Smoking Mirror.
4. Look at the pictures on pages 50 and 56. Who are the people shown in each picture? What does each picture tell about life in America at the time? Why might someone want to visit these places today?
5. Prepare a bulletin board display about the Vikings. It could have pictures of Viking sailing ships, clothing, and types of homes. You might also include maps of Viking trips to North America.
6. Imagine that you were a sailor on the ship of Dias or da Gama. Write a letter to your parents describing the voyage. You might mention the places you visited during the journey and your feelings about the trip.

3 Becoming a Nation

Unit Preview

The British started many colonies in North America. Some colonists came to the Americas to find religious freedom. Others came for adventure and to find riches. Soon there were 13 colonies. They formed three geographic groups—the New England Colonies, the Middle Colonies, and the Southern Colonies. Most of the colonists were farmers.

After a war with the French, the British gained almost all of France's empire in North America. To pay for the war, however, the British began to tax the colonists for products such as paper, tea, sugar, and stamps.

The colonists tried to gain their rights from Great Britain. They even wrote to King George III about their problems. The king did not answer the letter. The colonists then decided to break away from Britain. They issued a Declaration of Independence on July 4, 1776. In order to win their independence, however, the colonists had to fight a war. Fighting had begun at Lexington in 1775, and it ended when the British surrendered at Yorktown in 1781.

Many Europeans helped the Americans to fight the British. After the battle of Saratoga, the French openly came to the aid of Americans. Women and black Americans also played important parts in winning the Revolution.

Things to Discover

If you look carefully at the picture map, and time line, you can answer these questions.

1. The map shows the 13 colonies in North America. What ocean borders these colonies? How can you tell where one colony ends and another begins?
2. The picture shows colonists marching in Massachusetts. How can you tell that the marchers are not British soldiers?
3. When was Connecticut founded?
4. How long after Maryland was Pennsylvania founded?
5. How long after the Boston Massacre did the Boston Tea Party take place?
6. When did the First Continental Congress meet? How long after this meeting was the Declaration of Independence adopted?

Words to Learn

You will meet these words in this unit. As you read, you will learn what they mean and how to pronounce them. The Word List will help you.

assembly	Parliament
boycott	Patriots
democracy	plantations
indentured servants	repealed
independence	representative
Loyalists	treaty
militia	

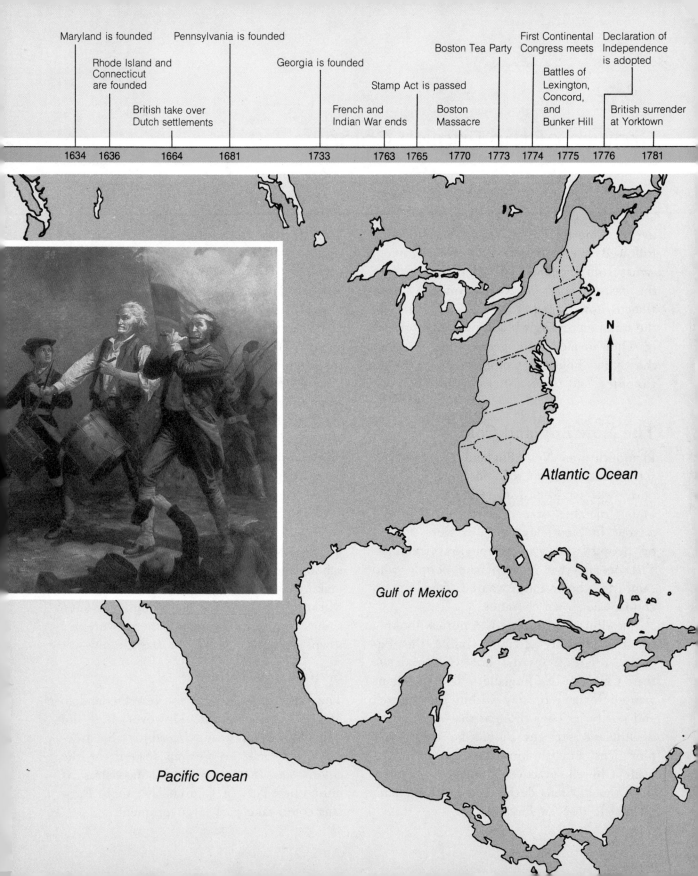

Maryland is founded

Rhode Island and
Connecticut
are founded

British take over
Dutch settlements

Pennsylvania is founded

Georgia is founded

French and
Indian War ends

Stamp Act is passed

Boston
Massacre

Boston Tea Party

First Continental
Congress meets

Battles of
Lexington,
Concord,
and
Bunker Hill

Declaration of
Independence
is adopted

British surrender
at Yorktown

1634 1636   1664   1681   1733   1763 1765   1770   1773 1774 1775 1776   1781

Atlantic Ocean

Gulf of Mexico

Pacific Ocean

N

1
Growth of the English Colonies

Once a few colonists had proved they could live in America, more people from Europe followed them. Most of the newcomers came from England. They settled all along the eastern coast of North America, from what is now Canada to Florida. As a result, the number of English colonies grew quickly. They formed three geographic groups—the New England Colonies, the Middle Colonies, and the Southern Colonies.

The New England Colonies

Plymouth was New England's first lasting settlement. As you read in Unit 2, Plymouth was started for religious reasons. Many of the other colonies that were started in New England also were started by people who wanted religious freedom. That means that most of the people who came to the region wanted freedom to choose their own churches.

The Puritans came to America looking for freedom of religion. Unlike the Pilgrims, the Puritans did not want to leave the Church of England. The Puritans wanted instead to stay within the Church and purify it. They thought that the Church of England services should be made simpler. The English king, however, did not want Church practices "purified." Therefore, the Puritans decided to leave England and settle in New England.

Founding Massachusetts Bay Colony

The English king gave the Puritans the right to settle in Massachusetts, north of Plymouth. This group of Puritans called itself the Massachusetts Bay Company, and promised to trade with England.

The first Puritans arrived in Massachusetts in 1628 and started the fishing village of Salem. However, many of the colonists grew ill from the damp air. When 1,000 more Puritans arrived in 1630, they decided to look for a healthier spot. Under Governor John Winthrop they sailed farther south. They chose a place where a clear stream flowed into Massachusetts Bay. There the Puritans built a new community —Boston.

The Puritan settlement of Boston grew quickly. Many of its colonists had gone to school and were used to giving orders and making choices. Many others were skilled workers who could make things and keep things running. By 1640 there were 22 towns in the Massachusetts Bay Colony.

Settling Rhode Island

The Puritans had come to New England to find religious freedom. However, they did not allow other groups to enjoy this freedom. Instead, the Puritan leaders of the colony said that everyone in Massachusetts must obey Puritan Church law. Only Puritans could take part in government.

A young Puritan minister named Roger Williams did not agree with the Puritan leaders. He believed that all people should be free to worship as they wished. He also said that the Puritans had taken land unfairly from the Indians. Williams thought that the colonists should have paid the Indians for the land.

The Puritan leaders planned to send Williams back to England. However, Williams escaped one cold winter evening. He stayed for a while with the Narragansett (nar′ə gan′sit) Indians. Then in the spring of 1636 Williams founded the settlement of Providence, on Narragansett Bay. He had bought the land for the colony from the Indians.

Roger Williams soon was joined by others from Massachusetts Bay who also had spoken out against Puritan practices. In 1644 Williams received a charter from the king of England for the colony, which was called Rhode Island.

Anne Hutchinson

The second settlement of Rhode Island was Portsmouth. It was started near Providence by Anne Hutchinson and others. She was born in England in 1591 and came to Massachusetts Bay Colony in 1634 with her husband, William. Although she had 14 children, Anne Hutchinson found time to take part in many community activities.

Anne Hutchinson did not agree with the Puritan leaders of Massachusetts Bay. She

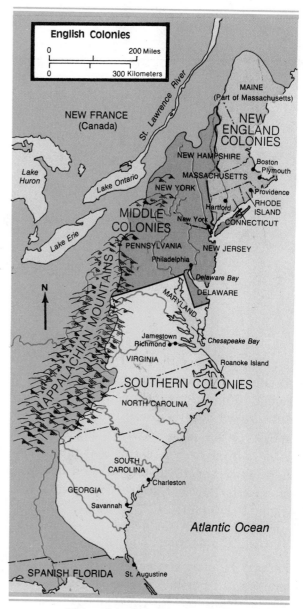

Most of the colonies were not sure where their land ended on the west. The Appalachian Mountains formed the western frontier.

Anne Hutchinson was brought before the Puritan leaders of Boston. At her trial, she refused to give up her beliefs.

held her own religious meetings and told her listeners that they did not always have to look to Church leaders for answers to religious questions. All people could find answers within themselves, she said. She spoke for her ideas so well that the Puritan leaders brought her to trial and then drove her away. Anne Hutchinson then left Massachusetts Bay and started her own settlement, Portsmouth.

Settling Connecticut

Thomas Hooker was another Puritan minister who did not like the strict Puritan laws of Massachusetts. In 1636 he and a group of men, women, and children built a town on the banks of the Connecticut River where Hartford now stands. Other towns

soon were built along the river and along the Atlantic Coast south of Massachusetts and Rhode Island. In 1662 these towns received a charter from the king. They became the colony of Connecticut.

New Hampshire and Maine

You read in Unit 2 that even before the Pilgrims arrived in New England, Europeans had come to this part of North America to fish. Some had settled along the coast north of Massachusetts. For a while these people lived under Massachusetts rule. Then they, too, grew unhappy with the harsh Puritan laws and left. They settled in New Hampshire, which became a separate colony under control of the English king. Some people went to live in land that is now Maine. However, Maine remained part of Massachusetts until 1820.

Life in New England

At first, most of the colonists in New England tried to make their living by farming. This was hard to do because much of the soil of the area is thin and rocky. The growing season is short. As a result, the farms were small. Their owners raised only enough for their own use.

Luckily, the ocean waters off New England were filled with fish. New Englanders began to make their living from the sea. Many fishing villages soon grew up along the Atlantic Coast. Some of the coastal towns became shipbuilding centers. The

Key

1. Church
2. Town Hall
3. Farm
4. Mill
5. Covered Bridge
6. Carpenter Shop
7. General Store and Home
8. Inn
9. School
10. Town Common, or Green

Most New England towns were built along the same plan. Use the key to help you find the different buildings in the town.

rich forests of New England had the wood and other materials needed to build ships.

Other New Englanders became skilled craftspeople. They made the goods that everyone needed—tools, furniture, and dishes, for example. New Englanders began to sell their products to other colonies and to England. Many colonists became traders and merchants. New England's growing trade helped to make Boston a trade center and a large city.

New Englanders had quickly formed their own kind of town government. At first, the colonists had gathered in town meeting houses to talk over the problems and needs of the townspeople. The meeting house also was used as a church. As towns grew larger, however, New Englanders

built town halls in which to hold meetings. Here local laws were made and town officials were chosen. Not all the townspeople could take part in the voting, though. Only white male adults who owned land could hold office and vote.

Religious faith was strong in New England, especially among the Puritans. Each Sunday the whole family went to church. They sat for three hours, singing hymns and listening to a long sermon. Sometimes people fell asleep during these sermons. When they did, church members were awakened by having a feather rubbed under their noses by someone watching them.

The Puritans thought that everyone should be able to read the Bible. Therefore, they taught their children to read and

Many colonial children used a hornbook to help them learn how to write the alphabet.

write at home. A law was passed saying that every New England town with more than 50 families had to have a school. School children learned reading, writing, and arithmetic. Schooling ended for all of the girls and most of the boys after about three grades. Some boys then went on to "grammar schools." There they learned Latin, Greek, mathematics, and other subjects. A few boys went on to Harvard, the first college built in the English colonies.

The Middle Colonies

Settlers from England kept on coming to the colonies, hoping to make a new start in life. England thus needed more land for its settlers. As you read in Unit 2, the land to the south and to the west of New England belonged to the Dutch. To the south of New Netherland was New Sweden. This colony had been taken over by the Dutch in 1655.

Establishing New York

England had wanted to take New Amsterdam, the capital of New Netherland, for some time. The city of New Amsterdam was desired because it had the best harbor on the Atlantic Coast. One day in 1664, four English warships sailed boldly into New Amsterdam harbor. Their commander sent a message to the Dutch governor, Peter Stuyvesant (stī′və sənt). The message demanded that Governor Stuyvesant surrender, or give up his hold over, New Amsterdam.

Governor Stuyvesant did not want to surrender, but the Dutch colonists refused to fight for him. Stuyvesant had ruled badly, and the colonists did not like him. The English therefore were able to take New Amsterdam, and all of New Netherland, without a fight.

The English king, Charles II, gave New Netherland to his brother James, Duke of York. James kept part of the land as a colony for himself. He named it New York.

Founding New Jersey

The Duke of York gave another part of the land taken from the Dutch to two friends, Lord John Berkeley and Sir George Carteret. This land became New Jersey colony.

Berkeley and Carteret were not much interested in running New Jersey and soon sold some of the land. In 1702 the English king took over the colony of New Jersey.

Founding Pennsylvania

To the west of New Jersey was a large area claimed by King Charles II. An Englishman named William Penn longed to have this land for a colony. Penn was a member of a religious group called the Quakers (kwā′ kərz). Many of the beliefs of the Quakers were unpopular in England. For example, the Quakers did not believe in churches that had many officials or too many kinds of services. They did not believe they should fight in wars. Their beliefs caused this group to be treated badly in England.

Penn looked to America as a place where he might start a colony. The Quakers would be able to practice their beliefs freely there. Luckily for the Quakers, Charles II owed Penn's father a large amount of money. When Penn's father died, Penn tried to collect this debt. Instead of money, he asked for the land west of New Jersey. In 1681 the king gave Penn a charter to the land west of the Delaware River. The heavily wooded land came to be called Pennsylvania, which means "Penn's Wood."

Like Roger Williams, Penn believed that the Indians should be paid for their land. Therefore, Penn bought the land from the Delaware Indians. He and the Indians also signed a *treaty* (trē′tē), or agreement between groups of people or nations. In the treaty, the Pennsylvania settlers and the Indians promised to live in peace.

Pennsylvania colony was an immediate success. Penn offered religious freedom to all religious groups, not just to Quakers. He also advertised his colony in papers all over Europe.

Settling Delaware

The area that became the colony of Delaware had passed from Swedish to Dutch to English owners. Soon after the Duke of York gained this land, he sold it to William Penn. It then became part of Pennsylvania. But the people of Delaware wanted to be separate from Pennsylvania. In 1704 Penn allowed Delaware to have its own *assembly* (ə sem′blē), or lawmaking body.

William Penn and the Delaware Indians signed a *treaty* of friendship. Penn and the Quakers were so fair to the Indians that the Indians never attacked the Pennsylvania colony.

A

Colonial Life

Life was hard for the colonists at first. Settlers had to build homes, clear the land, and plant crops (C). Some families started their homes in the wilderness, where there were no stores. Therefore, they looked forward to visits from peddlers, who traveled from place to place to sell their goods (A). Peddlers also brought news from town.

By working hard, many colonists succeeded in making a better life for their families. A number of people in the New England, Middle, and Southern colonies were able to build large farms. Merchants, such as the northern mill owner Moses Marcy, also owned fine homes (E). Their children wore beautiful clothes and had many toys (B).

By the early 1700s, seaports such as Baltimore, Maryland, were growing quickly (F). In the towns, colonists worked at many jobs and crafts. They made silverware, furniture, clothes, and other items. Later, when the colonies became states, craftworkers put scenes of colonial life on what they made. The ride of Paul Revere (D) was favorite scene shown by proud Americans. ■

E

B

C

D

F

New York City was a busy seaport by 1697. Buildings along the waterfront were large and sturdy. Many docks were needed for ships.

Life in the Middle Colonies

Settlers came to the Middle Colonies in search of a better life. Most people were not disappointed. Those who came to farm found rich soil, long and deep rivers, and a fairly long growing season. Farming conditions were much better there than in New England.

The major crop in the Middle Colonies was wheat. Much of the wheat and wheat flour was shipped to other colonies. The area therefore soon became known as the "breadbasket" of America.

A number of farmers in the Middle Colonies grew wealthy. They used their money to buy all kinds of fine goods. Hoping to share in this wealth, craftspeople came in great numbers to the Middle Colonies. Everything from carriages to silverware to wigs poured out of craftspeople's shops.

Such shops lined the streets of the port cities of New York and Philadelphia. Soon merchants were shipping crafted goods as well as agricultural products to other colonies and overseas.

The Middle Colonies had the greatest mix of people and religions of all the colonies. New York still had a large Dutch population. William Penn's advertisements had brought many people from Germany, France, Denmark, Sweden, and Norway. There also was a very large Scotch-Irish population. The families of these were settlers had long ago left Scotland to settle in Ireland. Black settlers were first brought to the area as slaves by the Dutch, in about 1650. A slave is a person who is the property of another person. Some slaves in Middle Colonies were soon given their freedom.

The Southern Colonies

The first of the Southern Colonies to be settled was Virginia. It grew up around the settlement at Jamestown, which you read about in Unit 2. Within its first 75 years, Virginia had become a wealthy tobacco-growing colony. It was to be joined by four other Southern Colonies—one to its north and three to its south.

Founding Maryland

Like many other religious groups, the Roman Catholics were not allowed to practice their religion freely in England. Finally George Calvert, the first Lord Baltimore, decided to try and help the Catholics.

The Calverts were a noble and wealthy family in England. They became Catholics in 1625, and soon afterwards George Calvert asked King Charles I for a charter to start a colony in America. Catholics would be able to worship freely there. Before the king could sign the charter, Calvert died.

The king granted the charter to Calvert's son Cecil, who received 10 million acres (4 million ha) of land north of Virginia. The colony was called Maryland, in honor of Queen Henrietta Maria, the wife of King Charles. In the spring of 1634, 200 settlers reached Maryland. They built the town of St. Mary's at the mouth of the Potomac River.

Settling the Carolinas

Florida, on the southeastern Atlantic Coast, was held by Spain. England and Spain both claimed the land between Virginia and Florida, but no one had settled this land. In 1663 King Charles II gave eight English nobles much of the land between Virginia and Florida. The region came to be called Carolina. This name honored King Charles, whose name in Latin was Carolus.

During the next few years, many settlers came to Carolina. Those who lived in the northern part of the colony soon became tobacco growers. They also cut down and sold the tall pine trees of the area to shipbuilders.

The southern part of Carolina had many swampy lands. Rice grew well in these hot, damp places. So did indigo (in'di gō'), a plant used to make blue dye for cloth. It was Eliza Lucas who was responsible for successfully growing indigo in southern Carolina. Rice and indigo brought wealth to the southern part of the colony. Charleston rapidly became a leading port city.

The owners of Carolina gave the colonists few rights. Many settlers, therefore, chose to live in other colonies. In 1719 the owners sold Carolina to the king. Ten years later the colony was divided into two parts —into the colonies of North Carolina and South Carolina.

Settling Georgia

The first colonies had been founded mainly to make money for their owners or as places where settlers could enjoy religious or political freedom. Georgia, however, was started by James Oglethorpe (ō'gəl

1. Mansion
2. Formal Garden
3. Overseer's House
4. Smokehouse and Kitchen
5. Pastures
6. Carpenter and Blacksmith Shops
7. Stables and Barns
8. Slave Cabins
9. Spinning House
10. Orchards

Many Southern *plantations* were very large. The key will help you understand what made up the plantation.

thôrp') for a different reason. He wanted a settlement for people who were in English prisons for owing money.

At that time people in England who could not pay their debts were put in prison. They were forced to stay there until they could pay. Since they could not earn money while they were in prison, many debtors had no chance of ever getting out of prison.

King George II granted Oglethorpe land in America to set up a colony for debtors. In 1733 Oglethorpe brought 30 families to America. In honor of the king, these settlers named their colony Georgia. They called their first settlement Savannah.

Life in the Southern Colonies

The first land settled in the Southern Colonies was the Atlantic Coastal Plain. This wide, lowland area has rich soil and many rivers running through it to the sea. It was possible for the settlers to build large farms called *plantations* (plan tā'shənz). Each plantation grew one main crop, such as tobacco, rice, or indigo. The plantations generally were built near a river, so planters could ship their own crops to markets along the Atlantic Coast or overseas.

Each plantation made most of what it needed. It grew its own food crops and raised its own animals. It also preserved its own food. The plantation usually had blacksmiths, carpenters, and other craftspeople to make tools and other goods. Also, a plantation could not run without many hands to do the work. Where could the planters find the many workers they needed? They decided to use black slaves.

Slavery in the English colonies began in 1619. At that time a Dutch ship brought 20 Africans to Jamestown. At first the blacks were treated as *indentured servants* (in den'chərd sur'vənts). These were people who worked for a few years for the person who paid for their passage to the colonies. Then the indentured servants were given their freedom. There were already many white indentured servants in the colonies. Some blacks also became free. But as time went on blacks were not freed. Instead they became slaves, the permanent property of their owners.

Not all Southern farmers owned plantations. Most worked much smaller pieces of land by themselves. Only a few of these small landowners owned slaves.

Governing the Colonies

The colonies were under the rule of England. Therefore the colonists set up governments that were much like those in England. Each colony had a lawmaking body, called an assembly. The assembly was made up of *representatives* (rep'ri zen'tə tivz), people who act for those who elect them. The colonial representatives were men who were elected by the white male landowners of the colonies. The first assembly to meet in the colonies was the House of Burgesses (bur'jis əz). Burgess is another word for representative. The House of Burgesses became Virginia's assembly in 1619. This first elected lawmaking body in America was an important step in the growth of American *democracy* (di mok'rə sē), or rule by the people.

In addition to an assembly, each colony also had a head of government called a governor. The governor had a council, which gave advice. Almost all of the colonial officials were men. However, a few women, such as Margaret Brent of Maryland, played important roles in colonial government. When Governor Cecil Calvert of Maryland died, Margaret Brent acted as governor for a time. She also demanded a vote in the Maryland assembly.

Do You Know?

1. Which colonies made up the New England Colonies? The Middle Colonies? The Southern Colonies?
2. Why did Roger Williams leave Massachusetts?
3. Who started Pennsylvania? Why?
4. What is a plantation? In which group of colonies were there plantations?
5. What was the first elected assembly in the English colonies?

Before You Go On

Using New Words

treaty   indentured servants
assembly   representative
plantation   democracy

The phrases below explain the words or terms listed above. Number a paper from 1 through 6. After each number write the word or term that matches each definition.

1. A person who acts for a group
2. A very large farm on which one or more main crops are grown
3. An agreement among groups of people or nations
4. People who worked for others for a few years, in return for payment of their passage to the colonies
5. Government by the people
6. A lawmaking body

Finding the Facts

1. What colony was started by each of the following people: Thomas Hooker, William Penn, Lord Baltimore, James Oglethorpe?
2. How were the views of Roger Williams different from those of most Puritan leaders in Massachusetts Bay Colony?
3. Why did Anne Hutchinson leave Massachusetts?
4. What were two major ways of making a living in the New England colonies?
5. What law passed by the Puritans shows that education was important to them?
6. How did England gain control of New Netherland?
7. Why were the Middle Colonies called the "breadbasket" of America?
8. How did Eliza Lucas help southern Carolina gain wealth?
9. Near what natural feature were most early southern plantations built? What were some of the jobs that were done by plantation workers?
10. Did most southern farmers own plantations?
11. What was the House of Burgesses? Who went to its meetings?
12. Who was Margaret Brent?
13. How were indentured servants different from slaves?

2
Road to Independence

By 1750 more than 1 million English colonists lived along the Atlantic Coast. Within 20 years that number doubled. As a result, new colonists moved west, where the land was still unsettled. They went across the Appalachian Mountains into the Ohio River Valley. There they ran into trouble.

Both France and England (now called Great Britain) said they owned the land between the Appalachians and the Mississippi River. Here, the French had built up a rich fur trade with the Indians. France did not want to lose its land or its trade. Relations between France and Britain grew worse.

The French and Indian War

The French built a number of forts in the Ohio Valley, beginning in 1753. This angered the British. In 1754, therefore, the governor of Virginia sent the *militia* (mi lish'ə) to stop the French from building more forts. The militia was a group of colonists who served as soldiers when they were needed. Led by 21-year-old George Washington, the Virginia militia was quickly defeated by the French.

The British government acted quickly. It sent over 1,500 troops to attack the French again. Britain and France now were at war. Because several groups of Indians helped the French, this struggle came to be called the French and Indian War.

At first the war went badly for the British and the colonists. After a while, though, British-American forces were able to drive the French out of much of the Ohio Valley. Under General James Wolfe, the British captured the important Canadian settlement of Quebec. The British took Montreal in 1760.

In 1763 Britain and France signed a peace treaty. France gave to Britain all its lands between the Appalachians and the Mississippi River.

Many battles of the French and Indian War were at sea. Here, the British and French fight near an Indian fort on the St. Lawrence River.

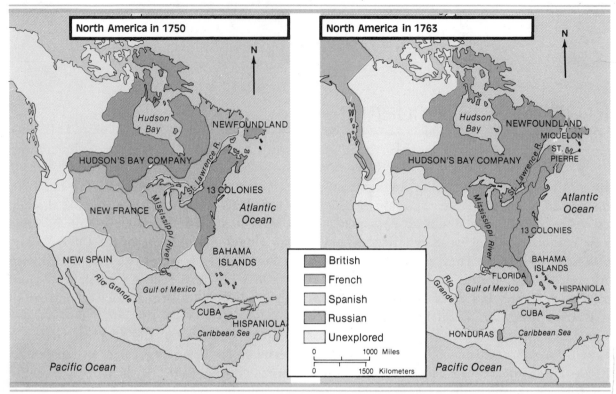

North America in 1750

North America in 1763

Hudson Bay

NEWFOUNDLAND

HUDSON'S BAY COMPANY

St. Lawrence R.

13 COLONIES

Atlantic Ocean

NEW FRANCE

Mississippi River

BAHAMA ISLANDS

NEW SPAIN

Rio Grande

Gulf of Mexico

CUBA

HISPANIOLA

Caribbean Sea

Pacific Ocean

Hudson Bay

NEWFOUNDLAND

MIQUELON

ST. PIERRE

HUDSON'S BAY COMPANY

St. Lawrence R.

Atlantic Ocean

Mississippi River

13 COLONIES

BAHAMA ISLANDS

FLORIDA

Rio Grande

Gulf of Mexico

HISPANIOLA

CUBA

HONDURAS

Caribbean Sea

Pacific Ocean

British
French
Spanish
Russian
Unexplored

0   1000 Miles

0   1500 Kilometers

Three European nations claimed large parts of North America in 1750. Which nation had lost vast areas of land by 1763?

Trouble Between Britain and the Colonies

The colonists had hoped to settle in the lands won in the French and Indian War. But the British king, George III, refused to allow this. Instead, he made the Proclamation of 1763, which said that no more settlers could move west of the Appalachian Mountains. This land was to remain the home of the Indians. King George wanted to protect the fur trade there. Settlers would drive away both the Indians and the animals.

Then the British government took a step that made Americans even angrier. It began to pass new tax laws for the colonies. Taxes are money that citizens pay the government

to keep it running. The French and Indian War had cost Great Britain a great deal of money. Britain needed money to pay its war debts. The British government said that the colonists must help to pay the debt. The colonists felt this was unfair. They said they already had helped pay for the war. But *Parliament* (pär′lə mənt), the British lawmaking body, passed the new tax laws anyway.

New Tax Laws

Parliament passed the Sugar Act in 1764. This act made colonists pay a tax on sugar and other imported goods brought into the colonies. The next year Parliament passed the Stamp Act. Colonists now had to buy stamps to put on all newspapers, business papers, and even on playing cards.

The colonists argued against such tax laws. They said that Parliament did not have the right to tax them. They pointed out that the colonists had no representatives in Parliament. Since they had no part in passing tax laws, the colonists should not have to obey them.

"Taxation without representation is tyranny!" the colonists cried. Tyranny is the cruel and unfair use of power by a ruler. Groups such as the Sons and Daughters of Liberty were formed to protest, or show that they were not in favor of, the new laws. The colonists also attacked some of the stamp collectors and destroyed the stamps. Finally in 1766, Parliament gave in and *repealed* (ri pēld'), or did away with, the Stamp Act.

The colonists may have thought they had won, but they had not. The next year Parliament passed the Townshend Acts. These acts, or laws, placed taxes on such commonly used items as glass, lead, paints, paper, and tea imported from Britain. The colonists then fought back with a *boycott* (boi'kot). They refused to buy, sell, or use any goods from Britain. British troops were sent in to protect the tax collectors.

The Boston Massacre

It was not long before fighting broke out between the colonists and the British troops. Trouble started on a wintry day in Boston in March of 1770. A redcoated British soldier was standing guard at the tax collection building. Colonists began throwing snow and ice at him. Other soldiers came to his aid. In the mix up that followed, the "redcoats" opened fire. When the shooting ended, five colonists lay dead. The first to fall had been Crispus Attucks, a former slave who had worked as a sailor aboard a whaling ship.

Anger against the British quickly spread throughout Boston. "Massacre!" the colonists called the shooting. They demanded that the British troops leave Boston. The British did not leave. But Parliament repealed the hated Townshend Acts.

Colonists Take Action

The happenings in Boston caused Samuel Adams, a leader of the Sons of Liberty, to take action. He believed that the colonists should join in their stand against the British tax practices. Sam Adams set up committees in many parts of Massachusetts. These committees wrote to, or corresponded with, one another. They told one another about the actions of the British. Soon there were committees of correspondence in all the colonies.

The Boston Tea Party

Even with the repeal of the Townshend Acts, the British believed in the need for a tax on tea. In 1773 Parliament passed the Tea Act. Now the colonists could buy their tea only from the British East India Company.

Once against the colonists protested. In the dark of night on December 16, 1773, a group of "Indians" climbed aboard three British tea ships in Boston Harbor. Actually, they were Samuel Adams and some other Sons of Liberty dressed as Indians. They surprised the British crew and threw 340 chests of tea into the harbor.

News of the "Boston Tea Party" spread down the Atlantic Coast. It gave colonists from Boston all the way down to Charleston the courage to refuse to buy British tea.

The Intolerable Acts

Parliament was very angry, and passed a number of new acts to punish the citizens of Boston. One act closed the port of Boston. No ships were allowed to enter or leave Boston harbor. The city now faced being short of food. Another act placed the people of Massachusetts under a British governor instead of their local governments. Still another act ordered the colonists to supply housing and food for 10,000 British troops.

Shocked Americans called these harsh acts the "Intolerable Acts." The colonists joined in smuggling food and other sup-

At the Boston Tea Party, colonists dressed as Indians threw British tea into the sea. They cried, "Boston Harbor a teapot tonight!"

plies to the people of Boston. The colonists also began to unite against British rule. Many Americans said that the colonies should gain *independence* (in'di pen'dəns) from Britain. Independence is not being under the power of another country.

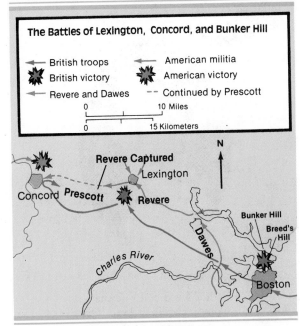

Paul Revere and William Dawes were not able to finish their rides because they were captured. Dr. Samuel Prescott escaped to warn other colonists about the British.

The First Continental Congress

Several colonial assemblies called for a meeting of representatives of all the colonies. All but Georgia agreed. On September 5, 1774, 56 American representatives met in Philadelphia. The meeting became known as the First Continental Congress.

The representatives decided to send a letter to King George III asking for the repeal of the Intolerable Acts. They also asked that the colonists alone be allowed to decide on their taxes. Finally, the letter said that the colonies would not trade with Britain until the king agreed to these requests. The king did not answer the letter.

Moving Toward Independence

Before the representatives left the First Continental Congress, they agreed to meet again in May 1775. Meanwhile, American relations with Britain grew worse. Britain sent more troops to Massachusetts. British warships sailed into Boston harbor.

The colonial leaders told the people of Boston not to give up hope. They also said they should be prepared to fight. The colonists formed military units and drilled on

village greens. They called themselves minutemen because they promised to fight "at a minute's notice."

Fighting at Lexington and Concord

Spies for the British told the military commander of Massachusetts, General Thomas Gage, about the preparations of the colonists. Gage learned that the colonists were hiding guns and gunpowder in Concord, Massachusetts. Gage also found out that Samuel Adams was hiding in Lexington. John Hancock, another leader of the Sons of Liberty, was hiding nearby. Gage ordered 700 British soldiers to take the two leaders and the hidden supplies.

The colonists also had spies. When the colonists heard of Gage's order, they made their own plan. The colonists set up a watch to find out when the British troops

Esther Reed believed that American women should help win the Revolution by giving money for troops.

would leave Boston. A man stationed in the tall steeple of Boston's Old North Church was to signal by lantern when the British started to leave. Riders chosen to carry word of the British actions were then to ride across the countryside with their warning.

Late on the night of April 18, 1775, lanterns flashed in the steeple. The British troops were about to cross the Charles River and begin their march. The riders, Paul Revere and William Dawes, took off from different starting points. "The British are coming! The British are coming!" they shouted as they raced down country roads.

At dawn the British troops reached Lexington's village green, where they found a small group of minutemen waiting for them. Badly outnumbered, the minutemen began to move back. Suddenly, a shot rang out! More shots were fired. At the end, 8 colonists were dead and 10 were wounded.

The British soldiers then moved on to Concord. There they fought a short but bitter battle with minutemen at the North Bridge. Under heavy fire from the colonists, the British troops began to return to Boston. They had failed to capture Adams and Hancock or the colonists' supplies. Revere's warning had helped the two leaders to escape.

No one knows who fired that first shot at Lexington. But it set off events so important that it is sometimes called "the shot heard around the world."

The Second Continental Congress

The Second Continental Congress met in Philadelphia in May 1775. The members had learned of the fighting at Lexington and Concord. They also heard that fighting was continuing around Boston. Congress asked each colony to send military units to help the Massachusetts minutemen. It named one of its members, George Washington, to take command of the American forces in Boston.

The Battle of Bunker Hill

While Washington was on his way to Boston, another battle broke out there. Minutemen from all over New England had arrived to help the colonists in Boston. They had planned to fight from Bunker Hill, but instead left some soldiers there and moved on to nearby Breed's Hill. On June 17, 1775, General Gage ordered more than 2,000 British soldiers to take Breed's Hill.

That afternoon the British redcoats began to climb the hill. American rifle fire and cannon balls rained down on them. Row after row of the British soldiers fell. Those still standing had to retreat. After regrouping, they again tried the dangerous climb. Again, the British were shot at, but they climbed on. By this time the Americans were running out of ammunition. Now the minutemen had to retreat from both hills. They left behind nearly 450 killed, wounded, or captured troops.

The British won both hills, but more than 1,000 British troops had been killed or wounded. As one of their generals said, another such victory "would have ruined us." This battle, which was called the "Battle of Bunker Hill," showed the British that they were fighting a strong people who meant to win.

The Declaration of Independence

Even after the battles of Lexington, Concord, and Bunker Hill, many Americans still wanted to remain part of Great Britain. They were loyal to the British king. All they wanted was to have the rights that they thought Britain was not giving them.

By the end of 1775, however, the colonists began to change their minds. King George III continued to say that the colonists were in rebellion against Britain. The king also sent more troops to attack the "rebels." As a result, more colonists began to speak out in favor of independence.

Patrick Henry was a well-known lawyer in Virginia. He became famous for his speeches while he was in his late twenties.

A colonist named Thomas Paine wrote a pamphlet called *Common Sense,* which quickly became popular. In this booklet Paine explained why Americans should make the final break with Britain. Another colonial leader, Patrick Henry, also spoke out for freedom. This fiery speaker from Virginia said that for him the choice was clear—"Give me liberty or give me death."

Finally, in June 1776 the Continental Congress decided to take action. It named a committee of five members to write a paper to declare, or formally say, that the colonies "are, and of right ought to be, free and independent states." The oldest member of the group was Benjamin Franklin of Pennsylvania. Others were John Adams of Massachusetts, Philip Livingston of New York, and Roger Sherman of Connecticut. The final and youngest member was Thomas Jefferson of Virginia. It was Jefferson who wrote most of the paper.

In Philadelphia, *representatives* of the thirteen colonies accepted and signed the Declaration of Independence.

In early July this paper, called the Declaration of Independence, was presented to the Continental Congress. It stated in moving terms that Americans were breaking their ties to Britain. It also told why:

"We hold these truths to be self-evident, that all men are created equal, that they are endowed (given) by their creator with certain unalienable Rights (rights that cannot be taken away), that among these are Life, Liberty, and the pursuit of Happiness. . . .

"That to secure (make safe) these rights, Governments are instituted (set up) among Men, (getting) their just powers from the consent of the governed. . . .

"That whenever any Form of Government becomes destructive of these ends, it is the Right of the People to alter and abolish (do away with) it, and institute (set up) a new Government. . . ."

On July 4, 1776, the Continental Congress adopted the Declaration of Independence. All the members lined up to sign it, to show they accepted it. At his turn, John Hancock wrote his name very large. "There," he said, "the King of England can read it without his glasses!"

Do You Know?

1. What caused the French and Indian War?
2. Why did the British tax the colonists after the French and Indian War?
3. When did the Continental Congress adopt the Declaration of Independence?
4. Why did the colonists declare their independence from Great Britain?

3
The Revolutionary War

The colonists had declared their independence. Now they had to fight to win it. The war that was fought between 1776 and 1781 has several names. The most common ones are the War of Independence and the Revolutionary War. It is often called the Revolutionary War because the Americans had revolted, or turned against, British rule.

Winning the Revolutionary War

How could the American colonists possibly win a war against Britain? The British had one of the most powerful armies in the world. Their navy was known as "the ruler of the seas." Moreover, the king was making British fighting power even stronger. He hired about 30,000 German soldiers, called Hessians (hesh′ənz), to fight the Americans. Then, too, the British had a solid base in Canada. From there they could send both their army and their navy to attack the colonists.

Not all colonists were in favor of the war. Probably only about one third of the colonists believed in independence strongly enough to fight for it. These colonists were called *Patriots* (pā′trē ətz). Another third of the colonists were against the war. These *Loyalists* (loi′ə listz) wanted to keep their ties to Britain. The remaining colonists did not feel strongly one way or the other.

Nevertheless, the war had started. The American army, or Continental Army as it was called, had to be formed and trained. With General George Washington in command, these tasks began.

Fighting in the Northeast

In March 1776 George Washington's soldiers were able to drive the British out of Boston. Washington then moved the Continental Army to Long Island in New York. He expected a British attack. When the attack came, the much stronger British force drove the Americans out. Over the next several months Washington had to retreat across New York and New Jersey. By late 1776 his army had only about 3,000 soldiers. They camped in Pennsylvania.

Across the Delaware River, at Trenton in New Jersey, the British and Hessians had set up winter camp. Washington needed guns, ammunition, and food for his soldiers. Therefore, he planned a surprise attack on the camp at Trenton. On Christmas night Washington and his soldiers crossed the icy waters of the Delaware River. At dawn they attacked the sleepy Hessians and took at least 1,000 prisoners. More important, the Americans captured needed supplies. Then Washington's soldiers moved on to nearby Princeton and captured more enemy supplies.

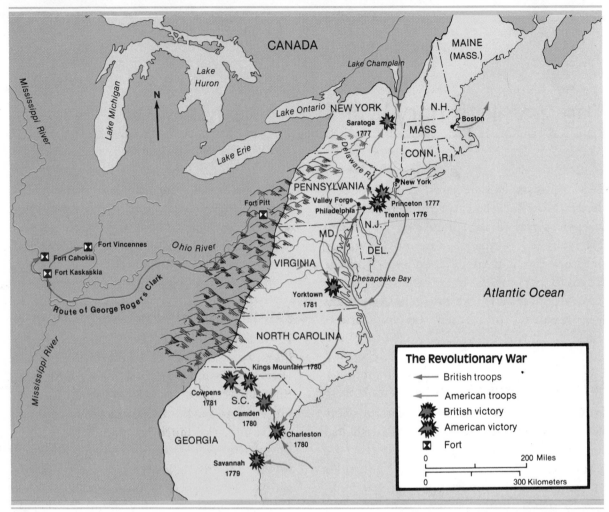

Most of the battles of the Revolutionary War were fought near the coast. Which important battles were fought in the West?

Battle of Saratoga

The defeats at Trenton and Princeton angered the British. They decided to try to end the war quickly in 1777. Their plan for victory was to cut off New England from the rest of the colonies. To do this they planned to send three British armies toward Albany in New York from different directions. Luckily for the Americans, one British army never began its move. Another ran into swamps and deep forests, and its general was killed. The Continental Army met the third British army at Saratoga, north of Albany. There the Americans won a major victory.

The Battle of Saratoga marked the turning point of the war. It gave new hope to the Patriots. It also helped decide France to enter the war openly on the side of the Americans. Before the battle of Saratoga, France had helped the Americans only in secret.

Harsh Winter at Valley Forge

The events in Pennsylvania were not so good. Washington's army was not able to stop the British from taking Philadelphia. Disappointed, Washington set up winter camp at Valley Forge, which is not far from Philadelphia.

The winter of 1777–1778 was perhaps the worst time of the war for the Americans. Crowded into whatever housing they could find or put together, the soldiers suffered from illness, lack of food, and the cold. Yet through all the hardships, they trained and drilled. Baron von Steuben (bar'ən von stoo'bən), a trained soldier from Germany, helped those who made it through the winter at Valley Forge to become a stronger and better-trained army.

Fighting in the West

The Revolutionary War was not fought only along the Atlantic Coast. It was also fought west of the Appalachians, in the valleys of the Ohio and Mississippi rivers. The British already had forts there to protect their trade with the Indians. Now the British were arming the Indians and trying to get them to attack American settlers in this land.

Virginia believed that it owned this land. Therefore, a Virginia Patriot named Captain George Rogers Clark led a small band of frontier fighters west. His plan was to capture the British forts that were arming the Indians. In several surprise attacks,

Clark succeeded. His forces drove the British troops out of this area.

Fighting at Sea

There was no American navy at the beginning of the war. Therefore, private ships called privateers offered to help. The privateers were able to destroy many of the British ships that were bringing supplies to their soldiers. Often the Americans sailed almost to Britain's shores to attack its shipping. Meanwhile, the Americans slowly put together a small navy.

John Paul Jones was one of America's boldest and most courageous naval captains. He commanded an old warship called the *Bonhomme Richard* (bən əm' rē shar'), which the French had given the Americans. Sailing close to the British coast one day in 1779, Jones met a British warship, the *Serapis* (sə rā'pis). The two ships fought for several hours. Then the *Bonhomme Richard* started to sink.

"Have you struck your colors?" (meaning, "Are you ready to surrender?") shouted the British captain. "I have not yet begun to fight!" shouted Jones. Then his forces leaped aboard the *Serapis* and captured it just as the *Bonhomme Richard* sank.

Final Victory in the South

In 1778 the British decided to take the war to the South. They named General Charles Cornwallis to take charge of the war there.

At first the British were successful. They easily captured the port cities of Charleston in South Carolina and Savannah in Georgia. But as they moved inland, the British ran into trouble. Hit-and-run fighters under the command of South Carolina's "Swamp Fox," Francis Marion, kept up their raids on the redcoats. American forces under

American and French troops surrounded the British at Yorktown. Why couldn't the British escape by sea?

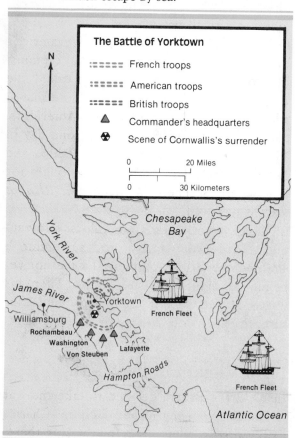

The Battle of Yorktown

:::::: French troops
:::::: American troops
:::::: British troops
▲ Commander's headquarters
☢ Scene of Cornwallis's surrender

0 ____ 20 Miles
0 ____ 30 Kilometers

N

York River
Chesapeake Bay
James River
Yorktown
French Fleet
Williamsburg
Rochambeau
Washington
Von Steuben
Lafayette
Hampton Roads
French Fleet
Atlantic Ocean

Generals Nathanael Greene and Daniel Morgan caused still more British losses.

Finally, Cornwallis ordered his army back to the coast to wait for help. He made his way up to Yorktown, Virginia, which is on Chesapeake Bay.

Washington saw his chance to trap Cornwallis. He asked French ships to sail up to Chesapeake Bay to stop British ships from reaching Cornwallis. Then Washington led his army and some French soldiers south from New York to Yorktown. There they were joined by more French troops.

Cornwallis was surrounded on land and cut off from by sea. He could not escape. On October 19, 1781, he surrendered his army of 7,000 troops.

After the surrender at Yorktown, the Americans and British met in Paris to talk about the terms of peace. According to the treaty signed in 1783, Britain agreed that the United States was a "free, sovereign (having complete authority), and independent nation." Great Britain also gave the land between the Appalachians and the Mississippi River to the United States.

How the War Was Won

How did a small group of Patriots defeat one of the world's most powerful nations? The United States had many things in its favor. The new nation had several talented leaders. George Washington, for example, was a brilliant commander of the armed forces. Political leaders such as John Adams helped to guide the nation. Benjamin Franklin gained the respect of many Europeans while serving as American minister, or representative, to France. He helped talk the French into joining the American cause.

Friends from Europe

Help also came from France and from other European countries. A young Frenchman, the Marquis de Lafayette (mär kē′ də laf′ē et′), offered his services as an officer to Washington. So did Comte de Rochambeau (kônt də rō′sham bō). Both French officers led armies in the final battle at Yorktown.

From Germany came Baron von Steuben. Another German officer, Baron de Kalb, fought bravely and died for the Patriots' cause. From Poland came the engineer Thaddeus Kosciusko (thad′ē əs kos′əus′kō), who helped Americans build defenses. The Polish officer Casimir Pulaski (kaz′ə mēr pōō las′kē) died in battle.

Women in the War

The new nation also could not have won the war without the help of its women. With 200,000 men fighting in the Continental Army, American's farms could have stopped producing food and its stores could have closed down. Instead, women stepped in and took over. Abigail Adams ran the family farm in Massachusetts while her husband, John Adams, worked in Congress.

Thousands of women also helped by making shot, gunpowder, and bandages.

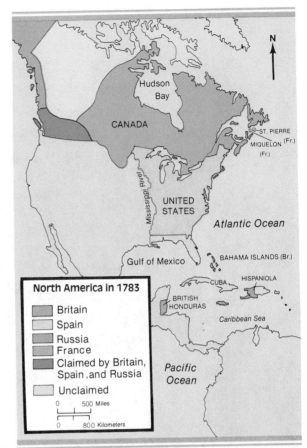

North America in 1783

- Britain
- Spain
- Russia
- France
- Claimed by Britain, Spain, and Russia
- Unclaimed

0 500 Miles

0 800 Kilometers

In 1783 a new nation, the United States, appeared in North America. What natural feature formed its western boundary?

They took care of the wounded. Women sometimes acted as spies for the American side. One of them was Lydia Darragh (dar′ō). The British took over her home in Philadelphia to use as their headquarters. She listened to what the officers said and reported their plans to General Washington. Nanye hi (nan yē′ hē), a Cherokee woman, served as both scout and spy.

There were also times that women took part in the fighting. Mary Hays McCauley, a Patriot from New Jersey, went to war to help her husband by bringing soldiers pitchers of water. This earned her the nick-

95

Mary McCauley was one of the few women to fight in the Revolutionary War. She fired her husband's cannon after he died.

name "Molly Pitcher." One hot day her husband was shot and fell. Mary McCauley took over his cannon and kept it firing.

Black Americans in the War

Black Americans also helped bring about the American victory. At least 5,000 black Americans joined the Continental Army. They fought in every major battle from Lexington and Concord to Yorktown. Some who were slaves were granted their freedom after the war.

Do You Know?

1. Who were the Patriots? Who were the Loyalists?
2. Who won the Battle of Trenton?
3. Why was Saratoga called the turning point of the Revolutionary War?
4. What part did women play in the Revolutionary War?

96

To Help You Learn

Using New Words

militia   independence
Parliament   Patriots
repealed   Loyalists
boycott

The phrases below explain the words or terms listed above. Number a paper from 1 through 7. After each number write the word or term that matches each definition.

1. American colonists who fought for independence during the Revolutionary War
2. Cancelled, or ended, a law
3. Citizen-soldiers who serve when they are needed
4. American colonists who were against independence from Great Britain
5. The lawmaking body of Great Britain
6. A refusal to buy, sell, or use certain goods
7. Freedom from control by others

Finding the Facts

1. Which of the English colonies were started by people looking for religious freedom?
2. Which group of colonies had the greatest mix of people coming from different countries and who believed in different religions?
3. Which group of colonies had the best conditions for growing indigo, rice, and tobacco?
4. Which group of colonies had large fishing and shipbuilding industries?
5. Why after the French and Indian War did Great Britain decide to make the colonists pay taxes?
6. What were the committees of correspondence? Why did the colonies start these committees?
7. How and where did the Revolutionary War begin? Who was chosen to command the American army?
8. Who wrote most of the Declaration of Independence?
9. How did the following people help the Americans to win the Revolutionary War: Benjamin Franklin, George Rogers Clark, the Marquis de Lafayette, Baron von Steuben, Lydia Darragh, Molly Pitcher?
10. About how many Americans were on the side of the Patriots?

Learning from Maps

1. Turn to the map of the Battle of Yorktown on page 94. How does the map show that Cornwallis was surrounded? Whose headquarters are shown on the map? What symbol is used to stand for the French fleet?
2. Most maps have a scale of miles and kilometers. The scale helps you to know how far one place is from another. Look at the scales on the two maps below.
   - Use the scale on map 1 to measure the coastline of the Southern Colonies.
   - Use the scale on map 2 to find out how far Jamestown is from Charleston.
   - Which map shows more land—Map 1 or Map 2?
   - Which map has more details—Map 1 or Map 2?
3. Turn to the map of North America in 1783, which is shown on page 95. Which natural features formed the eastern and western boundaries of the United States? Which country controlled the most land?

Using Study Skills

1. **Time Line:** The following events are not listed in the order in which they happened. Find the date for each in Unit 3. Then write the events in the right order on a time line. Start in 1600 and end in 1785.
Battle of Saratoga

Map 1

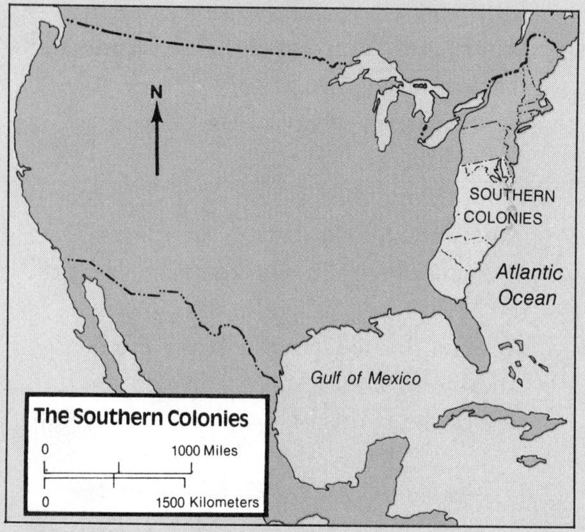

Map 2

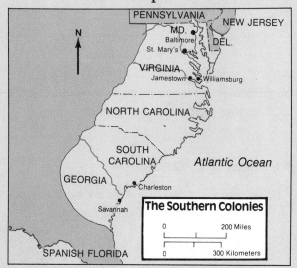

William Penn and Quakers arrive in
  Pennsylvania
Great Britain gives up 13 colonies
Dutch surrender New Netherland
First Continental Congress meets
French and Indian War begins

2. **Diagram:** Turn to the diagram of a New England town on page 73. What types of buildings did the town have? Does one building seem to be more important than the others? If so, which one? What do you think the town common, or green, was used for? What kind of work do you think people in this town did?

Thinking It Through

1. Americans owe much to colonial leaders, such as Anne Hutchinson and William Penn. What freedoms do Americans enjoy today because of the brave acts of these two people?
2. Why was the House of Burgesses in Virginia important in American history?
3. Explain how the colonists, with little training and few weapons, were able to win against the larger, better-trained British army.

Projects

1. "Yankee Doodle" was a song that was first sung during the War of Independence. Find the words of the song. Then study them to find out what the song meant. Learn to sing this and other Revolutionary War songs that you might have come across in your search.
2. The Research Committee might look for more information about one of the Revolutionary War leaders or battles in the text.

   The Explorers' Committee might prepare a map that shows where the armies fought in the battle.
3. Imagine that you are an early settler. Write a letter to someone in your family who did not come to America. Describe how you spend your days. Also tell about some of the interesting things that have happened to you.
4. The Reading Committee might ask the librarian for books about life in the colonies and for books about the War of Independence.
5. Make an outline map of the United States by tracing the map on pages 6 and 7. On the map, write in the names of the 13 colonies and of the important rivers, lakes, and settlements. Label the Atlantic Ocean. The map of early settlements on page 71 will help you. Keep the outline map for use as you study more sections of the text.
6. Turn to the pictures of colonial life on pages 74 and 77. What do the pictures show about the life of colonial children? Would life in the colonies seem to be different from life today? Explain.

4 Forming a New Government

Unit Preview

The United States and Great Britain signed the treaty giving the United States its independence in 1783. It was not easy for the new nation to set up a government. The states did not want to give up their rights. Therefore, American leaders formed a central government under the Articles of Confederation that was weak. It had no power to tax the states for money. It could not form a sound system of money or make the states obey laws and treaties. A rebellion in Massachusetts finally made Americans decide they needed a better government.

American leaders met in Philadelphia to improve the Articles of Confederation. However, they soon agreed to write a new plan of government, or Constitution. The leaders formed a strong central government. Power was divided among three branches, or parts. They were the executive, legislative, and judicial branches. The leaders also planned for the future by making it possible for the Constitution to be changed. Some states would not accept the Constitution until leaders agreed to add a Bill of Rights later.

George Washington was elected the first President of the nation. Congress set up several departments to help him govern the nation. The heads of these departments formed the Cabinet. A place was chosen to build a home for the federal government.

Things to Discover

If you look carefully at the picture, map, and time line, you can answer these questions.

1. The map shows that the area to the west of the 13 states did not have any state boundaries. Why did this part of the United States not have state boundaries?
2. The picture shows George Washington taking the oath of office in Federal Hall, New York, in 1789. How can you tell that the President is taking an oath?
3. When were the Articles of Confederation drawn up? How long after this did representatives meet to change the Articles?
4. When was the Constitution adopted?

Words to Learn

You will meet these words in this unit. As you read, you will learn what they mean and how to pronounce them. The Word List will help you.

amendments
Articles of Confederation
Bill of Rights
Cabinet
compromise
Constitution
convention
delegates
executive branch
federal system
House of Representatives
judicial branch
legislative branch
ratified
republic
Senate
Supreme Court
veto

100

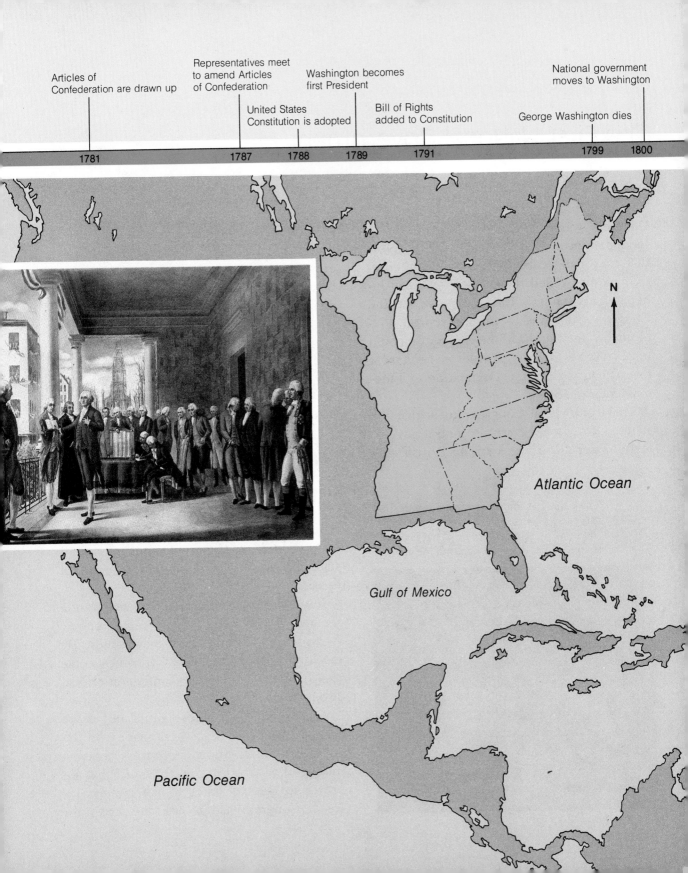

Articles of
Confederation are drawn up

Representatives meet
to amend Articles
of Confederation

Washington becomes
first President

National government
moves to Washington

United States
Constitution is adopted

Bill of Rights
added to Constitution

George Washington dies

1781   1787   1788   1789   1791   1799   1800

N

Atlantic Ocean

Gulf of Mexico

Pacific Ocean

1

The First National Government

The first job of the Second Continental Congress was to write the Declaration of Independence. This it did in 1776. Now that they had declared their independence, the colonies called themselves "free and independent states." The next task of the Congress then was to form a central government under which the 13 states could unite. However, this proved to be harder to do than writing the Declaration of Independence.

The Continental Congress knew that the states did not want a strong central government. After all, it was a strong British gov-

ernment that they were rebelling against. It took the Continental Congress nearly a year and a half to agree on a plan of government. It then took the states more than three years to accept the plan of government.

The Articles of Confederation

The new plan of government was called the *Articles of Confederation* (kən fed′ə rā′shən). It became the law of the land in 1781. The Articles of Confederation joined the 13 states into a confederation, or league. Under the Articles of Confederation, the central government was made up of a Congress. This Congress was formed of representatives from all the states. Each state had one vote in Congress. Nine of the 13 states had to vote for a law in order for it to pass.

For a while the Articles of Confederation seemed to work. Fighting a common enemy —the British—united the new states. By the time the war ended, it had become clear that the Articles of Confederation had several weaknesses.

For example, Congress could not make the states obey the laws it made for the country. In addition, Congress needed money to govern the country, but it had no power to tax the states to get money. Instead, Congress had to ask the states for

The eagle has long stood for strength. In this early painting, the eagle is carrying a shield of the United States. What is on the shield? What does the painting mean?

the money and hope to receive it. For another example, Congress had the power to make trade treaties with other countries. However, Congress had no power to make the states follow these treaties.

Money Problems Under the Articles

During the Revolutionary War, Congress needed money to fight. Therefore, it borrowed money from other countries and from American citizens. When the war ended Congress did not have the money to pay its debts. It could not even pay the wages it owed the Revolutionary War soldiers. Without the power to tax, Congress had no way to raise money.

America's trade was hurt by the money owed. To do well, American businesses had to be able to sell both raw materials and manufactured goods to other nations. However, many countries had not been paid the money that they had loaned the United States during the war. These countries now did not want to do business with Americans.

The nation's trade and business also were hurt for another reason. Some of the money being used was worthless. During the war Congress had printed large amounts of paper money. But after the war Congress had no gold or silver to make its paper money worth anything. Also, each state printed or coined its own money. Much of this paper money also was worthless. Even the coins caused problems. Often one state's coins were not given full value in

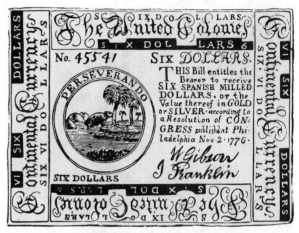

This six-dollar bill is only one kind of paper money used by Americans in 1776. Who issued the money? What could the person who handed the bill in to a bank get in return?

another state. For example, a coin made in New Jersey valued at 12 cents might be accepted as only 9 cents in another state. Yet Congress had no way to make a sound money system for all the states.

The power of the states to control their own trade and taxes also made it hard for states to do business with one another. The states placed taxes on each other's goods and quarreled over the use of roads, rivers, and bridges.

Shays' Rebellion

Everyone was badly hurt by the nation's money problems. Business owners did not have enough trade. War veterans suffered because they still had not been paid their wages. Many farmers suffered too. The

Farmers fought with the state militia at Springfield, Massachusetts, on January 25, 1787. The farmers were led by Daniel Shays, and they soon were forced to flee.

states often placed high taxes on farmers' land. Those who could not pay these taxes lost their farms.

The hard times of the farmers were especially severe in western Massachusetts. Finally, farmers decided to help themselves. Led by Revolutionary War veteran Daniel Shays, the farmers attacked the state arsenal at Springfield, Massachusetts. They wanted guns so they could stop the state from taking any more farms. The state militia easily put down the rebellion. But the fact that the rebellion happened showed many people that the national government created by the Articles of Confederation was weak.

A Call for New Government

Shays' Rebellion proved to George Washington that the Articles were not working. "I predict the worst consequences (see the worst outcome for the future) from a half-starved, limping government, always moving upon crutches and tottering at every step . . . ," he said. Other leaders also worried about the weaknesses of government created by the Articles. In 1785 and 1786 several states sent representatives to meetings to try to repair the Articles. They were not able to solve the problems.

One leader, James Madison of Virginia, thought that all the states should meet to try to solve the problems. Alexander Hamilton of New York talked Congress into calling a meeting. Congress set the meeting for the second Monday in May 1787, at Independence Hall in Philadelphia. This *convention* (kən ven′shən), or special meeting, was given the job of changing the Articles to make them work.

Do You Know?

1. When did the 13 colonies become 13 states?
2. What were the Articles of Confederation?
3. What weaknesses did the national government have under the Articles of Confederation?
4. Why did Daniel Shays lead the farmers of Massachusetts to rebel?

Before You Go On

Using New Words

Articles of Confederation   convention

The phrases below explain the words listed
above. Number a paper 1 and 2. After each
number write the word that matches the
definition.

1. A special meeting, usually held for many
   people
2. Law setting up the first central government
   of the United States

Finding the Facts

1. What was the first important job carried
   out by the Second Continental Congress?
2. What is a confederation?
3. How long did it take for the states to
   accept the Articles of Confederation?
4. How were laws made under the Articles of
   Confederation?
5. Why did the states not want a strong
   central government?

6. Why do you think the Congress set up by
   the Articles of Confederation could not
   make the states obey the law?
7. Why did Congress need money after the
   Revolutionary War?
8. Why is it important for Congress to have
   the power to raise taxes?
9. Why did other countries not want to trade
   with the United States after the
   Revolutionary War?
10. Why was American paper money
    worthless after the Revolutionary War?
11. Why was it hard for the 13 states to do
    business with one another?
12. How did money problems hurt everyone
    after the Revolutionary War?
13. What did Shays' rebellion show about the
    Articles of Confederation?
14. Why was a convention held in Philadelphia
    in 1787?
15. In what building in Philadelphia did the
    convention meet?
16. Why did Shays' Rebellion cause George
    Washington to worry?

2
The Constitution of the United States

It was raining as 55 representatives, called *delegates,* (del′ə gātz) gathered in Philadelphia in May of 1787. The delegates knew that they did not have much time to make the nation's plan of government stronger. Every day more problems seemed to arise. The delegates also worried that other nations would use the weakness of the United States to gain their own ends. If this happened, the American people might lose the freedom they had fought so hard to win.

Patriots and Leaders

Among the leaders meeting in Philadelphia were some of the most talented and respected people in the country. Many of them had become famous during the Revolution. One of these leaders was George Washington, who was quickly named president of the convention. Although Benjamin Franklin was 81 years old and sick, he came because he wanted to be part of so important a meeting. The youngest member was

The *delegates* who met at the *convention* in Philadelphia worked very hard. They agreed not to talk about their work to others.

James Madison, who kept a daily record of the meetings. Another young delegate, Alexander Hamilton, had been Washington's aide during the Revolution.

Several leaders of the American Revolution were missing, though. Thomas Jefferson was in France serving as the United States minister there. John Adams, the United States' minister to Great Britain, was in London. Patrick Henry refused to take part in the meeting. He said that he "smelled a rat." Henry was bitterly against a strong central government. He feared that the convention would form a strong government that would take away the rights of the states.

At first the delegates tried hard to carry out their plan—to make some changes in the Articles of Confederation. It soon became clear that this would not be enough. They saw that they would have to begin all over again and write a completely new *Constitution* (kon′stə tōō′shən), or plan of government. The meeting then became the Constitutional Convention.

Benjamin Franklin— Leader, Printer, and Inventor

Benjamin Franklin had worked hard to help the United States gain its freedom. Now he wanted to help the nation form the government it needed. Franklin was already loved as one of America's greatest Patriots. He had signed the Declaration of Independence and the treaty ending the Revolu-

As a boy, Benjamin Franklin learned how to make up pages for printing. He is carrying the frames that hold type used for printing words.

tionary War. Franklin also was a well-known author and a scientist. He invented such items as the lightning rod and bifocal (bī fō′kəl) glasses. These eyeglasses help people to see both close-up and afar.

Born in Boston in 1706 of a poor family, Franklin went to work in his brother's print shop at the age of 12. In his spare time Franklin taught himself by reading every book he could find. He even memorized whole pages of some books. The result was that Franklin owned his own newspaper by the time he was 30 years old. He also was the author of *Poor Richard's Almanac,* a book with information on yearly events.

When he was about 30 years old, Franklin decided to enter politics in Philadelphia. He wanted to solve some city problems. He soon was drawn into the important national issues of the day. He spent the next 40 years helping Americans to gain their rights as colonists and as citizens

In an experiment with a kite flown during a storm, Benjamin Franklin proved that lightning was a form of electricity.

of a new nation. To do this, he lived for several years in London and in Paris. While he was there, Franklin's belief that all Americans should have a say in their government grew stronger. He worked to gain this end until his death at the age of 84.

Planning a New Government

The delegates at the Constitutional Convention had many important decisions to make. What kind of government would the new Constitution set up? Should they describe their government in great detail or just give an outline of it? Throughout the hot and humid Philadelphia summer, the delegates talked over questions such as these. They came up with many answers.

First, the delegates believed that the nation should be a *republic* (ri pub′lik). In a republic people control their government by electing representatives to the government to look after their interests.

Second, the delegates believed that the new government had to have power in order to do its job. It had to have power to tax. It had to have the power to print and coin money and to make a single, sound money system for all the states. The government had to have the power to make laws for trade among the states and with foreign countries. It also needed a President who would see that the laws were obeyed.

The New England, Middle, and Southern states had different needs because of their different ways of making a living. Therefore their delegates had many arguments during the summer of 1787. To settle the arguments, the delegates had to *compromise* (kom′prə mīz′). That is, each side gave up a little of what it wanted. Then both sides agreed to accept a plan that gave them at least part of what they wanted.

Making Compromises

One of the things the states did not agree about was the kind of Congress that the nation should have. States with many people believed that they should have more representatives in the Congress than states with few people. The smaller states believed that each state should have the same number of representatives in the Congress.

The compromise that was worked out divided Congress into two parts, or houses. In one house, called the *Senate* (sen′it), each state would have two representatives, called Senators. In the other house, called the *House of Representatives,* large states would have more representatives than small states. This solution came to be called the Great Compromise.

Three Branches of Government

The Constitution divides the government into three parts, or branches. The first branch is Congress, which is made up of the Senate and the House of Representatives. Congress forms the *legislative branch* (lej′is lā′tiv branch′), which makes laws.

The Government of Our Nation

Legislative Branch (Congress) passes the laws.

Executive Branch (President) carries out the laws.

Judicial Branch (Supreme Court) makes judgments about the laws.

109

The second branch is the *executive* (eg zek′yə tiv) *branch*. It carries out the laws that Congress makes. The executive branch is headed by the President. The third branch is the *judicial* (jōō dish′əl) *branch*. Its job is to explain the meaning of the laws. The judicial branch has a system of courts that decides when laws have been broken. At the head of the judicial branch is the *Supreme Court* (sə prēm′kôrt′). This court has nine justices, or judges who serve for life. The head of the Supreme Court is the Chief Justice.

Checks and Balances

The delegates had a good reason for dividing the government into three branches. They did not want the new national government to grow too strong. By dividing the government's powers, the framers of the Constitution hoped to keep any one branch from gaining too much power.

For the same reason, the delegates also set up a system of checks and balances. Each branch of government has its own powers. But each also has ways to check, or stop, another branch from using too much power.

For example, laws are made by the two houses of Congress. A law is first called a bill, or a proposed law. To become a law, a bill passed by Congress must be signed by the President. Suppose that Congress passes a bill that the President does not want. The President can *veto* (vē′tō), or refuse to approve, the bill by not signing it.

The President, then, has checked the power of Congress. But suppose a very large number of members of Congress still want that law. They can overcome the President's veto by voting again. If two thirds of both houses vote for the bill, it becomes a law. Congress, then, has checked the power of the President.

A Federal System

The Constitutional Convention found still another way to limit the power of the government. It divided power between different levels of government. The central, or national, government was given certain powers in matters that are shared by all the states. For example, the central government can coin money, make treaties, and oversee trade. But certain other powers were left to the states. For example, each state has say in education, marriage laws, and other state matters.

This dividing of government powers between the national government and state governments is called the *federal system* (fed′ər əl sis′təm). Each citizen of the United States lives under both a national and a state government.

Making Amendments

The delegates wanted to form the best plan of government they could. However, they knew that they could not plan for everything. Also, they knew that the nation

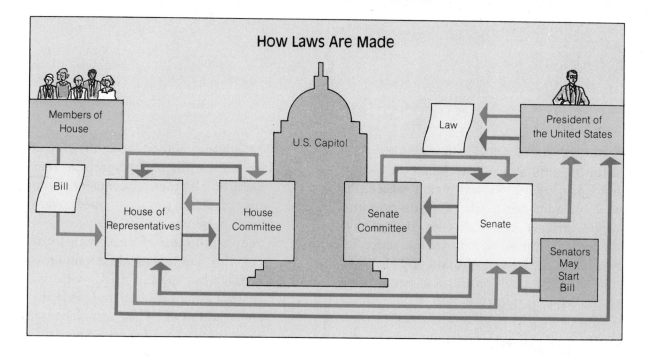

How Laws Are Made

Members of House

Bill

House of Representatives

House Committee

U.S. Capitol

Senate Committee

Senate

Senators May Start Bill

Law

President of the United States

would change in the future as it grew and faced new problems. Therefore, they made it possible to make changes in the Constitution. Changes in the Constitution are called *amendments* (ə mend′məntz). In order for an amendment to be added to the Constitution, it must be *ratified* (rat′ə fīd), or accepted by vote, in most of the states.

Approving the Constitution

Four long and hard months after it began, the Constitutional Convention finished its work. The Constitution was ready. But before it became "the law of the land," two things had to happen. First, most of the delegates had to sign the Constitution. Second, at least nine of the 13 states had to ratify it. Neither of these steps would be easy. Many Americans were not sure about setting up the government the Constitution outlined.

Benjamin Franklin gave perhaps the best reasons for accepting the Constitution. He

asked the Convention delegates to sign it, stating:

"I am sure of this: that the combined wisdom of so many thoughtful men is certain to be sounder as a whole than anything any one of us could have written alone. So I hope each of you will join me . . . and show your approval of the whole effort by signing it, and supporting it before the people."

Thirty-nine delegates signed the Constitution. Then it was sent to the states for their vote. Each state set up a convention to study the Constitution. At these state conventions many delegates spoke for and against the new plan of government. People against the Constitution thought that it did not have enough in it to protect the rights of the people. These speakers reminded everyone how Parliament had acted without thought to the rights, or liberties, of Americans by passing such acts as the Intolerable Acts. They did not want an American government ever to do the same.

Several states refused to ratify the Constitution until a way was found to protect individual rights. It was finally agreed to add amendments to the Constitution that would protect the rights of the people. Once this promise was made, the states began to ratify the Constitution. By the summer of 1788 the Constitution was the law of the land.

The Bill of Rights

The first ten amendments were added to the Constitution in 1791. They are called the *Bill of Rights*. These amendments list the rights that the government cannot take away from the American people. They promise that:

1. Congress may not make any laws that take away freedom of religion, freedom of speech, freedom of the press, freedom to meet together peacefully, or freedom to question government actions.
2. The people have a right to keep and bear arms, or weapons.
3. The government cannot make people give food and housing to soldiers in peacetime.
4. The government cannot search people or homes without good reason.
5. People charged with grave crimes have the right to trial by jury. They also cannot be tried for the same crime twice and cannot be made to give evidence against themselves.

Americans cannot have their lives, liberty, or property taken from them unfairly. If the government needs any of their property, the government must pay for it.

6. People who are charged with breaking the law have the right to a speedy and public trial, with witnesses. They must be told what they are accused of. They also have the right to be defended by a lawyer.
7. In almost all cases that come to trial, people have the right to be tried by a jury.
8. Punishments for breaking the law must not be cruel or unusual.
9. The fact that the Constitution does not give a certain right to people does not mean the people do not have that right.
10. If the Constitution does not give certain powers to the national government and does not forbid them to state governments, then the state governments or the people have those powers.

Do You Know?

1. What is a republic?
2. What was the Great Compromise?
3. Why did the Constitution divide the national government into three branches?
4. What is the Bill of Rights?

3

Our Government Begins

There was never any question about whom the American people would choose as their first President. "First in war, first in peace, and first in the hearts of his country" described George Washington. In April 1789 he made his way from Virginia to New York City, the nation's capital at that time. There he took the oath of office:

> "I do solemnly swear that I will faithfully execute (carry out) the Office of President of the United States, and will, to the best of my ability, preserve, protect, and defend the Constitution of the United States—so help me God."

The President's Cabinet

Never before had a nation set up the kind of government the United States had planned. Therefore, the founders had to try new things. They had to experiment.

It soon became clear that President Washington would need help to "faithfully execute the Office of President." Congress therefore formed three departments of government to help the President. The head of each department is called a secretary.

The nation's first executive department was the Department of State. This department is responsible for the way the United

In April of 1789, George Washington entered New York Harbor in a gaily decorated boat. How did New Yorkers greet him?

States deals with foreign countries. President Washington named Thomas Jefferson to head it, as Secretary of State.

The second executive department set up was the Department of the Treasury. It was given the hard job of straightening out and managing the new nation's money problems. President Washington named Alexander Hamilton as Secretary of the Treasury. Third came the Department of War, to take care of the nation's defense. A former Revolutionary War general, Henry Knox, became the first Secretary of War.

Benjamin Banneker was born free in Maryland. Besides helping with the plans for Washington, Banneker wrote books, studied mathematics and the stars, and was a landowner.

Two more executive offices were formed while Washington was President. An Attorney General was made the nation's chief law officer. The first Postmaster General had to set up and run the nation's postal service.

The President called on these executive officers for advice in handling the nation's affairs. Soon they came to be called the President's *Cabinet* (kab′ə nit). Over the years new departments have been added to the executive branch, as the need for them arose.

A New and Permanent Capital

The new nation needed a capital city where the government could meet and carry out its duties. In 1790, President Washington chose a piece of land for the capital on the banks of the Potomac River. It was located in about the center of the 13 states, midway down the Atlantic Coast. Since the Potomac River flowed between Virginia and Maryland, each state gave up part of its land for the new city. Plans began to be made for Washington, as the new capital was called.

President Washington asked a French citizen who had fought in the Revolution to plan the capital city. Pierre L'Enfant (pē er′ län fän′) promised to make the capital "magnificent enough to grace (honor) a great nation." Benjamin Banneker, a black mathematician and astronomer, was hired to help L'Enfant.

Before the capital of Washington could be built, the land had to be measured and cleared. What river is in the background?

L'Enfant planned a beautiful city. He placed the Capitol, the building in which Congress meets, at the center of the city. It stood on high ground, where it could be seen easily from afar. Under L'Enfant's plan the streets were to spread out from the Capitol like the spokes of a wheel. The President's home, which is called the White House, and other important government buildings were to be near the Capitol. There were to be many parks and squares.

Unfortunately, L'Enfant often quarreled with people. He was asked to leave the job in 1792. Banneker remembered L'Enfant's plans, however, and was able to finish work on the city. In 1800 the government was finally able to move to Washington from Philadelphia, which had served as the nation's capital after New York. The American government was home at last. In 1871 the capital gained its full name—Washington, District of Columbia (D.C.).

George Washington

It seemed only right that the nation's capital should be named after Washington. George Washington had served his country unselfishly and well.

Washington was born in Virginia on February 22, 1732. When he was only 12, he had to help manage his family's land.

115

A

Washington Monuments

Every year, millions of people from all over the country and the world visit Washington, D.C. The capital of the United States has been known for its beautiful places for almost 200 years. Throughout the city are parks and white buildings.

All of the major buildings of the federal government are in Washington. As you can see in this old painting, the White House and the Capitol were among the first buildings to be put up in the city (B). Every American President except for George Washington has lived in the White House (A).

From the beginning, Washington, D.C., has stood for freedom. The Supreme Court (C) reminds Americans of the importance of law. Among the most loved sights in the city are its monuments. These special buildings honor the country's greatest Presidents. The Washington Monument (D), for example, can be seen from many parts of the city. The Jefferson Memorial (E) was built in the style of building that Thomas Jefferson loved. On the Lincoln Memorial are carved speeches made by Abraham Lincoln (F).

F

116

B

C

E

D

117

George and Martha Washington are shown with their two grandchildren and a servant. What is the family doing?

Washington's father had just died. Four years later Washington left home to seek adventure in the wilderness to the west. He learned to be a surveyor, a person who measures land.

When Washington was 20 years old, he inherited a family plantation, Mount Vernon, in Virginia after his brother died. A few years later, in 1759, he married a wealthy widow, Martha Custis. Washington then turned to farming. At Mount Vernon he raised crops, cattle, and fine horses.

Though he loved Mount Vernon, Washington often left home to defend his land. You read in Unit 3 that he fought in the French and Indian War. Then he served as commander-in-chief during the Revolutionary War. Next he served as president of the Constitutional Convention. Finally, Washington was elected the nation's first President, and he served two terms. When his second term ended in 1797 Washington returned to Mount Vernon. He died there two years later. The entire nation mourned his loss.

Do You Know?

1. What is the President's Cabinet?
2. What is the job of the Secretary of State?
3. Who planned the capital city of the United States?
4. What is the Capitol building?

To Help You Learn

Using New Words

The phrases below explain the words or terms listed above. Number a paper from 1 through 16. After each number write the word or term that matches each definition.

1. The highest court in the United States
2. Approved by vote in most of the states
3. The part of Congress that has the most members
4. Laws that are added to the Constitution
5. Settlement of an argument by having each side agree to give up part of what it wants
6. The dividing of governing powers between the state governments and the national government
7. A nation in which the people govern through their chosen representatives
8. A group of people, chosen by the President, to help with the duties of the executive branch
9. The part of Congress that has two members from each state
10. People chosen to represent their states
11. Lawmaking branch of government
12. The first 10 amendments to the Constitution
13. A written plan of government
14. Branch of government that explains the meaning of laws
15. A President's refusal to approve a bill
16. Branch of government that carries out the laws

Finding the Facts

1. What are the three branches of the United States government? What is the main job of each?
2. Give two examples of the system of checks and balances in the government.
3. How can the Constitution be changed?
4. Why was the Bill of Rights added to the Constitution?
5. Who was the first President of the United States? Who did he choose to be Secretary of State?
6. What is the job of the Secretary of the Treasury?
7. Where is Washington, D.C., located?

Learning from Maps

The map on this page shows part of Washington, D.C. On it are some of the important buildings, parks, and other places in the city. It also shows some of the main streets. Study the map and do the following exercise:

- Locate the Capitol, the building where Congress meets, and the Supreme Court building. In which direction would you go to get from the Capitol to the Supreme Court building?
- The President lives in the White House. Which street connects the White House and the Capitol?
- With your finger, trace the route you might take from the Capitol to the Washington Monument.

Using Study Skills

1. **Flow chart:** Turn to the chart on page 111. This kind of chart is called a flow chart. It shows the steps that must be followed for something to happen. This flow chart shows the steps that are needed for a bill to become a law.
   - What is the first step in making a law?
   - What is the last step in making a law?
   - Charts sometimes use symbols to stand for people or things. In this chart what does the building in the middle stand for? What symbol is used to stand for a law? What do the arrows show?
2. **Table:** Look closely at the table on page 121. It gives information about the members of Congress and the President.

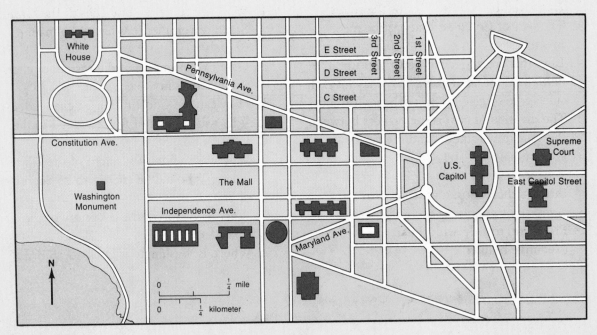

Congress and the President

Officials	Length of Term	Age Needed to Run for Office	Citizenship
Senators	6 years	at least 30 years old	American citizen for at least 9 years
Representatives	2 years	at least 25 years old	American citizen for at least 7 years
President	4 years	at least 35 years old	native-born American citizen

- How old must a person be to become a Senator? To become President?
- When could an immigrant from Mexico become a Representative? A President?
- The "Length of Term" is the number of years for which a person is elected to be in office. After each term is over, the person must be elected again. How long is a Senator's term? A Representative's term? A President's term?

Thinking It Through

1. The Articles of Confederation set up a weak national government. This caused many problems for the government and for the states. Name two of these problems. Then explain how the new Constitution solved them.
2. Think about what you have learned about George Washington and his life. Tell why you think he is sometimes called the father of his country.
3. Turn to page 112 and reread the list of rights in the Bill of Rights. Why did the states want these rights? What problems could arise today if Americans did not have these rights?

Projects

1. The Explorers' Committee might want to learn more about the many important buildings in Washington, D.C. Students could start their search by looking at the pictures on page 116 and 117 for ideas. Then they might make a large map that shows where some of these buildings are found. The committee also could plan a sightseeing trip through Washington, D.C., and prepare a tour-guide book that describes the important sights on the trip.
2. Have the Research Committee find out more about the approval of the Constitution by the states. Which states quickly approved the new plan? In which states did people worry about accepting the Constitution? What problems did these people find in the Constitution?
3. Have the Reading Committee find copies of *Poor Richard's Almanac* or other books by Benjamin Franklin. They might read some interesting or amusing parts of these books to the class.

5 A Growing Nation

Unit Preview

The United States grew quickly. Americans began to cross the Appalachians and to settle the Ohio Valley. Soon there were several states between the mountains and the Mississippi River.

The young nation still had to face problems, though. Indians in the territories did not want to give up their homes to settlers. Britain gave weapons to the Indians. The British also stopped American ships at sea and seized sailors. As a result, the United States fought a second war with Great Britian in 1812. No one won the war, but America won the respect of many countries.

The United States gained land farther west. France sold the Louisiana Territory to Americans. Texas joined the Union, which led to a war with Mexico that gave Americans all of the Southwest. Many settlers went there and to Oregon and Utah. After the discovery of gold in California, however, thousands of people went West to strike it rich.

Americans built roads and canals to make travel easier. They also made speedier ways to travel and keep in touch.

New inventions changed the way many Americans made their living. People began to work in factories. The cotton gin, reaper, and other new machines made work on farms easier. However, these changes made slavery grow and brought problems for workers.

Things to Discover

If you look carefully at the picture, map, and time line, you can answer these questions.
1. The map shows you the size of the United States in 1853. What do the black lines in the different parts of the country show you? What country borders the United States on the north? On the south?
2. The picture shows pioneers going west. The name of the picture is "Ships of the Plains." Why do you think these wagons crossing the grasslands were called ships?
3. When were the first textile machines built in America?
4. Louisiana was bought in 1803. How long after that did Lewis and Clark start their trip?
5. How long after the opening of the Erie Canal was the locomotive built?

Words to Learn

You will meet these words in this unit. As you read, you will learn what they mean and how to pronounce them. The Word List will help you.

abolish	industry
abolition movement	pioneers
canal	reforms
cash crop	territory
frontier	turnpikes
impressment	

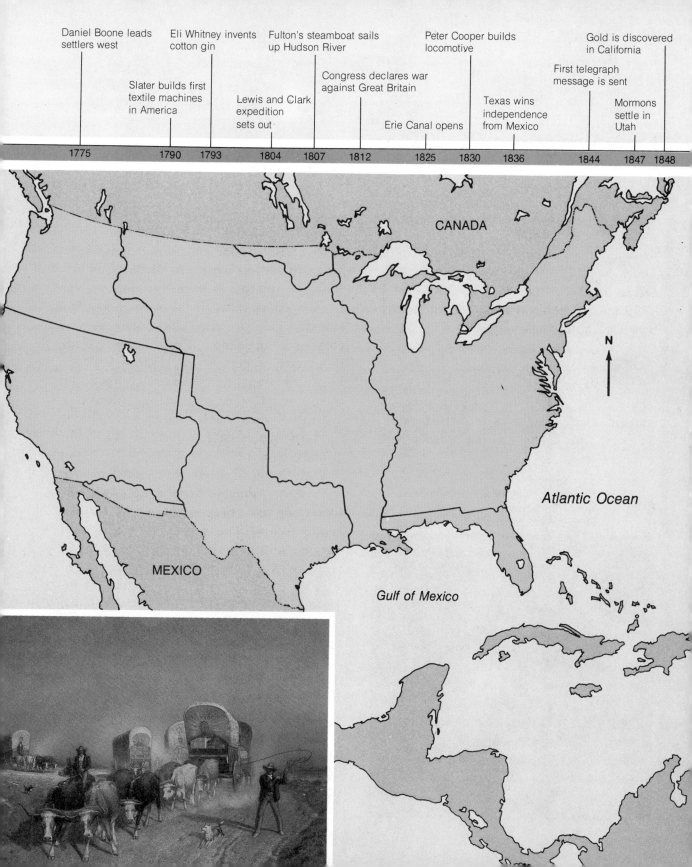

Daniel Boone leads settlers west

Eli Whitney invents cotton gin

Fulton's steamboat sails up Hudson River

Peter Cooper builds locomotive

Gold is discovered in California

Slater builds first textile machines in America

Lewis and Clark expedition sets out

Congress declares war against Great Britain

First telegraph message is sent

Texas wins independence from Mexico

Mormons settle in Utah

Erie Canal opens

1775   1790 1793   1804   1807 1812   1825 1830 1836   1844   1847 1848

CANADA

N

Atlantic Ocean

MEXICO

Gulf of Mexico

1
New Frontiers

The national government settled into Washington, D.C., in 1800. At that time no one dreamed that within 50 years the United States would stretch from the Atlantic Ocean all the way to the Pacific Ocean. In 1800 most Americans lived east of the Appalachian Mountains.

Crossing the Appalachians

There is an old Chinese saying that "the longest journey begins with just one step." The first step in the exciting journey westward of the United States was the crossing of the Appalachian Mountains. In March 1775 Daniel Boone and some friends led a group of settlers west through the Cumberland Gap in southwestern Virginia. A gap is an opening through the mountains, or a narrow valley that travelers could follow to cross the highlands. Even before 1800, thousands of settlers had followed Boone westward along the Wilderness Road, his trail through the Appalachian Mountains and to the west. These settlers were able to form the states of Kentucky in 1792 and Tennessee in 1796.

The Western settlers were called *pioneers* (pī′ə nērz′). Pioneers are people who do something first, preparing the way for others to follow. The western pioneers were the first settlers to live on the *frontier* (frun tēr′). A frontier is the area that lies at the edge of a settled region. Beyond it is unsettled land. Often the pioneers traveled in covered wagons and followed old Indian trails. Some came by boat along the Great Lakes or along the Ohio River.

Pioneer Life

Pioneers had to have great courage to move to the frontier. They also had to be willing to work very hard. First, people had to cut down trees to build houses for their families. Often their houses were one-room log cabins. There were no stores on the fron-

Among the first *pioneers* to settle in Kentucky were the families who followed Daniel Boone across the Appalachians.

Many *frontier* settlements started as forts. They included high fences, lookouts for guards, and places for soldiers to stay. What other buildings did these settlements have?

tier in which to buy food and other needed items. Therefore, pioneers had to make many things for themselves.

Living on the frontier was often lonely. Farms were built far from one another. The pioneers quickly found ways to fight loneliness, though. They came up with reasons to join together. One reason was "barnraising." When a farm needed a new barn, families from miles around would gather there to help. Then it was time for picnicking, dancing, and playing games. Families met also to form quilting bees. While the children played, the women made warm bed quilts for the cold nights. The men talked about their lives on the frontier.

Pioneer children did not have much time to go to school or to spend studying. If there were any schools, children often had

to walk far to get to them. Children were lucky if they could take time from their chores, or work, to learn to read, write, and "do sums." Pioneer children often had only three or four years of schooling.

New States of the Frontier

Thousands of pioneers went to live in the unsettled land between the Appalachian Mountains and the Mississippi River. This land was then known as the West. Land that was part of the United States but did not have enough people to be a state was called a *territory* (ter′ə tôr′ē). The land to the west of the Appalachian Mountains was divided into two territories. The Northwest Territory was the land north of the Ohio River and east of the Mississippi River. In a few years the settlers had formed five states out of the Northwest Territory. They were Ohio (1803), Indiana (1816), Illinois (1818), Michigan (1837), and Wisconsin (1848).

Many other pioneers went from the Old South west to the territory called the Old Southwest. The Old Southwest was the land south of the Ohio River and east of the Mississippi River. Besides Kentucky and Tennessee, the states of Mississippi (1817) and Alabama (1819) were formed out of this territory.

About 4,000 of the 14,000 Cherokees who set out on "The Trail of Tears" died. The long trip to the Indian Territory (present-day Oklahoma) began in 1838.

Removing the Indians

When George Washington became President in 1789, Indians lived in about half the land that was then the United States. Many Indians had long since left the original 13 states along the Atlantic Coast. They had gone west to find new land on which to live.

Now, though, the pioneers also were going west. When more trouble between the settlers and Indians arose, the settlers asked the American government to remove the Indians from the lands between the Appalachian Mountains and the Mississippi River. Often the government made treaties with the Indians to buy their land. However, this did not stop the pioneers from moving to land that belonged to Indians.

The Indians did not want to lose more of their homeland. A Shawnee Indian chief named Tecumseh (ti kum'sə) tried to unite the Indians to stop the pioneers. In 1811 United States troops led by William Henry Harrison defeated Tecumseh's forces at Tippecanoe (tip'ē kə noo') Creek in Indiana. The Americans soon were able to drive most of the Indians out of the Northwest Territory.

The Indians and settlers also fought in the Southeast. In 1826 the American government made a treaty with the Creek Indians for their land, and the Creeks agreed to move west of the Mississippi River. But their neighbors, the Cherokees, refused to make a treaty to sell their land in Georgia.

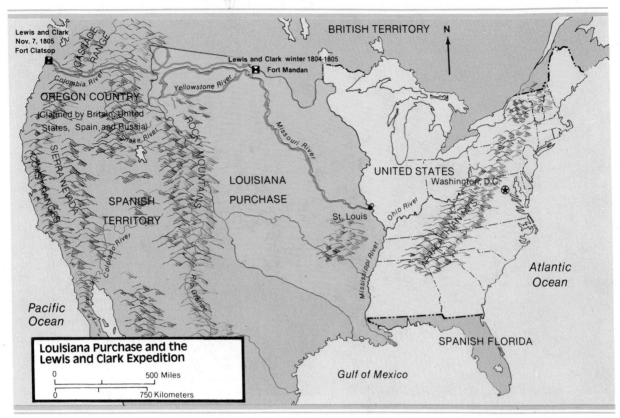

When the United States bought the Louisiana Territory it moved its frontier westward to the Rocky Mountains.

The government took the Cherokee land anyway and offered it for sale to settlers. The army then forced the Cherokees to move west. Nearly one fourth of the Indians died on the long, hard march to the West. Their heartbreaking journey has come to be called "The Trail of Tears."

The Louisiana Purchase

For a long time the land west of the Mississippi River had been claimed by the French. This land, called Louisiana, stretched from the Mississippi River west to the Rocky Mountains and from the Gulf of Mexico north to Canada. The Louisiana Territory was about the same size as all of the United States at that time.

In 1803, while Thomas Jefferson was President of the United States, the French offered to sell this land to the United States. The head of the French government, the Emperor Napoleon (nə pō′lē ən), was fighting wars in Europe and needed money to keep on fighting. He therefore offered to sell the Louisiana Territory to the United States for 15 million dollars.

President Jefferson jumped at the chance. This was the greatest land bargain in history. With the Louisiana Purchase, the United States doubled its size for only a few cents an acre.

Near the end of their trip, Lewis and Clark traveled along the Columbia River. Their guide, Sacajawea, spoke for them with the Pacific Northwest Indians and other groups they met.

The Lewis and Clark Expedition

What kind of land had the nation bought? What grew there? What Indian groups made it their home? President Jefferson wanted answers to all these questions.

Jefferson chose two men to lead an expedition to go and study the land. One leader was Jefferson's secretary, Meriwether Lewis. The other was William Clark, a former army officer. With them went a party of about 40 people.

In May 1804 the group left St. Louis, Missouri, and followed the Missouri River northwestward. The group set up winter camp in what is now North Dakota to wait for spring. There the explorers hired a

French-Canadian fur trader named Charbonneau (shär bə nō′) and his wife Sacajawea (sä kä jä wē′ə) to act as their guides. A Shoshone (shə shō′nē) Indian, Sacajawea could understand the Indian languages. Her job was to speak for the explorers to the Indians they met.

Sacajawea was a great help to Lewis and Clark. She knew much of the land they were going through. At one point she is thought to have saved everyone's lives. They met a group of Shoshones who seemed ready to destroy the newcomers. But then their chief and Sacajawea caught sight of each other. It turned out that they were brother and sister! As a child Sacajawea had been kidnapped and carried far away from her home. This was the first time since then that brother and sister had seen each other. After the happy meeting, the Shoshone chief gave the explorers the pack animals and guides they needed to go on.

Lewis and Clark kep heading westward over the Rocky Mountains and all the way to the Pacific Ocean. As they traveled, the explorers wrote down what they saw. They drew maps showing the land and the rivers. They reported on the kinds of animals they saw.

In all, the Lewis and Clark expedition traveled through 8,000 miles (12,800 km) of wilderness. The explorers returned to St. Louis two years, four months, and nine days after they had left. People were surprised to see them. The expedition had been gone so long that everyone throught that its members had died. President Jefferson welcomed Lewis and Clark back with pleasure.

Thomas Jefferson—Man of Many Talents

President Jefferson studied the findings of Lewis and Clark with great interest. For in addition to being a great national leader, Jefferson was also a scientist. In Virginia, where he had been born in 1743, Jefferson had studied everything around him. Growing plants, weather patterns, the movement of the stars, the workings of ma-

chines—all drew his attention. So did the writings of great thinkers.

Jefferson's ability to think clearly and to explain his thoughts to others was soon put to good use. The Declaration of Independence shows to all how well he wrote. His home in Virginia, called Monticello (mon'tē sel'ō), was filled with things he invented. Among them were the swivel chair, or a chair that turned easily, and a dumbwaiter. The dumbwaiter was a small elevator that was used to carry food and other small items from one floor to another.

Thomas Jefferson was the third President of the United States. He also spent many years in France as an American representative.

After Jefferson left the Presidency in 1809, he persuaded the Virginia government to open the nation's first state university. Jefferson served as the first head of the University of Virginia and designed several of its buildings.

Jefferson died on July 4, 1826. This was exactly 50 years after the Declaration of Independence was adopted. In the words he wrote for his own tombstone, Jefferson tells us what he thought his greatest actions were:

"Here lies buried Thomas Jefferson, author of the Declaration of Independence, of the Statute (law) of Virginia for religious freedom, and father of the University of Virginia."

This scarf has eight scenes from the War of 1812. Among the scenes are important naval battles.

The War of 1812

When Napoleon turned over the Louisiana Territory to American officers in Paris, he said a very interesting thing. "You will fight England again," he told them. Just a few years later, events proved that Napoleon was right.

Causes of the War

Great Britain and France had been fighting each other for years. When Washington was President, both nations began to stop or take American ships at sea. They wanted to cut off each other's trade with the United States. Neither wanted the other nation to have the use of American goods.

Then British ships took a further step. Besides stopping American ships and boarding them, the British also took away some of the sailors. They said that these sailors were British citizens. This taking of sailors by force was called *impressment* (im press'mənt).

The United States government told Britain to stop taking sailors from American ships. Impressment was an attack on the American right to freedom of the seas. But the United States Navy had only a few ships and could not stop these unfriendly British acts.

When James Madison became President in 1809, he soon had to face another problem with the British. They again began stirring up the Indians along the frontier. After the Revolutionary War, the British had agreed to give up their forts in the Northwest Territory. Instead of leaving, they were arming the Indians!

Beginning in 1811, some members of Congress demanded that the United States go to war with Britain. They said that war was the only way to stop the unfriendly British acts. They also believed that if it went to war, the United States could win Canada away from Britain. These members of Congress soon came to be called "War Hawks."

President Madison was won over to the War Hawks' side. On June 1, 1812, he sent Congress a message which called for war against Great Britain. Congress then declared war on Britain.

Fighting the War of 1812

The War Hawks believed that the Canadians would join the American side. This would make it easy for the Americans to win the war. However, both the Canadians and the Indians under Tecumseh helped Great Britain. As a result, the American army lost its early battles.

The war at sea was more successful than the war on land. The main reason was that the United States had several powerful warships. One of them, the *Constitution,* took on the British warship *Guerrière* (gwer rē ār') soon after the war began. After only 30 minutes of fighting, the *Guerrière* sank. Cannon balls seemed to bounce off the thick wooden hull of the American ship, however. Its wooden sides seemed to be as

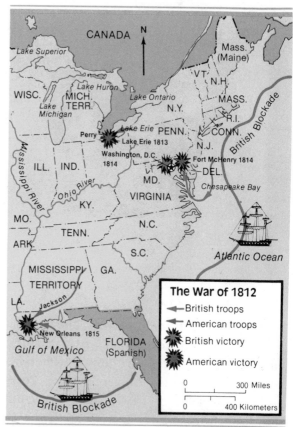

The battles of the War of 1812 were fought on land and on sea. Which battles were won by the Americans? By The British? Where was the British naval blockade set up?

strong as iron. The thankful crew members proudly nicknamed their ship "Old Ironsides."

In 1813 another naval battle won by the Americans was the turning point of the war. The British had gained control of the Great Lakes and had placed six warships on Lake Erie. The British used Lake Erie as a

131

This painting is of the battle of Fort McHenry. It shows the "bombs bursting in air" that Francis Scott Key saw during the fighting.

supply route for their troops. The Americans planned to destroy the British ships. In September 1813 a young American naval captain named Oliver Hazard Perry led a small fleet of newly built ships out into Lake Erie.

For three hours the British and Americans fought. Finally, Perry was able to make his report. "We have met the enemy, and they are ours," he said proudly. The Americans had cut off the British troops from their supplies. The American army then was able to defeat the Canadians and the Indians.

The Burning of Washington

British warships still controlled the Atlantic Coast, though. A year after Perry's victory, a British force of 1,500 troops sailed into Chesapeake Bay and marched to Washington, D.C. The British defeated the soldiers defending the nation's capital.

President James Madison and his wife Dolley fled the city. When Dolley Madison escaped from the White House, she carried with her a valuable painting of George Washington. When the British troops entered the White House, they ate the meal that had been prepared for the President and his Cabinet. The troops then set fire to the White House, the Capitol building, several other buildings, and all of the city's bridges.

"The Star-Spangled Banner"

The British ships then headed for Baltimore. To take the city, the British had to get past Fort McHenry, which guarded the entrance to the harbor. About 1,000 American troops defended the fort. On the morning of September 13, 1814, British ships began their attack on Fort McHenry. Their cannons and rockets kept firing all that day and through the night.

A young American lawyer, Francis Scott Key, was on an American ship held by the British. He watched the battle with fear and with hope. As dawn broke on September 14, his hope was rewarded. The American flag still flew above Fort McHenry! This sight made Key so happy that he wrote a poem, quickly, on the back of an envelope:

> "And the rockets' red glare, the bombs
>   bursting in air,
> Gave proof thro' the night that our flag
>   was still there."

These and the rest of his words in "The Star-Spangled Banner" were soon put to music. It became America's national anthem, or song of praise.

The Battle of New Orleans

The last battle of the War of 1812 was fought in New Orleans. Built at the mouth of the Mississippi River, New Orleans was an important American shipping port. In January 1815, 8,000 British troops were sent to capture the city.

General Andrew Jackson was in charge of the defense of New Orleans. His force of Kentucky and Tennessee soldiers reached New Orleans before the British did. The Americans began to dig trenches, from which they would fire at the British. Jackson's troops were joined by fighters from the Gulf Coast, many of them former pirates.

By the end of the battle 2,000 British soldiers had fallen. The American force counted only 13 dead. News of the American victory raced through the nation.

The Peace Treaty

Actually, the Battle of New Orleans need never have been fought. The war had already ended! Representatives of Britain and the United States had met in Belgium in Europe. There on Christmas Eve, 1814, they had signed a peace treaty. However, news took a long time to cross an ocean. Americans did not learn about the peace treaty until several weeks later—at about the same time they heard of the victory at New Orleans!

Do You Know?

1. How did the pioneers deal with the lonely life of the frontier?
2. What was the Louisiana Purchase?
3. What caused the War of 1812?
4. Why did Francis Scott Key write the "Star-Spangled Banner"?

Before You Go On

Using New Words

frontier   pioneers
impressment   territory

The phrases below explain the words listed above. Number a paper from 1 through 4. After each number write the word that matches the definition.

1. People who first do something, such as settle in a new place
2. Taking sailors from a ship that belongs to another country
3. Land that belongs to the United States but that is not a state
4. Unsettled land at the edge of a settled area

Finding the Facts

1. In what part of the United States was the Northwest Territory?

2. Who was Tecumseh? What important battle did he lose?
3. What was the "Trail of Tears"?
4. Why was the Lewis and Clark Expedition important to the nation?
5. Name at least two things for which Thomas Jefferson is remembered.
6. Why did the United States go to war with Great Britain in 1812?
7. Name two battles of the War of 1812. Describe one of them.
8. What is the national anthem of the United States? Who wrote it?
9. Why didn't the Battle of New Orleans have to be fought?

2
Reaching the Pacific

The War of 1812 made the United States proud of itself. No one had won the war, but once again Americans had stood up to a strong European nation—Great Britain. In doing so, the United States had won the respect of several other countries.

Proud Americans then decided they wanted to expand their nation, or make it even larger. Out west beyond the Louisiana Territory was a land where few American settlers lived. It stretched from the Rocky Mountains all the way to the Pacific Ocean.

The Birth of Texas

In the western land were the areas we call Texas and the Southwest. They once had been under Spanish rule. When Mexico became independent of Spain in 1821, these areas remained part of Mexico.

The Mexican government decided to invite people from other nations to settle this territory. First, Mexico offered large pieces of land in Texas to settlers. In 1821, 300 pioneer American families led by Stephen Austin arrived. More pioneers followed.

The Mexican government soon began to fear it would lose Texas. It therefore said that no more Americans could settle there. Moreover, the Americans who lived in Texas had to obey Mexican laws. The Mexican government then sent troops into Texas to make sure the settlers obeyed the

laws. The Texans grew angry and decided that they wanted to be independent of Mexico. Mexico wanted to keep Texas, however. Fighting finally broke out between the Texans and the Mexican troops.

"Remember the Alamo!"

On October 2, 1835, the two sides fought a battle in the town of San Antonio. The Texans won and took many prisoners. This angered the Mexican president, General

Most of the battles of the Texas War for Independence took place near the Gulf of Mexico. Which battles were won by the Texans? By the Mexicans?

135

Antonio López de Santa Anna. He led a large army to crush the rebels.

In February 1836 fewer than 200 Texans gathered in an old San Antonio mission called the Alamo (al'ə mō'). They prepared to defend themselves, to the death if need be. Their leader, Colonel William B. Travis, sent a message out from the Alamo:

"To the people of Texas and all Americans in the world: I call on you in the name of liberty, of patriotism, and everything dear to the American character to come to our aid. . . . If this call is ne-glected, I am determined to sustain myself (keep myself alive) as long as possible and die like a soldier who never forgets what is due to his honor and that of this country. Victory or death!"

Travis's plea was not answered. At dawn on March 6, 1836, Santa Anna's army of 3,000 soldiers attacked the Alamo. The two sides fought until every defender of the mission was dead. One of them was Davy Crockett, the frontier fighter.

Just four days before this battle, delegates from all over Texas had met and de-

The Alamo in San Antonio, Texas, has become a symbol of freedom. It stands for people who are willing to die for their beliefs.

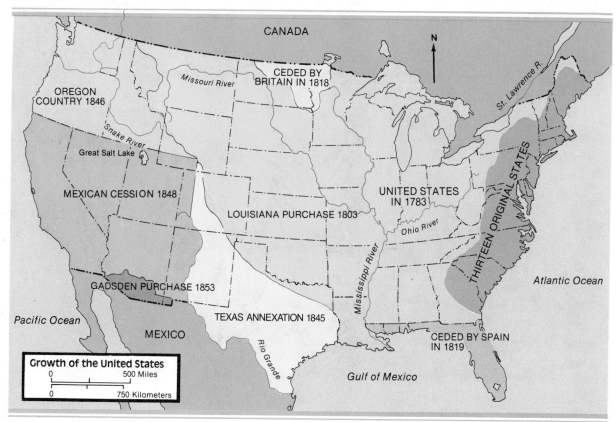

The United States started with thirteen colonies along the Atlantic Coast. The country added land until it reached the Pacific Ocean.

clared Texas to be independent of Mexico. They had said that Texas was now a republic, which they called the Lone Star Republic. Sam Houston was its first president.

Six weeks later, the Texans met the Mexicans in the Battle of San Jacinto (sän jä sēn′tō). With the cry of "Remember the Alamo!" ringing in their ears, the Texans attacked. Santa Anna was taken prisoner, and the Mexican army returned across the Rio Grande.

The Mexican government still did not admit that all of Texas was lost to Mexico. Therefore, when Texas became part of the United States in 1845, the Mexican government grew angry.

War with Mexico

The quarrel between the United States and Mexico grew worse because Texas and Mexico did not agree about where the border between them was. Texas said that its southwestern border was the Rio Grande. Mexico said that land far to the north and east of that river was part of Mexico. The American President, James K. Polk, ordered American army troops to go to the Rio Grande. There in April 1846, Mexican troops attacked the American army. The next month the United States declared war on Mexico.

The war with Mexico did not last long. American forces under Generals Zachary

137

Americans learned much about ranching from Spaniards who lived in the Mexican Cession.

Taylor and Winfield Scott attacked Mexico by land and by sea. Other troops marched westward to California. Americans there quickly defeated the Mexicans. The fighting ended in 1847, when the Americans captured Mexico's capital, Mexico City.

The Mexican Cession

President Polk wanted the Southwest to become part of the United States. When he had tried to buy this land, Mexico had refused to sell. Now that the United States had won the Mexican War, Mexico accepted the Rio Grande as Texas's southwestern border.

Mexico also granted the United States all of the Southwest in return for 15 million dollars. The land that the United States gained from Mexico is called the Mexican Cession (sesh′ən). It included what are now New Mexico, Arizona, Utah, Nevada, and California.

Trails to the Far West

The Mexican Cession was called the Far West. American settlers had started moving there to live years before the war.

Several well-used wagon trails to the West led from Missouri. One of them was the Santa Fe Trail. It took pioneers into what is now New Mexico. Another route was the Mormon (môr′mən) Trail leading to Utah. The Oregon Trail was taken by settlers who wished to go to the Oregon country in the Northwest. All of these trails joined other trails leading to the Southwest, to Oregon, and to California.

Moving to the Oregon Country

The Oregon Country was on the West Coast, north of California. Settlement of the Oregon Country began after two missionaries went there in the 1830s. They were Marcus and Narcissa Whitman. Through the Whitmans and other missionaries, word of the riches of Oregon reached the East. "Oregon fever" swept the nation.

The Oregon Country was claimed by both the United States and Great Britain. The two nations had agreed to share it, but by the 1840s Oregon had many more Americans than British. As a result, the two nations signed a treaty in 1846. It gave the United States the Oregon Country as far north as what is now Canada. In a few years this territory became the states of Oregon, Washington, and Idaho.

The Mormons and Utah

Utah was settled by a religious group called the Mormons. They belonged to the Church of Jesus Christ of Latter-day Saints. This group was started in the 1820s by Joseph Smith in New York State.

The Mormons built prosperous communities wherever they settled—first in Ohio, next in Missouri, and then in Illinois. But many people around the Mormons did not like their religious beliefs. For example, at that time the Mormons believed a man could have more than one wife. In 1844 a mob attacked the Mormons in Illinois and killed Joseph Smith.

Brigham Young became the new Mormon leader. He decided that the Mormons would have troubles in any settled part of the United States. Therefore, he decided that the Mormons should go west.

In 1846 Young led 5,000 Mormons westward. On July 24, 1847, the weary travelers looked down from a mountain into a great valley. There, in the Great Salt Lake Valley in what is now Utah, the Mormons started to build their new home. By the end of the 1800s Utah was a state.

Settlement of California

Fur traders first arrived in California in the 1820s. Other groups of Americans arrived there soon afterward. Then, shortly after the war with Mexico began in 1846, Americans who had settled in California declared it a republic independent of Mexico. The Californians then raised their own flag, which showed a grizzly bear and a lone star. It was the flag of the "Bear Flag Republic."

During the war with Mexico, both the American army and the American navy helped the Californians to drive the Mexicans out of California. As you have seen, California then became part of the United States.

This drawing made fun of the fortyniners and the many ways they thought of reaching the gold fields of California.

The Gold Rush

At that time something happened that caused people from all over the world to race to California. On January 24, 1848, a worker who was building a lumber mill near Sacramento noticed something shining in the water nearby. Gold, it was gold! The owner of the mill, John Sutter, wanted to keep the find a secret. But news of gold at Sutter's mill spread quickly.

"Gold fever" soon took hold of California. By 1849 tens of thousands of gold seekers, or "fortyniners," left their homes in other states to go to California. Some boarded ships that sailed all the way around the tip of South America and up to California. Others sailed south to Panama. There they crossed the land and took ships that sailed north. Still others went overland.

By 1849 nearly 80,000 "fortyniners" had reached California. Few of them ever "struck gold." But the California gold rush caused California to boom, or grow quickly. In 1850 California became the nation's thirty-first state.

Do You Know?

1. Why did Texas want to be independent of Mexico?
2. What caused the war between the United States and Mexico?
3. What trails did the pioneers follow to the Far West?
4. Who were the Mormons? Where did they finally settle?
5. Who were the fortyniners?

3
Improving Transportation and Communication

The United States had grown rapidly. In 1782 it was a small nation east of the Appalachian Mountains. By 1803, it had doubled its size with the Louisiana Purchase. In 1848 the nation stretched across the continent.

As the nation grew its people needed more and better ways to move about. Therefore, new methods of transportation were invented. People who lived far apart also needed ways to keep in touch with one another. As a result, new means of communication were made. All of these methods not only brought people closer together. They also completely changed the way Americans lived.

Building Roads

As the nation grew larger, people tried to find ways to make travel easier. At first, settlers had used the rough trails of the Indians. The dirt roads that took their place were full of holes and stones. Most of these roads were short. Then in 1811 the American government built a new and better road west, from Maryland all the way to Illinois. It was called the Cumberland, or National, Road.

Private companies also built roads. They charged people tolls to use the roads. Every few miles along such a road, there was a gate, or pike. The traveler had to pay a toll, or fee, to have this pike opened or turned.

As a result, such roads came to be called *turnpikes* (turn′pīkz).

Soon, private and public roads joined farms to towns and towns to cities. Covered wagons, carts carrying trade goods, and stagecoaches filled the roads at all times of day and night.

Using the Rivers

Whenever it was possible, Americans shipped their goods by water because it was cheaper. Ships on the oceans used sails. Flatboats were used on rivers. The flatboats were like rafts—flat pieces of wood nailed together. Pioneers would load their furniture on the flatboats and sail down the river, with the current, or in the direction the water flowed. When they reached their stop, the pioneers unloaded their belongings. Then they used the wood from the flatboats to build their houses.

Traders also used flatboats. They, too, loaded their goods on flatboats and sailed downriver. At some port, they sold their goods. The traders sold the wood from the flatboats for lumber. Then they made their way home by going overland.

Flatboats were useful, but there was one big problem in using them. They could not sail upriver, against the current. In 1807 a new kind of boat suddenly made travel by river easier.

Fulton's Steamboat

For years a young American named Robert Fulton had been interested in steam engines. He wanted to make a ship that was powered by a steam engine. He finally decided to put the steam engine into a large riverboat. People laughed at his strange boat—this steamboat. "Fulton's Folly," they called it.

They stopped laughing one August morning when Fulton's steamboat, the *Clermont* (klar'mont), left New York City. It sailed *up* the Hudson River, against the current. Thirty-two hours later, it reached Albany, 150 miles (240 km) upstream. Fulton was able to report happily:

"The power of boats run by steam is now fully proved. The morning I left New York, there were not perhaps 30 persons in the city who believed that the boat would ever move 1 mile (1.6 km) per hour or be of the least use."

Building Canals

The success of the steamboat gave New York merchants an idea. Their businesses had grown, now that it was easy to ship goods upstream on the Hudson River. Their businesses would grow even more if they could find a way to ship goods farther inland, to the Great Lakes. Why not dig a *canal* (kə nal') across the state of New York, from the Hudson River to Lake Erie? A canal is a waterway that people build to connect two bodies of water.

The Erie Canal

Governor DeWitt Clinton of New York agreed that such a canal should be built upstate. New York State agreed to put up 7 million dollars in tax money to pay for it. Taxpayers who thought the canal was foolish called it "Clinton's Big Ditch."

Work on the canal began in 1817 and continued for eight years. Thousands of workers were needed to dig the deep trench. They dug through farmland, rock, and swamps for nearly 360 miles (576 km). The trench was then filled in with water to make a kind of artificial river. Flatboats could then be floated along the canal. They would be pulled by ropes drawn by horses or mules walking along the towpath on the side of the canal.

The Erie Canal was opened in 1825. It made money from the start. The canal both lowered the cost of shipping and cut down on the time of travel. It was then possible to ship goods from New York City all the way to Buffalo, New York, for only one and a half cents a mile (one cent a kilometer). The boats traveled about one and a half miles (2.4 km) an hour.

The Coming of the Railroads

Americans of the early 1800s found that they needed even faster means of traveling about. Someone had thought of pulling carriages along tracks, or rails. At first these cars were pulled by horses. The American inventor Peter Cooper decided to try to

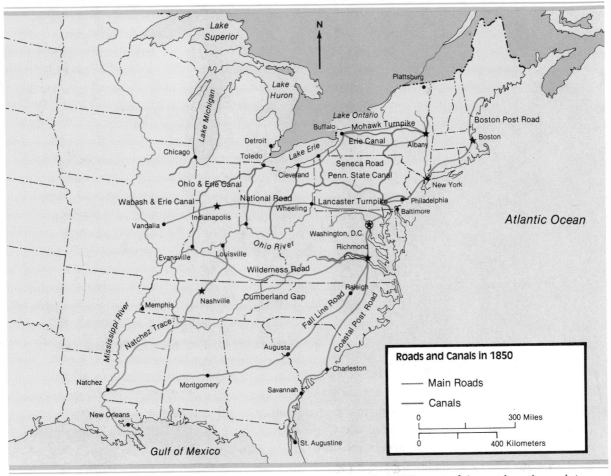

In 1850 most of the roads and *canals* in the United States were east of the Mississippi River. Which road ran from Maryland to Vandalia, Illinois? Which canals were near the Great Lakes?

improve on work done by the British. They were trying to use a steam engine to draw the cars. In 1830 Cooper made a steam locomotive (lō'kə mō'tiv), a train engine that moved by steam power. This locomotive was so small that it was named the *Tom Thumb.*

Like "Fulton's Folly," the *Tom Thumb* was made fun of at first. Could a steam locomotive outrun a railcar pulled by strong horses? A race was set up. A railroad car pulled by Cooper's locomotive had to race against a car pulled by a horse along the Baltimore and Ohio tracks. The *Tom Thumb* did well until it broke down. The horse then raced on to victory.

The victory did not last long. Steam locomotives soon were improved and took the place of horses on railroads. Within 20 years railroads crossed the eastern United States in many directions. They traveled at the speed of 30 miles (48 km) an hour.

A

Early Ways of Travel

Travel became easier for Americans during the first half of the 1800s. Large, strong wagons, such as the Conestoga wagons, were made (A). These wagons were safer to use than smaller wagons. They also had more room for riders to carry things on long trips. For shorter trips, lighter carriages with better springs made the ride less bumpy. This picture of a New York street (D) shows some of the kinds of carriages that were used in cities.

C

Ships were still the fastest and most comfortable way to travel. Business leaders began to build canals to join one waterway to another. Barges were pulled by mules through the Erie Canal (B).

Steam engines changed travel the most at this time. Robert Fulton's steamboat, the *Clermont,* made it possible to sail up and down rivers (E). The locomotive *Tom Thumb* was famous for losing its race to a horse (C). But it proved that railroads could be a speedy way to travel.

D

144

B

E

Samuel Morse was both a painter and an inventor. He is best known for his invention of the telegraph, which is shown on the table.

Messages by Telegraph

In 1832 Samuel F. B. Morse, a poor young artist, was sailing back to the United States after studying in Europe. While aboard the ship *Sully,* Morse heard of a new discovery. Someone had found out how to send electricity through a length of wire. For the rest of the voyage Morse thought about ways to send electrical messages by wire. As he left the ship, Morse said to the captain, "When you hear of the telegraph one of these days as the wonder of the world, remember the discovery was made on the good ship *Sully.*"

Morse began to try out his ideas. He strung wires all over his room. He learned how to send long and short bursts of energy through them. That is, some bursts of energy lasted for a short time and others a little longer time. Morse also worked out a system of using short and long signals to represent letters of the alphabet. These "dots and dashes" made up the Morse Code.

In 1843 Morse was able to get money from the government to build a telegraph line. A wire was strung from Washington, D.C., to Baltimore, 37 miles (59.2 km) away. On May 24, 1844, the first message was sent from Baltimore to the Supreme Court in Washington. Morse tapped it out: "What hath God wrought?" ("What has God made?") A message that would have taken six hours by horseback had been received in only seconds.

Soon telegraph wires connected many parts of the United States. By 1860 there were more than 50,000 miles (80,000 km) of telegraph lines uniting the country.

Do You Know?

1. How did Americans improve their roads during the early 1800s?
2. Why was the steamboat so important to the development of water transportation?
3. Who designed the *Tom Thumb?* How did it help to improve America's transportation system?
4. What was the Morse Code? How does it work?

4
Changing Ways of Life

Americans were pleased with all the new ways to travel and keep in touch. However, they did not know that they were taking part in a very important change in the nation's history. This change was so great that it is sometimes called the Second American Revolution. It was the Industrial Revolution (in dus'trē əl rev'ə lōō'shən). This revolution was a complete change in the way people made their living. It was brought about by the making of new machines and new kinds of power.

The Industrial Revolution

An *industry* (in'dəs trē) is all the businesses that take part in making an item, such as sugar. During the nation's early days Americans had only a few industries. Yet some of these industries were large. The textile, or cloth, industry, for example, was a large industry. Goods were made by hand. Women made the cloth for clothing by spinning the thread from flax or cotton and then weaving it.

Later, machines were made that could do some of the work that had been done by hand before. The British made machines that could spin thread and weave cloth at least 10 times faster than workers using the old spinning wheels and hand looms could. This made Great Britain the world leader in textile manufacturing. To stay ahead, Britain ruled that no plans or models of its textile machines could be taken out of the country.

Beginning of the Factory System

A young British weaver named Samuel Slater found a way around this rule. He memorized the plans for the new machines! Then he sailed for the United States. Americans were eager for his knowledge.

Slater built the first textile machines in Pawtucket (pô tuk'it), Rhode Island, in 1790. There, on the machines built from memory, cotton yarn was soon made in large amounts. Many textile factories sprang up in the Northeast. These early factories had to be built next to rivers or streams. The rushing water was needed to run the machines. Soon New Englanders also began to build factories making other goods—guns, ready-made clothes, and furniture, for example.

Increasing Immigration

At first most of the factory workers came from the farms of the Northeast. In early factory towns such as Waltham and Lowell in Massachusetts, the workers often were young girls. As the factory system grew, however, more workers were needed.

At this time, many Europeans were eager to come to the United States to find work.

In the 10 years after 1820, more than 125,000 immigrants arrived. During the next 10 years the number of immigrants grew to over half a million. Between 1840 and 1850 more than one and a half million immigrants arrived on American shores.

Growth of Cities

The growth of the factory system and of the number of immigrants led to the growth of American towns and cities. Old cities grew larger. Sometimes factories were built in open spaces. New towns and cities grew up around these factories. Soon the North had several large cities. By 1850 Boston had over 130,000 people. New York had nearly 600,000 people, and Philadelphia had about 340,000.

The Cotton Gin Changes the South

While more and more factories were being built in the North, the South remained a land of farms. Plantations and smaller farms

Population of Largest Cities 1850	
New York	515,547
Philadelphia	340,045
Baltimore	169,054
Boston	136,881
New Orleans	116,375

continued to grow large amounts of tobacco and rice. Along the damp coasts of southern South Carolina and Georgia, some cotton was grown. It was much in demand from British and Northeastern textile manufacturers.

Americans did not raise much cotton, though. It was too costly to prepare for market. Before cotton could be sold, the many seeds had to be removed from the cotton plant. This job had to be done by hand. It took a whole day to clean just 2 pounds (.9 kg) of cotton.

Cotton suddenly became an important Southern crop. In 1793 Eli Whitney invented a machine to clean the cotton. His "cotton gin" had long teeth that tore the fibers away from the seeds. A person using the cotton gin could clean 25 times as much cotton as before. As a result, more land in the South was used to grow cotton.

Increase of Slavery

The cotton gin gave the South an important new *cash crop*—a crop that is raised mainly to make money. It also caused slavery to grow in the South. Slaves were used to plant and take care of the cotton. Before the cotton gin appeared, 700,000 slaves lived in the South. Some people believed that slavery there might even die out in time. But after the invention of the cotton gin, the number of slaves grew. There were 2 million slaves in the South by 1820 and 4 million by 1850. Cotton became "king" in the South.

New Farm Machinery for the West

In the early 1800s the nation's "bread basket" moved from the Middle Atlantic states to the Middle West. There the rich, gently rolling prairie lands of Indiana and Illinois and of Iowa were good for growing corn and wheat.

It took a long time to harvest, or gather, crops in the very big farms of the West. Crops had to be cut by hand, which was a slow and backbreaking job. Then, in 1831, Cyrus McCormick built the mechanical reaper. This horse-drawn machine cut crops cleanly. With a reaper, it was possible to harvest crops five times faster than by hand.

Another invention made farming easier in the lowlands of the Mississippi River and later in the flat plains to the west of the river. The land near the mouth of the Mississippi was wet and heavy. To the west of the river, the soil was covered with sod—a mat of long, tangled grass. Wooden plows often broke when farmers tried to loosen the sod. This changed after 1837, when John Deere made a steel plow. The new steel plow was tough enough to cut through both the muddy soil and the sod.

Calls for Reform

Americans of the 1800s were proud of their nation. But they still wanted to make it better in every way. Many Americans tried to improve the lives of the poor, the

The company started by Cyrus McCormick sold farm machinery. What machines are shown in the company's ads?

mentally ill, and the handicapped, for example. Other people worked toward helping everyone enjoy their full rights as citizens.

Soon many groups of people began to call for *reforms* (ri fôrmz'), or changes to correct these problems. They worked to pass laws that made it possible for more Americans to take part in their government.

The Growth of Democracy Under Jackson

In 1828 Andrew Jackson ran for President. His slogan, or phrase telling everyone what he stood for, was "Equal rights for all. Special privileges for none." After Jackson won the election, he saw to it that more people gained the right to vote. In many places men no longer needed to own property to vote. As a result of such changes, the number of voters doubled during the time Jackson was President.

Rights for Women

No reforms were made for women, however. They still did not have the right to vote or hold public office. In many states married women were not allowed to own property. Any property that they owned when they were single became the property of their husbands when they married. In addition, women could not go to schools of higher learning.

One of the Americans who tried to gain equal rights for women was Margaret Fuller. She explained what women wanted: "We would have every path laid open to women as freely as to men." In 1848 Elizabeth Cady Stanton and Lucretia Mott called together 300 delegates at Seneca Falls, New York. This was the first women's rights convention in history.

Equal rights for women were slow in coming, however. A few colleges began to accept women students. Some states gave women more rights over their own property. But women would not gain the right to vote for another 70 years.

Sarah and Angelina Grimké

Many of the people who wanted equal rights for women also wanted to *abolish* (ə bol′ish), or do away with, slavery. Sarah and Angelina Grimké (grim kē′), for exam-

ple, began to take part in the women's movement because of the *abolition movement* (ab′ə lish′ən moov′ment). They had tried to speak out in public against slavery. But they were often shouted down before they could say very much. Both sisters learned quickly that many people thought women should not speak in public.

The Grimké sisters knew much about slavery. Sarah had been born in 1792 and Angelina in 1805 to a wealthy slave-owning family in South Carolina. They saw the many ways in which slaves were treated unfairly. The Grimkés' dislike of slavery grew so strong that they decided to leave Charleston. They moved north to Philadelphia and made it their home.

Both sisters traveled through the North, speaking to people. They explained that slavery had no place in a democratic country. They also spoke in favor of equal rights for women.

Do You Know?

1. What was the Industrial Revolution?
2. Where was Slater's mill built? What kind of mill was it?
3. How did the cotton gin change the South?
4. What reforms were started in the United States during the early 1800s?

To Help You Learn

Using New Words

abolish ✗

abolition movement

canal ✗

cash crop ✗

industry ✗

reforms

turnpikes ✗

The phrases below explain the words listed above. Number a paper from 1 through 7. After each number write the word or term that matches the definition.

1. Improvements or changes for the better
2. A waterway people make to connect two bodies of water
3. To do away with something
4. A farm product, such as cotton, that is raised mainly to make money
5. All the businesses that make one kind of product, such as cloth
6. Roads on which a traveler has to pay a fee
7. The actions taken by people to try to end slavery

Finding the Facts

1. What was the National Road?
2. Where was the Erie Canal built? How did the canal improve shipping?
3. How did the telegraph make it easier for Americans to keep in touch with one another?
4. How did the Industrial Revolution start in the United States?
5. Why did American cities grow during the 1800s?
6. How did the cotton gin make it easier to clean cotton?
7. Did women have the same rights as men in the 1800s?
8. What important meeting was held at Seneca Falls, New York, in 1848?
9. How did Sarah and Angelina Grimké work to end slavery?

Learning from Maps

1. Turn to the map on page 127. It shows the land that was part of the Louisiana Purchase and the route followed by Lewis and Clark. Look closely at the map and answer these questions.
   - What symbol does the map use to show the route of Lewis and Clark?
   - Along which rivers did Lewis and Clark travel?
   - When did Lewis and Clark reach the Pacific Ocean?
2. Look closely at the map of the War of 1812 on page 131. Then answer these questions.
   - What symbol is used to show the British blockade of the United States?
   - Where were the important battles of the war fought? Who won each battle? How can you tell who won?
   - Where did Perry fight the British?

3. Turn to the map on page 135. It shows important battles of the Texas War for Independence. Look closely at the map and answer these questions.
   - Where did the important battles take place?
   - What color is used on the map to show land claimed by both Texas and Mexico?
   - What bodies of water formed the natural borders of Texas?

Using Study Skills

1. **Table:** Turn to the table on page 148. It lists the five largest cities in 1850. Which city had the most people? Which city had the third largest population?

   Make a bar graph with the information shown on the table. Begin by writing the names of the five cities along the bottom of the graph. Then number the left-hand side of the graph from zero to 600,000 people. Next, draw bars to show the number of people in each city. Compare the table and bar graphs. Which shows the differences in size of population at a glance? Is it easier to use a table or a bar graph to find the exact number of people in the population?

2. **Outline:** Making an outline can help you organize information. It also can help you remember what you read. Use these phrases and terms to complete the outline that follows.

   > Washington
   > Bought from Mexico in 1848
   > Settlement begun by missionaries, such as the Whitmans
   > Louisiana Purchase
   > Idaho
   > Santa Fe Trail

   The Growth of the United States

   I.
   A. Bought from France in 1803
   B. Explored by Lewis and Clark
   II. Mexican Cession
   A.
   B. Some trails used by settlers traveling to the area
   1.   2. Mormon Trail
   III. Oregon Country
   A. Given to United States by treaty with Great Britain in 1846
   B.
   C. States formed from area
   1. Oregon   2.   3.

Thinking It Through

1. Name one invention important to the Industrial Revolution. How did this invention change life in America?
2. Compare the War of 1812 with the Mexican War. For each war, make a list of (a) causes and (b) results.
3. If gold were found in California today, how would people travel to the gold fields? Would anyone today use the same means of travel as those used by people going west in 1849?

Projects

1. During the 1800s many people worked to make life in America better. Among them were: Horace Mann, Gerrit Smith, Susan B. Anthony, Dorothea Dix, and Theodore Weld. Read about one of these people or a person mentioned in the text. What did the person you chose do to reform America?
2. Find out more about the trip of Lewis and Clark. Write a diary for the trip. Tell about the groups of American Indians, the animals, and plants you saw along the way.
3. The Explorers' Committee might find information about Zebulon Pike, who also helped to explore the Louisiana Purchase. The committee should use an outline map of the United States to show the routes Pike followed from 1805 to 1807.
4. Prepare a poster or bulletin board display that will show how America's transportation improved during the 1800s. It might have pictures of early railroads, canal boats, steamboats, and stage coaches. You might also write a few sentences telling about an imaginary trip you took on each type of transportation. Place what you wrote beside each picture.
5. The Research Committee might find out more about immigrants who came to the United States during the Industrial Revolution. Which nations did most of these immigrants come from? Why did the immigrants come to the United States? Where did they settle? How were the immigrants treated by other Americans?
6. Turn to the pictures on pages 138 and 140. Study them closely. Then write a story or short play about the people and things shown in one of the pictures.

6 Conflict and Growth

Unit Preview

Different ways of living had formed in the North and South. The growth of slavery and a movement to end slavery made the differences worse. They finally led to Civil War.

After Abraham Lincoln became President in 1861, several southern states left the Union and set up their own government. The fighting that broke out lasted until 1865, when the North won. This saved the Union and ended slavery.

The South had been ruined by the war. During Reconstruction, or the time of rebuilding, new state governments were formed in the South. Some Northerners and blacks were in these governments.

America's frontier ended after the Civil War. Many people went west looking for gold. Others started farms and cattle ranches on the Great Plains. Cowhands drove the cattle to stops on the railroads that were being built across the country. Some railroad stops and mining towns grew into large cities.

The move to the West ended the way of life of many Indians. Buffalo herds were killed, and the settlers fought with the Indians for their land. When the Indians lost, they were made to live on reservations.

At this time, the United States also added lands that were not joined to the rest of the country. They were Alaska and Hawaii.

Things to Discover

If you look carefully at the picture, map, and time line, you can answer these questions.

1. The map shows the states that were in the Union and the Confederacy during the Civil War. It also shows the Southern states that stayed in the Union. Why do you think these states were called the Border States?
2. The picture shows cotton plants. How did the growth of cotton help to cause the Civil War?
3. In what year was the Missouri Compromise passed?
4. Did the Civil War begin before or after the Homestead Act was passed?
5. When was the Emancipation Proclamation signed?
6. What event happened during the same year that the Civil War ended?

Words to Learn

You will meet these words in this unit. As you read, you will learn what they mean and how to pronounce them. The Word List will help you.

carpetbaggers   scalawags
Confederacy   secede
discrimination   segregation
homestead   sharecropping
reservation   tariffs

154

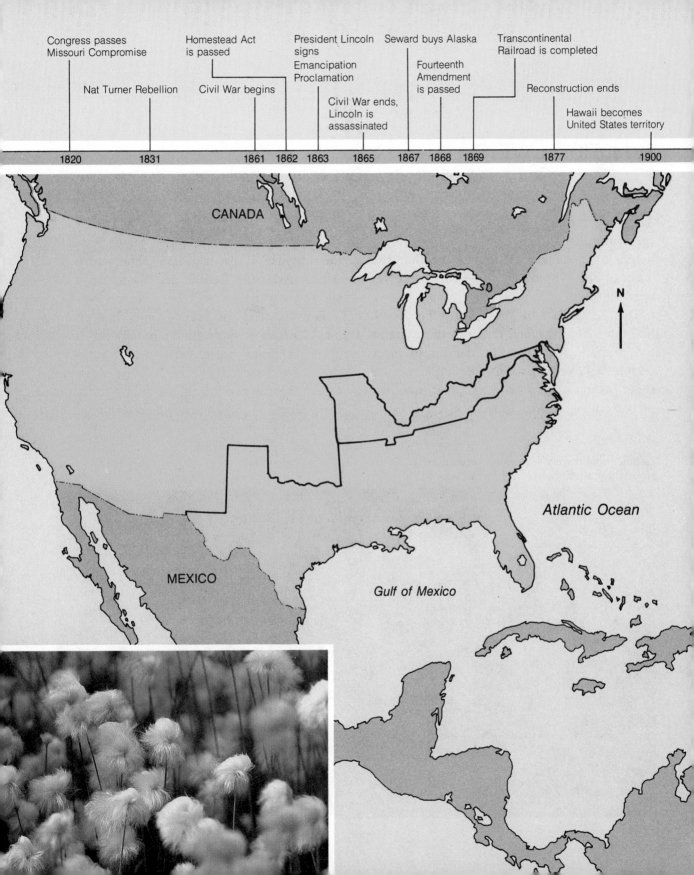

Congress passes
Missouri Compromise

Nat Turner Rebellion

Homestead Act
is passed

Civil War begins

President Lincoln
signs
Emancipation
Proclamation

Civil War ends,
Lincoln is
assassinated

Seward buys Alaska

Fourteenth
Amendment
is passed

Transcontinental
Railroad is completed

Reconstruction ends

Hawaii becomes
United States territory

1820   1831   1861 1862 1863   1865   1867 1868 1869   1877   1900

CANADA

N

MEXICO

Gulf of Mexico

Atlantic Ocean

1

A Nation Divided

The movement to get rid of slavery caused the United States to become divided. Arguments over slavery made it clear that the ways of the North and the South were far apart.

By the middle of the 1800s, the North had few slaves. In fact, most northern states did not allow slavery. In the South most people believed that they needed slaves on their plantations to produce great amounts of cotton, sugar, and tobacco.

The System of Slavery

In the early 1800s the United States was not the only nation that had slaves. Many parts of Africa, Asia, and Central and South America allowed slavery.

For hundreds of years people had taken black Africans from their homeland. The black Africans were then loaded aboard ships. In chains, they crossed the Atlantic Ocean. Probably 9 million black African men, women, and children made their jour-

Families who were sold at slave auctions were afraid they would be split up by the sale.

This slave family in the South is in front of their cabin. Slaves often were given only one new set of clothes a year.

ney under terrible conditions. Probably one third of these Africans died during the trip.

Life as a Slave

Two things were true in the life of all slaves in the United States. First, they were owned by the person who bought them. Second, slaves had no legal or human rights. Slaves could not travel anywhere without permission. They could not even marry without permission. Their owners could break up slave families, by selling a wife, a husband, and their children to different buyers. In many states slaves were not allowed to learn to read and write.

The lives of the slaves were not all the same. Slaves with skills were more valued than slaves who worked only with their muscles. Life was hardest for the field slaves. Men, women, and children had to

work from sunup to sundown in the fields for six days a week.

Most slaves lived in one-room cabins made of rough boards. These cabins had dirt floors and no windows, just small openings in the walls for windows. Each week the slaves received a few pounds of corn meal and perhaps a little meat or fish. Vegetables came from the small gardens the slaves grew behind their cabins.

Life usually was easier for the slaves who worked in the owner's house. House slaves cleaned, cooked, took care of the owners' children, and waited on the family. These slaves often were given better clothes to wear and were better fed than field hands.

Slaves who had been trained in a craft were treated the best of all the slaves. On plantations there were slaves skilled as blacksmiths, carpenters, and bootmakers.

Harriet Tubman, on the left, was a conductor on the Underground Railroad. She helped many slaves escape to freedom in the North.

Rebellion and Escape

During the 1800s, there were several slave rebellions. Perhaps the most famous one was led by the preacher Nat Turner in Virginia in 1831. Turner and about 70 other armed slaves planned to kill their owners to win their freedom. But Nat Turner's rebellion ended like all the rest. He and his followers were caught and put to death.

Thousands of slaves slipped away by night. They walked north, following the North Star. Once in the North, the runaway slaves hoped to reach Canada. In Canada, they could not be taken and returned to their owners.

In time a system was worked out to help slaves travel north to freedom. It was called the "Underground Railroad." This "railroad" had no tracks or railroad cars. It did have "stations," however. Each station was a friendly house where an escaping slave could rest and get food.

"Conductors" played an important part in the Underground Railroad. These people led escaping slaves to friendly houses along the way. Probably the most successful conductor was Harriet Tubman. At the age of 29 she had escaped her own slavery in Maryland. Then, time and time again, she returned to the South. Each time she led a few slaves to freedom—more than 300 slaves in all. A reward of 40,000 dollars was offered for her capture. With well-earned pride, Tubman could later say, "I never ran my train off the track, and I never lost a passenger."

Free Blacks

Some blacks were freed by their owners. In some places slaveowners would free slaves who had earned enough money to buy their freedom. This usually happened to slaves in the cities. By 1850 about a half million free blacks lived in the United States.

North and South Grow More Divided

As the United States grew larger, slavery spread to other areas besides the Old South. This was the name given to the Southern states that had been original colonies. Many of the settlers going west took their slaves with them to work on the plantations they planned to start. As a result, several new states entered the Union as slave states. By 1819, for example, Alabama, Mississippi, and Louisiana had entered the Union as slave states.

The Missouri Compromise

The free states of the North did not want to be outnumbered by the slave states. By 1820 there were 22 states in the Union— 11 were free states and 11 were slave states. Then Missouri wanted to enter the Union as a slave state. This would end the even numbers of free and slave states in the Senate. There would then be 12 slave states and 11 free states.

After much arguing in Congress, Senator Henry Clay of Kentucky came up with a compromise. Clay said that Missouri should enter as a slave state. At the same time Maine should also enter—but as a free state. Then the balance would remain even —12 slave states to 12 free states. Clay also said that in the future slavery should not be allowed in any other states made out of the Louisiana Territory.

Congress agreed to this plan, known as the Missouri Compromise. But it knew that the Compromise would not end the arguments over slavery.

The Abolitionist Movement

The abolitionist movement began to grow stronger during the 1830s. At that time William Lloyd Garrison began a newspaper called the *Liberator,* which was against slavery. Garrison wanted more people to learn about the fight to end slavery.

At this time also, free blacks began to use other methods to bring an end to slavery. Some blacks, for example, became lecturers. Their words explained what slave life was like, first-hand.

Sojourner Truth and Frederick Douglass

One of the most popular people to speak against slavery was Sojourner Truth. She was born a slave in New York State in about 1797. Her name then was Isabella Baumfree (bôm'frē). In 1828 New York

Frederick Douglass, on the left, and Sojournor Truth both helped the *abolition movement*. They spoke against slavery in many places.

ended slavery in the state, and she became free.

Isabella Baumfree decided that she had a great task to perform in life. Instead of staying at home, she should travel from place to place. At each place she would stop for a while, or take a sojourn (sō′jurn). During this stay Baumfree would tell people she met the truth about the evils of slavery. Isabella Baumfree then took on a new name—Sojourner Truth.

Another powerful speaker against slavery was Frederick Douglass. While still a youngster, Douglass secretly learned to read and write to prepare himself for freedom. When Douglass was 21 years old, he saw his chance. His owner had sent him to work in the shipyards of Baltimore. There he sneaked aboard a train and reached the North without being discovered. Douglass

then made his way to Massachusetts.

In the North, Douglass came upon a copy of the *Liberator*. He found Garrison's words "full of holy fire." Douglass then met Garrison, who told Douglass he should speak out against slavery. Like Sojourner Truth, Douglass traveled from place to place talking about the need for abolition. He placed himself in danger by doing this. If he were caught, Douglass could be returned to his owner.

The Compromise of 1850

In the years following the Missouri Compromise of 1820, the number of free and slave states remained even. By 1850 the number stood at 15 states each. At that time, however, California was asking to be admitted into the Union as a free state.

Congress again became the scene of bitter arguments. Northerners and Southerners did not agree over other matters besides California. Once again Senator Henry Clay of Kentucky came forward with a compromise. By this time he had come to be called "the Great Compromiser." Clay's new plan said that Congress would:

(1) Admit California as a free state.
(2) Allow slavery in other parts of the Southwest only if the settlers there voted for it.
(3) End the slave trade in Washington, D.C.
(4) Pass a strong fugitive slave law. This would help owners of runaway slaves to get back their slaves.

Clay worked for six months to get his compromise accepted by Congress. Finally, the Compromise of 1850 won the votes it needed to pass.

The Fugitive Slave Law

The new Fugitive Slave Law allowed sheriffs to come to the North and take slaves who had run away. It offered government help in getting the sheriffs and their captured slaves back to the South.

Many Northerners thought the new law was a shame to the nation. Abolitionists openly did not obey the law. Citizens who saw a fugitive slave being taken often tried to stop the action. Federal troops sometimes had to be called in to protect the sheriffs from angry citizens.

Tale of a Runaway Slave

The Fugitive Slave Law caused one author to write a tale about the evils of slavery. *Uncle Tom's Cabin* was the work of Harriet Beecher Stowe (stō). After reading about the life of a slave who had run away, Stowe wrote a story of kindly slaves who were mistreated by a cruel overseer named Simon Legree (lə grē′).

Uncle Tom's Cabin by Harriet Beecher Stowe turned many of its readers in the North against slavery. How much did the book cost with illustrations, or pictures? How else was the book sold?

135,000 SETS, 270,000 VOLUMES SOLD.

UNCLE TOM'S CABIN

FOR SALE HERE.

AN EDITION FOR THE MILLION, COMPLETE IN 1 Vol., PRICE 37 1-2 CENTS.
"   "   IN GERMAN, IN 1 Vol., PRICE 50 CENTS.
"   "   IN 2 Vols., CLOTH, 6 PLATES, PRICE $1.50.
SUPERB ILLUSTRATED EDITION, IN 1 Vol., WITH 153 ENGRAVINGS,
PRICES FROM $2.50 TO $5.00.

The Greatest Book of the Age.

Uncle Tom's Cabin was an immediate success in the North. Within 16 months, it had sold a million copies. The book was also made into a play. *Uncle Tom's Cabin* was even talked about among members of Congress.

The book made Southerners angry. They said *Uncle Tom's Cabin* was unfair to slavery. Most slaveowners did not treat their slaves so cruelly. However, the book made many Northerners sure that slavery had to be ended.

Quarrel over Tariffs

Slavery was not the only issue dividing the country. North and South also disagreed about *tariffs* (tar′ifs). A tariff is a tax placed on goods brought into or sent out of a country. They most often are placed on imports. A tariff is a way for the government to take in money.

A tariff also can help a country's industries grow. This kind of tariff is called a protective (prə tek′tiv) tariff. A tariff raises the price of foreign goods, making them cost more. If the foreign goods are no longer cheaper, more people will buy the items made in their own country. The industry at home will then grow.

But why did tariffs divide North and South? As you have seen, the North had many factories and wanted its industry to grow. The South, however, did not have many factories. Instead the South made money by selling farm goods—rice, tobac-co, cotton, sugar. High tariffs did not help the Southerners earn money. These taxes only raised the prices that Southerners had to pay for imported manufactured goods. Southerners, therefore, wanted tariffs to be low.

Crisis over Kansas and Nebraska

The division between North and South grew worse in 1854. The Missouri Compromise had forbidden slavery in the remaining parts of the Louisiana Territory. But in 1854 the Kansas-Nebraska Act changed this. It allowed slavery in Kansas and Nebraska, if the people there voted for it. Once again those who were for slavery argued bitterly with people who were against slavery.

Do You Know?

1. How was the life of a field slave harder than the life of a house slave?
2. What was the Underground Railroad?
3. What argument did the Missouri Compromise solve?
4. Why did the abolitionists cause the North and South to grow farther apart?
5. Why did the North want high tariffs?

2
The Civil War

It became clear that the quarrels between the North and the South soon would cause the nation to break apart. Could such a break be peaceful? The answer was no. With the break came war—the Civil (siv′əl) War. Civil War is a war between different parts of a country.

Moving Toward a Split

Groups within the North and South had been growing farther apart over the slavery question for several years. Meanwhile, a new political party, the Republicans, was formed in 1854. Its members had joined together because of the Kansas-Nebraska Act. They wanted to end slavery in the territories. Many abolitionists eagerly joined the new Republican Party. One of the people to join the Republicans was a lawyer from Illinois named Abraham Lincoln.

Abraham Lincoln

Abraham Lincoln was born on February 12, 1809, in a small log cabin in Kentucky. He lived there until he was seven years old. Then Lincoln's family moved farther west to Indiana. Lincoln learned to read and write, but he spent most of his time helping his father to farm. Lincoln loved to read, and he borrowed books to study from neighbors.

When Lincoln was 21 years old, his family moved again, this time to Illinois. There Abraham Lincoln worked at many jobs. During these years, Lincoln kept on reading. Among the books he read were many law books. Lincoln later became a lawyer and opened an office in Springfield, Illinois.

Elected to the state legislature, Lincoln served there for eight years. Next, the vot-

Even though he was very busy during the Civil War, President Lincoln found time to be with his children. Here, he is reading with his young son, Tad.

The South Secedes

The southern states knew that Lincoln was against the spread of slavery. Even before the election of 1860, some of the southern states said they would *secede* (si sēd′), or withdraw, from the Union if Lincoln won.

Just one month after the election, on December 20, 1860, South Carolina seceded. By February 1861, Mississippi, Florida, Alabama, Georgia, Louisiana, and Texas had left the Union.

In that same month of February, representatives from the seceded states met in Montgomery, Alabama. They formed the Confederate States of America. The representatives elected Jefferson Davis, a Senator from Mississippi, to be the President of the *Confederacy* (kən fed′ər ə sē). By May, Virginia, Arkansas, Tennessee, and North Carolina had joined the Confederacy. Richmond, Virginia, became its capital.

The shots fired at Fort Sumter in South Carolina saddened many of the people who watched from nearby rooftops.

Shots Are Fired at Fort Sumter

When the southern states seceded, they took control of local federal forts. Taking one of those forts caused the first shots of the war to be fired. South Carolina decided to take over Fort Sumter in Charleston harbor. However, the United States commander there refused to surrender.

In April President Lincoln ordered badly needed supplies to be sent to Fort Sumter. The Confederacy decided to take the fort before the supplies could arrive. On April 12, Confederate guns began to fire at Fort

ers of Illinois elected him to the House of Representatives. Lincoln ran for the Senate in 1855. During his campaign he made clear his views on slavery. He believed that slavery was wrong in every way. But Lincoln did not say that slavery had to be ended. He said that slavery should not be allowed in the territories.

Lincoln lost the 1856 election. However, the Republican Party made Lincoln its candidate for President in 1860. Lincoln won the election, and became the sixteenth President of the United States.

Sumter. Two days later the federal troops gave up and President Lincoln asked Congress to declare war. The Civil War began.

War Between the States

A civil war is one of the worst kinds of wars. It divides the citizens of a country and forces them to become enemies of one another. It often separates members of a single family. Robert E. Lee, for example, fought as a Confederate general. His cousin Samuel Lee fought as an officer in the Union navy. Henry Clay's family was also split. Four of Clay's grandsons fought for the South. Three other grandsons fought for the North.

Both states and territories in the United States were divided over the question of slavery. Which slave states did not *secede* from the Union? Which territory or territories joined the Confederacy?

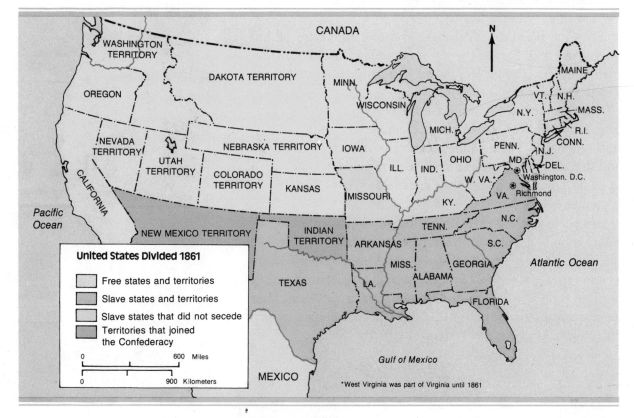

United States Divided 1861
- Free states and territories
- Slave states and territories
- Slave states that did not secede
- Territories that joined the Confederacy

0   600 Miles
0   900 Kilometers

*West Virginia was part of Virginia until 1861

A

Life in the Mid-1800s

Many of the changes that took place in America during the mid-1800s started during the Civil War. In the battle at New Orleans, for example, Union gunboats used iron to protect them from gunfire (E). The iron worked so well that it was used in ships after the war.

The Civil War brought changes in sports also. Baseball had started in 1839. During the war it became a favorite sport of many soldiers. The players shown here are Union prisoners in North Carolina (F).

Many women worked to make life better for Americans after the Civil War. A number of them learned their skills during the war. These women took care of wounded soldiers and thought up ways to get medicine to troops. Women such as Sallie Tompkins joined the Confederate Army. She is remembered for her bravery (C).

After the war, life changed in all parts of the country. The South rebuilt. The North changed as more factories were opened (A). Men, women (D), and children left their farms to work in these factories. Families from both the North and the South left their homes to make a new start in the West. Miners went west to strike it rich. All of these people helped western cities such as San Francisco to grow quickly (B). ■

E

B

C

D

F

167

Northerners gave food and housing to volunteers for the Union army. They also cheered them as they left for battle.

Conditions in the North and South

Which side in 1861 was better prepared to fight a war—the North or the South? The North had more things in its favor than the South. The North had more people and many more factories than the South. Its shops and factories were able to make more weapons and supplies for northern troops. With its many railroads, the North could send troops and supplies easily to the battlefields.

The South had some advantages, too. It had many well-trained military leaders. Most of the Southerners who joined the army knew how to shoot and ride horses. This made them very good soldiers. Both Northerners and Southerners strongly believed in their causes. But Southerners were fighting to save their way of life.

The Early Battles

The northern, or Union, army immediately set out to capture the Confederate capital, Richmond, Virginia. They hoped that this would quickly destroy the South's government.

The northern troops began their march toward Richmond on a pleasant July day.

About 36,000 bluecoated Union soldiers left Washington, D.C., to march into Virginia. In almost a party mood, picnickers and news reporters went along with the army. To get a good view of the action, these onlookers settled on a hill. It overlooked a stream called Bull Run. The visitors then waited for the attack to begin. They were certain that the Union could easily defeat the Confederate troops.

At first the Union troops fought well. They soon were stopped by a "stone wall" of graycoated Confederate troops, however. The southern commander who planned this action won the nickname of "Stonewall" Jackson. It caused the frightened northern troops to run back to Washington.

Never again after this first Battle of Bull Run would anyone go into battle in such light spirits. One year later, in 1862, the Union again tried to take Richmond. Once more it was stopped—in the Second Battle of Bull Run. Two more tries to take Richmond, one in 1862 and the other in 1863, also failed.

To help win the war, the Union navy set up a blockade along the South's Atlantic Coast. A blockade is a line of ships stationed along the coast to keep ships from sending goods to foreign countries. The blockade also kept foreign countries from bringing goods to the South. The loss of trade was a great blow to the South. Southerners had hoped to pay for much of the war by selling cotton overseas.

The Emancipation Proclamation

President Lincoln had declared war in order to preserve the Union, that is, to keep it together. He did not call for war in order to end slavery. "The Union must be preserved," he said, "with or without slavery." As the war dragged on, however, President Lincoln decided that the South must free the slaves.

On January 1, 1863, Lincoln issued the Emancipation Proclamation (i man′sə pā′shən prok′lə mā′shən). It stated that all slaves who lived in the Confederate states were now free. The Union could not then really free the slaves in the Confederacy. It was not in control in the South. However,

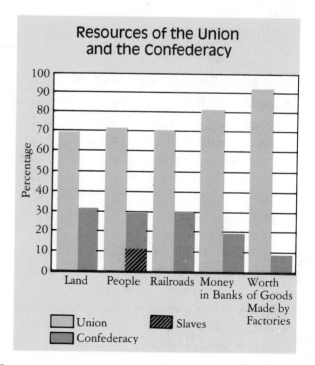

Resources of the Union and the Confederacy

Percentage: Land, People, Railroads, Money in Banks, Worth of Goods Made by Factories

☐ Union ▨ Slaves ▨ Confederacy

169

This Civil War poster asked black Americans in Pennsylvania to join the Union army. It reminded people that the flag of the Union stood for freedom.

the Emancipation Proclamation made it clear that the slaves would be freed if the North won the war.

Blacks Fight for the Union

Blacks had offered to help the Union at the beginning of the war. They worked as cooks, carpenters, drivers, nurses, and spies for the Union forces. Nevertheless, they were not allowed to join the Union army or navy as fighters. The law did not allow it. In the summer of 1862, though, this law was repealed, or done away with. As a result, many black Americans joined the armed forces, even though they knew they would not be treated as equals.

In the army and navy, black troops suffered *discrimination* (dis krim′ə nā′shən), or unfair treatment. Blacks could not be offi-cers. Instead, regiments were led by white officers. Black troops also were not paid as well as white troops. In spite of these hardships, blacks fought bravely in almost all battles. One black regiment, the Massachusetts 54th, was very courageous. It was ordered to take Fort Wagner in Charleston harbor. Nearly 100 black soldiers fought their way toward the top of the fort wall. Every one of the black soldiers was killed.

More than 180,000 blacks served in the Union army. Nearly 30,000 served in the Union navy. Twenty-one blacks won the Congressional Medal of Honor, which is the nation's highest military award.

The Turning Point— Vicksburg and Gettysburg

For the first two years of the war, neither side was clearly ahead. Then in the summer of 1863, two Union victories tipped the balance in favor of the North.

One of these battles was fought at Vicksburg, Mississippi. Vicksburg is a port on the Mississippi River. The Union knew that if it captured Vicksburg, it would control the whole Mississippi River. General Ulysses S. Grant was in charge of the Union troops. After trying several times, his Union troops surrounded Vicksburg. For 47 days the people of Vicksburg held out. Finally, the constant Union firing and the lack of food wore out the city. On July 4, 1863, Vicksburg surrendered.

At that same time, another battle was being fought to the east, in Pennsylvania. This was one of the few times that there was any fighting in the North. General Robert E. Lee had marched into Pennsylvania. President Lincoln sent Union troops under General George G. Meade to stop him. The two armies met at Gettysburg (get'iz burg') on July 1, 1863. Lee tried three times to defeat the Union troops. Each time the Union troops fought off the charge. Lee could do nothing but take his tired army back to Virginia. This date of

July 4, 1863 was the beginning of the end for the South.

Robert E. Lee

Robert E. Lee was a colonel in the United States Army when the war began. President Lincoln asked Lee to take command of the Union army. But Lee felt that he had to refuse. He felt great loyalty to his home state of Virginia. He also believed he must stand by his state and the Confederacy. Jefferson

Most of the fighting of the Civil War took place in the South. In which southern states were many battles fought?

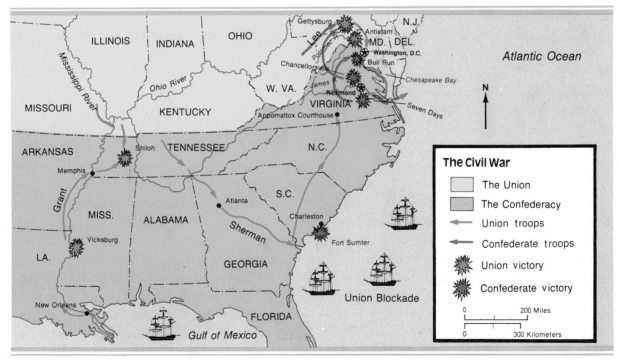

Ulysses S. Grant, on the left, led the Union forces during the Civil War. Robert E. Lee was in command of the Confederate Army.

Davis made Lee commander of all the Confederate forces.

Lee was born in Virginia in 1807, to an old Virginia family. At 18 years of age, Lee entered the military academy at West Point in New York. He was a very good student and graduated first in his class. Lee soon proved to be a brilliant soldier. Following service in the war with Mexico, he became head of West Point.

Ulysses S. Grant

Ulysses S. Grant also attended West Point. He went to school there 14 years after Lee. Born in Ohio in 1822, Grant was named Hiram Simpson Grant. But because of an error, he was listed at West Point as Ulysses Simpson Grant. That is the name Grant kept.

Grant, like Lee, served well in the war with Mexico. After the war, he left the army and moved to Illinois. There he worked at a number of jobs, including farming and running a hardware store.

When the Civil War started, Grant joined the army again. He rose to the rank of general. In 1864 President Lincoln made Ulysses S. Grant commander of all the Union armies.

The War Ends

On April 9, 1865, Lee and Grant met at Appomattox (ap'ə mat'əks) Courthouse in Virginia. The South knew it could not keep on fighting. The Union blockade had caused southern trade to stop. The Union troops of General Philip Sheridan and General William Sherman had destroyed southern farms, bridges, and anything else they saw as they marched through the South. Lee asked Grant for terms of surrender. The Civil War was over at last.

Death of Abraham Lincoln

When the number of deaths from the war was added up, the total was shockingly large. More than 600,000 troops had been killed. One out of every four who had fought was dead. Five days after the war ended, yet another name was added to the list of dead—Abraham Lincoln.

On Friday evening of April 14, 1865, the President had gone to Ford's Theater in Washington, D.C. He went to see a play called *Our American Cousin.* As President Lincoln sat in the theater, a man sneaked in behind him. Suddenly a shot rang out! Lincoln sank down in his seat. The man who had shot him, an actor named John Wilkes Booth, ran across the stage. Booth wanted to punish Lincoln for the defeat of the South. President Lincoln died the next morning. People wept as Lincoln's funeral train took him back to Illinois.

Reuniting the Nation

The loss of President Lincoln was a great blow to the whole nation. Lincoln had wanted North and South to join together in a spirit of forgiveness and cooperation. Without Lincoln this task would be harder to do.

Many parts of the South were badly damaged during the Civil War. In some cities, few buildings were left standing.

The southern states needed new leaders and new governments. These governments had to be accepted by Congress. The years from 1865 to 1877, when the North and South were being reunited, was called Reconstruction (rē′kən struk′shən).

Problems of the South

The South had been totally crushed and now lay in ruins. Returning soldiers found their homes burned and their fields crushed. People in the South did not know what the future held for them. Businesses

The Fifteenth Amendment gave black Americans the right to vote. The picture shows many of the freedoms the blacks were working for.

and farms had been destroyed and their owners did not have the money to start again. Moreover, Southerners had lost their unpaid labor force—the slaves. In 1865 the Thirteenth Amendment freeing the slaves had been added to the Constitution.

Blacks were given their freedom, but they had little else. Most freedmen, as the freed men, women, and children were called, had no money, no property, and few friends to help them.

Some blacks stayed on at their old plantations. After the war many plantation owners began to farm their land by a method called *sharecropping* (shār′krop′ing). Under the sharecropping system, plantation owners bought seeds and tools. They gave these to blacks, and sometimes to whites, along with use of the old slave cabins. In return, the sharecroppers farmed the land, giving part of what they raised to the owners.

Freedmen's Bureau

Congress tried to help the freedmen make a new start. It set up the Freedmen's Bureau to give food and clothing to the blacks who needed them. It also set up schools for people of all ages.

At one time the Freedmen's Bureau had said that any abandoned land would be given to the blacks. This statement was more of a wish than a fact, but many people came to believe that the government would give all blacks "forty acres (16 ha) and a mule." The rumor was totally false, but it made white Southerners angry at the Freedmen's Bureau. These Southerners said that many blacks would not work for whites because they were expecting to get their own land.

Black Codes

White Southerners wanted to keep blacks as farm workers. They also did not want the blacks in the South to have much freedom. As a result, southern state governments did not give blacks citizenship or the right to vote.

Southern governments also passed laws called the black codes. Under the black codes, a black who did not have a job could be arrested. He or she could then be made to work for a white employer. Some black codes said it was against the law for blacks to learn a craft, to own guns, or to stay outdoors past a certain hour in the evening.

Congress Helps the Blacks

Congress decided to give the Freedmen's Bureau more power, so that it could protect the freedom of the blacks. Also, in 1868 Congress passed the Fourteenth Amendment to the Constitution. This amendment gave full citizenship to all the former slaves. Later, the Fifteenth Amendment gave all black men the right to vote.

Once black men could vote, several blacks began to run for office. In the years just after the Civil War, 22 blacks from the South were elected to Congress. Many more blacks also were elected to state governments in the nation.

White Southern Reaction

Many white Southerners thought that Congress should leave the South alone and allow it to rebuild itself. Many Southerners also were bitter over the power certain groups had gained in the South.

One group that Southerners did not like was made up of Northerners who had come to the South after the war. Some of the Northerners had come to work for the Freedmen's Bureau. Other Northerners had come south to start up new businesses there. Several of the newcomers had unfairly gained money in the South. White Southerners called these Northerners *carpetbaggers* (kär′pit bag′ərz) because many of them had come south carrying their belongings in a piece of luggage made of carpet.

The second group that angered the South was made up of white Southerners who worked closely with northern officials. These people were thought of as traitors to the South. *"Scalawags"* (skal′ə wagz′), their neighbors angrily called them.

Some southern whites turned to violence to show their anger at the changes that Reconstruction was making in the South. These Southerners formed secret societies such as the Ku Klux Klan. The aim of these groups was to frighten blacks to stop them from voting and using their rights as citizens. The secret societies also frightened whites who were friendly with blacks.

End of Reconstruction

As time wore on the North lost interest in Reconstruction. It became clear that some problems in the South would take a long time to correct. Also, the North had its own problems to find answers to. In 1877 Congress called for the federal troops that had been sent to the South to be brought home. Reconstruction ended.

The southern states soon began to take steps to take away more of the freedom of the blacks. They made it harder for blacks to vote. Local laws also were passed to keep blacks separated from whites. This separation is called *segregation* (seg′rə gā′ shən). Blacks had to sit in certain parts of trains or theaters, away from whites. Blacks could not eat in the same restaurants or go to the same schools as whites. Segregation caused bitter feelings to remain between black and white Americans.

Do You Know?

1. What advantages did North and South each have during the Civil War?
2. What is the Emancipation Proclamation?
3. Which battles were the turning point of the war?
4. What was Reconstruction?
5. Why were black codes started in the South?

Before You Go On

Using New Words

carpetbaggers   secede
Confederacy   segregation
discrimination   sharecropping
scalawags   tariffs

The phrases below explain the words or terms listed above. Number a paper from 1 through 8. After each number write the word or term that matches each definition.

1. To leave or to withdraw from the Union
2. A farming system in which a landowner supplies seeds and tools to a farmworker who, in return, gives part of the crop to the landowner
3. Unfair treatment, usually of a small group, by members of a larger group
4. Taxes on foreign goods brought into a country
5. Southerners who worked with northern officials in the South during Reconstruction
6. Name of the South during the Civil War
7. Separation of blacks and whites
8. Northerners who went to the South during Reconstruction

Finding the Facts

1. Give one example of the ways in which slaves had to live without freedom.
2. Who was Nat Turner?
3. How did Harriet Tubman help fight slavery?
4. How did each of these people work to end slavery: William Lloyd Garrison, Sojourner Truth, Frederick Douglass?
5. What did the Compromise of 1820 do to settle the slavery problem in the Louisiana Territory?
6. Why did *Uncle Tom's Cabin* anger Southerners?
7. Why did the South want low tariffs?
8. Who was President of the Confederacy?
9. Why did many Northerners think the Union army could easily defeat the Confederate army?
10. Were black Americans in the Union army and navy treated equally to others in the military? Explain.
11. What problems did the South face after the Civil War?
12. What was the Freedmen's Bureau?
13. Give one example of the black codes.
14. What was the Ku Klux Klan?

3
The Nation Expands

For four years Americans had used much of their energy fighting the Civil War. When the war ended in 1865, they happily put this energy to other uses. Now Americans could seek new ways to make their fortunes. It was at this time that pioneers be-

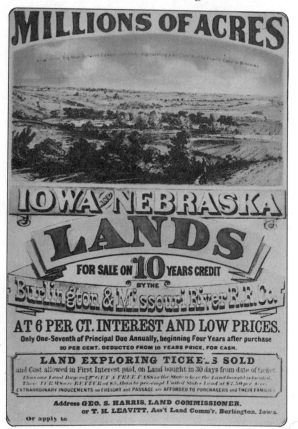

This poster advertised land in the West that was for sale. In what part of the country was the land that was being advertised?

gan to settle the central part of the United States. This area was called America's Last Frontier.

On their way to the Pacific Coast, settlers had crossed the grassy lands between the Mississippi River and the Rocky Mountains. However, few people chose to stay in the country's "Last West." Parts of this area were so dry that many people called it "the Great American Desert."

Another reason settlers did not want to stay in the Last West was that many Indians lived there. Some groups of Indians had long made this land their home. Others had been driven there more recently from the East and Far West.

The Last West is Settled

The Last West was made up mostly of the Great Plains. This broad flat land had few trees, and its ground was covered with a tough sod. In many places the grass grew very high. Summers were very hot, and insects were everywhere at this time of year. Winters were very cold.

The other parts of the Last West that began to be settled in the middle 1800s were the valleys of the Rocky Mountains and of other western mountains. Many people chose to make a living there after gold, silver, and other metals were found in the mountains.

Thousands of Chinese helped to build the transcontinental railroad. They had to work in all kinds of weather.

Transcontinental Railroad

By the 1860s many railroads had been built in the East. Now that the Pacific Coast was settled, Americans wanted to build a railroad that would run across the continent. Such a transcontinental (trans′kon tə nent′ əl) railroad, or one running across the country, would link the East with the West.

Congress took steps to build a transcontinental railroad during the 1860s. It voted to loan million of dollars to two railroad companies—the Union Pacific and the Central Pacific. These companies then began work on a railroad running from Omaha, Nebraska, to Sacramento, California.

Actually, the two railroad companies were taking part in a contest. The Central Pacific began laying track in Sacramento, California, and built eastward. The Union Pacific began laying its tracks in Omaha, Nebraska, and built westward. Each company was paid for the miles of track it put down.

The work was backbreaking, especially in the mountains. There, tunnels had to be blasted. Uneven ground had to be leveled. Even where the land was already level, bridges had to be built to cross rivers. All of this work had to be done with pick and shovel.

This hard work was done mainly by immigrants. The Central Pacific hired 6,000 workers from China. It also hired Mexican Americans. The Union Pacific employed thousands of immigrants from Ireland. These workers were able to lay about 1 mile (1.6 km) of track a day across the Great Plains.

The two railroad teams met in Promontory, Utah. On May 10, 1869, the presidents of the two companies met there for a ceremony. They drove a golden spike in the rails, the last spike to link the railroads. The Atlantic Coast now was linked by rail to the Pacific Coast. It was possible to cross the country in only seven days.

179

Boom Towns

In the 1850s gold, silver, and other ores were found in the Rocky Mountains. Americans and foreigners alike rushed to the area. They wanted to make their own "strikes," or discoveries.

In 1859 gold was discovered at Pikes Peak in what is now Colorado. Soon thousands of covered wagons were headed there. These wagons often had signs such as "Pikes Peak or Bust" on them. Few miners found gold at Pikes Peak, though.

In the same year, 1859, the greatest of all mining strikes was made. A very large amount of gold and silver was found in what is now Nevada, at the Comstock Lode. It was the richest deposit of gold and silver ever discovered. Within only four years, it produced 15 million dollars worth of ore. In a few more years, more than 300 million dollars worth of ore had been mined. During the 1860s Montana, the Dakotas, Arizona, and New Mexico all rang with cries of "Gold!" and "Silver!"

In many areas, towns sprang up near the mines almost overnight. Such quickly growing towns are called boom towns. Virginia City near the Comstock Lode, for example, grew to a town of 20,000 people in just a few months. As soon as the ore ran out, many boom towns became "ghost towns" such as Tombstone, Arizona, and Dewey, Idaho. Some of the new cities in the Rockies, however, grew into important cities. Denver, Colorado, became an important trade center. In the same way, Last Chance Gulch became Helena, Montana's capital.

The Cattle Industry

Soon another industry appeared in the Last West. Americans found that the grassy plains could be used to fatten cattle. In the 1860s millions of longhorned cattle ran wild in southern Texas. These cattle had first been brought over by the Spaniards. The cattle often had escaped the ranches and learned to live in the grasslands. With the transcontinental railroad, cattle could be caught and then sent east by rail to be sold.

Americans began to start cattle ranches in the Last West. The cowhands who rounded up the cattle came from all parts of the nation. Skilled whites, blacks, Indians, and Mexican Americans worked together to drive the cattle northward to the new railroads. This journey was called the long drive.

Some cowhands drove their herds along the Goodnight-Loving Trail, from Texas north to the train stop at the town of Cheyenne, Wyoming. Or they drove them up the Chisholm Trail to Abilene, Kansas. The Western Trail led to Dodge City, Kansas.

Cattle drives sometimes took as long as three months. When the cowhands finally reached town, they often made up for the weeks of constant, often dull, work. Towns such as Abilene and Dodge City soon became well-known as rough, lawless places.

Many of the *homesteaders* who settled the Great Plains lived in sod houses. The house shown here was built into the hillside.

Homesteading

The settlers who came to farm the Great Plains were different from the ranchers and miners. They usually came as families. Families had been encouraged to come to the Great Plains by the Homestead Act of 1862. This act offered a settler 160 acres (65 ha) of land free. The settlers had to build a home and work the land for five years. At the end of that time, the farm, or *homestead* (hōm'sted'), was owned by the settler, after paying a small fee. The homesteader also could buy the land from the government after working it for six months.

Life on the Great Plains was very hard. Because there were few trees, pioneers often had to dig out hillsides to make their homes. They also cut up the tough sod into squares shaped like bricks. Houses made of these sod bricks were dark and damp.

Farming the land was very hard work. Plowing was made a little easier after John Deere invented the steel plow. The climate also worked against the farmer. At times there was no rain, and farmers and animals suffered during these times of drought. At other times, torrents of rain would fall suddenly and flood homes and fields.

Some homesteaders gave up because they lost hope or were too lonely. Others, however, found out how to pump water from deep out of the ground. They worked out better ways to farm. As the homesteaders grew more grain, they were able to buy wood from other places. Then, sod houses were replaced with better houses.

Indians Lose Their Land

The spread of the mining, cattle, and farming industries in the Last West destroyed the way of life of the American Indians. The rest of the United States was settled. There now was no place else for the Indians to go.

End of the Buffalo Herds

Most of the Indians of the Last West lived by hunting the buffalo herds of the Great Plains. Large herds of these animals had moved freely across the grasslands for hundreds of years. Now homesteaders were turning grazing land into farms. Settlers also were killing off the buffalo herds. At first sharpshooters killed the buffalo for the railroad building crews to eat. Once the railroads were built, eager buffalo hunters climbed aboard the railroad trains and shot buffalo from the moving cars. By the late 1800s, buffalo skins had become valuable.

As the buffalo died out, so did the Plains Indians' way of life. With the loss of the buffalo, the Indians lost an important source of food.

Settlers and Indians Clash

Angered by the actions of the settlers, the Indians began to attack them. The settlers then demanded that the government protect them from the Indian raids.

The government decided that the Indians should live on *reservations* (rez'ər vā'shənz). A reservation is land set aside for Indian use. The Indians were not supposed to leave the reservation. Only Indians were supposed to enter the reservation or use its land.

Then gold and other minerals were discovered on Indian land. Miners began to take this land for themselves. They also asked the government to back up their actions. Fights soon broke out between the settlers and the Indians. Settlers attacked Indians whose land they wanted. Both Indians whose land was taken and Indians who refused to live on reservations attacked settlers. The government sent in the army.

In just five years, from 1869 to 1874, more than 200 battles were fought. One Civil War general, Philip Sheridan, told why the Indians fought so fiercely. "We took away their country, their means of support, broke up their mode (way) of living, their habits of life," he said. "It was against this that they made war. Could anyone expect less?" he asked.

One of the most famous of the Indian battles was "Custer's Last Stand." In 1876, about 650 army troops under the command of General George Armstrong Custer were sent to put down an Indian uprising in Montana. Three chiefs—Sitting Bull, Crazy Horse, and Rain-in-the-Face—had put together a force of about 2,000 Indians. Although Custer's group was much smaller, Custer was sure he would win, and led his troops against the Indians at the Little Bighorn River. Custer and his soldiers died.

This was the last big victory for the Indians. They fought during the 1880s, but the

Only the Indian *reservations* in the West are shown on this map. Which states had the largest reservations in 1890?

buffalo were now almost completely destroyed. Many of the Indians were tired of being chased from place to place.

Chief Joseph of the Nez Percé (nez'purs') Indians explained why the Indians had to give up. "Our chiefs are killed," he said. "The little children are freezing to death. My people, some of them, have run away to the hills and have no blankets, no food. . . . I am tired. My heart is sick and sad. . . . I will fight no more forever."

Life on the Reservation

To Indians used to moving about freely, life on a reservation was a complete change. Instead of choosing their own way of life, the Indians had to stand in line waiting for the government to give them food. The government hired white agents to run the reservations. Often these agents were dishonest. They spent only part of the government money they received on the Indians. Agents kept part of the money for their own use.

The United States government tried more than one plan to improve the life of the Indians. But the government made mistakes. It did not really understand that many Indians wanted to keep their own culture. Soon the Indians were caught between two ways of life. One way was their old one which could not be saved. The other way of life was the American one, which was very different. The difference between the two ways was often too great for the Indians. Many died on the reservations.

183

New American Territories

Americans had wanted their nation to stretch across the whole continent. By the middle of the 1800s that goal was reached. Then some Americans decided that the United States should reach overseas.

Alaska—"Seward's Folly"

Russia had long owned Alaska, which is across the Bering Strait from Russian Siberia. During the Civil War, Secretary of State William Seward learned that Russia wanted to sell Alaska. Seward wanted to buy Alaska to remove Russia from North America. Buying Alaska would give the United States much new land.

Congress did not really want to buy Alaska. What use could this huge cold area be to the United States? Some members of Congress thought it was foolish. "Seward's Folly," they called it. Other members of Congress called Alaska "Seward's Icebox." But Seward finally convinced Congress. The United States bought Alaska in 1867 for 7,200,000 dollars—two cents an acre.

Thirty years later gold was discovered in Alaska. This discovery started a gold rush. Then, in the 1950s, great amounts of oil were found in Alaska. Seward had not been so foolish after all.

Hawaii—Far Out in the Pacific

During the early 1800s, several Christian missionaries left New England to go to the Hawaiian Islands. They were later joined by other American settlers. The settlers found that certain crops grew well in Hawaii. Within a few years the Americans in Hawaii had become the owners of giant sugar and pineapple plantations. They sold their crops to the United States.

In 1891 a new ruler came to the throne in Hawaii. She was Queen Liliuokalani (li lē ə wō kə län′ ē). The Queen did not want Americans to be so powerful in her country. She believed in a "Hawaii for the Hawaiians."

The American planters did not want their businesses to be harmed. They and the other Americans on the islands, therefore, made the Queen give up her throne. Later, they asked the American government to take control of Hawaii. After the annexation in 1898, the United States made Hawaii an American territory in 1900.

Do You Know?

1. Where was the Last West located?
2. Why did the building of the transcontinental railroad help the Last West to be settled?
3. What is a boom town? A ghost town?
4. What is homesteading?
5. Why did the Indians finally stop fighting with the settlers?
6. What other areas besides the Last West did Americans settle during the late 1800s?

To Help You Learn

Using New Words

homestead   reservation

The phrases below explain the words or terms listed above. Number a paper 1 and 2. After each number write the word or term that matches each definition.

1. A farm for which many settlers worked five years to own
2. Land set aside for Indians to live on

Finding the Facts

1. Why was Henry Clay called the "Great Compromiser"?
2. How were the careers of Lee and Grant the same? How were they different?
3. How did some blacks become free before the Civil War?
4. Why did the North and South not agree about tariffs before the Civil War?
5. Why did some Southern states secede after Lincoln was elected President?
6. Which slaves were freed by the Emancipation Proclamation?
7. What rights did the Thirteenth, Fourteenth, and Fifteenth Amendments give to blacks?
8. How did Southern states treat blacks after the end of Reconstruction?
9. Why did so few people settle in the Last West before 1860?

10. From what countries did many of the workers on the Transcontinental Railroad come? Why was it hard to build the railroad?
11. How did the Homestead Act of 1862 help the Great Plains to be settled?
12. What did the end of the buffalo herds do to the way of life of the Plains Indians?
13. Why did so many Indians find it hard to live on the reservations?

Learning from Maps

1. Look closely at the map on page 165. What color is used to show free states? Name one slave state that did not secede. What city was the Confederate capital? What city was the Union capital? About how far apart are these two cities?
2. Look at the map of the Civil War on page 171. In what part of the country did most of the fighting take place? Where was the northernmost battle fought? Where did the Battle of Shiloh take place? Who won the Battle of Shiloh? Which general led Union troops on a march across Georgia?
3. Turn to the map of Indian reservations on page 183. Find the largest reservations. Then turn to the climate map on page 11. Study the two maps together. What kind of climate did each of the reservations you chose have?

Next turn to the map on page 14 showing land use and mineral resources. What kinds of land did the reservations you chose have? What resources were nearby?

Using Study Skills

1. **Bar graph:** Turn to the bar graph on page 169. It shows resources of the Union and Confederacy at the beginning of the Civil War. Study the graph and answer these questions: What color is used to stand for Union resources? About what percentage of the nation's money was held in southern banks? Which part of the country had more railroads?

2. **Pictures:** Study the pictures on page 166 and 167. What do the pictures tell you about life in different parts of the United States during the middle of the 1800s and during the Civil War?

3. **Graph:** Look at the circle graph on this page. It shows the number of people who worked in some of America's largest industries in 1860. Which industry had the most workers? Which had the fewest workers? What percentage of people worked in the iron industry?

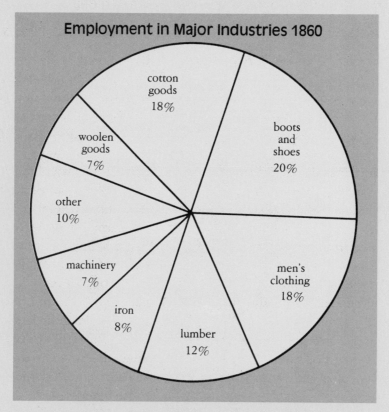

Employment in Major Industries 1860

cotton goods 18%

boots and shoes 20%

woolen goods 7%

other 10%

machinery 7%

men's clothing 18%

iron 8%

lumber 12%

Thinking It Through

1. Why is a civil war worse than some other kinds of wars?
2. What do you think was the main cause of the Civil War? Why?
3. Each of the CAUSES listed below brought about something listed under RESULTS. Match the causes with the correct results.

CAUSES
A. Congress passed the Homestead Act.
B. The Missouri Compromise was passed by Congress.
C. Gold was discovered in Alaska.
D. Congress passed the Compromise of 1850.

RESULTS
1. Many people rushed to Alaska.
2. California entered the Union as a free state.
3. The question of slavery was settled in the Louisiana Territory.
4. Pioneers went west to settle free land offered by the government.

Projects

1. The United States has had many flags during its history. Groups of students might find out about some of these flags. They might look for information about: the American flag at the time of the Constitution, the American flag of 1818, the Great Star flag, the Union flag during the Civil War, and four Confederate flags used during the Civil War.

   Make pictures of the flags and label each for a classroom display.
2. Your class might learn some songs that were sung by the cowhands in the days of the long drive. Books that have many of these songs are *Cowboy Songs* by John and Alan Lomax and *The American Songbag* by Carl Sandburg.
3. The Reading Committee might ask the librarian to find some exciting stories about the settlement of Oklahoma or about cattle ranching in the 1860s. Have the committee read a story on one of these subjects and report on it to the class.
4. Have the Research Committee make a report on the Alaska Pipeline. When was it built? Why was it built? Why did many Americans think the pipeline would harm the land around it?
5. Prepare a newspaper about the Civil War. It should have news articles about major battles. It should also have stories telling about the changes the war made in many families. You might also draw cartoons or other illustrations for the paper.

7 A Modern Nation

Unit Preview

The United States grew into a major world nation during the late 1800s and the 1900s. American industry grew. So did cities, as people moved from farms and towns. Immigrants also settled in the cities to work.

Cheap steel, electricity, the telephone, the automobile, and the airplane were a few of the many inventions that changed the lives of Americans. Now people were able to put up tall buildings and talk to those far away. They no longer had to live near their work.

Some Americans grew wealthy as a result of new industries and businesses. Workers formed unions and asked the government to end unfair business practices. After a time of growth, the country went through a Great Depression. Many people lost jobs, businesses, homes, and savings.

After a war with Spain, Americans gained land in the Caribbean Sea and Pacific Ocean. During the 1900s the United States also took part in two world wars and two Asian wars.

More Americans gained their rights as citizens in the 1900s. Women won the right to vote and moved toward full equality in every part of American life. Black Americans, Spanish-speaking Americans, senior citizens, and the handicapped also gained more of their civil rights. The lives of many people were made easier by computers, lasers, and other kinds of new technology.

Things to Discover

If you look carefully at the picture, map, and time line, you can answer these questions.

1. The areas highlighted on the map show major centers of population in the United States. In what part of the country are the largest centers?
2. The picture shows an astronaut testing machinery in space. Why would it be important for Americans to be able to leave their spaceships while in space?
3. Did World War I end before or after the opening of the Panama Canal?
4. When did women gain the vote?
5. When did President Nixon visit the Soviet Union?

Words to Learn

You will meet these words in this unit. As you read, you will learn what they mean and how to pronounce them. The Word List will help you.

alliance	muckraker
assembly line	neutral
civil rights	pollution
Cold War	slums
communism	stocks
concentration camps	strike
conservation	technology
depression	tenements
dictator	trust
holocaust	

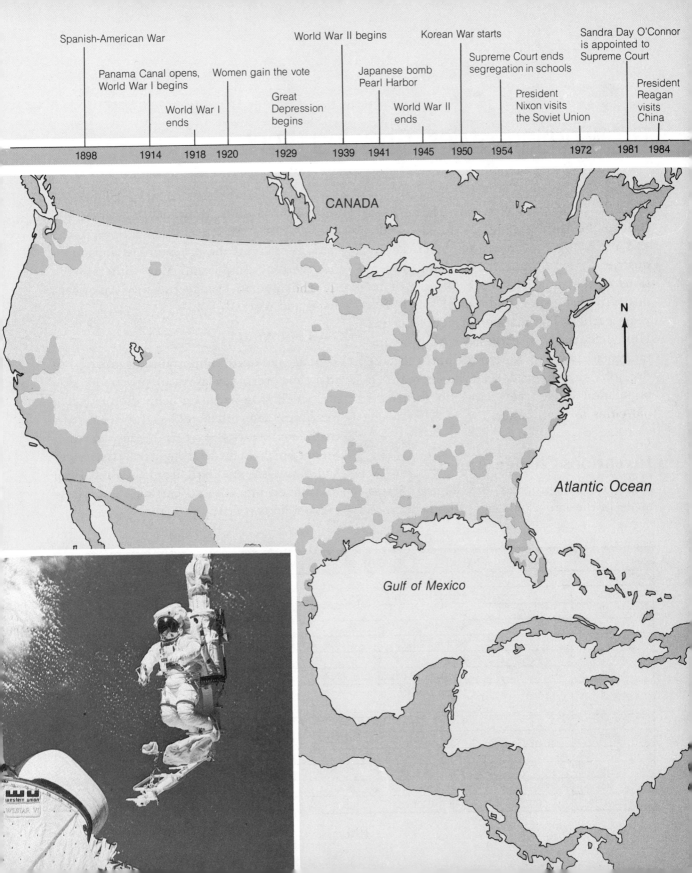

Spanish-American War

Panama Canal opens,
World War I begins

World War I
ends

Women gain the vote

Great
Depression
begins

World War II begins

Japanese bomb
Pearl Harbor

World War II
ends

Korean War starts

Supreme Court ends
segregation in schools

President
Nixon visits
the Soviet Union

Sandra Day O'Connor
is appointed to
Supreme Court

President
Reagan
visits
China

1898   1914   1918   1920   1929   1939   1941   1945   1950   1954   1972   1981   1984

CANADA

N

Atlantic Ocean

Gulf of Mexico

1

Growing Industries, Growing Cities

Growth—that was the word that best described the United States in the late 1800s and early 1900s. Almost all American industries grew during these years. Inventions of the time led to the forming of industries that were undreamed of a few years earlier. The number of people in the United States also increased rapidly as immigrants rushed to American shores to take the jobs that opened up. The increase in population caused new cities to form and old cities to grow larger.

Inventions Change America

Much of the progress the United States made in the late 1800s came about because of new inventions. Between 1875 and 1900 there were a million new inventions in the nation. Many of these new items and methods were not important. Many others, however, helped to change the way Americans lived and worked.

Iron into Steel

Among the most important discoveries of this time were new ways of producing iron and steel. Iron had long been used to make machines and other tools. But iron rusts easily and cracks if it is made too thin. Steel, which is made from iron, is stronger and easier to bend that iron. Steel also can be thinned into a sharp cutting edge. However, steel was costly to make.

Important Inventions and Inventors		
1793	Cotton Gin	Eli Whitney
1831	Horse-drawn Reaper	Cyrus McCormick
1837	Steel Plow	John Deere
1840	Morse Code	Samuel Morse
1846	Sewing Machine	Elias Howe
1852	Elevator	Elisha Otis
1868	Railroad Airbrake	George Westinghouse
1873	Barbed Wire	Joseph Glidden
	Typewriter	Christopher Sholes
1876	Telephone	Alexander Graham Bell
1879	Light Bulb	Thomas Edison
1884	Fountain Pen	Lewis Waterman
1899	Vacuum Cleaner	John Thurman
1903	Airplane	Wright Brothers
1930	Computer	Vannevar Bush

Then in the 1850s and 1860s new methods were invented to make steel quickly and cheaply. These discoveries came at the time the transcontinental railroads were being built. Steel rails and railway bridges made railroads safer to use. Soon steel also was being used to build a new type of building—the skyscraper. The steel industry quickly became a major industry in the United States. By 1900 the United States was making more steel than any other nation in the world.

Putting Electricity to Use

People had known about electricity for hundreds of years. In the 1700s Benjamin Franklin proved that lightning and electricity were one and the same. Now, in the 1800s, inventors began finding new ways to put electricity to work.

The possible uses of electricity greatly interested a teacher of the deaf in Boston. Alexander Graham Bell hoped that he might make a machine that would send the human voice over electric wire. Bell worked on his invention for 10 years before he made it work in 1876.

At first, the telephone was thought of as an amusing toy. But Bell and others knew that it could be useful in business and in private life. At that time a message had to be carried from one place to another, or sent by telegraph. Now the same message, spoken, could be sent in an instant by electric waves. With the telephone, an age of instant communication was born.

Thomas Edison made more than a thousand inventions. He is shown here with an invention that photographed things that can be seen through a microscope.

Thomas Edison—Wizard of Menlo Park

Probably no inventor worked longer and harder than Thomas Edison, who made more than 1,100 different new items. Many of these inventions used electricity. Edison did not think of himself as being especially gifted, though. "Genius is 1 percent inspiration and 99 percent perspiration," he said. "There is no substitute for hard work."

Edison first became interested in electricity as a young telegrapher working on the railroad. He made his first major invention in 1868, when he was only 21 years of age. It was an electric vote counting machine. At the age of 24, Edison quit his job and became a full-time inventor. One invention followed another from his laboratories in Menlo Park, New Jersey, and elsewhere. Edison's three most famous inventions probably were the phonograph, the electric light bulb, and the motion picture.

Big Business

Talented inventors helped make new businesses possible. However, it was daring business leaders who helped businesses to grow larger. So many big businesses appeared in the late 1800s that it was called an Era of Big Business.

John D. Rockefeller was one of America's first giants of big business. He began with an oil refinery in Ohio. Americans had just discovered how to bring crude oil, or petroleum, up from deep in the ground. The oil was then treated and used for lighting and heating and for oiling machinery. Rockefeller thought he could make more money from oil. He bought all the oil refineries he could. Then he combined, or joined, them together into one giant company—Standard Oil. This company became the nation's leader in producing and selling oil.

Andrew Carnegie was another giant of American business. In 1873 he built a steel mill near Pittsburgh, Pennsylvania. In the years that followed, Carnegie built many more steel mills. He bought land that had large deposits of iron ore. He also bought coal mines because coal is used in making steel. In addition, Carnegie built ships and railroads. By 1900 Carnegie had built a giant steel company that was made up of many businesses that took part in the making of steel. In 1901 Carnegie sold his company to J. P. Morgan for hundreds of millions of dollars. Morgan thought he had gotten a bargain!

Regulating Big Business

Big business was helping the nation to grow wealthy. Yet a number of people began to question the methods used by some businesses. Reformers said that many people and businesses were being hurt. Soon magazine and newspaper writers called *muckrakers* (muk'rāk'ərz) began to report about big business. The writers said that big business took many unfair and harmful actions. For example, writers said that Rockefeller paid the railroads less to ship his oil than other shippers did. The muckrakers said that such practices killed free competition. Smaller businesses that could not compete had to go out of business.

Many Americans were very worried by a form of big business called a *trust*. Sometimes several companies would join together to control a whole industry. This trust would then set very low prices on its products. Small companies could not compete and had to close their doors or sell their company to the trust. To end some unfair practices, Congress passed the Sherman Antitrust Act in 1890.

Rise of Labor Unions

The growth of big business and industry caused another problem. Many workers in the booming industries often had to work 70 to 80 hours a week. In addition, working conditions often were unsafe. For example, machines often did not have coverings to protect the people who used them. Workers sometimes lost fingers or arms or received other injuries as a result. Even though they worked hard, most Americans earned very little money. Wages were sometimes less than 20 cents an hour.

Some workers began to form groups called labor unions. These unions demanded shorter working hours, safer working conditions, and higher pay. At first labor unions gained little that they asked for. Employers said the unions were trying to tell them how to run their businesses. Business owners often fired workers who joined unions.

The unions began to take actions to gain their demands. One of the actions the

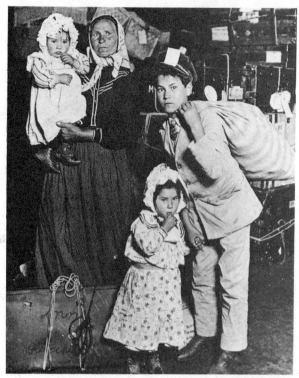

This Italian family had just arrived at Ellis Island in New York. They were among the many immigrants from Southern Europe who came to the United States to build a new life.

unions often used was the *strike* (strīk). In a strike, workers stop working and refuse to go back on their job until employers meet their demands. Several of the early strikes led to bloodshed.

Little by little, though, labor unions were accepted. The American Federation of Labor (A.F.L.) became one of the strongest of the early unions. Workers won shorter work weeks, safer working conditions, and higher wages.

New Waves of Immigrants

Before the Civil War most immigrants to the United States came from Northern and Western Europe. They came mainly from

England, Ireland, Scotland, Germany, Norway, and Sweden. Immigrants continued to come from these countries after the Civil War. However, in the 1800s growing numbers of immigrants came to the United States from Southern and Eastern Europe. These people came mostly from the countries of Italy, Greece, Russia, Poland, and Austria-Hungary.

At this time immigrants also began to come from nations in Asia, mostly from China and Japan. Still other immigrants came from countries in Central America, from Mexico, and from the islands of the Caribbean Sea.

The number of immigrants grew quickly. Before 1880 fewer than half a million immigrants arrived on American shores each year. By 1905 more than 1 million immigrants were arriving each year.

Why the Immigrants Came

Most of the immigrants came to the United States to make a better living for themselves and their families. Many of the newcomers had been farmers in Europe who could no longer make their small farms pay. Some immigrants were craftsworkers whose skills were no longer needed as Europe industrialized.

Some immigrants came for other reasons. A number of Europeans, for example, were looking for religious freedom and escape from the wars that often broke out in Europe. All these new immigrants looked to the United States as a place where they and their families could make a new start in life.

Problems the Immigrants Faced

For many years the United States welcomed immigrants. The nation needed more people to work in its new factories and to help settle the Last West. These early immigrants were not very different from the original settlers. However, the immigrants who came later did not receive the same welcome. In time, most immigrants succeeded in making a better life for themselves and their families in the United States. First, though, they faced many problems.

One problem that the new immigrants faced was language. Earlier immigrants from England, Ireland, and Scotland spoke English. Many of the new immigrants did not speak English, however. This made it hard for them to get along in the country. Housing was another problem. It was hard to find living places for a million new people each year.

Finally, there was the problem of religious prejudice. Immigrants from Southern and Eastern Europe had hoped to leave such prejudice behind. But many native-born Americans were Protestants, and some of them did not like Catholics or Jews. Roman Catholics from Ireland had suffered from unfair treatment for some time. Now Catholics from Italy and Jews from Russia and Poland also were faced with religious prejudice.

Changing Immigration Policy

Americans began to grow more unfriendly toward the immigrants for a number of other reasons also. Many Americans thought that there were too many "strangers" coming among them. They disliked the "different ways" of the newcomers and feared that so many "foreigners" would change the United States. American workers also were worried about the new immigrants. They believed that immigrants would accept low pay to get jobs. If this happened, American-born workers would have to work for less pay also.

To end these fears, Congress began to limit immigration. It ended Chinese immigration entirely. An agreement between the United States and Japan in 1907 stopped Japanese immigration also. Then Congress passed laws to limit the number of immigrants allowed to enter the United States each year. These laws favored immigrants from Northern and Western European countries over those from other countries.

During the early 1900s, lower New York City was crowded with people and carts selling food, clothing, and other items. *Tenements* were built close together.

Cities Grow and Change

Most of the new immigrants chose to live in the cities, where there were factories. More people also were leaving their farms to live in cities. Fewer and fewer people lived on farms. As a result, more than half of Americans lived in cities by 1920.

Some cities grew rapidly in population. In the years between 1870 and 1910 the number of people in Baltimore, Philadel- phia, and St. Louis more than doubled. The number of people in New York and Pittsburgh tripled. Cleveland and Detroit grew six times larger in population. Chicago's number of people grew seven times larger.

Problems of Rapid City Growth

Such rapid growth of cities caused many problems. Cities could not build houses fast enough to keep up with the need for them. As a result, too many people were crowded closely together.

Many areas were not taken care of. It was in these *slums* (slumz), old areas that were falling apart, that the poor and many of the new immigrants lived. At the heart of many slums were buildings called *tenements* (ten'ə məntz). These were narrow, uncared for buildings of five or six stories. The rooms were often small, and hallways and stairways often were dark and dirty.

Some buildings might have only one water faucet. Everyone in the building, perhaps 100 people or more, had to share it.

The Special Work of Jane Addams

Reporters began printing stories about the problems of poor city dwellers. Photographers showed pictures of the slums. This caused many citizens to begin to try and improve the living conditions of poor people.

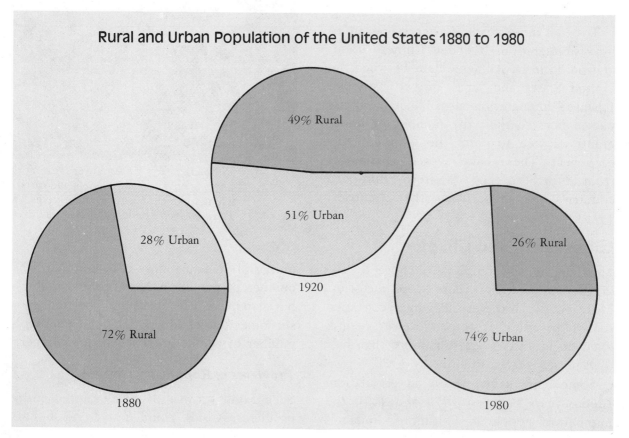

Rural and Urban Population of the United States 1880 to 1980

49% Rural

51% Urban

1920

28% Urban

72% Rural

1880

26% Rural

74% Urban

1980

Jane Addams gave much of her time to help the children and older people who went to Hull House for help and advice.

Jane Addams was one of the Americans who decided to help the poor in cities. She has been born to a well-to-do family in Illinois in 1860. From childhood, Addams believed that there was some "special work" that she should do in life.

Jane Addams went to work among the poor in a Chicago slum. It was there that she founded Hull House, which was a settlement house, or a kind of neighborhood center. Immigrants from the neighborhood came there to learn English. Working mothers brought their children to stay there during the day. People also came to talk about the problems their neighborhood faced—poor housing and unhealthy conditions, for example.

Improving Cities

Following the example of Jane Addams, settlement houses were started in poor neighborhoods in several cities. City governments also began to improve living conditions. For example, city health departments were set up to take care of poor people who were ill. Health departments also worked to get rid of disease. Cities passed laws to make buildings more healthful and safer.

In many cities, spaces were set aside for parks and playgrounds. These places gave city dwellers somewhere to take their children and to enjoy their free time. Improvements in public transportation also made cities less crowded. Trolley cars, for example, made it possible for people to live farther away from their jobs.

Do You Know?

1. What new industries helped the United States to grow during the late 1800s?
2. What did John D. Rockefeller achieve? Andrew Carnegie?
3. Why did some Americans want to reform big business?
4. Why were labor unions formed?
5. What problems did the new immigrants face?
6. How did Jane Addams help poor people in Chicago?

2

Looking Beyond the Nation's Borders

The growth of the United States during the late 1800s made Americans take a greater interest in what was happening in other parts of the world. American businesses and farms were producing more goods than the American people needed. Therefore, these industries needed to sell their products overseas. As a result, the United States looked outward.

Gaining New Land

The United States was very interested in Cuba, just 90 miles (144 km) from the

The United States had gained many overseas territories by 1900. Name some of these areas.

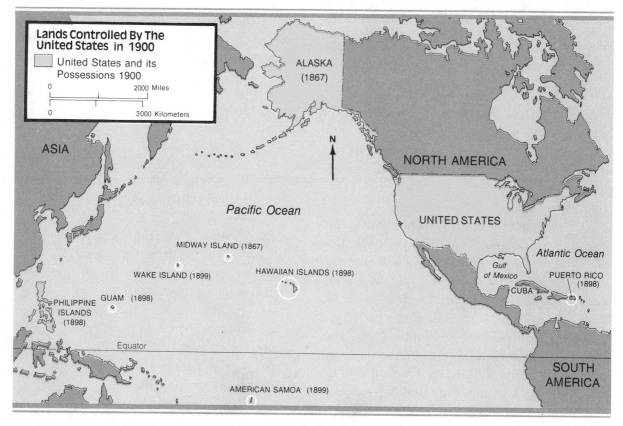

Lands Controlled By The United States in 1900

☐ United States and its Possessions 1900

0 — 2000 Miles
0 — 3000 Kilometers

ASIA

ALASKA (1867)

NORTH AMERICA

N

Pacific Ocean

UNITED STATES

MIDWAY ISLAND (1867)

WAKE ISLAND (1899)

HAWAIIAN ISLANDS (1898)

GUAM (1898)

PHILIPPINE ISLANDS (1898)

Atlantic Ocean

Gulf of Mexico

PUERTO RICO (1898)

CUBA

Equator

AMERICAN SAMOA (1899)

SOUTH AMERICA

coast of Florida. Cuba had been settled by the Spaniards. In 1895 Cuban rebels began fighting a major battle with the Spaniards for their independence.

Most Americans hoped that the Cubans would win. However, the United States stayed out of the fighting at first. Then in 1898 the United States government sent the battleship USS *Maine* to Cuba. The ship was sent to protect Americans who lived or worked in Havana, Cuba.

On February 15, 1898, the *Maine* was in Havana Harbor. A bugler aboard had just sounded "Taps," signaling the end of the day. The next moment an explosion ripped through the battleship. Nearly 260 of the 350 officers and crew aboard were killed. Americans immediately demanded that the United States to go to war with Spain. "Remember the *Maine*!" they cried.

War with Spain

Two months later Congress declared war on Spain. The fighting took place in the Pacific Ocean as well as in the Caribbean Sea.

Just a few days after the nation went to war, American naval ships sailed into the port of Manila, the capital of the Philippines. The Philippine Islands in the Pacific Ocean were then under the control of Spain. Commodore George Dewey led the American attack on the Spanish ships in Manila harbor. Within a few hours the Spanish fleet was destroyed.

Soon after, in June, 17,000 American ground troops landed on Cuba and defeated

Teddy Roosevelt led the Rough Riders who had volunteered to fight in Cuba in 1898.

the Spaniards there. Cuba could now become an independent nation. In the peace treaty that followed, Spain turned over to the United States its control of Puerto Rico in the Caribbean and of the island of Guam in the Pacific. Spain also agreed to give the Philippines to the United States.

One of the heroes of the war was Theodore Roosevelt. Before the war, he had been Assistant Secretary of the Navy. Believing that war would soon come, Roosevelt had sent Commodore Dewey to the western Pacific. That put Dewey in a place to attack the Spaniards at Manila as soon as the war began. Before the war started, Colonel "Teddy" Roosevelt also had organized his own cavalry. The "Rough Riders," as this group was called, fought bravely in the battle for Santiago, Cuba. The popularity that "Teddy" Roosevelt won as a result helped to make him President in the early 1900s.

Building the Panama Canal

The war made it clear to the United States that it had to be able to move ships quickly and easily between the Atlantic and Pacific oceans. The only way a ship could move from the Atlantic to the Pacific was to sail all the way around South America.

A shorter route was possible, though. Part of Central America is very narrow. At the Isthmus of Panama, for example, only 50 miles (80 km) separates the Pacific Ocean from the Caribbean Sea. A canal through this isthmus would shorten the journey from ocean to ocean by 7,000 miles (11,200 km).

In 1878 a French company had tried to build a canal across Panama. It gave up when thousands of workers died from yellow fever and malaria. In the early 1900s, though, President Theodore Roosevelt was determined to have a canal dug across Central America.

Panama was part of the South American nation of Colombia at the time. President Roosevelt offered Colombia 10 million dollars and a yearly rent of 250,000 dollars for the right to build and run the canal. Colombia said no. Angry, Roosevelt gave backing to rebels in Panama who

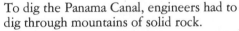

To dig the Panama Canal, engineers had to dig through mountains of solid rock.

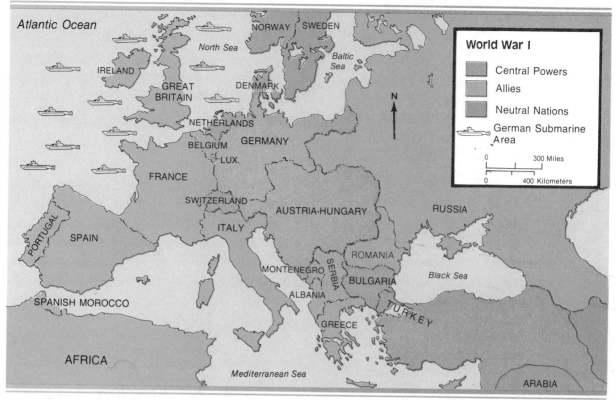

During World War I, the United States fought on the side of the *Allies*. Which European nations were the Allies?

wanted to throw off the control of Colombia. Then President Roosevelt recognized Panama as an independent nation. Panama, in turn, allowed the United States to build the canal.

Work on the canal began in 1904. First, the United States had to rid the area of yellow fever and malaria. It sent to Panama Colonel William Gorgas. He and Doctor Walter Reed had learned in Cuba that yellow fever and malaria were caused by the bite of infected mosquitos. The army sprayed the swamps where the mosquitos lived to kill the insects.

The canal finally was completed after 10 years of hard work digging through swamps, jungles, and mountains. The cost was almost 400 million dollars. On August 15, 1914, the first ship sailed through the locks of the Panama Canal. The locks were needed to raise and lower ships across the different levels of land.

World War I Begins

While the canal was being completed, war broke out in Europe. Several nations there had long been trying to gain new land for themselves overseas. Great Britain, France, Germany, Italy, Russia, and other European nations had claimed land in Asia and Africa. Each nation wanted to gain more land than the other European nations. They tried to gain power in other ways also.

They competed to have the strongest army and navy. They tried to gain the most trade and raw materials. All of this competition caused hatred and fear among the nations of Europe.

A System of Alliances

To protect themselves from one another, European nations began to form *alliances* (ə lī′əns əz), or agreements, of friendship. Nations belonging to an alliance agreed not to attack the other nations in the alliance. They also promised to fight for any member of the alliance that was attacked by another nation.

Before 1914 two powerful alliances had formed in Europe. One was the Triple Alliance. Germany, Austria-Hungary, and Italy—the three countries that formed this alliance—were called the Central Powers. The second alliance was called the Triple Entente (än tänt′). Its members were Great Britain, France, and Russia, and they were called the Allies (al′īz).

The war that everyone feared finally broke out. In June 1914 an Austro-Hungarian royal couple were riding in a parade. A shot rang out and then a second shot. Both husband and wife were killed. The murder of the royal couple led to war. Because of all the alliances the war spread throughout Europe. The war even reached as far as the European possessions in Africa and Asia. So many nations and areas took part in the war that it was called a World War.

The United States Enters World War I

The United States tried to stay out of the war by remaining *neutral* (nōō′trəl). That is, the United States did not want to take sides. As the war went on, however, it became very hard for Americans to stay neutral. Germany was using submarines to attack ships. These U-boats ("U" stood for *u*ndersea boat) sank many ships of the Al-

Many American women worked in weapons factories during World War I. They took the jobs of men who went to fight in Europe.

lies. Since Americans were aboard these ships, they, too, were killed.

In 1917 a letter written by a member of the German government to a German official in Mexico was discovered. The letter told the official to see if Mexico would go to war against the United States. Americans angrily demanded war. In April 1917 President Woodrow Wilson asked Congress to declare war against the Central Powers. The United States entered the war on the side of the Allies.

The Allies greatly needed American help. They had been fighting for nearly three years. The United States immediately began to send troops and supplies to the Allies. Nearly 3 million Americans joined the military. More than 1 million American troops went to Europe to fight, mostly in France.

To help fight the war, women took over jobs left by men who joined the military. As a result, women learned many new skills. They became factory mechanics and trolley car conductors. They even became barbers. To help fill all the jobs in war factories, many thousands of black Americans began to leave the South for northern cities. Many of these families never returned to the South.

Searching for World Peace

By 1918 the Central Powers were losing the war. Eager American troops gave fresh hope to the Allies. The joined forces finally caused the Central Powers to surrender. At 11:00 A.M. on November 11—the eleventh hour of the eleventh day of the eleventh month—the war ended.

President Wilson had called the fight "a war to end war." So much suffering led the President to look for ways to stop such a war from happening again. To bring about a lasting world peace, he wanted to form a "League (lēg) of Nations." Meeting together, nations of the world could talk over their problems peacefully.

The nations of Europe accepted Wilson's plan for a League of Nations, and the League was founded in 1920. Many members of the United States Congress, however, did not want the United States to join the League. They were afraid that this world body would try to control the foreign affairs of the United States. As a result, the United States did not join the League of Nations.

Do You Know?

1. Why did the United States go to war with Spain in 1898?
2. Why was the Panama Canal built?
3. What nations belonged to the Central Power during World War I? The Allies?
4. Why did the United States enter World War I?
5. What was the League of Nations?

Before You Go On

Using New Words

alliance   strike
muckrakers   tenements
neutral   trust
slums

The phrases below explain the words or terms listed above. Number a paper from 1 through 7. After each number write the word or term that matches each definition.

1. Apartment buildings that were uncared for and that often had dark, dirty hallways and small rooms
2. Taking no side in an argument
3. A business arrangement in which several companies join together to end competition in an industry
4. An agreement among nations to work together for a common goal
5. Old run-down areas in a city
6. The action taken by workers who refuse to work until their employers meet their demands
7. People, especially writers, who pointed out that some of the actions taken by big business were unfair

Finding the Facts

1. Why was a better way of making steel important to American industry?
2. Name two of Thomas Edison's inventions.
3. Why did Congress pass the Sherman Antitrust Act?
4. Why did many workers want to form labor unions?
5. From which countries were many of the immigrants to the United States in the late 1880s?
6. Why did Congress begin to allow fewer immigrants into the United States?
7. What problems did the rapid growth of cities cause?
8. What was Hull House?
9. What did the United States gain from its war with Spain?
10. Why was it hard to build the Panama Canal?
11. How did European nations compete with each other in the early 1900s?
12. What event led to the start of World War I?
13. Why did the United States not join the League of Nations?

3

Good Times and Bad

After World War I, people in the United States turned away from Europe to look to their own needs. During war, people often have to do without things in order to supply the nation's troops. Now that the fighting had ended Americans wanted to forget the suffering of war. They wanted to buy the things they had gone without and to have a good time.

The Roaring Twenties

One American writer called the 1920s "the Era of Wonderful Nonsense." People of the time seemed to enjoy trying to do new things, even if they were silly. Everyday life was freer. During the "Roaring Twenties," as these years were called, the American people looked to the future with great hope.

Women Gain the Vote

Women finally gained the vote in 1920. This happened partly because of World War I. Women had filled many jobs in which they had to manage or to do hard physical labor during wartime. The admiration of the nation led many Americans to agree to a Constitutional amendment giving women the right to vote.

The Nineteenth Amendment giving women the vote is sometimes called "the Susan B. Anthony Amendment." It is named after a woman who worked hard for the amendment to be passed. Unfortunately, Susan B. Anthony did not live to see women gain the vote. She had died in 1906.

Spread of Automobiles

Making an automobile cheap enough for many people to buy put millions of American families "on wheels" in the early 1900s. Automobiles had been around long before the 1920s, but they were very costly. In 1906 Henry Ford had figured out a way to make cars cheaply.

One method Ford introduced to car making was the *assembly* (ə sem′blē) *line*. The assembly line is a way of putting something together by using a line of workers. Each worker adds something to the product. What Ford did was to design a moving belt that held the car frame. The belt moved slowly past a line of workers. Each worker added one piece to the car frame. For example, one worker added the steering wheel, another the wheels, and so on. By the end of the assembly line, the car was completed and ready to be driven away.

Ford's car was called the Model T. By 1927 Ford was making one Model T every 10 seconds. The price was 290 dollars. Other car makers quickly followed Ford's lead and used the assembly line to make more cars quickly. In 1920 there were 9 million cars on American roads. During the next 10 years, 32 million more cars were made in the United States.

Coming of Airplanes

In 1903, the same year that Ford began his company, another great improvement was made in transportation. Two brothers, Orville and Wilbur Wright, made an airplane.

The Wright brothers hoped to build a motor-powered airplane. In their shop they finally made a flying machine that looked as if it would fall apart. They took their machine to the windy beaches of Kitty Hawk, North Carolina, to test it. On the morning of December 17, 1903, the plane flew for 12 seconds before returning to the ground. The Wright brothers had made the first motor-powered flight in history. Soon many inventors were at work on airplanes.

At the beginning of the 1920s, pilots competed to be the first person to fly alone across the Atlantic Ocean. A young airmail pilot named Charles A. Lindbergh was the winner. On the rainy morning of May 20, 1927, his single-engine plane, the *Spirit of St. Louis,* took off from Long Island in New York. A little more than 33 hours later, the plane landed at Orly Field, outside Paris, France. "Lucky Lindy" became a hero overnight.

New Fields of Entertainment

Another industry that grew quickly during the 1920s was entertainment. Two inventions especially—the radio and the motion picture, or movie—greatly changed the way Americans spent their free time.

An Italian inventor named Guglielmo Marconi (gōōl yel′mō mär kō′nē) had discovered how to send electric messages through the air in the 1890s. Other inventors improved on his work. By the 1920s, radio sets appeared in living rooms across the nation. The 1920 Presidential election was the first event reported over the radio. Within a few years, news as well as programs of music, drama, comedy, and sports were heard by Americans daily in different parts of the country.

Motion pictures also quickly grew popular at this time. Hollywood, California, became "the movie capital of the world." At first movies were silent. There was no sound to go with the film. Then new inventions made "talking pictures" possible. The first talking movie was *The Jazz Singer.* Within months, silent movies were dead. More and more people started going to the movies.

Booming Business

During the 1920s, American industries produced twice as much each year as they had in earlier years. Why did American businesses do so well? New inventions led to new industries, and new industries led to more jobs. Also, taxes were lowered during this time. This gave Americans more money to spend. Americans spent some of their money to make more money. For instance, they spent their money to buy *stocks* (stokz). Stocks are shares of ownership in a company. Shareholders receive part of the money earned by companies. Since American businesses were making large profits during the 1920s, many people wanted to buy stocks.

The Great Depression Strikes

By the end of the 1920s, problems were beginning to form in the nation. Farmers who grew more crops than they could sell often ended up losing their farms. Factory owners who produced more goods than they could sell began to lay off workers.

In 1929 the nation entered a period of *depression* (di presh'ən). A depression is a period of hard times, when there is little business and when fewer people have jobs. People without jobs do not have money to buy things. Businesses that cannot sell their goods cannot stay open. The depression then gets worse. The hard times that began in 1929 were so terrible that these years became known as the "Great Depression."

Life During the Great Depression

One fourth of the nation's workers could not find work during the Great Depression. Many families went hungry or had no place to live. Large numbers of farm families packed everything they owned in cars and headed west. Some people without homes built huts out of old boxes to live in.

At this time, there were almost no gov-

Many families lost their homes during the Great Depression. They walked the highways looking for jobs and a place to live.

ernment programs to help those without jobs. Some people believed the government should do more to help the poor. In 1932 Americans elected Franklin D. Roosevelt as President. He promised government programs that would give Americans "a new deal."

The New Deal

President Roosevelt had been born into a wealthy New York family in 1882. He became a lawyer and later entered politics. Suddenly, when he was 39 years old, Roosevelt was struck with the crippling disease of polio. It looked as though Roosevelt's political career was over. But he gathered his strength and went back to politics.

As President, Roosevelt got Congress to pass programs to help Americans hard hit by the Depression. He also started programs to try to end the Depression. New

Deal programs offered government loans to farmers and also tried to raise crop prices. Other programs tried to help businesses and factory workers by getting industries to create more jobs for workers. The government also made new jobs. One program sent young men to American forests. There they worked to conserve, or save, the forests. They also created parks for all the people to enjoy.

The New Deal helped many Americans. Nevertheless, large numbers of people remained jobless. Then, at the end of the 1930s, the nation faced new problems.

World War II Begins

The Great Depression hurt not only the United States, but also countries around the world. In some countries the people turned to strong leaders to guide them out of their time of trouble. Some of these leaders turned out to be *dictators* (dik′tā′tərz). A dictator is a ruler who completely controls a country. A dictator has power over people, the government, and the armed forces.

Rise of Dictators

One of the countries that was ruled by a dictator was Germany. Adolf Hitler had come to power there in 1933. Italy also had a dictator, Benito Mussolini (bə nē′tō moos′ə lē′nē). Both Hitler and Mussolini built up the military strength of their nations. Japan was another country that was

ruled by dictators. A group of military leaders had taken over the government. They too built up the nation's military strength.

All three of these nations wanted to become more powerful. They hoped to do this by taking the land of other nations. In the middle of the 1930s, Germany, Italy, and Japan became partners. They were called the Axis (ak′sis) powers. Italy then invaded part of Africa. Japan invaded China. Germany took control of Austria and next began to take over other countries in Europe.

In September 1939 Germany marched into Poland. However, Great Britain and France had a treaty of friendship with Poland. Both nations had promised to fight for Poland if it was attacked. These nations now declared war on Germany. Because of the attack on Poland, one group of nations faced another group of nations. World War II began.

The United States Enters World War II

The United States tried to stay out of the fighting. Then on December 7, 1941, everything changed. At dawn on that Sunday, Japanese airplanes and submarines made a surprise attack on the United States naval base at Pearl Harbor in Hawaii.

The next day President Roosevelt asked Congress to declare war on Japan. Japan's partners, Germany and Italy, then went to war with the United States. Americans now faced fighting a war across the Atlantic

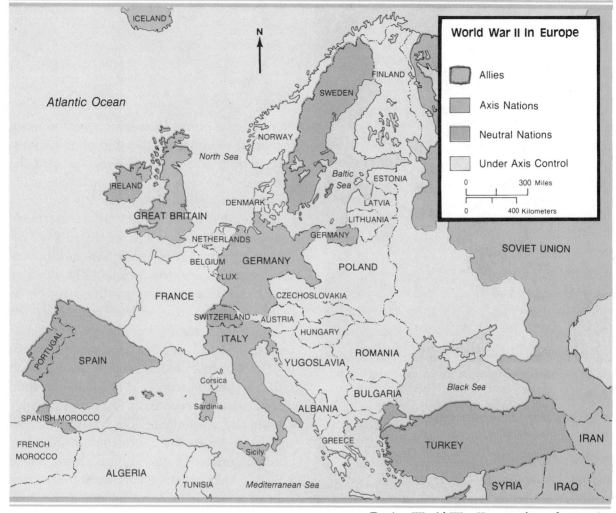

During World War II, a number of countries were attacked by Germany and placed under Axis control. Name three of them.

and Pacific oceans. The United States joined the Allies—Britain, France, the Soviet Union (formerly Russia), and several other countries that were fighting the Axis powers.

Fighting the War

Millions of American men and women entered the military services. By the end of the war, about 13 million people were in the military. Millions of Americans went to work in war factories to make the war supplies that were needed. Even the children helped. They collected materials that could be reused for the war effort. Among these items were old tires, pieces of metal, and grease left over from cooking.

Japanese Americans

After Japan attacked Pearl Harbor, many Americans on the West Coast began to fear the Japanese who lived there. Many of the Japanese were American citizens. Yet

Japanese Americans were taken by bus to special camps during World War II. More than 100,000 Japanese had to live in these camps. They often lost both homes and businesses.

many Americans feared that these people would act as spies for the Japanese government.

The result was that the Japanese Americans were made to leave their homes. They were sent to special camps where they lived during the war. Later the United States government apologized to the Japanese for this unfair action. None of the people placed in the camps was ever found to be a spy. Many Japanese Americans had fought bravely in the war.

Ending the War in Europe

The war in Europe finally ended in May 1945. American, British, and French forces fought their way east across Europe toward Germany. At the same time the forces of the Soviet Union, on the side of the Allies, fought their way toward Germany from the opposite direction. The Allied forces came together and crushed Germany.

When the Allies closed in on Germany they saw what many had heard rumors of. The Germans had rounded up millions of men, women, and children and placed them in *concentration* (kon′sən trā′shən) *camps,* or prison camps. Most of the people in the concentration camps were Jews. Hitler had unfairly blamed the Jews for all of Germany's problems. Many Germans believed Hitler's unfair words. The concentration camps held Jews and other people Hitler thought of as enemies. They came from all the lands taken by Germany. Millions of people, including 6 million Jews, were killed in these camps. This terrible destruction of a people came to be called the *holocaust* (hol′ə kôst′).

Ending the War in Asia

The war in Asia kept on after the fighting stopped in Europe. The United States had plans to attack Japan. However, American leaders worried that fighting in Japan would cause the deaths of many more Americans.

The result was that the United States decided to use a new and terrible weapon. On August 6, 1945, an American plane dropped a single atomic bomb on the Japanese city of Hiroshima (hēr′ō shē′mə). Three days later another atomic bomb was dropped on the city of Nagasaki (nä gə sä

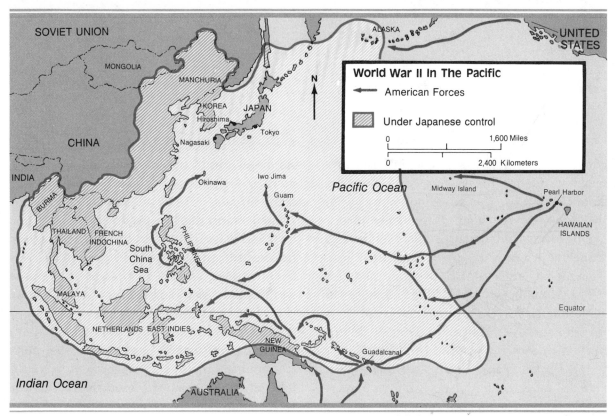

Many of the islands in the Pacific Ocean had been taken by Japan during World War II. How does the map show you the areas that Japan had taken? What are some of these areas?

kē). The loss of life from the bomb blast and from the rays given off by the bomb was so great that the Japanese surrendered on August 15.

Founding of the United Nations

Before World War II ended, leaders of the Allied nations planned to try to stop such a war from happening again. They talked about setting up an organization of nations that would peacefully settle disagreements among nations.

The representatives of 51 nations met in San Francisco on April 25, 1945. They signed an agreement setting up the United Nations. The representatives also promised to work for peace through the United Nations. The United States was a member of the new organization.

An Uneasy Peace

The United States and the Soviet Union had fought as Allies during World War II. After the war, however, the United States and the other Allies found it hard to remain friends with the Soviet Union. The Soviet Union had set up a very different form of government from that of the other Allied nations. The aims of these two kinds of governments began to clash.

Communism in the Soviet Union

The Soviet Union has a Communist government. Under the system of *communism* (kom′yə niz′əm), the government owns all property—all the land, businesses, farms, and factories. Individual people cannot own property. Moreover, the Communist government has great control over the people.

The republic of the United States, on the other hand, has a democratic form of government. As you read in Unit 3, democracy is rule by the people. In a democracy, people have many more freedoms than they do under communism. In a democracy, people are free to own property and to choose their jobs. Americans also have the freedoms guaranteed by the Bill of Rights.

The Cold War

After World War II, the Soviet Union wanted to spread communism to other countries. It set up Communist governments in many nations of Eastern Europe. The Soviet Union also tried to get nations in other parts of the world to become Communist. In 1949 China became a Communist nation. Cuba became Communist in 1959.

The United States and many nations of Western Europe wanted to stop the spread of communism. Instead of fighting with guns and bombs, though, the Western nations and the Communist nations fought each other with angry words and threats. This struggle was given a name—the *Cold War*.

Hot War in Korea

At times the Cold War heated up. Then guns and bombs took the place of words and threats. However, even then the United States and the Soviet Union did not fight each other directly. Instead they backed different sides in the war.

One place where a hot war broke out was in the Asian nation of Korea. After World War II Korea had been divided in two. North Korea had a Communist government, and South Korea remained non-Communist. In June 1950, however, North Korean troops attacked South Korea. South Korea immediately asked the United States for help. The United Nations sent South Korea a military force, which was made up mostly of Americans. Communist China then sent a military force to help the North Koreans.

After three years, North Korea and South Korea agreed to stop fighting. However, Korea still was divided into a Communist North Korea and a non-Communist South Korea.

The Vietnam War

After World War II, another Asian nation —Vietnam—also was divided into a Communist north and a non-Communist south. North Vietnam wanted to take control of South Vietnam and make all of Vietnam Communist.

The United States promised to help South Vietnam fight the Communists. At first, the United States helped by sending guns, tanks, and other war supplies. Then it began sending a few military forces. During the middle 1960s many more troops were sent. Still the war went on, year after year. The fighting caused great loss of life and property to both the Vietnamese people and to Americans.

In the early 1970s the United States government began to take its troops out of Vietnam. Americans hoped that South Vietnam could carry on the fight alone. By 1975, however, South Vietnam had fallen. All of Vietnam was united under a Communist government.

Efforts for Peace

While these wars were being fought, the United States kept trying to find ways to make the world a peaceful place. In 1961, for example, President John F. Kennedy formed an organization called the Peace Corps. President Kennedy asked Americans to offer their services to help other countries. He called mostly for teachers, farm experts, health experts, and engineers. Members of the Peace Corps have served in nearly 60 countries.

During the Cold War, many world leaders grew worried about the arms race that had come about. Many nations, worried that they might be attacked, wanted to own atom bombs and other nuclear weapons. Beginning in the 1960s, the United States and the Soviet Union met several times to talk about cutting down on the number of these weapons and their testing.

The United States has long tried to bring peace to the Middle East. In 1948 the new Jewish nation of Israel was founded in the Middle East. The neighboring Arab countries do not want Israel to exist. This had caused the Jews and the Arabs to go to war several times. In 1979 President Jimmy Carter helped the leaders of Egypt and Israel work out a peace treaty. But the Middle East remains a place of unrest.

The United States tried to bring about peace in other ways also. In 1972 President Richard M. Nixon visited both China and the Soviet Union. It was the first time an American President had visited either of these countries while in office. In 1984, the year President Ronald Reagan was reelected, he also visited China.

Do You Know?

1. What amendment to the Constitution gave women the vote?
2. What is an assembly line? In what industry was it first used?
3. What was the Great Depression?
4. How did dictators start World War II?
5. Why did the United States enter World War II?
6. What was the Cold War? Where did it heat up into hot wars?

A

Presidents Work for Peace

America's Presidents have worked hard to bring about world peace. During the 1900s they have made trips to many parts of the world to meet with other world leaders. President Woodrow Wilson, for example, went to France to sign the treaty ending World War I (F). Even before World War II ended in 1945, President Franklin D. Roosevelt met with Prime Minister Winston Churchill of Britain (seated, left) and Soviet Premier Joseph Stalin (seated, right) in the Soviet Union (G). They talked about Europe's problems.

D

Many world leaders have visited the United States. President Dwight D. Eisenhower invited Soviet Premier Nikita Khrushchev in 1959 (B). President Houphouet-Boigny of the Ivory Coast was welcomed by President John F. Kennedy in 1962 (C). President Jimmy Carter invited Prime Minister Menachem Begin of Israel and President Anwar Sadat of Egypt to America to help them to make peace in 1979 (E).

America's Presidents also have made treaties of friendship with other countries. When President Richard Nixon visited the Soviet Union in 1972, the two countries signed a treaty limiting the nuclear weapons they would make (D). President Ronald Reagan visited China in 1984 and signed a treaty in which the United States agreed to help China with nuclear energy (A).

E

214

B

C

F

G

215

4

Looking Ahead with Confidence

On July 20, 1969, an American astronaut named Neil Armstrong became the first person to walk on the moon. Americans were proud of reaching the moon. Reaching this goal gave the American people renewed belief that other American goals also could be reached. One of these goals is equality of freedom and opportunity for all Americans. Another goal is protecting the environment. Still another goal is improving the quality of life.

Equality of Freedom and Opportunity

Equality has been a goal throughout the nation's history. The writers of the Constitution wanted all Americans to have equal justice before the law. That is, the writers wanted to make sure that the nation's laws would treat all people in the same way.

Movement for Civil Rights

Black Americans have tried to gain the *civil* (siv'əl) *rights* that were denied to them. Civil rights are the rights of all citizens to be treated equally under the law.

As you have read, most black people in the United States were slaves until the Civil War. After the Civil War, black codes in many states made it hard for blacks to vote. These codes also segregated, or kept apart, blacks and whites. Finally in 1954, the Supreme Court made a far-reaching decision. It said that segregated schools were unequal and that school segregation had to be ended.

Blacks immediately tried to end segregation in public places, such as buses and restaurants. Different means were used. In Montgomery, Alabama, in 1955 a woman named Rosa Parks refused to give her seat in the bus to a white rider. She was then arrested. Dr. Martin Luther King, Jr., a minister in Montgomery, led a boycott of Mongtomery buses to protest segregation. Black people refused to ride the buses. In 1956 the Supreme Court said that segregation on buses had to end.

Blacks entered restaurants for whites and refused to leave until they were served. These "sit-ins" also often were successful. Restaurant segregation was ended.

Dr. Martin Luther King, Jr., became the leader of the black civil rights movement. He led many marches of blacks and whites protesting segregation. He was put in jail several times for his actions. In 1963 Dr. King led a "March on Washington." More than 200,000 Americans from all over the nation took part. Their aim was to tell Congress that it must pass new laws guaranteeing full civil rights to blacks.

More gains were made in civil rights during the 1960s and 1970s. The fight for rights went on in the 1980s. Laws were

Martin Luther King, Jr., center, hoped to gain *civil rights* for blacks by peaceful actions.

passed that strengthened black voting rights. Laws also gave black Americans equal chances for housing and jobs. Black Americans held many important jobs in the government and throughout the nation.

Women's Liberation Movement

Equality of men and women was another goal of the 1960s, 1970s, and 1980s. American women long had received less pay than men for doing the same jobs. Women had fewer chances than men to get better paying jobs.

In 1966 the National Organization for Women, or NOW, was founded to gain equal opportunity for women. Laws were passed giving women more opportunities. One law said that women must be given equal pay for equal work. Another law said that women must be given equal rights to jobs. However, these laws did not correct all the ways that men and women were treated unequally. Women, therefore, wanted an Equal Rights Amendment added to the Constitution. Many men and women, however, did not believe the new amendment was needed. The Equal Rights Amendment was not approved by the needed number of states by 1982 as a result.

Today there are many more women in important jobs in business, politics, and the military services. In 1981 Sandra Day O'Connor became the first woman Justice of the Supreme Court. Sally Ride became the first American woman astronaut in space in 1983. Nonetheless, women still do not always have the same chances as men. The struggle for equal rights for women goes on.

Toward Equality for All

Other groups besides blacks and women also have worked for equality. American Indians and Hispanic Americans, for example, have long tried to gain their full civil rights. Hispanic Americans include Americans who came to the United States from Puerto Rico, Mexico, Cuba, islands in the Caribbean, and Central and South America. The handicapped and senior citizens are other groups that have worked hard to share equally in our nation's many opportunities.

The equal rights movement has made many gains. The movement will continue until all the people in the United States enjoy full equal rights.

Many Americans enjoyed greater opportunities during the 1970s and 1980s. Among them were women, minority and ethnic groups, the handicapped, and senior citizens.

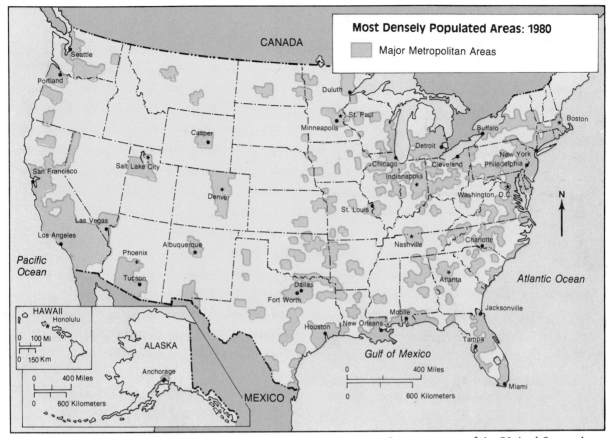

Most Densely Populated Areas: 1980

Major Metropolitan Areas

In many parts of the United States, large cities are near each other. Such places have little room for farms.

Conserving Our Environment

Americans have come to realize that they must conserve, or save, their natural resources. *Conservation* (kon'sər vā'shən) will make it sure that Americans of the future have enough resources to live well.

The government began its conservation efforts more than a hundred years ago. At that time the government started setting aside large areas of land as national parks. The first national park was Yellowstone National Park, in 1872. Since then more than 40 national parks have saved great areas of natural beauty for the use of all Americans.

Today a major goal of the United States is conservation of the environment—our air, land, water, plants, and animals. Over the years factories and automobiles have brought about *pollution* (pə lōō'shən). Pollution is making the environment dirty. Factories and cars have poured smoke and gasses with harmful chemicals into the air. Factories sometimes have poured waste products from manufacturing into waterways.

In 1970 Congress created a new government office, the Environmental Protection Agency. The agency was given the task of trying to get rid of pollution and to protect

219

Students in classrooms throughout the country are using computers to help learn mathematics, English, and other subjects.

the natural resources of the United States. This task cannot be carried out unless all Americans do their part to use resources wisely.

Improving Life for All

Today Americans live longer and are healthier than ever before. One reason that Americans are healthier is that they eat better. Improved health also has been brought about by gains in medicine. New medicines cure illnesses that once would have brought death. New methods of surgery also improve health and make it possible for people to live longer. One new method of surgery uses a beam of light called a laser (lā′zər) beam to correct sight problems.

Many of these gains in medicine were made possible because of advances in *technology* (tek nol′ə jē). Technology is the ability to make and use tools. Inventions such as the telephone, television, and space rockets were advances in technology.

The gains made in technology are still changing many of the ways we live and work. Computers, for example, can store a great deal of information. These machines are used by banks and other businesses to keep records. Computer games can entertain us. Computers also make it possible to solve problems in seconds that once would have taken weeks or months. Moreover, computers offer people more chances to find jobs.

Gains in technology mean longer, healthier lives for all Americans. Better methods and machines also mean that Americans will have more free time in the future. If used well, that free time can be used to create more opportunities and richer lives.

Do You Know?

1. What ended segregation in American schools? Segregation in busing?
2. Name two causes of pollution.
3. What are some of the reasons Americans live longer today than in the past?
4. What is technology? How is it changing the way we live?

To Help You Learn

Using New Words

assembly line	depression
civil rights	dictator
Cold War	holocaust
communism	pollution
concentration camps	stocks
conservation	technology

The phrases below explain the words or terms listed above. Number a paper from 1 through 12. After each number write the word or term that matches each definition.

1. The struggle carried on with words between Communist and Western nations
2. The ability to make and use tools
3. Hard times during which many businesses close and many people lose their jobs
4. A system of making goods in which each worker adds one part to an item as it passes by on a belt
5. Making the environment dirty
6. Shares of ownership in companies
7. Prison camps where large numbers of people are held and often killed
8. Rights of citizens to be treated equally under the law
9. The term given to the terrible destruction of the Jewish people during World War II
10. Saving of natural resources
11. Ruler with total control over a country
12. A system where the government owns all property

Finding the Facts

1. How did the United States government try to control big business during the late 1800s?
2. What were two important inventions that helped American industry to grow in the late 1800s?
3. What problems did cities have in the early 1900s?
4. How did Theodore Roosevelt help the United States to (a) win the war with Spain, and (b) gain control of the Panama Canal?
5. How did alliances of European countries lead to World War I?
6. What was the goal of the League of Nations?
7. When did women gain the vote?
8. How did Henry Ford help to make automobiles that cost less?
9. Who was Charles A. Lindbergh?
10. How was life hard for Americans during the Great Depression?
11. What was the New Deal?
12. How did World War II begin?
13. Why did the United States decide to use the atomic bomb on Japan?
14. How is the government of the Soviet Union different from the United States government?
15. What is one reason for the unrest in the Middle East?

Immigrants to the United States 1890-1939

Each figure stands for 500,000 people

1890-1899	🚶🚶🚶🚶🚶🚶🚶
1900-1909	🚶🚶🚶🚶🚶🚶🚶🚶🚶🚶🚶🚶🚶
1910-1919	🚶🚶🚶🚶🚶🚶🚶🚶🚶🚶🚶🚶
1920-1929	🚶🚶🚶🚶🚶🚶🚶🚶
1930-1939	🚶🚶

16. Name two methods that people have used to gain more civil rights for blacks.

17. Why did some people favor the Equal Rights Amendment? Why were others against it?

18. What is the job of the Environmental Protection Agency?

Learning from Maps

1. Turn to the population map on page 219. What color is used to show the most densely populated areas in the United States? Which cities along the West Coast are in densely populated areas? Are any parts of your state in the most densely populated areas? If so, where? If not, where is the nearest densely populated area?

   "Boswash" is a name given to the crowded area between Boston and Washington, D.C. Use the map of the United States on page A-5 to identify the major cities within "Boswash." Make a list of them.

2. Use a world map or a globe to answer these questions. What four large islands make up Japan? On which island is each of the following cities: Hiroshima and Nagasaki? On what continent are North Korea, South Korea, and Vietnam? What countries are next to Israel?

3. Compare the maps on pages 201 and 209. Which countries shown on the map of World War I were no longer there at the time of World War II? Which new countries were formed between World War I and World War II?

Using Study Skills

1. **Graph:** Look closely at the picture graph on this page. It shows the number of immigrants who came to the United States during 1890 to 1939. How many people does each figure on the graph stand for? During which period did the most immigrants come? About how many immigrants came from 1910 to 1919? About how many immigrants came between 1920 and 1929? Can you think of a reason why the number of immigrants to the United States was so low between 1930 and 1939?

2. **Chart:** Look at the list of Presidents of the United States on page 576. Who was President during these times: end of World

War I, bombing of Pearl Harbor, start of the Korean War, the passage of the Civil Rights Act of 1964?

3. **Time Line:** The following events are not listed in the order in which they happened. Copy the statements in the right order. Look through Unit 7 again to find the dates you need.

> Panama Canal is opened
> President Nixon visits China
> World War II ends
> Franklin D. Roosevelt is elected President
> Peace Corps is started

Thinking It Through

1. Why is conservation important to the country? What can you do to help conserve natural resources?

2. During the 1970s many immigrants arrived from Vietnam. In 1980 many immigrants arrived from Cuba. Many of these immigrants were placed in camps until Americans were found who would sponsor, or be responsible for, them for a few years. Imagine that you sponsored an immigrant. How might you help that person to get settled in the United States?

Projects

1. The Research Committee might find out what each person below invented or discovered. Use books from your school library.

Isaac Singer	Wernher Von Braun
Garrett Morgan	George Eastman
Lewis Latimer	Anna Baldwin
Barbara McClintock	Vladimir Zworykin
Jan Matzeliger	Charles Drew

2. Work in two groups. One group can find out more about World War I. The other can find out more about World War II. Each group might find out about leaders, important battles, and organizations formed to deal with wartime problems. Each group might also make a map showing major battles of the war.

3. Many people have helped groups to gain civil rights. The Reading Committee might like to find a book or story about the following people:

William E.B. Du Bois	Gloria Steinem
Max Cleland	Vine Deloria
César Chávez	Maggie Kuehn

4. List five ways in which computers touch your life. Decide whether each of the ways the computer is used makes your life better or worse. Be prepared to discuss your reasons with the class.

5. Study the pictures on pages 217 and 218. They show something about life in present-day America. Think of three words or phrases that describe life as it is shown in the pictures.

    Now turn to the pictures on pages 76 and 77. How was life different at that time? Are there any ways in which life then was the same as it is today?

8 The Northeastern States

Unit Preview

The Northeast has two regions. In the New England section, there are Maine, New Hampshire, Vermont, Massachusetts, Connecticut, and Rhode Island. In the Middle Atlantic states, there are New York, Pennsylvania, New Jersey, and Delaware.

The settlers in the northeastern states were skilled at making things, and there were rivers to provide power for mills, and later, factories. The rivers also helped to develop trade among settlements, and later, among cities. American manufacturing began in the Northeast, and it has remained an important manufacturing region.

Improved methods of transportation developed in the Northeast. The Erie Canal was built to connect New York City and the Great Lakes region. Steam power was used to run boats and trains. Railroads linked cities of the Atlantic Coastal Plain with midwestern cities like Chicago.

New York City, the largest city in the United States, is in this region. Other large cities are located in the Northeast. These cities grew as industries developed. Immigrants came from many countries to live and work in the cities.

Fishing, lumbering, quarrying, and farming are occupations of the northeastern states today. But their manufacturing and mining make the northeastern states a great industrial and commerical region of the United States.

Things to Discover

If you look carefully at the picture, map, and time line, you can answer these questions.

1. How many states are in the Northeast?
2. What ocean borders the states of the Northeast?
3. The picture shows Pittsburgh, a large northeastern city in Pennsylvania. What natural feature might explain why the city grew up there?
4. When did the Erie Canal open? How many years later did the St. Lawrence Seaway open?
5. When was the first oil well drilled in the United States?
6. What country borders some of the northeastern states?

Words to Learn

You will meet these words in this unit. As you read, you will learn what they mean and how to pronounce them. The Word List will help you.

anthracite	quarry
bituminous	shaft mining
coke	slag
electronics	smelt
export	spinning jenny
import	strip mining
lignite	suffrage
locomotive	textile
merchant marine	tourist

Samuel Slater's
spinning mill built

Erie Canal opens

First American steam
locomotive built

First oil well drilled
in United States

National Woman Suffrage
Association founded

Philadelphia begins
urban renewal

St. Lawrence Seaway opens

Winter Olympics held
in Lake Placid

1793   1825 1830   1859 1869   1945 1959   1980

CANADA

Atlantic
Ocean

Pacific
Ocean

MEXICO

Gulf of
Mexico

N

1

Geography of the Northeastern States

The Northeast has two regions. The first to be settled was New England. This name is a reminder that its earliest settlers came from England. The New England States are Maine, New Hampshire, Vermont, Massachusetts, Connecticut, and Rhode Island.

The other region, the Middle Atlantic, gets its name from its location. Look at the eastern coastline of the United States on the map on page A-7. You can see that the Middle Atlantic states are about midway between the north and south ends of the Atlantic coast. These states are New York, New Jersey, Pennsylvania, and Delaware.

Both regions have irregular coastlines, a broad coastal plain, mountains, valleys, and flat lowlands. The Northeast has a rich source of water power in its hundreds of lakes, streams, and rivers.

Land Surface

The surface of the Northeast is not level. The soil is thin and covered with rocks. A great glacier, or sheet of ice, caused this. Thousands of years ago this glacier covered the northern part of North America. For years it was very cold there, and the land lay under the great sheet of ice. Slowly, very slowly, the glacier moved southward. As it moved, it wore down the tops of mountains, carrying rocks and soil with it.

The weather grew warmer. The ice and snow began to melt. Water filled the hollow places scooped out by the glacier. It formed rivers and lakes. Millions of large rocks were left where they were dropped by the melting ice.

The Piedmont

The map of the Northeast on page 227 shows the land surfaces or natural regions. A map which shows the natural regions is called a physical map. A physical map uses different colors to represent the different natural regions. The key, or guide, is in the upper lefthand corner. What color represents plains, or lowlands? The lowland along the Atlantic coast is called the Atlantic Coastal Plain. Where are there more lowlands? West of the Atlantic Coastal Plain are hills and mountains called the Appalachian Highland. What color is used to show the highland? What color means high mountains? Where are high mountains found on the map of the Northeast?

West of the Atlantic Coastal Plain is the Piedmont region. A piedmont, as you remember, is an upland region between a plain and mountains. The Piedmont in North America lies between the Atlantic Coastal Plain and the Appalachian Highland. It extends from the Hudson River south to central Alabama.

The Appalachian Highland

West and north of the Piedmont the land rises to form the Appalachian Highland. It is made up of many mountain ranges with gentle slopes and rounded peaks. Forests cover most of the

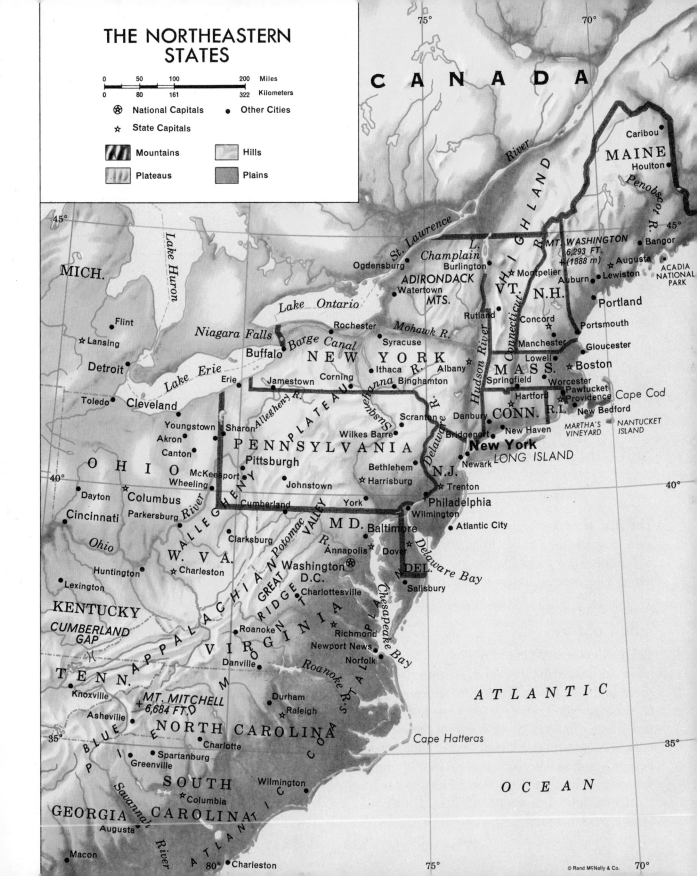

THE NORTHEASTERN STATES

| | 50 | 100 | | 200 Miles |
| 0 | 80 | 161 | | 322 Kilometers |

⊗ National Capitals   • Other Cities

☆ State Capitals

▨ Mountains   ▨ Hills

▨ Plateaus   ▨ Plains

CANADA

MICH.

MAINE

Caribou

Houlton

Penobscot R.

Bangor

St. Lawrence River

L. Champlain

Ogdensburg

Burlington

MT. WASHINGTON
6,293 FT.
+(1888 m)

Augusta

ACADIA
NATIONAL
PARK

ADIRONDACK
MTS.

Watertown

Montpelier

VT.

N.H.

Auburn

Lewiston

Lake Huron

Flint

☆ Lansing

Lake Ontario

Rochester

Niagara Falls

Barge Canal

Syracuse

Mohawk R.

Rutland

Concord

Portland

Portsmouth

Detroit

Buffalo

NEW YORK

Ithaca

Albany

Manchester

Gloucester

Lowell

☆ Boston

Erie

Lake Erie

Jamestown

Corning

Binghamton

Springfield

Worcester

MASS.

Pawtucket

Toledo

Cleveland

PLATEAU

Allegheny R.

Susquehanna R.

Scranton

Hartford

Providence

Cape Cod

Hudson River

Connecticut R.

CONN.

R.I.

New Bedford

Youngstown

Sharon

Wilkes Barre

Danbury

New Haven

MARTHA'S
VINEYARD

NANTUCKET
ISLAND

Akron

PENNSYLVANIA

Bridgeport

Canton

Pittsburgh

Delaware R.

New York

OHIO

McKeesport

Bethlehem

Newark

LONG ISLAND

Dayton

Columbus

Wheeling

ALLEGHENY

Johnstown

Harrisburg

N.J.

Trenton

Cincinnati

Parkersburg

River

Cumberland

York

Philadelphia

Clarksburg

VALLEY

M D.

Wilmington

Atlantic City

Ohio

W. VA.

Potomac R.

Baltimore

APPALACHIAN

Annapolis

Dover

Delaware Bay

Huntington

☆ Charleston

GREAT

Washington
D.C. ⊗

DEL.

Lexington

RIDGE

Charlottesville

Salisbury

KENTUCKY

VIRGINIA

Richmond

Chesapeake Bay

CUMBERLAND
GAP

Roanoke

Newport News

ATLANTIC

TENN.

Danville

Norfolk

Knoxville

MT. MITCHELL
6,684 FT.

Roanoke R.

OCEAN

Asheville

Durham

BLUE

NORTH CAROLINA

Raleigh

Charlotte

Cape Hatteras

RIDGE

Spartanburg

COASTAL

Greenville

Wilmington

SOUTH

☆ Columbia

GEORGIA

CAROLINA

Savannah River

ATLANTIC

Augusta

Macon

Charleston

© Rand McNally & Co.

Appalachians. The highest New England peak, Mount Washington, is in New Hampshire. It is more than 6,000 feet (1,800 m) above sea level. Mount Washington is snow-covered during the winter.

Good farmland is found in the wide valleys of the Appalachian Highland. The largest, most fertile area is the Great Valley. This valley extends south from eastern Pennsylvania.

2
Settling the Northeastern States

The first settlers came to the northeastern region of the United States from many countries of Europe. They wanted a chance to earn a good living. They wanted to live in freedom.

The Colonies

The earliest settlements in the Northeast were made in Massachusetts. The Pilgrims landed there in 1620. Neighboring Rhode Island and Connecticut were settled a few years later. Before they established governments of their own, New Hampshire and Maine were under the rule of Massachusetts for many years. Vermont was claimed by both New Hampshire and New York until it became a state in 1791. Maine became a state in 1820.

New York was originally a Dutch colony. Later it was divided into three colonies—New York, New Jersey, and Delaware. People from Sweden were the first to settle in Delaware. Pennsylvania was settled by William Penn, an English Quaker.

After the Revolutionary War, the colonies developed a new plan of government. They became the states we are studying now.

Transportation

The rivers and lakes of the Northeast helped the region become a manufacturing center. Manufacturing means making goods by machines. Water power ran the early factories. The lakes and rivers provided excellent transportation.

By the early 1800s, the lands around the Great Lakes were being settled. The new settlers there needed the goods that were manufactured in New York. They wanted to trade their farm products for the things they needed.

But in those days it took a long time to move products from one place to another. And it was very expensive. What was needed was a cheap means of transportation.

Water has always been the cheapest means of transportation. The region had plenty of waterways. How could the settlers living around the Great Lakes make the best use of them? How could they get their farm products and raw materials to New York City in the cheapest and easiest way?

New York City is located at the mouth of the Hudson River. People who settled to the north took their products down the Mohawk and Hudson rivers to New York City. Steamboats were a popular means of river travel after Robert Fulton proved that steam power could run boats. Fulton tested his steamboat, the *Clermont,* on the Hudson River.

The Erie Canal

"A canal between the Hudson River and Lake Erie would give us a waterway connecting the Great Lakes with the Atlantic Ocean." So spoke Governor Clinton of New York in 1817.

In 1825 the first boat moved along the Erie Canal and down the Hudson. The Erie Canal provided an easy, cheap means of transportation between the Great Lakes region and New York City. Find the Erie Canal on the map of early transportation routes on page 309.

A *locomotive* steams swiftly along the New Portage Railroad near Cresson, Pennsylvania. Train connections between faraway areas made the world seem smaller.

The Early Railroad

Sending goods by water is slow. Soon people wanted faster means of transportation. Hard roads had been built to connect the cities of the Atlantic coast with the lands west of the Appalachians. Carriages and wagons carried passengers and freight along these roads. But vehicles drawn by horses are also slow.

Then English inventors built a railroad steam engine which could move on its own power. It was called a *locomotive* (lō'kə mō'tiv). In 1829 a locomotive was brought from England to the United States. Peter Cooper, an American, improved it. The following year he built *Tom Thumb,* a small steam locomotive which could pull a train of coaches.

Soon railroads were built connecting the cities of upper New York State with New York City. Boston, Philadelphia, and other eastern cities also built railroads. By 1861 most cities of the Atlantic Coastal Plain were connected with Chicago and other cities west of the Appalachians. In 1869 the Atlantic and Pacific coasts were joined together with iron rails. Today railroads connect all parts of the country.

Other Waterways

Trains are fast, but water transportation is cheaper. Manufacturers of heavy machinery wanted the cheaper water transportation. So New York State built an improved waterway called the New York State Barge Canal. The canal extends 800 miles (1,280 km) from Lake Champlain and the Hudson River to Lakes Erie and Ontario. This system of canals, rivers, and lakes includes the Erie Canal. Heavy goods are sent on flatbottomed boats called barges.

Until recent years large ocean-going ships could sail up the St. Lawrence River only as far as Montreal. West of Montreal canals had been built to carry smaller ships around the rapids in the river. A large modern ship could not use the canals.

A ship traveling from Erie, Pennsylvania, to Montreal, Quebec, on the St. Lawrence Seaway passes under eight bridges. How many locks does it go through? Where is the water level highest? Where is it lowest?

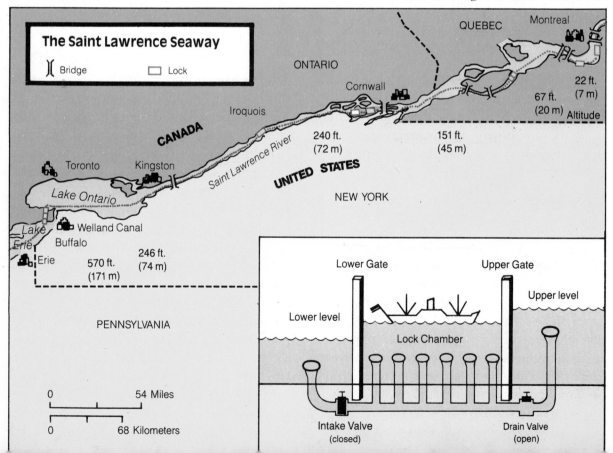

The Saint Lawrence Seaway

)(Bridge   ☐ Lock

QUEBEC   Montreal

ONTARIO

Cornwall

Iroquois

22 ft. (7 m)

67 ft. (20 m)   Altitude

CANADA

Saint Lawrence River

240 ft. (72 m)

151 ft. (45 m)

Toronto   Kingston

UNITED STATES

NEW YORK

Lake Ontario

Lake Erie   Welland Canal

Buffalo

Erie

570 ft. (171 m)

246 ft. (74 m)

PENNSYLVANIA

0   54 Miles

0   68 Kilometers

Lower Gate   Upper Gate

Upper level

Lower level

Lock Chamber

Intake Valve (closed)   Drain Valve (open)

Life was often difficult for immigrants who came to the United States at the turn of the century. Many lived in apartments and earned money at low-paying jobs. This family is making artificial flowers.

Canada and the United States decided to work together and widen these canals and deepen the river channel. The St. Lawrence Seaway was opened in 1959. Now ocean ships can reach Buffalo and cities farther west on the Great Lakes.

Growth of Industry

Industry refers to manufacturing as well as other businesses. It also means the making of, or working with, certain kinds of products. Examples are the automobile industry, the coal industry, and the *tourist* (toor'ist) industry. A tourist is a person who travels for pleasure. Still another meaning of industry is any kind of work which provides us with what we want or need. Mining, building, farming, and transportation are all industries. Later in this unit, you will read about the chief industries of the Northeast.

The Northeast became a region of rapidly growing industries for two reasons. The first reason was that improvements in transportation lowered the cost of sending goods. The lower cost made it possible for industries to produce more goods. The second reason for the growth of industry was that a large number of workers lived in the northeastern states. Industries need many people to work in factories and provide services. More workers meant an increase in the production of goods.

During the 1830s more and more iron was needed for farming tools and railroad tracks. By the middle 1800s the iron industry, especially in Pennsylvania, had grown very large. The United States began trading its iron products with other countries of the world. By the late 1800s our country had become one of the largest industrial countries in the world.

Growth of Cities

As industries in the northeastern states grew, more people were needed to work in factories. So the population of the cities grew. Improved farm machines meant that fewer farmers were needed to supply the same amount of food. So many farmers moved to cities to become factory workers.

A large number of immigrants arrived in our country from Europe in the nineteenth and twentieth centuries. These people came in ships that often landed in New York City first. Many stayed there while others settled in Boston, Philadelphia, and Pittsburgh. The immigrants often crowded into run-down parts of cities. They could not afford better housing.

During the 1900s a large number of blacks also moved to the northeastern states and other northern states. At that time these states had more industries than southern states had. The blacks wanted to find jobs in industries of the Northeast. So they too settled in cities.

Women's Rights

As you remember, during the first half of the 1800s people began to work together for equal rights for women. They demanded that women be given the same opportunity for an education as men. They resolved to organize and work for women's *suffrage* (suf′rij), or right to vote.

A large meeting was held in Worcester, Massachusetts, in 1850. It was organized by Lucy Stone and Paulina Wright Davis. Men as well as women attended. They came from nine states. It was the first national meeting held to discuss equal rights for women.

Susan B. Anthony, Leader for Women's Rights

Susan B. Anthony was born in Adams, Massachusetts, in 1820. She became a teacher. She was interested in working for change in our country. Anthony felt strongly that women must be given rights equal to those of men.

Anthony began to make speeches across the country. She published a weekly paper on women's rights. In 1869 Susan Anthony and Elizabeth Cady Stanton founded the National Woman Suffrage Association. The Association was against the Fifteenth Amendment of the Constitution. This amendment gave black men the right to vote. But it did not give black or white women this right. The National Woman Suffrage Association believed that all women should have the right to vote, just as men had.

Susan B. Anthony wrote and spoke convincingly for women's *suffrage*. Though she did not live to see the results of her work, her efforts were successful.

In 1872 Anthony voted in New York. It was her way of testing the Fifteenth Amendment. She was arrested, tried, and fined for breaking the law. But Anthony refused to pay the fine because she felt that the law was wrong. She was not put into jail.

All her life Susan B. Anthony worked for the right of women to vote. She died in 1906. Fourteen years later, the Nineteenth Amendment was added to the Constitution. This law gave women the right to vote. In 1979 the United States government issued the Susan B. Anthony coin in her honor.

Do You Know?

1. What advantage does water transportation have over trains? What advantage do trains have over water transportation?
2. What three groups of people moved to cities in the Northeast to work in factories?
3. What right was given to women by the Nineteenth Amendment?

Before You Go On

Using New Words

locomotive   suffrage
tourist

The phrases below explain the words listed
above. Number a paper from 1 through 3.
After each number write the word that
matches the definition.
1. The right to vote
2. A person who travels for pleasure
3. An engine which can move on its own
   power

Finding the Facts

1. How did the glacier that moved over
   North America long ago change the surface of the northeastern states?
2. What is a piedmont?
3. Where is the highest mountain peak in
   New England?
4. In which present-day northeastern state
   were the earliest settlements made?
5. Who started the colony of New York?
6. When did the Erie Canal open? What did
   it provide?
7. What American built a small steam
   locomotive which could pull a train of
   coaches?
8. Why did New York State build the New
   York State Barge Canal?
9. What two countries worked together on
   the St. Lawrence Seaway?
10. Name two reasons why industries grew in
    the northeastern states.
11. What caused cities in the northeastern
    states to grow?
12. Where was the first national meeting on
    equal rights for women held? Who
    organized the meeting?
13. What did Susan B. Anthony work for
    most of her life?

3
Living and Working in New England

Maine, New Hampshire, Vermont, Massachusetts, Rhode Island, and Connecticut make up the New England states. The population map of the United States on page 518 shows that many people live in Massachusetts, Connecticut, and Rhode Island.

Manufacturing

Manufacturing is the leading industry of New England. Thousands of people make a living by working in mills and factories. The chief products are made from cloth, metal, leather, and lumber. New England is also a leader in the manufacturing of electronic equipment.

Textiles

Weaving cloth is called *textile* (teks'tīl) manufacturing, or the textile industry. This was an early industry in New England. At first spinning was done by hand. Only one thread was spun at a time. By 1793 Samuel Slater had a *spinning jenny* (jen'ē) set up in a mill on a river near Pawtucket (pô tuk'it), Rhode Island. A spinning jenny could spin many threads at a time. Machine-made thread could be sold more cheaply.

Then power looms, or weaving machines, were invented. The first power loom in our country was built in Waltham (wôl'tham), Massachusetts, in 1814. Thread could then be spun and cloth woven by power machines in textile mills or factories.

The first spinning and weaving machines were run by water power. Mills were built at waterfalls and rapids. Then steam replaced water power. Coal from Pennsylvania began to be used in furnaces to make steam. Now most textile machines are run by electricity.

Textile mills need raw materials such as linen, silk, cotton, and wool. The early settlers of New England raised sheep for wool. Today New England mills need more wool than their farms can supply. They get wool from our Rocky Mountain states and other lands.

For years, New England had more textile factories than any other part of the United States.

At *textile* mills giant mechanical looms weave cloth from thread at very high speeds. Mill workers keep the machines supplied with spools of thread.

But during the 1800s manufacturers began building textile factories in the South to be closer to the cotton region. The factories provided jobs, and the number of workers increased. By the 1940s the South had more textile mills than New England. But the textile industry is still important in the New England states today.

Metal Products

Many New England settlers were skilled metal workers. They made small articles such as jewelry and watches. Today articles of iron, copper, brass, gold, and silver are made in Connecticut cities. More production of metal articles has helped to make up for lost business in textiles. It has also created jobs for more workers.

Typewriters, brushes, and machinery for mills and factories are made in New England. Some cities also make articles of sterling silver. Sterling is the name for fine, almost pure, silver.

Leather Products

Colonial shoemakers cut, shaped, and sewed every pair of shoes they sold. The hides and skins they used came from the animals raised nearby. The leather they used was made in small factories called tanneries. There the hides were treated, or tanned, with the juices of wood and the bark of certain trees to soften them. Later they were dyed.

Today large factories take the place of shoemakers and village factories. Hides and skins reach New England by truck and railroad from our West. Ships bring more from South America. Goods brought in, or imported, from other

These leather pieces have been tanned and dyed. They may be cut and sewn to make jackets, coats, shoes, or boots.

countries are called *imports* (im'pôrts).

Leather articles are still manufactured in parts of New England. Massachusetts ranks second and Maine sixth in the nation in leather manufacturing. Shoes are the leading leather product. Some of the region's leather products are sent to other countries. Goods sent out of a country are called *exports* (eks'pôrts).

Forest Products

New England has large forests in certain areas. Spruce, pine, hemlock, birch, ash, and maple are some of the trees in these forests. Spruce logs make good paper. Lumber, made from other kinds of trees, is used to make ships, toys, and other articles. New England's forests furnish lumber for everything from ships to toothpicks to paper products.

In colonial times Bangor, Maine, was a great lumber market. Maine is still famous for its lumber, ranking sixth in the nation. Today Maine has many very large paper mills.

Much of New England's paper is used in books, magazines, and newspapers. Towels, napkins, and wrapping paper are also made.

Do you like maple syrup and maple sugar? These products are made from the sap, or juice, of the sugar maple tree. The Indians taught the settlers how to bore small holes into the trunks of the trees and to put spouts into the holes. Then they hung buckets under the spouts to catch the sweet, flowing sap. The sap is boiled to make maple syrup. With longer boiling it becomes maple sugar. Vermont is still famous for fine maple sugar and syrup.

Electronics

New England has many factories that produce electronic products. *Electronics* (i lek tron'iks) is a branch of the science of electricity. It has made possible such inventions as television, radio, sound motion pictures, tape recorders, and small calculators. It has also made possible radar, X-ray machines, and computers. When you make a long-distance telephone call, electronic

An *electronics* worker assembles the wires for a device that will guide airplanes by remote control. Working with electronic circuits is detailed and complicated.

devices amplify, or strengthen, your voice. When a door opens as you walk toward it, photoelectric cells are at work. All such modern wonders are based on electronics.

Stone Quarrying

Granite, marble, and slate are used for buildings. These valuable kinds of building stone are found in New England. Many people make a living by cutting these stones. The open pit where stone is cut is called a *quarry* (kwôr'ē).

Stone used for building is found in huge solid layers. Great pieces must be loosened by blasting with dynamite. Special saws run by machinery can then cut them into blocks. The blocks are too large and heavy to be hauled far. So quarries must be near rivers or railroads.

Vermont is among our country's leaders in quarrying granite, marble, and slate. The largest granite quarries in the United States are near Barre, Vermont. Granite is a good, hard material for building monuments and public buildings. Marble comes in a variety of colors. Slate is used for floors, shingles, and roofs. Other important minerals dug from quarries in New England are clay, sand, and gravel.

Farming

New Englanders can raise only a small part of the food they need. Most of the farms are small because the land is hilly and the soil is rocky.

In the early days farmers tried to raise grains, vegetables, fruit, livestock, and poultry. They tried to supply people with all kinds of foods. That is, they engaged in mixed farming. More and more people went to work in factories. Farmers had to feed many more people. So each began raising just a few crops to sell in city markets. Such farmers did what is called specialized farming.

Farmers began to do specialized farming for two reasons. The first reason was that they realized some crops grew better than others. Farmers could raise more of these than of other crops. The other reason was that city people would buy more of certain foods than of others.

Farms near large cities, called truck farms, raise vegetables and fruits for city markets. These farms are small. Produce is grown out of doors in summer and in greenhouses in winter. In winter tomatoes, lettuce, celery, and strawberries are grown in these greenhouses.

Dairy farming is an important business. It provides milk, cream, butter, and cheese. Vermont is the leading dairy state in New England. The hillsides of New England have pastures for dairy cattle. Hay and corn are grown on the less hilly parts. Much of the corn is cut while it is still green and stored in tall buildings, called silos. Corn from the silos and hay are used to feed the cattle all winter.

Poultry farms specialize in raising chickens, eggs, ducks, and turkeys. The hundreds of poultry farms in Connecticut, Vermont, Rhode Island, and Massachusetts send their products to cities in New England and New York.

Fruit orchards dot the hilly New England landscape. Fruit trees will grow on hilly land where farm machinery cannot be used. Apple trees are not easily killed by frost. Apples are the most important fruit crop in New England where frost comes early.

Potatoes grow well in sandy soil and cool, moist summers. The soil and climate of Aroostook (ə roos′ took) County, in northern Maine, are just right for them. On their large potato farms Maine farmers use machinery to plant and harvest crops.

Tobacco, too, needs good soil and special care. In New England, only the Connecticut River Valley is suited to its growth. A leaf tobacco good for cigar wrappers is grown there.

Cranberries will grow only in wet lands. Maine, Cape Cod, and the nearby islands of Nantucket and Martha's Vineyard are famous for cranberries.

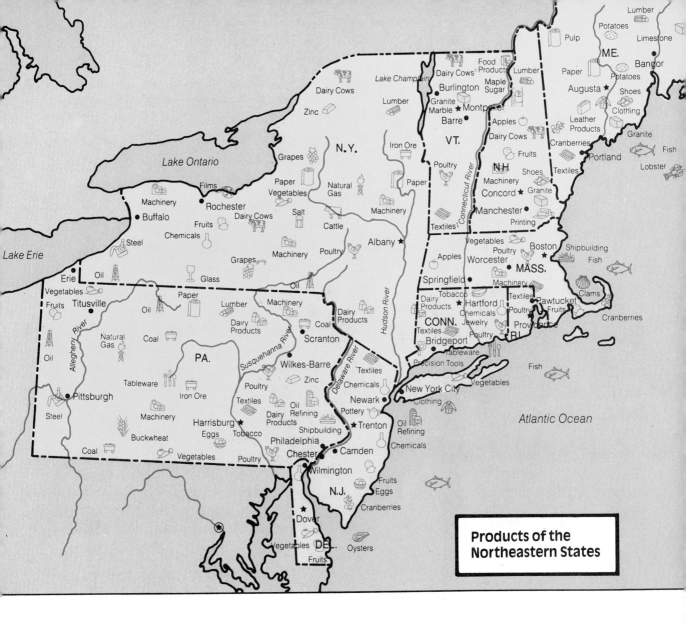

Products of the Northeastern States

Fishing

Even before the settlers arrived, people came to New England to fish. The shallow waters off the coast of New England are fine places to fish. Billions of small fish come to these waters to feed on sea plants. Larger fish, like cod, halibut, and haddock, come to eat the smaller fish. The large fish are caught and sold in many city markets. While most fish is sold fresh, some fish is frozen and shipped to other places.

Some of the fishing areas are far from the coast. Fishing there is called deep-sea fishing. Fishing fleets leave coastal cities to do deep-sea fishing early in spring. There are boats with both sails and motors in the fleet. Each ship carries several small rowboats, called dories. Every morning fishers leave the ship in dories. At sunset they return to the ship. The day's work is done when the fish is packed in ice or stored in ice-cold, or refrigerated, rooms. When these

239

Fishers from New England may spend weeks at a time on deep-sea fishing boats like this one. Why do you think sea gulls follow the boats?

rooms are filled, the fishing fleet returns to its port.

Many countries have laws to protect their fishing waters. The United States has laws stating that no other country can fish within 200 nautical miles (370 km) of our shore without permission.

Inshore fishing means fishing within 2 or 3 miles (3 or 5 km) of the coast. Inshore fishers go out in their small motorboats. They bring in the catch each night.

In the quiet waters of New England's bays and inlets several kinds of shellfish, or animals that live in shells, are found. Clams, oysters, crabs, and lobsters are shellfish. Massachusetts furnishes many clams. Maine is famous for its lobsters.

Lobsters are caught in traps, called lobster pots. The pots are made so that lobsters can swim into them, but they cannot get out. Fishers usually bait the pots with fish. Because so many are being caught along our eastern coast, lobsters are now raised to replace those caught. The eggs are gathered and kept in quiet, inland ponds until they hatch. The baby lobsters are then put into bays and into the mouths of rivers. They grow there until they are large enough to catch.

Two other products of inshore fishing are scallops and clams. Scallops swim by moving their shells. They grow in beds off the southern shore of New England. Scallops are scooped up with dredges or gathered with rakes. Clams live in the sands along the seashore. Today clams, too, are growing scarce. According to a Massachusetts law, clams can now be dug only at certain times.

Recreation

Would you like to spend a vacation in New England? Many people do. The beaches along the coast are fine places to go. New England has beautiful mountains, forests, lakes, and rivers. Hunters and skiers visit these spots in the winter. People like to go there in summer to camp and fish.

The states and our national government have set aside large parks, forests, and seashores for the people's recreation. New England has many such recreation areas. White Mountain National Forest, in New Hampshire, and Green Mountain National Forest, in Vermont, are two of these. Acadia (ə kā′dē ə) National Park, situated along the coast of Maine, has many summer visitors. Cape Cod, Massachusetts, was named a National Seashore in 1961.

People interested in the history of our coun-

A wooden lobster pot usually is baited with fish. One end of the pot has a net shaped into a funnel. The lobster can go through the funnel to reach the fish but cannot find the opening again to escape.

try visit New England, where many events in our early history took place. Some landmarks still remain. Furniture, tools, and costumes of early days may be seen in museums.

Major Cities

New England is an industrial area, and manufacturing is a major activity of its cities. The seaports of this region are centers for shipbuilding, fishing, and transporting goods. Lumber mills, quarries, and textiles are still important industries, as they were in colonial times.

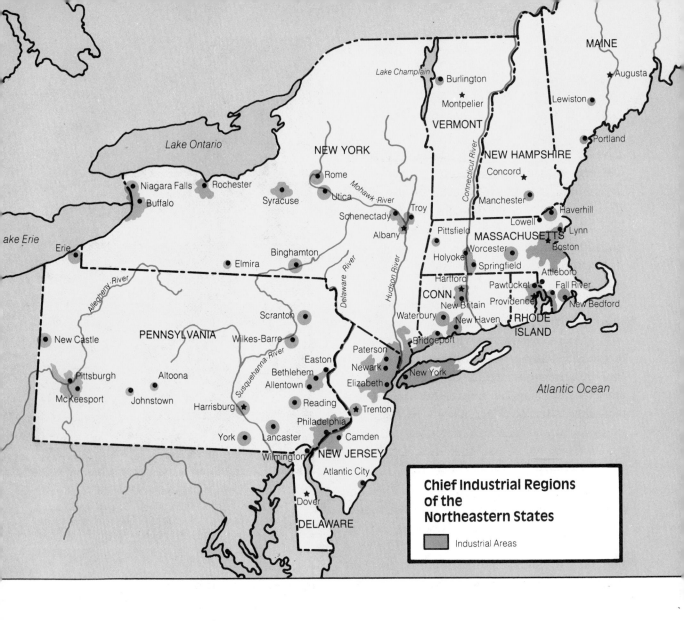

Chief Industrial Regions of the Northeastern States

Industrial Areas

Boston is the largest city in New England and the capital of Massachusetts. As the largest industrial center in New England, Boston has many factories. Making machinery, medical instruments, and processed foods are important industries. Printing, publishing, banking, and insurance firms are also there. Boston is second among the world's busiest wool markets. It is a major fish market. The Port of Boston is the busiest in New England.

Providence (prov′ə dəns) is the capital and largest city of Rhode Island. It is a major manufacturing center and seaport in New England. Providence is one of the world's most important centers for the making of costume, or inexpensive, jewelry. Machinery, metals, silverware,

Factories, office buildings, and homes all line the waterfront of Boston. Many people enjoy sailing boats on the Charles River.

and textiles are also made in Providence.

Hartford is the capital of Connecticut. So many insurance firms are located in Hartford that it is often called "Insurance City." Factories of Hartford make aircraft equipment, machinery, metal products, and chemicals. Bridgeport is the largest city in Connecticut. Machine tools, brass products, and electrical equipment are made there. It has a port on the Pequonnock (pi kwon′ək) River.

The capital of Maine is Augusta. It has shoe factories as well as cotton, paper, and lumber mills. Printing and poultry-processing are carried on there. Processing means preparation. In Augusta, poultry is prepared for sale.

Portland is Maine's largest city. Its factories make printed material, clothing, metal products, electronic parts, and processed foods. Portland's harbor is the closest in the United States to Europe. It is the second busiest oil-shipping center on the Atlantic. It is a fishing fleet base, and a center for shipping seafood and potatoes.

Concord, the capital of New Hampshire, has granite quarries and printing plants. Its factories make electronics, leather, and wood products. The largest city in New Hampshire is Manchester (man′ches′tər). It is the state's chief manufacturing center. Boots, shoes, and cotton and woolen goods are made there.

Vermont's capital is Montpelier (mont pēl′yər). It has insurance firms, granite industries, and printing plants. Plastics and machinery are made there. The largest city in Vermont is Burlington. Its factories make cereal and aircraft equipment.

Do You Know?

1. What is mixed farming?
2. What products come from New England's forests?
3. What is meant by the textile industry?
4. How are hides tanned or made into leather?
5. Name three products of the electronics industry.

243

4
Living and Working in the Middle Atlantic States

New York, New Jersey, Pennsylvania, and Delaware make up the Middle Atlantic states. The Middle Atlantic area has good harbors and important trade centers.

Do you know how many people live in the United States? About one-sixth of them live in the Middle Atlantic states. The many large cities tell us that the Middle Atlantic states are one of our most important manufacturing regions. Find this section on the population map of the United States, page 219, and the map of industrial regions of the Northeast on page 242. Comparing these maps shows that a large population and industry go together.

Mining

What a treasure chest of natural resources the Appalachian Highland is! See the map of land use and resources on page 14. Iron ore, coal, copper, and some natural gas are found there. Early settlers discovered iron ore. They used charcoal as fuel to *smelt* (smelt) the iron ore. Smelting means separating the iron metal from its ore by heating.

Later, coal was found close to the iron ore. Coal then took the place of charcoal in smelting iron. The United States leads the world in coal production.

The Story of Coal

In the early days of Pennsylvania, so the story goes, two people were hunting near where Wilkes-Barre and Scranton now are. Night came, and they built a small fire between two black stones.

"This will scare wild animals away and keep us warm," they said. "The stones will keep the fire from spreading."

In the night the hunters began to feel very warm. "How strange!" they said. "Our fire should be out by this time."

Instead of a small fire they saw a large blaze! Puzzled, they went closer. "The black stones are burning," the hunters said. "They must be coal." The hunters were right. They had discovered a large field of *anthracite* (an'thrə sīt'), or hard coal.

Two other important kinds of coal are *bituminous* (bī too'mə nəs), or soft, coal, and *lignite* (lig'nīt), or brown coal. The map on page 245 shows where these two kinds of coal are found in our country. Do we have more bituminous coal or more lignite coal? In what states is lignite found?

Methods of Mining

Two methods are generally used to mine coal. One method is *strip* (strip) *mining*. This method is used when the coal beds lie close to the earth's surface. Giant power shovels or other earth-moving equipment remove the layer of earth covering the coal. The coal is broken up, usually by explosives, and loaded into trucks.

Some coal lies in the ground in layers separated by rock. A deep shaft has to be cut through the rock to reach the coal. Elevators

built in the shafts lower miners and machinery to tunnels, which lead to the coal. These tunnels are lighted with electricity. Small electric trains run on tracks in these tunnels. They carry workers, tools, and coal to and from the elevators. This kind of mining is called *shaft* (shaft) *mining*.

Most of the work in mines today is done by machinery. Miners use large machines run by electricity to cut the coal into squares. Holes are made with electric drills, and dynamite is put into them. The dynamite blasts the coal out in lumps. Usually machines load the lumps into cars, and the electric train hauls them to the shaft. In the early years of mining, this hard work was all done by people and mules. Some mines are still old-fashioned and dangerous.

Strip mining has been used to mine coal here. This way of mining is a good way to get coal, but it causes problems. Notice how bare and empty the earth looks. With no plants growing in it the soil easily can be blown or washed away. The places where coal is found in the United States are shown on the map below. In which states of the Northeast is *bituminous* coal found?

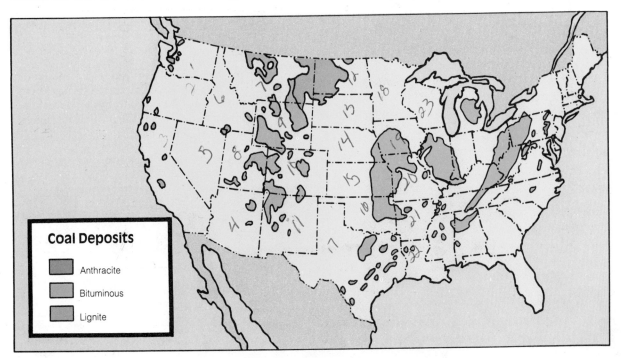

Coal Deposits

- Anthracite
- Bituminous
- Lignite

245

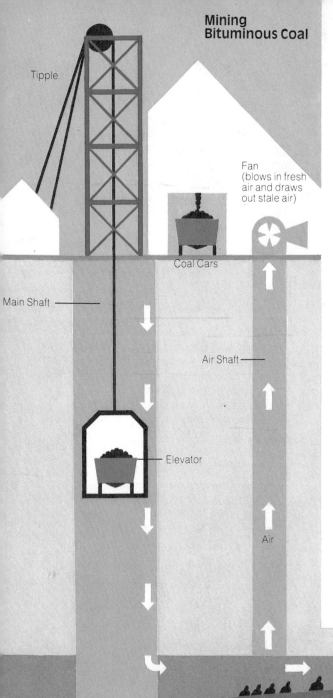

Mining Bituminous Coal

Tipple

Fan
(blows in fresh
air and draws
out stale air)

Coal Cars

Main Shaft

Air Shaft

Elevator

Air

Work Car

Cutter

Shuttle Car

Loader

When the coal reaches the surface, it is separated from the rock, washed, and broken up. The lumps are sorted according to size. Coal is shipped by freight cars, trucks, or boats. At freight yards and docks it is loaded into trucks, which carry it to homes, factories, and stores in many parts of our country. As other sources of energy are becoming scarce and expensive, people are beginning to use more coal. Scientists are trying to find new ways to use coal as fuel.

Uses of Coal

The largest deposits of anthracite are found in the eastern part of Pennsylvania. People who heat their houses with coal like to use anthracite because it burns with little soot or smoke. In the past, factories also liked to use hard coal because it is excellent for making steam and electricity. Hard coal is more expensive than other

An elevator takes workers and equipment down into the coal mine and brings them up again. Miners get from the elevator to the coal on a train. What other machines are used in mining coal?

kinds of coal because it is scarce. How does this help to explain why anthracite is rarely used in industry today?

Until recently bituminous coal from the Allegheny Plateau was used to run most of the manufacturing machinery of the Northeast. It makes more soot and smoke than hard coal. But it is cheaper. Bituminous coal is the main fuel in power plants. It is used as fuel in some homes and furnishes power to thousands of factories. Tar, pitch, and dyes are made from bituminous coal. It can be changed into products such as cement, perfume, and paint.

Oil and Gas Production

Oil is very important today. The first oil well in the United States was drilled in Titusville (tīt′əs vil), Pennsylvania, in 1859. The discovery of oil caused great excitement. Soon other wells were drilled. Gas was also found with the oil. For many years the Allegheny Plateau furnished more oil and gas than any other part of our country. Today this region supplies only a small part of the oil and gas that we use.

Where does most of our oil come from today? The map of oil fields on page 362 will show you. Name some uses of oil.

Shipbuilding

Shipbuilding was important along the Atlantic coast from the time the first settlers arrived. Ships then were sailing vessels and were made of wood. Lumber was plentiful in the American forests.

The swiftest, most beautiful of sailing vessels was the clipper ship. The first clipper ships were built in the 1840s. Because clipper ships had very large sails, they could travel at a fast "clip," or speed. The long, slender ships cut through the water with ease. The nation's *merchant marine* (mur′chənt mə rēn′) first became important in the time of the clipper ships. The merchant marine is the fleet which carries on the trade of a nation. It delivers goods to ports around the world. The United States Merchant Marine Academy is at Kings Point, New York.

But the fastest clipper ships could not keep up with steamships, which were driven by engines. Next, steel replaced wood for ships. Shipbuilding remained important in cities like Philadelphia, which was near coal and iron-ore fields. Camden, New Jersey, and Chester, Pennsylvania, are also important shipbuilding centers.

Textiles

People in the crowded industrial areas east of the Appalachians needed textiles. Eastern Pennsylvania had fuel and water power. But there were few raw materials at hand. The many railroads and rivers made transportation easy. "It would pay us to bring in the raw materials if we built textile mills here," said manufacturers.

Today textile mills are found in New York, Pennsylvania, and New Jersey. These three states are among the top ten textile-producing states in our country. In addition, factories in these states make much clothing, which is sold in stores throughout the world.

Manufacturing

The Middle Atlantic states are among the leading industrial states in our country. Industries grew there because the region had many natural resources, a good location, and a large number of workers.

About one-third of the population in the Middle Atlantic states works in manufacturing. Pennsylvania manufactures iron and steel, machinery, transportation equipment, and metal products. New York and New Jersey manufacture food products and clothing. Many food products are manufactured in Delaware as well. The Middle Atlantic states manufacture chemicals, electrical equipment, paper, and paper products. Much printing and publishing are done there.

Iron and Steel Milling

The making of iron and steel and of iron-and-steel products became the leading industry of the highlands of Pennsylvania. This area has hundreds of rivers for transporting goods. It once had abundant deposits of coal and iron ore. Today, however, Pennsylvania's mines can no longer supply its factories with enough raw material. Iron ore is brought from the region around Lake Superior and from western South America.

Iron is the basic ingredient used in the steel industry. Which northeastern states have large amounts of iron? How does this relate to the large number of steel mills in the area? Where are our copper deposits?

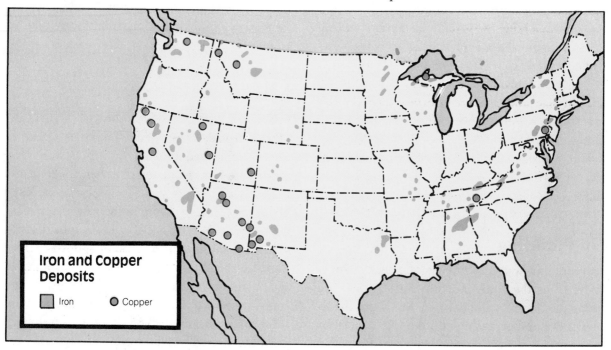

Iron and Copper Deposits

Iron Copper

The Story of Iron and Steel

Smelting iron ore and making steel are two different industries. Smelting, as you know, means heating the ore to separate the iron metal from its ore. At one time charcoal and coal were used as fuel to melt the ore. Today *coke* (kōk) and limestone are used in smelting iron ore. Coke is made by slowly heating soft coal in airtight ovens to take out the gas, tar, and oil. What is left is coke. Coke, when used as fuel, produces much greater heat than coal does.

The ore is smelted in tall, round buildings called blast furnaces. They are made of steel and lined with brick. Iron ore, coke, and limestone are poured into a blast furnace. As these minerals slowly pass down the furnace, blasts of hot air are blown into it. The coke burns with great heat and the ore and limestone melt. The melted rock joins with the limestone, forming *slag* (slag). The slag, when melted, is lighter than the melted iron, so it floats on top.

The melted iron is drawn from the bottom of the furnace and poured into molds. The iron cools in the molds and hardens into bars. The iron can be made into usable articles. It is also made into steel. Steel is tougher and harder than iron.

To make steel, the bars of iron are melted again, or the hot liquid is used before it hardens. Small amounts of carbon are added. Metals such as nickel or chromium may be added. This is all melted in a large furnace. The hot liquid steel is run off into molds to harden into ingots (in′gəts), or bars.

Do you know why the steel industry is so important in the United States? The manufac-

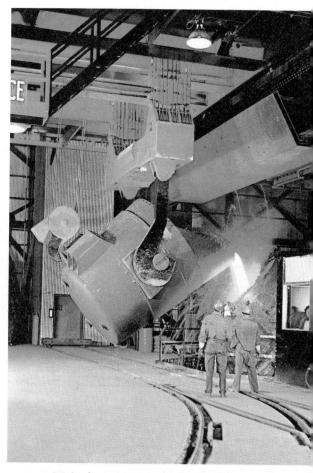

Melted steel is poured from the furnace. It is liquid and white-hot. Workers must wear protective clothing. Later, the molten metal will be formed into sheets or bars.

ture of automobiles, airplanes, ships, and locomotives depends on the steel industry. Skyscrapers are built with steel for the framework. Trains run on steel rails. Today the steel industry in the United States is modernizing. It is doing this to meet competition from the steel industry in Europe and Japan.

249

Philadelphia
An Old City with a New Face

The year was 1682. A group of people led by William Penn met together to plan a city called Philadelphia. The plan called for straight streets and many parks. More than 260 years later another group of people met together to replan the same city. Philadelphia had changed a great deal in 260 years. Narrow streets had become jammed with traffic. Many people no longer came into the city to shop. Large areas had become run-down.

Philadelphia was one of the first large cities to do something about its urban problems. Streets were widened, and travel into the city was made easier. Neighborhoods were rebuilt according to a special plan. The plan called for more than tearing down old buildings and putting up new ones. Many old buildings were left standing and were restored. New buildings were designed so they did not look out of place in old neighborhoods.

Philadelphia has much to be proud of. It is the largest city in Pennsylvania. Our Declaration of Independence was signed there. Our Constitution was written there. For a while the city was our nation's capital.

Philadelphia's location near water helped it become a busy seaport. Woolen mills and shipyards were built. Later it became a leading manufacturer of railroad engines. Today the city's factories turn out iron and steel products, textiles, and chemicals. It is near the largest oil-refining region on the Atlantic coast. ■

251

Oyster fishers pour their catch into storage bins for the trip to market.

Farming

Crops grow well on the Atlantic Coastal Plain, in the Hudson Valley, on the Piedmont, and on the Lake Plain south of Lakes Ontario and Erie. These regions have good soil and a mild climate. Their farms help to supply city people with the fresh food they need.

Two important kinds of farming in the Middle Atlantic states are dairy farming and poultry farming. New York and Pennsylvania rank among the top ten states as producers of dairy cattle. Pennsylvania ranks among the top ten states in the production of eggs. Peaches, pears, and apples are grown in New Jersey and Delaware. Farmers in western New York grow fruits and grapes.

The sandy soil and mild climate of the Atlantic Coastal Plain are well suited to truck farming, or the raising of produce for market. The melons, strawberries, tomatoes, and other vegetables of New Jersey, Delaware, and Long Island are famous in the Northeast.

Truck farms on Long Island specialize in potatoes, cabbage, and other vegetables. Cranberries grow on New Jersey marshes. Eastern Pennsylvania produces tobacco. Why do each of these areas specialize in certain crops?

Fishing

You know that both deep-sea and inshore fishing are carried on all along the coast. But in the shallow, quiet waters off Long Island and Delaware a special kind goes on—fishing for oysters. When oysters are first hatched, they swim about looking for something to which they can cling. Baby oysters fasten themselves to rocks and shells. Often thousands of them are found growing close together at the bottom of a bay or a sound. Such places are called oyster beds.

There is a large market for oysters. So many people make a business of raising them. They collect thousands of eggs in large tanks. When the baby oysters hatch, they are put into shallow waters. Here they grow to full size. This takes 3 to 4 years. Then they are ready for market. Other shellfish come from this region. Long Island waters produce fine scallops. New Jersey has many clams, lobsters, and crabs.

Some oyster fishers go out in small boats and gather the oysters with long-handled rakes. Others have boats which are fitted with strong iron dredges run by machinery. Dredges scoop up great bagfuls at a time. Oysters are packed in ice and shipped to inland cities and towns.

Major Cities

The cities of the Middle Atlantic region are important manufacturing centers. Products are made from steel, paper, chemicals, and textiles. Banks, insurance firms, and printing plants provide services for our country and the world. With its airports and harbors, this area is part of a great transportation network.

Buildings tower above New York City, a center of art, industry, fashion, music, and literature. It is also a busy international port.

New York City is the largest city in the United States and one of the five largest cities in the world. The people of this great city come from many different ethnic backgrounds.

Publishing books and magazines is an important industry. There are more printing plants in New York City than in any other city in our nation. As a world financial center, many corporations and banks have their headquarters in New York. New York City is also known as a center of fashion. The clothing and textile industries employ many people. Other industries include food products, furniture, chemicals, paints, and paper products.

Many tourists visit this city to enjoy its museums, theaters, and art galleries. The Port of New York is one of the world's largest and busiest. New York City also has two major airports.

Albany is the capital of the state of New York. It is one of the state's leading transportation centers. Its busy port on the Hudson River makes it an important industrial and shipping center. Many people in Albany have government jobs. Others work in factories that make brass products, medicines, and paper products.

More cameras and film are made in Rochester (roch′es′tər) than in any other city in the world. Other factories in Rochester make instruments, dental equipment, electronic equipment, food products, clothing, and textiles.

Pittsburgh, Pennsylvania, is a river port. It stands where the Monongahela (mə non′gə hē′lə) and Allegheny rivers join to form the Ohio River.

Pittsburgh is Pennsylvania's second largest city. Nearby coal mines and iron ore deposits helped Pittsburgh become one of the world's greatest steelmaking centers. It is one of the world's largest makers of aluminum, machinery, and safety equipment. Plate glass, used for windows, is another important product of the Pittsburgh area. Glass is made from certain sands. The sand and clay in this area are exactly right for making glass. Dishes, bricks, and tile are manufactured from clay found near Pittsburgh. A number of Pittsburgh's products are transported on its rivers.

The capital of Pennsylvania is Harrisburg. A large number of people there work for the government. Many others work in clothing and shoe factories. Steel is also an important industry, as it is in Pittsburgh.

New Jersey's capital is Trenton. It has many factories. Making electrical goods, metal products, machinery, and rubber products are leading industries. Trenton is also a printing and publishing center. About one-third of the people there work for the government.

Newark is New Jersey's largest city. It is the third largest insurance center in the United States and a major banking center. Newark has many factories. The chief industries make electrical equipment, metal products, and processed foods. Newark is a leading New Jersey port and air cargo center.

Wilmington is Delaware's largest city. It is one of our country's largest chemical and petrochemical centers. A petrochemical is made from petroleum or natural gas. Wilmington's factories make automobiles, steel, plastics, dyes, textiles, and rubber and leather products. Dover, the capital of Delaware, is in a rich farming region. Its chief industries are canning, airplane repairing, and rubber products.

Recreation

Many people visit the Middle Atlantic states each year. Like New England, the Middle Atlantic states have beautiful mountains, forests, lakes, and rivers. People visit these spots in the winter to hunt and ski. Many people attended the Winter Olympic Games held at Lake Placid in New York State in 1980.

People go to the Middle Atlantic states in the summer to camp, fish, and enjoy boating. The beaches along the Atlantic coast have many vacationers. Both the states and the federal government have set aside lands for parks, forests, and recreation. One such area is the Allegheny National Forest in Pennsylvania.

Tourists enjoy the Middle Atlantic states because of an interest in our country's history. This region played an important part in colonial times, during our war for independence from Great Britain.

Do You Know?

1. What is the difference between iron and steel? What are some uses of steel in our everyday life?
2. What are the chief products of Pennsylvania?
3. What are two kinds of farming in the Middle Atlantic states?

To Help You Learn

Using New Words

slag
bituminous
anthracite
coke
imports
merchant marine
exports
quarry
locomotive

shaft mining
smelt
lignite
spinning jenny
electronics
strip mining
textile
suffrage

The phrases below explain the words or terms listed above. Number a paper from 1 through 17. After each number write the word or term which matches the definition.

1. Brown coal
2. The right to vote
3. Woven cloth
4. Goods and products brought in from another country
5. A way of mining coal when it is close to the earth's surface
6. An early machine which could spin many threads at a time
7. An open pit from which stone is cut
8. Goods and products which are shipped out of a country
9. A special branch of electricity used in industry
10. Ships which carry on the trade of a nation
11. Heating ore to separate the metals from the ore
12. What is left after the iron is smelted
13. Soft coal
14. Coal from which gas has been removed
15. Hard coal
16. A way of mining coal through a deep hole
17. An engine which can move on its own power

Finding the Facts

1. What highland is located in the northeastern states?
2. In what state is the Erie Canal?
3. What has always been the cheapest means of transportation?
4. What did Peter Cooper build?
5. Who founded the National Woman Suffrage Association in 1869?
6. What is the leading industry of New England?
7. Which New England state is famous for lumber? Which is famous for maple sugar?
8. Where are the largest granite quarries in the United States?
9. What is the capital of each New England state? What is the largest city of each?
10. Where are the largest deposits of anthracite? What are two methods of mining coal?
11. What are some uses of bituminous coal?
12. What helped industries grow in the Middle Atlantic states?
13. What are two important kinds of farming in the Middle Atlantic states?

14. What is the largest city in our country?
15. What is the capital of each Middle Atlantic state? What is the largest city of each?

Learning from Maps

1. Study the map of the northeastern states on page 227. Which natural regions extend through the whole Northeast? Which do not? What country lies north of the northeastern states? What ocean is at the east? Which of the Great Lakes border this region?
2. On the map of the United States on pages A-6– A-7 locate the northeastern states. Between what parallels of latitude do the northeastern states lie?
3. Look at the map of forest regions of our country on page 427. What kinds of forests are in the northeastern states? Which kind of forest grows along the coast between Massachusetts and Delaware?
4. Look at the map of iron and copper deposits on page 248. Which northeastern states have deposits of iron? Which have copper deposits?

Using Study Skills

1. **Graph:** What does the graph on page 257 show?

   About how many tons of coal were produced in 1974? Was this more or less than the amount produced in 1972?

   In what year was the least amount of coal produced?

   Did the amount of coal produced between 1973 and 1976 increase or decrease? About how much less coal was produced in 1972 than in 1976?
2. **Diagram:** Look at the diagram showing coal mining on page 246. What kind of coal does the diagram show being mined? What machines do the miners use in the mine? How does fresh air get into the mine and stale air get out?
3. **Chart:** Make a chart like the one for Maine below, for the other northeastern states. Find the population figures and the capital for each state on pages 580– 583. Find the date admitted to the Union, the largest city, and the chief occupations of each state by using your text, an almanac, and encyclopedias.

State	Population	Capital	Admitted to Union	Largest City	Chief Occupations
Maine	1,133,000	Augusta	1820	Portland	lumbering, leather goods, farming, fishing

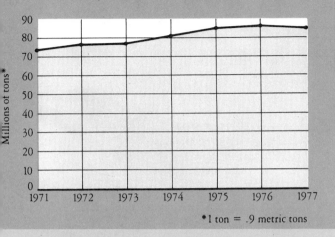

Production of Bituminous Coal in Pennsylvania, 1971-1977

Millions of tons*

90
80
70
60
50
40
30
20
10
0

1971 1972 1973 1974 1975 1976 1977

*1 ton = .9 metric tons

Thinking It Through

1. You remember that coal and iron ore were found together in eastern Pennsylvania. There were also many swift streams in this area. Can you explain how these things helped manufacturing to grow rapidly in this region?

2. Industries grew in the northeastern states for many reasons. If you could start a new business, what kind of business would you like to start? Where would you like to start your business? What things would you consider before choosing a location?

3. People who are interested in the history of our country visit buildings and landmarks in the northeastern states where events in our early history took place. Why is it important to save historical buildings and landmarks? Explain your answer.

4. Philadelphia was one of the first large cities to do something about its urban problems. If you could work on a committee to replan your city, what would you want done? Why?

Projects

1. Have the Reading Committee ask the librarian for help in finding books about life in the northeastern states. There are many interesting books about early settlers, American Indians, cities, and industries.

2. The Explorers' Committee might find out more about the clipper ships and the fast runs they made to China. They should try to find pictures of particular ships, such as the *Flying Cloud* or the *Sea Witch*.

3. The Research Committee might find more information about coal. What steps are being taken to make coal mining safer and to make coal burn more cleanly? What is being done to develop America's coal reserves? You might write the Department of Energy in Washington, D.C.

4. Many people from the northeastern states have made important contributions to our country. Work in small groups. Have each group find out about one of the following people: Edmund Muskie, Beverly Sills, Calvin Coolidge, Bella Abzug, Washington Irving, Reggie Jackson, Shirley Chisholm, Molly Pitcher, Mary Cassatt, and Howard Pyle. What contribution did each person make? Share what you find with the class.

5. If you cannot get a large outline map of the United States, make one by tracing the map on pages A-6 and A-7. Write in the names of the northeastern states, the important rivers, lakes, and cities. Label the Atlantic Ocean. Show the capital of each state with a star.

9 The Southeastern States

Unit Preview

The southeastern region of the United States is a vital agricultural and growing industrial area. The southeastern states in this region are Virginia, West Virginia, Maryland, North Carolina, South Carolina, Georgia, Kentucky, Tennessee, Alabama, Mississippi, and Florida.

The first lasting English settlement in America was made in this region. English people kept coming to the Southeast long after the first settlement. Spanish people were the first settlers in Florida. As the coastal lands became more populated, pioneers moved inland. The Indians of the region were forced to give up their land. The government had many Indian groups moved to places farther west.

Before the Civil War the southeastern states were called the "land of cotton." Today many products besides cotton are shipped from the Southeast. Forests grow fast in the warm climate of the Southeast, and lumbering is an important industry. After iron and coal were found near Birmingham, Alabama, it became a steel center. Many other industries have developed in the Southeast. The government project called TVA has helped to develop some industries as well as farming.

With all its industry, the Southeast remains a major farming region. But farming has changed too. Cotton and tobacco fields now share the land with orchards and with fields of soybeans, peanuts, corn, sweet potatoes, and other crops.

Things to Discover

If you look carefully at the picture, map, and time line, you can answer these questions.
1. What ocean borders some southeastern states? What body of water is south of these states?
2. What white fluffy crop shown in the picture grows well in the southeastern states?
3. When did the United States buy Florida?
4. What happened to the Cherokees in 1838?
5. How many years after the first airplane flight did the first people land on the moon?

Words to Learn

You will meet these words in this unit. As you read, you will learn what they mean and how to pronounce them. The Word List will help you.

basin	growing season
bauxite	legume
boll	naval stores
cannery	phosphate
citrus fruit	rayon
cotton belt	reservoir
crop rotation	sharecropper
cultivator	soil erosion
dam	soybean
dehydration	subtropical land
flood plain	tenant farmer
frontier	tung oil
gap	

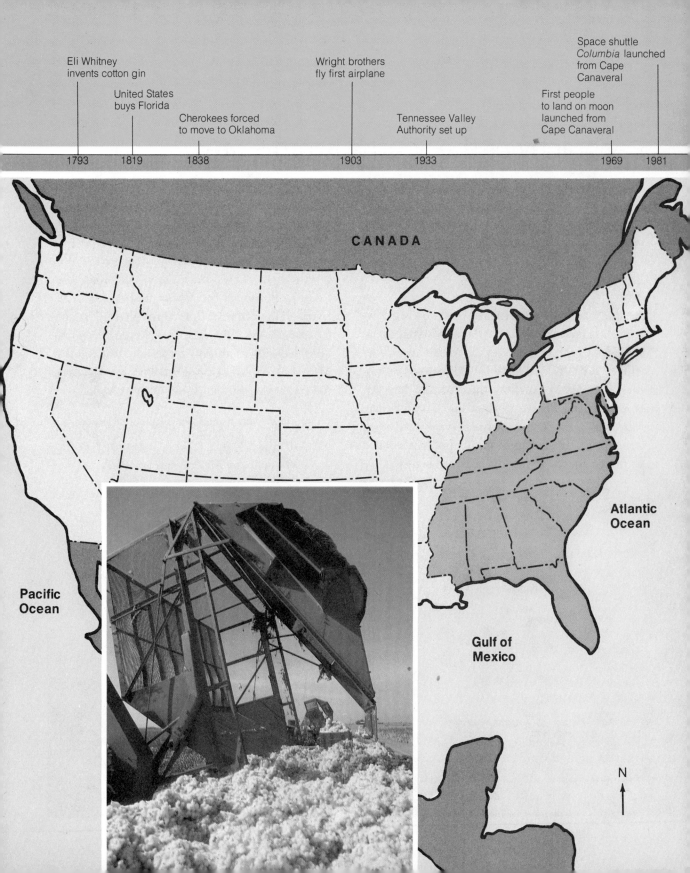

Eli Whitney
invents cotton gin

United States
buys Florida

Cherokees forced
to move to Oklahoma

Wright brothers
fly first airplane

Tennessee Valley
Authority set up

Space shuttle
Columbia launched
from Cape
Canaveral

First people
to land on moon
launched from
Cape Canaveral

1793   1819   1838   1903   1933   1969   1981

CANADA

Pacific
Ocean

Atlantic
Ocean

Gulf of
Mexico

N

1
Geography of the Southeastern States

The southeastern states have an irregular coast-line, and hills and mountains inland.

The Lowlands

A large part of the southeastern states is a low-land. It is made up of the Atlantic Coastal Plain, the Gulf Coastal Plain, and the Mississippi *Flood* (flud) *Plain.* A flood plain is land covered by water when rivers overflow their banks. The Atlantic Coastal Plain and the Gulf Coastal Plain join in Florida. These two plains are really one large plain. It stretches along the eastern and southern coasts of the southeastern states.

The only way to tell where the Atlantic Coastal Plain ends and the Gulf Coastal Plain begins is by seeing which way the rivers flow. On the map of the southeastern states opposite find the Potomac, the James, and the Savannah rivers. These rivers flow through the Atlantic Coastal Plain. The Alabama River drains the Gulf Coastal Plain and flows into the Gulf of Mexico. The Mississippi River is the largest of the rivers that flow into the Gulf of Mexico.

Flat-bottomed boats called barges carry heavy loads of products on the Mississippi River. These goods are delivered to cities along the Mississippi *Flood Plain.*

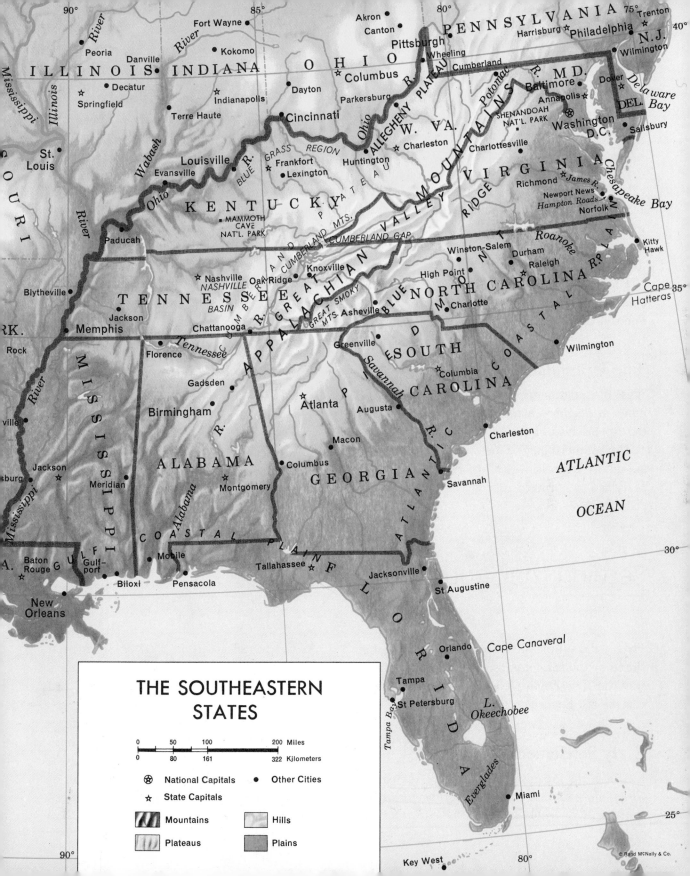

THE SOUTHEASTERN
STATES

0	50	100		200	Miles
0	80	161		322	Kilometers

⊗ National Capitals   ● Other Cities

☆ State Capitals

Mountains   Hills

Plateaus   Plains

© Rand McNally & Co.

Find the Blue Grass Region and the Nashville Basin on the map. These low, fertile regions are separated from each other by the western stretches of the Appalachian Highland. Because they are surrounded by higher lands, they are called *basins* (bā′sinz).

The Great Valley lies in the heart of the Appalachian Highland. It extends from eastern Pennsylvania to central Alabama.

The Uplands and Highlands

West of the Atlantic Coastal Plain is the Piedmont. It becomes higher as it stretches toward the Appalachian Highland.

The southern part of the Appalachians forms an almost unbroken chain of mountains from Maryland to northern Alabama. The mountains west of the Blue Ridge Mountains and the Great Valley are the Cumberland Mountains. These mountains have a *gap* (gap), or narrow valley through which it is easy to travel. The gap is known as Cumberland Gap.

The northern part of the Appalachian Highland is sometimes called the Allegheny Plateau. The southern part is the Cumberland Plateau.

Do You Know?

1. What states make up the Southeast?
2. What three plains make up the lowland of the southeastern states?
3. What is the northern part of the Appalachian Highland called? The southern part?

2
Settling the Southeastern States

Five of the southeastern states were among the thirteen original colonies of our country. One was the first English colony settled. Another was the last English colony settled.

Early Settlements

In 1565 the Spanish founded St. Augustine (ô′gəs tēn′), Florida, the oldest permanent white settlement in the United States.

As you have learned, in 1607 colonists from England settled Jamestown in Virginia. Maryland was settled in 1634 by an Englishman, Lord Calvert.

The colony called Carolina was quite large. It was later divided into North Carolina and South Carolina. In 1733 the colony of Georgia was founded by James Oglethorpe. It was the last of the English colonies. These five colonies were among the first thirteen states.

Growth of the Southeastern States

Settlers continued to come to the southeastern colonies from England, Scotland, Ireland, and Germany. The rapid growth of the coastal areas led settlers to move inland to the Piedmont.

To the west was the Appalachian Highland. Land companies bought large tracts of land beyond the mountains from the British government. The companies offered pioneers large sections of land for low prices.

Main Routes to the West

The long, high ridges of the Appalachian Highland were hard to cross. But the pioneers found and used four natural routes to the West, as shown on the map of these routes on this page.

In New York, the Hudson and Mohawk rivers provided a route through the mountains. This route led to the Lake Plain and the Great Lakes waterway.

In Pennsylvania and Maryland, pioneers followed the crude traces of roads—cut by Britain's armies—to the forks of the Ohio.

In Virginia and North Carolina, the pioneers followed rivers to their sources in the Appalachians. Once through the mountains, pioneers found themselves in the Great Valley. They traveled along this valley and river bottoms to the Cumberland Gap. It offered easy passage to the hilly uplands of Kentucky and Tennessee.

In South Carolina and Georgia, pioneers followed the coastal plain westward around the Appalachian Highland. However, this route led them through territory claimed by Spain.

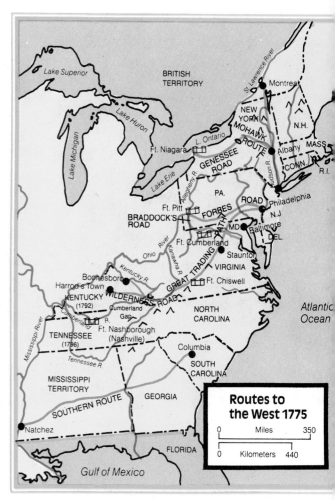

Follow the main early routes to the West. Locate the rivers on the map. Which routes followed rivers part of the way? What route crossed the mountains?

Settling the Frontier

As the Coastal Plain, the Piedmont, and the Great Valley became more densely populated, many pioneers decided to move west. They constantly moved onward to the everchanging

263

Pine-covered mountains rise steeply above the deep valleys and ridges of Virginia. Settlers found rich farmland in the valleys of the Appalachian Highland.

frontier (frun tēr'). The settled region of a country lying along the border of an unsettled region is called a frontier.

Daniel Boone and James Robertson led the first groups of settlers through Cumberland Gap. They settled the land west of the Appalachian Highland. At first, these new settlements were claimed by Virginia and North Carolina. Soon after our country became independent,

Kentucky and Tennessee became states of the United States. Kentucky became a state in 1792, Tennessee in 1796.

Settling Alabama and Mississippi

Cotton grew well in Georgia and the Carolinas. The factories of old England and of New England needed raw cotton. So southerners planted cotton on most of their land. Because they did not know how to use fertilizer, their land wore out. A search for new cotton lands led the planters into what are now Alabama and Mississippi.

Planters rushed to the cotton-growing region between Georgia and the Mississippi River. At first, Congress ruled this region. When enough people had settled here, two new states were formed. In 1817 Mississippi became a state. In 1819 Alabama became a state.

Indians of the Southeastern States

The Creek Indians lived in what are now Alabama and Georgia. When settlers began to move onto Creek lands, the Indians became angry. They attacked Fort Mims in Alabama. United States soldiers, led by Andrew Jackson, fought back. They defeated the Creeks who were then forced to move to present-day Oklahoma.

The Seminole (sem'ə nōl') Indians lived in what is now Florida. When they heard about the Creeks, the Seminoles decided to take action to keep their lands. This decision started the First Seminole War. Jackson led some soldiers across the border of Florida and took several Spanish forts. He forced Spain to give up its claim to the territory. In 1819 Spain decided to sell Florida to the United States for 5 million dollars. But Jackson did not conquer the Indians.

Several years later, the Second Seminole War broke out. After 2 years of fighting, Osceola (äs'ē ō'lə), the Seminole's chief, was captured. The Seminoles continued to fight until they were nearly ruined. Many of the survivors moved to Oklahoma. Others stayed in Florida.

The Cherokee (cher'ə kē) Indians lived in the Carolinas and Georgia. Following the War for Independence, settlers began to move onto Cherokee lands. More settlers arrived after gold was discovered there. Georgia asked the United States government to force the Cherokees off their lands. The Cherokees asked for help from the United States Supreme Court. But the Court ruled against the Indians. The Court stated that the Indians lived on the land, but did not own it.

Later, Congress made a treaty forcing the Cherokees to be moved to what is now the state of Oklahoma. The 1838 march of the Cherokees became known as the "Trail of Tears." Almost 4,000 people died because of starvation and disease. Look at the map of Indian removal on page 300. Trace the route the Cherokees followed to the West.

The Story of Cotton

In colonial times the rice and indigo plants were the chief money crops in South Carolina and Georgia. Then cotton-spinning mills were built in the North. The mill owners there and in England wanted more cotton. They bought all the cotton southerners sent to market and wanted more. Before long cotton was the chief money crop in the South. Plantation owners wanted more slaves to work in the fields.

But the cotton had to be free from seeds before it was sold. Removing the seeds from the cotton by hand was slow work.

Eli Whitney, a young New England schoolteacher, was visiting a Georgia plantation in 1793. Whitney realized that if a machine could be invented that would remove the seeds from the cotton, much more cotton could be cleaned in a shorter time. Whitney invented such a machine, called a cotton gin. It cleaned as much cotton in a day as 50 people could by hand.

What a change that invention caused! Planters as far north as Virginia began to raise cotton. Still the factories wanted more. Planters then moved to cotton lands west of the Appalachian Highland. The cotton-growing region became known as the *cotton belt* (belt). Find the cotton belt on the map on page 272.

Again demands for more slaves increased. Slave traders brought more blacks to the South to provide cheap labor. Many farmers felt that they could not make money from growing cotton without the cheap labor provided by slaves. So slavery continued. Disagreements about it became one of the causes of the Civil War.

Sharecroppers and Tenant Farmers

Before the start of the Civil War, planters had no trouble getting workers. As their plantations grew, they bought more slaves. After the war there were no slaves. There were few workers to be hired on farms. Besides, the planters had little money to pay the workers. How could they run their plantations?

The system that developed was called sharecropping. A planter's land was divided. The planter kept part and divided the rest into small farms which were rented. The planter gave each renter a cabin, a mule, a plow and other farming tools, and food. In return, the workers tended the planter's land. After the harvest, workers shared all the crops with the owner of the land. Such workers came to be known as *sharecroppers* (sher′krop′ərz).

A planter often also had *tenant* (ten′ənt) *farmers* on the land. Tenant farmers, too, were given small plots to work. But they owned their tools and work animals. They paid their rent with either crops or money.

George Washington Carver, Plant Expert

George Washington Carver was born near Diamond Grove, Missouri, about 1861. He was the son of slaves. He worked while in college to earn money for his education. After college Carver became a teacher of agriculture at Tuskegee (tus kē′gē) Institute in Alabama.

The land in Alabama was worn out. It had been used only for growing cotton. Carver restored minerals to the soil by planting other kinds of crops.

Carver found that peanuts, sweet potatoes, and pecans grew well in the Alabama soil. He then taught farmers what he had learned. Carver found how to make more than 400 products from peanuts and sweet potatoes, and more than 75 products from pecans. His improvements completely changed agriculture in the Southeast.

Carver continued to work at Tuskegee, studying ways of better farming. After his death in 1943, Congress set aside January 5 as a day to honor George Washington Carver.

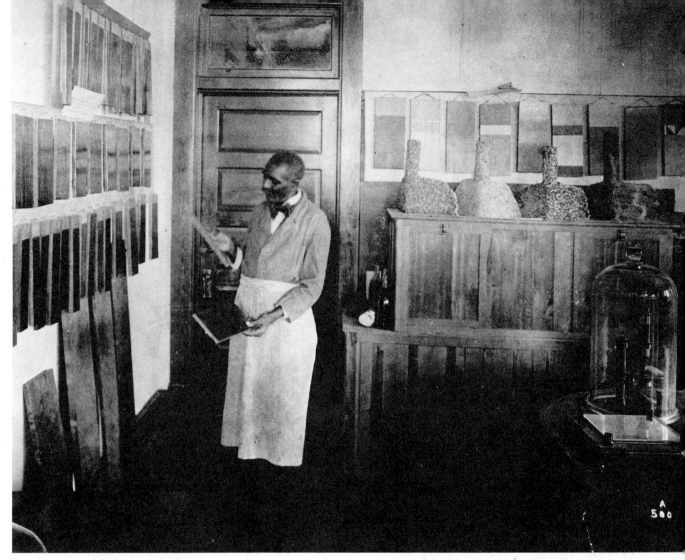

George Washington Carver had a laboratory at Tuskegee Institute. Here he worked many hours each day to carefully test all of the products he made from pecans, sweet potatoes, and peanuts.

Growth of Transportation

As the southeastern states grew, transportation improved. Better roads and more railroads were built. They helped carry raw materials to the North. They carried food grown in the West to the South where food was needed.

Then a new kind of transportation developed. In December 1903, Wilbur and Orville Wright came from Dayton, Ohio, to make the first successful airplane flight at Kitty Hawk, North Carolina. They chose Kitty Hawk because it was one of the windiest places in the country. It had sandy hills which were free of bushes and trees. The work of the Wright brothers led to the air travel we enjoy today.

During the 1950s and 1960s our country became interested in space exploration. Scientists worked with engineers to design long-range

Orville Wright had to lie flat on the frame to control the airplane he and his brother built. The Wright brothers' plane is now in a museum in Washington, D.C.

missiles. Launchings were made from a missile-testing center at Cape Canaveral on Florida's Atlantic coast. The climate there allows launchings to be made all year long. Nearby islands provide bases for stations to track launched spacecraft. In 1969 the first people to land on the moon were launched from Cape Canaveral at the John F. Kennedy Space Center.

Do You Know?

1. Why did settlers use the Cumberland Gap?
2. Why did more and more landowners plant cotton?
3. What is Cape Canaveral?

Before You Go On

Using New Words

tenant farmer   frontier
flood plain   cotton belt
sharecropper   basin
gap

The phrases below explain the words or terms listed above. Number a paper from 1 through 7. After each number write the word or term that matches the definition.

1. Any low region surrounded by higher lands
2. The region of a country lying along the border of an unsettled region
3. Lowland that is often covered by water when rivers overflow their banks
4. A person who pays rent for farmland with either crops or money
5. A narrow valley in mountains
6. Area in the South where cotton grows well
7. A person who works on another's farm and shares crops with the landowner

Finding the Facts

1. What kind of coastline do the southeastern states have?
2. In which state do the Atlantic Coastal Plain and the Gulf Coastal Plain meet?
3. How can you tell where the Atlantic Coastal Plain ends and the Gulf Coastal Plain begins?
4. Where is the Great Valley?
5. Where is the Cumberland Gap?
6. Which five southeastern states were among the thirteen original states of our country?
7. Who led the first groups of settlers through Cumberland Gap?
8. How was Florida added to the United States?
9. What Indian tribe was forced to move to Oklahoma in a march known as the "Trail of Tears"?
10. What did Eli Whitney invent?
11. What crops did George Washington Carver introduce to the southeastern states?
12. How did railroads help the southeastern states?
13. Who made the first successful airplane flight in 1903? From where was it made?
14. From where were the first people to land on the moon launched?
15. Where did the Creek, Cherokee, and Seminole Indian groups live? Where did many of them have to go?

3

Living and Working in the Southeastern States

The population maps on pages 219 and 518 show that almost one-fourth of America's people live in the Southeast. Beginning in the 1950s, more and more people have found jobs in the new industries of the Southeast. Some people work on farms, in forests, or in orchards.

The Tennessee Valley Authority

The Tennessee Valley is the land drained by the Tennessee River and its tributaries. It once had good soil, forests, minerals, and navigable rivers. But poor farming methods robbed the soil of plant food. Many trees were cut or burned down. Heavy rains caused floods which carried off the topsoil. Fertile fields became barren. They were cut by gullies, or ditches. This washing away of soil is known as *soil erosion* (i rō′zhen). Our government sent scientists to see what could be done to save the valley.

In 1933 the government set up an organization known as the Tennessee Valley Authority, usually shortened to TVA. The TVA had offices in Knoxville, Tennessee. TVA planned ways to prevent floods, stop soil erosion, plant trees, and make better use of the natural resources.

The work of the TVA was started by building more *dams* (damz). A dam is a wall or bank built across a river to stop its flow. Wilson Dam, at Muscle Shoals in Alabama, had been built in

1925, before this experiment began. The dams hold back the waters so the rivers do not overflow their banks and cause floods. *Reservoirs* (rez′ər vwärz′), or lakes, are formed behind the dams. Water from the reservoirs is allowed to flow into the streams when the rivers are low. This makes them navigable at all times. Power plants were built at the foot of some dams. These plants generate (jen′ə rāt′), or make, electricity. The electricity generated in the plants supplies power and light to factories, towns, and farms in a 200-mile (320 km) area.

Trees were planted on the bare slopes. These new forests help check soil erosion and prevent floods. Experts showed farmers how to plow land in order to keep soil from being carried away in heavy rains. They showed farmers how to fertilize the land and rotate crops. TVA has done much to improve farming methods in the Tennessee Valley.

TVA has also brought electric power to the valley and helped it change into an industrial region. Factories and factory towns have grown up throughout the farming sections. The TVA project has saved millions of dollars by preventing floods. It has helped develop water power in many states of the South.

Farming in the Southeast

Most of the land in the Southeast is coastal plain. Only a small area is too rugged for farming. The climate and rainfall there are favorable

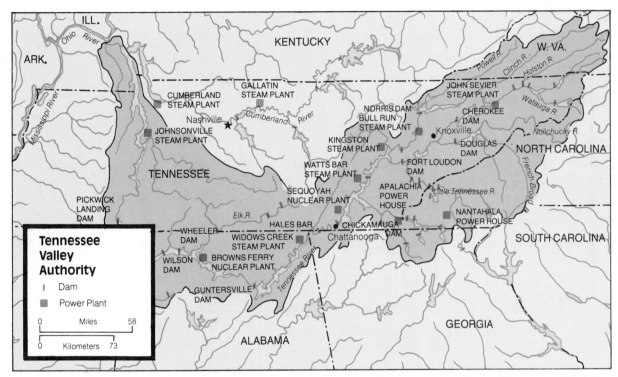

The Tennessee Valley Authority (TVA) built *dams* to control floods and power plants to generate electricity along the Tennessee River. What states benefit from TVA?

for farming. Most of the Southeast has mild or warm winters and warm summers, (See the climate map on page 11.) The surface and climate make it possible to grow many different crops.

The Cotton Belt

Cotton must have certain conditions to grow. Cotton needs a very special climate. It must have a *growing season* (sē'zən) of at least 200 days. The growing season is the part of the year when crops can be grown outdoors. It is the time between the last killing frost in the spring and the first killing frost in the fall. Most farm crops do well with a shorter growing season than cotton must have.

Cotton must also have between 20 and 60 inches (51 and 152 cm) of rainfall. If the plants get too much rain, they rot. With too little, they wither and die. The rain must come in spring and early summer. Rain in late summer or early fall rots the cotton fiber. It makes harvesting the cotton a difficult task.

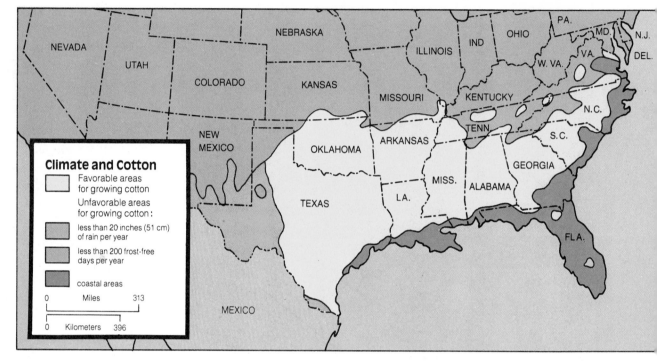

The map legend reads:

Climate and Cotton

- Favorable areas for growing cotton
- Unfavorable areas for growing cotton:
  - less than 20 inches (51 cm) of rain per year
  - less than 200 frost-free days per year
  - coastal areas

Miles 0 — 313

Kilometers 0 — 396

The area where cotton is the leading crop is called the *cotton belt*. What kind of climate does cotton need? How many states are in the *cotton belt?*

Today small farmers usually own the land they work. Instead of raising the same crops on the same land year after year, they practice *crop rotation* (rō tā′shən). That is, if they have raised cotton for 2 or 3 years, they plant a different crop. Some crops, like cotton, rob the soil by using up its richness. Other crops, like soybeans and peanuts, put plant food back into the soil. By rotating crops, a farmer builds up the soil. However, cotton is still grown on many farms in the Southeast.

From Planting to Market

Part of the Southeast is near the tropics. See the physical map of North and South America, pages A-9 and A-11. We speak of land near the tropics as *subtropical* (sub trop′i kəl) *land.* In the subtropical part of the cotton belt, planting can begin in February. Farther north it is April before danger from frost has passed.

After the soil is plowed and broken up, seeds are sown by drills. Later, machines called *cultivators* (kul′tə vā′tərz) are used to loosen the soil and uproot the weeds. Cultivators are pulled between the rows of cotton by tractors.

Eight or ten weeks after the seeds are planted, the cotton belt is a sea of blossoms. At first the blossoms are white, then pink, and then red. In a few days the blossoms fall off. Small seed pods, called cotton *bolls* (bōlz), form in their places. Late in August the cotton bolls start to burst open, showing white, fluffy fibers.

Cotton picking begins when the first bolls open. Long ago people picked the cotton. Today almost all the cotton is picked by machines.

Near most large cotton fields is a large building where the seeds are taken out of the cotton. The machine that separates the fiber from the seeds is a cotton gin. Another machine presses it into bales, wraps the bales in heavy cloth, and ties them with steel bands.

A bale of cotton weighs about 500 pounds (225 kg). Before they are shipped, the bales are put into another machine which presses the cotton together tightly. This makes the bales much smaller and easier to handle. They are then stored in warehouses ready to be shipped.

Uses of the Cotton Plant

Years ago people learned to make cloth from cotton fibers. Now useful products are also made from cotton seeds. Cottonseed oil is used in cooking, in making soap, and as salad oil. Cottonseed cake makes excellent cattle feed. It can be ground up to make a cheap fertilizer.

Short cotton fibers sometimes stick to the seeds. These fibers are too short to make good cotton cloth. They are often used in making *rayon* (rā′on). Rayon is a type of cloth that looks and feels much like silk. The stalks of the cotton plant are used in making paper.

Tobacco

The first money crop raised in our country was tobacco. The method of growing and preparing the crop has not changed very much. Raising tobacco is hard work. The tiny seeds must be started in seedbeds. Each plant is then set out in the field by hand or by machine. The growing plants are carefully tended. When ripe, the leaves are picked and taken to barns or sheds for curing, or drying. This prepares the leaves for market.

Tobacco is usually cured in one of two ways. Sometimes the leaves are hung in sheds. These sheds either have walls made of slats or no walls at all. Tobacco dried this way is "air-cured." In the Carolinas tobacco is often dried by stoves or furnaces. Tobacco treated this way is "heat-cured." The dried tobacco is taken to market towns. It is sold at a public sale to buyers from tobacco factories.

North Carolina and Virginia make up one of the chief tobacco regions in the country. North Carolina's farms produce more tobacco than those of any other state. Another tobacco region is in Kentucky and northern Tennessee.

Mixed Farming

In recent years southern farmers have turned to new kinds of farming. They still grow cotton and tobacco. They also raise many kinds of grains, fruits, and vegetables for market. They keep farm animals and poultry and raise feed for them. The crops and animals they raise on mixed farms help to build up worn-out soil.

Certain plants, like peas and beans, which grow in pods, are called *legumes* (leg′yoomz). Legumes are grown on many farms in the South.

An important legume is the *soybean* (soi′bēn′). The first soybeans were brought here from China. Many uses have been found for

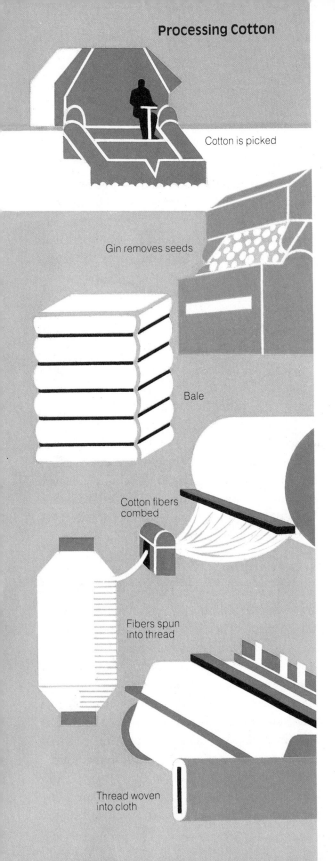

Processing Cotton

Cotton is picked

Gin removes seeds

Bale

Cotton fibers combed

Fibers spun into thread

Thread woven into cloth

Production of Cotton in the United States 1975-1982

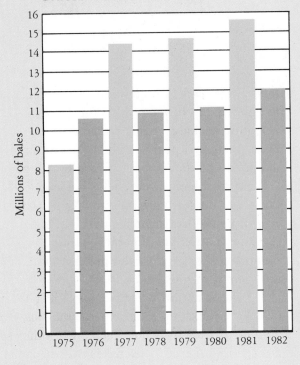

Millions of bales

1975 1976 1977 1978 1979 1980 1981 1982

The graph above shows how cotton production has changed from year to year. What are some causes of these changes? The steps in processing cotton are shown in the diagram at the left. Which of these steps would take place inside a textile mill?

soybeans. They are ground into flour and used in cakes and bread. Soybean oil is used to make a variety of paints, varnishes, and plastics.

Peanuts are also legumes. They have pods which grow and ripen underground. The low, sandy coastal plain of southeastern Virginia and of North Carolina is fine for growing peanuts. They also grow well in Alabama and Georgia. As you remember, George Washington Carver introduced the growing of peanuts to farmers in the region.

Many pecans are raised in the Southeast. Tall pecan trees grow wild along the Gulf Coast.

This is a farm in Tennessee. In plowing the fields, the farmer has followed the natural curve, or contour, of the land's surface. This will help prevent *soil erosion.*

They are cultivated in only a few southern states. Pecan nuts have thin shells. This makes it easy to get the meat out. Bags of pecan nuts are shipped to all parts of our country.

The tung tree is a native of China. The trees are also grown in the United States for needed *tung* (tung) *oil.* Tung oil is pressed from the seeds found in tung nuts. This oil is used in making paint, varnish, and plastics. Large groves of tung trees grow in Mississippi and Florida. They supply most of the tung oil used by manufacturers in the United States.

Fruits and Other Special Crops

Almost every kind of fruit you can think of grows in the Southeast. South Carolina raises and ships more peaches than any other state except California. Fine peaches also grow in Georgia and Alabama and in the Great Valley in Maryland and Virginia. The Great Valley in Virginia is famous for apples as well as peaches. There are also many apple orchards in West Virginia.

Not many parts of our country are warm enough to raise oranges, grapefruit, lemons, and

275

limes. These *citrus* (sit′rəs) *fruits* need a tropical or subtropical climate. More than one-half of all the citrus groves in the United States are in Florida. They produce more than two-thirds of our citrus fruits.

The owner of a citrus grove is always worried until the fruit is ripe. One frost can ruin an entire crop. Lemons and limes are most easily killed.

Huge packing sheds are built near the citrus groves all through the citrus-growing regions. Some of the fruit is washed, sorted, packed in boxes, and shipped to big cities. Tampa and Orlando are cities in Florida where citrus fruits are packed and shipped. Juices are prepared for market too. Plants for processing canned frozen juice are often located near citrus groves.

Other special crops of the southeastern states are sweet potatoes, sugarcane, and rice. Growing sweet potatoes began to pay after the work of George Washington Carver. He made bread, starch, glue, candy, plastics, and other things from sweet potatoes. Then farmers in Mississippi, Alabama, and other states in the region could make money by growing sweet potatoes. Drying sweet potatoes is also an important industry.

Sugarcane needs a hot, wet climate and fertile soil. Find the Everglades on the map of the Southeast on page 261. These great swamplands in southern Florida are being drained. Sugarcane grows well in these wet lands and is an important crop in Florida.

Some rice is grown along the Gulf Coast. The swampy, warm conditions on this coastal plain are good for rice-growing.

Livestock Raising and Dairy Farming

Southerners have always raised livestock. Today numerous farms in the Southeast have pigs. Many farmers also raise poultry, cattle, horses, sheep, and bees.

Raising horses was a paying business before the automobile was invented. The Bluegrass Region of Kentucky is still famous for fine racing and riding horses. Fine horses are also raised in Virginia.

Dairy farming is an important industry in most of the Southeast, especially in the northern part. There are many dairy farms east of the Appalachians. The coastal plain of Maryland has large dairy farms. The Piedmont of Maryland and Virginia and the Great Valley are other important dairy regions. The hilly sections of West Virginia supply dairy products to nearby cities.

Raising beef cattle is becoming important in Kentucky, Georgia, and Florida. The largest beef-cattle ranches east of the Mississippi River are in Florida. Cowhands care for great herds of cattle on the grasslands north of Lake Okeechobee (ō′kə chō′bē). Hog raising is important in South Carolina and Georgia.

Many mules are raised in the Southeast. Mules are smaller, tougher, more sure-footed, and cheaper than horses. They are used on some farms and in mines.

Large flocks of sheep graze in Virginia, West Virginia, Tennessee, and Kentucky. Sheep are raised for meat and wool.

Poultry is raised in the Southeast. Many of the chickens raised for eating come from the Southeast.

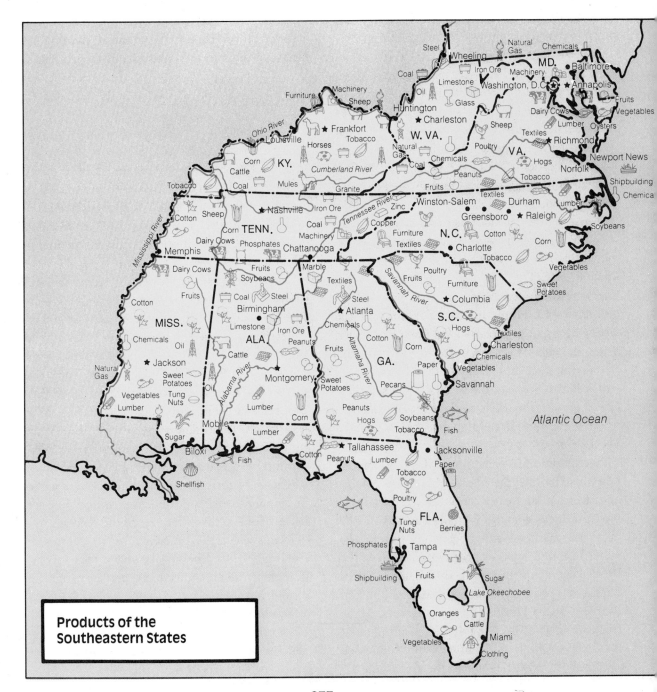

Products of the Southeastern States

Truck Farming

Spring comes early to the Atlantic Coastal Plain of Maryland and Virginia. The light, sandy soil warms up quickly. Farmers have made it an important vegetable-growing area. Cabbages, tomatoes, onions, lettuce, sweet corn, potatoes, strawberries, and melons are grown. They are planted early in spring. As soon as one crop is picked, the fields are plowed and another crop is planted. Two or three crops can be raised each season.

Most of the produce is sold in large cities close by. Today fresh vegetables and fruits can be shipped in refrigerator cars and trucks without spoiling. They can also be kept from spoiling by canning, freezing, or *dehydration* (dē'hī drā'shən). Dehydration means taking out the water by a special process. When water is added later, the vegetables and fruits are ready to eat.

Maryland is in the heart of this region of truck farms. Some of the vegetables raised there are shipped to markets elsewhere. But many of them are canned in canning factories, or *canneries* (kan'ər ēz).

Refrigeration has made truck farming important on all parts of the coastal plain in the Southeast. Refrigerated trucks and railroad cars transport products quickly. Farmers can supply the northern markets with vegetables during the winter. Florida supplies about one-fourth of the fresh vegetables eaten in the United States during the winter. Southern Mississippi and Alabama share Florida's winter markets. Many truck farms in Florida specialize in raising potatoes and strawberries. Kentucky and Tennessee also grow strawberries for northern markets.

Some southern farmers still raise one or two money crops. The change to mixed farming has made farming in the Southeast more profitable.

Fishing

Many people in the southeastern states make a living by fishing. Along the Atlantic Coast and the Gulf Coast the continental shelf is more than 75 miles (120 km) wide. Hundreds of kinds of fish come to these warm, fairly shallow waters to feed. Each year fishers there catch about one-fourth of all the fish caught in the United States.

Many people like to eat oysters, shrimp, crabs, and clams. That is why there is a big market for shellfish. Oysters grow best in warm, quiet waters. The greatest oyster beds in the Gulf of Mexico are off the coast of Mississippi. Chesapeake Bay and Delaware Bay are the chief oyster areas on the Atlantic Coast. Baltimore, Maryland and Biloxi (bə läk'sē), Mississippi are important oyster-packing and shipping cities. Shrimp, too, like warm waters. Shrimp boats are a common sight in the Gulf of Mexico. Oysters and shrimp are packed in ice to be shipped fresh, and some are frozen. They are usually sent to the cities east of the Rockies.

Clams and crabs are caught off the shores of Delaware and Chesapeake bays. Sea trout, flounder, mullet, and red snapper are caught in southern waters.

Some people fish for sport or fun. Game fish live in the waters around the peninsula of Florida. People who like to fish for sport go there and to other parts of the Gulf.

Large machines help workers load logs on trucks. The trucks deliver the logs to nearby mills or to railroad cars to be carried to other parts of the United States.

Lumbering

What a huge forest most of the Southeast was when the first colonists arrived! Coastal lands were covered with softwood trees, chiefly yellow, or southern, pine. Oak, hickory, maple, and other hardwoods grew on the cooler uplands. Gum, sycamore, and cottonwood grew along the rivers and in the bottom lands of the Mississippi. Cypress was found in the swamps. What is now our Southeast was once the largest stretch of forest lands in our country. It is still a fine forest region.

Trees grow easily in the Southeast because of the warm climate and abundant rain. Forests grow faster in that section than in other parts of our country. Today one-fourth of our lumber comes from the forests of the Southeast. To replace those that are cut down, new trees are planted.

Cutting Lumber

Most lumbering in the Southeast is done on the coastal lowlands. Look at the product map on page 277 to see what states have important lumber industries.

Roads and railroad tracks are run into the forests to the lumber camps. Logs are loaded on flat cars or on trucks and carried to the mills. Because of the mild climate, lumbering goes on in these forests of the Southeast in both winter and summer.

The logs are sawed and made into boards in mills close to the lumber camps. For many years the boards were sent to factories in the North or exported. Today the Southeast has its own factories for the making of furniture and other wood products. But the forests still supply much of the lumber used in other parts of the United States.

Inside a lumber mill, special machines cut logs into boards and neatly stack them for shipment. Most of the lumber will be used later by the construction industry.

Uses of Lumber

The gum of the pine tree is made into turpentine, tar, and resin. In colonial days these products were known as *naval* (nā′vəl) *stores*. Naval stores were used in shipbuilding at that time. Today the gum of the pine tree is used in making linoleum, paper, and soap. Tar is used for paving and roofing. Turpentine is used to mix paints. The pine forests of northern Florida, southern Georgia, and Alabama supply most of the naval stores now needed.

Tall, straight pines make good telephone poles and boards for building purposes. Yellow pines can be turned into wood pulp. Wood pulp is made by grinding wood and mixing it with water. Wood pulp is used to make paper, especially newsprint, the paper used in newspapers. Wood pulp is also used to make rayon.

Oak, maple, and other hardwood trees from the Appalachians make excellent lumber for houses and furniture. Gumwood is shaved into thin layers and made into berry boxes, fruit baskets, and barrels.

The forests of this region supply the furniture-making factories, pulp and paper mills, and rayon plants of the Southeast with lumber. They also send lumber to factories in other parts of the world.

Mining

The Southeast has many natural resources. For 200 years the land was used chiefly for farming. Mining is now an important industry in the Southeast.

Coal, Oil, and Gas

The coal-deposits map on page 245 shows that a bituminous coal field lies under almost the whole Appalachian Highland. This is the largest coal field in the world. It extends into Kentucky, West Virginia, Virginia, Tennessee, and Alabama. Kentucky and West Virginia mine the largest amounts of coal each year.

Many mining towns have grown up in these states. Much of the coal mined is used to make electricity for power in factories of the southeastern states. Some coal is shipped north or exported. Often, coal is sent by water because it is cheaper to ship heavy goods by water than by railroad. Norfolk and Newport News, Virginia's largest seaports, export more coal than any other cities in the United States.

The oil and natural-gas fields of the Appalachian Highland also extend into West Virginia and Kentucky. These fields help furnish power and fuel for the glass and chemical factories of West Virginia. Oil fields are also located in the Gulf coastal area. Some oil is pumped from offshore deposits in the Gulf. Look at the map of oil deposits on page 362.

Other Minerals

You have learned that iron ore, coal, and limestone are used in making steel. Large amounts of all three are found close together in northern Alabama. The Great Valley near Birmingham is one of the richest iron-ore areas in our country. You know that coal is mined in this region and that limestone is found throughout the Great Valley. Much limestone lies near Birmingham. With these resources Birmingham has become a great iron-and-steel city.

The Southeast has other minerals in addition to coal, oil, gas, and iron. One of these is phosphate (fos′fāt). Phosphates are minerals needed for growth by plants and animals. Worn-out soil often lacks phosphates. Southern farmers use a great deal of fertilizer, some of which is made from phosphate rock.

Large amounts of phosphate rock are found in Tennessee and Florida. The world's largest deposits of this rock lie near Tampa Bay, in Florida. Here the rock is so near the surface that it can be scooped up with power shovels. Not all the phosphate rock is made into fertilizer. Some is made into a substance that puts "fizz" in soft drinks. One kind of baking powder also contains phosphate.

Building stones, mainly marble and granite, are quarried in Georgia, Tennessee, Virginia, and Alabama. In northern Georgia is a bed of building stone 60 miles (96 km) long and several miles wide. Pure white and pink marble is quarried there. This marble is in great demand for statues and public buildings. Granite is used for large buildings, bridges, monuments, and curbstones because it is so hard.

Graphite, zinc, and lead are mined in the Southeast, too. Graphite is a soft, black, greasy mineral. It is chiefly used in making "lead" pencils. Tennessee has many deposits of zinc.

Manufacturing

Until the middle 1900s most of the people in the Southeast made their living by farming. The map on page 285 shows that all the southeastern states now have industrial regions.

The Southeast has rich raw materials, a good climate, good transportation, and a great number of workers and markets. Industries need all

Machine parts are made from metal in this manufacturing plant in Tennessee. Workers use precise cutting machines to shape each part to exact measurements.

these. That is why many northern factories moved to the Southeast during the 1900s.

A few factories were moved before the 1900s. Among them were textile mills from New England. Small towns grew up around the early mills and factories. At first each town manufactured just one kind of article, depending on the kind of raw materials nearby. Some southern towns still specialize in one or two products. However, large factories in the Southeast now makes many kinds of goods.

One leading industry today is the manufacture of chemicals. Another leading industry is food processing. Other industries manufacture textiles, furniture, clothing, iron and steel, and paper products.

Vacationing

Many people visit the Southeast each year. They enjoy the beaches along the Atlantic and Gulf coasts. They vacation among the beautiful mountains, forests, lakes, and rivers.

Four national parks have been set aside in the southeastern states. The parks are visited by hundreds of people. Everglades National Park is in southern Florida. It is the largest subtropical wilderness and swamp in the United States. The Great Smoky Mountains National Park stretches along the border between North Carolina and Tennessee. It is a wooded highland. Mammoth Cave National Park, in Kentucky, is a huge cave with miles of passageways and an underground river. It has beautiful natural formations and lakes. Shenandoah National Park, in Virginia, is part of the Blue Ridge Mountains.

The Lincoln Memorial, Washington Monument, and Capitol are points along a line through the central area of Washington, D.C. Museums and other government buildings are close by.

People interested in our country's history visit the Southeast. Many important events of the past took place in these states.

Washington, D.C.

Washington, D.C., is the capital of the United States and the center of our national government. Members of Congress, members of the Supreme Court, and the President work in Washington, D.C. This city has many museums and interesting buildings. Washington, D.C., is an attraction for visitors from all over the world. Many businesses and organizations are located in this important city.

The great dome at the top of the Capitol can be seen from almost every part of Washington. Congress meets in the Capitol to make laws for the whole United States.

Near the Capitol is the Library of Congress, one of the finest libraries in the world. On the other side of the Capitol is the National Archives (är′kīvz) building, where our nation's records are kept. The Declaration of Independence and our Constitution are kept there. They are in a case covered with a special kind of glass to protect them.

For many years, the Supreme Court met in a special room in the Capitol. Now the Court meets in a white marble building with eight graceful columns.

On Pennsylvania Avenue, about one mile (1.6 km) from the Capitol, stands the White House. Our President lives and works in the White House while in office. The President's house is a fine building with deep porches surrounded by rolling lawns and shady trees.

Most of the people in Washington work in the government. They help in the task of running the country. Government is the main business of the capital.

Washington is also a city of monuments. The most famous of these are the Washington Monument and the Lincoln Memorial. The Jefferson Memorial, the newest of the three, is also a well-known Washington landmark.

The Washington Monument is a tall shaft made of marble and granite. It rises more than 500 feet (150 m) above the ground. From the windows near the top there is a fine view of the city.

A wide lawn slopes from the Washington Monument to a clear, deep pool. Its waters reflect the Washington Monument and the Lincoln Memorial, which stands at its other end. Wide marble steps lead to a hall in the Lincoln Memorial. Here is a large statue of President Abraham Lincoln. A ray of light seems always to fall on the quiet marble figure seated on the marble chair. People seldom talk as they look at this statue. Lincoln's eyes are kind and his smile friendly. He seems to say, "Come closer. I like people. Come and talk with me."

The head of Jefferson's huge statue almost touches the ceiling in the Jefferson Memorial. Everything else seems small next to this statue. It reminds visitors of Thomas Jefferson's belief in democracy, the idea that all people are created free and equal. Visitors leave thinking of the kind of democracy Jefferson wanted when he wrote the Declaration of Independence.

Washington, D.C., has many other points of interest. The Museum of African Art is located in Washington. The Smithsonian (smith sō′ nē ən') Institution is one of a number of other museums. Ford's Theater is the place where President Lincoln was shot. Plays, music, and dance are enjoyed at the Kennedy Center for the Performing Arts.

Chief Cities

Three of the twenty largest cities in the United States are in the Southeast. These cities are Baltimore, Maryland; Washington, D.C.; and Memphis, Tennessee.

Coast Cities

In early colonial times towns were built along the Atlantic Coast. Many of the towns started then are important cities today.

Baltimore, Maryland, on Chesapeake Bay, became an early trade center. Today it is the largest city in the Southeast. Baltimore ranks next to Birmingham in making iron and steel. Baltimore's factories make everything from heavy machinery and airplanes to railroad cars, chemicals, and food products. Fruit, vegetables, and seafood are canned there. The factories make the cans for these foods. Almost every kind of industry is found in Baltimore.

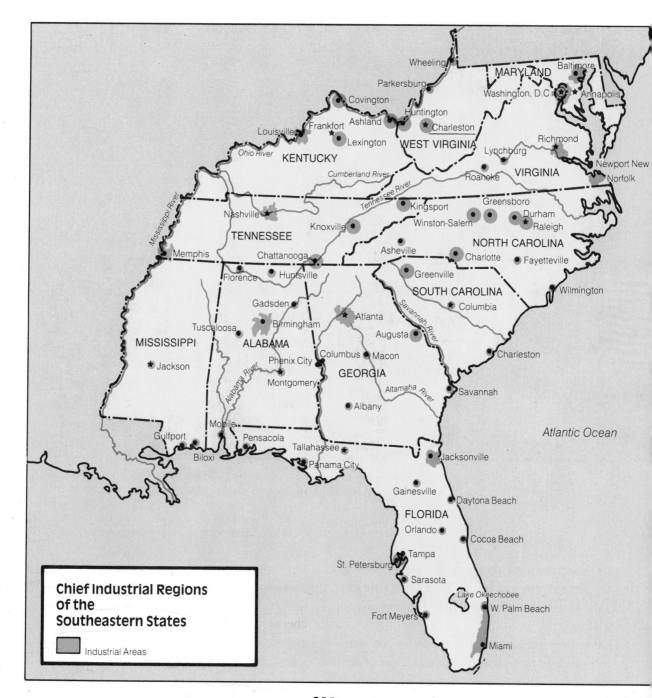

Chief Industrial Regions of the Southeastern States

Industrial Areas

285

Miami Beach has many hotels along the Atlantic coast. People from northern states enjoy visiting here during winter months. The weather is warm enough for swimming and outdoor sports.

There are many dairy farms near Annapolis (ə nap′ə lis), the capital of Maryland. Annapolis is the home of the United States Naval Academy.

The physical map of the southeastern states on page 261 shows that Chesapeake Bay is connected with the Atlantic Ocean by a narrow neck of water called Hampton Roads. This is one of the nation's busiest waterways. Norfolk and Newport News, in Virginia, are on Hampton Roads. Together they form the nation's largest shipbuilding center. Norfolk is the largest city in Virginia. It is the site of the biggest naval base in the United States.

To the south are Charleston, South Carolina, and Savannah (sə van′ə), Georgia. They are shipping and manufacturing cities. Both produce cotton textiles, wood pulp, other wood products, and fertilizer.

Jacksonville and Tampa, in Florida, are manufacturing and trade centers. Jacksonville, on the Atlantic Coast, makes cigars, articles of wood, and naval stores such as tar, pitch, and turpentine. It is Florida's largest city. Tampa's manufacturing plants package processed food. Phosphate ore is mined and exported from the port of Tampa.

Miami (mī am′ē), on the eastern coast of Florida, is a famous tourist city, which is also important for its ready-to-wear clothing factories. Many people fled to Miami from Cuba in the late 1950s and 1960s. Many Cubans settled in Florida.

Mobile (mō′bēl), Alabama, on Mobile Bay has one of the finest harbors on the Gulf Coast. From Central America comes *bauxite*, (bôk′sīt), the ore from which aluminum is made. Aluminum, fertilizer, cotton, and lumber products are exported. Mobile is the port for Birmingham.

Appalachian Cities

Birmingham, Alabama, is the chief manufacturing center of the southern Appalachian area. Birmingham and its neighboring cities form a large industrial region. This is a region of mining and quarrying, coking and smelting, making steel, and manufacturing iron-and-steel goods. Birmingham, Alabama's largest city, produces chemicals, transportation equipment, and processed food.

Chattanooga (chat′ə nōō′gə) and Knoxville (noks′vil′), in eastern Tennessee, manufacture heavy machinery, as well as smaller articles. These cities also produce cotton goods.

Wheeling, West Virginia, and Charleston, the capital of West Virginia, are railroad centers and river ports. They are on the Appalachian Highland, where coal and oil are found. They manufacture products from oil and iron and steel. Charleston is noted for making chemicals.

Piedmont Cities

Many industrial cities in the Piedmont are old market towns. They turned to manufacturing because they were close to raw materials and had water power.

Richmond, Virginia's capital, is one of the oldest manufacturing cities of the Southeast. Richmond's factories make tobacco products, cotton goods, rayon, and paper.

Winston-Salem and Durham (dur′əm), in North Carolina, lead the world in tobacco products. Greensboro (grēnz′bur′ō), North Carolina, also started by making tobacco products. Today it is a cotton textile center, too.

Charlotte (shär′lət), the largest city in North Carolina, is the center of a group of busy towns. They specialize in cotton textiles, rayon, and knitted goods. Columbia, the capital and largest city of South Carolina, produces textiles and fertilizers.

High Point, North Carolina, was one of the first southern cities to manufacture furniture on a large scale. Today it remains a leading furniture-making center. It also makes textiles, hosiery, mirrors, paints, and shipping containers.

Atlanta
A Modern Boom Town

Few southern cities suffered more in the Civil War than Atlanta, the capital and largest city of Georgia. In the battle of Atlanta, the city was burned to the ground and all but destroyed. But Atlanta rose from its ashes. Today it is a booming business capital of the southeastern states.

More than 1,500 factories are located in Atlanta. They make everything from iron-and-steel goods to chemicals and textiles. Canneries in Atlanta can peaches and other southern farm products. In addition to industry, many large nationwide businesses have established their headquarters there.

Atlanta is an inland city far from the coast. No navigable river is nearby. Yet it is a transportation center. In 1837, Atlanta was chosen as the location of the southern end of a railroad. Atlanta developed as a transportation and trade center. Many farm and factory products go through Atlanta. It has one of our country's busiest airports.

Atlanta's mild climate and booming industries attract many people to the city. With the help of the national government, the city set up neighborhood centers to help people find jobs. ■

River Cities

Louisville (loo′ē vil′), Kentucky, and Memphis (mem′fis), Tennessee, are river ports. They were both market centers in early times. Now they are manufacturing and trade centers. Each is the largest city in its state. Louisville, on the Ohio River, early became a market for the products of neighboring regions. Tobacco products, furniture, paints, and varnishes, electrical goods, bricks, and tile are made there. Louisville also makes baseball bats.

Memphis, Tennessee, is a large Mississippi River port. It began as a shipping port for cotton from the nearby farms and lumber from the surrounding bottom lands. Now it has many factories too. The factories make cotton goods and cottonseed products. Memphis is the world's largest market for cotton and hardwood.

Huntington, West Virginia, is a port city on the Ohio River. It is the largest city in the state.

Montgomery (mont gum′ər ē), the capital of Alabama, is also a river port. Jackson, the capital and largest city of Mississippi, lies on the Pearl River. Both cities are manufacturing and trade centers. Many oil companies have offices in Jackson because of the nearby oil fields. Montgomery also makes lumber products.

Other Cities

Nashville, the capital of Tennessee, lies in the center of the Nashville Basin. Dairy farmers in this region sell their products in Nashville.

Horses are bought, sold, and traded in Lexington, Kentucky, and in Frankfort, the state capital. Raleigh, the capital of North Carolina,

is a research center. The capital of Florida is Tallahassee (tal′ə has′ē). Many of the people there have government jobs. Tallahassee is also a trading center for dairy foods, fruits and nuts, and lumber.

In some places in the Southeast, entirely new cities have been built. They are called "satellite (sat′əl īt), communities" because they are on the edge of large metropolitan areas like Washington, D.C. However, they do not depend on the metropolitan areas. These communities have their own industries and are self-sufficient. One famous satellite community is Reston, Virginia. It is a carefully-planned small city with parks, lakes, and other recreation areas. Another similar community is Columbia, Maryland.

Do You Know?

1. Why did the government set up the Tennessee Valley Authority?
2. Why do farmers in the Southeast states practice crop rotation?
3. Why do trees grow easily in the southeastern states?
4. What minerals are found in the southeastern states?
5. What cities in Virginia form a large shipbuilding center?

To Help You Learn

Using New Words

bauxite   phosphate
boll   cultivator
dam   crop rotation
gap   growing season
rayon   citrus fruit
legume   subtropical land
cannery   dehydration
soybean   naval stores
reservoir   soil erosion
frontier   cotton belt
tung oil

The phrases below explain the words or terms listed above. Number a paper from 1 through 21. After each number write the word or term which matches the definition.

1. A place like a lake, formed behind a dam, where water is stored
2. A narrow valley in mountains
3. A mineral needed for growth by plants and animals
4. The region of a country lying along the border of an unsettled region
5. The ore from which aluminum is made
6. Turpentine, tar, and resin made from the gum of the pine tree
7. A wall or bank built across a river to stop the flow of water
8. The washing away of soil by heavy rains or floods
9. Area in the South where cotton grows well
10. The time of year when crops can be grown outdoors
11. Land that lies near the tropics
12. A way of building up the soil by planting different crops on the same land every 2 or 3 years
13. A kind of legume first brought to this country from China
14. A vegetable, such as peas or beans, that grows in pods
15. A machine used to loosen the soil and uproot weeds
16. Small seed pod of the cotton plant
17. Oil made from the nuts of a tree
18. The removal, or taking out, of water by a special process
19. Oranges, lemons, and grapefruit
20. A cloth that looks and feels like silk
21. A factory where food is prepared and canned

Finding the Facts

1. What plains make up the lowland of the southeastern states?
2. What highland forms an almost unbroken chain from Maryland to Alabama?
3. Describe the land in the Bluegrass Region and the Nashville Basin.
4. What four routes did pioneers use to cross the Appalachians?
5. What crop caused planters to rush to present-day Mississippi and Alabama?

6. Why did the Creek Indians attack Fort Mims in Alabama? What was the result?
7. How are tenant farmers and sharecroppers alike? How are they different?
8. Why was the cotton gin so important?
9. Who improved agriculture in the southeastern states?
10. What did Orville and Wilbur Wright do in 1903? Why did they choose Kitty Hawk?
11. How has the Tennessee Valley Authority helped conservation?
12. What are some uses of the cotton plant?
13. What was the first money crop raised in our country?
14. What legumes, nuts, and fruits are grown in the Southeast?
15. Why are the southeastern coastal states a good fishing area? What shellfish are shipped to other parts of the country from the Southeast?
16. What different products are obtained from trees in the southeastern states?
17. What is phosphate used for?
18. Why did many northern factories move to the southeastern states?
19. What are some famous monuments in Washington, D.C.?
20. What is the capital of each southeastern state? What is the largest city of each?

Learning from Maps

1. On the map of the United States on pages A-6– A-7 locate the southeastern states. Between what parallels of latitude do the southeastern states lie?

2. Turn to the map of the southeastern states on page 261. What body of water borders the southeastern states on the east? What body of water borders them on the south? Where are mountains found? What is the highest peak? Which southeastern state is entirely plains?
3. Look at the map of the TVA on page 271. What river flows through this area? What dams are in Alabama?
4. Look at the map of chief industrial regions of the southeastern states on page 285. Which states have industrial areas along their coast? What state has the least amount of industry?

Using Study Skills

1. **Time Line:** Arrange the following events in the correct order. Your text will help you find when each event took place.
   Kentucky becomes a state
   Alabama becomes a state
   Atlanta chosen as railroad location
   Tennessee becomes a state
2. **Chart:** Make a chart of the southeastern states like the one you made for Unit 5, page 256.
3. **Graph:** Look at the graph on page 274. In which year was the least amount of cotton produced? In which year was the greatest amount of cotton produced?
   Did the amount of cotton produced between 1977 and 1978 increase or decrease? Did the amount produced between 1981 and 1982 increase or decrease?

How much cotton was produced in 1976? About how much more was produced in 1979 than in 1978?

4. **Diagram.** Look at the diagram showing cotton processing on page 274. Arrange the steps below in the correct order.

Gin removes seeds

Cotton is picked

Fibers are spun into thread

Threads are woven into cloth

Cotton fibers are combed

Thinking It Through

1. After the invention of the cotton gin slavery developed rapidly. If the gin had not been invented, do you think slavery might have gradually disappeared? Why or why not?

2. During the 1900s many northern factories moved to the southeastern states. How did this change the southeastern states? What might this region be like if factories had not moved there?

3. Birmingham, Alabama, is often called the "Pittsburgh of the South." How do you explain this?

4. Many Americans are moving to the "Sunbelt." The southeastern states make up part of the "Sunbelt." Why do you think people choose to move to this area?

Projects

1. You might like to make a classroom movie which tells the story of cotton. To do this, you need a roll of narrow shelfpaper. On the paper draw pictures one under the other, beginning with the planting of cotton seed and ending with pictures of finished goods made from cotton. Write short captions. Fasten each end to a short stick and show your movie.

2. Many historical buildings are still standing in the Southeast. Find as many pictures of these as you can in magazines and newspapers. Make a scrapbook or put them on a bulletin board and put labels under them.

3. The Research Committee might find out more about the Indian groups mentioned in this unit. How did the Indians live before they were forced to leave their lands? How did their lives change when they moved?

4. Pretend you work for the government of a southeastern state. Make a pamphlet explaining why a certain factory should set up a plant in your state. Include pictures in the pamphlet. Decide which state you work for and what factory you desire.

5. The Reading Committee might ask the librarian for books about the southeastern states. Try to get books about the pioneers, the Indians, the TVA, and the people you read about in this unit.

10 The North Central States

Unit Preview

In 1783 the United States reached from the Atlantic Coast to the Mississippi River. Most people lived near the Atlantic Coast. But pioneers already were looking westward.

Part of today's North Central region was, in 1783, the Northwest Territory. Five North Central states were carved from this region: Illinois, Indiana, Ohio, Michigan, and Wisconsin. After the Louisiana Territory was bought, seven other North Central states were formed from this territory: Minnesota, Iowa, Missouri, North Dakota, South Dakota, Nebraska, and Kansas.

The government set up a plan so sections of the territories could become states. Many people moved into the territories to get the free land offered by the government.

Settlers found in the region of the North Central states some of the world's best corn and wheat lands. It has remained so, but it has also become a great industrial region. The discovery of iron ore opened up this area to industrialization.

Good transportation systems have helped industries and farms in the North Central states. The Mississippi River provides a waterway for shipping products to the sea. Barges can move the products south to New Orleans. The St. Lawrence Seaway, connected with the Great Lakes, also offers access to the sea. Ocean-going ships can move between the Great Lakes and the Atlantic Ocean.

Things to Discover

If you look carefully at the picture, map, and time line, you can answer these questions.

1. How many states are in the North Central region?
2. When did Congress set up a plan of government for the Northwest Territory?
3. What important type of work done in the North Central states is shown in the picture?
4. What natural features form part of the border for some North Central states?
5. How was travel made easier after 1811?
6. What important raw material for industry was discovered in the region? When?
7. Marietta, Ohio, was the first settlement in the Northwest Territory. When was it founded?
8. When was the Louisiana Territory purchased?

Words to Learn

You will meet these words in this unit. As you read, you will learn what they mean and how to pronounce them. The Word List will help you.

bran	reaper
combine	seed drill
disk harrow	sod
expedition	sterilize
linseed oil	surplus product
open-pit mining	taconite
pasteurize	territory
prairie	threshing machine
processing	toll

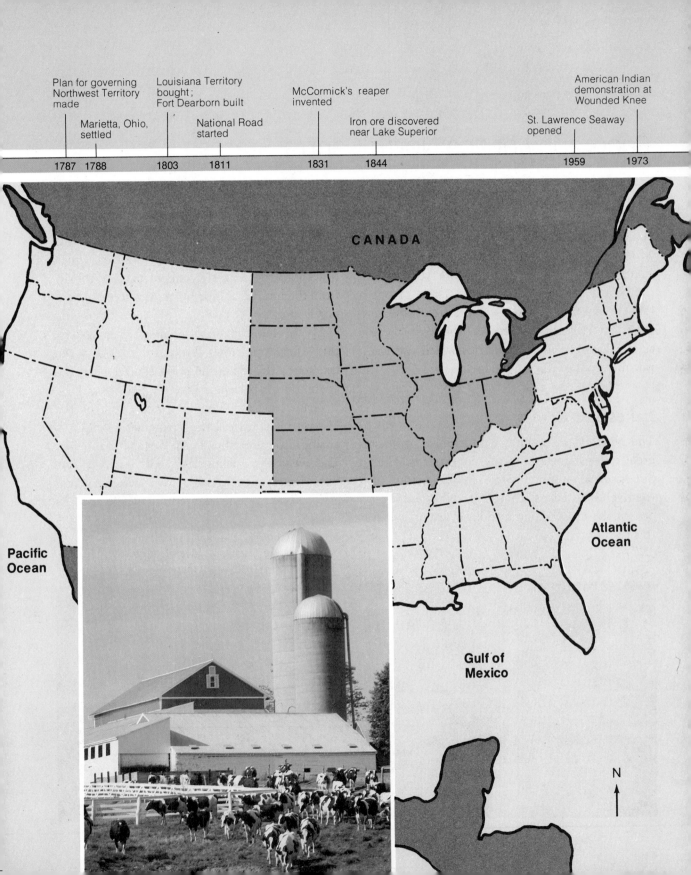

Plan for governing Northwest Territory made

Marietta, Ohio, settled

Louisiana Territory bought; Fort Dearborn built

National Road started

McCormick's reaper invented

Iron ore discovered near Lake Superior

St. Lawrence Seaway opened

American Indian demonstration at Wounded Knee

1787 1788   1803   1811   1831   1844   1959   1973

CANADA

Pacific Ocean

Atlantic Ocean

Gulf of Mexico

N

1
Geography of the North Central States

The North Central states are Ohio, Michigan, Indiana, Illinois, Wisconsin, Minnesota, Iowa, Missouri, Kansas, Nebraska, and North and South Dakota. Almost everywhere you go in the North Central states you see farms of one kind or another. These twelve states produce food for millions of people. Some of these states also have great industries which use the raw materials of the region.

Lakes and Rivers

The North Central states are fortunate to have great water highways. In these states are Lakes Superior, Michigan, Huron, and Erie, four of the five Great Lakes. These busy lakes make up one of the most important inland waterways in this country.

The Great Lakes are connected with each other by small rivers and lakes. They are also connected with the St. Lawrence River, which flows into the Atlantic. This forms a waterway from the middle of North America to the Atlantic Ocean.

Much of our nation's greatest river system, the Mississippi, flows through the North Central states. It drains the wide central plain between the Appalachians and the Rockies.

Giant concrete dams have been built on the Missouri River, the largest tributary of the Mississippi. Behind the dams are artificial lakes. These dams and lakes help control floods, furnish electric power, and provide water for irrigation. The Missouri River is navigable as far as

Chicago, Illinois, is on the west side of Lake Michigan. It is the largest city in the North Central states.

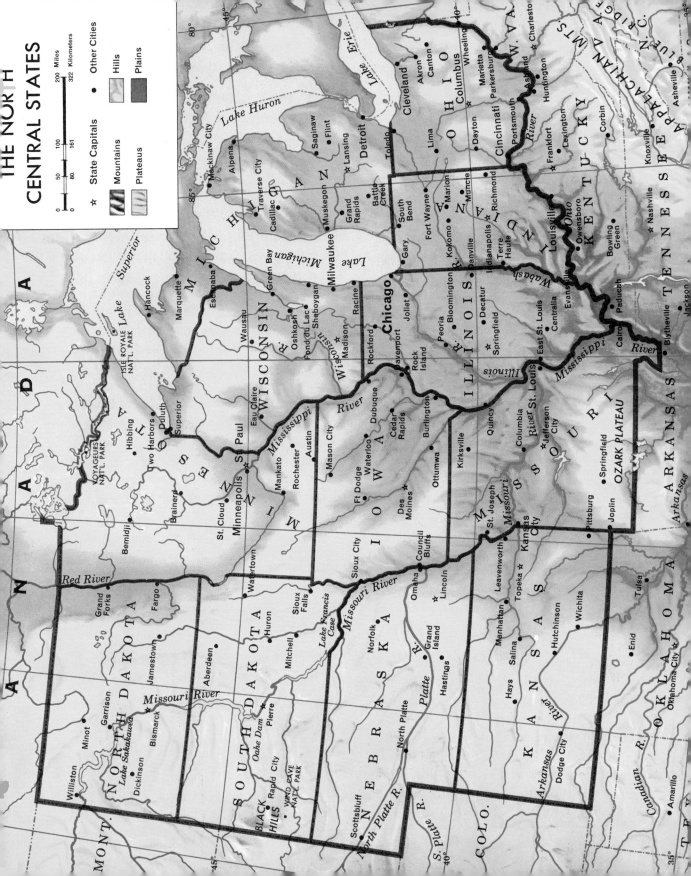

Sioux City, Iowa. It flows into the Mississippi just north of St. Louis.

At Cairo, Illinois, the Ohio River joins the Mississippi. Starting at Pittsburgh, the Ohio River is navigable its entire length. The Ohio and Missouri rivers help make the Mississippi a mighty river.

Soil and Surface

Thousands of years ago the great glacier that covered northern North America covered much of the North Central states. As it moved southward, it left thin soil, bare rocks, and hills in some places. For the most part it left deep, rich soil and stretches of level and gently rolling land. Because of the deep, rich soil farmers there can grow good crops. The level and gently rolling land makes it easy for farmers to use machinery. It also keeps the soil from being washed away easily by rain.

Most of the North Central states is lowland. These states are part of a plain that stretches for more than 1,000 miles (1,600 km) from the Appalachians to the Rockies. See the map of these states on page 297 and the map of the United States on pages A-6–A-7.

A rough, hilly region extends southward from Canada into Michigan, Wisconsin, and Minnesota. This is a region of lakes, forests, and rocks. Eastern Ohio is part of the Allegheny Plateau. Southern Missouri is part of the hilly Ozark Plateau. In southwestern South Dakota, the Black Hills break the stretch of rolling plains. These hills are higher than the Appalachians but lower than the Rockies.

Climate

The North Central states have a favorable climate for farming. The summers are usually hot and the winters cold. But the northern part of this region has longer, colder winters and shorter, cooler summers than the southern part. The growing season is about 4 months long in the northern part. In the southern part it is 6 months long. This is long enough for wheat, corn, and oats to grow and ripen.

The rainfall of these states is also favorable for growing many kinds of crops. Most of this region receives between 20 and 40 inches (51 and 102 cm) of rainfall each year. A few places receive more than 40 inches (102 cm). Western North Dakota, South Dakota, Nebraska, and Kansas receive less than 20 inches (51 cm) a year. Farmers there plant crops that need small amounts of rain to grow, or they irrigate their crops.

The differences in the growing season, rainfall, and temperature make parts of the North Central states better suited to one crop than to another. Because of these differences it is possible to raise a variety of crops and livestock.

Do You Know?

1. What are the twelve North Central states?
2. What is the surface of the North Central states like?
3. What great waterways are in these states?

2

Settling the North Central States

George Rogers Clark and those with him, you remember, captured the Northwest Territory from the British during the Revolutionary War. This territory stretched from the Ohio River north to the Great Lakes and as far west as the Mississippi River. Find this area on the map of the Northwest Territory on this page.

The Northwest Territory

The Northwest Territory was first claimed by France. Then the British defeated the French and gained control of it. After the Revolutionary War it became part of the new nation, the United States of America.

Several eastern states claimed part of the Northwest Territory. It had been granted to them, they said, in their colonial charters. But Maryland, which had no western lands, did not favor these claims.

"We are now under one government," Maryland declared. "All western lands should belong to the national government, not to the states."

New York led the way by giving up its claims to the western lands. One by one, the other states gave up their claims, too. The land then became a *territory* (ter'ə tor'ē) of the United States. A territory is a settled area, not yet a state, which is governed by Congress.

Plan of Government

In 1787 Congress made a plan of government for its new land. By this plan the Northwest Territory, as the whole land was called, was to be divided into smaller areas which could become states. The plan had three steps.

At first the whole territory would be controlled by Congress. A governor, secretary, and three judges would make the laws and see that they were carried out.

When there were 5,000 voters in an area, the settlers could elect their own assembly. They could make their own laws and raise money by taxes. They would also elect a representative who would advise Congress about their affairs. An area so organized became a territory.

Five states were formed from the Northwest Territory. What are they? What rivers border this territory? How do you think it got its name?

When such a territory had 60,000 free inhabitants, it could become a state. The people would write their own constitution. When Congress approved it, the territory would join the Union as a new state. It could then send a representative to Congress to help make the laws. Best of all, the new state would have the same rights that the old states had. The plan also promised the settlers certain rights in helping to govern themselves.

This plan of government was very successful.

Indians lost their land when settlers moved west. From what part of the Northwest Territory did the Indians first move? The Trail of Tears is the path the Cherokees took to Oklahoma.

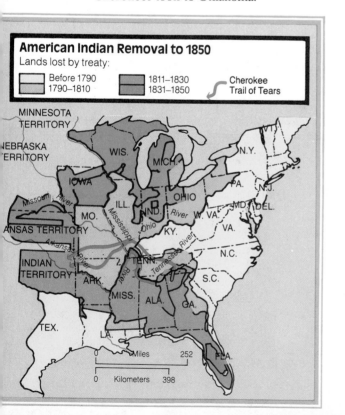

American Indian Removal to 1850

Lands lost by treaty:

Before 1790	1811–1830
1790–1810	1831–1850

Cherokee Trail of Tears

MINNESOTA TERRITORY

NEBRASKA TERRITORY

WIS.

MICH.

N.Y.

IOWA

ILL.

OHIO

PA.

N.J.

MO.

IND.

River

MD. DEL.

W. VA.

Missouri River

Mississippi

Ohio

KY.

VA.

ANSAS TERRITORY

Arkansas River

TENN.

Tennessee River

N.C.

INDIAN TERRITORY

ARK.

S.C.

MISS.

ALA.

GA.

TEX.

LA.

FLA.

0   Miles   252

0   Kilometers   398

It was used as a pattern in all new territories of the United States. *North west*

Settling the Northwest Territory

Besides making a plan for governing the Northwest Territory, Congress had to decide how the land was to be settled. Should it be sold or given away to settlers? The struggling young nation needed money. So it sold large tracts of land to people who formed land companies. These companies would make money by selling the land to settlers.

First settlements in Ohio

One of the first land companies was formed by a group of citizens in Boston. They bought 1,500,000 acres (600,000 ha) of land along the Ohio River. General Rufus Putnam, who fought in the Revolution, was their leader.

General Putnam and those with him made their settlement at the mouth of the Muskingum River in 1788. They named it Marietta. It was the first settlement in the Northwest Territory under the new plan.

Another settlement made on the Ohio River was Cincinnati. Later Moses Cleveland made a settlement on Lake Erie. Find these towns on the map of the Northwest Territory, page 299.

War with the American Indians

As people moved into the Northwest Territory, they settled on lands that belonged to the American Indians. The Indians fought to keep their lands. The British, who hoped to get back the Northwest Territory, also urged the American Indians to fight the settlers. President Washington sent General Anthony Wayne to protect the settlers. At the battle of Fallen Timbers, General Wayne defeated a group of American Indians made up of the Shawnees (shô nēz'), Ottawas (ot'ə wəz), Chippewas (chip'ə wäz), and Potawatomis (pot'ə wot'ə mēz). The American Indians were forced to move from most of the Ohio region.

Settlers kept moving westward taking more American Indian lands. Tecumseh (ti kum'sə), a Shawnee chief, worked to help American Indians keep their lands. But soldiers led by William Henry Harrison defeated a group of Shawnees at the battle of Tippecanoe. The Indians were forced to move from what is now Indiana.

The last fighting in the Northwest Territory that involved the Indians was the Black Hawk War. The Sauk (sôk) and Fox Indians were defeated. They were forced to leave what is now Illinois and move to a reservation in Iowa.

Routes to the Western Lands

Settlers now poured into the region north of the Ohio River. There were four main routes used by the pioneers to get beyond the Appalachian Mountains. Beyond the mountains, the Ohio River became the great highway to the Northwest. Tens of thousands of settlers used this river to reach the western lands.

Look at the map of routes to the west on page 263. Pioneers followed the Great Valley, through the Cumberland Gap, to the Kentucky River. They followed this river northwest to the Ohio River. From the Great Valley, pioneers also followed the Kanawha River to the Ohio.

Two rough roads across Pennsylvania and Maryland led pioneers to Fort Pitt, now Pittsburgh, on the Ohio River.

Pioneers from New England and New York traveled west along the Hudson and Mohawk rivers to Lake Erie. Some continued westward along its southern shore. Others traveled on the lake. This route provided the easiest way through the mountains. After the Revolutionary War, this lowland route became important. Pioneers traveled on foot, on horseback, by covered wagon, and by boat.

Transportation by Boat

One kind of boat used by the pioneers was a flatboat. It was a flat-bottomed boat with square ends. Another kind of boat that carried pioneers was a keelboat. It was longer and narrower than a flatboat. It had a narrow platform on each side. People walked along the platform and pushed the boat through the water with long poles. Some keelboats had masts and sails that could be used too.

Moving in Covered Wagons

Those who traveled by covered wagon had to plan carefully. Heavy furniture had to be left behind. But the wagon was big enough to carry household goods and farming tools. It could carry seed corn and enough food for the long journey west.

Covered wagons were shaped like boats. They were higher at both ends than in the middle. The wheels were large. Over the tops of the wagons were curved bows which supported white canvas covers. Strong oxen pulled the

301

Covered wagons were a good way for families to move their belongings. These settlers are crossing the plains to the West. What animals did they take with them? Why?

wagons slowly. The rough roads made the wagons sway from side to side.

Life in a New Settlement

The pioneers had to find a place to live. Some wanted to settle in villages and towns. Others looked for farms.

Farmers often settled near a river or stream. Fine crops could be grown on the rich, level land of the river valley. The river could be used for travel.

Some farmers chose a spot where large trees grew. They thought the soil was fertile because trees grew there. Besides, trees furnished wood for building houses and fences. They also supplied fuel for the fireplace.

Other settlers were happy when they found a grassy meadow or an open place in the forest.

Here crops could be planted with little trouble. The land did not have to be cleared of trees and bushes.

As soon as possible, they planted a small patch of corn. Corn was the pioneers' best crop. It could be eaten by people as well as by animals. Corn husks were made into mattresses for the beds. The cobs were often used for fuel.

A House-Raising

Food and shelter were the things settlers needed most. Their first shelter was often a log hut with only three walls. The other side of the hut was open. The roof sloped to the ground. Such log huts sheltered many pioneers until they could build a better home.

Good neighbors were very important in helping build a more permanent home. People were glad to help new neighbors get settled.

There was much work to be done. Trees had to be cut down and underbrush, or thick bushes, cleared away to make room for the new home. Logs had to be carefully chosen, trimmed of branches, and cut to the right lengths.

The neighbors began to arrive early in the morning. They chopped down trees and rolled the logs to the clearing. Then they cut the logs to the right length and notched them so that they would fit together. Four logs were laid to form a foundation. Walls were made by putting one log on top of another to a height of 7 or 8 feet (2.1 or 2.4 m). The roof was made by placing poles to form a gable. The poles were then covered with shingles.

Willing hands made the work go fast. By sunset the one-room cabin was finished. The family was glad to have their new home.

Husking and Quilting Bees

Neighbors helped one another with other jobs that were too big for one family to do alone. Sometimes neighbors gathered for a husking bee. Husking meant taking the husks or outside leaves from the ears of corn. Two teams would race to husk a pile of corn. After the husking bee everyone would enjoy supper. Later everyone would enjoy a lively square dance.

A quilting bee provided another occasion for neighbors to get together. Quilts are bedcovers. The top covers of quilts are usually of patchwork, or small bright scraps of cloth sewed together. The bottom cover is often a piece of plain cloth. Layers of cotton or wool are placed between covers. Then the covers are quilted, or stitched together in lines or patterns.

Pioneers could build a log house in one day. Everyone helped. Men and women had many things to do until the job was done. What activities do you see?

Marketing Goods

By the early 1800s thousands of people had settled in the Northwest Territory. Fields of grain and pasture lands had taken the place of forests. Villages and towns had sprung up.

More corn, tobacco, hogs, sheep, and wheat than the settlers could use, or *surplus products* (sur′plus′ prod′əkts), began to be raised on the farms. People in towns and cities of the East wanted to buy these surplus products. But it cost too much to send them across the Appalachians to the eastern cities.

The pioneers in the Northwest Territory found a way to solve their problem. Many of their farms were along the Ohio River, or along the streams flowing into it. Transportation on it was easy and cheap.

"Our corn, tobacco, and pork can be loaded at our own landing," they said proudly. "Our boats can float downstream on the Ohio to the Mississippi and on down to the port of New Orleans.

"Ships come to New Orleans from Europe, the West Indies, and cities along our Atlantic Coast. We can get a good price for our products by sending them to New Orleans."

As time passed, settlers in the Ohio Country sold more and more of their products in New Orleans. They bought manufactured goods and other things they needed. So trade grew up between the Ohio settlers and the merchants of New Orleans, the great Mississippi River port.

The Louisiana Purchase

No sooner had the farmers found a place to sell their surplus products than they faced another problem. New Orleans and the land west of the Mississippi belonged to Spain.

While Washington was President, Congress made a treaty with Spain. With this agreement settlers could send their products down the Mississippi. They could land their goods at New Orleans without paying a tax.

Then the news came that Spain had given New Orleans and all the Louisiana Territory to France.

France was a great, powerful nation. It could stop the trade at New Orleans if its leader wished.

President Jefferson greatly feared that this might happen. He was also afraid that the farmers might even try to capture New Orleans themselves. That would mean war with France!

President Jefferson sent James Monroe to France to join our representative there. He hoped they could persuade France's leader to sell New Orleans and the land around it. To everyone's surprise, France offered to sell not only New Orleans but all the Louisiana Territory. This vast plains region stretched from the Mississippi River to the Rocky Mountains.

The United States agreed to buy the Louisiana Territory. It would pay 15 million dollars for the region.

When the United States bought Louisiana Territory in 1803, it doubled the size of the young nation. Much of the region of our North Central states was part of this territory. The great Mississippi River system and the rich land it drained became part of our nation.

Exploring the Louisiana Territory

Little was known about this huge region west of the Mississippi. President Jefferson asked Meriwether Lewis to lead an *expedition* (eks'pə dish'ən), or exploring party, into the region. See the map of this expedition, page 305.

Young Meriwether Lewis was President Jefferson's private secretary. He asked William Clark to go with him on this important expedition. William was the younger brother of George Rogers Clark.

The President asked Lewis and Clark to trace the Missouri River to its source, or beginning. He also wanted them to cross the mountains and find a way to the Pacific Ocean. As they traveled, they were to take careful notes about the soil, climate, animals, plants, and minerals.

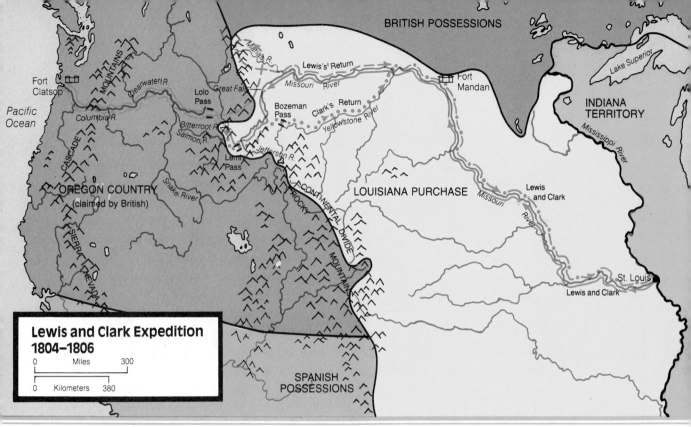

Meriwether Lewis and William Clark explored the Louisiana Territory for two years. Why do you think the explorers took separate routes back?

The President also hoped they would gain the good will of the Indians living in the region.

The reports and maps that Lewis and Clark brought back gave much information. People began to realize what a huge, rich country lay beyond the Mississippi. They called it the new West. The journey of Lewis and Clark also gave our country a claim to the land between the Rocky Mountains and the Pacific Ocean. This was known as the Oregon Country.

New States: Ohio, Indiana, Illinois

By 1803 so many people lived in Ohio that Congress allowed it to enter the Union as a state. Ohio was the first state to be made from the Northwest Territory. Because the plan of government for the Northwest Territory did not permit slavery, Ohio came in as a free state. Within the next 15 years Indiana and Illinois also came in as free states.

Problems in the New West

Pioneers kept moving west. When they found much of the land in the Northwest Territory taken up, they settled in Louisiana Territory.

In 1818 Missouri asked to join the Union. It had been settled by people from the South who had slaves. So Missouri wanted to come in as a slave state. As yet no law had been made about slavery in the Louisiana Territory. Also our country had the same number of slave states as free states. This balance would be upset if Missouri became a slave state.

The Missouri Compromise

For 2 years Congress quarreled over how Missouri was to come into the Union. The Missouri Compromise finally settled the quarrel. A compromise is an agreement in which each side gives up something that it wants. Under this compromise Missouri was to be admitted as a slave state. Maine, far to the north, was to be admitted as a free state. The number of slave and free states would still be equal. The North and the South would have exactly the same number of members and votes in the Senate.

The compromise also decided the question of slavery in the Louisiana Territory. The southern boundary of Missouri was to be the dividing line between slave and free states. All new states formed north of this line except Missouri were to be free states. New states formed south of this line would be permitted to have slaves.

Kansas and Nebraska

For a while the slavery question in the Louisiana Territory appeared to be settled. Two states had been formed in this region. Each had entered the Union as the compromise stated.

Arkansas was admitted in 1836 as a slave state. It was south of Missouri. Iowa came in as a free state in 1846. It was north of Missouri. People thought the Missouri Compromise would continue to work. They were disappointed.

In 1854 a new law was presented to Congress. This law stated that the land bordering Missouri on the west and lying just north of its southern boundary would become two territo-ries. The southern part was to be called Kansas Territory. The northern part was to be the Nebraska Territory.

No one objected to this part of the law. But another part caused much trouble. It stated that the settlers in each territory had the right to decide whether or not to permit slavery.

People began taking sides at once. "Kansas and Nebraska are north of the line agreed upon in the Missouri Compromise," said Northeners. "The slavery question in this territory was settled by that compromise. It must stand."

Southerners were in favor of the new law. It gave a chance for another slave state and more Southern senators.

Slavery became more of a problem than ever. Even the members of Congress quarreled about it. But they finally passed the law.

People soon learned what the new law meant. Neither Northerners nor Southerners were concerned about Nebraska. Everyone thought it would be a free state. In Kansas the story was different. Find Kansas on the map of the North Central states on page 297.

Since the settlers themselves could decide whether the state was to be slave or free, the race was on. Northern settlers rushed in hoping to make it a free state. Southern planters hurried there to win it for slavery. For almost 7 years there were bitter quarrels and arguments between the two groups. At last Kansas came into the Union as a free state.

Quarrels of this kind led to bitter feeling between the North and the South. As you know, the difference of opinion over slavery led to the Civil War.

Cyrus McCormick invented a *reaper* that helped farmers cut grain faster than they could cut it by hand. Cyrus is shown behind his reaper when it was tried out in 1831. People were surprised and delighted to see that the reaper really worked.

Farming on the Prairies

When the pioneers went beyond the Mississippi, they found a new kind of land. They saw miles of gently rolling plains covered with tall, thick grass. These grassy plains were called *prairies* (prer′ēz). On and on the prairies stretched. Trees were few, except along the rivers.

Some settlers chose land for their farm along the streams where there were trees. Others settled on the open prairies. It was hard work breaking the thick *sod* (sod). Sod is the part of the soil containing grass and its roots. The pi-

oneers raised fine crops from the rich prairie soil. The prairie grass made good hay for pasture. Logs were scarce. Many pioneers built their homes of sod.

Cyrus McCormick, Inventor

When people learned that fine crops could be grown on the prairies, more settlers came. But harvesting had to be done by hand. It was slow, hard work. A *reaper* (rē′pər) was needed for cutting grain. Such a harvesting machine was built by Cyrus McCormick.

Cyrus was born in Virginia in 1809. There he watched his father try many times to make a reaper. Cyrus, too, began to work on the machine. He finally succeeded in 1831.

Then Cyrus McCormick moved to Chicago, Illinois, so that he could be near the prairie farms where wheat was grown. Cyrus built a factory in Chicago that made reapers.

Many farmers began to use the McCormick reaper because it saved time and money. Later, a new and strong steel plow was invented. With it the tough prairie sod could be plowed more easily. Then people by the thousands came to these grassy plains.

Free Land to Settlers

The United States doubled in size when it bought Louisiana Territory. When people wanted any of the new land, they had to buy it from the government. After a while they began to say, "The United States owns a great deal of land. Much of it has no settlers. The government should give some of it to us."

In 1862, during the Civil War, Congress passed the Homestead Act. This was a law that permitted a person to select 160 acres (64 ha) of government land. At the end of 5 years the land belonged to the person if that person planted crops on it and lived on it.

When the Civil War ended, thousands of soldiers returned to their homes. Some wanted to begin a new life on land of their own. The Homestead Act helped them. Many families went west and lived on this government land. Some blacks also went west after the Civil War. Most settled in Kansas and started farms.

Losing More Land

Once again as people moved westward they took American Indian lands. Fighting between the American Indians and the soldiers took place. Each side won some battles. The Sioux (soo) defeated General George Custer at the battle of Little Bighorn in Montana. But later, Sitting Bull and other Sioux were trapped by the soldiers at Wounded Knee Creek in South Dakota.

Many American Indians live in the North Central states today. Most live in South Dakota. During the 1970s some American Indian groups demanded the return of some of the lands taken from them in the past. In 1973 at Wounded Knee, South Dakota, the American Indian Movement drew attention to the Indians' problems and demands. This group held the town against federal agents for 71 days. Finally the government promised to study their complaints.

Travel by Road

Today it is easy for us to travel. The pioneers were not so fortunate, however. They had to find ways to get from one part of the country to another.

The first roads followed paths made by the American Indians or wild animals. Some pioneers blazed trails through the forests. Later, these trails were widened and improved. New roads were also built. On some, logs were laid side by side. Others were made of boards or thick planks. Still others were built of stone and gravel.

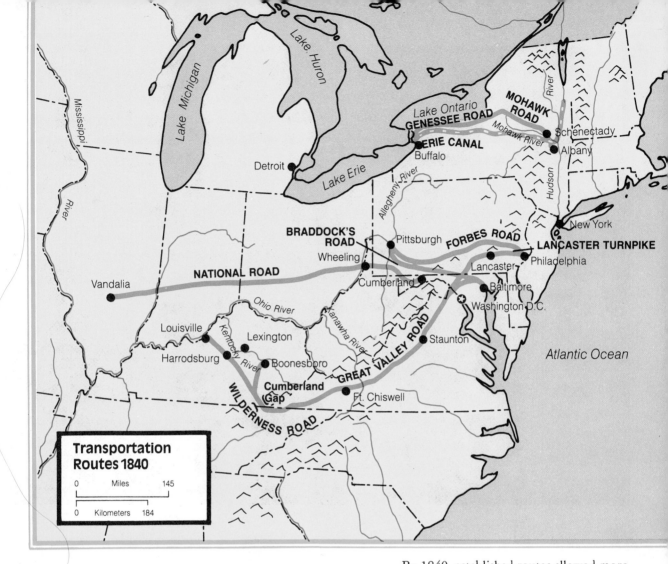

By 1840, established routes allowed more people to move to the West. Settlers beyond the Appalachians used these routes to send their products east.

The National Road

One of the best and most important highways of its time was built by our government. This fine road was about 30 feet (9 m) wide. It was built of broken stone with stone bridges across the streams. Because the government built it, it was called the National Road.

The National Road began at Cumberland, Maryland, and went to Wheeling, on the Ohio River. It was extended westward across Ohio,

Indiana, and Illinois to Vandalia. Later, another road was added to extend the National Road to St. Louis on the Mississippi River. This was the first time our government had built a road. Find this road on the transportation map on this page. It is part of U.S. 40 today.

Travel was heavy on the National Road. Big covered wagons pulled by powerful teams of horses moved freight on it. Over it rolled farm wagons, market wagons, and buggies. Cattle,

The Erie Canal was built through towns and under road bridges. Travel along the canal brought trade to towns and helped them grow. How did boats move through the canal?

sheep, and hogs were driven to market over the road, and thousands of pioneers used it to travel westward. Later, railroads extended westward. As the railroads were built, the National Road became less important.

Toll roads

Many of the improved roads were built by business people to make money. They charged a *toll* (tōl), or money, for using the road. There are toll roads today run by governments.

Travel by Water and Rail

For years people wondered, "Can boats be moved without sails or oars?" When the steam engine was invented, people began to try to run boats with steam power.

The Clermont

In 1807 Robert Fulton proved that steam power can run boats. His boat, the *Clermont,* started in New York and puffed its way up the Hudson. The *Clermont* reached Albany in 32 hours. Here at last was a boat that did not depend on the wind. It was moved by steam power. It could even travel against the wind. This made up-stream travel faster and easier. Within a few years steamboats traveled on all the important waterways.

The Erie Canal

Travel by water is cheaper than travel by land. Where there were no waterways, people often dug canals to connect bodies of water. Many canals were built during the first half of the 1800s.

The most famous was the Erie Canal, which connected the Hudson River with Lake Erie. See the transportation map, page 309. It was an all-water route between the Great Lakes and the Atlantic Ocean. Eastern merchants and manu-facturers used it to send goods and supplies to the North Central states. Meat, lumber, and grain from these states went through the canal to eastern cities. Thousands of pioneers traveled part of the way to the West on the canal.

Early Railroads

By the 1830s railroads were coming into use. The first railroads were built in the East. They usually joined one town with another.

Passengers rode in cars built like stage-coaches. These early trains were uncomfortable and not very safe. The windows had no glass. The cars swayed, and it was hard for passengers to keep their seats. Sparks and cinders some-times burned holes in clothes.

As time passed, safer, longer railroads were built. Towns and cities grew up along the rail-road tracks.

The St. Lawrence Seaway

The Great Lakes and the St. Lawrence River are shared by Canada and the United States. Ships of the two countries use the lakes, their canals, and connecting rivers.

For years the people of Canada and the United States hoped to make the St. Lawrence River a seaway. To do this both the river and the waterways between the Great Lakes had to be deepened and widened. Then ocean-going vessels could sail from the Atlantic Ocean directly to cities on the Great Lakes.

In 1959 their dream came true. The two governments worked to make the St. Lawrence and the waterways between the lakes usable for larger ocean-going ships. Narrow places were widened and shallow places deepened. Canals and dams were built. It was like adding a new seacoast to many cities of the United States.

Do You Know?

1. Where was the Northwest Territory? What states were made from it?
2. What plan of government did Congress set up for this territory?
3. Why did pioneers need a Mississippi port?
4. What was the Louisiana Purchase?
5. What was the Missouri Compromise? How did the law of 1854 change it?

Before You Go On

Using New Words

sod   territory
toll   expedition
prairie   surplus product
reaper

The phrases below explain the words or terms listed above. Number a page from 1 through 7. After each number write the word or term that matches the definition.

1. A settled area, not yet a state, that is governed by Congress
2. An exploring party
3. That which is left when needs are satisfied
4. A small sum of money paid for use of a road
5. A grassy plain
6. The part of the soil containing grass and its roots
7. A machine for cutting grain

Finding the Facts

1. Why are the North Central states an important farming region?
2. When would a territory become a state?
3. What Shawnee chief worked to help American Indians keep their lands?
4. What purchase did the United States make in 1803 that doubled the size of our country?
5. What agreement decided the question of slavery in the Louisiana Territory?
6. Why did Cyrus McCormick build a reaper factory in Chicago, Illinois?
7. How did the Homestead Act help to settle the West?
8. What road began in Cumberland, Maryland, and extended to St. Louis?
9. Who built the first successful steamboat?
10. Why was the Erie Canal important?
11. What is the St. Lawrence Seaway?

3

Living and Working in the North Central States

Farming is a very important business. It helps to feed people throughout the world. Rich farmlands make the North Central states a valuable part of our country. A large number of people make their living on farms in these states.

Important Crops

The greatest corn-growing region of our country is in the North Central states. It is called the corn belt. It stretches from Ohio to the central part of Nebraska. Find it on the map of the corn belt on page 314. Here you will find more fields of corn than of any other crop.

Throughout the corn belt the growing season is at least 5 months long. Most kinds of field corn need this much time to grow and ripen before the heavy frosts come. A heavy frost usually kills plants or stops their growth. The hot summer days and nights of the corn belt are good for corn. There are frequent showers, especially in May and June. The rich soil, the level and gently rolling land, the long growing season, and plenty of rain are just right for corn. These things combine to make the corn belt the best corn-growing region in the world.

Harvesting corn is an easy job with the help of a mechanical picker. This machine picks the corn, removes the husks, and drops the corn in a wagon.

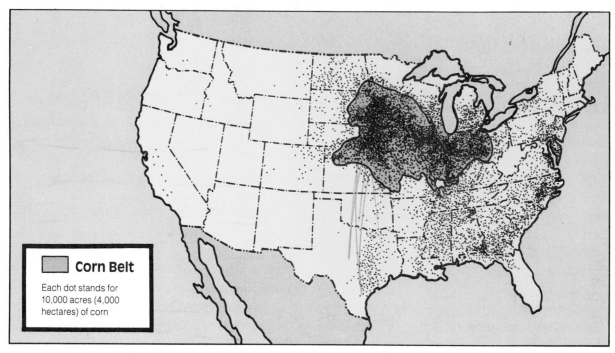

The area shaded in orange is commonly known as the corn belt. Other states grow corn too, but conditions for growing corn are best in the North Central states. Does corn grow where you live?

Besides corn, you will see fields of soybeans, oats, wheat, and hay. The farmer sells most of these crops. Soybeans are made into oil, soybean flour, and other products. A large percentage of oleomargarine comes from soybean oil. The cake left after the oil is pressed out of the beans is used to feed livestock. Iowa usually leads in growing corn in our country. Illinois is first in soybeans. Many other states in the region also raise soybeans.

Many corn-belt farmers raise cattle, hogs, and poultry to supply their own families. Indiana leads the North Central states in egg production. There are many dairy farms in the corn belt. Fresh milk and butter are sold in cities nearby. Cheese making is also a big industry.

More hogs are raised and fattened in the corn belt than in any other part of our country.

Many farmers also raise beef cattle. They send them to meat-packing centers. Some centers are Omaha, Kansas City, East St. Louis, St. Paul, St. Joseph, Des Moines, Sioux City, Cincinnati, and Ottumwa.

Uses of Corn

Most of the corn and some of the other kinds of grain are fed to animals. Instead of selling the grain, the farmers fatten their animals with it and then send them to market. Meat brings a higher price than does grain. The corn belt is the greatest meat-producing area of our country. Can you see why it is sometimes called the "meat belt"?

Corn is also made into corn bread, hominy, or mush. Breakfast cereal, syrup, and corn starch are other corn products. Paper and wall-

314

board are made from the stalks and leaves. Even the cobs are ground and used.

Farm Work

In spring a farmer uses a tractor to plant crops. Attached to the tractor is a *disk harrow* (har'ō). The harrow has sharp steel disks shaped like saucers with cutting edges. These sharp disks make the soil fine and smooth. Using a disk harrow is faster than plowing.

Sometimes fertilizer is spread across the fields. It adds richness to the soil and brings a bigger yield of corn. Then the corn planter attached to the tractor makes furrows in the ground and drops the seeds at the same time. The cultivator loosens the soil so that rain can soak in. It also digs up the weeds.

During the summer the farmer cuts the alfalfa. This plant makes good hay. After it dries in the sunshine for several days, it will be baled and hauled to the hay barn. The farmer also harvests the oats. A *combine* (kom'bīn) cuts the ripe oats and separates the grain from the straw and chaff at the same time. The farmer uses a combine to cut all the grain on the farm.

In fall the farmer drives the tractor down the rows of corn. Behind the tractor the corn picker gathers the big yellow ears of corn. The corn picker husks the corn and puts it into the wagon.

Our Nation's Breadbasket

Every day millions of Americans eat bread made of wheat grown in the fields of the North Central states. The greatest wheat-growing region in our country is in these states. It is sometimes called our nation's "breadbasket" because so much wheat is grown there.

Wheat was not grown in America until the seed was brought from Europe. In colonial days it was grown in the northeastern part of our country. As the pioneers moved west, wheat growing spread with them. When farmers moved into Ohio, Indiana, and Illinois they found that wheat grew well in these states.

Later, when settlers reached North Dakota, South Dakota, Nebraska, and Kansas, they found good wheat land there. The soil was rich, the land was cheap, and the climate was fine for wheat. Because there was less rain than farther east, this region was better for wheat than for corn. Wheat soon became the most important crop in that region.

Wheat Farming Develops

In early days farmers in the North Central states did not have machinery to help them. Much of their work was done by hand. The farmers worked as much land as they could plant and harvest. Wheat must be harvested as soon as it is ripe; so most wheat farms were small.

During the 1800s the reaper and other new and better farm machines were put on the market. In the 1840s planting machines, called *seed drills* (drilz), were invented. These seed drills planted the seed faster and more evenly. They planted many rows at a time.

By this time, also, the iron plow had replaced the wooden plow. Still later, plows were made of steel. The steel plows easily broke up the tough sod of the prairies.

Harvesting was speeded up by the invention of the *threshing* (thresh′ing) *machine*. The threshing machine separated the kernels of wheat from the stalks. Before this time threshing had been done by beating the stalks or by driving animals over them. With a threshing machine a few people could do the work of many. Work that had once taken several days could be done in a few hours.

These new and improved machines brought about changes in farming. Work on the farm began to be done by machines pulled by horses. Later the farmers used tractors. Farms grew larger. Farmers did not have to work as hard as when they did all work by hand.

Wheat farms today are very large. Many are 300–400 acres (120–160 ha) in size. Some farms are 500–1,000 acres (200–400 ha). Many are even larger.

Today's Wheat Lands

The map of the wheat belt on this page shows that wheat is grown in many parts of the North Central states. This is called the wheat belt. Notice that the dots are closest together in Kansas and North Dakota. These are the two leading

The wheat belt stretches across the United States. What state lies completely in a shaded area? Where is most winter wheat grown? Can you name the state that grows the most spring wheat?

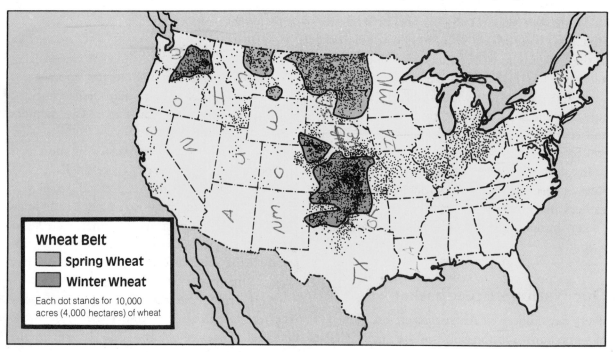

Wheat Belt
- Spring Wheat
- Winter Wheat

Each dot stands for 10,000 acres (4,000 hectares) of wheat

Farmers using *combines* can harvest many acres of wheat in a day. These machines can even cut wheat on hilly land.

wheat-growing states. Bismarck, the capital of North Dakota, is a shipping center for nearby wheat farms and cattle ranches. Topeka is the capital of Kansas. It is one of the wheat belt's shipping centers. Topeka has flour mills, meat-packing plants, and railroad shops which are among the world's largest.

The wheat-growing region around Kansas is called the winter-wheat region. It extends into Nebraska, Colorado, Oklahoma, and Texas. Winter wheat is sown in autumn and harvested in summer.

Two important manufacturing centers in the winter-wheat area are Omaha and Lincoln. Omaha is one of the largest wheat-storage areas in the United States. Lincoln, the capital of Nebraska, has large flour mills.

North Dakota is the center of the spring-wheat region. This region extends into Minnesota, South Dakota, Montana, and also into Canada. Winters there are too long and too cold for wheat to be sown in the autumn. Instead it is sown in spring and harvested in late summer.

Pierre, the capital of South Dakota, is a trade center for nearby farms. A railroad center and the second largest city in South Dakota is Rapid City. The largest city in South Dakota is Sioux Falls. This city is a trade center. It also has large meat-packing plants.

A Wheat Farm

Autumn is a busy time of year in the winter-wheat region. The farmer drives the tractor across the broad, level fields. Attached to it is a harrow. When the ground has been cut into very fine pieces, the farmer will sow the wheat.

The farmer attaches the tractor to the seed drill to sow the wheat. In the long box across the top of the drill are both seed wheat and fertilizer. As the tractor pulls the drill, the seeds

317

and fertilizer slide down the many little tubes to the ground. A small disk at the bottom of each tube makes a furrow into which the seeds and fertilizer fall. Chains dragging behind the drill pull the loose topsoil over the seeds.

The wheat seeds sprout in a short time. The broad fields soon grow green and look as though they are covered with grass. Wheat plants are several inches tall by the time cold weather comes.

Toward the end of June the wheat is ready for harvest. The farmer harvests the wheat with a combine. The combine cuts the wheat and threshes it at the same time. It cuts the heads from the wheat stalks and shakes out the kernels of wheat. The chaff and the straw are left on the field. Later the straw will be tied into bundles or bales by another machine. The threshed wheat is stored in a bin in the combine. When the bin is full, the golden grain is dumped into a truck.

The wheat is hauled to town to be stored in the grain elevator. This tall building is called an elevator because the wheat is carried up, or elevated, to the top and dumped in. Buckets on a moving belt carry the wheat up.

The grain elevator is a good place for storing wheat to keep it dry, fireproof, and away from mice and rats. Later, the wheat will be shipped to grain markets or to flour-milling cities.

Farmers in the wheat region carry on mixed farming. This means they do not depend on one crop for their living. They use some of the land for pasture and some for crops to feed and fatten the livestock. The crops are usually wheat, corn, oats, and alfalfa and other hay crops. If the farm is farther west, where there is less rain, the farmer would raise sorghum in place of corn. Sorghum is a canelike grass raised for grain and feed. It does not need as much moisture as corn.

There are many risks in farming. Farmers cannot always depend on the weather. Winter snows act like a blanket. They protect the wheat plants. But too little snow may allow the roots of the wheat to freeze. Dry weather in spring keeps the wheat from growing well. If there are hot, dry winds while the kernels are forming, the kernels shrink. Heavy rains at harvest time may knock the seeds from the heads and beat the stalks to the ground. Grasshoppers and other insects may destroy the wheat. A plant disease called wheat rust may attack it. If any of these things happens, the wheat crop is poor, and the farmer loses money.

Raising Spring Wheat

In Montana, North Dakota, South Dakota, and Minnesota spring wheat is raised. Wheat grows well in the deep, rich soil of this almost level land. The rainfall is light, but there is enough for wheat. The rain comes in the spring and early summer when the wheat needs it more than at other times.

The work in the spring-wheat region is much like that in the winter-wheat region. In autumn farmers plow and prepare their fields for planting. When spring comes, they plant the wheat as fast as possible.

Spring-wheat farmers often raise oats, barley, and hay, as well as wheat. Some raise flax. The flax in this area is raised for its seed. From the crushed flaxseed *linseed* (lin′sēd′) *oil* is made.

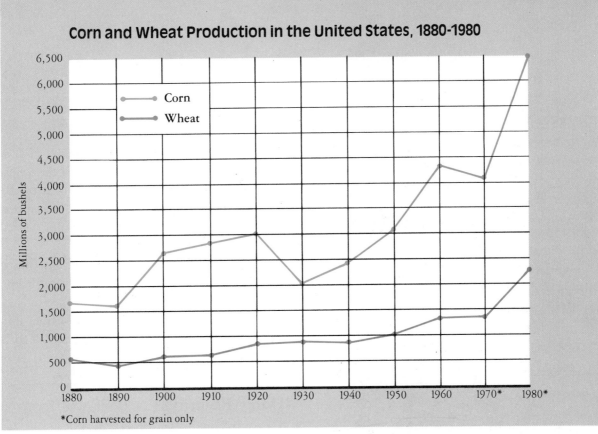

Corn and Wheat Production in the United States, 1880-1980

*Corn harvested for grain only

This graph compares the production of corn and wheat over a long period of time. Which crop has always given more bushels? During which two periods did corn production fall?

Linseed oil is used to make paint and varnish. Many farmers, especially in the eastern part of the spring-wheat region, keep dairy cows.

Flour Milling

In the early days, farmers took their grain to millers for grinding into flour. The mill was usually built beside a stream or river. The moving water turned the big wheel on the outside of the mill. This wheel was connected with the millstones inside. As the big wheel went round and round, the heavy millstones ground the wheat into flour.

Today, most flour mills are run by electricity. Wheat from hundreds of small elevators is shipped to modern mills in big cities. It is stored there in giant elevators. A wide, moving belt carries the grain from the elevators to the top of the nearby mill. Then pipes take it from floor to floor. On the way down it passes through many machines.

From the time the wheat enters the mill until it leaves as flour, machines do all the work. Machines clean and wash the wheat and remove any dirt, sticks, or stones mixed with it. Other machines grind the wheat into flour.

In a modern mill the wheat passes between many sets of steel rollers. Each time it passes through a set of rollers it is ground a little finer. After each grinding, it is sifted. The fine silk

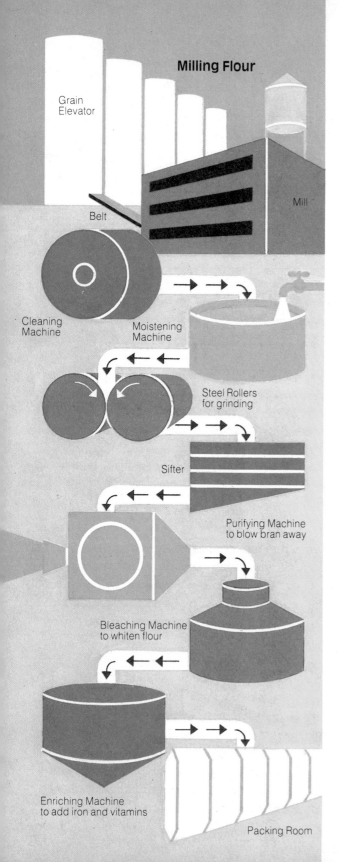

Milling Flour

Grain Elevator

Mill

Belt

Cleaning Machine

Moistening Machine

Steel Rollers for grinding

Sifter

Purifying Machine to blow bran away

Bleaching Machine to whiten flour

Enriching Machine to add iron and vitamins

Packing Room

cloth of the sifters takes out the pieces of *bran* (bran). Bran is the dark outer coat of the wheat seed. When whole-wheat flour is made, this outer coat is left in. When white flour is made, the bran is taken out. The bran is not wasted but is used for chicken and cattle feed.

When the flour is very fine and smooth, it goes to the packing room. Machines put it into bags, sacks, or boxes.

Workers load the sacks and bags of flour into trucks or freight cars. The flour goes to all parts of our country and to other lands.

Dairy Farming

You can see by the map of dairy farms on page 321 that the North Central states have many dairy farms. Wisconsin produces more milk than any other state. It is also first in cheese making. Madison, the capital of Wisconsin, is in the heart of Wisconsin's dairy region.

Minnesota has many dairy farms. It leads the nation in butter making. Minneapolis is the largest city in Minnesota, and St. Paul is the capital.

Iowa is also a leading butter producer. The capital and largest city of Iowa is Des Moines (də moin'). Des Moines is a trade and manufacturing center. It makes farm machinery and cereal products and has meat-packing plants. Many farm magazines and business papers and journals are published there.

Wheat grains go through many stages to become flour. Grinding rollers break up the kernels. What does the bleaching machine do?

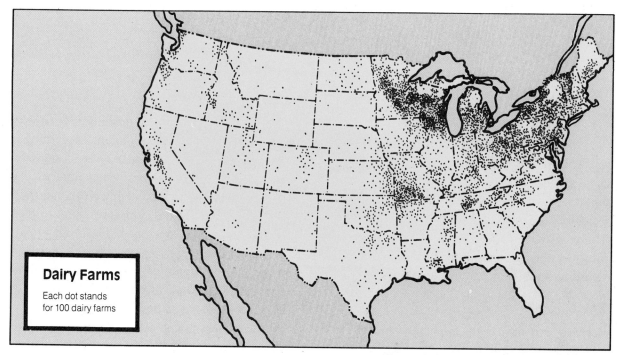

Dairy Farms

Each dot stands
for 100 dairy farms

Dairy farms are found in all the states. Where are the densest areas of dairy farming? Locate these areas on the map, page 11. Describe the type of climate most suitable for dairy farming.

The dairy-region land is not as level as the land in the corn belt. Some parts are hilly and rough. Others are swampy or have many lakes. Winters are longer and colder than in the corn belt. Much hay is grown there. Dairy cows instead of beef cattle graze in the grassy pastures. There are creameries and cheese factories instead of grain elevators and stockyards in the towns. But the dairy region is as important as the corn belt.

A Dairy Farm

Sometimes there is a stream flowing through a dairy farm. Cows need plenty of water to drink. There are hayfields, cornfields, and fields of oats or other grains. Cows need grain as well as grass and hay to give rich milk.

Hay is cut green and allowed to dry in the sun before it is stored for winter feed. Oats and other grains are also raised for winter feed. The straw left after these grains are threshed is used as bedding for the cows.

The tall, round building that looks like a tower is the silo. Winter feed for the cattle is stored in the silo. Corn, clover, and alfalfa are cut while they are still green. A machine chops up the cornstalks, clover, and alfalfa into little pieces. It blows the pieces through a pipe into the silo.

The milkhouse is near the barn. This building is kept spotlessly clean. Today most dairy farmers use milking machines to milk their own cows. Anna Baldwin, a United States farmer, made the first suction milking machine. Later a Scottish inventor made a milking machine like those used today.

On large farms glass or stainless steel pipes carry the milk from the milking machines to the milkhouse. The milk runs out of the pipes into cans or into large, refrigerated tanks in the milkhouse.

Dairy farmers have work to do every day. The cows have to be milked morning and evening. In spring and summer crops have to be raised to feed the cows throughout the year.

The Dairy Plant

Perhaps you have seen large refrigerator tank trucks carrying milk to the city. They can carry milk long distances. They keep it cold until it reaches the dairy plant. Milk is also carried by railroad cars. Huge glass-lined tanks inside these cars keep the milk cold and clean.

Many people and many machines work with the milk at the dairy plant. There everything is done to keep the milk clean, pure, and safe. Most of the work is done by machinery. The glass bottles must be thoroughly clean and then *sterilized* (ster′ə līzd′) to kill germs before they go to bottle-filling machines. The milk is *pasteurized* (pas′chə rīzd′) or heated, to kill certain germs. Then it is cooled and put into the bottling machines. Each clean, sterilized bottle is filled with milk and capped at once.

Some milk is put into paper containers. This milk is pasteurized also. The containers are sterilized before they are filled. Then they are

Swiss cheese is made from fresh, sweet milk. Cheesemakers separate the solid parts of the milk from the liquid part to form the cheese.

dipped in hot paraffin, a kind of wax. Paraffin makes them strong and keeps them from leaking. When the containers are filled, they are put into wooden boxes, ready to be sent to grocery stores or to your home.

Some dairy farmers live too far away to send fresh milk to the city. Some of them separate the rich, yellow cream from the milk and sell it to creameries. There it is made into butter. Farmers sometimes sell their fresh milk to cheese factories.

Dairying in the Past and Today

When our country was first settled, most farmers carried on general farming. They raised grains and other crops. They kept a few cows to furnish milk, butter, and cheese for themselves. Sometimes they had more than they could use. At the village store they traded what they did not need for groceries and other supplies. Other farmers kept a few extra cows. They sold their surplus milk and butter to regular customers in towns and cities.

After a while farmers became interested in dairying as a business. They brought good breeds of dairy cattle from Europe. These cows gave more and richer milk. The invention of the cream separator made it easier for them to separate cream from milk. A test for butterfat helped farmers decide which cows were giving the richest milk. They received a better price for the milk which had more butterfat in it. Refrigerator cars made it possible to send dairy products longer distances. Milking machines made it easier for farmers to have large herds. Milk and cream are used in many ways. The

milk may be used fresh. It may be made into ice cream, cottage cheese, butter, and cheese, or into evaporated, condensed, or powdered milk. Many products have been made from milk by treating it in special ways. These products include paint, cloth, glue, and plastics.

Vineyards and Orchards

Many people think of the Great Lakes only as a fine water highway. Fruit growers along the shores of Lake Michigan and Lake Erie value them for another reason. The lakes help to make these shores a fine fruit region.

Winds in the northern part of the United States come mostly from the west. Before these westerly winds reach the fruit lands, they have been blowing over water. In spring the water of the lakes is cold. The winds are cooled by blowing over this cold water. This slows down the blossoming of the fruit trees until there is little danger of frost. If frost kills the blossoms, the trees will bear no fruit.

During the summer the water in the lake is heated by the sun. In the fall the water stays warm long after the land has cooled. Winds blowing over this warm water take the warm air with them. This protects the orchards and vineyards until the fruit ripens. Find the fruit-growing region on the products map on page 324.

Lumbering

When settlers first came to the Northwest Territory, forests covered most of the land east of the Mississippi River. The pioneers cut down

Products of the North Central States

the trees. They built their homes, barns, and fences of them. From trees they made flatboats, keelboats, and canoes. They used some for fuel. Many trees were cut down to make room for fields of grain or just to clear the land.

The settlers did not realize they were ruining our forests. So far as they knew, there were trees enough to last forever. They could not know that a time would come when people would need to conserve, or save, the forests of the United States.

Lumbering was an important industry in the region around the Great Lakes by the time the Civil War ended. In the winter lumberers cut down trees and sawed them into logs. They hauled them in wagons to the frozen rivers and streams. Sometimes oxen or horses dragged them over icy roads. In spring the ice in the riv-

ers melted. Then the lumberers moved the logs down the rushing rivers to the sawmills.

The mills were usually built where rapids or falls in the river furnished power. Factories using wood to make carriages, furniture, and wagons often grew up near the mills.

Lumber from these forests helped build many cities and towns along the Great Lakes. It helped build new settlements on the treeless plains of Missouri and Kansas, too.

Like the pioneers, lumberers seemed to think these forests would last forever. Often they cut down all the trees in a region but used only the best timber. The rest was left on the ground to rot.

Once these forests produced much lumber. Today only a little lumbering is done in the Great Lakes region. Other forests there have been set aside as national forests so they are protected. Through careful cutting and the planting of young trees, the Great Lakes region may again be an important source of lumber.

Mining in the North Central States

The North Central states contain mineral riches the pioneers never dreamed were there. These mineral resources are important for this region, and for the whole country.

The United States, as you have read, is one of the world's leading manufacturing nations. But manufacturing would not be possible without plentiful supplies of such minerals as coal, iron, lead, petroleum, and zinc.

Lead, Zinc, and Other Minerals

Missouri leads our country in the production of lead. This soft, heavy, bluish-gray metal is used to make storage batteries, paint, and pipes. It is also used around electric wires and in nuclear energy plants to protect people from the deadly rays. There are many lead mines in the Ozark Plateau. Find this plateau on the map of the North Central states on page 297.

The Ozark Plateau also produces zinc. Zinc is used in electric batteries and in paint. It makes a good coating for iron, because it does not rust easily.

Lead and zinc are two important mineral resources. What North Central states have deposits of these metals? Much lead and zinc is found farther west, but it is used by industries of the North Central states.

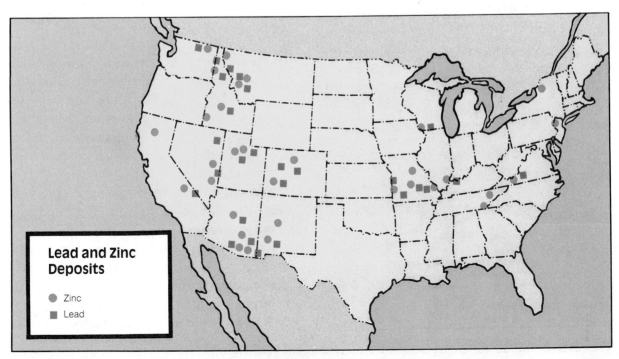

Lead and Zinc Deposits

- ● Zinc
- ■ Lead

The oil fields here supply some of the gasoline, fuel oil and natural gas needed in the North Central states. Look at the map of oil fields and pipelines on page 362. In which states might you expect people to make a living in the oil industry today?

The coal map on page 245 shows that bituminous coal is found in these states. The fields in Indiana, Illinois, and eastern Ohio are among our nation's leading coal fields. They supply fuel to run factories and to heat homes and offices. Some coal is sent to lake ports for shipment. Deposits of brown-black coal, a soft coal known as lignite, are found in the Dakotas.

South Dakota leads our nation in gold production. At Lead, in the rich Black Hills region, is the largest gold mine in the United States.

This is what natural copper looks like before it is *processed.* Copper is dark gold in color and is made into many different things. Jewelry is sometimes made with copper. What coin is entirely made of copper?

Limestone, sand, and clay are also found in this region. Limestone, as you know, is used to make cement and iron. Sand is used in making glass. Clay is made into bricks and pottery.

Long before Europeans came to this country, American Indians mined copper in northern Michigan. When the French came, they were more interested in looking for furs. They did nothing with the copper.

Years afterward the Michigan copper mines became the most important in our country. Today Michigan does not produce as much copper as it once did.

Iron Ore, a Great Mineral Resource

Our nation's greatest iron-mining region is near the western end of Lake Superior. See the iron and copper map on page 248. This great deposit of ore has helped make our nation one of the greatest producers of iron ore in the world.

Chance led to the discovery of iron in this region. One day surveyors were measuring land near Lake Superior. Their compass needle began to act strangely. Nothing they did could make it act right. When they tried to find what caused the trouble, they discovered large deposits of iron ore.

News of this discovery spread. People were pleased to find so much iron. They formed a mining company and began to mine the ore.

Some of the ore is buried deep in the ground. It is reached by shafts and tunnels, which make it expensive to mine. Some of the ore lies near the top of the ground. It is mined cheaply, for the layers of earth and gravel which cover it are

Open-pit mining is used to mine iron ore in parts of Minnesota. The ore is taken by trucks or railroad cars to docks on Lake Superior. Ships carry the ore to iron and steel centers.

easily stripped off. Large power shovels scoop up the ore. As they dig deeper and deeper into the ground, they make a huge pit or hole. This method of mining is called *open-pit mining* (mī'ning). The largest open-pit mine in the world is in Minnesota, about 70 miles (112 km) northwest of Duluth.

Most of the ore from this region is shipped from the lake ports of Duluth and Superior. Find them on the map of the Great Lakes waterway system on page 328. Long trains of freight cars loaded with reddish-brown ore move from the mines to these ports. They move out on the great loading docks high above the water and then dump the ore into bins beneath the tracks. For 8 months of the year the Great Lakes are free of ice. During this time freighters carry the ore to such iron-and-steel centers as Gary, Indiana; Detroit, Michigan; and Cleveland, Ohio. From Cleveland and other places on the Great Lakes some of the iron ore is sent to Pittsburgh. What route does it follow?

Miners know that the rich ores around Lake Superior cannot last forever. After long, hard work they learned how to take the iron out of certain kinds of rock. One of these iron-bearing rocks is called *taconite* (tak'e nīt).

Taconite has small amounts of iron scattered through it. To use the iron in a blast furnace, it must be removed from taconite rocks in a special way. After the rock is mined, it is ground and crushed into a powder as fine as flour. The iron is removed and formed into small balls of nearly solid iron. When the balls are baked, they are ready to go into blast furnaces. There is a good supply of taconite in Michigan, Wisconsin, and Minnesota. The Lake Superior region can supply iron for many years to come.

Many workers are needed to mine these ores and process them. Mining companies have built houses, shipping centers, churches, schools, power plants, and other buildings near their plants. In this way whole new towns have grown up.

A Trip Through the Great Lakes

The Great Lakes are one of the world's busiest and most important inland waterways. They provide cheap transportation for shipping. Let us follow a freighter with a cargo of iron ore as it goes down the Great Lakes from Duluth to Cleveland.

On lake freighters the space between the pilot house and engine room is called the hold. Cargo is carried in the hold. We can look down through the hatches, or openings in the deck, into the hold.

The ore-loading dock rises above us as our ship anchors by it. Steel chutes, or tubes, from bins in the dock are let down through the openings into the hold. Soon reddish-brown ore comes rumbling and thundering down the chutes. Within a few hours the last of the ore thunders into the hold. Then all of the hatches are covered. The freighter is ready to leave.

Rapids, Locks, and Canals

The map on this page shows the Great Lakes and the rivers and other narrow waterways that connect them. Rapids and waterfalls in the connecting waterways made it hard to travel on the lakes in early times. The Welland Canal was dug around Niagara Falls so that boats could go be-

The map shows some of the routes used to take products from the Great Lakes to the sea. The diagram below shows the different altitudes of the Great Lakes. How do ships move to another level?

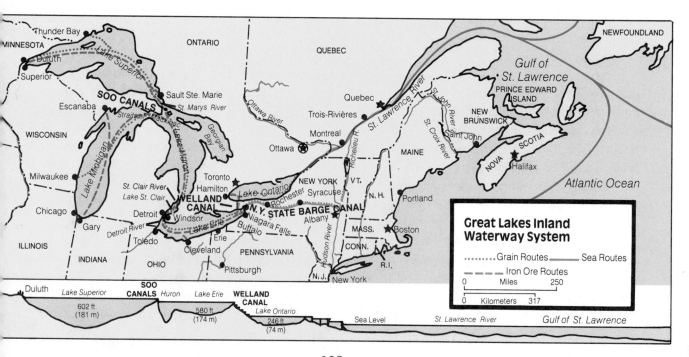

Great Lakes Inland Waterway System

.... Grain Routes ——— Sea Routes
— — — Iron Ore Routes

0   Miles   250
0   Kilometers   317

This freighter on Lake Superior near Silver Bay, Minnesota, is filled with iron ore. It will travel the Great Lakes Inland Waterway System to its final destination.

tween Lake Erie and Lake Ontario. The Soo Canals were built around the rapids in St. Marys River, which joins Lake Superior and Lake Huron. One canal is on the United States side of the river. The other is on the Canadian side.

Lake Huron is 22 feet (7 m) lower than Lake Superior. Ships passing through the canals are lifted or lowered that distance. This is done by giant locks. Locks are large boxes set up in the canal. They are made of concrete with a gate at each end. The locks are part of the canal.

Through the Soo Canals

The freighter enters Lock No. 3. The water in it is at the level of Lake Superior. Slowly our ship glides into the lock. We notice that the gate in front of us is closed. Then the heavy gate behind us swings shut. We are cut off from the rest of the canal. Slowly the water is let out of the lock. The freighter sinks lower and lower.

We see more and more of the walls of the lock. At last the water in the lock is level with the water in St. Marys River. The big gate in front of us swings open. With a short blast of our whistle we steam out of the lock. We continue on our way down the quiet, tree-lined St. Marys.

From St. Marys River we steam across Lake Huron. Then we pass through the St. Clair River and Lake St. Clair.

Delivering the Iron Ore

The freighter passes through the Detroit River and into Lake Erie. We soon enter Cleveland's outer harbor. There we pull alongside a row of huge machines. These are cranes with giant scoops attached to them. Each scoop takes about 20 tons (18 metric tons) at a bite. The hatch covers come off. The freighter will be unloaded in a few hours.

Vacation Lands

The Great Lakes and the lands around them are good places for rest and play. The sandy beaches and the beautiful scenery along the lakes attract thousands of summer visitors. They stay at motels, hotels, and tourist camps along the shores.

Some people like to take a cruise on the big passenger ships. Others find pleasure in sailing boats or using speedboats on these lakes. Still others find good fishing in the region. Sand dunes in Indiana and Michigan also attract visitors to the Great Lakes region.

Each year many people visit the national parks of the North Central region. Isle Royale National Park is a Michigan island in northern Lake Superior. Its woods have many animals and plants. Voyageurs National Park in northern Minnesota is known for its fishing. Wind Cave National Park is located in the Black Hills of South Dakota. The park has American Indian sites in addition to an interesting cave.

Cities, Manufacturing, and Trade

The North Central states are one of the important manufacturing regions of the country. From their forests, mines, and farms come raw materials to be made into usable products in their factories.

Many factories in the North Central states get power from oil or natural gas. The map on page 362 shows the main oil pipelines. The region's factories use electricity, too. In many places, coal is burned to make this electricity. Electricity is also made in nuclear energy plants.

Beautiful Birch Lake near Ely, Minnesota, is fine for canoeing and fishing. Besides the Great Lakes, the North Central states have many smaller lakes people can enjoy.

Chief Industrial
Regions
of the
North Central
States

Industrial Areas

Tens of thousands of people in this region earn their living by *processing* (pros′es sing) food. Processing means preparing food for marketing. Meat packing is a leading industry in many cities and towns. Flour mills are scattered throughout the wheat lands. Illinois, Michigan, and Minnesota have canneries, where vegetables are canned or quick-frozen.

Factories making farm machinery have also grown up in these states. Transportation costs are less when this heavy machinery is made near farms where it is used.

Manufacturing and Trade Centers

Many cities of the North Central states have gained importance through manufacturing. But they also serve as trade centers for the people of the area. Farmers take their products to nearby cities and sell them. In the cities they buy the things they need. People from smaller communities also shop in cities near them.

Many other mills and factories in this area depend upon iron and steel for the products they make. Indianapolis, the capital of Indiana, needs iron and steel for its automobile parts, trucks,

Like most major cities in the North Central states, Milwaukee, Wisconsin, has large railroad yards.

airplane motors, and heavy machinery. Indianapolis also makes chemical products and has meat-packing and vegetable-canning plants.

Wichita, Kansas, is an important farm machinery and airplane manufacturing center. This city, which lies in the oil fields, also makes oil-well equipment.

Milwaukee, Wisconsin's largest city, manufactures much heavy machinery. Because it is on Lake Michigan, it has cheap water transportation for its shipping. Some of Milwaukee's leading products are automobile frames, large gas engines, power shovels, and tractors. The people of Milwaukee also manufacture food products, leather goods, paper products, and other goods.

Some industries in the North Central region get their raw materials from other parts of our country or even from foreign lands. The rubber industry of Akron, Ohio, gets its natural or crude rubber from across the ocean. Akron is often called the rubber capital of the world because so many rubber products are made there. The leading product is automobile tires.

Columbus, the capital of Ohio, is another trade and manufacturing city in this area. It makes much mining machinery. It has machine shops, meat-packing plants, and other factories. Cincinnati, on the Ohio River, is well-known for its soap, machine tools, and other products.

Omaha, on the Missouri River, is another river port. It is the largest trading and manufacturing city in Nebraska. To it come products from the surrounding farms. Omaha has become one of the largest livestock markets in the nation. It is also an important grain market. Most of its manufacturing is connected with the processing of food. There are also many insurance companies located in Omaha.

The North Central states have many very large cities. All are important in manufacturing. Let us look at the largest of these cities.

Chicago, Great City on Lake Michigan

Chicago, near the southern end of Lake Michigan, is one of the three largest cities in our country. Both France and England once claimed the land where Chicago now stands. In 1783 this land became part of the United States. Twenty years later Fort Dearborn was built at the mouth of the Chicago River. When steamboats and railroads came, Chicago grew rapidly.

Many settlers from the East journeyed to Chicago by boat and made their homes on the nearby prairies. In a few years they were sending their surplus grain and cattle to Chicago. Some of these products were used in Chicago, but many were shipped to busy cities in the East. In exchange, these cities shipped manufac-

The trading and industrial city of Detroit, Michigan, is built out to the very edge of the Detroit River. Recently the people of Detroit rebuilt this waterfront area.

tured goods to Chicago. This growing city soon became the trading center for the rich farming region around it. Today it is the most important marketing center in the North Central states.

Chicago is the greatest railroad center and air center in our nation. It is also easily reached by trucks, river barges, and lake freighters.

In the Chicago area many foodstuffs are prepared for market. Corn is made into all kinds of corn products. Chicago is the center for this industry. It is also a busy grain market. Chicago leads all our cities in the manufacture of farm machinery. It is also an important iron-and-steel center. Chicago's position on the Great Lakes provides cheap transportation for bringing raw materials to its factories. The finished products can also be shipped out cheaply to all parts of the world.

Detroit, the Motor City

When the French were in the Northwest, they built a fort and trading post on the narrow river between Lake Erie and Lake St. Clair. Today the city of Detroit stands where the old fort stood. It is one of the country's largest cities.

Detroit's good location on the Great Lakes makes it a fine industrial and trading center. Detroit ranks first in the manufacture of automobiles. So many automobiles are made in Detroit that it is called the Motor City. Other important products of Detroit's factories are machinery, brass and bronze products, tools, chemicals, medicines, and paints.

Automobiles and their parts are also manufactured in the Michigan cities of Flint, Pontiac, and Lansing. Lansing is the capital and trade center for surrounding farms.

St. Louis
Gateway to the West

St. Louis, Missouri became the "Gateway to the West" after the Louisiana Purchase. Wagon trails led out from St. Louis. Steamboats once docked at St. Louis. Major overland trails to the western lands also began in St. Louis. Western products were sent to St. Louis to be distributed over the country by river and land. St. Louis was an important Missouri and Mississippi River port.

Today St. Louis is still the Mississippi River's most important inland port. Diesel-powered towboats push barges up and down the river between St. Louis and New Orleans. The barges are loaded with products. Do you remember why shippers like to send heavy materials by water?

The Missouri River, too, continues to help St. Louis. Look at the map on page 331 showing the industrial regions of the North Central states. What cities shown here are on the Missouri River? Why is St. Louis a good outlet for their river trade?

As in the past, the city is still a major railroad center. Airlines and good highways make reaching St. Louis easy. They also help make St. Louis an important center for receiving and shipping goods. Why does St. Louis attract industries?

Look at the picture of the Gateway Arch. Can you tell why the Arch is a monument to the present as well as to the past importance of St. Louis? ■

Cleveland, Ohio, depends a great deal on the iron and steel industry. These ships are delivering steel mill supplies. The city's skyline is seen in the background.

Cleveland, Largest City on Lake Erie

Iron ore and coal help many people make a living in the cities along Lake Erie's southern shore. The map of the North Central states on page 297 shows how close these cities are to the important coal fields of the vast Appalachian Plateau.

Cleveland is important as a manufacturing and trading center and port on Lake Erie. You have already seen that it is among the world's largest receiving ports for iron ore. The St. Lawrence Seaway also gives it a large overseas trade. Cleveland was laid out at the mouth of the Cuyahoga (kī ə hô′gə) River in 1796 by Moses Cleveland. From a trading post, it has grown to be the largest city in Ohio, and one of the largest cities in the United States.

Much of Cleveland's work is carried on in the wide, flat valley of the Cuyahoga River. Here are railroad tracks, lumber yards, power plants, blast furnaces, steel mills, and docks. Cleveland's factories make a variety of products. But iron and steel and the products made from them are the most important manufacturing done in this lake city.

More than 2 million people live in the metropolitan area around Cleveland. The city's industries and other activities provide most of these people with jobs.

Toledo, a Lake and River Port

Toledo is another important port on the southern shore of Lake Erie. It is also at the mouth of a river. Along its banks are docks, factories, and railyards.

Thousands of cars of coal come into Toledo each year. They bring coal from mines in Ohio, Kentucky, and West Virginia. At Toledo's coal docks huge machines pick up the coal cars and lift them into the air. They turn them upside down and dump the coal into the holds of waiting lake freighters. The freighters carry the coal up the lakes to Detroit, Milwaukee, Gary, Chicago, and Duluth. Toledo is a major shipper of soft coal, or lignite. Leading industries make automotive parts and glass. Oil refining and the making of food and metal products are among its other industries.

Kansas City, Two Cities on the Missouri

Kansas City, Missouri, and Kansas City, Kansas, began as river towns. Today Kansas City, Missouri, is the larger. These cities are so close together they are like one big city.

Kansas City is one of our largest livestock markets and an important meat-packing center. Good railroads make it easy to send the meat products to markets in all parts of our nation. This district is also an important grain market and one of our country's leading flour-milling centers.

There are other kinds of mills and factories in the Kansas City area. But most people earn their living doing work connected with livestock from western ranches and wheat from farms in the surrounding country.

Another trade center on the Missouri River is Jefferson City, the capital of Missouri. Jefferson City handles the products of the surrounding farms.

Minneapolis and St. Paul, Twin Cities

Minneapolis and St. Paul, Minnesota, are often called the Twin Cities. St. Paul is on the eastern bank of the Mississippi River. Minneapolis, on the western bank, is a few miles upstream from St. Paul. Barges can now go up the river right into the heart of Minneapolis. Barges carry great loads of oil, gasoline, coal, and machinery to this city. St. Paul is the capital of Minnesota. But both cities share in the trade and other business of the region around them. On the map of the North Central states on page 297 find these Mississippi River cities.

Minneapolis, now the larger of the twin cities, grew up at the Falls of St. Anthony. The falls supplied water power for the early settlers to saw logs from the nearby forests. Later wheat became important on the western plains. Then the power of the falls was used to grind grain. Flour mills were built close to the falls. Minneapolis became an important flour-milling center. Today along with Buffalo and Kansas City it is one of our nation's leading flour-milling cities.

The Minneapolis-St. Paul district has stockyards and meat-packing plants. Of the dairy products produced, butter is the most important. Farm tools are also made there.

The North Central states have fertile land, a climate good for farming, and important minerals. These states have some of the largest cities in our country. In them the products of farms, mines, and forests are sold, processed or manufactured, and shipped out. This region is one of our country's chief farming, mining, and manufacturing areas.

Do You Know?

1. What is the corn belt?
2. Name the North Central winter wheat belt states.
3. What industry developed in the Great Lakes region by the time the Civil War ended?
4. What are the chief minerals of this area?
5. What are some of the largest cities in the North Central states? How many are lake and river ports?

337

To Help You Learn

Using New Words

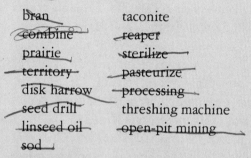

bran
combine
prairie
territory
disk harrow
seed drill
linseed oil
sod

taconite
reaper
sterilize
pasteurize
processing
threshing machine
open-pit mining

The phrases below explain the words or terms listed above. Number a paper from 1 through 15. After each number write the word or term that matches the definition.

1. A machine with sharp, curved steel blades, used to break up lumps of earth
2. A machine which cuts grain and separates kernel from straw
3. To kill germs in milk by means of heat
4. The darker, outer coat of a wheat seed
5. A machine which separates kernels of grain from stalks
6. A machine used to plant wheat or other small grains
7. To kill germs
8. A product made from crushed flaxseed
9. Preparing food for marketing
10. Mining done on the surface of the earth
11. An ore-bearing rock with iron in it
12. Settled area, not yet a state, governed by Congress
13. A wide, grassy plain
14. A machine used to cut grain
15. The part of the soil containing grass and its roots

Finding the Facts

1. What twelve states are called the North Central states?
2. What is the climate of the North Central states like?
3. Why was the plan of government set up for the Northwest Territory important?
4. What was the Louisiana Purchase?
5. How did the government provide free land to settlers?
6. How has the St. Lawrence Seaway helped cities along the Great Lakes to grow?
7. Why is farming a big business in the North Central states? What do most farms in this region grow or raise?
8. What happened to the forests which the North Central states once had?
9. Below is a list of persons whom you met in Unit 7 and descriptions of these people. Match the persons with their descriptions.

   Clark   Jefferson
   McCormick   Baldwin
   Putnam

   a. I was President when the Louisiana Territory was bought by the United States.
   b. I captured the Northwest Territory from the British.

c. I invented a harvesting machine, called a reaper.

d. I helped to found the first settlement in the Northwest Territory.

e. I made the first suction milking machine.

10. What minerals are mined in this region?

11. Why are these cities important: Chicago, Cleveland, Detroit, St. Louis?

Learning from Maps

1. On the map of the United States, on pages A-6– A-7, find the North Central states. Between what parallels of latitude do these states lie? Which states border the Great Lakes? Which border the Mississippi? The Missouri? The Ohio?

2. Use the scale of miles on the map of the North Central states on page 297 to find the distance between: (a) Cincinnati and Chicago; (b) St. Louis and Cleveland; (c) Minneapolis and Chicago; (d) Milwaukee and Kansas City.

3. Look at the map of transportation routes on page 309. What road was used to travel from Philadelphia to Pittsburgh? What three cities did the National Road connect?

4. Study the map of chief industrial regions of the North Central states, on page 331. What state capitals are in industrial areas?

5. Use the Great Lakes map on page 328 to trace a cargo of iron ore from Duluth to Cleveland. Name the lakes, rivers, and canals through which it travels.

Using Study Skills

1. **Time Line:** Make a time line for this Unit. Put in the dates for these events: Fulton makes steamboat; railroads come into use; Congress passes the Homestead Act.

   Put in the date when each North Central state was admitted to the Union. Use an almanac or encyclopedias to help you.

2. **Chart:** Make a chart of the North Central states like the one you made for Unit 5, page 256. Use the chart on pages 580–583, your text, an almanac, and encyclopedias.

3. **Outline:** Make an outline of the development of wheat farming. The outline has been started for you below.

Wheat Farming Develops
I. In early days
   A. Work done by hand
   B. Most farms small
II. During the 1800s
   A. New and better farm machines
      1. reaper
      2.
      3.
      4.
      5.
   B. Horses pull machines
   C. Farms larger
III. Today
   A.
   B.

4. **Diagram:** Look at the diagram on page 320. What does this diagram show? How does wheat get from the grain elevator to the mill? What does the first machine do to the wheat? What does the purifying machine do? What machine makes the flour white?

5. **Graph:** Look at the graph on page 319. What does this graph show? Which crop did the United States produce more of each year between 1890 and 1980? Did the production of corn increase or decrease between 1920 and 1930? Did the production of wheat increase or decrease between 1910 and 1920? About how many more bushels of corn were produced in 1960 than bushels of wheat?

Thinking It Through

1. Each of the events in the first list was the cause of an event in the second list. Match the causes and the results.

   Causes

   A. George Rogers Clark captured the British forts in the Ohio Valley.

   B. Congress passed the Homestead Act.

   C. The American Indians were forced to move from most of the Ohio region.

   D. President Jefferson bought the Louisiana Territory from France.

   E. The Missouri Compromise was passed by Congress.

   Results

   a. The question of slavery was settled in the Louisiana Territory.

   b. The area of the United States was doubled.

   c. The Northwest Territory became a part of the United States.

   d. Pioneers went west to settle on free land.

   e. Settlers moved into the Northwest Territory in great numbers.

2. Why are rivers an important means of transportation, even in the jet age? What kinds of goods usually go by water?

3. On what river is St. Louis situated? Why did industries like those shown in the pictures on page 331 grow up there?

4. Why did Detroit become the leading automobile city? Why do you think Kansas City became a meat-packing center? What is the leading industry in your city? Why did that industry become important?

Projects

1. Chicago is the meeting place for more lines of transportation than any other city in our country. Railroads, waterways, bus lines, and air routes serve the city. The Explorers' Committee might secure maps showing the lines of travel which make Chicago the greatest transportation center in our country.

2. Several large cities in the North Central states grew up on spots where forts or trading posts once stood. The Research Committee might find out about the early history of some of these cities. Use the encyclopedia and start with Chicago. Be sure to include St. Louis, Detroit, and Cincinnati also.

3. Draw pictures of the pioneers as they moved westward on their way to settle the Northwest Territory or of the pioneers at an activity that drew neighbors together.

4. Collect pictures of farm machines from magazines or newspapers for your scrapbook. Find out how each works.

5. Find out what articles are made or what foods are processed in your town or city. Make a list of the articles and foods.

6. The Explorers' Committee might show principal routes the pioneers used to travel west by land and by water.

7. The Reading Committee might ask the librarian to help them plan an exhibit of stories and poems of pioneer days.

11 The South Central States

Unit Preview

The four South Central states are Arkansas, Louisiana, Oklahoma, and Texas.

When the United States became independent, New Orleans and all lands west of the Mississippi were claimed by other nations. Later, in 1803, the United States purchased New Orleans and the Louisiana Territory from France.

When Mexico became independent of Spain, Texas was part of Mexico. Soon Texas became an independent nation. Nine years later, Texas became part of the Union.

Oklahoma was once known as Indian Territory. The government set aside lands there for the Indians. In 1889, the area was opened to settlers.

Most of the people who rushed to Oklahoma were looking for land to farm. Farming is still important in all the South Central states. The eastern part of this region is like the Southeast. It has the same climate and crops. Cotton, rice, and sugar are important products. In the drier western part of the South Central states cattle and sheep are raised.

But the region's greatest wealth lies under the ground. Bauxite, from which aluminum is made, and petroleum are its most important minerals. The development of these natural resources has given the South Central states many fast-growing cities. Houston is the largest city in this region.

Things to Discover

If you look carefully at the picture, map, and time line, you can answer these questions.
1. When did the United States gain New Orleans?
2. How many states are in the South Central region?
3. The picture shows the Alamo as it looks today. When was a battle fought there?
4. When did Texas become a state? How many years was this after the battle of the Alamo?
5. What body of water forms the southern border of some South Central states?
6. What country borders a state in this region?
7. What important natural resource was found in Texas in 1901?
8. When did settlers begin going to Oklahoma?

Words to Learn

You will meet these words in this unit. As you read, you will learn what they mean and how to pronounce them. The Word List will help you.

delta	levee
derrick	mission
drill	mohair
dry farming	raw sugar
feed lot	refinery
flowing well	reservation
gusher	sulfur
helium	

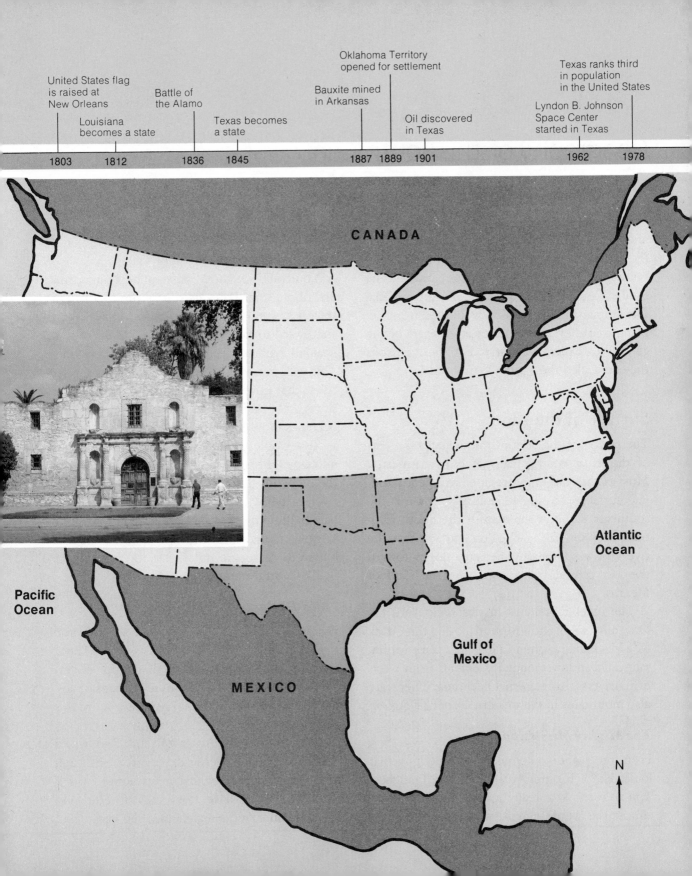

United States flag
is raised at
New Orleans

Louisiana
becomes a state

Battle of
the Alamo

Texas becomes
a state

Bauxite mined
in Arkansas

Oklahoma Territory
opened for settlement

Oil discovered
in Texas

Lyndon B. Johnson
Space Center
started in Texas

Texas ranks third
in population
in the United States

1803   1812   1836   1845   1887 1889 1901   1962   1978

CANADA

Pacific
Ocean

MEXICO

Gulf of
Mexico

Atlantic
Ocean

N

1
Geography of the South Central States

Would you like to take a jet plane and fly high above the earth? If you did, you would see that the South Central states lie about halfway between our eastern and western coasts. The South Central states are Arkansas, Louisiana, Oklahoma, and Texas. You would see from the plane that they are in the southern part of the central area of our country. For these reasons they are called the South Central states.

Surface of the Land

The region of the South Central states is a part of the great central plain of North America. Most of the land in this region has a gently rolling surface. It slopes generally toward the southeast. Look at the map of the South Central states on page 345. You can see that the rivers flow southeast. The land slopes toward the low coastal plains bordering the Gulf of Mexico.

The chief mountains in this region are the Ouachita (wäsh′ə tô′) Mountains and the Ozark (ō′zärk) Plateau, often called the Ozark Mountains. These low mountains extend from western Arkansas to eastern Oklahoma. There are also mountains in the western corner of Texas.

The Mighty Mississippi

From the plane you would see something that looks like a big tree with spreading branches. The tree trunk is really a huge river. It flows almost the whole length of our country from north to south. The river is the Mississippi, the longest river in the United States. The region it drains is called the Mississippi Valley.

You could see the Mississippi begin in northern Minnesota. From its source the Mississippi travels more than 2,000 miles (3,218 km) southward to the Gulf of Mexico. As it flows, it changes from a clear stream to a muddy one. This is because it receives dirt, or silt, from the rivers that flow into it. Gradually, too, the river slows down as it becomes broader and the land becomes more level.

You would see that the Mississippi divides into several branches near its mouth. The land the branches flow through at the mouth of the river is the Mississippi *delta* (del′tə). A delta is land built up by mud and sand brought down by a slow river. The Mississippi delta covers hundreds of square miles. See the map of the South Central states, page 345.

Flood Plains

From the plane you would also see several large rivers flowing into the Mississippi. These are the tributaries of the Mississippi River. Two of these tributaries—the Arkansas and the Red rivers—join the Mississippi in this region.

The Mississippi, Arkansas, and Red rivers have flood plains because they flow through low, flat land. A river that flows between high banks does not have flood plains. The land along such a river is higher than the water, and

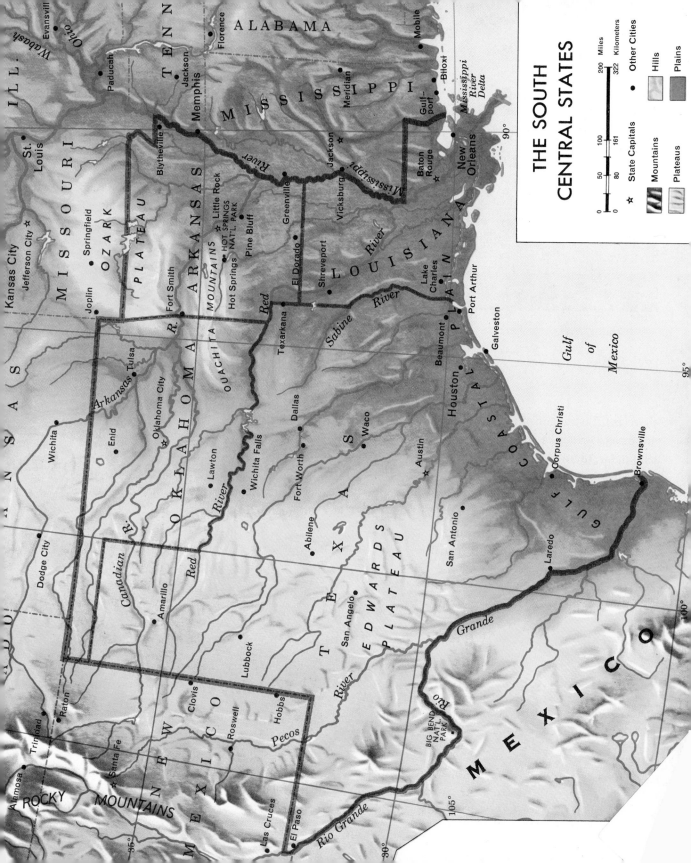

THE SOUTH CENTRAL STATES

Legend

★ State Capitals
• Other Cities

Mountains
Plateaus
Hills
Plains

Miles 0   50   100   200
Kilometers 0   80   161   322

ILL.
Evansville
Wabash
Ohio
Ohio
Paducah

ALABAMA
Florence
Mobile
Biloxi
Gulfport
Mississippi River Delta

TENN.
Jackson
Memphis

MISSOURI
St. Louis
Jefferson City ★
Springfield
Joplin

MISSISSIPPI
Blytheville
River
Meridian
Jackson ★
Vicksburg
Mississippi

OZARK PLATEAU
ARKANSAS
Little Rock ★
HOT SPRINGS NAT'L. PARK
Hot Springs
Pine Bluff
Greenville
Baton Rouge ★
New Orleans
Gulf of Mexico

Fort Smith
OUACHITA MOUNTAINS
El Dorado
Shreveport
LOUISIANA
River
Lake Charles
Port Arthur

KANSAS
Kansas City
Wichita
Dodge City

OKLAHOMA
Arkansas River
Tulsa
Oklahoma City ★
Enid
R.
Red River
Texarkana
Sabine River
Red River
Beaumont
Houston
Galveston

Amarillo
Canadian River
Lawton
Wichita Falls
Dallas
Fort Worth
Waco
GULF COASTAL PLAIN
Corpus Christi
Brownsville

NEW MEXICO
Trinidad
Raton
Santa Fe ★
Alamosa
ROCKY MOUNTAINS
Clovis
Roswell
Lubbock
Hobbs
Pecos
Red
San Angelo
Abilene
TEXAS
EDWARDS PLATEAU
Austin ★
San Antonio
Laredo
River
Rio Grande
BIG BEND NAT'L. PARK
Rio Grande
Las Cruces
El Paso

MEXICO

90°
95°
100°
105°
85°
30°

When the Mississippi River reaches its *delta* below New Orleans it divides into several branches. These narrow waterways flow through swampland into the Gulf of Mexico.

there is little danger of overflow. But these rivers have low banks and often overflow the flat land near them. For thousands of years each flood has left much rich soil on the land it covered. Today some of the richest farmland in our country is in these flood plains.

When these rivers overflow, they sometimes cause great damage. Mounds of earth, or *levees* (lev'ēz), have been built along the banks to hold back the water. The levees are made of earth strengthened by metal cables or concrete. During heavy floods people work day and night piling sandbags around the levees to strengthen them and help them hold.

Climate of the South Central States

Most of the South Central region has a mild climate. The short winters are sometimes chilly because of cold winds from the north. But in most of this region warm, moist winds blow in from the Gulf of Mexico. The farmers usually get enough rain to grow good crops. See the climate map of North America, page 11.

The Gulf Coast gets much rain and is swampy. But western Texas and Oklahoma are too far inland to get much rain from the Gulf of Mexico. The winds from the Gulf usually blow toward the east and northeast. Moist winds do not reach this western area to bring it much rain. But there is enough moisture for grazing. The area west of the Pecos River receives very little rain. Crops can be raised there through irrigation.

Do You Know?

1. What four states are called the South Central states? Why?
2. What sections of the South Central states receive the most rainfall? Which receive the least rainfall?

2
Settling the South Central States

The explorers of Spain and France played important parts in the early history of what is now Louisiana and Arkansas. The flags of both countries have flown over this region.

The Spanish Explorers

De Soto was one of the most famous of the Spanish explorers. He and those with him explored parts of North America while looking for treasure. Their travels took them into the low Mississippi Valley, but they found no gold.

De Soto did find hot springs, the waters of which were said to have some healing powers. Several groups of Indians used these springs long before the Spanish arrived. Today Hot Springs is an important city in Arkansas. Each year many people visit the famous health resort there.

The French Explorers

About 140 years after De Soto's visit, the French explorer, La Salle, traveled the Mississippi River. When La Salle reached the mouth of the river, he claimed the whole Mississippi Valley for King Louis of France. It was called the Louisiana Territory.

Other French came later. They wanted furs. They found many fur-bearing animals in this region. They built trading posts and settlements there. The first trading post was Arkansas Post, near the mouth of the Arkansas River.

La Salle dreamed of making the Mississippi River Valley a French colony. He named the region Louisiana in honor of King Louis of France.

The Founding of New Orleans

Pierre d' Iberville (pē yer′ dē′ber vēl) was born in New France, as Canada was then called. From his parents, who were French, he learned to love France.

Pierre made a trip to France to see the king. He asked for permission to strengthen France's claims to the Mississippi River Valley. "To do this," he said, "we need a colony at the mouth of the Mississippi."

"You are loyal to France," the king answered. "I shall give you ships and supplies to build the settlement."

Two hundred soldiers and colonists sailed from France with Pierre and his half brother, Jean de Bienville (zhän′ də byan′vēl′).

The brothers chose a good location for a settlement. There they founded a colony. Pierre left Jean to govern the colony and then sailed back to France.

In 1718 Jean founded New Orleans, which later became the capital of the colony. He was its governor for many years.

The Founding of Little Rock

"Far to the north is a green mountain which sparkles in the sun," says an Indian to a group of French explorers. "That must be the mountain I am searching for," answers one of the explorers. He was Bernard de la Harpe. He explored part of Arkansas in a search for the green mountain. La Harpe did not discover the mountain, but he found a good place for a settlement.

During part of this journey La Harpe traveled on the Arkansas River. While on this river, he noticed a huge mass of rock rising from one of the shores. Farther on, he saw a second great rock. La Harpe called these two masses of rock Little Rock and Big Rock.

An Indian camp was near the smaller of the rocks. There La Harpe started a fur-trading post. This trading post grew into the city which today is called Little Rock.

Under Three Flags

Near the end of the French and Indian War, in 1762, France gave some of the Louisiana Territory to Spain. The territory was a gift to Spain for its help during the war. Spain held Louisiana for about 40 years. During this time, the United States had an agreement with Spain. That agreement allowed settlers near the Ohio River to send products down the Mississippi to the port of New Orleans.

In 1800 France took possession of the territory again. Now the settlers were afraid France would close the port.

President Jefferson decided to try to buy New Orleans from the French. France had been at war and needed money. The French ruler offered to sell the whole Louisiana Territory to the United States.

Louisiana, a State

So, in 1803, the United States bought the Louisiana Territory. See the map on page 137. Settlers were soon moving into the southern part of it. Just 9 years later the southeast part had enough people to become a state. Louisiana was admitted to the Union in 1812.

Arkansas, a State

Arkansas was settled more slowly. After purchasing the Louisiana Territory, the United States government sent soldiers there. The soldiers built Fort Smith in Arkansas and other forts also. These forts provided protection for the settlers.

Settlers now began to flock into Arkansas in large numbers. Most of the people who went there in the early days settled along the rivers. In 1836 Arkansas had enough people to become a state.

The French and Spanish heritage of the South Central states can be seen today. Balcony railings in New Orleans are like those in France. The Spanish built the San José *mission* near San Antonio, Texas.

Early History of Texas

The Spanish began to explore the region that is now Texas soon after Columbus discovered America. They built a few forts and *missions* (mish′ənz), or church settlements, in Texas to hold their claims to the territory.

Soon after La Salle claimed the Mississippi Valley for France, the French began to build forts along the Texas coast. The king of Spain became worried. So he sent more soldiers to the region and built more forts. The Spanish also built more missions. A few Spanish settlers followed. In this way Texas became Spanish.

Texas under Mexican Rule

After a while Spain began to have trouble with its colonies in the Americas. These colonies wanted to be independent. One of the colonies that rebelled and won its independence was Mexico. At that time Mexico included most of what is now Texas. Very few people were living in Texas then. So the Mexican government invited Americans to go there.

The first settlers from the United States went to Texas under the leadership of Stephen Austin (ôs′tin).

Three hundred families were in the group. They arrived in 1821. Because he led the first United States settlers to Texas, Stephen Austin has sometimes been called the "Father of Texas."

People from many parts of the United States soon began arriving in Texas. Farmers from the Southeast moved to Texas to find new fields in which to grow cotton and tobacco. Cattle ranchers also drove their herds to the fresh grazing lands of Texas.

The number of settlers from the United States continued to grow. Mexico soon began to fear that it would lose Texas. So it declared that it would accept no more settlers from the

Santa Anna ordered his Mexican troops to storm the walls of the Alamo on the last day of fighting.

United States. Mexico also passed a law forbidding slavery in Texas. But the cotton planters kept the slaves they had brought to work on their new plantations.

The Texas Revolution

When General Santa Anna became the leader of Mexico, the trouble grew worse. There were a few armed fights. Then some Texans banded together. They set up their own temporary government and captured San Antonio.

Later Santa Anna marched his troops into San Antonio. They met a group of about 200 Texans who were determined to fight for their independence gathered inside the Alamo (al′ə mō). The Alamo was an old walled mission in San Antonio. Santa Anna had a large army and many cannons. He demanded that the Texans surrender. They refused.

Santa Anna's forces stormed the mission walls and forced their way inside. Within the chapel of the mission the little band of Texans fought bravely. The battle lasted 13 days. When it ended, no Texas soldiers were left alive.

When the fighting was taking place at the Alamo, Texas declared its independence from Mexico. David G. Burnet was chosen as the president of the new provisional government, and Manuel Lorenzo de Zavala (sä vä′lä) as the vice-president. Sam Houston was made commander of the Texas army.

Later, Sam Houston and a group of Texans attacked the Mexican army at San Jacinto (sän jä sēn′tō). Cries of "Remember the Alamo!" split the air as the Texans rushed into battle. They defeated Santa Anna and the Mexican army. The victory ended the war. Mexico gave up its claim to Texas, and Texas won its independence.

In 1836 the Texans set up a republic. Sam Houston was president. Their flag had one large star on a blue field and two stripes, one white and one red. Today Texas is called the Lone Star State.

Becoming a State

After Texas won freedom, many Texans wanted to join the United States. So Texas sent a request to Washington asking to become a state.

The government of Mexico did not recognize the independence of Texas. Some

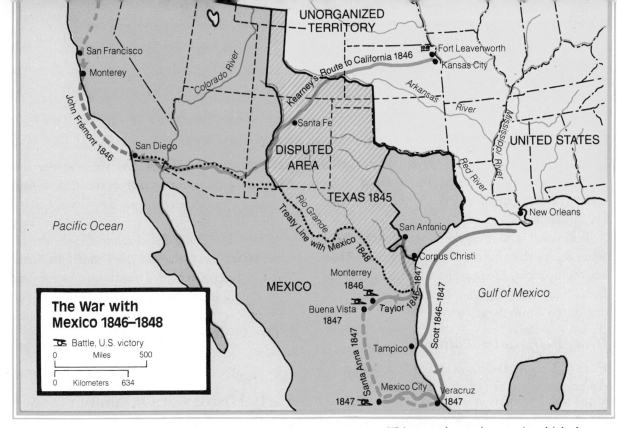

The War with
Mexico 1846–1848

Battle, U.S. victory

| 0 | Miles | 500 |
| 0 | Kilometers | 634 |

This map shows the area in which the war with Mexico was fought. Which Mexican cities were major battle sites? What river forms the border between Texas and Mexico?

Americans feared that Mexico would declare war if Congress admitted Texas.

Most northerners feared that Texas would come in as a slave state. The northerners did not want Texas to join the United States. But most of the leaders in the United States government wanted to admit Texas. They said, "A strong European country might take Texas if we do not make it part of our nation. We do not want a European power on our border." In 1845 Congress voted to make Texas a state.

War with Mexico

When the United States admitted Texas into the Union, Mexico was not pleased. A quarrel developed over boundaries between Texas and Mexico. The United States sent troops to Texas to protect Texas from Mexican soldiers. But Mexico also wanted to protect its land. A Mexican force defeated the American troops. The United States then declared war on Mexico. The United States soldiers met and defeated Santa Anna's army. The United States troops were led by General Zachary Taylor.

During this time General Winfield Scott led a group of United States soldiers across the Gulf of Mexico. One of the captains was young Robert E. Lee. They landed at Veracruz (ver'ə krōōz') and captured it. See the map on this page. Then they marched on and captured Mexico City on September 14, 1847. That ended the war.

Under the peace treaty Mexico gave up its claim to land north of the Rio Grande. The United States paid Mexico 15 million dollars for this land.

Texas was a part of the South in the Civil War. So six flags have waved over Texas. They are the Spanish, French, and Mexican flags, the Lone Star flag, the Stars and Stripes, and the flag of the Confederacy.

Henry B. Gonzalez, Political Leader

Henry B. Gonzalez (gôn sä′lās) is a Mexican-American from San Antonio, Texas. He was born there in 1916. After college, Henry worked for a while with his father. Then he held several positions in the local government of San Antonio. Henry Gonzalez ran for the

Congressman Henry Gonzalez works in Washington, D.C., on behalf of people living in Texas.

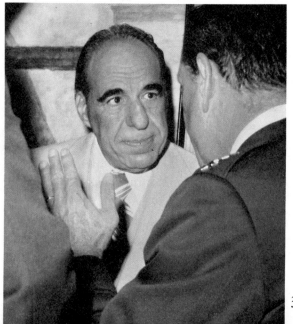

Texas State senate in 1956. He was the first Mexican-American to serve in the state senate. In 1961 he was elected to the United States House of Representatives.

While in Congress, Henry Gonzalez has worked for laws that support small business. He has fought for civil rights protection and better education for minorities. He has also written several magazine articles about the problems of Mexican-Americans in the United States.

Early History of Oklahoma

The first explorers to reach part of what is now Oklahoma were the Spanish. They did not find gold in this region. But they did find different groups of Indians.

La Salle never explored the Oklahoma region, although he traveled down the Mississippi River. But the French claimed Oklahoma as part of the Louisiana Territory.

American Indian Reservations

During the first half of the 1800s more and more people settled in the eastern part of the United States. In doing this, they claimed more and more land that belonged to the Indians. Most of the Indians fought to keep their land. But, because the United States soldiers had superior weapons, the Indians were defeated.

The United States government attempted to provide for the Indians. It set aside for their use land in various parts of the United States. Such land set aside by the government is called a *reservation* (rez′ər vā′shən).

352

Thousands of people rushed to get land when the Indian Territory in Oklahoma was opened to settlers. Riders on horses were among the first to make claims.

The government passed a law that forced many Indians in the eastern United States to move to reservations in present-day Oklahoma. This region, north of Texas, became known as Indian Territory. By the late 1800s, most Indians in the United States had been forced to move to reservations west of the Mississippi River. See the map of American Indian removal on page 300.

The Oklahoma Land Rush

People asked the government to open the unsettled part of the Indian Territory to settlers. After a time the government bought from some Indians a large area in what is now Oklahoma. A great land rush took place when the government opened this land to settlers.

Settlers would get the land free. It would go to those who got there first and set out stakes to mark their claims. But everybody had to wait until noon on April 22, 1889. Let us try to imagine that we are there.

Many thousands of people have taken their places at the Kansas border. They have come in covered wagons, in carts, on horseback, and on foot. The eager pioneers have to be held back by United States troops until the hour of the opening. As the morning passes, people push their way closer to the border line.

At exactly twelve o'clock the pistol shot rings out clearly. The troops hardly have time to get out of the way. The rush of settlers into Indian Territory begins.

The people move in to stake their claims. Cities of tents appear by nightfall. The area has 50,000 people in it within 24 hours of the opening. Guthrie and Oklahoma City are suddenly cities of 10,000 people each.

Oklahoma, a State

In a short time all the free land was taken. Within a year enough people had settled in Oklahoma for it to become a territory. A few years later, in 1907, Oklahoma became a state.

Many Indians live in the South Central states today, especially in Oklahoma. The United States government is trying to improve conditions for Indians on reservations. It is also trying to help those who move to cities. The government has made laws to protect the rights of the Indians. They are now United States citizens and can live and work wherever they wish. The Indians continue to fight for their rights but the battles are now in courts of law.

Some Indians in Oklahoma continue to practice traditional crafts. Others have moved their families to cities to find work in business and industry.

Do You Know?

1. Why were Fort Smith and other forts built in Arkansas?
2. How did the location of New Orleans lead to our buying the Louisiana Territory?
3. How did the war with Mexico end?
4. Why is Texas called the Lone Star State?
5. What happened as more and more people settled in the eastern part of the United States?
6. What is a reservation?
7. How was Oklahoma settled? When did it become a state?

Before You Go On

Using New Words

levee   mission

delta   reservation

The phrases below explain the words listed above. Number a paper from 1 through 4. After each number write the word that matches the definition.

1. A church settlement built by Spaniards in the Americas
2. An area set aside by the government for the use of American Indians
3. Land built up by mud and sand brought down by a slow river
4. A bank of earth built along a river to keep it from overflowing its banks and flooding the land

Finding the Facts

1. How long is the Mississippi River? Where does it begin? Where is its mouth? What large rivers flow into it in the region of the South Central states?
2. Why do people pile sandbags around levees during heavy floods?
3. Why don't western Texas and Oklahoma get much rain from the Gulf of Mexico?
4. Who started a fur-trading post that grew into the city now called Little Rock?
5. Why did Pierre d'Iberville think it was important to found a French colony at the mouth of the Mississippi River? Who founded New Orleans in 1718?
6. What large piece of land did the United States buy from France in 1803?
7. Why did the United States government send soldiers to what is now Arkansas during the early 1800s?
8. How did the Spanish try to hold their claims to the territory that is now Texas?
9. Who led the first settlers from the United States to Texas in 1821?
10. What happened at the Alamo? What happened at San Jacinto? Who headed the Texas army and later became the president of Texas?
11. What two generals helped the United States defeat Mexico in the war that took place shortly after Texas became a state?
12. To which branch of Congress was Henry Gonzalez elected in 1961?
13. Why did the Indians in the eastern United States lose their land during the first half of the 1800s?
14. What present-day state was once known as Indian Territory?

3
Living and Working in the South Central States

Let us take a boat trip down the Mississippi River from St. Louis to New Orleans. Most travel on the Mississippi today is on barges which carry freight up and down the river. But a few river boats carry passengers.

This chart lists the major crops and livestock in the South Central states. What major crop is grown in all four states? Which states raise sheep?

Farming Products and Livestock in the South Central States

	Major Crops	Other Crops	Livestock
Arkansas	soybeans, rice, cotton	tomatoes, strawberries, wheat	chickens, hogs, cattle, turkeys
Louisiana	rice, sugarcane, soybeans, cotton, sweet potatoes	corn, strawberries, melons, nuts	cattle, hogs, chickens
Oklahoma	wheat, peanuts, cotton, sorghum	hay, soybeans, pecans, barley, oats	cattle, sheep, chickens, hogs, turkeys
Texas	cotton, rice, sorghum, wheat	barley, oats, vegetables, nuts, citrus and other fruits	cattle, sheep, hogs, chickens, goats, turkeys

Farming in the South Central States

The captain hands us a chart showing some of the farming products and livestock found in the South Central states.

The captain tells us this region has much rich farmland. Farming is one of the chief ways of earning a living in the South Central states. Some of this rich land is on the Mississippi flood plains.

Cotton, a Leading Crop

"The chief crop of the South Central states is cotton," the captain says. This region has about half the cotton land in the country. Texas is the leading cotton state in our country. Many people here make their living from cotton. See the map of climate and cotton on page 272.

The Story of Rice

Our captain tells us that another important crop of the South Central states is rice. Most of our country's rice is grown on the flood plains in Arkansas and on the coastal plain of Louisiana and Texas. Rice is a thirsty plant, and the fields must be kept under water most of the time. Low levees are built to keep the water in the fields.

Most rice is planted by low-flying airplanes which scatter the seeds onto flooded fields. Workers keep 2 to 6 inches (5 to 15 cm) of water on the rice fields. Workers also keep

Rice fields in Texas are irrigated by canals. Low *levees* help keep water on the fields. Later the rice will be stored in silos until trucks or trains carry it to market.

weeds out of the fields. The rice plants grow and cover the fields like thick grass. After a few months, the leaves begin to turn yellow. The fields are drained. It is now time to harvest the ripened grain. Most of the rice is harvested with large farm machines called combines. This machine is like the combines that reap and thresh other grains. First, the machine cuts off the stalks. Next it beats the stalks to separate the straw from the grain. The grain is then sent to mills, where it is hulled and usually polished, then packaged. New Orleans and Houston are the rice markets of the South Central states.

Other Crops

Our captain says that farmers in this region grow many other crops besides cotton and rice. Look at the chart on page 356. In addition to strawberries and tomatoes, peaches and grapes are some of the many fruits grown in Arkansas. One section of Louisiana is known for its fine strawberries. Fine citrus fruits are grown in Texas in the Rio Grande Valley. Texas is also noted for its peaches, watermelons, other fruits and vegetables, pecans, and peanuts.

Northwest Texas and western Oklahoma do not get much rain. Winter wheat is the chief crop of this area. Some farmers practice *dry farming* (drī′ färm′ing). Dry farming is a way of conserving the moisture in areas where little rain falls. On these fields crops are planted every other year. The weeds are kept out so that none of the precious moisture in the soil is wasted. In this way enough moisture is stored so that a crop can be raised every 2 years.

The Story of Sugar

Do you know how much sugar you eat in a year? The average person in this country eats almost 100 pounds (45 kg) of sugar each year. Most of the sugar that we eat comes from lands outside the United States. Sugarcane needs rich, moist soil and a hot, sunny climate. The Coastal Plain and the Mississippi Flood Plain of Louisiana have such a climate. About one-fourth of the cane sugar grown in our nation is from Louisiana.

Sugarcane grows tall like corn. But unlike corn, it is not usually grown from seed. Short pieces of cane stalk are planted. Farmers use machines to plant pieces of cane stalk in furrows, or ditches, and cover them with dirt. Soon green shoots push up through the loose earth. In 7 to 22 months the stalks are 7 to 15 feet (2 to 5 m) high. They are filled with sweet juice.

When machines are used to cut the cane, the leaves and tassels are first burned off. Fire does not hurt the cane stalks because they are too full of juice to burn.

When sugarcane is cut by hand, the workers use long, sharp knives. Each knife has a long hook on the back which the worker uses to strip off the cane leaves.

The cane stalks are loaded onto trucks which take them to the sugar mill, or *refinery* (ri fī′nər ē), where raw materials are purified. The cane stalks must be taken to the refinery immediately because they dry out quickly.

The sugar refinery with its tall smokestack is one of the largest buildings in the towns of the sugar country. Here the stalks are washed as they are carried along on a moving belt. Then large rollers squeeze the sweet juice from the sugarcane. The juice is treated to purify it and cooked into a syrup. The syrup is boiled to form a brown mass of molasses and crystals. Then a machine spins most of the molasses out of the syrup. The sticky brown crystals that remain are called *raw* (rô) *sugar*. Some of this raw sugar is packaged. But most of the brown sugar is further treated to make it white. It is then shipped to all parts of the country.

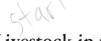

Livestock in the South Central States

Some of the cattle raised by early American settlers in the South Central states were the Texas longhorns. The first settlers found these cattle roaming wild. The cattle were descended from stock brought by the Spanish explorers.

Cattle, together with hogs and other livestock, are still raised in all the South Central states. See the chart on page 356. Western Texas and Oklahoma have the largest farms, or ranches. Ranchers there travel by jeep, truck, and helicopter, as well as on horseback. Many ranchers graze their cattle on the range. After a while, the ranchers take the cattle to a *feed lot* (fēd lot). This is a pen where cattle are given special feed to fatten them for market.

Texas has more cattle, sheep, and goats than any other state. It has fine saddle horses and race horses. Texas leads in producing wool and *mohair* (mō′her′). Mohair is a special cloth made from the long, silky hair of a certain kind of goat.

The Edwards Plateau lies in southwestern Texas. See the map of the South Central states on page 345. This plateau is almost as large as the state of Pennsylvania. The chief occupation there is raising cattle, sheep, and goats.

The King Ranch, the largest in Texas, is on the Gulf Coast. It is larger than the state of Rhode Island. Many thousands of cattle and fine horses for racing are raised on this ranch.

An important new kind of cattle has been bred on the King Ranch. In long periods of hot

Modern cowhands still ride horses when they herd cattle. Today they may also use trucks and helicopters to do much of the same work on a ranch.

weather cattle become sick and die. On the low Gulf Coast there are many insects. Cattle are troubled by these insects. But the Brahman cattle of India, a country in Asia, are not bothered by heat or insects. Some of these cattle were brought from India to Texas and bred with the best Texas shorthorns. The Texas shorthorns are fine cattle for beef because they grow large and heavy.

The result of crossing the two kinds of cattle was successful. The new breed of cattle is known as the Santa Gertrudis (sant'ə gertrood'əs). Like the shorthorns, it is good for beef. It is not troubled by heat or insects.

Lumber, Fish, Furs

Our trip down the Mississippi River continues. As we move farther south, the trees grow thicker and thicker. The swampy delta region is covered with thick, tall grass and forests of cypress trees. Because of the warm climate and heavy rainfall, trees grow faster here than in most other parts of our country.

The captain tells us that the tall, straight cypress trees make fine lumber. Their tough wood does not rot easily. Forests cover about half the area of Louisiana and Arkansas. Eastern Texas and eastern Oklahoma also have much lumber.

We pass many small fishing boats moving up from the Gulf. The boats are filled with shrimp and oysters. The Louisiana waters supply much of the shellfish in our country. The shrimp are either canned or frozen for shipment, but the oysters are packed in ice and shipped in refrigerator cars. Probably you have eaten shrimp or oysters caught in Louisiana waters.

Trappers often take their furs to market by boat. Their catch may include mink, opossum, muskrat, and raccoon skins. These animals live in watery places. Many skins come from fur farms, where people make a living by raising the animals.

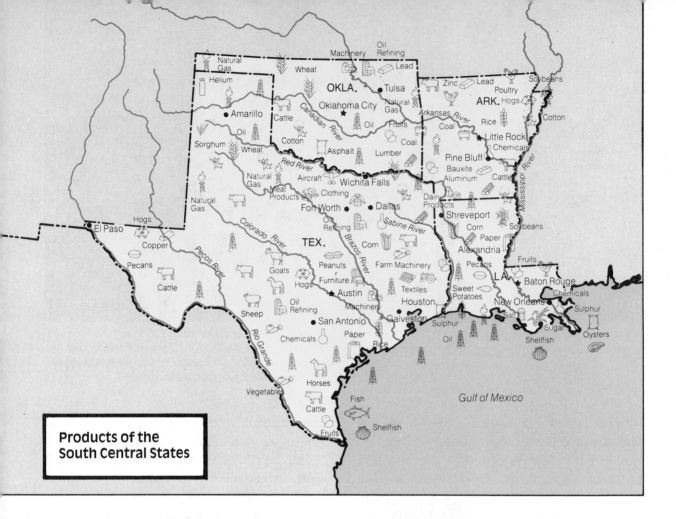

**Products of the
South Central States**

Mining in the
South Central States

Three South Central states—Texas, Louisiana, and Oklahoma—rank among the leading oil-producing states of our country. Some oil fields in this region are on land. Others are offshore in the Gulf of Mexico. Petroleum, or crude oil, is often called "black gold." Can you explain this?

The Story of Oil and Natural Gas

Can you imagine our living without the automobile and the airplane? These are only two of the machines that we probably could not use without the products of petroleum. From petroleum we get gasoline, kerosene,

fuel oils, lubricating, or smoothing, oils, and many other useful products. Natural gas is often found with petroleum.

Texas and Louisiana rank among our leading states in the production of natural gas. Natural gas is a very good fuel. It leaves no dirt and is easy to use.

Petroleum is found deep down in the earth. Thousands of years ago plants and animals were buried in mud and sand. As they were pressed down under many layers of sand and rock, they decayed. This decayed matter formed oil and natural gas.

Early settlers in North America sometimes found oil while drilling, or digging, for salt. But they had no use for oil. The settlers were annoyed when they found oil instead of salt. Later it was found that kerosene, which is made from petroleum, could be burned in lamps to give light. The demand for kerosene oil began to grow.

In 1859 Edwin Drake was hired by a company in Pennsylvania to get oil by digging wells. He used a tool for boring holes, called a *drill* (dril) to dig down into the earth. The drilling was hard and slow. Then at about 70 feet (21 m), Drake struck oil. Word of Drake's success soon spread. Others began to drill for oil in many parts of the country. They found it in great amounts, first in eastern Texas, in 1901, and later in other South Central states. See the map of oil fields on page 362.

Most oil wells must be dug much deeper than 70 feet (21 m). Deep oil wells may go down many thousand feet. A few go 4 miles (6 km) into the earth. Sharp, heavy tools are used to drill the wells. Huge steel frameworks, called *derricks* (der'iks), are built to support the drilling tools. The derricks often are more than 100 feet (30 m) high.

A drill is forced down into the earth. When the drill reaches oil, the gas that is often found with the oil tries to escape to the upper air. If there is a large amount of gas to be set free, it shoots upward with great force. As it does so, it pushes the oil up too. Sometimes oil and gas shoot high in the air. Such a well is called a *gusher* (gush'ər). Gushers were allowed in the

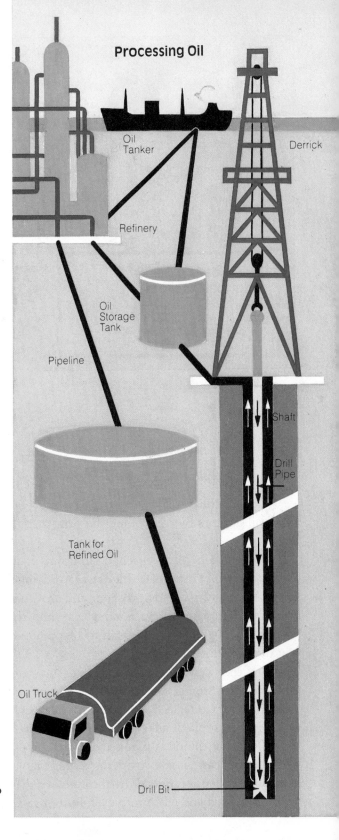

Processing Oil

This diagram of oil processing shows the major stages and places oil goes through on the way to market. How does it get to market after it has been processed?

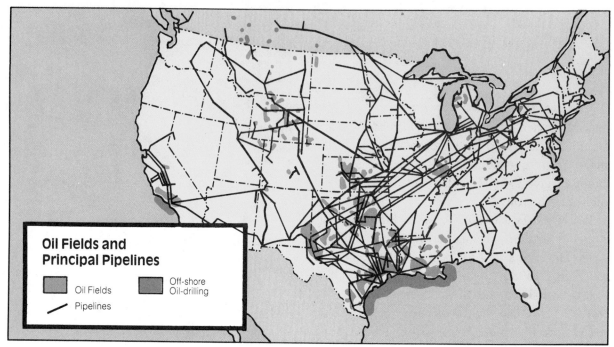

Oil Fields and Principal Pipelines

- Oil Fields
- Pipelines
- Off-shore Oil-drilling

The major areas where oil is found are shown on the map. What states have the most oil fields? What areas of the country get oil through pipelines?

early days. Today oil workers try to prevent wasteful gushers by controlling the flow of the oil.

Usually when oil is reached, it flows in a steady stream. This is called a *flowing* (flō′ing) *well*. After a while most gushers and flowing wells stop flowing because no gas is left to push the oil up. Then the oil has to be pumped out of the well.

From the wells the oil is carried through pipes to huge storage tanks. Some oil is shipped from the storage tanks by railroad tank cars and some in boats called tankers. But in the United States most of the oil is pumped through pipelines. In any case, it goes from the storage tank to a plant called a refinery. At the refinery the oil is processed and made into useful products.

Offshore Drilling

Petroleum is sometimes found beneath the water offshore. To reach it, oil workers use drilling platforms which are towed out to sea. The legs of the platforms are lowered until they rest on the bottom. The platforms hold the derricks and drilling machinery which can drill to depths of 20,000 feet (6,000 m). The oil is pumped through underwater pipes into tankers which carry it to refineries on land.

Sometimes offshore drilling causes problems. The oil may be accidentally dumped into the water. Large tankers may collide, or an underwater pipe might leak. The oil floats on top of the water. Then it spreads out, creating a slick which pollutes the water. In 1979, an oil well blowout in the Gulf of Mexico created a slick

Oil workers on platforms drill for oil under the Gulf of Mexico. Underwater pipelines will take the oil to *refineries* on land. Piles of sulfur are loaded into railroad cars that will carry the sulfur to large chemical plants. There it will be processed into many useful products.

so large that it washed up on the shores of Texas. Many fish and shore birds were killed, and the water was unfit to use. Oil workers are trying to prevent this from happening again.

The Story of Sulfur

Much of the world's supply of *sulfur* (sul′fər) comes from the Louisiana and Texas Gulf Coast. Sulfur is a yellow mineral found deep in the ground below 500 to 1,500 feet (152 to 457 m) of gravel, sand, and clay. It lies in a hard, solid layer. For many years it could not be mined cheaply. Then Herman Frasch (hur′man fräsh), an American scientist, found a good way to mine the sulfur.

Today the sulfur is mined according to Frasch's plan. A derrick similar to that used in drilling oil wells is built. Four hollow pipes,

one inside the other, are run down to the sulfur bed. Hot water is forced down the two outside pipes. The hot water melts the sulfur, because sulfur melts at a relatively low temperature. Then air is forced through the fourth or smallest pipe. This pushes the melted, or liquid, sulfur to the surface through the third pipe. A pipeline carries away the liquid sulfur and empties it into a huge storage bin. When the sulfur cools, it hardens into a solid block. Such blocks break up easily into fine powder, which is easy to process.

Sulfur is important in the making of many things, from explosives and steel to newsprint and rayon. It is used in tanning leather, in bleaching, dyeing, and making ink and paper. Powdered sulfur is used in preparations that kill insects on plants. Sulfuric acid, used in making explosives, fertilizers, and medicines, is also made from sulfur.

Salt Quarrying

Besides petroleum and sulfur, the Gulf Coast of Louisiana yields salt. For almost 100 years, Louisiana has been a leading salt producer. The salt lies underground in thick beds of rock salt. Salt mines are like quarries under the ground. Oklahoma and Texas also produce salt.

Do you know that there are more than 1,000 uses for salt? The most common use of salt is in the kitchen and at the table to season food. But the largest amounts of salt are used in industry. Salt is used in meat-packing plants and in factories that process hides and leather. Bakers, cereal producers, and butter and cheese manufacturers use huge amounts. Farmers feed salt to livestock.

Bauxite Mining

Arkansas has some of the largest deposits of bauxite in North America. Bauxite is the ore from which aluminum is made. Bauxite, which looks like clay, is mined from open pits. The ore is washed and crushed. Then the bauxite is taken out and melted.

Aluminum is a strong, light metal which is important in the building of airplanes. Kitchen utensils are also made from aluminum.

Helium Fields

Helium (hē′lē əm) is found in Texas in large quantities. Helium is a very light gas which does not burn or explode. It is used in the blimp, which is a kind of balloon airship. A blimp is a gas bag that has no metal frame and collapses when the gas is taken out. Helium is used in rocket launchings and in some welding.

A major helium field lies near Amarillo, in the Texas Panhandle. Texas is shaped somewhat like a large pan. The "handle" of the pan is the area that extends northward from the rest of Texas. See the map of the South Central states on page 345. This field can produce helium for the United States for many years. The helium plant there is the largest in the country.

Lead and Zinc

The Ozark–Ouachita Mountains are rich in lead, zinc, coal, and other minerals. Lead and zinc are also found in Oklahoma. These two minerals are usually found and mined together. Lead is used to make water pipes, paints, bullets, and many other things. Articles made of iron and steel are coated with zinc to prevent their rusting. Zinc is also used in making refrigerators.

Chief Cities of the South Central States

The cities of this region are chiefly trade and transportation centers. In some cities, however, much manufacturing is done. The large cities are railroad and airplane centers. Some are also ports. The city of Houston is a center for our country's space program.

Cities of Louisiana

Shreveport lies on the Red River in northwestern Louisiana. It is the chief market for the gas, lumber, cotton, and oil produced in this part of the state. Shreveport has cotton mills, lumber factories, and oil refineries. But it ships most of the lumber, raw cotton, and crude oil to other parts of our country.

The capital of Louisiana is Baton Rouge (bat'ən roozh') a Mississippi River port. Baton Rouge is the trade and shipping center of a rich farming region. One of the largest oil refineries in the world is at Baton Rouge. Petroleum products are shipped to ports all over the world.

New Orleans is the chief trade and shipping center for the lower Mississippi Valley. It is about 100 miles (160 km) above the mouth of the river. Gulf storms seldom reach its harbor. Cotton, sugar, rice, lumber, furs, and oil are shipped from New Orleans to northern industrial cities. But some oil and sugar refining, rice milling, furniture and paper manufacturing, and shipbuilding are done in New Orleans. Early fruits and vegetables, shrimp, and oysters are shipped in refrigerated cars to large cities in other parts of our country.

Mississippi River traffic has grown in recent years. Products from the North Central states are sent down the Mississippi to New Orleans. From New Orleans they are shipped overseas by freighter.

Freighters from the Northeast bring manufactured goods to New Orleans. Vessels from Central America and South America bring coffee, bananas, lumber, and many other things. These products are sent from New Orleans to various parts of the United States and to foreign countries.

Trumpeter Louis Armstrong plays for his wife, Lucille, in their New York home. Louis was a famous jazz musician from New Orleans.

Louis Armstrong, Jazz Musician

New Orleans is the birthplace of a kind of music known as jazz. New Orleans is also the birthplace of Louis Armstrong. He was a great jazz trumpet player and singer.

Louis, also known as "Satchmo," first learned to play the cornet. He played in New Orleans and on riverboats. Then he joined a jazz band in Chicago, Illinois. Two years later, Louis joined a band in New York City. The leader of this band had Louis switch from the cornet to the trumpet. He played the trumpet from then until his death in 1971.

During his life, Louis Armstrong led both large and small bands. He began to sing in addition to playing. Soon his singing became as excellent as his trumpet playing. Louis made a large number of recordings. He performed in many European cities. He also made several films. Louis "Satchmo" Armstrong helped to make jazz an important part of American music.

365

Houston
Skyline of the Southwest

In 1962, pasture land southeast of Houston, Texas, was chosen as the place to build the nation's space center. People at the space center develop and test space vehicles. Astronauts train at the space center. In the control center are people who take charge of every space flight from launch to splashdown.

Founded in 1836, Houston began as a trading center for cotton farmers and cattle ranchers. It became and still remains a leading cattle market. Then, in the early 1900s, oil was discovered in Texas. Railroad cars would not do for shipping oil. Houston needed a port for ocean tankers. Look at the map of the South Central states on page 345. Notice the channel that shows how Houston made itself a port by bringing the sea to its door.

With an ocean port, Houston's industries grew rapidly. Because oil, natural gas, and sulfur are found nearby, huge chemical factories and oil refineries have grown up. Factories also turn out farm machinery and oil-field equipment. ■

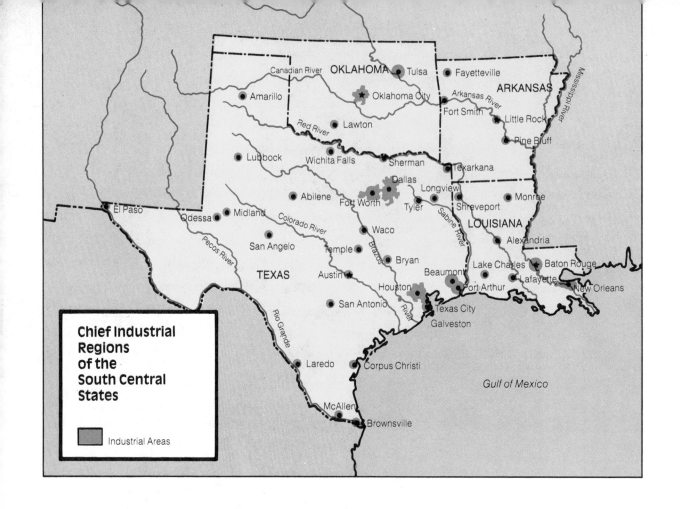

Chief Industrial Regions of the South Central States

Industrial Areas

Cities of Texas

Texas is so large that great distances separate most of its cities. However, all of the larger cities like Houston have airports. Excellent roads and highways connect cities with farming and marketing areas. Texas also has about 15,000 miles (24,140 km) of railroad.

Amarillo is the chief trade and shipping center of the Texas Panhandle. Most people in Amarillo earn a living by handling the wheat, oil, cattle, and sheep of the Panhandle area.

El Paso, in the western corner of Texas, is the main trade center of western Texas and northern Mexico. This area produces oil, wheat, cotton, and cattle. El Paso is also a center for refining copper.

In south central Texas are the cities of San Antonio and Austin. Both were capitals of the area now known as Texas. San Antonio was the capital while the area was under Spanish and Mexican rule. After Texas won its independence, Austin became the capital. Many tourists visit these cities each year. They come to see the many historic sites. What famous mission is in San Antonio?

Austin is the trade and shipping center of a large farming and grazing region. Its industries include manufacturing brick, tile, and furniture.

San Antonio is a trade and shipping center for cotton, oil, livestock, wool, grain, vegetables, and citrus fruits. San Antonio has oil refineries, meat-packing plants, flour mills, and factories where clothing, pottery, tile, brooms, and refrigerators are manufactured.

Dallas is the headquarters for several oil firms and is a leading cotton market. Other important industries include aircraft parts, and food products, banking, insurance, and fashions center.

In early days Fort Worth was an important trading and supply center for cattle ranchers. Today it is one of the largest meat-packing cities in the South. Aircraft factories and large oil refineries are located in Fort Worth. The city is also one of the principal grain-milling centers of the South Central states. Many oil companies and insurance firms have offices in Fort Worth.

Galveston is a busy Texas port on an island off the Gulf Coast. A bridge about 3 miles (5 km) long connects Galveston with the mainland. Many people spend their vacations on the island's beaches.

Cities of Arkansas and Oklahoma

Little Rock, which is on the Arkansas River, is the capital and largest city of Arkansas. It is a trading center. It ships cotton, lumber, rice, soybeans, and minerals to other states. Some people work in factories that turn out wood products or food products. Others work in clothing or aluminum factories.

Have you ever seen a city with oil derricks? Oklahoma City, the capital and largest city of

Oil companies drill for oil wherever it may be found. These *derricks* are in front of the Oklahoma state capitol.

Oklahoma, has oil wells on front lawns, in schoolyards, and even on the state capitol grounds. This city is also a major trade and shipping center. It has one of the largest cattle stockyards in the world.

The city of Tulsa turned into a boom town with the discovery of oil beneath a cornfield. Tulsa has continued to grow. Today some of the biggest oil companies in our country are in Tulsa. This modern, bustling city is the chief trade center for northeastern Oklahoma.

Do You Know?

1. What are some of the chief crops of the South Central states?
2. What kinds of livestock are raised in the region?
3. What kinds of minerals are important in the region?

To Help You Learn

Using New Words

helium	sulfur	dry farming
drill	derrick	flowing well
gusher	refinery	reservation
mohair	levee	raw sugar
delta	feed lot	

The phrases below explain the words and terms listed above. Number a paper from 1 through 14. After each number write the word or term that matches the definition.

1. An oil well from which the oil shoots high into the air
2. A building in which raw materials are changed into finished products
3. The brown crystals that form when the juice of sugarcane is boiled and allowed to cool
4. The framework built to support the machinery needed to drill an oil well
5. A tool used to bore holes in the ground
6. Cloth made from goat hair
7. A very light gas which does not burn or explode
8. An oil well which produces oil in a steady stream without being pumped
9. A yellow mineral
10. A way of conserving moisture in dry areas by growing only one crop every 2 years on the same plot of ground
11. A pen where cattle are fed special feed to fatten them for market
12. An area set aside by the government for the use of Indians
13. Land built up by mud and sand brought down by a slow river
14. A bank of earth built along a river to keep it from overflowing its banks and flooding the land

Finding the Facts

1. What four states are called the South Central states? What is the capital city of each of these states?
2. What rivers in the South Central states have flood plains?
3. What city did Jean de Bienville found in 1718?
4. Why was the battle at San Jacinto important to Texas?
5. What caused the war between the United States and Mexico after Texas became a state? What change took place under the peace treaty after the war ended?
6. Why did the United States government set up reservations for Indians in the first half of the 1800s?
7. In what year did each of the South Central states become a state?
8. Which state is the leading cotton state in the United States?
9. What crop grown in Arkansas, Louisiana, and Texas must be kept under water most of the time?

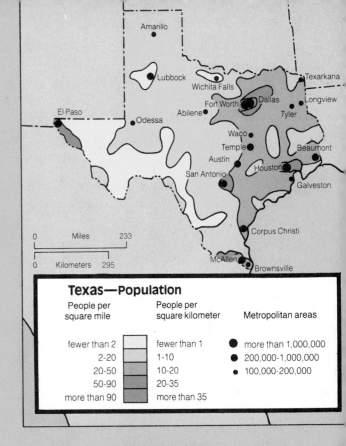

Texas—Population

People per square mile	People per square kilometer	Metropolitan areas
fewer than 2	fewer than 1	● more than 1,000,000
2-20	1-10	● 200,000-1,000,000
20-50	10-20	• 100,000-200,000
50-90	20-35	
more than 90	more than 35	

10. In which South Central state is sugarcane grown?

11. When were great amounts of oil first found in Texas? What are some products made from petroleum? Why is natural gas a good fuel?

12. What are the chief uses of sulfur? Of bauxite? Of helium? Of lead? Of zinc?

13. What are the chief cities of Louisiana? What is made in these cities? Which city is the birthplace of jazz?

14. What are the chief cities of Arkansas and Oklahoma? For what industries are these cities known?

15. What are the chief cities of Texas? For what industries are these cities known?

Learning from Maps

1. On the map of the United States on pages A-6–A-7 locate the four South Central states. Between what parallels of latitude do they lie? What kind of climate would you expect to find in them? Locate the capitals of these states.

2. On the same map trace the Mississippi River from its source in Minnesota down to the Gulf of Mexico. Of what states does it form the boundary? What important tributaries of the Mississippi drain the South Central states?

3. Look at the key to the map of the South Central states on page 345. What kind of land makes up most of the region? Where is the Edwards Plateau?

4. This map is a population map of Texas. It shows where many people live and where few people live in Texas. In which part of Texas do most people live?

Which city, Houston or Amarillo, has the most people living there? Which two large cities are so close that they almost look like one large city on the map?

Where is the largest area in which the fewest number of people live?

Which cities are surrounded by areas with fewer than two people per square mile? By areas with more than 90 people per square mile?

What are some of the largest cities in Texas? Look at the map of chief industrial regions of the South Central states on page 368. Which of these cities are industrial areas? Explain your findings.

371

5. On the map of the War with Mexico on page 351 trace the route of General Taylor. How did General Scott and his army reach Mexico City?

6. Study the products map of the South Central states on page 360. What is the most important product of this area? Which states have important fisheries? Which state has large quantities of helium? Sulfur? Bauxite?

7. The map on page 362 shows the location of the oil fields in the United States. Which states have the most pipe lines carrying oil to market?

8. The map on page 525 shows cattle trails of the West about 1870. In which South Central state did the four cattle trails shown on the map begin? Trace the route of each trail.

Using Study Skills

1. **Chart:** Look at the chart on page 356. In which state are sweet potatoes a major crop? Where are peanuts a major crop? Where is sorghum a major crop? Which crop is a major one in all four states? In which state are tomatoes grown? Where are strawberries grown? What crops are raised in Texas? In which state are goats raised? Where are cattle and hogs raised? Where are chickens raised?

2. **Diagram:** Look at the diagram of processing oil on page 361. What are some of the parts of an oil drill? What happens to the oil before it reaches the refinery? What happens to the oil after it has been through the refinery?

Thinking It Through

1. When our country bought the Louisiana Territory, the land size of the United States almost doubled. The United States became the owner of New Orleans, the Mississippi River, and a large piece of land west of the Mississippi. How did this purchase help our country?

2. Parts of the South Central states are on a flood plain. What are the advantages and disadvantages of living on a flood plain?

3. Look at the photograph of the Lyndon B. Johnson Space Center, page 366. What makes the Center look like a separate city? The Center has only a few thousand employees, yet it has created tens of thousands of jobs. Why?

4. Discuss in your class what would happen to our homes, factories, and transportation if all the oil wells suddenly ran dry. Here are some points to think and read about first: What products are made from petroleum? How do we use these products? What other kinds of energy and lubrication do we have?

Projects

1. Make a model of a delta. Try to borrow a sand table and make your model in sand. Show how a river or stream deposits soil at its mouth.

2. The Research Committee should find out how the coming of the railroads and the invention of refrigerator cars helped the meat industry grow.

3. Your class might learn some songs which were sung by the cowhands in the old trail-driving days. Books which contain many of these songs are *Cowboy Songs* by John and Alan Lomax and *The American Songbag* by Carl Sandburg.

4. The Reading Committee may find books on these subjects: the settlement of Oklahoma; Texas and the war with Mexico; the Mississippi River; the Louisiana Purchase. The committee might ask the librarian to find some exciting stories about western cattle ranching in the 1860s. Read a book or story on one of these subjects and report on it to the class.

5. Many people have played an important part in the growth of the South Central states. Divide into small groups. Have each group find out about one of the following people: Davy Crockett, Juan Cortina, Barbara Jordan, Van Cliburn, Hattie Caraway, Maria Tallchief, or Stand Watie. Tell your story in the form of a play.

6. The Mississippi River and its tributaries form the largest inland waterway in the United States. Members of the Explorers' Committee might collect information about the waterway and report to the class. Let them use a map to show how barges and boats travel from New Orleans to St. Paul and Minneapolis, to Chicago, and to cities in Ohio. They should also tell what products the boats and barges carry.

7. Oklahoma, which became a state in 1907, is one of our youngest states. Find out which states of our nation are newer than Oklahoma. When were they admitted to the Union?

12   The Rocky Mountain States

Unit Preview

The Rocky Mountain states are Colorado, Montana, Wyoming, Idaho, Nevada, Utah, Arizona, and New Mexico.

Spanish explorers were the first to venture into this region. The Spanish made settlements in the southern part of this area. One of the earliest was Santa Fe. It was founded in 1610. Missions, or church settlements, were also built.

American Indian groups were living in the Southwest many years before the Spanish came. The Pueblos, Navajos, and Apaches used their skills to develop the resources they found.

The United States sent its first explorers to this region in 1806. Later, trappers and fur traders wandered throughout the area. Then wagon trains of settlers rumbled across the Rockies heading to the Far West. But few settlers came to stay in the Rocky Mountain region until after the discovery of silver and gold there.

Mining is still important in the Rockies. Besides silver and gold, copper, uranium ores, and other minerals are also mined. These minerals are important raw materials.

Farming is also important in the Rocky Mountain states, but rainfall is uncertain. Farms in some areas must be irrigated with water from dammed-up rivers. The dams are also useful for controlling the rivers and providing hydroelectric power for industry.

Things to Discover

If you look carefully at the picture, map, and time line, you can answer these questions.

1. How many states are in the Rocky Mountain region?
2. Whom did the United States send to explore this region in 1806? What famous landmark did this person discover?
3. When did Santa Fe become a capital?
4. How long after Pike's explorations was one of the main western trails opened?
5. What discovery brought a rush of settlers to the mountain country in 1859?
6. Dams have been built on many rivers in the Rocky Mountain states. The water is used for irrigation and to provide hydroelectric power. What is another way rivers are used, as shown in the picture?
7. How long after the Hoover Dam was completed was the Fort Peck Dam completed?

Words to Learn

You will meet these words in this unit. As you read, you will learn what they mean and how to pronounce them. The Word List will help you.

Continental Divide	oil shale
fleece	pueblo
geyser	ridge
hogan	shearing
international	

Coronado explores
the Grand Canyon

Santa Fe made
capital of New Mexico

Zebulon Pike
finds Pikes Peak

Sante Fe Trail opened

Salt Lake City
started by
Mormons

Comstock Silver
Lode opened

Yellowstone
made national
park

Hoover Dam
completed

Fort Peck
Dam completed

United States studies
oil shale production

Nevada
becomes
the fastest
growing state

1540   1610   1806   1821 1847 1859 1872 1936   1940   1970s 1980

CANADA

Atlantic
Ocean

Pacific
Ocean

MEXICO

N

1

Geography of the Rocky Mountain States

The plains region in the central part of our country extends westward to the Rocky Mountains. Many different plants and animals thrive in the Rockies. However, it is too cold for trees to grow on the snowy tops of these mountains.

Surface of the Land

The Rocky Mountains begin in New Mexico. They stretch north through Colorado, Utah, Wyoming, Idaho, and Montana. From there they reach on into Canada and Alaska.

East of the Rockies—in Montana, Wyoming, Colorado, and New Mexico—the Great Plains begin. The Great Plains are a part of the level or rolling region that stretches from the Rockies to the Appalachians. The map of the United States on pages A-6– A-7 shows how wide this plains area is.

The map of the Rocky Mountain states on page 377 shows that a huge plateau lies west of the southern Rockies. A plateau is a high but rather level area. This plateau is called the Colorado Plateau. It covers much of Arizona and Utah and smaller areas of Colorado and New Mexico.

Northwest of the Colorado Plateau is a huge basin, or lower area surrounded by mountains. It is called the Great Basin. Western Utah and most of Nevada are in the Great Basin.

The Rocky Mountain region thus has a great variety of scenery. There are rugged mountains and plains, deep valleys, canyons, and rivers.

The Continental Divide

The peaks of the Rockies rise so high that they form a dividing line on the North American continent. All the rivers on one side of the *ridge* (rij), or long and narrow chain of hills or mountains, flow to the east.

On the other side of the ridge the rivers flow to the west. This ridge is called the *Continental* (kon'tə nent' əl) *Divide.* The Continental Divide separates the rivers that flow east from those that flow west.

Four important rivers, the Arkansas, the Rio Grande, the Colorado, and the Platte, begin in the Rocky Mountains. Because of the Continental Divide, some of these rivers, such as the Arkansas, tumble down the eastern slopes of the Rockies. Then they flow eastward to the Mississippi River, southward to the Gulf of Mexico, and finally to the Atlantic Ocean. The Colorado River, however, runs down the western slopes of the Rockies to the Gulf of California, which empties into the Pacific Ocean.

Climate of the Mountain States

Moist, warm winds blow eastward from the Pacific Ocean. The winds lose much moisture as they rise to cross the mountains in the states next to the ocean. For this reason most parts of the Rocky Mountain states are very dry. Land at high altitudes thus receives more rain and snow than does lower land. The western sides of the mountains are better watered than the eastern.

THE ROCKY
MOUNTAIN
STATES

| 50 | 100 | 200 Miles |
| 80 | 161 | 322 Kilometers |

★ State Capitals   • Other Cities

Mountains   Hills

Plateaus   Plains

© Rand McNally & C.

The Rocky Mountains in Colorado have snow near their peaks even during the summer. The air is much colder at the tops of these mountains than at their bases.

In the highest ranges, rains and melting snows feed mountain streams. In some areas the people of these mountain states can use water from the rushing streams to irrigate land. The water is stored in reservoirs, or artificial lakes. From the reservoirs water is taken through canals and ditches to irrigate dry fields in the nearby area. Through irrigation the fields can produce good crops. The reservoirs also supply water for nearby cities.

The temperature of the Rocky Mountain region varies according to the altitude of the land. At lower levels much of the region has hot summers and cold winters. But the mountains stay cool even in the summer. There are stretches of hot, dry desert in parts of New Mexico, Arizona, Nevada, and Utah.

The temperature in these states also varies according to latitude. Places near Canada are much colder than are places near Mexico. The region near Mexico is usually warm all year because Mexico is closer to the equator.

Do You Know?

1. What eight states are called the Rocky Mountain states?
2. What kinds of climate do the Rocky Mountain states have?
3. How do the mountains provide water for the people who live near them?

2
Settling the Rocky Mountain States

"Far to the north are seven golden cities," said an American Indian to a group of Spanish explorers.

"I must find these golden cities," declared the Spanish adventurer Francisco Coronado. "Then I will fill Spain's treasury and win fortune for myself."

Spanish Explorations

Coronado marched north from Mexico hoping to find treasure. With him were many Spanish soldiers and a large number of American Indians. These Spaniards were the first Europeans to explore the region that is now Arizona and New Mexico.

Months of hard travel followed. Many of the Spaniards grew ill and died. Then one day Coronado saw a city in the distance which looked bright and beautiful in the sunshine. But when he finally reached it, he found that the city was a group of American Indian villages. The Spanish found plenty of food in the villages, but there was neither gold nor silver. They were greatly disappointed. Still they pushed on, searching for treasure.

Coronado and the soldiers broke up into several groups. One of these groups made a great discovery. While following the Colorado River, they came to the Grand Canyon. This is a deep, wide valley worn away by the swift waters of the Colorado River. The Spaniards were amazed by the great size and beauty of the canyon.

Coronado and the soldiers found no treasure and left no settlements in the mountain country. But they did explore and claim a large part of the area for Spain. And they discovered the Grand Canyon of the Colorado.

Southwest American Indians

American Indians were living in the southwestern part of the country long before the Spanish arrived. One of these Indian groups lived in apartment houses built close together. The

Francisco Coronado led Spaniards through large areas of the Rocky Mountain region. They saw many beautiful places in present-day New Mexico and Arizona.

houses were made of stone or clay and had several stories. The Spanish called such Indian villages *pueblos* (pweb′lōz).

The Pueblo Indians

The Indians living in pueblos became known as Pueblo Indians. Most of the Pueblo Indians were farmers. They grew corn, beans, and squash.

The Spanish tried to teach Christianity to the Pueblos. But the Indians wanted to keep their own religion. The Pueblos drove the Spanish away. Later the United States gained the lands on which the Pueblos lived. The government then let the Pueblos keep their old ways of life.

María Martínez, a Pueblo Indian, with one of her famous black-on-black pots. The brilliant shine of this type of pottery is produced by firing.

Many of the Pueblo Indians of today live in pueblos in New Mexico and Arizona. Some farm. Others work in nearby cities. Still others have become well known for their art.

María Martínez, Pottery Maker

María Montoya Martínez (mär tē′nās) was born in 1887 at San Idlefonso Pueblo, New Mexico. María and her husband Julian began making black-on-black pottery in the early 1900s. This special type of pottery had been made by the Pueblo Indians a long time ago. But no one remembered how to make it. Then María and Julian made some tests and found how to make the black-on-black pottery. After Julian died in 1943, Mariá continued the work.

María used materials from the earth to make the pottery. She formed each pot by hand. The pots were perfectly shaped. Then each pot was heated a certain way to get the black finish.

Over the years the Martínez pottery became well known. María was invited to show her works at world's fairs. She was invited to the White House by four Presidents. She also received a number of awards and honors for her work. María died in 1980, but her children, grandchildren, and great-grandchildren continue to make the famous pottery.

The Navajo Indians

Another group of American Indians living in the southwest at the time the Spanish arrived were the Navajos (näv′e hōz′). They lived in houses called *hogans* (hō′gänz). The dome-shaped hogans were built of poles, tree bark, and mud.

Sand painting is one of the ceremonies of the Navajo religion. These ceremonies may be related to farming or to curing sickness and preserving health.

At first the Navajos hunted for much of their food. Then the Pueblo Indians taught them to farm. After the Spanish brought livestock to the area, many Navajos became sheep ranchers.

During the middle 1800s many settlers started ranches on Navajo lands. The Navajos fought to keep their lands. Manuelito (män wä lē′tō), a Navajo, helped lead several attacks against the settlers. Then Kit Carson and a group of United States soldiers captured thousands of Navajos. The Navajos were forced to march several hundred miles to what is now New Mexico. This march became known as the "Long Walk." In 1868 the Navajos agreed to settle on a reservation that covered parts of present-day Arizona, New Mexico, and Utah.

Today the Navajos are the largest group of American Indians in the United States. Most live in Arizona, New Mexico, and Utah. Some raise crops or tend sheep. Others own or work in businesses. Still others are craft-workers or artists.

The Apache Indians

The Apache (ə pach′ ē) Indians also lived in the Southwest at the time the Spanish arrived. Some Apaches lived in thatched huts made of brush. Others lived in tepees made of animal skin.

The Apaches hunted for most of their food. They learned some farming from the Pueblo Indians, just as the Navajos had.

When the early Spanish settled on the Indian lands, the Apaches often raided them. In time other people settled on Apache lands. The Apaches, led by Cochise (kō chēz′) and Geronimo (jə rän′ ə mō′) fought to keep their lands but were defeated by United States soldiers.

This old Spanish mission, San Xavier del Bac, in Tucson, Arizona, is a reminder of the Spanish heritage of the Southwest.

The Apaches were then placed on reservations. In 1886 Geronimo led a group of Apaches from a reservation in a final attack on the soldiers. He was defeated and again placed on a reservation.

Many Apache Indians of today live in Arizona and New Mexico. Some raise sheep. Some work in the lumber or cattle business owned by Apaches.

Mission Settlements

Two priests who came to the West in early times were Father Eusebio Kino (ā o͞o sā′ vyō kē′nō) and Father Junipero Serra (hoo nē′pə rō ser′ə). They came to teach Christianity to the American Indians. Father Kino started a mission in 1700 in what is now Arizona. Father Serra founded at least nine missions farther west, in California. Several other church settlements were built by followers of the two priests.

For many years the West had few settlements besides missions. Let us visit one of the mission settlements in Arizona in those early days.

A Visit to a Mission

We enter this mission settlement through a gate in a thick stone wall. The wall has been built around the settlement to protect the people inside. A fort and soldiers guard the settlement.

Many American Indians are at work. Some are tanning hides. Others are making jewelry of silver set with brightly colored stones. We see a priest teaching a group how to make candles. Some are tying wicks onto a wooden rod. Others are dipping wicks into a large pot of warm animal fat. The wicks will then be hung on a frame to cool. They will be dipped again and again until enough layers of fat cover each wick to form a candle.

Clang, clang, clang! A blacksmith is working before a great fire. He is making horseshoes and wagon wheels. Farther on, we see carpenters making benches for the church and chairs and tables for their homes.

We come to a group of people working near a stone oven. They are baking loaves of wheat, corn, and barley bread. Some are kneading dough on large, flat stones. Others are taking brown loaves out of the oven.

Farther along we pass a building where women are weaving cloth. Sheep are grazing in the fields of this mission settlement. From the sheep the Indians get wool for cloth. Besides sheep, this settlement has horses, cows, and oxen. The grazing lands are outside the wall.

As we leave, we see that the farmlands of this mission settlement also lie outside the stone wall. A canal has been dug from a nearby stream to irrigate these fields. Oranges, lemons, limes, and figs grow in orchards. Grains and vegetables grow in the fields.

The Santa Fe Trail

After the Louisiana Purchase in 1803, some traders from the United States began to make the long journey to Spanish settlements in Arizona and New Mexico. They traveled over a route called the Santa Fe Trail.

The city of Santa Fe was founded in 1610 as the capital of the Spanish province of New Mexico. Notice on the map of western trails on

All the routes to the West followed large rivers for part of the way. Why do you think this was so? From what city did most of the trails start? What natural barriers did settlers on the trails have to face?

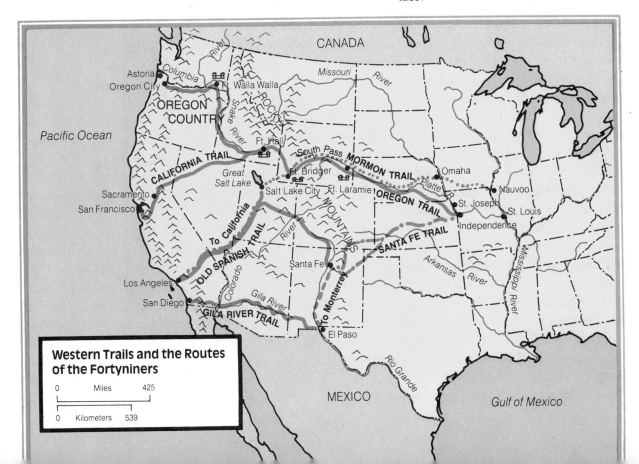

Western Trails and the Routes of the Fortyniners

0   Miles   425

0   Kilometers   539

Traders traveled on the Santa Fe Trail in covered wagons pulled by oxen. What kinds of manufactured goods do you think the traders took to Santa Fe?

page 383 that Santa Fe was the meeting point of two other trails. The Old Spanish Trail led to Los Angeles. Another trail led south along the Rio Grande to Monterrey and other Mexican cities.

In 1821, William Becknell was the first trader to use the Santa Fe Trail. After that, many traders used it to carry manufactured goods from the United States to Santa Fe. These manufactures were exchanged for the mules, furs, gold, and silver of Mexico.

The traders started from Independence, near the Missouri River. Then they journeyed southwest across the wide, flat plains to a point on the Arkansas River. Here the trail divided. The shorter, more dangerous route crossed a wide desert where there was no water for 60 miles (96 km). The longer, safer trail went through part of the Rocky Mountains. The two trails joined again before Santa Fe, New Mexico, was reached. Follow the route on the map of western trails on page 383. The trail covered almost 800 miles (1,287 km). The Santa Fe Trail was once an important trade route.

Because of the dangers on this trail, traders on the Santa Fe Trail traveled in large groups. At first they used pack mules to carry the goods. Then as the trail grew wider with use, they traveled in covered wagons. Each wagon was pulled by ten oxen or mules and could carry a load of 6,000 pounds (2,721 kg). A wagon train could go about 15 miles (24 km) a day along the Santa Fe Trail.

After a time stagecoaches carried passengers on their westward journeys. Then the trip from Independence, Missouri, to Santa Fe, New Mexico, took about two weeks.

The Mormons in Utah

One of the most important routes to the West was the Oregon Trail. Near that trail, in what is now Utah, is Salt Lake City. This city was built by a religious group called Mormons. These people were looking for land on which to settle.

The Mormons were searching for a place where they could worship as they wished. First they had tried to settle in Ohio. Then they moved on to Missouri and later to Illinois. But wherever they tried to settle, neighboring people objected to what the Mormons believed.

The Mormons decided that they would have to find a new region where there were no people to object to their ways of worship. So they made up their minds to move out of the United States.

Brigham Young was determined to lead his people to an area where they could worship in peace. The Mormons built a successful settlement in the desert of Utah.

Brigham Young, Mormon Leader

The leader of the Mormons in their westward travels was Brigham Young. Under his leadership about 200 Mormons started west in the winter of 1846. They traveled 1,000 miles (1,609 km) to the shore of the Great Salt Lake. This land then belonged to Mexico. No other settlers were living there. It was a very dry area where only desert shrubs grew.

The Building of Salt Lake City

All the Mormons worked together under Brigham Young's leadership to build a new settlement. They dug ditches to irrigate the land. They plowed the land and planted the crops. They built barns, houses, and a church, which they called a temple. They laid out wide, straight streets.

In their second year their crops were threatened by a huge swarm of Rocky Mountain grasshoppers. But before the grasshoppers destroyed the crops, flocks of sea gulls appeared and ate the grasshoppers. The Mormons were so grateful that they set up a statue of the sea gulls.

Within a few years several thousand other Mormons joined this settlement. Everyone worked hard. Today Salt Lake City is one of the major cities of the Rocky Mountain states.

Settlement of Nevada and Colorado

In 1848 the discovery of gold in California drew thousands of people westward. Some who reached California failed to find gold there and left. Their search for mineral treasures took them to the Rocky Mountain region.

The Comstock Lode

Ten years after the gold rush to California, a huge deposit of gold and silver was discovered in western Nevada. This mine was called the Comstock Lode. News of it brought many adventurers to Nevada.

One adventurer who went to Nevada in the days of the Comstock Lode became a well-known writer. His real name was Samuel Clemens, but he used Mark Twain as a pen name. His stories, published in a newspaper, tell us

Reaching the top of Pikes Peak is a challenge for many visitors to the Colorado Rockies. Some walk, others ride horses, and some ride a train to the top.

much about the early days in Nevada. Later Mark Twain became famous as the author of *The Adventures of Tom Sawyer* and *The Adventures of Huckleberry Finn*.

Pikes Peak or Bust

When the Comstock Lode was discovered, gold was also found in the Pikes Peak region of Colorado. Hundreds of people came to Colorado. Some traveled on foot. Some rode on horseback. Others went in covered wagons. Many covered wagons had signs reading "Pikes Peak or Bust" printed on them. When some of these wagons went home later, their covers carried the word "Busted." Today a highway and a rail-way run to the top of Pikes Peak. Many people travel up the mountain every year to enjoy the wonderful scenery.

Becoming a Part of the United States

The map showing the growth of the United States on page 137 shows how the United States obtained the territory between the Mississippi River and the Pacific Ocean. It shows that parts of Colorado, Wyoming, and Montana lie within the region that was gained from France through the Louisiana Purchase.

Arizona, Nevada, and Utah are within the region that once belonged to Mexico. Some land that now lies within Wyoming, Colorado, and New Mexico also belonged to Mexico.

To the north was the Oregon Country, which was shared by the United States and Great Britain until 1846. After it was divided and more people settled there, new states were carved out of it. One of these was Idaho. Part of Wyoming and of Montana also belonged to the Oregon Country in the early days.

Do You Know?

1. What areas did Coronado and the Spaniards with him explore?
2. Who founded missions in Arizona?
3. Who led the Mormons in their westward travels?
4. What was the Comstock Lode?

Before You Go On

Using New Words

pueblo   Continental Divide
hogan   ridge

The phrases below explain the words or terms listed above. Number a paper from 1 through 4. After each number write the word or term that matches the definition.

1. A dome-shaped American Indian house built of poles, tree bark, and mud
2. A long, narrow chain of hills or mountains
3. A dividing ridge in the Rockies which separates the rivers flowing east from the rivers flowing west
4. An Indian village like apartment houses built of stone or clay

Finding the Facts

1. What different types of land surfaces make up the Rocky Mountain region?
2. Why don't all rivers that form in the Rocky Mountains flow in the same direction?
3. Why are most parts of the Rocky Mountain states very dry?
4. How is the temperature of the Rocky Mountain region affected by altitude and latitude?
5. What is the Grand Canyon? By whom was it discovered?
6. What three American Indian groups were living in the southwestern part of the country at the time the Spanish arrived? Which group is the largest today?
7. For what did María Martínez receive a number of awards and honors?
8. Why did Father Kino and Father Serra come to the West in early times? In which present-day state did Father Kino settle? Where did Father Serra build missions?
9. Why was the Santa Fe Trail an important route during the 1800s? How did travel on the Santa Fe Trail change as time passed?
10. Why did the Mormons journey westward? What city did they build?
11. How did the Comstock Lode help to bring settlers to Nevada?
12. What discovery brought many settlers to Colorado?
13. What foreign countries once owned parts of the region that now makes up the Rocky Mountain states? To which country did most of the land in this region once belong?

3

Living and Working in the Rocky Mountain States

Many people who live in the plains region of the mountain states earn their living by farming and livestock raising. The leading crops are wheat and cotton. Cattle and sheep feed on the tough grass that covers much of the land.

Grazing and Farming Lands

Most of the land west of the Rockies has little rain. Some regions are covered with short, coarse grass. The grasslands are used mainly for cattle and sheep grazing. Many more sheep than cattle pasture there, however. Sheep can live on less water and poorer grass than cattle can. Sheep also climb more easily and can graze on mountain slopes.

Sheep like salt in addition to the grass they eat. Sheepherders make sure salt is part of their diet. Sheep are marked so sheepherders know which sheep are theirs.

Raising Sheep

During the winter the sheep grow a thick, warm wool coat called a *fleece* (flēs). In spring the sheep are rounded up and their fleeces are clipped off. This is called *shearing* (shēr′ing) the sheep. Ranch workers bring the animals to a shearing shed. Each worker throws a sheep to the floor and holds it down. With large electric clippers the worker quickly and painlessly cuts off the sheep's coat of wool.

In the spring ranchers wait until there is no danger of a late snowfall on the mountainsides. Then the sheepherders go with the sheep to the fresh pastures. Each sheepherder must keep the flock from grazing in one place more than three days. In this way the sheep do not eat the grass so close that it will not grow again. In the late fall the sheepherders take the sheep back to the ranch for winter feeding.

Farming in the South

The dry land in Arizona and New Mexico has irrigation water for only a very small part of its area. The Elephant Butte Dam on the Rio Grande provides water for some of New Mexico's dry land. The irrigated land produces corn, wheat, and onions.

Some of the finest cotton in the world comes from Arizona. Arizona's cotton farmers get irrigation water from Roosevelt Dam, on the Salt River. Arizona is also known for its lettuce, melons, and citrus fruits. Some of these crops grow on land irrigated by water from Hoover

Dam, on the Colorado River. The reservoir made by this dam is called Lake Mead.

Lake Mead stores water to irrigate parts of Nevada as well as Arizona. Nevada is one of the driest states in the nation.

In much of Colorado the Rocky Mountains make farming difficult. Without irrigation farming would be hard in the rest of this state. Some lands are irrigated by water from streams formed by melting snow from the nearby Rocky Mountains. The farmers there grow sugar beets, potatoes, fruit, and grains.

Utah raises these crops also. It has very little rainfall except in the Wasatch Mountains, a range of the Rockies. Most farming is in the valleys near these mountains. More than 1,000,000 acres (404,854 ha) have been irrigated in Utah.

Farming in the North

Much of Montana and eastern Wyoming lies in the Great Plains. These states get very little rain except in the Rockies. Some of the land near the foot of the Rockies can be irrigated. Water from streams formed by melting snow in the Rockies irrigates ranches near these mountains.

The largest earth dam in the United States is on the Missouri River at Fort Peck, Montana. People in this plains area earn a living by raising cattle or sheep on the irrigated land.

Many sheep are also raised in the valleys on the lower slopes of the Rockies. Montana and Wyoming are among the leaders in raising sheep and in wool production.

Montana is one of our leading wheat states also. Much of the wheat is raised by dry-farming methods. Dry farming is a way of conserving moisture. It is used where there is little rain and no supply of water for irrigation. Crops are planted on part of the land during one year, while the rest of the land has no crops. This land is allowed to rest and is able to hold its moisture for the whole season. The next year crops will be planted on it, while the first area rests.

Many dams control the Missouri River. They help prevent floods in the area. Also, the dams provide water for irrigation and electricity.

The waters of the Snake River are used to irrigate much farmland in southern Idaho. This watered land grows sugar beets, wheat, fruit, and potatoes. Idaho is one of the chief potato-growing states in the United States. Idaho's vegetables are grown not only to produce food but also to produce seeds.

Mining in the Mountain States

The Rocky Mountains are rich in minerals. Gold and silver are still mined in every state in the region. Other new mineral treasures have also been found, including petroleum and uranium. The uranium mined on the Colorado Plateau is used in nuclear energy plants.

Most Rocky Mountain states produce copper. Copper is used to make water pipes, pans, faucets, and pots. It is used in telephone, telegraph, and electrical wiring. Arizona is the largest copper-producing state.

Large copper mines are also located near Bingham Canyon, Utah, and in Butte, Montana. See the map of copper deposits on page 248. The Bingham Canyon mine is a great open pit,

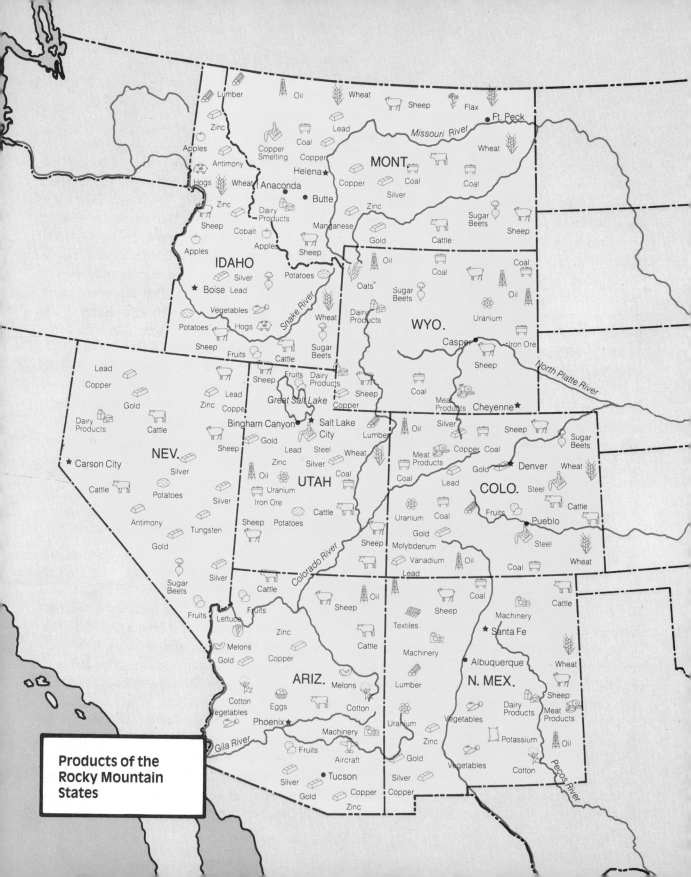

Products of the
Rocky Mountain
States

in which power shovels mine the copper. Under Butte, Montana, people work in tunnels to mine the copper. Above ground are huge smelters. Some of the copper is refined there. But most of the ore is sent to be smelted in Anaconda (an'ə kon'də), Montana.

Utah has coal and iron mines. Colorado, New Mexico, Montana, and Wyoming also have coal. Lead and zinc are found in Utah, Arizona, Colorado, Idaho, and Montana. See the map of lead and zinc deposits on page 325. Wyoming has much petroleum. Other states with petroleum and natural gas are Colorado, Utah, Montana, New Mexico, and Arizona.

Lumbering in the Mountain States

Lumbering is not a leading industry in the Rocky Mountain states. But Montana, Idaho, and Colorado have sawmills that produce lumber products.

Most of the wooden match sticks we use are made from Idaho white pine trees. The slopes of the Rocky Mountains in Idaho yield much of the white pine cut in the United States. White pine is a soft wood that is easy to work with. It is used for making furniture, shingles, matches, and other wood products.

Energy Sources in the Mountain States

Although the mountain states produce some petroleum and natural gas, there is a shortage of these substances. Plans are being made to use more solar, or sun, energy as a source of power. People are studying better ways of collecting and storing energy from the sun. The energy is used to heat and cool homes and other buildings. People are also studying ways of changing solar energy into electricity.

People in the mountain states and elsewhere have built houses that can be heated by solar energy. Such houses have special roofs with collectors that trap the sun's heat.

Coal is another important source of energy used in the United States. Some coal fields are in the Rocky Mountain states. Look at the map of coal deposits on page 245 to find the states where these coal fields are located.

Some people in our country think that *oil shale* (shāl), a type of rock, may be a source of oil. But the cost of making oil from oil shale is great. So oil shale has not been used much. Large amounts of oil shale can be found in Colorado, Utah, and Wyoming.

Scenic Wonders

Many tourists visit the Rocky Mountain states to enjoy their beautiful scenery. Some regions of great natural beauty have been set aside as national parks.

National Parks in the South

One of the greatest wonders of the world is the Grand Canyon in Arizona. The canyon has been carved out by waters of the Colorado River. Another national park in Arizona is the Petrified Forest. It is strewn with logs of an old woodland now turned to stone.

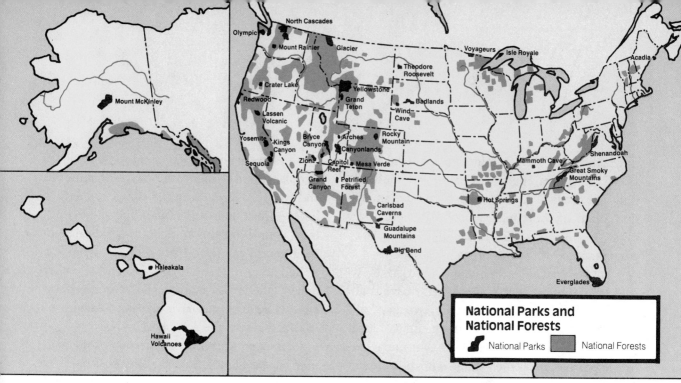

The United States has set aside many parks as places of great natural beauty. National forests are areas of timberland where wildlife is protected. Several large parks and forests are in the Rocky Mountain states.

Carlsbad Caverns National Park is in New Mexico. It is a series of huge caves with interesting rock formations.

Colorado has two national parks. Rocky Mountain National Park has many high peaks. Mesa Verde National Park is a site of Pueblo Indian cliff dwellings.

Utah has five national parks. They are Arches, Bryce Canyon, Canyonlands, Capitol Reef, and Zion. Each has interesting rock formations.

National Parks in the North

Our oldest and best-known national park is Yellowstone. Most of this park is in northwestern Wyoming, but it also reaches into Idaho and Montana. Yellowstone is one of the greatest *geyser* (gī′zər) regions in the world. A geyser is a spring which throws shafts of hot water and steam high into the air. People visiting Yellowstone are thrilled by Old Faithful, the geyser that sends water upward every 60 to 70 minutes. The park also has canyons, waterfalls, and a wide variety of plants and animals.

South of Yellowstone in Wyoming is the Grand Teton National Park. It has beautiful mountain scenery.

Another famous park in the Montana Rockies is Glacier National Park. It has many glaciers and lakes. Just north of it, Canada has made part of the Canadian Rockies into a public park. The two parks, one in Canada and one in the United States, together form a great *international* (in′tər nash′ən əl) park. "International" means belonging to, or having to do with, two or more nations.

A

B

C

These are some of the beautiful and unusual sites of national parks in the Rocky Mountain states: "Queen's Garden Trail" in Bryce National Park (A); clear blue lakes among jagged mountains in Glacier National Park (B); "Cliff Palace" in Mesa Verde National Park (C); the deep, long gorge of the Grand Canyon (D); and the geyser called "Old Faithful" in Yellowstone (E). Can you find these national parks on the map on page 392? Which park would you most like to visit? Why?

E

D

Denver
A Vital Center of Trade

In 1869 the people of Denver were worried. The first transcontinental railroad was finished. Trains could now go from coast to coast. But the railroad went through southern Wyoming. It did not go through Denver, the capital of Colorado. Denver then, as today, was important because it was a trade center. Why did people worry that Denver would become a "ghost town" after the transcontinental railroad bypassed it?

The city did not become a "ghost town." It built its own railroad line north to join the transcontinental railroad in Wyoming. Other railroads leading to Denver were built also. Today, the city is a major transportation center for the Rocky Mountain region.

Denver serves as a trade center for two regions. The city is a gateway to the Rocky Mountain region. It also serves the plains region east of the Rockies.

Many of the goods that Denver supplies to nearby areas are manufactured in other parts of the nation. However, some machinery and other goods are made in Denver's own factories.

Denver was a gateway to the mining country of the mountains before it became a plains center. The city was founded during the Pikes Peak gold rush. Then silver strikes touched off another boom.

Later the United States government built a mint in Denver for making coins. What metals are used in coins? Why was Denver a good place to build a mint?

By 1900, however, the ranches and farms of the plains were as important to Denver as the mines of the mountains. The mining booms were over. But today the mountains have given Denver another kind of boom, a tourist boom.

Look at the picture on page 378. What makes Denver a tourist center? Turn to the map of the Rocky Mountain states on page 377. What national park is located nearby? People once flocked through Denver on their way to find gold and silver in the Rockies. Even greater numbers of people go today to enjoy the region's beauty. ■

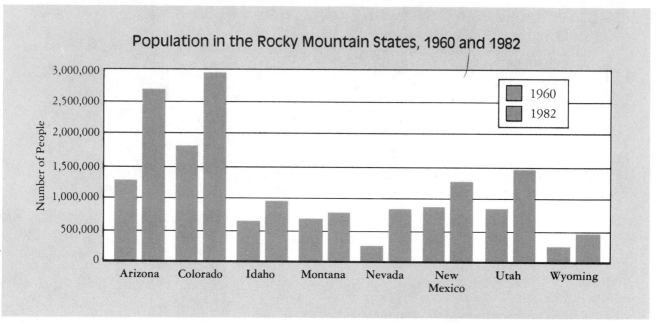

Population in the Rocky Mountain States, 1960 and 1982

Legend: 1960, 1982

Y-axis: Number of People (0 to 3,000,000)

X-axis: Arizona, Colorado, Idaho, Montana, Nevada, New Mexico, Utah, Wyoming

This graph shows how the population of each Rocky Mountain state grew between 1960 and 1982. Which two states grew the most between those years? Which two states grew the least?

Cities in the Mountain States

Turn to the map of the United States on pages A-6–A-7. Notice how great an area is occupied by the Rocky Mountain states. Their area is large, but they are not densely populated. In recent years, however, their population has been growing more rapidly. As you might suppose, much growth has taken place in the cities.

The Cities of Colorado and Utah

South of Denver in Colorado is the large steel center of Pueblo. At Colorado Springs is the United States Air Force Academy. Here the Air Force trains young men and women as officers.

In Utah the capital and major city is Salt Lake City. North of this city is Ogden. It is near the meeting place of the first railroad to cross the country. Ogden is an important railroad town.

South of Salt Lake City is Provo. It lies in a valley of rich farmland. It is known as the "Steel Center of the West" because of the nearby Geneva Steel plant.

The Cities of New Mexico and Arizona

Albuquerque is the largest city in New Mexico. Because of its healthful climate Albuquerque has many hospitals and rest homes. New Mexico's second largest city is Santa Fe. Santa Fe is the capital of New Mexico and the oldest city west of the Mississippi River. Santa Fe has many reminders of its Spanish history.

In Arizona, Tucson is the trade center of the copper-mining region and of irrigated farms. Phoenix, the capital of Arizona, is the heart of a farming area irrigated by Roosevelt Dam. Yuma is another desert garden spot. Its water is piped from the Colorado River.

The Cities of Nevada and Idaho

The chief trade center in Nevada is Reno. This city handles the products of the farms and mines at the foothills of the Sierras. Near Reno is Carson City, the capital of Nevada. It was named in honor of Kit Carson. A rapidly growing city of Nevada is Las Vegas. It is not far from Hoover Dam, in the southeastern part of the state.

Boise, in southwestern Idaho, is the capital of this state and its chief city. In southeastern Idaho, Pocatello is the leading city. Both Boise and Pocatello are trade centers for farming areas irrigated by water from the Snake River.

Lewiston is the trade center for mountainous northern Idaho. It was named for the famous explorer, Meriwether Lewis. It ships lumber and minerals.

The Cities of Montana and Wyoming

The largest city in Montana is Great Falls. Butte, a copper-mining center, ranks next in size. Anaconda also produces copper. The state capital is Helena. It is a trade center for Montana's mountainous western region.

Cheyenne, in southeastern Wyoming, is the capital and largest city of this state. It is also

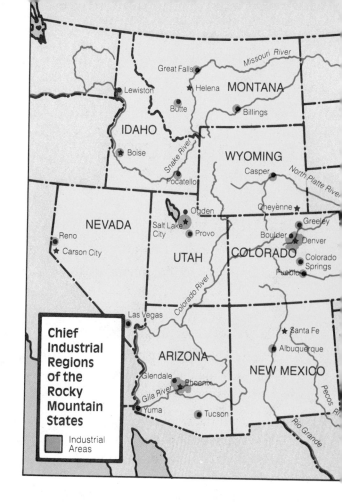

the trade center for a large grazing area. From Cheyenne, cattle are sent east to meat-packing centers. Located on the Platte River, near the center of Wyoming, is Casper. It is the trade center for this part of the state.

Do You Know?

1. Why do many farmers of the Rocky Mountain states practice irrigation?
2. What are some of the minerals found in the Rocky Mountain states?

To Help You Learn

Using New Words

Continental Divide	hogan
fleece	international
shearing	oil shale
geyser	pueblo

The phrases below explain the words or terms listed above. Number a paper from 1 through 8. After each number write the word or term which matches the definition.

1. Cutting off the wool of sheep
2. The thick wool of a sheep
3. Belonging to, or having to do with, two or more nations
4. A spring which throws hot water and steam high into the air
5. A type of rock that may be a source of energy
6. A dome-shaped Indian house built of poles, tree bark, and mud
7. An Indian village like apartment houses built of stone or clay
8. A ridge in the Rockies which separates rivers flowing east from rivers flowing west

Finding the Facts

1. What eight states are called the Rocky Mountain states? What is the capital city of each?
2. How was the Grand Canyon formed? What group of people discovered it?
3. How was the way of life of the Pueblo Indians in the early days different from the way of life of the Navajo Indians and the Apache Indians?
4. Who started a mission in what is now Arizona in 1700? Why did this person start a mission?
5. Why did traders use the Santa Fe Trail?
6. Who was the leader of the people who built Salt Lake City? Who were these people? Why did they go west?
7. Why did many settlers go to Nevada in the late 1850s? Why did many go to Colorado?
8. Why are so many sheep raised in the Rocky Mountain states?
9. What are three ways in which dams help the people in the Rocky Mountain states?
10. Below is a list of persons you met in Unit 12 and descriptions of them. Match the people and the descriptions.

Martínez	Coronado	Young
Kino	Twain	Pike

a. I started several missions in Arizona.
b. I led the Mormons to Salt Lake City.
c. I rediscovered how black-on-black pottery is made.
d. I discovered the great mountain in Colorado now named in my honor.
e. I wrote stories about the early days in Nevada.
f. A group of my soldiers discovered the Grand Canyon.

11. Where is some uranium found? What is one use of uranium?

12. What are some uses of copper? Where is copper mined?

13. What national parks are found in the Rocky Mountain states? In which states are they found?

14. What is the largest city in New Mexico? In Montana?

Learning from Maps

1. On the map of the United States, on pages A-6– A-7, locate the Rocky Mountain states. Find the great Rocky Mountain chain. What rivers drain the eastern slopes of these mountains? The western slopes? In what part of this region are the highest peaks? What is the Continental Divide? Where is it?

2. Find the climate map on page 11 and the map of the Rocky Mountain states on page 377. How many climate regions are there in this area? What kinds of seasons do people living in the Rocky Mountain states have?

3. Turn to the map of industrial regions, page 397. Which state has the most industry?

4. One of the most useful kinds of maps is a road map. Here is a part of a road map which shows a part of the city of Phoenix, Arizona. Phoenix is a large city. It is shown in solid yellow on the map. What smaller city is also shown?

   What kinds of roads on the map are shown in green lines? In red lines? How are Interstate roads marked? How are U.S. roads marked? How are state roads marked?

How can you tell from the map that Phoenix is the capital city of Arizona? How can you tell that many American Indians may have lived in the area where Phoenix is? What place does Phoenix have to help Indians?

5. Turn to the products map on page 390. What minerals are found in this region? What animals are raised? Where are sugar beets grown?

6. Look at the map of national parks and forests on page 392. What national parks are in the Rocky Mountain states? Which of the Rocky Mountain states have national forests? Why does the government set aside these large areas?

7. Study the map of western trails and the routes of the fortyniners on page 383. What trail was used to get from El Paso to San Diego? In which western cities did the trails end?

8. Look at the map of forest regions on page 427 to see what kinds of forests are found in the Rocky Mountain states.

State	Area (Sq. Mi.)	Capital	Dams	National Parks	State Flower
Arizona	113,909	Phoenix	Hoover Roosevelt	Grand Canyon Petrified Forest	Saguaro cactus
Colorado					Rocky Mountain columbine
Idaho		Boise			
Montana					
Nevada					
New Mexico	121,666		Elephant Butte		
Utah		Salt Lake City			
Wyoming		Cheyenne		Grand Teton Yellowstone	

Using Study Skills

1. **Chart:** Make a chart like the one above telling some important facts about the Rocky Mountain states. Some of the information has been filled in for you. Use the maps in this unit, the Reference Tables on pages 580–583, and an almanac or encyclopedia to help you.
2. **Time Line:** The following events are not listed in the right order. Copy the statements in the right order and place them on a time line. Use the time line on page 375 to help you.
   The founding of Salt Lake City
   The first use of the Santa Fe Trail
   The discovery of Pikes Peak
   The discovery of the Grand Canyon
   Comstock Silver Lode opened for mining
   Gold discovered in California
   First transcontinental railroad completed
   Father Kino starts a mission in Arizona
3. **Graph:** Look at the graph on page 396. Which state had the largest population in 1960? Which had the largest in 1982? Which state had the smallest population in 1960? Which state, Idaho or New Mexico, had the larger population in 1982? Which state, Nevada or Utah, had the smaller population in 1960?
   About how many more people lived in Arizona in 1982 than in 1960? Do you think that the population of the Rocky Mountain states will continue to grow? Why?
4. **Map:** Study the map of climate regions on page 11. Which Rocky Mountain states have mild winters, hot summers and are very dry? Which states have cold winters, cool summers and are wet?

Thinking It Through

1. The American Indians first saw the Spanish in the 1500s. What might the way of life of the Indians have been like if they had been left alone?
2. If the pioneers of 100 years ago could see the Rocky Mountain states today, what would most attract their attention? What ways of earning a living would be familiar to the pioneers? What ways would be new and strange to their eyes?
3. Many boom towns sprang up during the gold and silver strikes in the West. But as soon as the gold or silver ran out, they became ghost towns. Why did this not happen to Denver?
4. The desire for gold and silver brought people to Colorado, Nevada, and Wyoming and helped settle these states. Later, many other minerals were discovered in the Rocky Mountain states. Among these minerals were copper, zinc, iron ore, petroleum, lead, coal, uranium, and oil shale.

   Which of these minerals are important energy sources? Why is it important that the United States has these natural resources? What other energy source holds much promise for the future?
5. Review the information about national parks on pages 391–392. How do you think areas preserved as national parks have produced an industry? Describe how this industry affects the way people make a living in communities near the parks.
6. Look at the picture on page 382. Discuss the picture, relating it to what you have read in this unit about an early mission.
7. "The wilderness shall be glad, and the desert shall blossom as the rose." These are the words of a person who lived long ago. How have these words come true in the Rocky Mountain states?

Projects

1. Collect and put on your bulletin board pictures showing some of the huge dams which provide irrigation water in the Rocky Mountain states.
2. The Research Committee might find out more about these early explorers and settlers in the Rocky Mountain states: Francisco Coronado Father Eusebio Kino Zebulon Pike Brigham Young The students could pretend to be these people as they tell their stories.
3. The Explorers' Committee should show on a map the routes these people traveled and where the first settlements were.
4. The Reading Committee will find these books interesting: *The Santa Fe Trail,* by S. H. Adams; and *Waterless Mountain,* by L. Armer. Read one of these books and report on it to the class.

13 The Pacific States

Unit Preview

Much of our country's history is a story of people moving west. Finally, they reached the Pacific. The five Pacific states are California, Oregon, Washington, Alaska, and Hawaii.

Captain Robert Gray established the United States's claim to the Pacific Coast in 1792. President Jefferson sent Lewis and Clark overland to the Pacific Coast in 1804. But American settlers were not quick to follow these explorers. The Oregon country was not settled until 1843. The first large rush of Americans to California was in 1849, about a year after gold was discovered. In 1849, however, so many people went there that California became a state a year later.

People have not been quick, however, to move to Alaska. It is the largest state in area, but one of the smallest in population. In 1977 an 800-mile pipeline was built across Alaska to transport oil to port cities.

Alaska and Hawaii became states in 1959. Hawaii was an independent nation before that time.

To the government in Washington the Pacific region once seemed to be far away. The invention of the telegraph helped to bring the West Coast closer. A transcontinental railroad was completed in 1869. Today air travel makes Hawaii and Alaska hours, not days, away from Washington, D.C.

Things to Discover

If you look carefully at the picture, map, and time line, you can answer these questions.

1. The picture shows a scene on the Alaskan coast. What industry would make use of the boats in the harbor?
2. What form of communication began to be used in 1861?
3. Alaska and Hawaii are Pacific states, but they lie beyond the area shown on the map. How many Pacific states are shown?
4. What mineral was discovered in California in 1848?
5. When did the United States buy Alaska? How many years later did Alaska become a state?
6. What means of transportation helped people cross the mountains after 1869?

Words to Learn

You will meet these words in this unit. As you read, you will learn what they mean and how to pronounce them. The Word List will help you.

aqueduct	inlet
conveyor	Interior
current	lava
earthquake	sound
extinct	spawning
fault	trade wind
fortyniner	transcontinental
great circle route	volcano

402

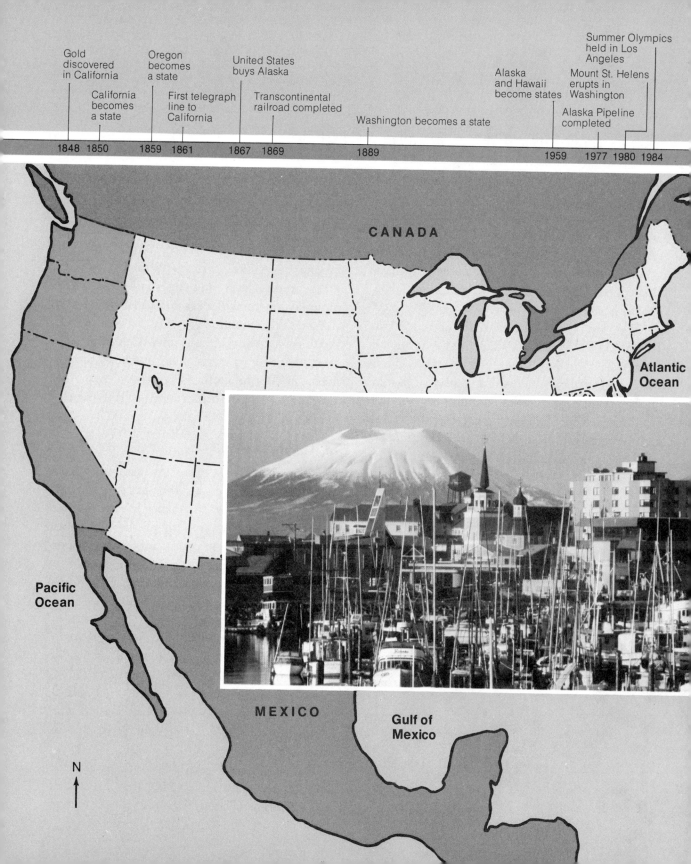

Gold discovered in California

California becomes a state

Oregon becomes a state

First telegraph line to California

United States buys Alaska

Transcontinental railroad completed

Washington becomes a state

Alaska and Hawaii become states

Summer Olympics held in Los Angeles

Mount St. Helens erupts in Washington

Alaska Pipeline completed

1848 1850 1859 1861 1867 1869 1889 1959 1977 1980 1984

CANADA

Atlantic Ocean

Pacific Ocean

MEXICO

Gulf of Mexico

N

Geography of the Pacific States

The Pacific states are alike in important ways. All have coasts on the world's largest ocean. All have fine natural resources such as fertile land, minerals, and good fishing areas. All have high mountains, green valleys, sparkling lakes, and other beautiful scenery.

The five states, however, differ in certain ways. Alaska, our largest state, lies farther north and west than any other part of the United States. Hawaii is located so far south that part of it lies in the tropics. Washington, Oregon, and California, which are on the coast of the mainland, reach from Canada to Mexico. Located so far apart, the five states have a variety of climates.

In northern California sandy beaches and grasslands border the Pacific Ocean. Forests and mountains are nearby.

Surface of the Coast States

The map of Washington, Oregon, and California on page 405 shows long ranges of mountains extending from north to south. In these three states and in Alaska also, the mountains near the ocean are called the Coast Range. The mountains lying farther inland in Washington, Oregon, and California are divided into two parts. The northern mountains, in Washington and Oregon, are the Cascade Range. To the south, in California, is the Sierra (sē er′ə) Nevada.

In Washington and Oregon

The Coast Range is quite low in Washington and Oregon. It is broken at two places. These are at Puget (pyoo′jit) Sound, in the north, and near the mouth of the Columbia River. A *sound* (sound) is a body of water like a large bay extending into the land. See the map of Washington, Oregon, and California on page 405.

Between the Coast Range and the Cascades lies a lowland. North of the Columbia River it is called the Puget Sound Lowland. South of the Columbia it is called the Willamette Valley. This entire lowland is called the Willamette-Puget Sound Valley. The Coast Range is low enough to let rain clouds reach this valley.

To the east, between the Cascades and the Rockies, are high tablelands. They are called the Columbia Plateau and the Snake River

Before Mount St. Helens erupted, the mountain was 9,677 feet (2,950 meters) above sea level. It now stands at about 8,400 feet (2,560 meters). Billions of tons of matter were blown away.

Plateau. They get their names from the Columbia River and its chief tributary, the Snake River.

Mount St. Helens is in the Cascade Range. It is a *volcano* (vol kā′ nō), or opening in the earth's surface through which steam, ashes, and hot, melted rock, or *lava* (lä′ və) flow. In 1980 trapped gases blew the top off Mount St. Helens and hot ashes were forced out.

In California

Low mountains make up the Coast Range of California. Between the Coast Range and the ocean there are only a very few narrow plains.

East of the Coast Range is the Central Valley of California. The Central Valley ends at the Si-

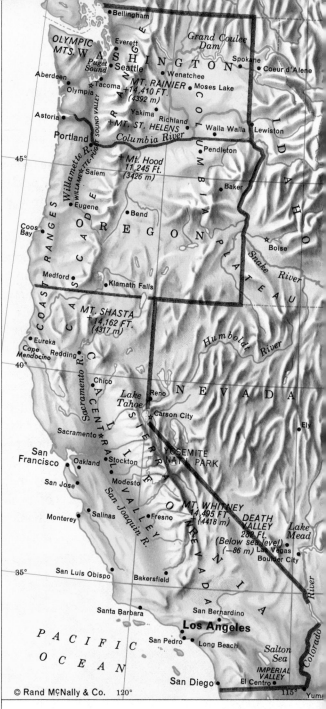

WASHINGTON, OREGON, AND CALIFORNIA

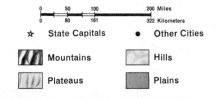

405

erra Nevada, in eastern California. These mountains are higher and narrower than the Rockies. Mount Whitney, the highest mountain in California, is in the Sierra Nevada.

Sometimes *earthquakes* (urth′kwāks′) take place in California. An earthquake is a movement of a part of the earth's surface. It can be caused by a sudden shift of rock along a *fault* (fôlt) or by volcanic or other disturbances. A fault is a break in a rock mass.

What Alaska Is Like

Alaska's greatest river is the Yukon. Find it on the map of Alaska on this page. The Yukon River and its valley divide Alaska into two parts.

The region south of the river has many high, snow-capped mountains. One group of peaks makes up the Alaska Range. Mount McKinley,

the highest mountain in North America, is in the Alaska Range.

Rugged mountains also rise along the southern coast of Alaska. Narrow waterways cut into the mountainous coast. Near the shore are many rocky islands. Near the middle of the southern coast is Cook Inlet. An *inlet* (in′let′) is a narrow strip of water which reaches far inland. Just beyond Cook Inlet is the fertile Matanuska (mat ə nōō′skə) Valley.

North of the Yukon River lies another range of mountains. It is called the Brooks Range. The northern mountains gradually slope down into flat coastlands. The coastlands end at the Arctic (ärk′tik) Ocean.

Alaska also includes a long chain of islands which curve westward into the Pacific. They are the foggy, barren Aleutian (ə lōō′shən) Islands.

Alaska is becoming an important center for

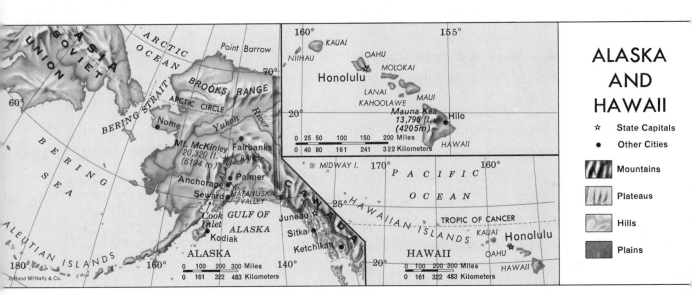

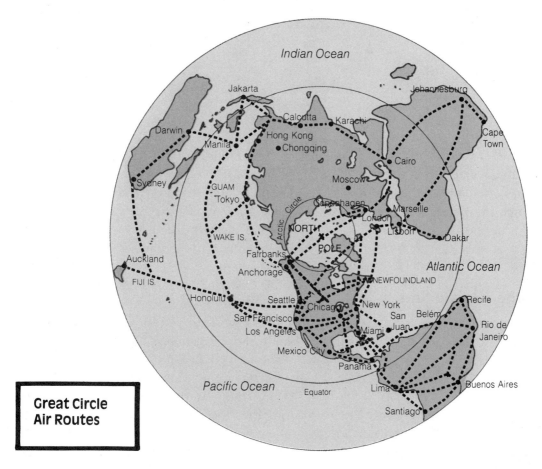

Great Circle Air Routes

Airplanes save many miles by flying "polar routes" over the top of the world. On the map find two routes from San Francisco to London. Which is shorter?

air travel. The most direct air routes from some west-coast cities to Europe or Asia are over the northern lands of North America. To prove this, use a piece of string on your classroom globe.

First, find Seattle, Washington, and Tokyo, Japan, on the globe. Next, put one end of the string on Tokyo. Now stretch it across the globe to Seattle. Be sure to place the string so that it curves around the globe at the shortest distance between these two cities. Pull the string tight. Did the route pass over some part of Alaska?

The route that you laid out on the globe is a

great circle route (root). A great circle route is the most direct and the shortest route between two places on the globe. Compare it with the airplane routes on the map on this page. How many of these airplane routes pass directly over Alaska?

What Hawaii Is Like

The islands of the state of Hawaii are the tops of old volcanoes which rise above the ocean. Lava from some of these volcanoes sometimes boils up and overflows down the mountainsides.

Most of these mountainous islands have lowlands along the coast and in the river valleys. Lava which once flowed from the volcanoes has made the soil rich in important minerals. The minerals have made the soil good for growing crops.

Climate of the Pacific States

The Pacific states have a wide variety of climates. Some regions are hot and dry. Others are cooler and have much rain.

The Climate of California

Moist, warm winds from the Pacific Ocean bring the coastal area of California enough rain for farming. The rain falls during the winter season. The summers are dry.

The warm winds from the ocean give the coast mild winters and cool summers. The Central Valley has cooler winters and warmer summers. The valley also receives much less rain than the coast does. For this reason its fields need irrigation.

The western side of the Sierra Nevada receives the last of the moisture from the rain clouds that move inland from the Pacific Ocean. The lands east of the mountains are dry and the temperatures are lower.

The Climate of Oregon and Washington

Many people enjoy the pleasant climate of the coast of Oregon and Washington. The breezes from the Pacific keep the winters mild and the summers cool. East of the Cascades, however, the summers are hot and the winters are cold.

The coastal region has one of the heaviest rainfalls in our country. This is because the winds from the Pacific carry much moisture. The moisture is turned into rain or snow by the cold air of the mountain ranges. Winter is the wet season.

The Cascade Mountains keep the moist Pacific winds from reaching the plateaus east of this range. Most of the plateau section is too dry to farm without irrgation.

The heavy rains and melting snow from the mountains form rivers and streams in this area. Among these is the Columbia River. Water from the streams irrigates ranches near the mountains.

Many dams have been built to irrigate large areas. One is the Grand Coulee (koo'le) Dam, on the Columbia River. The water from this dam can irrigate more than a million acres of land. The dams also supply electric power for factories and homes.

The Climate of Alaska

Southern Alaska has a mild, rainy climate. Its summers are warm but not hot. Its winters are cool but not cold. Ships can enter the harbors of Ketchikan (kech'i kan'), Juneau (joo'no), and Seward (soo'ərd) all year. These waters never freeze over.

Winds from the ocean help make the climate pleasant. On their way to Alaska they blow over a warm ocean *current* (kur'ənt). A current is a stream of water flowing through the ocean. Winds blowing toward Alaska become warm as they pass over the current. Because of this

Dog sleds have long been used to cross the snow-covered land of Arctic Alaska. Here Eskimo youths race their sleds.

current the temperature of southern Alaska almost never falls below 0°F (−18°C) in winter. The ocean winds bring heavy rainfall.

The part of Alaska through which the great Yukon River flows is often called the *Interior* (in tēr′ē ər). Interior means an area which lies inland, or away from the border and the coast. The winters of this region are long and very cold, with long nights and short days. Its summers are short and warm, with many hours of sunlight. The Yukon Valley has less rain than southern Alaska.

Arctic Alaska lies north of Interior Alaska. Its winters are long and cold. In winter the sun does not rise for days. That is because the tilt of the earth causes Arctic Alaska to be far from the sun in the winter.

The summer season in Arctic Alaska is very short. Only a foot or two (30 or 60 cm) of the frozen ground softens during the brief summer. Moss, grass, flowers, and small bushes grow in this tundra. The tundra is a treeless plain found in Arctic regions.

The Climate of Hawaii

Find Hawaii on the map of the United States, pages A-6–A-7. Notice that the islands are north of the equator and south of the Tropic of Cancer in the low latitudes. Steady winds that blow toward the equator from the northeast, called *trade* (trād) *winds,* make the climate of Hawaii pleasant. As these winds blow over the Pacific, they gather much moisture. When they reach the islands, they rise and are cooled. They drop most of their moisture on the northeast slopes. The southwestern slopes are dry. Crops must be irrigated there. South of the equator, the trade winds also blow toward the equator, but from the southeast.

Do You Know?

1. How are the Pacific states alike? How are they different?
2. What is the surface of Alaska like?
3. Why does Hawaii have such rich soil?

409

2
Settling the Coastal States

The first European settlements on the Pacific coast were made by the Spanish in what is now California in 1769. Missionaries came and built more than 20 missions along the coast. These missions became large estates, supported by American Indian labor. There were also some small farming settlements, known as pueblos, occupied by Mexicans.

American settlers started moving to California about 1840. They sent back glowing reports of the easy life there. As more and more Americans moved to California, the Mexican government began to regard the new American settlers as a threat to its rule.

Exploring California

The United States government became interested in the region and sent John C. Frémont, a young explorer, to learn about the Far West. Frémont's guide was the famous scout and trapper, Kit Carson. He carried Frémont's messages from California to Washington, D.C.

On his last trip, Frémont went as a captain in the United States Army. He reached California just before our war with Mexico. Frémont aided a rebellion of American settlers in California against Mexican forces. Without consulting anyone, the settlers decided to set up the Republic of California.

They made a flag by painting a bear and a star on white cloth. Then they raised the "Bear Flag" over their camp. When Frémont heard that war with Mexico had begun, he took down the Bear Flag. In its place he raised the Stars and Stripes.

As you remember, the war ended with the defeat of Mexico. Mexico lost not only Texas but also much land to the west of Texas. On the map of the growth of the United States on page 137, find the land given up by Mexico. After this war the United States stretched from the Atlantic to the Pacific.

The Rush to California

In 1848, just before the end of the war with Mexico, gold was discovered on Captain John Sutter's ranch in California. This large ranch was at the foot of the Sierra Nevada, near the present city of Sacramento. Find Sacramento on the map of California, page 405.

It was James Marshall, one of Captain Sutter's workers, who discovered the gold. He saw the shining grains while building a mill on a river that flowed through Sutter's land.

The Fortyniners

News traveled slowly in those days. Almost a year passed before the East heard of this discovery of gold in California. When the news finally reached the East, people went wild with excitement. Thousands left their homes to go to California. Since this rush began in 1849, the gold seekers were called the *fortyniners* (fôr′tē nī′ nərz).

410

The fortyniners used three main routes to California. Some gold seekers used the all-water route. They sailed from ports on the Atlantic Coast, around South America, and north along the Pacific Coast to San Francisco. This was a long voyage.

Others went by ship to Panama. Then they traveled on foot through the hot jungles of the isthmus to the Pacific. After this they took a ship to California. Trace these two water routes on the map on page 412.

The third route was along the overland trails to California. The gold seekers faced burning

Early gold seekers shoveled earth and rocks into a trough filled with water. The water washed away the earth. Sometimes miners found gold in the rocks that were left.

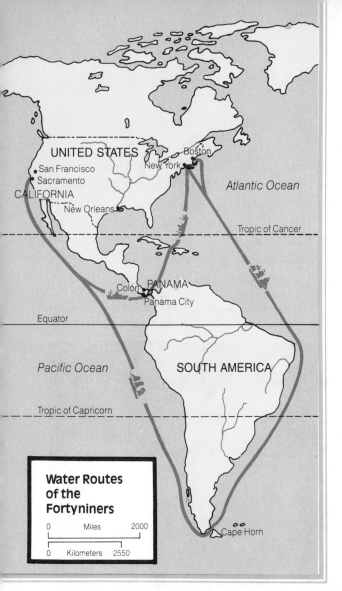

Water Routes of the Fortyniners

| 0 | Miles | 2000 |
| 0 | Kilometers | 2550 |

People who left their eastern homes to join the California gold rush faced a long journey. If you were a *fortyniner*, which water route would you take? Why?

deserts, snowstorms in the mountains, and American Indians who were protecting their lands.

Most land travelers to California used the Oregon Trail. See the map of western trails, page 383. The travelers started at Independence, Missouri. At Fort Hall the trail divided. The part that went southwest became known as the California Trail. Travelers to Los Angeles used the Santa Fe Trail and the Old Spanish Trail.

California Becomes a State

Gold seekers kept flocking to California. Cities were built overnight. Less than 2 years after Marshall's discovery, California had enough people to become a state. The people wrote a constitution. In this constitution they said that there was to be no slavery in California. In 1850 California joined the Union as a free state.

Connecting East and West

In the days of the gold rush it took months for mail sent from the East to reach the West. After California became a state, it was necessary to find faster and better ways to send mail. To speed up the mail, the United States government started an overland mail service.

Transcontinental Mail Service

By the new plan the mail was taken to St. Louis by train, where it was placed on stagecoaches. The coaches, carrying passengers and mail, traveled day and night. The journey from St. Louis, Missouri, to San Francisco, California, took about 25 days. This was our first *transcontinental* (trans'kon tə nent'əl) mail service. Transcontinental means across the continent.

Still mail was not fast enough for many people in the East and in California. So the pony express service was started. The pony express riders carried the mail from St. Joseph, Missouri, where the railroad ended, to Sacramento, California, in 10 days' time. See the Overland Mail and Transcontinental Railway map on this page. The pony express lasted for 19 months. Then a faster means of communication—the telegraph—put an end to it.

The Invention of the Telegraph

Samuel F. B. Morse invented the telegraph in 1844. The telegraph was a system of sending and receiving messages over a wire.

After working on his invention for 10 years, Morse asked Congress to help him. Congress granted Morse $30,000 to build a telegraph line to test his invention. The line stretched from Baltimore to Washington, a distance of 40 miles (64 km).

Soon telegraph lines were built all over the country. In October 1861, the first telegraph line joining California and the East replaced the pony express.

The First Transcontinental Railroad

Soon after the telegraph reached California, two railroad companies decided to extend the railroad to the west coast. Two crews of workers started laying tracks from opposite directions and worked toward each other. The workers on the Central Pacific Railroad pushed eastward from Sacramento, California. Many of these workers were Chinese. Workers on the Union Pacific Railroad worked westward from Omaha, Nebraska. Many of these workers

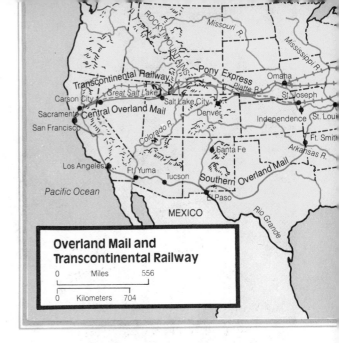

Overland Mail and Transcontinental Railway

0 Miles 556

0 Kilometers 704

Between 1858 and 1869 connections between California and the East improved. Why do you think this was so important? Which of the routes shown on this map was the fastest?

were Irish. Find the routes from Sacramento and from Omaha on the map on this page.

Both crews faced great difficulties. For almost 7 years thousands of workers used axes, picks, and shovels to lay mile after mile of track. Central Pacific workers pushing eastward dug tunnels through the high Sierra Nevada. Union Pacific crews pushing westward across the plains were always in danger of attacks by Indians protecting their lands. When they reached the Rockies, they had problems like those of the Sierra Nevada workers.

On May 10, 1869, the tracks finally were joined at a point near Ogden, Utah. A large crowd of people traveled great distances to see the railroad completed.

If we could join the crowd, we might hear the crews boasting and joking. Each crew is trying to prove that it has done the best job. Then all talk stops. A Union Pacific officer and a Central Pacific officer take turns hammering

413

Officers from the two railroads shook hands at the place where the Union Pacific and Central Pacific lines met.

into place the last spike, a gold one. The Union Pacific locomotive and the Central Pacific locomotive draw together until they touch. The telegraph flashes the news to the whole country. Now East and West are joined by the transcontinental railroad. Westward expansion is speeded up.

Exploring Oregon and Washington

In the early days of Spanish exploration several Spanish sea captains, sailing northward, may have gone as far as Oregon. In 1579 an English sea captain, Sir Francis Drake, sailed along the coast of Oregon. About 200 years later a famous explorer, Captain Cook, did the same. Both were looking for a passage through North America from the Pacific to the Atlantic. These explorers gave England its claim to the territory.

After the War for Independence, United States ships began to sail far north on the Pacific Coast. Robert Gray, an American sea captain, was in charge of a trading vessel that was bound for China.

After he reached the Pacific, Captain Gray sailed along the coast of Oregon and Washington. He found the mouth of a broad river which emptied into the Pacific Ocean. He named this river the Columbia for his ship, the *Columbia*. Through the discovery of this river Captain Gray gave the United States a claim to the whole country drained by its waters. But many years passed before the country was explored and settled.

The Lewis and Clark Expedition

"The United States now owns the Louisiana Territory," said President Jefferson in 1803. "I will send people to explore the Missouri River and all the lands west of the Mississippi River."

President Jefferson chose Meriwether Lewis to lead an exploring party to the distant West. William Clark was picked as the second leader.

In the spring of 1804 Lewis and Clark with about 40 people started their journey from St. Louis, Missouri. They kept daily records of everything they saw and of what happened along the way. They took notes about the soil, plants, animals, and climate. They also drew maps of the rivers, lakes, and plains that they passed.

Late in October they reached a place in North Dakota where they set up a winter camp. During the winter they met Sacajawea (sä kä jä wē'ə), a Shoshone (shə shō'nē) Indian, and her husband Charbonneau (shär bə nō'), a French trapper. As a child, Sacajawea had been stolen from her family and tribe and taken east. She wanted to see her old home. So Sacajawea and Charbonneau served as guides for the expedition.

In the spring the exploring party took boats to the end of the Missouri River. Then they met some Shoshone Indians. Among them was Sacajawea's brother.

Lewis and Clark were able to buy horses from the Shoshones so that they could travel across the mountains. They left their boats behind. After crossing the mountains, they came to the Snake River. They cut down trees

Sacajawea guided the Lewis and Clark Expedition through lands she knew from her childhood. A river, a peak, and a mountain pass have been named after her.

and built boats. In the boats they went down the Snake River and followed it to the Columbia River. They traveled to the mouth of the Columbia and finally reached the Pacific Ocean. Trace their route on the map, page 305.

In two and one-half years Lewis and Clark had traveled thousands of miles through unknown lands. They brought back maps and records of these lands. Although they discovered a route to the Oregon Country, it was never used as a trail to the Far West. Blackfoot Indians protecting their lands along the upper Missouri made the trail too dangerous. Years later many settlers journeyed to the Oregon country because of the reports of Lewis and Clark, but by other routes.

The Founding of Astoria

Lewis and Clark's reports of fur-bearing animals interested a New York fur trader named John Jacob Astor. Astor sent a group of trappers to the Oregon Country. Near the mouth of the Columbia River they built a trading post called Astoria. Here Indians and other trappers brought their furs to exchange for supplies.

Astoria was the first United States settlement in the Oregon Country. A few years later the Hudson's Bay Company, an English group, also built trading posts in the Oregon Country. For many years, English and American fur trappers and trading companies shared this rich land. It extended far north into Canada.

The Rendezvous System

Another businessman, Henry Ashley, also sent out trappers to bring back furs. Instead of setting up trading posts, Ashley organized the rendezvous (rän′də voo′) system in 1826. Each year trappers went into the mountains to get furs. One year later, they carried their furs to one agreed-upon place. Meanwhile, to this place Ashley brought pack trains loaded with supplies. At these "rendezvous," usually held in Wyoming in July, the Mountain Men, as the trappers came to be called, traded their pelts for Ashley's' supplies. Then the trappers went off hunting for another year. The pack trains took the furs to St. Louis.

By 1840 the fur trade was dead. The Mountain Men had disappeared or become scouts for wagon trains. Some, such as the well-known black Mountain Man James Beckwourth, discovered mountain passes that helped settlers go west.

The Oregon Trail

In 1836 two missionaries journeyed to the Oregon Country in a covered wagon. These missionaries were Marcus and Narcissa Whitman. They taught the Christian religion to the Indians there.

The Whitmans urged others to come to the Oregon Country. The settlements they helped to start there strengthened the claim of the United States to the region. The route that these early pioneers took became known as the Oregon Trail. It ended in Oregon City.

The Oregon Trail was more than 2,000 miles (3,200 km) long. See the map of western trails, page 383. An exploring party sent out from Astoria was the first group to follow the whole length of the Oregon Trail. Trappers and traders used it. When settlers started moving to Oregon, the Oregon Trail was an established route to the Far West. The first large group of settlers went to Oregon in 1843. About 1,000 persons were in this group.

Each spring other groups followed. Each family had a covered wagon drawn by horse or oxen. To travel in safety families would band together. A train of 40 or 50 covered wagons would set out from Independence, Missouri, or some point on the Missouri River. They took with them some household goods, seeds, farm tools, food, and guns.

The first large wagon train to travel on the Oregon Trail is depicted on the walls of Oregon's capitol. The Cascade Mountains in the background were difficult to cross.

A scout, or guide, went with each wagon train. The scout would ride ahead on horseback to look for water and for signs of Indians. The wagons were often attacked by Indians who were fighting to keep their hunting grounds.

As the pioneers traveled westward, they had to cross hot, dusty prairies and high mountains. Snowstorms raged in the mountains. Often wagons became stuck in huge snowdrifts. At times the food and water supply ran low. Many of the pioneers became sick, and some of them died. Finally, after several months, the wagon train reached the Oregon Country.

Clipper Ships to Oregon

Some other pioneers went to the Oregon Country by ship. Starting from the East, they sailed around South America, then up the Pacific Coast to the mouth of the Columbia River. In shipyards of the East a new, faster kind of sailing ship, called a clipper ship, was developed. This fast, graceful sailing vessel had a long, slim body, high masts, and large sails.

By the 1840s many clipper ships visited the coast of the Oregon Country on their way to China. They brought manufactured goods from the eastern part of the United States. They traded the goods for shiploads of furs to be sold in China. On the return trip these clipper ships carried silks, tea, finely carved woods, and other Chinese goods. The captain of a clipper ship could always get good prices for these Chinese goods in Boston.

By the 1870s the clipper ships were replaced by steamships. But they had been useful in trade and settlement.

Government in the Oregon Country

In 1843 a large group of people from the United States came overland to the Oregon Country. They settled in the northern part of the Willamette Valley. These settlers realized they would need some kind of government.

Adopting a Democratic Plan

Let us look in upon a group as they meet to decide on the laws under which they will live.

A tall, sunburned farmer stands up. "We need laws to live by," he says. "The Pilgrims met in the cabin of the *Mayflower* to make a compact before they settled Plymouth."

Another pioneer rises to say, "Texas set up its own government for its republic. We, too, should make laws for protection and to keep peace among ourselves."

And so the meeting went. Everyone was free to speak, and the group listened to what each one had to say. After they had agreed upon the laws under which they were to live, they wrote the laws down. In this way the early settlers of Oregon learned to govern themselves.

Becoming a Part of the United States

For almost 30 years Great Britain and the United States shared the Oregon Country. But in 1846 the two countries set a boundary at the forty-ninth parallel. Great Britain kept the northern part of the region, and the United States the southern. This boundary separates Canada from our Northwest to this day. The United States and Great Britain settled their claims peacefully.

Many people went to the Northwest. Soon there were enough people for the territory to become a state. In 1859 Oregon was admitted to the Union. In 1889 Washington became a state.

American Indians in the Coastal States

In the 1860s the Modoc (mōd'äk) Indians were placed on a reservation in northern California and southern Oregon. They could barely live on the poor land. So they escaped. After 6 months of fighting, the United States soldiers forced the Modocs to give up.

Chief Joseph, a Nez Percé Leader

Joseph, a Nez Percé (nez' purs') Indian, was born in Wallowa Valley of Oregon in about 1840. There he attended a mission school. Later, he became chief of the Nez Percé.

In 1855 the tribe agreed to live on a large reservation. The United States government promised that they could stay there. But in 1860, gold was discovered on the Indians' land. United States officials made a new treaty. It took away about three-fourths of the reservation. Chief Joseph would not accept the new treaty.

The government then ordered the Nez Percé to a reservation in Idaho. But the Nez Percé did not want to leave. Fighting broke out. Each side won some battles. But Chief Joseph knew that the Nez Percé could not defeat the soldiers. So he decided to move the Nez Percé to Canada. The Nez Percé traveled more than 1,000 miles (1,600 km).

When the Nez Percé were in Montana close to Canada, they stopped to rest. Chief Joseph thought that they were safe. But some soldiers found them. After a five-day battle, Chief Joseph decided to surrender. The Nez Percé were sent to Indian Territory, now Oklahoma. Later, Chief Joseph was sent to a reservation in Washington where he died in 1904.

Fishing Rights

Today American Indians are not forced to live on reservations. They live and work wherever they want. Some of the Indians make their living fishing salmon (sam′ən) in Puget Sound. The Indians claimed they had a right to half the salmon caught in Puget Sound. This upset other salmon fishers in the area. But in 1979 the United States Supreme Court ruled in favor of the Indians. The court stated that according to five treaties written during the 1800s, the Indians did have the right to half the salmon caught in Puget Sound.

Chief Joseph of the Nez Percé Indian tribe learned military strategy by watching United States soldiers. He was a determined leader who inspired his followers.

Do You Know?

1. By what three routes did gold seekers travel to California?
2. How was the route of Lewis and Clark on page 305 different from the route of the Oregon Trail on page 383?
3. How was the Oregon Country divided in 1846?

419

3
Early Days in Alaska and Hawaii

Long after the four nations of western Europe had explored and settled much of North America, another nation became interested. This nation was Russia.

Early History of Alaska

Russia was a large country. Its ruler wondered about the lands beyond the huge country. He sent Vitus Bering (bēr′ing), a Danish navigator, to find out what these lands were like.

On one of his voyages Captain Bering discovered the narrow waterway, or strait, which separates North America and Asia. The strait now bears his name. On a later voyage Bering saw the mainland of North America. This discovery, in 1741, gave Russia its claim to Alaska. Soon Russian fur traders traveled across the strait into Alaska to seek their fortunes.

Some Russians explored the North American continent as far north as the Arctic Ocean. Others made settlements or built trading posts as far south as northern California. Not long before George Washington became the President of the United States, the Russians made a permanent settlement in Alaska at Sitka (sit′kə).

As time went on, some people from the United States became interested in this far northern region. Whaling ships went to the Arctic Ocean to catch whales. Other United States vessels traded with the Russian settlements. There was talk that Russia wanted to sell Alaska. William Seward, our Secretary of State, was eager to buy this land. He thought it would become a valuable possession of the United States.

In 1867 the United States bought Alaska. We paid Russia more than 7 million dollars for this great piece of land in the northwestern corner of North America. Alaska was the first possession of the United States which was far distant from the rest of the Union. It was made a territory in 1912. In 1959 it became our forty-ninth state.

The Magic of Gold

About 30 years after we bought Alaska, gold was discovered in the Klondike region of Canada near the Alaskan boundary. Gold seekers rushed north as fast as they could. They went by dog team, on foot, or by boat on the Yukon River with their picks, shovels, and gold pans. Some became rich. Others found little gold or none. One gold seeker was Jack London, the well-known author. He found no gold, but he wrote many stories of life in the Yukon.

Settlement of Hawaii

It is believed that the first Hawaiians came from islands in the Pacific which we call Polynesia. These people sailed in giant canoes across the Pacific about 2,000 years ago. Later, a group of Polynesians from the island of

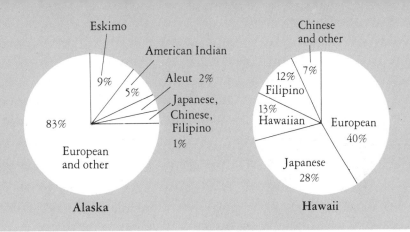

Groups of People in Alaska and Hawaii in 1980

Alaska
- Eskimo 9%
- American Indian 5%
- Aleut 2%
- Japanese, Chinese, Filipino 1%
- European and other 83%

Hawaii
- Chinese and other 7%
- Filipino 12%
- Hawaiian 13%
- European 40%
- Japanese 28%

The United States has always been the home of many different groups of people. These circle graphs show the groups that live in our newest states.

Tahiti (tə hē′tē) arrived. The Hawaiians got their food by fishing, farming, and gathering wild nuts.

Captain Cook in Hawaii

When the English explorer, Captain James Cook, arrived in Hawaii, the Hawaiians thought Cook was a god. Captain Cook was the first white explorer to discover the island. He was on his way to the Far North to look for a waterway between the Pacific and the Atlantic oceans. He stopped at the islands to get fresh food and water. The Hawaiians welcomed Captain Cook and the crew and treated them well.

On a later trip Captain Cook returned to the islands for ship repairs. This time a quarrel developed between the crew and the Hawaiians. Soon fighting broke out. In one of these fights Captain Cook was killed.

Settlers from Many Lands

As the years passed, other people came to the islands. Ships on their way to China often stopped to make repairs and to get fresh food and water. Sailors from these ships sometimes settled in Hawaii. From faraway New England missionaries came to the islands to teach the Christian religion. They opened schools, invented a way of writing the Hawaiian language, and helped the rulers of Hawaii to improve their government.

Then it was found that sugarcane grew well in the soil and climate of Hawaii. People from Europe and the United States came and laid out plantations. Workers from China, Polynesia, Japan, the Philippines, and other lands were brought to work in the cane fields. Many stayed to make their homes in Hawaii. Today people from the United States, Europe, and Asia live and work well together there.

Hawaii Under Our Flag

When Captain Cook came to Hawaii, there were many kingdoms on the islands. Each kingdom had its own ruler. Later King Kamehameha I (kə mā′ə mā′hä) became ruler of all the islands. After that, the islands were united under one ruler. Some of these rulers governed well. Others ruled poorly. After a while people grew tired of the corrupt leaders.

Lydia Liliuokalani was Hawaii's last queen. American settlers controlled much of Hawaii's wealth. Some objected to the queen's power over them and their businesses.

Lydia Liliuokalani, a Hawaiian Leader

Lydia Liliuokalani (li lē ə wō kə län′ē) was born in Honolulu in 1838. In 1891 she became queen of the Hawaiian Islands following the death of her brother the king.

During her reign, Queen Liliuokalani tried to increase her power as ruler. Many people, especially American settlers, became upset. They wanted to protect their businesses. A group of Americans, British, and Germans helped to remove the queen from office in 1893. A republic was then set up in Hawaii.

Liliuokalani spent part of her time writing books and songs. Her best-known song is *Aloha Oe (Farewell to Thee)*. It became the farewell song of Hawaii. Liliuokalani died in Honolulu in 1917.

Joining the United States

People from the United States who had gone to Hawaii to live wanted it to become part of our country. Leaders of the new government asked that Hawaii be made part of the United States. But the leaders of our government at first said, "No." Then the Hawaiians set themselves up as an independent republic.

Five years later Hawaii again asked to be allowed to join the United States. This time our government leaders were in favor of these islands being added to our country. In August 1898 the United States flag was raised over the Hawaiian Islands. Two years later, after a constitution had been adopted by the people of the islands, Hawaii became a territory. It remained a territory until 1959, when Congress voted to admit it to the Union.

Do You Know?

1. What did Bering find on his expedition?
2. Why did the Hawaiians welcome Captain Cook?
3. How did Alaska become a part of the United States?
4. How did Hawaii become a part of the United States?

Before You Go On

Using New Words

transcontinental	great circle route
current	fault
trade wind	lava
earthquake	inlet
forty-niner	sound
volcano	Interior

The phrases below explain the words or terms listed above. Number a paper from 1 through 12. After each number write the word or term which matches the definition.

1. A stream of water flowing through the ocean
2. An area of Alaska which lies inland, away from the border and coast
3. An opening in the earth's surface through which steam, ashes, and hot, melted rock, or lava, flow
4. A steady wind that blows toward the equator
5. A movement of a part of the earth's surface caused by a shift of rock or other disturbance
6. A narrow strip of water which reaches far inland
7. A person who went to California to seek gold
8. A break in a rock mass
9. Hot melted rock
10. Most direct and shortest route between two places on the globe
11. A body of water like a large bay, extending into the land
12. Across the continent

Finding the Facts

1. Where is the Coast Range? The Cascade Range? The Sierra Nevada?
2. Why does the temperature of southern Alaska almost never fall below zero in winter?
3. What forms the islands of Hawaii?
4. Whom did the United States government send to learn about the Far West and California?
5. What discovery on John Sutter's ranch caused people to flock to California?
6. Who invented the telegraph in 1844?
7. Who was Sacajawea?
8. What did James Beckwourth do to help settlers moving westward?
9. Where did the Oregon Trail begin? End?
10. Who tried to lead the Nez Percé Indians to safety in Canada?
11. What land did our country buy from Russia in 1867?
12. What discovery caused people to rush to Alaska in the late 1800s?
13. Who was Lydia Liliuokalani?
14. What happened to Alaska and Hawaii in 1959?

4

Living and Working in the Pacific States

California, Oregon, and Washington have thriving farms and busy industries. People who live in these states have many opportunities for making a living.

Farming in California

Fine crops are raised in the California valleys. But some places in the state lack water for farming.

Southern California

We visit Imperial Valley in southern California. This area was once a desert, but a canal was built to carry water from the Colorado River to irrigate it. Since then, this valley has become rich farmland. The Imperial Valley produces fine fruits and vegetables, cotton, sugar beets, and dairy products. The lettuce and melons you eat in winter may come from the Imperial Valley.

Oranges and lemons are grown on the lower slopes of the mountains in southern California. There they are protected from the cold air which settles on the floor of valleys. Southern California also produces olives, dates, figs, apricots, peaches, pears, almonds, and walnuts.

Field workers pick heads of lettuce and pack them in boxes. Railroad refrigerator cars carry the lettuce across the country.

The Central Valley of California

The Central Valley lies between the Sierra Nevada and the Coast Range. It is 400 miles (640 km) long and almost 50 miles (80 km) wide. Most of the Central Valley is used for farming. Because California gets its rain in winter, irrigation is needed in the valley only during the summer.

Irrigation water and electricity for the Central Valley come from dams on the Sacramento and the San Joaquin (san' wä kēn') rivers. The San Joaquin River flows north from the lower end of the valley. The Sacramento River flows south from the upper end of the valley. These rivers meet near the middle of the Central Valley and empty into San Francisco Bay.

The Central Valley is a fine cotton-growing area. It also produces potatoes, prunes, pears, peaches, grapes, sugar beets, tomatoes, asparagus, and grain. Some of the fruit and vegetables are shipped fresh and some are canned.

The Central Valley is famous for raisins. The land near Fresno is covered with grapevines. Raisins are sun-dried grapes. After the grapes are picked, they are placed on trays among the rows of grapevines. The grapes are dried into raisins by the hot, summer sun. This valley provides more than half the world's supply of raisins. The grapes are also used for making wine.

Coastal Valleys of California

California also has rich farmland in the valleys of the Coast Range. These valleys produce flowers, fruits, vegetables, dairy products, wheat,

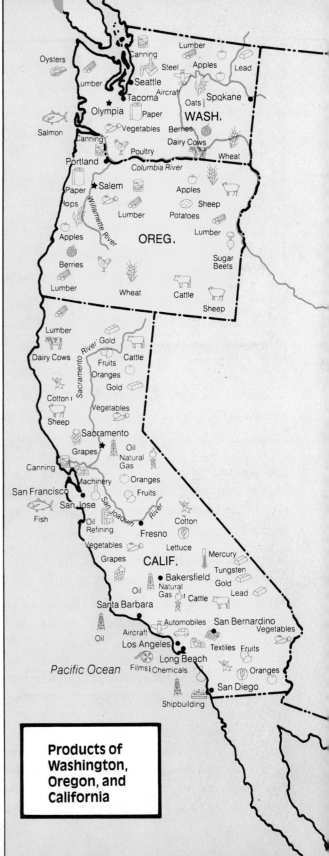

Products of Washington, Oregon, and California

425

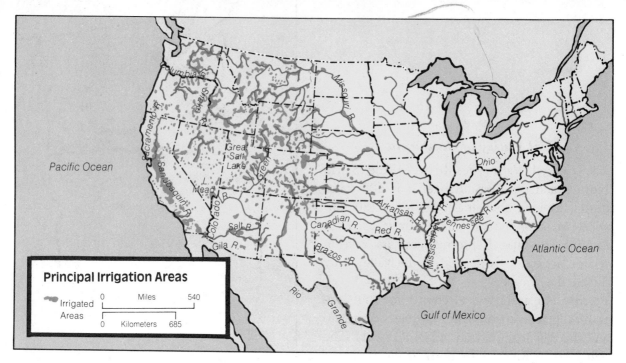

When dry or desert areas are irrigated they become productive farmlands. Many dams have been built on rivers in the western states to help prevent floods and to provide water for irrigation.

and poultry. One valley is famous for its fine prunes. Another is the greatest lettuce-growing area in the United States.

Manufacturing in California

Manufacturing is one of the chief industries of California. In the southern part of the state are large aircraft factories. The warm, dry climate suits this industry. It permits the flying and testing of planes in all seasons. For only about two weeks' time out of each year is the weather unfit for flying.

California also has factories that process foods, such as canned tuna, dried fruits, and frozen fruits and vegetables. There are plants that make machinery, cars, electronic equipment, rubber tires, and furniture. Shipbuilding is another important industry. Shipyards are located along the southern coast.

Farming in Oregon and Washington

Oregon is a great producer of fruit and berries, such as apples, pears, and strawberries. Its farmers also raise wheat, livestock, and poultry.

Washington is the chief apple-growing state in our nation. Washington is also the biggest producer of raspberries and blackberries. It is an important producer of pears and peaches. The chief fruit-growing areas in Washington are in the river valleys east of the Cascades. With irrigation, farmers in this area raise fine crops of apples, pears, plums, and other fruit.

Water from the Columbia River irrigates large parts of eastern and southern Washington. In areas where there is little water, wheat is grown by dry farming.

The Willamette Valley is famous for its apples, prunes, pears, and strawberries. It is one of the leading fruit- and vegetable-canning centers in our country. The Willamette Valley also has many poultry and dairy farms.

Some farmers in the Willamette Valley produce hops. Hops are plants used in the making of beer and of certain medicines. Seeds for vegetables and flowers are also grown in this area.

Lumbering on the West Coast

The western slopes of the Sierra Nevada, in California, have thick forests of towering white and sugar pines. Gigantic redwoods grow on the

Coast Range north of San Francisco. Many people in northern California earn their living by lumbering, working in sawmills, making furniture, and manufacturing wood pulp for paper.

Oregon is the leading lumber state in the whole United States. More timber is cut in Oregon than in any other state. Oregon's northern neighbor, Washington, also produces much lumber. In the forests of Oregon and Washington the trees are large, and they grow close together. Lumber is one of the leading products shipped from Oregon and Washington. Paper mills also are found in both states.

West Coast pine forests are very valuable. The Rocky Mountain states also have vast forests, but lumber is not a large industry there. Why do you think this is so?

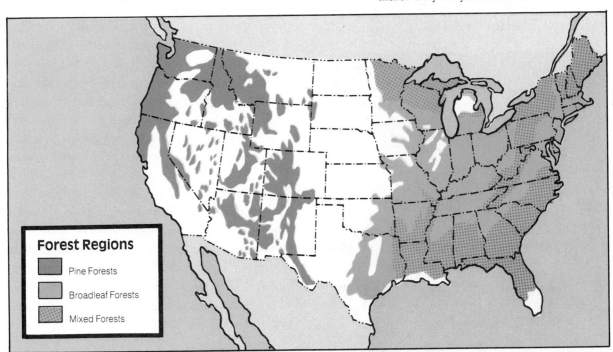

Forest Regions

- Pine Forests
- Broadleaf Forests
- Mixed Forests

Fishing on the West Coast

Many people on the California coast earn a living by fishing or canning fish. Fishing fleets set out empty from San Diego, San Pedro, and San Francisco and return filled with fish. Most of the tuna and sardines caught there are canned. But mackerel and crabs are eaten fresh.

Salmon is the most plentiful and the most valuable fish in Oregon and Washington. The people who earn a living by fishing also take halibut from the ocean and oysters from Puget Sound.

The salmon are found along the coast and in the rivers which empty into the ocean. Some of the salmon is shipped fresh in refrigerator cars to large cities throughout the country. But most of the salmon is canned. Many people work in the fish canneries.

Salmon Fishing

Each year millions of salmon swim in from the Pacific Ocean and enter the mouths of rivers there. The salmon make their way upstream, swimming against the current and leaping over waterfalls. The large dams on the Columbia River keep the salmon from swimming upstream. Fish ladders have been built to help the salmon get around these dams.

The salmon often swim hundreds of miles until they find a quiet *spawning* (spôn'ing), or nesting, place in fresh water. Here they spawn, or lay their eggs.

In 2 or 3 months the baby salmon hatch. At the end of their first year the young salmon are about 5 inches (12.7 cm) long. Soon they start to swim downstream toward the ocean. On the way many are eaten by birds or bigger fish. Some die in waters poisoned by waste materials from factories and cities. But thousands reach the ocean. The salmon spend the next 3 or 4 years in the ocean eating and growing. Then they return to spawn where they were born.

Most salmon fishing is done on the Columbia River, when the salmon begin their journey upstream. It is very easy to catch the salmon at this time. Laws now limit salmon fishing to keep too many salmon from being killed. The government has also set up places where baby salmon are hatched and taken care of.

Salmon swim up these fish ladders to their *spawning* places. Without the ladders, the fish could not get past the many dams built along the Columbia River and would die.

Mining on the West Coast

California is the chief mining state on the West Coast. It is one of our country's leading producers of petroleum and natural gas. See the map of oil fields and pipelines on page 362. Oil is found under the ocean off the coast of southern California. The lands in many parts of the Central Valley are rich in oil. California also has deposits of gold, mercury, and tungsten.

Mining is much less important in Oregon and Washington. But the two states do have some gold, silver, coal, copper, lead, iron ore, uranium, and clay.

Bridalveil Falls is one of the many breathtaking sights you can see in Yosemite National Park.

National Parks on the West Coast

Sequoia (si kwoi′ə) National Park in California is famous for its giant sequoia trees. Some of them are thousands of years old. Mount Whitney, in the Sierra Nevada, is in this park. East of Mount Whitney is the great desert known as Death Valley. This is the lowest land in the United States.

About 200 miles (320 km) east of San Francisco is Yosemite (yō sem′i tē) National Park. This beautiful park lies in the heart of the Sierra Nevada. It is noted for its waterfalls. One of these is famous for its rainbow colors. Another, which is called Bridalveil Falls, drops more than 600 feet (180 m) in a very slender column. Many tourists visit Yosemite National Park each year.

California has three other national parks. Kings Canyon National Park has many giant se-

quoia trees. Lassen Volcanic National Park has lakes, hot springs, a volcano, and steep domes of lava. Redwood National Park is located along the coast of California. It has the world's tallest redwood trees.

In southwestern Oregon is Crater Lake National Park. The lake, which is round, fills the crater, or opening, in the top of a once-active volcano. In Crater Lake is a small island, supposed to be the top of a volcano which fell in when the volcano erupted.

In Washington are three national parks, Olympic, Mount Rainier, and North Cascades. Olympic National Park has rugged mountains and thick forests of Douglas fir, spruce, hemlock, and cedar. The high, snow-covered top of Mount Rainier is the most beautiful sight in Mount Rainier National Park. North Cascades National Park is a mountainous region with many glaciers and lakes.

429

San Francisco
City by the Bay

San Francisco was founded in 1776 by the Spanish. Today San Francisco is the chief manufacturing, trade, and shipping center in northern California. San Francisco Bay is one of the best harbors in the world. It is large, deep, and safe from storms blowing in from the Pacific Ocean. The waterfront stretches for about 15 miles (24 km) around the bay. Dozens of ships lie beside large, crowded wharves. Lumber, canned fish, fruit, vegetables, and manufactured goods are loaded on these ships. Coffee, sugar, spices, and other items are brought in from foreign ports.

Much of San Francisco was destroyed by a terrible earthquake in 1906. But the people of San Francisco were quick to rebuild their city. Today, San Francisco is one of the largest cities in the United States. Among its more than half a million people are Americans of Chinese, Japanese, Mexican, and Philippine descent.

Charming cable cars help San Franciscans up and down many of the city's steep hills. But San Francisco also has a modern transportation system, called BART, which stands for Bay Area Rapid Transit. BART connects many of the cities in the bay area. The Golden Gate Bridge is one of the world's longest suspension, or hanging, bridges. This bridge connects San Francisco, which is on a peninsula, with the north coastal counties. Another suspension bridge, the San Francisco–Oakland Bay Bridge, connects San Francisco with the cities across the Bay. ■

Chief Cities Along the Coast

California, Oregon, and Washington have large, fast-growing cities. Each year thousands of acres of farms, gardens, and orchards are torn up. Land is needed for new homes, shopping centers, factories, streets, and freeways for the cities.

Farthest south along the coast is San Diego, one of the most rapidly growing cities in the United States. San Diego is an important port and naval base. Airplanes are also made there. Many tourists visit the city.

Los Angeles

Los Angeles is one of the three largest cities in the United States. Los Angeles is the chief industrial center of southern California. Oil refineries, automobile factories, clothing factories, and fish canneries are found there. The city is a leader in the manufacture of airplanes and equipment for space exploration. Hollywood, a part of Los Angeles, is the nation's capital for making films and television programs.

The area near Los Angeles receives little rainfall. The city had no water problem in 1781. It was only a small settlement then. But as Los Angeles grew, so did its problem of finding enough water. In 1913 the Los Angeles *Aqueduct* (ak′wə dukt) was built. An aqueduct is a pipe or channel that carries water over long distances. This pipeline brings water from the Sierra Nevada. In 1936 another aqueduct was built. The giant California Water Project began operations in 1972. It brings water from the Feather River, north of San Francisco.

The city's growth brought other problems. Los Angeles needed an ocean port for shipping its products. However, the ocean was 15 miles (24 km) away. San Pedro, a town on the coast, had a harbor. Los Angeles took in a strip of land to San Pedro and created the Port of Los Angeles. The harbor was dug out to make it wider and deeper. Then a great wall, or breakwater, was built. The breakwater was 2 miles (3.2 km) long and protected the harbor from high waves. Today the Port of Los Angeles is a busy west-coast port city.

Salem and Portland

Salem, the capital of Oregon, is located on the Willamette River. This city is about 50 miles (80 km) from the mouth of the Willamette, which flows into the Columbia. Salem is the trade and manufacturing center for the farmlands in this valley. Salem supplies lumber camps in the mountains with fruit, milk, butter, cheese, eggs, and poultry. Many people here earn their living in fruit canneries. Some people work in sawmills, where trees from the Cascade and Coast ranges are cut into lumber.

Portland is the chief trade and transportation center in Oregon. It is the gateway to the Willamette Valley and to the Pacific Ocean. When this city was founded, it lay just a few miles from the place where the Willamette River empties into the Columbia. Portland now extends all the way into the triangle of land formed by the joining of the Columbia and Willamette rivers. The Columbia River is deep enough for ocean liners to sail the more than 100 miles (160 km) from the Pacific Ocean to

Portland. Although it is quite far north, Portland's waterway does not freeze in the winter. Do you know why? See the map of the United States on pages 6–7.

Ocean steamships line the docks of Portland. Many carry away lumber from the Rockies, Cascades, and Coast Range. Some take away cargoes of canned salmon from the Columbia and other rivers. Other ships are loaded with grains and canned fruit from the Willamette Valley. Wheat, flour, and apples from irrigated parts of the Columbia Plateau are also shipped from Portland. Incoming ships bring farm machinery, automobiles, airplane parts, clothing, and other manufactured goods from California and the East.

Tacoma and Seattle

The cities on Puget Sound have deep, safe harbors. One of these cities is Tacoma. It is an important trade and manufacturing center. It has a huge copper refinery, large flour mills, railroad shops, machine shops, and woodwork factories. Tacoma is the chief lumber, pulp, and paper manufacturer in the Northwest.

Seattle, the leading port of the Northwest, is also on Puget Sound. Seattle started as a sawmill village at the mouth of a river which empties into Puget Sound. This village grew into a trade and shipping center for the lumber and fishing industries nearby. Then it became an important port and trade center in the days of the Alaska gold rush. Today Seattle is the chief city in Washington. It is one of the largest fur markets in this country. It also has a large aircraft industry.

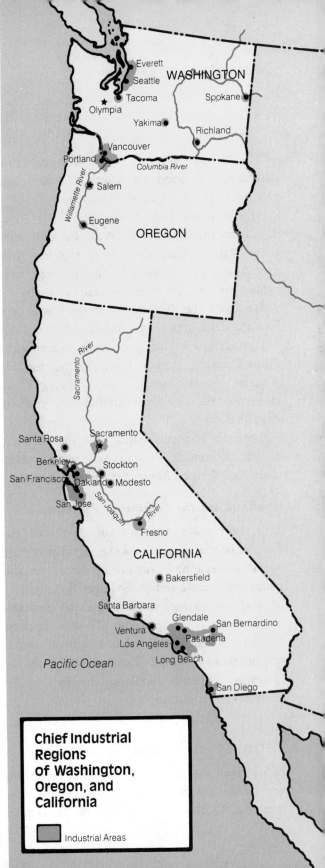

Chief Industrial Regions of Washington, Oregon, and California

Industrial Areas

433

The farms in the Coast Range valley produce fresh food for Seattle, Tacoma, and Olympia, the capital of Washington.

Seattle has a busy waterfront. Ships from Japan and other countries of the Far East bring many articles. Tankers carry petroleum from Los Angeles to Seattle. Farm machinery and other manufactured goods are brought by water from the Northeast. Both Seattle and Tacoma have large ship-building industries.

Lumber is a leading product in Washington. Ships carrying lumber leave Seattle for Los Angeles, South America, and Atlantic Coast cities. Seattle also ships lumber and grain to the Far East.

Railroads connect Seattle with the farmland of the Columbia Plateau and with eastern cities. Seattle is an important air center, too.

Spokane, on the Columbia Plateau

The chief trade and railroad center of the Columbia Plateau is Spokane. Railroads haul wheat and canned fruit from farms on this plateau to Seattle and other Puget Sound cities. Several important transcontinental railroads have stations in Spokane. This is because Spokane is near the only low mountain pass in the northern Rockies. Through the "Spokane Gateway" railroads run from the East to the cities on Puget Sound.

Farming in Alaska

Many Alaskans today make a living by fishing and by mining. Some trap or raise animals for their fur. Others farm or carry on lumbering.

Still others earn a living by caring for the tourists who visit Alaska each year.

The people of Alaska depend on the rest of the United States for much of their food. But farming in Alaska is growing in importance. As Alaska gains more people and new farms are started, the state will produce more and more food for its own population.

Alaska's leading farm region is the fertile Matanuska Valley, near the city of Anchorage. Cabbage, beets, lettuce, carrots, peas, and potatoes grow well in the long days of the short summers. Hay is also raised. There are many dairy farms. Farmers of this valley have good markets for their farm products. They send fresh milk and vegetables to markets in Anchorage.

The land along the Tanana River also is good for farming. Oats, barley, and spring wheat are grown there. Cabbage, peas, carrots, potatoes and other hardy vegetables are also raised. The growing season is short, but there are many hours of sunlight. In the middle of summer the sun shines more than 20 hours a day. Warm sunlight makes the crops grow fast. It makes the vegetables grow very large.

Lumbering and Mining in Alaska

Trees grow well in the mild, rainy climate of Alaska. The lower slopes of the mountains are green with thick forests of spruce and hemlock. Some lumbering is carried on, and it is becoming an important industry. As more people come to Alaska, lumbering and the making of wood pulp and paper will become even more important industries.

Mining is Alaska's most important industry. The leading mineral found there is petroleum. Oil was first produced in 1957 near Anchorage. Then, in 1968, huge quantities of oil were found in northern Alaska, between the Brooks Range and the Arctic Ocean. This region is known as the North Slope. See the map of oil fields on page 362.

Between 1974 and 1977, an 800-mile-long (1,280 km) pipeline was built across Alaska. It carries the oil from the North Slope to Valdez and other ports in the south that ships can use all year round.

Much natural gas was also discovered in the North Slope area. Many people think that even richer deposits of minerals are yet to be discovered in this northern area.

Gold, coal, copper, and uranium are also mined in Alaska, but in small quantities.

Alaska's Fishing Industry

Another important industry is fishing. Halibut, herring, cod, and king crabs are abundant in Alaskan waters. But salmon are the most important fish.

The Alaska Pipeline carries oil across the length of Alaska. The pipeline is above the ground because the earth is frozen in many parts of Alaska.

Every day boats bring their catch of salmon to canneries in Ketchikan and other cities along the coast. Much of the work at the canneries is done by machines. Machines unload the boats, placing the fish on a moving belt called a *conveyor* (kən vā′ ər). The conveyor carries the fish into a long cannery shed. Here the fish are cleaned, split open, washed and made ready for canning.

A machine cuts the fish into the right-sized pieces for each can. To make sure that each filled can is the right weight, a machine weighs the cans as they move along. Sealing machines close the cans, which are then taken to large pressure cookers. The salmon is cooked right in the cans. Later the cans are labeled and packed for shipment to all parts of the country. Salmon is Alaska's chief fish product.

Thousands of workers are needed to catch and can the salmon. Alaska does not have enough people to do all this work. So people come from Seattle and other nearby cities for the fishing season.

Government agents guard the fishing grounds by boat and by plane. They watch to see that Alaska's fishing laws are obeyed. They make sure that enough salmon reach the spawning grounds, where the baby salmon are hatched. Then there will always be a good supply of the fish.

Alaska's Fur Industry

Valuable furs have been shipped from Alaska ever since the days of the Russians. But the fur industry is no longer one of Alaska's main industries. Many people feel that it is not right to kill animals for their fur. People are worried, too, that certain kinds of animals will be completely killed off. They will become *extinct* (eks tingkt′). Extinct means no longer in existence.

The fur seals in Alaska were once in danger of becoming extinct. Find the Pribilof (prib′ə lof) Islands on the map of Alaska's products opposite. These tiny islands are the home of the fur seals. Their fine, silky furs

Products of Alaska

436

are used to make clothing. Every summer thousands of fur seals come to these rocky islands.

Hunters killed so many of these animals that the United States government stepped in and stopped the killing. When the main herd of seals had increased, hunters were once more allowed to kill them. But now only a certain number of seals may be killed each year.

Alaska's fur industry no longer depends on the killing of wild animals. Instead, there are fur farms where fur-bearing animals, especially mink, are raised.

Alaska's Scenic Beauty

Forest-covered slopes, snowy mountain peaks, rushing streams, waterfalls, and icy glaciers are part of Alaska's beauty. This beautiful scenery attracts thousands of visitors every year. Other visitors hunt wild game in the woods, fish in the many rivers and lakes, or camp in the mountains. Many visit Mount McKinley National Park to see Mount McKinley, with its snow-covered peak and glaciers. Taking care of tourists is an important way in which many Alaskans make their living during the summer months.

Cities in Alaska

The cities in Alaska are not as large as those in most other states. But some had a rapid growth as the oil industry developed in the 1970s.

Tourists go to Alaska by ship. Much of their journey can be made through the calm waters of the Inside Passage. Islands protect this passage from rough northern Pacific waters.

Ketchikan is the first Alaskan city reached by ships on the Inside Passage. The land is steep there. Some buildings and streets are built out over the water. In summer, the fishing boats come and go at the busy docks. Ketchikan is an important salmon-canning center. Some salmon are also frozen, smoked, or salted.

At Juneau, too, steep forest-covered mountains rise close to the coast. The city was built there because gold was discovered close by. But fishing, canning, and lumbering are the chief industries today. Juneau is the capital of Alaska. Government business gives work to many people. The city is connected by water and air with other parts of the nation.

Across the Gulf of Alaska is Seward. Find the gulf on the map of Alaska on page 406. Seward, an important port, is at the end of a railroad which runs to Fairbanks and to Anchorage.

Fairbanks is the leading city of the Interior. There is no other big town for hundreds of miles. Many people depend on Fairbanks for supplies. On its streets you see Indians, Eskimos, and military people from the large United States Air Force base at Fairbanks.

Fairbanks can be reached by airplane, train, and also by automobile. It is at the northern end of the Alaskan Highway. This highway is more than 1,500 miles (2,400 km) long. It connects Alaska with Canada. From Canada other highways go south to the rest of the United States.

Anchorage
A Modern Outpost

Getting off a plane at Anchorage's modern airport, you would hardly guess you were at a wilderness outpost. The heart of Anchorage is very modern. Yet nearby is some of the most rugged land left in the United States.

Alaska has the largest area of any state. But most of it is wild unsettled country. Only about 400,000 people live in the whole state. More than 40 percent of them live in or near Anchorage

Founded as a railroad construction camp, Anchorage today is a center for trains going into the Interior. Anchorage also has a port and major highway connections. Planes of all sizes land at Anchorage's airport, which is also an important international stopover. Why is air transportation so important to the people?

Anchorage is the main transportation center of Alaska. Why do you think Anchorage also became the main center for distributing goods? Why might it also be the natural place in Alaska for manufacturing to develop? ■

Farming in Hawaii

Hawaii, as you know, has a pleasant climate and rich soil. With these conditions, farming is one of the most important industries on the islands.

Sugarcane and pineapples are the two big money crops on the islands. The climate also favors the growing of tropical vegetable crops and coffee. Many people grow orchids and other flowers. The flowers are shipped to florists in the mainland states.

Workers harvest sugarcane with machines. You can see the color of Hawaii's rich soil where the sugarcane has been cut down.

Sugarcane, Hawaii's Largest Crop

The raising of sugarcane is a big business in Hawaii. Sugar is Hawaii's chief money crop. Most of it is grown on irrigated fields. Miles of tunnels and pipes bring water to the fields from the rainier sides of the islands. Sugar is a thirsty crop and needs much water.

It takes about 2 years for the cane to ripen. By careful planning, work on a large sugar plantation goes on all year long. Modern machinery is used to get the fields ready for planting, to plant the cane, and to harvest it.

Each plantation is like a complete town. Besides the sugar mills, there are homes, schools, churches, playgrounds, stores, and other services which the people need.

Most of the raw sugar from the sugar mills is sent to the mainland to be refined. A small part is kept in the islands.

Pineapples, Hawaii's Second Crop

Pineapples are Hawaii's second most important money crop. Like sugarcane, they grow best where it is warm all year.

As we ride through a large plantation, we smell the sweetness of the ripening pineapples. On both sides pineapple fields stretch for miles over hilly and gently sloping land. They look like a beautiful green carpet.

The rows of pineapples are planted across the slopes instead of up and down them. "Why have the pineapples been planted across the slopes?" we ask the manager.

"When we plow with the natural curve of the land, it helps to hold the soil in place. This keeps the rain from washing the soil away," the manager explains. "On steeper slopes we build terraces, or small flat hills of earth. These terraces help in holding back the water."

The manager stops the car so that we can see what a pineapple plant is like. We must be very careful not to go too close. The long leaves are like spikes and have sharp edges. For protection from the hot sun and the sharp spikes, the workers who are picking the pineapples wear dark eyeglasses and heavy gloves.

439

The black patches about the plants puzzle us. We look closer and see that the patches are paper! We are told that machines laid long strips of heavy paper across the fields before the pineapples were planted. The paper helps keep the soil warm and moist and prevents weeds from growing. It is left on the ground until it rots. The young pineapple plants are set out by hand through holes punched in the paper.

"About a year and a half after the pineapples are planted, the first fruit ripens," explains the manager. "We harvest the fruit chiefly in June, July, and August. But some are picked every month."

At harvest time workers put the ripe fruit on the long arm of a conveyor which reaches out across many rows of pineapple plants. A moving belt carries the pineapples to a bin on a truck. When the bin is full, the pineapples are rushed to the canneries. They are then canned, as fruit or as juice. Some are shipped as fresh fruit.

Workers harvesting pineapples need protection from the prickly fruit and the hot sun. What kinds of protective clothing do they use?

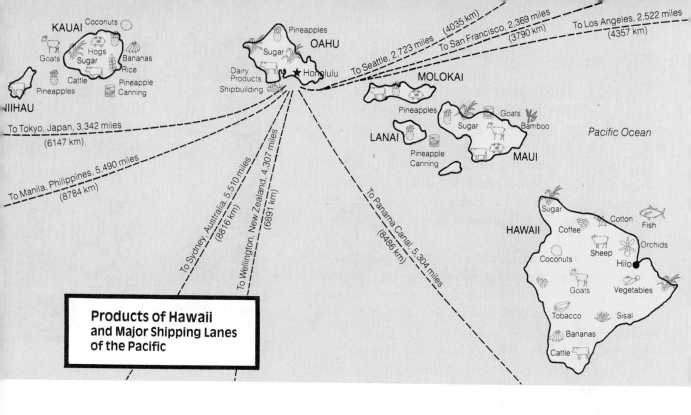

Products of Hawaii and Major Shipping Lanes of the Pacific

Hawaii's Industries

Hawaii's main industries are still based on its farm products. The processing of sugarcane and canning of pineapples are especially important. Coffee is grown and processed on the island of Hawaii. In addition, defense industries have long provided jobs. Many civilians work in or near military bases. The shipyards at Pearl Harbor employ many people.

Since Hawaii became a state, however, other industries have grown up. The construction industry has grown fast. New buildings have been built throughout the islands. Some building materials are now made in Hawaii. There are cement plants, a steel mill, and pipe manufacturing plants. An oil refinery has been built too. Hawaii's garment factories turn out popular Hawaiian shirts and dresses.

A Tourist Land

The beautiful scenery and pleasant climate of these tropical islands bring millions of visitors to Hawaii every year. Travelers enjoy the fine beaches, the mountains, and the brightly colored tropical flowers. December or June—no matter what time of the year it is—visitors are able to wear summer clothes. They can go horseback riding and play tennis or golf. They have fun at the beaches swimming, sun bathing, or riding the waves on a surf board. Some tourists like to visit the pineapple plantations and the canning factories. Others like to visit Hawaii's two national parks, Volcanoes and Haleakala (häl′ē äk′ə lä′) Crater. Taking care of tourists is a year-round business in Hawaii. Many Hawaiians earn their living that way.

Honolulu
An Island Metropolis

The ancient Hawaiians called Oahu the "Gathering Place." If you fly over the Hawaiian Islands today, you can see that Oahu is very crowded. The island's largest city, Honolulu, stretches out beneath you. Three-fourths of Hawaii's people live in or near this city.

Honolulu is the state capital and center of all government business. Pearl Harbor and other major military bases are close by. Also close by is Waikiki, the center of Hawaii's tourist business. In fact, almost all Hawaii's important business is centered in Honolulu.

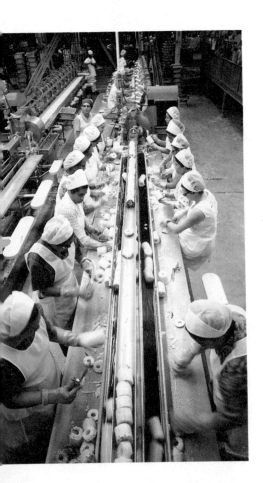

One reason Oahu and especially Honolulu became the islands' gathering place is Honolulu's excellent harbor. Why is shipping vital to the island? How does Honolulu's harbor bring industry?

But the city's future growth may be limited. Most of the other islands now have deep-water harbors, too. They are also developing tourist resorts and some industries. What effect might this have on Honolulu in the future? ■

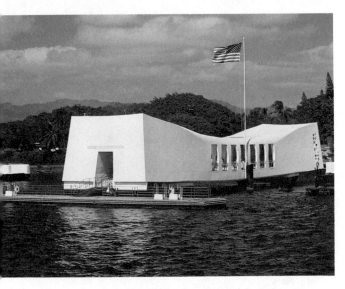

The U.S.S. *Arizona* Memorial floats on the water at Pearl Harbor. It marks the place where the ship *Arizona* sank in the 1941 bombing of the naval base.

Places where ways of travel meet and cross are often called crossroads. Hawaii is called the "Crossroads of the Pacific." Ships and planes on their way to and from Asia, Australia, and North America stop there to unload or take on mail, cargo, supplies, or passengers.

Many tourists like to visit Pearl Harbor on the island of Oahu (ō ä′hōō). It is a harbor where a very large number of United States ships are stationed. Pearl Harbor also has large airfields.

In 1941 war between Japan and the United States seemed close. But no one thought that the war would begin in Hawaii. At dawn on December 7, Japanese planes flew over Oahu, dropping bombs on the naval base and the airfields at Pearl Harbor. Many ships were sunk. Airplanes burned on the ground.

This was the beginning of World War II for the United States. The war lasted for nearly 4 years. The Hawaiian Islands were an important source of supplies in the Pacific during the war.

Because of its position on the crossroads of the Pacific, Hawaii is an outpost of defense for the United States. Pearl Harbor and other military bases on the islands are still very important.

Hawaii's location makes it important for other reasons too. It is a natural meeting place for peaceful contacts between representatives of America and Asia. The ancestors of many of Hawaii's people came from Asia.

Cities of Hawaii

Hawaii does not have many large cities. Honolulu is the largest. Hilo (hē′lō) is second in size. Hilo is on the island named Hawaii, the largest island in the group. Hawaiians call it the "Big Island." It has many sugar plantations and great cattle and sheep ranches. Hilo is the trade center and port of the "Big Island." The city is also an important tourist center.

Do You Know?

1. Where is California's Central Valley? What are some products raised there?
2. Why are there laws to regulate salmon fishing?
3. What minerals are found in Alaska?
4. What are Hawaii's most important crops?
5. Why is Hawaii important to the United States defense system?

To Help You Learn

Using New Words

volcano   spawning
conveyor   aqueduct
trade wind   great circle route
extinct   transcontinental

The phrases below explain the words or terms listed above. Number a paper from 1 through 8. After each number write the word or term which matches the definition.

1. Across the continent
2. An opening in the earth's surface through which steam, ashes, and hot, melted rock, or lava, flow
3. No longer in existence
4. Nesting place in fresh water
5. A steady wind that blows toward the equator
6. A moving belt which carries loads from one place to another
7. A pipe or channel that carries water over long distances
8. Shortest, most direct route between two places on the globe

Finding the Facts

1. What are the Pacific states? Why are these five states called the Pacific states? Which state is the largest? Which is the smallest?
2. What are the chief mountain ranges in the four coast states?
3. Where are the lowland areas in Washington and Oregon?
4. What is the highest mountain in North America? Where is it?
5. Where are the Aleutian Islands?
6. What is the climate of the five Pacific states like?
7. Who was John C. Frémont? Kit Carson? John Sutter?
8. Who were the fortyniners? By what three routes did they reach California?
9. Name three ways of sending messages that connected the East and West by the 1860s.
10. Who first discovered Alaska? From whom did we buy Alaska? When?
11. Who discovered Hawaii? When did Hawaii become part of the United States?
12. What crops are raised in California's Central Valley? In the Imperial Valley?
13. Why does southern California have so many airplane factories?
14. What is the leading lumber state in the United States?
15. Name two ways in which the Grand Coulee Dam serves the region in which it is located.
16. What fish are caught off the coasts of Oregon, Washington, and Alaska? Which kind of fish is the most valuable?
17. Why was a pipeline built across Alaska?
18. What national parks are in California?
19. What is the leading port city in the Northwest? On what body of water is it located? What are its most important industries?

20. Why is Hawaii a good place in which to grow sugarcane and pineapples?

Learning from Maps

1. Find the five Pacific states on a globe. In what direction is Alaska from Washington? Hawaii from Washington?

2. On the map of the United States on pages A-6–A-7, locate the Pacific states. Why are Alaska and Hawaii shown separately from the rest of the United States?

3. Look at the map of the Lewis and Clark Expedition on page 305, and trace the route of Lewis and Clark from St. Louis to the Pacific coast. What river did they follow most of the way? By what route did they return?

4. Trace the route of the Oregon Trail on the map of western trails on page 383. Through what different kinds of land would the settlers have to travel in going from Independence, Missouri, to Portland, Oregon? The map of the United States on pages A-6–A-7 will help you.

5. Study the map showing the products of the Pacific states on page 425 and answer these questions: What fruits are grown in these states? Where are the wheat lands? The lumber regions? What minerals are found in these states?

6. By using the map showing the growth of the United States on page 137, list the territories added to the United States between 1800 and 1860. Which Pacific state once belonged to Mexico?

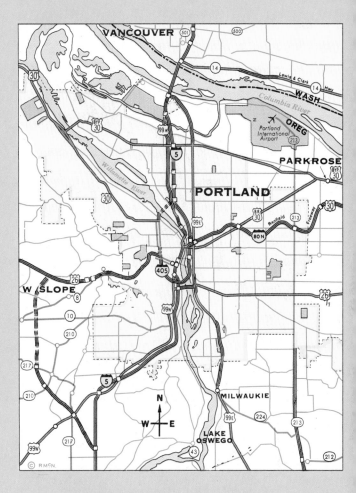

7. This road map shows the area around the city of Portland, Oregon. What roads are shown in green? What roads are shown in red? Why is State Route 14 called the Lewis and Clark Highway? What is the name of Interstate Route 80N? In which state is the city of Vancouver? What river would you cross to travel from Portland to Vancouver?

8. On the map of forest regions on page 427 locate the forest regions of Washington, Oregon, and California. What kind of forest is found in each of these states?

9. The elected Senators and Representatives travel to Washington to serve in the Congress. Show on a globe the shortest route Alaska's Congress members could take in traveling by airplane from Juneau to Washington, D.C.; Hawaii's Congress members from Honolulu to Washington, D.C. What large bodies of water would each group cross? What mountains would they cross? What states would they fly over?

Using Study Skills

1. **Time line:** Copy the time line on page 403. Put these other events on the time line in the right order.
   Morse invents telegraph
   Supreme Court grants fishing rights to Indians
   Bering Strait discovered
   Lewis and Clark Expedition begins
   United States and Great Britain divide Oregon Country
2. **Chart:** Make a chart of the Pacific states. List the states alphabetically beginning with Alaska. Use the chart in Unit 5 on page 256 as your model.
3. **Graph:** Look at the graphs on page 421. Which group of people made up 9% of the total population in Alaska in 1980? What percentage of the people in Alaska were American Indian in 1980? Which group of people made up the largest percentage? Which group made up the smallest percentage? Which group of people made

up 40% of the total population in Hawaii in 1980? What percentage of the people in Hawaii were of Japanese ancestry? Which group was larger—those of Japanese or those of Hawaiian ancestry?

Thinking It Through

1. Early settlers in the Oregon Country had to make their own laws because they were so far away from the national government. What kind of rules did they need? How was their experience like that of the Pilgrims who drew up the Mayflower Compact? Why do all groups need rules to live happily together?
2. If gold were discovered in California today, what means of transportation would people use to reach the gold fields? Would any of these be the same as those used by people who went west in 1849?
3. When the United States bought Alaska from Russia in 1867, many Americans did not know much about the new land. They thought the purchase of Alaska was foolish and called it "Seward's Folly." What is your opinion of this purchase?
4. Most early settlers and explorers did not turn back even though they faced many hardships. Why was it so important for them to continue their journey?
5. If you had been a fortyniner, which of the three routes to California would you have preferred to take? Why? You may wish to study the map of the geographical regions of the United States on pages 6–7 and the map of western trails

on page 383 before making your choice. Consider the danger, time, and cost of the route you choose.

Projects

1. Prepare an exhibit of the products of the Pacific states. Bring in sample products such as an apple, an orange, a pineapple, a can of salmon, and so on. In some cases you may have to use pictures.
2. Find a current event about one of the Pacific states and connect it with what you have learned in this unit.
3. Make a report on the Alaska Pipeline. When was it built? Why? Who built it? In what ways was it valuable? How did it affect the land around it?
4. The Research Committee might find information about Lewis and Clark's trip. Write a diary about the trip. Tell about the tribes of American Indians, the animals, and vegetation along the way.
5. The Explorers' Committee should use an outline map of the United States to show the route followed by Lewis and Clark and their exploring group in 1803–1805.
6. The Reading Committee will find these books interesting: *Narcissa Whitman, Pioneer Girl,* by Ann Warner; *Blue Willow,* by Doris Gates.

14 American Neighbors

Unit Preview

The United States has fifty states. It also has other lands. Some of these lands lie in the Atlantic Ocean. Others are in the Pacific.

To the north, the United States shares a long border with Canada. The French were the first to settle in Canada. The English came much later. The French and English went to war over North America. The war ended in favor of the English. Canada remained under English rule until 1867, when it became an independent nation.

The region south of the United States is called Latin America. Some of the countries in Latin America are clustered around the Caribbean Sea. Most of these Caribbean countries are independent nations. Some are colonies of European nations. Mexico is the Latin American country closest to the United States. The two nations share a border. In 1821 Spanish rule ended in Mexico.

Like their neighbors to the north, the countries of South America all began as colonies of European nations. Today all but one of these countries are independent. The countries of South America have important raw materials and farm products to sell to the rest of the world. All the countries want to do more than produce raw materials and farm products, however. South Americans want to develop new industries, and they have begun to do this.

Things to Discover

If you look carefully at the picture, map, and time line, you can answer these questions.

1. The picture shows the ruins of what was once a Mayan temple. The Mayas lived in Central America, the narrow strip of land between the American continents. What country is north of this region?
2. What country borders the United States on the north? On the south?
3. What ocean borders Canada on the north?
4. Which became independent first, Mexico, Cuba, or Brazil?
5. What form of government does Canada have?

Words to Learn

You will meet these words in this unit. As you read, you will learn what they mean and how to pronounce them. The Word List will help you.

asbestos	Latin America
balsam	llano
commonwealth	mestizo
confederation	missile
Creole	pampa
ejido	Parliament
estuary	pitchblende
gaucho	province
hacienda	selva
hurricane	tungsten
latex	vulcanizing

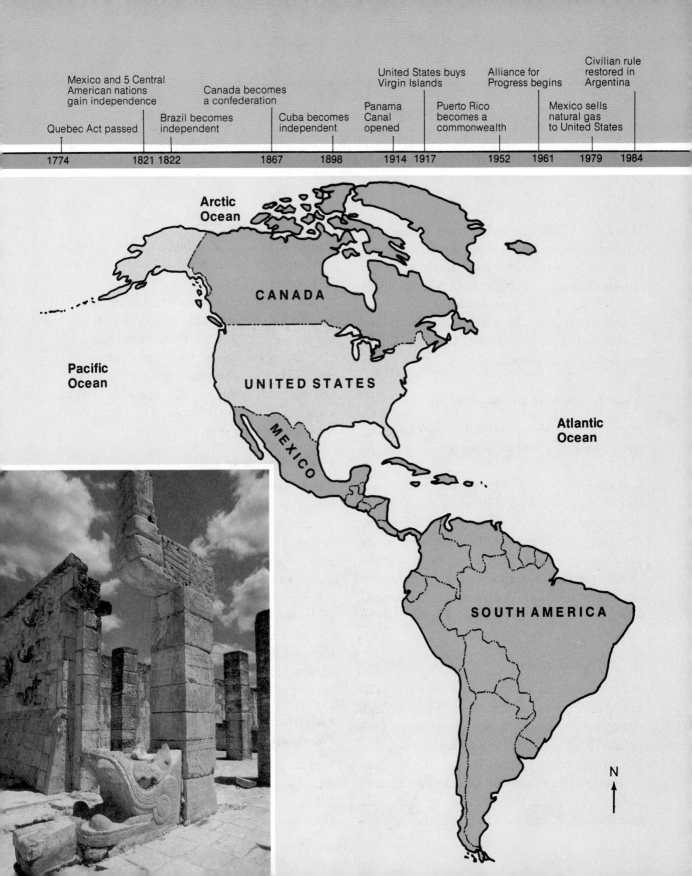

Quebec Act passed
1774

Mexico and 5 Central American nations gain independence
1821

Brazil becomes independent
1822

Canada becomes a confederation
1867

Cuba becomes independent
1898

Panama Canal opened
1914

United States buys Virgin Islands
1917

Puerto Rico becomes a commonwealth
1952

Alliance for Progress begins
1961

Mexico sells natural gas to United States
1979

Civilian rule restored in Argentina
1984

Arctic Ocean

CANADA

Pacific Ocean

UNITED STATES

MEXICO

Atlantic Ocean

SOUTH AMERICA

N

1
Other Lands of Our Country

The United States has other lands besides the fifty states that are part of our country. Two of these lands are Puerto Rico and the Virgin Islands. They lie in the Atlantic Ocean about 1,000 miles (1,600 km) southeast of Florida. They are part of the West Indies islands. American Samoa (sə mō′ə), Midway, Wake, and Guam are in the Pacific Ocean.

The Island of Puerto Rico

Puerto Rico is about 100 miles (160 km) long and 35 miles (56 km) wide. More than 3 million people live there.

Puerto Rico is mostly a land of hills and mountains with lowlands along the coast. It is in the tropics, where the growing season lasts the year round. As in Hawaii, the trade winds make the climate pleasant. They bring heavy rains to its northern and eastern slopes. For this reason, the largest of Puerto Rico's rivers and streams flow north toward the Atlantic. They are useful for water power and irrigation.

An Island on Guard

Puerto Rico has an important location. The only way to enter the Caribbean Sea is through passages between the West Indies islands. One passage is between Puerto Rico and the island of Hispaniola. This passage is one of the chief entrances to the Caribbean. Long ago the Spanish built a great, thick-walled fort at San Juan (sän hwän′), Puerto Rico's capital, to guard it.

Under Spanish Rule

Puerto Rico has had a long and interesting history. It is one of the many lands that Columbus discovered.

Juan Ponce de León (pōns dā lā′ōn), the first Spaniard to see Florida, made the first settlement on Puerto Rico. He was its first governor. For 400 years Puerto Rico was a Spanish colony. The people learned Spanish ways. After our war with Spain in 1898, the island became a part of the United States. The name Puerto Rico means "rich port."

Under American Rule

Changes were made in Puerto Rico after it became part of the United States. A public-school system like that in our states was set up. Roads, hospitals, dams, and hydroelectric plants were built. Most of the people worked on sugar plantations or in sugar mills owned by United States companies. Much of the money made by the plantations and mills went to the United States companies. Puerto Rico received little money. It was hard to make a living on the small, crowded island. Many left Puerto Rico to come to the United States mainland.

Luis Muñoz Marín, Puerto Rican Leader

Luis Muñoz Marín (loo ēs′ moo nyōs′ mä rēn′) was born in San Juan, Puerto Rico, in 1898. His father worked for Puerto Rico in Washington, D.C. So Luis went to school in the United

States. Later, he returned to Puerto Rico. There he worked on a newspaper which his father had founded.

In 1932 Luis was elected to the Puerto Rican Senate. Six years later he started a new political party, the Popular Democratic party. In 1948 the people of Puerto Rico were allowed to elect their own governor. They chose Luis Muñoz Marín as their first governor. He remained in office until 1964 when he decided not to run again. Luis died in 1980.

For more than 8 years as Senate President and later as governor, Luis worked hard to improve living conditions in Puerto Rico. He set up a series of programs known as "Operation Bootstrap."

As part of Operation Bootstrap the government of Puerto Rico bought large plantations. It divided them into small plots of land. The plots were sold at low prices to many farmers. Ways of farming were improved and better crops raised. Government irrigation projects provided water. Still, not all Puerto Ricans could be farmers. Puerto Rico needed industries to create more jobs for its people. As part of Operation Bootstrap the government helped by encouraging investors from the United States to build factories in Puerto Rico. Each new business was helped by not having to pay taxes for 10 years. New dams and power plants provided electricity for the factories. Government schools trained workers.

Operation Bootstrap brought electricity and an improved school system to all parts of the island. Old buildings were torn down and new ones were put up. A hotel was built, the first

Luis Muñoz Marín often traveled to Washington, D.C., when he was governor of Puerto Rico. He presented the interests of the *commonwealth* to the national government.

one in Puerto Rico. Tourists were invited to enjoy the island's fine climate. Many came and soon there were many hotels.

Puerto Rico as a Commonwealth

One of Luis Muñoz Marín's proudest moments came in 1952 when the United States Congress made Puerto Rico a free *commonwealth* (kom'ən welth'). A commonwealth is a form of government much like a state. As a commonwealth, it has its own constitution. Every 4 years Puerto Ricans elect their own governor and legislature.

Puerto Ricans are citizens of the United States and are free to move here. Many of them did so during the 1950s. Then almost 500,000 Puerto Ricans migrated to the mainland.

Puerto Rico's tie with the United States is of its own choice. Some day it may join the Union as a state. Or it may become an independent nation.

San Juan
Capital and Chief Port

San Juan is the capital and largest city in Puerto Rico. It has two parts. The older part of San Juan is on an island off Puerto Rico's northern coast. Along the busy, narrow streets are houses and shops of long ago. The newer part of San Juan is on the main island. In this new part of the city, buildings are as modern as any in the world. Bridges connect the two parts of the city.

San Juan was founded by followers of Ponce de León in 1521. The Spanish built forts and walls around the city to protect its harbor. The Spanish made San Juan a seat of government.

San Juan is the chief trade, manufacturing, government, and shipping center of Puerto Rico. The city's major industries make medicines, chemicals, fertilizer, and jewelry. Many people also make a living taking care of tourists. San Juan is the main port. Most of Puerto Rico's trade is with the United States. ■

Sugar, Tobacco, Fruit

About one-third of the people of Puerto Rico earn their living by farming. Sugar, the chief crop and leading export, is grown on the rich level coastland.

Tobacco is another important crop. It is grown on small farms in the valleys in the eastern mountain regions of this tropical island.

"I make most of my living raising and selling tobacco," a farmer says. "It keeps me busy from November, when it is planted, until March, when I harvest it. I also raise corn, beans, yams, or rice. After my tobacco is harvested, I plant other crops in the same field."

"Many things have changed in Puerto Rico since I was young," another farmer says. "Many farms now have electricity and running water. Irrigation is being used on the parts of the island where the rainfall is light.

"We grow pineapples on our farm. Some we market as fresh fruit. The rest we sell to the canneries."

Electrical power plants, like this one near San Juan, were built under Operation Bootstrap. The increased use of electricity attracted new industries to Puerto Rico.

Other crops grown in Puerto Rico are bananas, oranges, and coffee. Some farmers on the island also raise cattle, pigs, and chickens.

Puerto Rico's Industries

Many Puerto Ricans no longer depend on farming for a living. New factories have given work to thousands. They furnish many products which

Products of Puerto Rico and the Virgin Islands

once were imported. They also furnish products for export. Some of Puerto Rico's industries make chemicals, clothing, machinery, electrical equipment, food products, and petroleum products. The petroleum is imported mainly from Venezuela, a country in South America.

Tourism is another thriving industry. The island enjoys a year-round mild temperature, abundant sunshine, and refreshing breezes. Visitors come to see the deep forests, the flowering trees, and the mountains. They enjoy shopping in city streets that are more than 400 years old, and visiting museums, chapels, and craft shops.

United States Virgin Islands

If they could only speak, what stories the bays and inlets along the coasts of the Virgin Islands could tell! Some of these once hid pirate ships.

In 1917 the United States bought the Virgin Islands from Denmark, a country of Europe, for 25 million dollars. Their location makes these islands important. They are on ship routes to the Panama Canal. They are well located to help

The capital of the Virgin Islands is an important harbor. Charlotte Amalie Harbor overlooks a calm, clear, blue sea.

guard and defend this important canal. Prove this by the map on page 476.

Ten years after the United States bought the Virgin Islands, the islanders became United States citizens. In 1968 the islanders were given the right to elect their own governor. Three years later Melvin H. Evans took office as the first governor of the Virgin Islands. In 1979 voters in the Virgin Islands turned down a constitution that would have given them more self-government. The main reason they did so was that they feared more self-government would bring about tax increases.

Making a living on the Virgin Islands has never been easy. The soil is poor and rocky. Much of the land is hilly. Even on the flat land farmers cannot be sure of getting a good crop. Crops often fail because of dry weather.

Most Virgin Islanders make their living by raising cattle, growing cane, or taking care of tourists. Caring for tourists has become an important industry. Visitors enjoy the balmy climate, the white sandy beaches, and the beautiful tropical scenery. They like to go fishing, swimming, and sailing. Many tourist ships visit Charlotte Amalie (shär′lət ə mäl′ə) on the island of St. Thomas. This beautiful and interesting city is a free port, which means that goods can be received and shipped there without being taxed. Charlotte Amalie is built on hillsides overlooking the blue waters of its bay. It is the capital and largest town in the Virgin Islands.

Among the leading industries of the Virgin Islands are bauxite refining, petroleum refining, and cloth making.

American Samoa

The beautiful Samoa Islands are far to the south of Hawaii. Part of these islands belong to the United States. The rest is an independent nation. Our country has an important naval base in American Samoa. Ships and planes on their way to Australia and New Zealand find the islands good stopping places for supplies.

The Samoa Islands were discovered in 1722 by a Dutch explorer. In 1872 the United States Navy set up a naval base at Pago Pago (päng′ō päng′ō), the capital of American Samoa. For the first half of the 1900s the United States Navy managed the island. Then the United States government took over the management. The people of American Samoa make their own laws and elect their own governor.

Some people in American Samoa grow vegetables and fruits. Others take care of tourists, fish, and make crafts by hand. Tuna canning is another major industry of American Samoa. Much of the canned tuna is exported. Most American Samoan trade is with the United States and Japan.

Midway

Midway is an important link in the chain of our Pacific islands. For many years Midway has been a cable station. A cable is a telegraph wire which is laid under water. At the cable station on Midway messages are received and sent on to the United States and to places in Asia.

Two islands, Sand Island and Eastern Island, make up Midway. The islands are controlled by

Ships stop at Pago Pago, American Samoa, to refuel on their way across the Pacific Ocean. Passengers go ashore to enjoy good food and beautiful beaches.

the United States Navy. The Battle of Midway on June 4, 1942, marked the turning point of World War II in the Pacific. The United States defeated Japan when Japan tried to capture Midway.

Wake Island

Wake Island has been a United States possession since 1898. This tiny, lonely island is an important fueling station between Hawaii and Asia. Wake Island is also a cable station.

During World War II, Japan captured Wake Island. Japan held the island until the war ended in 1945.

Guam

Ferdinand Magellan discovered Guam in 1521 on a voyage around the world. This island was a Spanish possession until our war with Spain in 1898. Since then Guam has become one of our important air and naval bases in the Pacific.

The people of Guam are United States citizens. They make their own laws and choose their own governor.

Some people in Guam farm. They grow vegetables and fruits. They raise cattle, pigs, and chickens. Some people work on the air and naval bases. Others work in oil refineries or in factories that process food or make watches or clothing. Still others fish or take care of tourists.

For years the United States paid little attention to some of its island possessions in the Pacific. They seemed small and of little importance. But they are like steppingstones from the United States to Asia or to Australia and New Zealand. Most of our Pacific Island possessions are in the tropics, or low latitudes.

Today we realize how valuable these island possessions are. Because of their location, planes or ships can stop at these islands for supplies, fuel, or repairs. Many have submarine, air, or naval bases.

Do You Know?

1. What lands fly the United States flag in the Atlantic?
2. How did we get each of these lands?
3. What island possessions does the United States have in the Pacific?
4. In which climate belt do most of the islands lie?

2
Canada, a Northern Neighbor

Canada, our northern neighbor, is the second largest country in the world. Only the Soviet Union is larger.

Canada is made up of twelve *provinces* (prov'ins ez). In Canada a province is a region much like a state in our country. Nova Scotia (nō'və skō'shə), New Brunswick, Prince Edward Island, and Newfoundland are Canada's smallest provinces. Quebec (kwi bek') is Canada's largest province. It is about twice the size of Texas. Quebec is often called "the cradle of Canada."

Beautiful Moraine Lake is in the Canadian Rockies. The lake was formed by a glacier. It is filled with melted mountain snow.

Geography of Canada

Although Canada is large, it is thinly populated. Much of northern Canada has thick forests and frozen lands. So most Canadians live near the southern border.

Soil and Surface

The Appalachian Highland reaches into Canada. This is a region of low hills and fertile valleys. Some of Canada's best farmlands are in the lowlands along the Great Lakes and the St. Lawrence River.

The Laurentian (lô ren'shən) Upland covers almost half of Canada. It stretches from the Atlantic Ocean to the Arctic. Long ago a glacier moved over this region. As it moved, it took soil with it. It left behind rocky hills, lakes, and swamps. The region is not good for farming. But it has thick forests, many minerals, and swift rivers which furnish water power.

A wide central plain lies between the Laurentian Upland and the Rockies in the west. This fertile plain continues northward from the United States to the Arctic. Its level surface makes it easy to use machinery and to have large farms.

The Canadian Rockies are part of a region of high, rugged mountains. West of the Rockies are the Cascade Range and the Coast Mountains. Plateaus and narrow fertile valleys lie between the coastal mountains and the Rockies.

Southeastern Quebec is part of the Appalachian Highland. Southern Quebec lies in the

fertile St. Lawrence plain. Most of Quebec is on the Laurentian Upland.

Ontario has more people than any other province. Ontario's lowlands lie in the upper part of the St. Lawrence Valley and the plains along the Great Lakes. Find the natural regions of both provinces on the map of Canada on this page .

The provinces of Manitoba, Saskatchewan (sas kach′ ə won′), and Alberta lie between Ontario and British Columbia. They are part of the great central plain which extends northward from the United States. Its northern part

is covered with trees. Its southern part has a flat, grassy, almost treeless prairie, which gives these provinces their name. Most of the people live on this fertile grassy plain. The Laurentian Upland covers much of northern Manitoba and part of Saskatchewan. Western Alberta lies in the Rockies. Find these natural regions on the map of Canada on this page.

British Columbia is Canada's most western and most mountainous province. The towering snow-capped Rockies shut it off from the other provinces. The forest-covered Coast Ranges border its Pacific coast. Between these mountain ranges are other mountains, narrow, fertile valleys, and plateaus.

Canada's huge and valuable northland stretches west from Baffin Island and Hudson Bay to Alaska. It covers almost one-third of the country. It is divided into two territories, Yukon and Northwest Territories. See the map of Canada, page 459.

Climate

Because it lies in the high latitudes much of Canada has long cold winters. Parts of southern Canada have a climate which is much like that found in the northern United States. The winters are cold there but the summers are warm or hot. Look at the climate map of the United States on page 11.

British Columbia has extremes of climate. Its coastal lands have mild winters and cool summers caused by winds blowing over a warm ocean current. Inland the summers are hot, the winters cold. This province receives the heaviest rainfall in Canada. The warm winds bring heavy rain to the mountains along the coast. Inland, where the clouds have less moisture, the rainfall is light.

History of Canada

Eskimos lived in the far northern part of Canada long before Europeans arrived. Today Eskimos are scattered throughout Canada. They hunt, fish, and work for mining and transportation companies.

American Indians also lived in Canada long before Europeans arrived. The Indians lived mainly in the central and southern parts of the country. Today most Indians live on reserves, or reservations, set up by the Canadian government. They fish, farm, and work for lumbering and mining companies.

This chart compares Canada and the United States in several ways. Which country has more land? Which country has a greater population?

Canada and The United States

	Population	Area	Highest Point	Lowest Point	Largest Province or State	Smallest Province or State
United States	234,315,000	3,615,122 sq. mi. (9,363,123 sq. km)	Mount McKinley in Alaska 20,320 ft. (6,194 m)	Death Valley in California 282 ft. (86 m) below sea level	Alaska 586,412 sq. mi. (1,518,800 sq. km)	Rhode Island 1,214 sq. mi. (3,144 sq. km)
Canada	24,885,900	3,851,809 sq. mi. (9,976,139 sq. km)	Mount Logan in Yukon Territory 19,850 ft. (6,050 m)	Sea level	Quebec 594,860 sq. mi. (1,540,680 sq. km)	Prince Edward Island 2,180 sq. mi. (5,660 sq. km)

French and British Claims

Canada was discovered by Europeans trying to find a sea route to Asia. In 1534 Jacques Cartier (zhäk kär tē ā′) explored the Gulf of St. Lawrence. The next year he discovered and explored the St. Lawrence River. He claimed all the land drained by this river for France.

Samuel de Champlain (sham plän′) founded Quebec in 1608. This settlement was the first permanent French colony in America. Everywhere Champlain went he claimed the land for France.

French soldiers, fur traders, and missionaries continued to explore Canada. By the year 1700 the French had a firm hold in North America.

The British also explored Canada. Because of John Cabot's voyages in 1497 and 1498, they claimed all the eastern coast of North America. See the map of explorers' routes on page 54. They built forts and trading posts. Many of these grew into towns.

Important trading posts were also built in Canada by the Hudson's Bay Company. This English company was started in 1670. It was granted the huge area of land drained by all the rivers flowing into Hudson Bay. It was given the right both to trade in this region and to govern it. Even today this company has trading posts in northern Canada.

The French and Indian War

Time after time the British and the French fought for possession of North America. Their last struggle was called the French and Indian War. The war is known as the French and Indian War because many Indians helped the French.

The British won the war. The peace treaty, made in 1763, changed the map of North America. France gave up Canada and all its lands east of the Mississippi. Great Britain now controlled a large part of North America. The map of European claims in 1763 on page 84 shows how great this territory was.

British Government in Canada

The British wondered how they could rule their former enemies. There were many more French than British in Canada at that time.

In 1774 the British government passed the Quebec Act. By this law French Canadians were allowed to speak their own language and keep their own religion. Today about three out of every ten Canadians are descended from these early French colonists. Their language and many of their ways of living are much like those of the early settlers.

Since these early days Canada has had two languages—French and English. Money, stamps, and government papers are printed in both languages. In 1976, French was made an official language in Canada, equal in importance to English.

Settlers and Explorers

While the British were trying to solve their problems in Canada, trouble arose in their other North American colonies. After the War for Independence started, about 40,000 English colonists fled to Canada. They were welcomed by the British, who were glad to have more English-speaking settlers in Canada.

New settlers also came to Canada from Great

Britain. A large group from Scotland settled in Canada. The most famous of these was Alexander Mackenzie (mə ken′zē), a Scottish fur trader, who reached the Pacific in 1793. Mackenzie was the first European to reach the Pacific by traveling across Canada. Earlier he had explored the great river in northern Canada which now bears his name.

The Plan of Union

By 1837 Canada's colonists wanted more self-government. They rebelled. This revolt was soon settled, but the British government worried about losing its Canadian colonies. Lord Durham was sent to study the problem. His report urged more freedom and self-government for the Canadian colonies. The British government decided to accept his advice.

Within the next 20 years Great Britain's Canadian colonies grew. Colonists in some provinces talked of uniting the colonies under one government. At a meeting at Quebec the leaders worked out a plan for national government. They made a plan of *confederation* (kən fed′ə rā′shən), or union, that they took back to the colonies to be discussed. Later they sent representatives to London to discuss it with the British government. The plan of confederation was approved and made a law on July 1, 1867. This law, called the British North America Act, is Canada's constitution.

The new nation was made up of just four provinces: Nova Scotia, New Brunswick, Quebec, and Ontario. Manitoba was the fifth to join. Then British Columbia was added. The government promised to build a railroad to connect this distant region with eastern Canada. This railroad is now known as the Canadian Pacific Railway. Two years later Prince Edward Island joined Canada.

The building of railroads across Canada brought many settlers to the West. After 1900 settlers poured into this region from the United States, eastern Canada, the British Isles, and other parts of Europe. Then the provinces of Saskatchewan and Alberta became part of Canada.

Newfoundland, Great Britain's oldest colony, was the last to join. Canada now has ten provinces and two territories.

Canada's Government Today

In 1931 the British government passed a law saying that Canada was a fully independent nation. Since then Canada has governed itself. It makes its own laws, settles its own problems, and coins its own money. It makes treaties with foreign countries. It has chosen to be part of the group of nations called the British Commonwealth. These nations have agreed to work together. They have special trading and defense agreements. They recognize the British queen or king as their leader.

Canadians elect their officials in much the same way we do. They have a head of government, called the Prime Minister. He is much like our President. Their *Parliament* (pär′lə mənt), which makes laws for all Canada, is like our Congress. Parliament is made up of a Senate and a House of Commons. An official, called the governor-general, appoints the members of the Senate. The senators are chosen on

In Quebec many signs in stores and on the streets appear in both French and English. Why do you think this is so?

the Prime Minister's recommendation. The people elect House of Commons members.

Canada's People

Most people in Canada are English-speaking. But 80 percent of the population of Quebec is French. They speak French and maintain French ways of living. There is a movement among the French to separate from the rest of Canada and form an independent nation. In 1980, however, people of Quebec voted to remain with Canada.

During the late 1970s many Canadians were working for passage of a bill that would give women equal rights with men. In 1976 some Indians in Canada asked the government for their own province to replace the rights they lost long ago. Eskimos in Canada also asked for their own province. The government agreed to consider each request.

Living and Working in Canada

Canada's great natural resources make it a rich country. About one-sixth of its land is suitable for farming. Forests cover more than a third of it. It has many mineral resources. Rivers and waterfalls provide water power to make electricity. Most of Canada's industries use electric power. Ninety percent of the electricity comes from water power. Great new water-power projects are now underway.

Because Canada is so large, it has a wide variety of climates, soils, and land surfaces. People of different parts of Canada make their livings in different ways. In this section, you will read about the various regions of Canada. These are the Atlantic provinces, Quebec and Ontario, the prairie provinces, British Columbia, and the northland.

The Atlantic Provinces

Nova Scotia, New Brunswick, Prince Edward Island, and Newfoundland are the Atlantic provinces.

Many people in these provinces earn their living from the sea. The Grand Bank, one of the world's largest fishing grounds, is nearby. Find it on the map of Canada's products on page 411. Cod, haddock, halibut, herring, and mackerel are caught there. In the shallow waters near the shore, lobsters are trapped.

Some people build or repair boats. Others work in fish canneries or in quick-freezing plants. The by-products of fish provide work for others. Bones, heads, and tails are ground into meal for chickens and cattle. Oil is obtained from the livers.

Farming

Where the land is suitable, hay, oats, turnips, and potatoes are grown. These crops grow well in the cool, damp summers. Farmers also raise chickens, pigs, and keep dairy cows. Prince Edward Island and New Brunswick grow most of Canada's potatoes raised for seed. These seed potatoes are sold in Canada and other countries.

Strawberries, blueberries, apples, and other fruits are grown in the Atlantic provinces.

Fur Farming

Fur farming is now carried on throughout Canada. The first fur farm was started on Prince Edward Island.

A high fence surrounds the fox farm that we visit. Inside are pens made of strong, closely woven wire. Spring is an exciting time here. The pups, or baby foxes, are born then. The foxes are given good care. They are fed meat, fish, grass, and berries. They get fresh meat every day. Good food helps make a fine quality fur. The long, cold winters make the fur grow thick.

In December when the fur is thickest the foxes are killed and skinned. The skins are sent to Montreal, the largest fur market in Canada. Minks, raccoons, and skunks are also raised on farms for fur.

Lumbering

The forests of New Brunswick, Nova Scotia, and Newfoundland provide work for many people. Some trees are large enough to be made into boards. Others are made into wood pulp. Wood pulp is the ground-up wood from which paper is made. Rayon, plastics, and film are also wood products. Newsprint, the paper used in newspapers, and wood pulp are the most important products of Canada's mills. Canada supplies more than half the world's newsprint.

Mining and Manufacturing

Nova Scotia furnishes almost one-third of Canada's coal. Newfoundland has much iron ore.

Most of this ore is sent to Sydney near the coal fields in Nova Scotia. After it is made into iron and steel there, it is shipped to many countries. Labrador, the part of Newfoundland on the mainland, has rich deposits of iron ore. Ore from its mines is sent to mills in the United States and Canada.

Manufacturing is important in the Atlantic provinces. The factories and mills use the raw materials from the farms, the sea, the forests, and the mines. They produce wood pulp, paper, steel, butter, cheese, canned fruits, and lumber. Canned and frozen fish are also produced. Manufactured goods and processed foods are exported to the United States and many other countries.

Cities

The people of these provinces live mostly in small towns. Halifax, the capital of Nova Scotia, and St. John's, in New Brunswick, are the largest cities. Both are important seaports. When the St. Lawrence River freezes over, these ports are very busy. Their harbors remain open. Then they become the most important ports of eastern Canada. Cargo is brought to their ice-free ports and shipped inland by railroad.

Newfoundland's location is important for the air routes between North America and Europe. Planes flying the North Atlantic often stop at Gander, Newfoundland, for fuel or repair. Can you tell why?

After wood chips are washed and bleached, they go into a large tank. The tank cooks the chips in an acid mixture to make wood pulp. What happens next?

Making Paper From Wood

Paper Mill

Logs cut into short lengths

Drum removes bark from logs

Chipper cuts logs into chips

Chips cooked in acid mixture to make pulp

Pulp bleached after it is washed free of acid

Metal screen drains water

Heated rollers squeeze out water, dry pulp, and press it

Rolls of paper

Visitors to Quebec can watch the changing of the guard at the Citadel, an early British fortress. Today the Citadel is the summer home of Canada's governor-general.

Quebec and Ontario Provinces

Find the St. Lawrence River on the map of Canada on page 459. Notice the plain that lies on both sides of the river. This plain is the most important part of the province of Quebec. More people live on the St. Lawrence Plain than in any other part of the province.

The St. Lawrence Plain has rich soil and plenty of rain. Grass, hay, and potatoes grow well in its cool, moist summers. Dairy farming and the making of butter and cheese are carried on. Nearby is the Laurentian Upland. Its mines and forests furnish valuable raw materials. Its swift rivers furnish power for electricity and help Quebec produce more water power than any other province. The St. Lawrence River is closed by ice almost five months of the year. Yet it is Canada's most important water highway. With many raw materials, much water power, and good means of transportation the St. Lawrence Plain has much industry.

The Lake Plain

Most of Ontario's people live on the plain along Lakes Ontario, Erie, and Huron. Like the St. Lawrence Plain it has farms, factories, mills, cities and towns. Of Canada's twelve largest cities, four are on this plain. They are Quebec, Montreal, Ottawa, and Toronto.

This lake plain is farther south than the St. Lawrence lowland. It has the advantage of a longer growing season. Because it is near the lakes there is not so much danger from frosts in the late spring and early fall. The northern shore of Lake Ontario is one of Canada's important fruit regions. Mixed farming is carried on and many vegetables and tobacco are raised. Dairy farms supply milk and other dairy products to nearby cities.

Ontario is Canada's chief industrial province. It produces almost all of the farm machinery, automobiles, and bicycles made in Canada. Flour, breakfast food, canned vegetables and fruits, butter, and cheese are also products of Ontario. Ontario's waterfalls and rapids and United States coal furnish power to run its manufacturing plants. The Great Lakes are a fine water highway, used by both the United States and Canada.

The Laurentian Upland

The Laurentian Upland extends across both Quebec and Ontario. Notice on the map of Canada, page 459, how much of both these provinces it covers. Only a small part of this rocky, hilly upland has soil suited to farming. The growing season is short. But hay, oats, and other hardy crops grow well there.

The Laurentian Upland also has forests and fur-bearing animals. Quebec leads Canada in the manufacturing of paper.

Valuable Minerals

There are now mining towns in the Laurentian Upland where once forests grew. Gold, silver, copper, nickel, platinum, and other minerals are the reason. Platinum is a silvery white metal which is more precious than gold. Most of the world's supply of nickel comes from Ontario.

A mineral called *asbestos* (as bes′təs) is found in the Appalachian Highland. Since asbestos will not burn, articles made from it are said to be fireproof. Canada mines more asbestos than any other country.

Chief Cities

Quebec, a famous French city, is on the St. Lawrence lowland. This oldest city of Canada is built on two levels. Lower Town is crowded along the banks of the St. Lawrence. Here are warehouses, grain elevators, pulp mills, leather factories, stores, and docks. Many of the homes and churches are old. Upper Town is on a high cliff above the river. Many parks and historic spots are here. Quebec is the capital of Quebec Province.

Handling government business, caring for tourists, manufacturing, and shipping are ways in which people in Quebec make a living.

Ottawa (ot′ə wə), the capital city of Canada, is also on the St. Lawrence Plain. Ottawa began as a lumber town. It is still an important center for lumber, paper, and other wood products. Since it is Canada's capital, its most important work is carrying on government business.

Toronto is Canada's second largest city and the capital of Ontario. Like Chicago, it has a good location for trade on the Great Lakes. Hamilton, near Toronto, and Windsor, near Detroit, are other important cities on the lake plain.

Montreal
An Inland Port in the Heart of Canada

Most port cities are on the seacoast. But to reach Montreal, ocean ships travel up the St. Lawrence River 1,000 miles (1,600 km) inland. Find Montreal on the maps of Canada, pages 459 and 471. Montreal is in the heart of Canada. Why is its port important to nearby regions?

Montreal is an industrial city. Port and railroad services have helped Montreal's industries grow. The city's mills and factories produce flour, clothing, iron-and-steel goods, and electrical equipment. Find Montreal again on the map. How have the streams of the Laurentian Upland helped Montreal become an industrial city?

Montreal is named after Mont Real, or Mt. Royal, a hill in the city. The French explorer Jacques Cartier named this hill when he sailed up the St. Lawrence in 1535. Montreal was as far as Cartier's ship could go. On the map of the St. Lawrence Seaway, page 230, find how far inland ocean ships go today. Why has this made Montreal's port and industries busier than ever?

The Prairie Provinces

The prairie provinces are Manitoba, Saskatchewan, and Alberta. The prairies are Canada's most important farming lands. Their soil is deep and fertile, but the rainfall is light. Most of it comes during the short growing season. Millions of bushels of wheat are grown on these prairies every year.

Most prairie wheat goes eastward by train to Winnipeg (win'ə peg'), in Manitoba. There it is sampled and graded. It then goes by rail to Fort William or Port Arthur, on Lake Superior. Lake freighters carry it down the Great Lakes from huge grain elevators at these twin ports.

Some of the grain goes to mills in the United States. Some goes to the Pacific port of Vancouver (van koo'vər). Most of it goes to Montreal. There it is made into flour or shipped to other countries.

Western Saskatchewan and Alberta have large sheep and cattle ranches. There is too little rain for crops, but enough for grass. This region supplies meat for Canada and some for export. In certain areas fruits, sugar beets, and other crops are grown by irrigation.

Mining and Lumbering

About half of Canada's coal is mined in these provinces. Most of the oil and natural gas found in Canada comes from Alberta and Saskatchewan. Copper, zinc, gold, nickel, silver, and *pitchblende* (pich'blend') are also mined. Pitchblende is the mineral from which uranium is obtained.

Forests cover much of the Laurentian Upland in the prairie provinces. More than half of Canada's furs come from these provinces.

Chief Cities

Winnipeg is the largest city in the prairie provinces. It is Canada's third largest city and the capital of Manitoba. Much of the livestock and grain of the prairies is marketed there. Winnipeg is one of Canada's largest fur markets. It is an important railway center and manufacturer of railroad equipment.

Edmonton, the capital of Alberta, is an important airway center. The discovery of oil nearby brought many people and industries to this city. Calgary (kal'gər ē), in southern Alberta, has oil refineries and factories where foods are processed.

British Columbia

British Columbia leads all the provinces in fishing. Its most important catch is salmon from the Fraser River. Halibut, cod, and herring are also caught.

British Columbia is Canada's most important producer of lumber. Thick forests of cedar, fir, spruce, pine, and hemlock grow on the western slopes of the mountains. Many people work in the forests and in the saw, pulp, and paper mills.

Mixed farming, dairying, truck farming, and market gardening are carried on in the Fraser Valley. In the southern valleys apples, pears, peaches, and other fruits are grown by irrigation. The Peace River region grows much grain.

Mining and Manufacturing

Large deposits of gold, coal, copper, lead, zinc, and silver make mining British Columbia's sec-

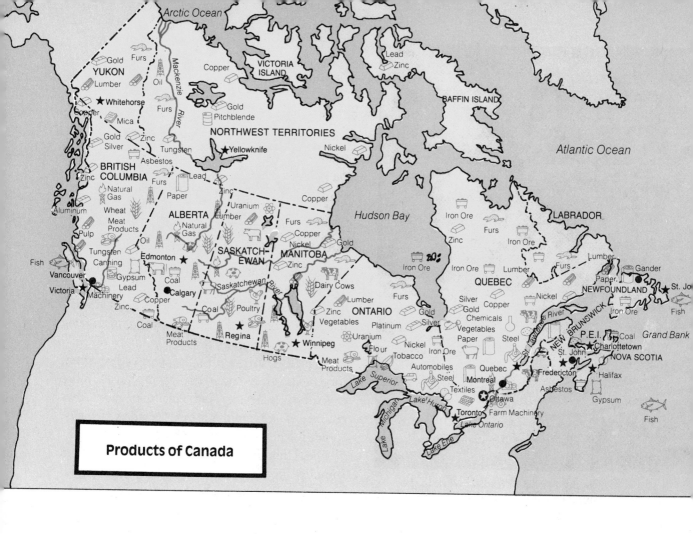

Products of Canada

ond largest industry. Many people earn their living by mining, smelting, and refining these minerals.

British Columbia has abundant water power from its many rushing mountain streams. At Kitimat, aluminum is made from ore brought from South America. Electricity, produced by water power, is used to refine this aluminum.

British Columbia ranks high in manufacturing. Its industries include fish processing, pulp and paper, petroleum products, meat packing, and aluminum.

Chief Cities

Vancouver is Canada's sixth largest city. Two railroad lines which cross Canada end there. Highway and airplane routes center on it. Vancouver's large, deep harbor is open all year round. It never freezes. Lumber, grain, newsprint, minerals, canned fish, and fruit are exported from Vancouver.

Victoria, on Vancouver Island, is the capital of British Columbia. Its mild climate, fine homes, and lovely English gardens attract thousands of tourists yearly.

471

Many people in Canada work in the lumber industry. This worker is sorting logs by kind of wood and size at the log pond of a sawmill.

Canada's Northland

Canada's northland is divided into the Yukon and Northwest Territories. Here and there is a trading post. Canada's northland has long been important for fine furs. Sometimes there is a mining town. Petroleum, gold, silver, lead, zinc, and uranium are mined there. When valuable ores are found, people settle in the northland and build towns and airfields.

Rivers and lakes are important summer highways in the Yukon and Northwest Territories. About four months each year steamers towing barges and rafts carry thousands of tons of heavy freight. Machinery, groceries, radios, and other needed supplies are taken to the towns. On their return trip they carry furs and products from the mines and oil fields.

Canada, Friendly Neighbor

Canada is rich in natural resources. It has fine forests, fertile farm lands, valuable minerals, and many lakes and rivers. It is a great trading nation and one of the important manufacturing nations of the world.

Canada is also one of the world's important food exporting countries. It produces more newsprint, asbestos, and zinc than any other country. The United States is Canada's best customer for newsprint, wood pulp, and minerals.

The United States and Canada have been friendly for a long time. The two countries worked to improve the St. Lawrence Seaway which is important to both countries.

Canada, like the United States, has set aside large areas as national parks. Banff and Jasper national parks are on the eastern slopes of the Rockies in Alberta. At these parks visitors enjoy the mountains, lakes, and forests.

Greenland and Iceland

Greenland and Iceland are Canada's island neighbors. Long before Columbus came to America, daring Norse explored and settled these islands.

Greenland

Greenland belongs to Denmark, a country of Europe, but rules itself. It is the largest island in the world. Most of its people are Eskimos.

Greenland is on a short, or great circle, route between North America and Europe. Planes flying the polar route often stop at Greenland to refuel. The United States has an air base at Thule (tōō′lē), on the west coast.

Greenland's weather station reports are important to the countries of northern Europe. Storms in Greenland usually mean that northern Europe will soon have the same kind of weather.

Much of Greenland is north of the Arctic Circle. Most of it is a high plateau covered with a great ice sheet. During the short summers the land along the coast is free of ice and snow. There, and on the rocky hillsides, grass and flowers grow.

Most Greenlanders make their living by fishing. Some raise sheep. Fish canneries and freezing and packing plants have been built by the Danish government.

The Republic of Iceland

Iceland lies east of Greenland about halfway between North America and Europe. Planes flying from North America to northern Europe often stop at Iceland's modern airport.

Iceland's first settlers were Norse. As the population grew, they chose a group of people, or council, to make their laws. Thus Iceland developed a system of self-government more than a thousand years ago. In 1944 Iceland became a republic.

Iceland is a land of great variety. Snow-covered peaks and icy glaciers stand side by side with hot springs, geysers, and volcanoes. Some volcanoes erupted in 1977, causing damage to a large electricity plant. The plant was rebuilt, but the volcano is still active.

The people in Iceland use their natural resources to good advantage. Pipes carry boiling water from the hot springs to heat homes and other buildings. Mountain streams and waterfalls produce electricity.

Potatoes, turnips, and hay grow well in the long, sunny days of Iceland's short summers. Sheep, cattle, and swift sturdy horses feed on the grass and hay. Cod, herring, and other kinds of fish are caught.

Iceland is a member of the North Atlantic Treaty Organization (NATO). As part of this defense system, Iceland allows the United States to maintain a naval and air base near Reykjavik (rāk′yə vēk′), the capital.

Do You Know?

1. What natural regions do Canada and the United States share? What water areas?
2. What are the chief ways that the people of Canada make a living?
3. What is the capital of Canada? Where is it located?
4. Why was July 1, 1867 an important day in Canada?
5. Why is Greenland important as a defense base and weather station?
6. How do Icelanders heat their homes?

Before You Go On

Using New Words

asbestos   province
commonwealth   Parliament
pitchblende   confederation

The phrases below explain the words listed above. Number a paper from 1 through 6. After each number write the word that matches the definition.

1. A plan for union of states or provinces
2. Mineral from which uranium is obtained
3. The body of lawmakers of Canada
4. A division of Canada somewhat like a state in our country
5. Mineral that will not burn
6. A form of government much like a state

Finding the Facts

1. Where are Puerto Rico and the Virgin Islands located?
2. What are Puerto Rico's land and climate like?
3. Who made the first settlement on Puerto Rico?
4. What changes were made in Puerto Rico after it became part of the United States?
5. Who was Puerto Rico's first governor elected by the islanders?
6. What are some crops grown in Puerto Rico?
7. What do some of Puerto Rico's industries produce?
8. How did the United States get the Virgin Islands?
9. Why is the location of the Virgin Islands important to us?
10. Why is farming difficult in the Virgin Islands?
11. What are some of the leading industries in the Virgin Islands?
12. Why is Midway important? Who controls Midway?
13. Why is Wake Island important?
14. Who discovered Guam?
15. How do people in Guam make a living?
16. How has American Samoa been managed during the 1900s?
17. How do people in American Samoa make a living?
18. How did the peace treaty of 1763 change the map of North America?
19. What was the British North America Act? When did it go into effect?
20. Name the Atlantic provinces. What are their capitals? In what ways do the people of these provinces make a living?
21. Why are Halifax and St. John's important winter ports of eastern Canada?
22. Why are forests important to Canada?
23. How has Toronto's location helped it become Canada's second largest city?
24. Name the prairie provinces. What are their capitals? In what ways do the people of these provinces make a living?
25. What makes Vancouver Canada's best Pacific port?
26. How are freight and supplies transported in the Yukon and Northwest Territories?

3
Mexico, Our Southern Border Neighbor

The region south of the United States is called *Latin* (lat'in) *America*. There Spanish, Portuguese, and French are spoken. These languages come from Latin, a language once spoken in southern Europe.

Our nearest Latin-American neighbor is Mexico. It shares an 1,800-mile (2,880-km) boundary with the United States. Mexico is larger than Texas, New Mexico, Arizona, California, and Nevada together. It has thirty-one states. It also has a federal district where Mexico City, the capital, is located. About three out of four Mexicans are *mestizos* (mes tē'zōs), or people of mixed Spanish and Indian ancestry. Most Mexicans speak Spanish and have Spanish ways and customs.

Geography of Mexico

Mexico has two coastal plains. One is along the Pacific coast. The other is along the Gulf of Mexico. Mexico shares the Gulf Coastal Plain with the United States. The map of Mexico, on page 476, shows that this eastern lowland widens out in the Yucatan (yoo kə tan') Peninsula. Note that it is wider than the western coastal lowland. Both coastal lowlands are hot. The eastern plain receives more rain.

Mexico has more highland than lowland. Ranges of high, rugged mountains rise from the lowlands along both coasts. Between these eastern and western ranges is the central plateau. This plateau is broken up into many valleys which are separated by hills and mountains. At its southern end it is more than 1.5 miles (2.4 km) high. Because of its altitude the climate is pleasant. The northern part receives less rain than the southern section.

South of the central plateau is a region of high mountains and many volcanoes. Some of Mexico's highest mountains are in this region. They are snow-capped the year round although they are in the tropics.

Mexico has two peninsulas. The peninsula of Lower California stretches southward from California. The Yucatan Peninsula stretches north and east into the Gulf of Mexico.

Because Mexico has lowlands, plateaus, and mountains, the climate patterns vary. Locate both Veracruz (ver'ə kroos') and Mexico City on the map of Mexico on page 476. These cities are in the low latitudes. But it is more comfortable to live in Mexico City than in Veracruz. That is because Mexico City is inland and higher above sea level.

Mexico also has great differences in rainfall. Some areas receive more than 80 inches (200 cm) a year, while others receive less than 10 inches (25 cm) a year.

History of Mexico

When the Spaniards arrived in Mexico they found the Aztecs (az'teks). The Aztecs were an Indian tribe that controlled most of central Mexico. But the Aztecs were not the first peo-

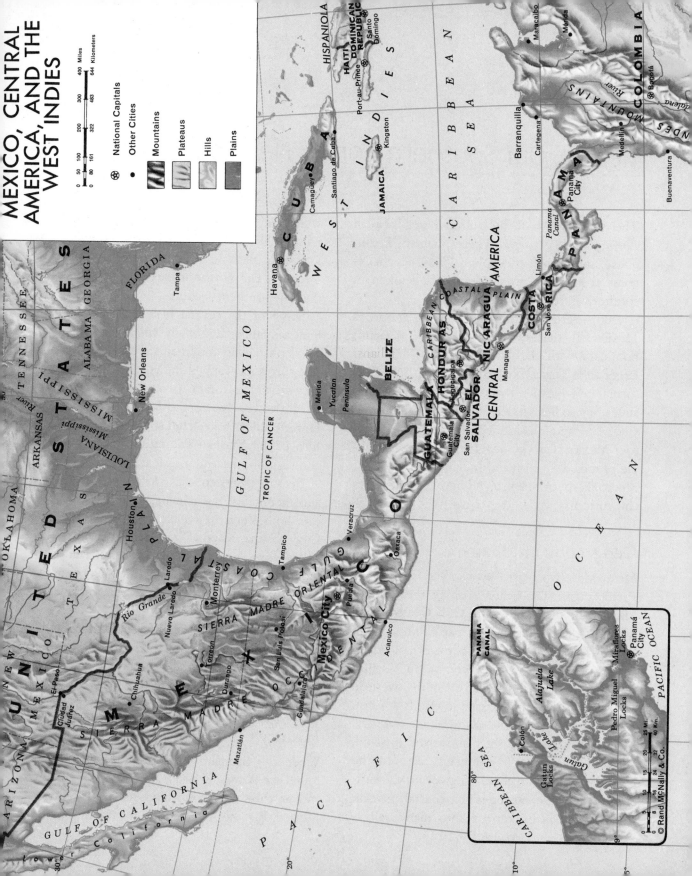

National Capitals
Other Cities

Mountains
Plateaus
Hills
Plains

Miles	Kilometers
0	0
50	80
100	161
200	322
300	483
400	644

UNITED STATES

ARIZONA
NEW MEXICO
OKLAHOMA
ARKANSAS
TENNESSEE
GEORGIA
ALABAMA
MISSISSIPPI
LOUISIANA
TEXAS
FLORIDA

El Paso
Ciudad Juárez
Chihuahua
Mazatlán
Durango
Torreón
San Luis Potosí
Guadalajara
Nuevo Laredo
Laredo
Rio Grande
Monterrey
Tampico
Houston
New Orleans
Tampa

SIERRA MADRE OCCIDENTAL
SIERRA MADRE ORIENTAL
COASTAL PLAIN
GULF COASTAL PLAIN

MEXICO

Mexico City
Puebla
Acapulco
Oaxaca
Veracruz
Mérida
Yucatán Peninsula

GULF OF MEXICO
TROPIC OF CANCER
GULF OF CALIFORNIA
Lower California

PACIFIC OCEAN

BELIZE
GUATEMALA
Guatemala City
EL SALVADOR
San Salvador
HONDURAS
Tegucigalpa
NICARAGUA
Managua
COSTA RICA
San José
Limón
PANAMA
Panamá City
Panama Canal

CARIBBEAN COASTAL PLAIN
CENTRAL AMERICA

CARIBBEAN SEA

CUBA
Havana
Camagüey
Santiago de Cuba

WEST INDIES

JAMAICA
Kingston

HISPANIOLA
HAITI
Port-au-Prince
DOMINICAN REPUBLIC
Santo Domingo

COLOMBIA
Bogotá
Barranquilla
Cartagena
Maracaibo
Mérida
Medellín
Buenaventura
ANDES MOUNTAINS
Magdalena River

PACIFIC OCEAN

PANAMA CANAL

CARIBBEAN SEA
Colón
Gatún Locks
Gatún Lake
Alajuela Lake
Pedro Miguel Locks
Miraflores Locks
Panamá City
PACIFIC OCEAN

Mi.	Km.
0	0
5	8
10	16
15	24
20	32
25	40

© Rand McNally & Co.

ple to live in this region. Scientists have found ruins and cave drawings painted about 1500 years before the Aztecs came to Mexico.

The Spaniards were dazzled by the wealth and great cities that the Aztecs had built. Within 3 years, the Spanish conquered the Aztecs. The Aztecs were the last in a series of great Indian civilizations in Mexico. The Spaniards forced the Indians to work in their mines or on their large farms. They took over most of the land. Only the poorer lands were left for the Indians.

The years passed. Many colonists became dissatisfied with Spanish rule. Spanish governors often treated the colonists unjustly. Colonists objected to the taxes and high prices.

Miguel Hidalgo y Costilla, Leader of Independence

Miguel Hidalgo y Costilla (mē gel′ ē däl′gō ē kōs tē′yä) was born in Guanajuato (gwän′ə wä′tō), Mexico, in 1753. He was the priest of a small Indian village. There he taught the people how to grow grapes, and how to make silk and bricks.

Father Hidalgo thought the Indians were being treated unfairly. He believed that they and other Mexicans would benefit if Mexico were free from Spain. In 1810 Father Hidalgo organized an independence movement.

Thousands joined Father Hidalgo's army. For a while they were successful against the Spanish troops. It seemed that Mexico would be freed. But then Father Hidalgo was captured and put to death in 1811.

Others took up the work of Father Hidalgo. In 1821 Mexico became independent.

Miguel Hidalgo y Costilla is called "The Father of Mexican Independence," although he did not live to see Mexico free from Spain. Monuments honoring Hidalgo are found in many Mexican cities.

After Independence

Independence brought few changes in life in Mexico. The descendants of the wealthy Spanish settlers continued to rule the country. The life of the Indians remained much the same. They toiled for the rich landowners or worked small patches of poor ground for themselves. Some people were very rich. Most were very poor.

On September 16 each year the people of Mexico celebrate their independence from Spain. The national cathedral in Mexico City is a center for the festivities.

"Why should we give up our large estates?" the wealthy landowners thought. Yet some leaders believed that most Mexicans would have a better life if these huge farms were broken up. They wanted the land divided among the Mexican farmers. Benito Juárez (bā nē′tō wär′ēs), a Mexican leader, believed in this idea.

Juárez became the head of Mexico about the time Lincoln was President of the United States. Like Lincoln, Juárez wanted to help the poor people. He worked hard to weaken the power of the wealthy landowners. He wanted to give the land back to the Indians so that they could farm it for themselves. He improved methods of farming. He became one of the most honored leaders of Mexico. But he died before many of his ideas could be carried out.

After Juárez' death, the wealthy landowners continued to hold the land. Many became more powerful than ever. The Indians and mestizos remained poor farm laborers or factory workers. But other leaders, who believed as Juárez did, carried out many of his ideas.

Changing Mexico

Many changes have taken place in Mexico since Juárez' time. Most of the large estates have been broken up and the land has been divided into small and middle-sized farms. Almost half the Mexican farmers own the land that they farm. But many farmers are poor. They have not learned new farming methods. Nor is there enough good land for all.

Some farms belong to an entire village. The land of these farms has been turned over to the farming village by the government. Such land is called an *ejido* (ā hē′dō).

In some ejidos the people farm the land as one large farm. All share in the work and in the crops. In other ejidos each family is given a piece of land. These families can use the land as long as they farm it and pay taxes on it. They cannot sell it or rent it.

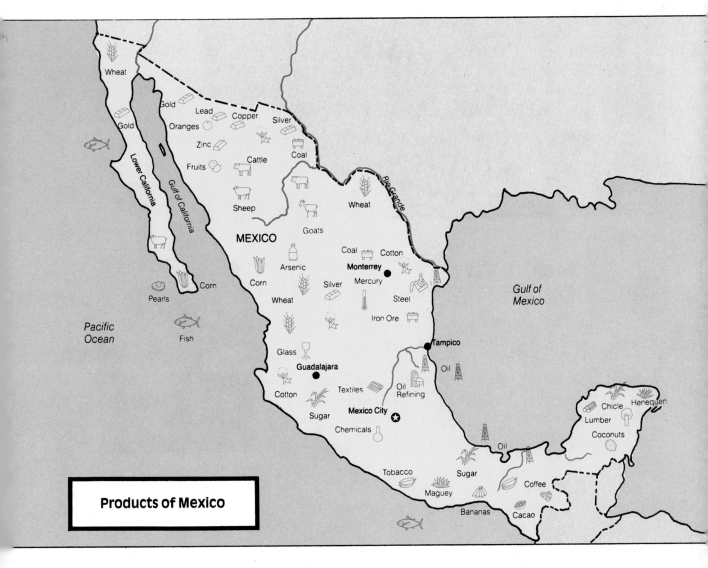

Products of Mexico

The government has tried to make available more land for farming. It has built dams and brought water to thousands of acres of dry land. It has set up a settlement plan. Farmers can become homesteaders on government land never farmed before. In 10 years, if their crops are good, they can own their home and 60 acres (24 ha) of land.

Education has greatly improved in modern Mexico. New schools have been built and new teachers have been trained. As in the United States, the law requires all Mexican children to go to school.

With new dams and hydroelectric plants, more electricity is produced. With new roads, railroads, and airports it is easier for Mexicans to travel.

Business is growing. New trades, businesses, and manufacturing have been started. In some factories, glass, cement, electrical goods, and shoes are made. There are automobile plants, tire plants, and chemical works.

Mexico City
Center of Mexican Life

Mexico City was the center of Mexican life before the Spaniards came. The city was called Tenochtitlán (tä nôch′tē tlän′) It was the capital of the Aztec Empire and the hub of Aztec activities. The Spaniards destroyed Tenochtitlán, but they built their new capital on the same spot.

Mexico City continues to show the early Spanish influence. In the huge central plaza, or square, are the beautiful old Spanish buildings. The great cathedral and the National Palace are built on Aztec ruins.

But the city shows the new Mexico too. Near the central plaza are tall modern office and apartment buildings. The country's big businesses are there. Over half the nation's industrial products are now made in or near Mexico City. Many people from the villages have crowded into the city to find jobs in industry. Mexico City is Mexico's largest city. It has the country's most pleasant climate. As the center of Mexican life, Mexico City shows the old and the new Mexico. ■

Living and Working in Mexico

The Indians who lived in Mexico when the Spaniards came were skilled workers. They made fine pottery, beautiful blankets, and beautiful articles of gold and silver. Today many Mexicans still take pride in making articles by hand. Caring for tourists also gives work to Mexicans. Three of every five Mexicans earn their living by farming. Mining gives jobs to others. More and more Mexicans now earn their living by working in factories and offices.

Farming in Mexico

The hot, rainy Gulf coast south of Tampico is a region of thick, tropical forests. Where the forests have been cleared, tropical crops such as sugarcane and bananas are grown. Coffee is raised on the mountain slopes.

Farther south, on the Yucatan Peninsula, much of the world's henequen (hen'ə kin) is grown. Henequen is a thorny cactus plant. From its leaf fiber, twine is made.

The northern Pacific coast is desert and mountains. Irrigation brings water for corn and cotton. Along the rainy southern coast, coffee and cocoa are raised.

The central plateau is where most Mexicans live. The climate is comfortable because of the altitude. Village houses are often made of adobe (ə dō'bē), a sun-dried clay. The chief crop is corn. It is made into thin, flat pancakes called tortillas. (tôr tē'yas) Tortillas and beans, called frijoles, (frē hō'lēs), are the main Mexican foods.

Minerals of Mexico

Mexico has large deposits of silver, gold, copper, lead, zinc, and petroleum. Vast new deposits of oil and gas have been found recently in Mexico. In 1979 the leaders of Mexico agreed to sell natural gas to the United States. In the same year, an oil well in the southern part of the Gulf of Mexico had a blowout. It caused one of the worst oil spills in the world. Some of the oil spread to the coast of Texas.

Mexico's Cities

Monterrey (mon tər rā'), in the northeast, is Mexico's most important city for heavy industry. Because of its steel mills, Monterrey is often called the Pittsburgh of Mexico. Both coal and iron are nearby. Railroads and roads pass through the city.

Guadalajara (gwäd'əl ə här'ə), Mexico's second largest city, is a manufacturing, farming, and cattle center. It is famous for its handmade glass and fine pottery.

Do You Know?

1. Where are Mexico's two coastal plains?
2. What language do most Mexicans speak?
3. What minerals are found in Mexico?
4. Who was Father Hidalgo? What did he do in 1810?
5. What did Benito Juárez want to do with the estates of wealthy landowners?

4
Central American and Caribbean Countries

The land between Mexico and South America is called Central America. In Central America are Guatemala (gwä′tə mä′lə), El Salvador (el′ sal′və dôr), Costa Rica (kōs′tə rē′kə), Honduras (hon door′əs), Nicaragua (nik′ə räg′wə), Panama (pan′ə mä), and Belize (be lēz′). Find them on the map of Central America on page 476. American Indians, mestizos, blacks, and people of Spanish-speaking descent make up most of the population.

The West Indies are a chain of thousands of islands stretching in a curve from Florida to northern South America. They separate the At-lantic Ocean from the Caribbean Sea. Most of them are the remains of volcanoes that erupted a long time ago. Some are too small for people to live on.

Cuba (kyōō′bə), Haiti (hā′tē), the Dominican (də min′ i kən) Republic, Jamaica (jə mā′kə), Trinidad (trin′ə dad′) and Tobago (tə bā′gō), the Bahamas, (bə hä′məz), and Barbados (bär bā′dōz) are among the populated islands. Most of the population is made up of blacks, mestizos, Indians, and people of Spanish, French, British, and Dutch ancestry.

Geography

The Central American countries all lie in the low latitudes. They share three natural regions—the Pacific Coastal Plain, the central highlands, and the Caribbean Coastal Plain. The mountains of the central highland have many active volcanoes.

Between the mountains lie valleys and plateaus. This region has a pleasant climate because it is high above sea level. Thick forests of tropical trees and plants grow in the hot, rainy Caribbean lowland. The Pacific coast has grasslands and forests. Rainfall is not so heavy there.

The West Indies lie in the tropics or low latitudes. Their climate is warm all through the year. Even the highest lands are not cool enough for frost. Crops can be grown there the year round. Often two or three crops are grown in a year.

The Pan American Highway connects Mexico, Central America, and South America. This area of the highway is in Costa Rica, just west of San José.

Ruins of a Mayan city can be seen at Chichén Itzá in Mexico. Temple walls and carvings in stone used in the service of the Mayan gods still stand.

Steady northeast trade winds help make the climate mild. They bring much rain. The northeastern slopes of the mountains have more rain than the southwestern slopes. Severe tropical storms, called *hurricanes* (hur′ə kānz′), can cause damage. During August, September, and October, these hurricanes sweep across the West Indies and even reach the United States. Their strong winds and heavy rainfall often destroy everything in their path.

The West Indies are important because they are on the sea routes to the Gulf of Mexico, Central America, and the Panama Canal. The location of the West Indies also makes them important in trade. Their tropical crops are sent to countries where such crops are scarce.

History of Central America

Indians had lived in Central America long before the Spanish came. The Mayas (mī′ yəz) were farmers. They were also great builders. They built large cities and beautiful stone temples in Honduras, Guatemala, and Mexico. The Mayas knew much about the stars and the movement of heavenly bodies. They created a calendar. They could write numbers up to a million and also had a form of picture writing. But the Spaniards conquered the Mayas.

After 300 years of Spanish rule, Guatemala, El Salvador, Costa Rica, Honduras, and Nicaragua declared their independence on September 15, 1821. At first these new countries were not sure what they wanted to do. When Mexico became free, they joined it. Then they broke away from Mexico and joined together as the United Provinces of Central America. This union did not last either. By the middle 1800s they were again independent countries.

On the eastern coast of the Yucatan Peninsula is Belize (formerly British Honduras). Belize was granted independence from Great Britain in September 1981. Thus Belize was the last country in Central America to gain its independence.

A steamship moves through the Panama Canal. There are locks in the canal which allow ships to be raised or lowered from one level to another.

Panama's History

North America is joined to South America by an isthmus. This land bridge between the two great continents is the Isthmus of Panama.

For years people talked about building a waterway through the isthmus. "Ships could take a short cut between the Atlantic and the Pacific," they said. The French were the first to try to build a waterway across the isthmus. But diseases, landslides, and floods caused the French company to fail.

After the war with Spain in 1898, the United States acquired possessions in both the Atlantic and the Pacific. The United States became interested in building a canal in order to get from one ocean to the other quickly. But Colombia, which owned Panama, refused to let the United States build a canal. The United States helped Panama to break away from Colombia and become an independent republic in 1903.

The Republic of Panama gave the United States permission to build the waterway. Panama also gave the right to rent a strip of land 10 miles (16 km) wide across the isthmus. This was the Panama Canal Zone, for which the United States paid Panama a yearly rent until 1978.

In 1904 Colonel William Gorgas was called to the Canal Zone to wipe out the mosquitos that caused fever and other diseases. Then came the great task of digging the canal through jungles, swampland, and mountains. After 10 years the waterway was completed. The two great oceans were united in 1914.

The Panama Canal is considered important for the defense of the United States. But for years many Panamanians felt that the United States should not exercise so much power in their country. They wanted a new treaty to replace the 1903 pact.

In 1978, a new treaty was signed between the Republic of Panama and the United States that gave Panamanians control of the Canal Zone. By the year 2000, Panama will have control of the canal. However, the United States keeps the right to defend the canal's neutrality, so that it can be used by all nations.

Living and Working in Central America

Rich soil, plenty of rain, and a long growing season aid farming. Farming is the chief work of the people. Crops that grow in a temperate climate as well as tropical crops are raised because of the differences in altitude.

Most manufactured products are used where they are made. Bananas, coffee, cacao, and sugar are grown for export. Valuable woods and other tropical forest products are exported. The United States is a good customer for all these products. In exchange, we ship machinery, clothing, and foods to Central America.

Guatemala, Land of the Mayas

Guatemala has the largest population of the Central American countries. More than half its people are descendants of the ancient Mayas. They live mainly in small villages in the highlands. They weave cloth, tend sheep, or make pottery. They farm their small fields of corn and beans or work on the large plantations.

Farming is the chief work in Guatemala. Corn, beans, rice, sugar, coffee, bananas, tobacco, and cotton are raised. Coffee and bananas are important exports.

Guatemala City, the capital, is the largest city in Central America. It is the manufacturing and transportation center of Guatemala. The city is also a tourist center.

Honduras

The people of Honduras make their living from farms, mines, and forests. Bananas are the chief export crop of Honduras. They are grown along the hot and rainy Caribbean coast.

Corn is the chief food crop, but wheat, beans, and other temperate-climate crops are also grown. Cattle are raised in the highlands. Coffee is the second most important export crop.

Tegucigalpa (tā goo′sē gäl′pä), the capital and largest city, has a pleasant climate because of its location. It is on a plateau at the foot of a mountain. Much of the city looks as it did in Spanish colonial days. Some streets are narrow and steep. But modern buildings and houses are also there. The old and the new are side by side.

Some people in Guatemala wash their clothes at a community washing area. The clothes are then spread out on the grass to dry in the sun. Other people use washing machines instead.

485

El Salvador, Pacific Land

El Salvador is the smallest and most thickly settled country of Central America. It is the only country that borders entirely on the Pacific.

Almost all the land in El Salvador is farmed even though much of it is mountainous. Coffee is the most valuable money crop. Sugar, henequen, cotton, rice, and *balsam* (bôl′səm) are also exported. Balsam is made from the sap of a tree which grows along the coast. It is used in making perfumes and some medicines. Corn, beans, and wheat are grown as food.

The government of El Salvador has helped farmers learn better ways to farm and save the soil. The government has improved the school system throughout the country.

Fine roads and railroads connect the capital, San Salvador, with other cities of the country. San Salvador is a busy modern city with parks and beautiful homes.

Nicaragua, Land of Lakes

Nicaragua has more lowland than any other country of Central America. It also has many lakes. Most of the people and most of the towns are in western Nicaragua.

Sugar, cotton, corn, and rice are grown on the lake plains in western Nicaragua. Coffee is raised in the central highlands. The fine grass on the highlands makes good pasture for cattle. Gold mining is also carried on in the highlands. Cotton, gold, coffee, and lumber are valuable exports.

Managua (mə nä′gwä), the leading city and capital, is an attractive city on the shores of a lake in western Nicaragua. It has many fine parks. Because of earthquakes which destroyed many old buildings, Managua has been rebuilt as a modern city.

Costa Rica, Panama, Belize

In Costa Rica many people, rather than just a few, own the land. Most of them are descendants of the Spanish settlers. Costa Rica's people have a share in their government.

Most Costa Ricans are farmers. On soil made rich by minerals from erupting volcanoes, they grow corn, beans, potatoes, and other temperate crops. Coffee is the leading crop and most valuable export. Bananas are also exported. San José, the capital, is a modern city.

The Panama Canal and the Canal Zone are only a small part of the Republic of Panama. The rest of the country stretches away from the Canal Zone in either direction. Farming is the chief occupation outside the Canal Zone. Corn and rice are the leading food crops grown on the small farms. Bananas and cacao are export crops grown on large plantations. Stock raising and mining are becoming important. Most of the people in cities near the Canal Zone earn their living from work connected with the canal. Panama City, the capital, is near the Pacific entrance to the canal. In its old section are colonial churches, narrow streets, and Spanish style houses. Its new section has modern houses, shops, and buildings. Because it is near the canal, it is a busy city. Much trade passes through this port and through Colón (kō lōn′), at the Atlantic entrance to the canal.

The main exports of Belize are the products

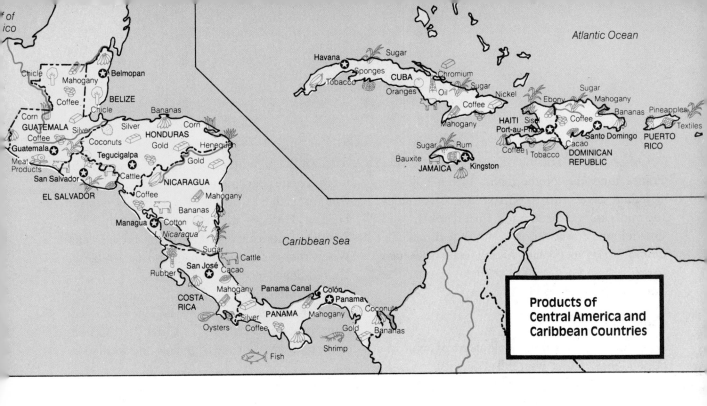

Products of Central America and Caribbean Countries

of its forests. Cedar, chicle (chik′əl), used for making gum, and mahogany are important exports. Mahogany is a beautiful hardwood used in making furniture. Most of the food has to be imported. Recently, bananas have become an important money crop.

History of the West Indies

The Spanish were the first Europeans to claim the West Indies. Then France, Britain, and the Netherlands began to seize some of the islands claimed by the Spanish. Denmark also took some. After a time many of the Spanish islands revolted and became independent.

Hispaniola (his′pən yō′lə) is the island where Columbus made his first settlement. Two nations, Haiti and the Dominican Republic, share the island. Hispaniola belonged to Spain for a long time. Spanish settlements were made in the eastern part of the island. Later, France gained control of the western part, now called Haiti.

Under French rule, western Hispaniola became a rich colony. Hundreds of black slaves were brought there to work on the plantations. After a while the slaves, led by Toussaint L'Ouverture (tōō san′ lōō vər tyōōr′), rebelled. The long struggle ended in independence for Haiti in 1804. Haiti was the first European colony of Latin America to become independent. The Dominican Republic gained its independence in 1844.

Jamaica, Trinidad and Tobago, Barbados, and the Bahamas are former British possessions. They now belong to the British Commonwealth. Jamaica and Trinidad and Tobago became independent in 1962, Barbados in 1966, and the Bahamas in 1973.

Other islands still belong to Great Britain, France, and the Netherlands. In 1978 Great Britain gave up control of Dominica (dō min′i kə). Martinique (mär ti nēk′) and Guadeloupe (gwäd əl ōōp′), a group of islands, belong to France. The Dutch control Aruba (ə rōō′bə) and Curaçao (koor′ə sou′) near the northern coast of South America.

Cuba's History

Long after Spain's other colonies had won independence, Cuba was still a Spanish possession. Many times the Cubans revolted against Spain's harsh rule.

In 1895 yet another revolution erupted. The United States became involved in the Cuban revolt when the battleship *Maine,* while lying in Havana Harbor, mysteriously blew up. The Spanish-American War lasted only a few weeks. When the war with Spain ended in 1898, the United States won control of Cuba.

The United States soon made Cuba an independent nation. But independence did not bring peace and stability to Cuba. In 1953 another revolution broke out. This one was led by

Havana, Cuba, has the largest population of all the West Indian capital cities. What are some of Havana's industries? Which capital city has the smallest population?

Countries of the West Indies

Country	Capital	Population of Capital	Some Industries and Products
Aruba and Curaçao	Willemstad	95,000	Oil refining, tourism, electronics, shipbuilding
Bahamas	Nassau	138,500	Tourism, banking, rum
Barbados	Bridgetown	8,789	Rum, molasses, tourism
Cuba	Havana	1,900,240	Textiles, wood products, cement, chemicals, cigars, sugar
Dominica	Roseau	20,000	Agriculture, tourism
Dominican Republic	Santo Domingo	1,300,000	Molasses, rum, cement, textiles, furniture
Guadeloupe	Basse-Terre	15,833	Agriculture
Haiti	Port-au-Prince	745,700	Rum, molasses, tourism
Jamaica	Kingston	671,000	Aluminum, rum, molasses, cigars, oil products, tourism
Martinique	Fort-de-France	98,807	Rum, tourism
Trinidad and Tobago	Port-of-Spain	250,000	Oil products, rum, cement, tourism

Fidel Castro (fē del′ käs′trō). He and his supporters kept on fighting until the dictator, Batista, went into exile.

Since 1959 Castro and his supporters have ruled Cuba. When they took over all foreign-owned businesses and properties, the United States government became concerned.

In 1960 the United States stopped buying Cuba's sugar. So Cuba began to trade with the Soviet Union and other communist countries. Then the United States broke off diplomatic relations with Cuba.

Many Cubans who did not want to live under Castro fled to the United States. These Cuban exiles tried to start a revolution against Castro. They were defeated at the Bay of Pigs.

A crisis erupted in 1962 when the United States discovered that the Soviet Union was installing *missiles* (mis′əlz) in Cuba. Missiles are weapons that are designed to be thrown or fired toward a target. The United States demanded that the missiles be removed. It set up an air and naval blockade of Cuba. After four days of tension, the Soviets agreed to remove the missiles and the crisis ended.

During the 1970s and 1980s many Cubans fled to the United States. A large number of them settled in Florida.

Living and Working in the West Indies

Most of the people in the West Indies make their living by farming or processing farm products. Sugar cane, cacao, bananas, coffee, and pineapples are grown. Most of these tropical

Some women of Barbados and other West Indian Islands are able to carry things gracefully on their heads. This custom requires good posture and balance.

crops are raised for export to the United States and Europe. Since colonial days, more land has been used to grow money crops than to grow food crops. Much of the food used by people in the West Indies must be imported.

Many island governments now want to set up new industries to provide more jobs for their people. More people can make a living from industry than from farming.

Beautiful scenery, ocean breezes, fine beaches, warm, sunny days, and different ways of living bring thousands of tourists to these islands. The money they spend there helps many islanders earn a living.

Do You Know?

1. Where is Central America?
2. What are some exports of these countries?
3. Where are the West Indies?
4. Which islands of the West Indies are independent? Which are under foreign control?

489

Before You Go On

Using New Words

balsam	hurricane
ejido	missile
Latin America	mestizo

The phrases below explain the words or terms listed above. Number a paper from 1 through 6. After each number write the word or term that matches the definition.

1. A person of mixed ancestry, usually Spanish or Portuguese and Indian
2. Land south of the United States, where Spanish, French, or Portuguese is spoken
3. A tropical storm with strong winds
4. Land turned over to a farming village by the government
5. The sap of a tree used in making medicines and perfumes
6. A weapon that is designed to be thrown or fired toward a target

Finding the Facts

1. Where in the Americas is Mexico?
2. Who organized a movement to set Mexico free from Spain?
3. Why is Benito Juárez remembered as one of Mexico's important leaders?
4. In what ways is the Mexican government helping its people today?
5. How do most Mexicans earn a living?
6. What countries make up Central America?
7. Where are the West Indies?
8. In what latitudes are the Central American countries and the West Indies?
9. What Central American countries declared their independence from Spain in 1821?
10. What and where is the Panama Canal?
11. How has Cuba been governed since 1898?
12. What are the chief money crops of each of the Central American countries?
13. How do most people in the West Indies make their living?

5
South America

South America is the fourth largest continent. It has thirteen countries. See the map of South America on page 492. Colombia (kə lum'bē ə) and Venezuela (ven'ə zwā'lə) are in northern South America. Colombia is as large as Texas, Oklahoma, and New Mexico put together. Venezuela is almost as large as Texas, Oklahoma, and Louisiana.

Ecuador (ek'wə dôr'), Peru (pə rōō'), and Chile (Chil'ē) border the Pacific Ocean. Ecuador, the Spanish word for equator, is about as large as Colorado. Chile is a very long and narrow country.

Brazil (brə zil'), Uruguay (yoor'ə gwā'), and Argentina (är gen tē'nə) border the Atlantic Ocean. Argentina is as large as the part of our country which lies east of the Mississippi River. Uruguay is about half as large as California. Brazil, the largest South American country, is almost as large as the United States.

Guyana (gī an'ə), Suriname (soor'ə nam), and French Guiana (gē an'ə) also border the Atlantic. Bolivia (bə liv'ē ə) and Paraguay (par'ə gwā') lie in the heart of South America. Paraguay is about the size of California.

Geography of South America

South America has a variety of land surfaces. The Andes Mountains stretch along the Pacific Ocean. They are the second highest mountains in the world. Melting snow trickles down the mountain slopes in streams used for irrigation.

Near the Atlantic coast are hills and low mountains called the Guiana and Brazilian highlands. The Guiana Highlands are shared by Venezuela, Guyana, Suriname, and French Guiana. The Brazilian Highlands stretch from northeastern Brazil almost to Uruguay.

In Bolivia the Andes Mountains divide into two chains. Between them is a high plateau. In the far south of Argentina is Patagonia (pat'ə gō'nē ə). Patagonia is a long, narrow plateau. Much of the central part, or interior, of Brazil is also plateau.

The *llanos* (lä'nōz) are grassy plains which stretch between the Andes and the Orinoco (ōr ə nō'kō) River in Venezuela. Colombia and Venezuela share the llanos. The *pampas* (pam'pəz), or treeless plains, stretch across central Argentina from the Atlantic to the Andes. North of the pampas lies the Chaco (chä'kō), a large area of grass and forests. Argentina's pampas are the flattest plains in the world. The interior of Brazil is also flat. The Atacama (ät ə käm'ə) Desert is in northern Chile. It is one of the driest deserts in the world.

Major Water Systems

The Amazon River in Brazil is the second longest river in the world. The Amazon Lowlands are drained by the Amazon River and its many tributaries. This basin includes almost half of Brazil.

The Parana (par ə nä'), the Uruguay, and the

CENTRAL
AMERICA

SOUTH AMERICA

| 0 | 100 | 200 | 400 | 600 Miles |
| 0 | 161 | 322 | 644 | 966 Kilometers |

⊛ National Capitals
☆ Other Capitals
• Other Cities

Mountains
Plateaus
Hills
Plains

Colón Panama Canal
Barranquilla
Maracaibo
Lake Maracaibo
Caracas
TRINIDAD AND TOBAGO
Port of Spain
10°
Medellín
Magdalena River
LLANOS
VENEZUELA
Ciudad Bolívar
Orinoco River
Georgetown
Paramaribo
Buenaventura
Bogotá
GUYANA
SURINAME
FRENCH GUIANA
Cayenne
COLOMBIA
GUIANA HIGHLANDS
EQUATOR
Quito
ECUADOR
Rio Caquetá
Rio Negro
Belém
Guayaquil
Iquitos
SELVAS
Amazon
Manaus
Madeira
Amazon River
Rio Tapajós
Fortaleza
Cape São Roque
Point Aguja
P
A
C
I
F
I
C
Rio
BRAZIL
Recife
Trujillo
PERU
0°
Lima
Callao
SELVAS
Rio
Rio Tocantins
Salvador
10°
São Francisco
Cuzco
Lake Titicaca
La Paz
Arequipa
Mollendo
Cochabamba
BOLIVIA
Cuiabá
BRAZILIAN
Brasília
Goiânia
Arica
Atacama Desert
Sucre
HIGHLANDS
Belo Horizonte
20°
Antofagasta
TROPIC OF CAPRICORN
PARAGUAY
Rio
São Paulo
TROPIC OF CAPRICORN
Rio Paraná
Asunción
Curitiba
Rio de Janeiro
Santos
Tucumán
O
C
E
A
N
Coquimbo
Córdoba
Santa Fe
Rio Paraná
Rio Uruguay
Pôrto Alegre
30°
Viña del Mar
Mount Aconcagua 22,834 ft.
Mendoza
Rosario
URUGUAY
Valparaíso
Santiago
Montevideo
Concepción
Buenos Aires
PAMPAS
Rio de la Plata
ARGENTINA
A
T
L
A
N
T
I
C
Bahía Blanca
40°
Puerto Montt
PATAGONIA
O
C
E
A
N
Comodoro Rivadavia
Falkland Islands
South Georgia
Punta Arenas
STRAIT OF MAGELLAN
Tierra del Fuego
Ushuaia
Rand McNally & Co.

50°

Paraguay rivers unite to form the Plata River system. This river system is smaller than the Amazon but more important for transportation. The rivers which unite to form it empty into an *estuary* (es'chōō er'ē), or arm of the sea, called the Rio de La Plata (rē'ō dē lä plä'tə). Argentina, Uruguay, and Paraguay share the land and the rivers.

Climate

Most of South America is in the tropics. The map of South America, page 492, shows the equator passing through the northern part of the continent. Because of the varied land surfaces, South America has some of the coldest and some of the hottest places on earth. The southern part of South America is in the middle latitudes. The climate is much like that of our country. South America has great differences in rainfall. The rainiest parts are in the Amazon basin. The driest parts are along the coast of Peru, in northern Chile, and in Argentina.

The *selvas* (sel'vəs) are the tropical rain forests of the Amazon. These deep forests have two seasons. One is a "rainy" season when it rains most of the time. The other is a "dry" season, which is not quite so rainy.

History of South America

The Incas (ing'kəz) were perhaps the greatest of the Indian civilizations in the Americas when the Spanish arrived. They lived in South America. At one time the empire stretched 2,000 miles (3,200 km) north to south along the Pacific coast of South America.

The Incas had a highly developed form of government. They were farmers and skilled builders. They built terraces so that they could farm the slopes of mountain villages, and canals to irrigate their crops. They built forts, temples, palaces, roads, and bridges. The Incas were also skilled metal workers. They had much gold and silver. But like the Aztecs and the Mayas, the Incas were conquered by the Spaniards.

For more than 300 years Spain ruled its colonies in the Americas with a firm hand. Taxes were heavy. Prices were high. Trade could be carried on only with Spain. Only Spaniards born

Large, broad-leafed plants thrive in the tropical rain forests of the Amazon. More than 80 inches (203 cm) of rain may fall there in a year.

493

in Spain could be high officers or hold the best jobs. The Spanish colonists were angry.

The Spaniards born in the Americas, who were called *Creoles* (krē'ōlz), were very unhappy. "Why are we not allowed to hold high offices?" the Creoles asked.

While Mexico and Central America were gaining their freedom, Spanish colonies in South America also were fighting for their independence. Simón Bolívar (sē mōn' bō lē'vär) led the fight for freedom in Venezuela, Colombia, Ecuador, Bolivia, and Peru. José de San Martín (hō sē' dē sän' mär tēn') was a leader in Argentina and Chile. He also helped Bolívar in Peru. Bernardo O'Higgins led the fight for freedom in Chile. He became its first president.

Bolivia was formed from part of Peru and part of Argentina. It was named for Simón Bolívar. Paraguay became independent without fighting. The Paraguayans asked their Spanish rulers to resign. The Spaniards agreed. Paraguay won its independence without war.

Brazil belonged to Portugal. The son of Portugal's king governed the colony. Brazilian colonists asked the king's son to declare Brazil an independent country and become its ruler. He agreed and in 1822 was crowned Brazil's ruler. Three years later, Uruguay, which had once been part of Brazil, declared its independence.

The English, the Dutch, and the French had settled the Guianas. Guyana (formerly British Guiana) gained independence in 1966, Suriname (Dutch Guiana) in 1975. French Guiana is the only part of South America that is not independent.

After all these countries had won their independence, they faced other problems. They fought against each other over boundaries. The citizens fought among themselves. About three out of every four persons were Indians or mestizos. Most of these people had little or no education. Powerful people, usually with the help of the army, were able to seize governments and rule as they pleased. The people suffered under these dictators. The countries remained poor.

Simón Bolívar is called "The Liberator." The United States honors people who fought for freedom in nations around the world. Bolívar's statue stands in Washington, D.C.

SIMON BOLIVAR
THE LIBERATOR

BORN JULY 24 1783
CARACAS VENEZUELA

DIED DECEMBER 17 1830
SANTA MARTA COLOMBIA

Even today military governments are common in South American nations. Brazil, Peru, Uruguay, Bolivia, and Chile all have military governments. Ecuador has often been under military control. But in 1979 voters elected a leader who did not belong to the military. Paraguay has had a series of dictators.

The governments of Argentina, Colombia, Venezuela, Suriname, and Guyana are among the few democracies in South America. Guyana is a member of the British Commonwealth.

Living and Working in South America

Many people in South America make their living by farming. Some of them work in mines, in industries, or in lumbering. Still others make their living by caring for tourists.

Colombia

Most of Colombia's people live in the Andean highlands. They farm on the plateaus and in the fertile valleys. Coffee is grown on the slopes of the Andes. It is Colombia's most important money crop. Colombia is one of the world's chief coffee producers.

Colombia produces platinum, a hard metal used for jewelry and dental work. Colombia is also an important source of gold. In addition, the nation's mineral exports include silver, emeralds, and copper.

Many of Colombia's large cities are in the highlands. Medellín (med'əl ēn') lies in a rich valley of the Andes. In its mills and factories

cotton and woolen goods, shoes, soap, sugar, watches, and jewelry are manufactured. Medellín is the center of a rich farming and mining region. Gold is mined nearby. It is refined in the government mint at Medellín. Barranquilla (bär'räng kē'yä), at the mouth of the Magdalena River, is Colombia's chief port. Barranquilla is also an important air center.

West of Barranquilla is the city of Cartagena (kär'tə jē'nə). Cartagena's chief business today is oil. Petroleum is piped from oil fields more than 400 miles (640 km) away. Petroleum is Cartagena's chief export. Colombia ranks second to Venezuela in the production of oil in South America.

Bogotá (bo'gə tä') is Colombia's capital, largest city, and the center of its art and music. It is on a high plateau in the eastern Andes Mountains. On the farms around Bogotá corn, wheat, potatoes, and barley are grown. Cattle and sheep supply food for the people of Bogotá and the coastal lowlands.

Venezuela

The Andean highlands are an important farming section of Venezuela. On the mountain slopes coffee is the chief crop. It is Venezuela's most important farm export. In the low valleys there are cacao plantations. Sugar, beans, corn, wheat, and potatoes are grown at different altitudes.

The hot, damp lowland near Lake Maracaibo (mar'ə kī'bō) brings much money to Venezuela. Oil derricks rise like a forest from the lake region. Pipelines are thick there. The most valuable product and export of Venezuela is oil.

Products of South America

Venezuela ranks fifth in the world in the production of oil.

Most of the oil from these fields is sent to the Dutch-controlled islands of Aruba and Curaçao. There, it is made into gasoline and fuel oil.

Oil has made Maracaibo Venezuela's second largest city. Iron ore, sugar, and coffee as well as petroleum are exported.

Near the old colonial city of Valencia cotton is raised. The cotton is woven into cloth in the textile mills there.

Most of Venezuela's people live in the cool, comfortable Andean highlands. Caracas (kə rä′kəs), the beautiful capital and largest city, is located in a high valley. It is an old city, yet a very modern one. La Guaira (lä gwī′rä) is the busy seaport for Caracas.

Guyana, Suriname, French Guiana

Farming is the most important work in Guyana and Suriname. The heat and heavy rainfall produce fine tropical crops for export and for home use. Sugarcane and rice are raised along the swampy coastal plain.

The most important export is bauxite. Guyana and Suriname rank among the top six countries in the world in bauxite production. As you know, aluminum is made from this ore. Aluminum is used in making airplanes, automobiles, and trains. The United States buys much of the bauxite.

French Guiana is the smallest and the poorest of the three Guianas. Many kinds of tropical crops could be grown there. However, only a

Some of Venezuela's largest oil deposits are beneath Lake Maracaibo. Oil wells are drilled from platforms on the water. The platforms are anchored to the lake bottom.

small part of the land is used for farming. The people import much of their food. Some gold is mined.

Brazil

The people of Brazil number more than 119 million. The first Europeans to settle there were from Portugal.

Working in the Amazon Valley

In Brazil are Indians who make a living by hunting and gathering. They live in the Amazon Valley. Some gather nuts. They pick up Brazil nuts which are delicious to eat and make a fine oil for cooking. They also gather tagua (ta′gwä) nuts which, when carved, are white and look like ivory. Other people dig the roots of the manioc (man′ē ok′) plant. Tapioca, used in puddings, is made from the root of this plant.

Some people make a living by collecting the sap of rubber trees. Pure rubber melts in hot weather and breaks in cold weather. Few uses were found for it at first. Then a way of treat-

Some of the heavy forest growth in the Amazon Valley is being cleared to make the land suitable for farming. The cool highlands are ideal for growing coffee. Here a worker cleans coffee beans.

ing rubber with sulphur, called *vulcanizing* (vul′kə nīz′ing), was discovered. Vulcanizing keeps rubber from melting, or hardening, whatever the weather may be.

Manufacturers began to make rubber raincoats, overshoes, and other things of vulcanized rubber. Then the automobile was invented. Millions of tons of rubber were needed for tires. Workers were hired to gather *latex* (lā′teks), the sap of the rubber tree.

Then planters in Asia began to grow rubber on plantations. Asian rubber was cheaper than wild rubber from South America. Later, people learned to make synthetic rubber from gas, coal, tar, and petroleum. The United States and the rest of the world now use more synthetic rubber than natural rubber. Synthetic rubber can be produced cheaply enough to compete with natural rubber.

Brazil continues to produce natural rubber. But its rubber plantations can supply only enough rubber for the tire industry in Brazil.

Farming, Mining, Manufacturing

The northern part of the Brazilian Highlands is a great desert. In spite of the lack of water and grass, cattle and goats are raised in the northern highlands. In irrigated areas cotton, sugarcane, vegetables, and fruits grow.

Carnauba (kär nou′bə) wax and babassu (bä′bə sōō′) oil are valuable products. The leaves of the carnauba palm are coated with wax. It is used in making floor and furniture polish, motion-picture films, and phonograph records. Oil from the babassu nut is used in soap, margarine, and cooking oil.

Some parts of the highlands receive heavy rains. There sugarcane, cotton, cacao, bananas, and other tropical crops are grown.

About three-fourths of the world's coffee is raised in Brazil. Most of Brazil's coffee comes from the central highlands. The coffee plant needs a cool climate, a long growing season, plenty of water while it is growing, and dry weather when it ripens.

Gold was Brazil's most important mineral product for many years. About 200 years ago diamonds were discovered in the highlands of Brazil. Most Brazilian diamonds are used for drill points and cutting tools. They are important to industry. Rich iron-ore fields lie north of Rio de Janeiro (rē ō dā jə ner′o). Most of this iron ore is exported.

Today Brazil has more factories than other South American countries. At first most of the factory products were used in Brazil. Now all kinds of goods are exported too. Automobile, steel, rubber, and meat-packing companies are found in large cities. Trained people from the United States work in these companies to help the Brazilians. Foreign aid and money have helped Brazil's industries grow.

Brazil's Cities

Manaus (mä nous′) and Belém (bə lem′) are the only large cities of the Amazon Valley. Manaus, an important river port and a market center, is inland. Belém, the chief rubber center of Brazil, is on one of the mouths of the Amazon River. It is the entrance to the Amazon Basin.

Salvador, a cacao port and railroad center, is built on two levels like many cities on Brazil's coast. Its latitude is only 12 degrees from the equator, so the heat in the lower city is almost unbearable. Most people live in the upper city, which is cooled by ocean breezes. Elevators carry them to and from work in the lower city.

Recife (rə sē′fə) is built partly on a peninsula and partly on islands. Many of its streets are canals. Recife is Brazil's chief sugar port and railroad center. It exports much cotton and tobacco. Recife's people work in cotton mills, tobacco factories, sugar refineries, on docks, and on boats. Fishing is also important.

The city of Rio de Janeiro, Brazil's old capital, is built on a bay which forms a fine harbor. In addition to being a seaport, Rio is a railway, highway, and airway center.

Because Rio de Janeiro lies between the ocean and the mountains, the city has no space to grow. Brazil's government wanted the people to move west, away from the coast. So Brazilians decided to build a new capital far inland. In 1961 government operations were moved to the new city, Brasília (brə zil′ē ə).

São Paulo
A Fast-Growing, Energetic City

São Paulo (sou pou'loo) is the largest city in Latin America. Coffee made São Paulo grow. The city spurted ahead after it became Brazil's main coffee-marketing center.

Between São Paulo and the sea are steep cliffs. The city's people overcame this barrier by hanging a railway on cables down to the port of Santos. Load after load of coffee goes down these cables. Santos is the world's busiest coffee port.

Today coffee is still São Paulo's main business. But new industries are growing. Much nearby land is now used to pasture livestock and grow cotton. What new industries do these two activities give São Paulo? Machinery and electronics equipment are made there.

To get power for new industries, São Paulo's energetic people dammed up rivers and pumped the water over mountains to make electricity. South America's first nuclear power plant was also built near São Paulo. The fast-growing city has entered the nuclear age. ■

Chile

Most Chileans make a living by farming. The most important farming region is Chile's Central Valley. On the haciendas of the Central Valley are acres and acres of winter wheat, rice, corn, rye, and barley. Beans, potatoes, and lentils are grown. Dairy cows graze in the pastures. Livestock and alfalfa to feed them are raised on the ranches. Juicy grapes hang in the vineyards. There are citrus fruit groves and orchards of apple, peach, and cherry trees.

Lumbering is important in southern Chile. The extreme southern tip is good for sheep raising.

One mineral found in Chile is nitrate of soda. Most of the nitrate is made into fertilizer. Some is used in chemicals, gunpowder, and other war materials. Iodine, used in medicine, is also made from nitrate of soda. More than half of the world's iodine comes from Chile.

Copper is now Chile's most important export product. Three important copper mines lie at the eastern edge of Atacama. One is the largest open-pit copper mine in the world.

Chile has enough coal to run its industries. Much of the coal lies below the ocean off the coast of central Chile. Tunnels where miners work, business offices, and restaurants have been built under the Pacific Ocean. Chile's growing industries need the coal from these undersea mines.

Chile's Cities

Valparaiso (val'pə rī'zō) has the best natural harbor in the country. Trade is important in Chile, and Valparaiso is its trade center. Woolen and cotton textiles and some iron-and-steel goods are manufactured. Leather, shoes, cans, wines, flour, and chemicals are made in the factories. Heavy machinery, however, must still be imported.

Santiago (san'tē ä'gō), the capital, is Chile's largest city and most important industrial center. It is the fourth largest city in South America. Its more than 3 million people work for the government and in factories, mills, stores, and offices.

Peru

Many persons in Peru make a living by farming. Sugarcane, cotton, rice, coffee, and tobacco are raised on the large haciendas of the coastal oases. Peru sells millions of pounds of raw sugar each year and even more cotton. Another important export of Peru is guano (gwä'nō). Guano is an excellent fertilizer. Guano is formed from the droppings of birds who live on the islands off the coast of Peru.

Fine cattle and horses are bred on the largest ranches of the grassy plains of Peru. Stock raising is also important on the cold northern plateau. Llamas, alpacas, and sheep grow thick coats in cold regions.

Mining is important in Peru. The land is rich in gold, silver, and other minerals. It ranks sixth in the world in lead production. Petroleum is found on the northern coastal plain. In the mountains northeast of Lima (lē'mə) are the richest copper mines in the world. Cerro de Pasco (ser'ro dā päs'kō) is the center of the copper-mining region. Cuzco (kōōs'kō), the old Inca capital, is the center of another mining re-

Peruvian Indians who live in cool mountain regions wear warm wool ponchos. Many of these colorful blankets are made to be sold at markets to tourists.

gion farther south. Peru is becoming a more industrial nation. A number of factories have been built in recent years. More are being built. The factories make petroleum into fuel oil, gasoline, and other products. They refine sugar. Some metal, cotton, and woolen goods are manufactured.

Peru has a large fishing industry. It ranks fourth in the world in tons of fish caught. Most of the fish are ground into meal in factories on the coast. Fish meal is used as feed for livestock.

Some manufacturing is still done by hand. Indians weave warm ponchos and other clothing from the wool of sheep, llamas, and alpacas. A poncho is a blanket with a slit in the middle so that the wearer can slip it over his or her head. Tourists buy many of these beautiful, handmade blankets.

The Spanish explorer Pizarro founded Peru's beautiful capital. Lima is the largest and most important city. Its factories, mills, and stores give work to thousands. Nearly half of its people work for the government. One of the oldest universities in the Americas is in Lima.

Lima is not on the coast. Highways connect Lima with Callao (kä yä′ ō), its port. Callao is the only seaport in Peru where ocean liners can dock. Airplanes connect Lima with Cuzco and other towns in the mountains.

Ecuador

Haciendas (hä′sē en′dəz), or large plantations, are found in the valleys of Ecuador. Cacao, coffee, sugar, bananas, cotton, rice, and tobacco grow on the haciendas there. Cacao beans are shipped to Europe and the United States, where they are made into chocolate. Bananas are also an important export.

The Eastern Lowland is part of the Amazon selvas. Few people live here. Two important trees grow wild in this region. Rubber is made from the sap of the rubber tree. Quinine (kwī′nīn) comes from the bark of the cinchona tree. Quinine is a medicine used in treating malaria, a tropical disease.

Many of the people of Ecuador live in the highlands. They make a living by raising dairy cows or growing potatoes and wheat. Valuable forests of rubber trees, balsa, and toquilla (tō kē′yä) palm trees grow in the foothills. Balsa logs are lighter than cork. They are excellent for making boats, airplanes, and life rafts. Toquilla palm leaves are used to make straw hats.

Guayaquil (gwī'ə kēl) is Ecuador's largest and most modern city. It has an excellent natural harbor on the Guayas River.

A railroad connects the coast city of Guayaquil with Quito (kē'tō), 9,000 feet (2,700 m) above sea level. This old city, the capital of Ecuador, now has modern apartment houses, factories, stores, automobiles, and electric streetcars. Colonial buildings, people in Inca costumes, llamas, and burros are common sights. Because of its altitude, Quito is much cooler than Guayaquil.

Bolivia

About three of every four persons in Bolivia live on the plateau. They raise barley, corn, wheat, and potatoes when there is enough rain or where irrigation is possible. Potatoes are their chief crop. The main food of thousands of Indians is chuño (chōōn'yō). Chuño is made by first freezing, then drying, potatoes. Fish from the waters of Lake Titicaca adds variety to the food eaten there.

Grains, vegetables, fruit, and sugarcane thrive in the mountain valleys and on the hills of the eastern slopes. The coffee and cacao grown there are exported. This pleasant region could produce enough to feed the people of the plateau. But transportation is poor. Products must be carried across the mountains on the backs of llamas and burros. Many kinds of food would spoil before reaching the markets.

Llamas, alpacas, and sheep mean clothing, food, and transportation to the people of the plateau. Cloth is made from the wool of the sheep, llama, and alpaca. Alpaca wool brings a good price.

Minerals are Bolivia's greatest natural resource. Bolivia has more tin than any other country in the Americas. It also produces more *tungsten* (tung'stin) than any other country in South America. Tungsten is a mineral that is mixed with steel to harden it. Nine-tenths of the country's exports are minerals. Most of the tin is shipped to the United States.

Bolivia's mineral deposits lie far from the coast on the plateau. Many of the mines are 12,000 to 20,000 feet (3,600 to 6,000 m) above sea level. It is very hard and costly to take machinery up so high. Because of this, mining is not fully developed in Bolivia. Besides, few workers can mine at such high altitudes.

Bolivians weave cloth and make jewelry and pottery by hand. There is no large-scale manufacturing in Bolivia. Most manufactured goods have to be brought from other countries.

Bolivia's Capitals

Bolivia has two capital cities. One capital is La Paz (lä päs'). The other is Sucre (sōō'krə).

La Paz lies in a valley on the plateau. It is the highest capital in the world. La Paz is the largest city in Bolivia and the center of the nation's manufacturing, business, and transportation. Railways connect it with the Pacific and Atlantic coasts. Most of Bolivia's imports and exports pass through La Paz.

Sucre is a much older city. However, Sucre has poor roads and is harder to reach than La Paz. So only the Supreme Court meets there. Other government business is carried on in La Paz.

Argentina

Farming and cattle raising are the chief occupations in all parts of Argentina. One-fourth of the world's meat, one-third of the hides, and one-fifth of the wheat come from Argentina's pampas. Other money crops are corn and flax. Sugarcane, grapes, and other fruits are also grown.

Argentina's largest sheep ranches are in Patagonia. *Gauchos* (gou′chōz), or cowhands, on horseback herd the sheep. The wool and some lamb and mutton are exported.

Forests are the chief source of wealth on the northern plains. Its most valuable tree is the quebracho (kā brä′ chō) tree. Quebracho wood is hard. It is used for railroad ties, paving blocks, and fence posts. Tannic acid is made from the sap of the quebracho tree. Tannic acid is used to make leather soft, firm, and strong. Leather factories of all kinds use much tannic acid.

Oil fields have been found in eastern Patagonia. The government is hoping these oil fields will help the country to pay its debts.

Argentina's Cities

Industry in Argentina is becoming more important than farming. The Plata shore between Buenos Aires and La Plata is the chief industrial region. The cities of this region are seaports, river ports, railroad, trade, and manufacturing centers. Meat packing, tanning hides and skins,

Gauchos herd sheep and cattle across the plains of Patagonia in Argentina. They do the same work as cowhands on the plains of the United States.

and milling grains are the most important industries. Most factories make goods needed in Argentina. Argentina has few minerals and not enough iron ore and coal for heavy industry such as making machinery. The people who live in the cities make a living mostly by trading with other lands.

Buenos Aires is the capital and largest city. It is also the greatest seaport and most important trading and manufacturing center in Argentina. Buenos Aires has many railroads and a livestock market. Some of the largest meat-packing houses in the world are in Buenos Aires.

Freighters sail 200 miles (320 km) up the Paraná River to Rosario, the grain port of Argentina. Rosario is also the flour-milling center of South America. The first public schools of Argentina were built in this city.

Bahía Blanca (bə hē′ə blän′kä) is the only large city of Argentina directly on the Atlantic Ocean. It handles the products of the pampas and Patagonia.

Uruguay

More than three-fourths of the land in Uruguay is used for stock and cattle raising. Cattle, sheep, pigs, horses, and mules are raised on huge ranches. There are also orchards and diary farms. Wheat, corn, oats, and flax are grown.

Uruguay exports more beef and mutton than any South American country except Argentina. Many of its almost 3 million people work in meat-packing houses.

Uruguay has no coal, fuel oil, or iron ore, so it has few factories. Articles for everyday use are made in these factories. Heavy machinery and other manufactured goods are imported.

A few people work in silver and copper mines. A larger number work in granite and marble quarries.

Montevideo (mon′tə vi dā′ō), the capital and largest city, has more than one million inhabitants. Montevideo is a seaport and the center of Uruguay's trade.

Paraguay

About 75 million acres (30 million ha) along the Paraguay River are just right for cotton. A bank in Asunción (ä soon syōn′) furnishes farmers with free cotton seeds. These farmers supply Asunción's mills with cotton.

Quebracho trees, wild orange trees, and holly bushes grow in the forests. From the leaves of a shrub that grows wild in Paraguay a hot drink called yerba maté (yer′bə mä tā′) is made. Yerba maté is often called Paraguayan tea. The bush is also grown on great plantations. Tannin from the bark of the quebracho, castor-oil beans, and leaves of the wild orange tree used for perfume are exports of Paraguay.

Asunción, the capital, is 1,000 miles (1,600 km) from the sea. Today it is the smallest of the Latin-American capitals.

Latin-American Problems and Progress

The people of Latin America face many problems. Some of these problems are geographic. Certain areas have hot, rainy, unhealthy cli-

505

Representatives from countries that belong to the Organization of American States meet regularly at the headquarters in Washington, D.C.

mates. Other areas are deserts. In many places, jungles and mountains make transportation difficult. Another problem is the lack of industry. But Latin Americans are making improvements. One improvement was made after World War II. This was the development of an organization called the Organization of American States, or OAS. Members of the OAS are like the members of the United Nations. They try to work out problems peacefully. The OAS supports trade, science, and education among its members.

Another improvement was the Alliance for Progress, which began in 1961. This program worked to raise living standards, increase industry, and encourage foreign trade. Members of the Alliance were twenty-two Latin American countries and the United States. Each Latin-American member decided what it could do for itself, and what help it needed from others. The United States agreed to help with money.

By 1971, many changes had been made. Today, some larges estates are divided into small farms. The governments are lending people money to buy these farms. Better housing is being built. Industry is increasing. Most important, education is improving throughout Latin America.

Do You Know?

1. What countries are in South America?
2. Why were South American colonists under Spanish rule angry and unhappy?
3. What was the Alliance for Progress?

To Help You Learn

Using New Words

commonwealth mestizo tungsten
vulcanizing   pampa   hacienda
Parliament   llano   selva
Creole   gaucho   estuary
Latin America   latex   hurricane

The phrases below explain the words or terms listed above. Number a paper from 1 through 15. After each number write the word or term that matches the definition.

1. A cowhand of the pampas
2. An arm of the ocean which extends into the land
3. Treeless plain
4. A form of government much like a state
5. A large plantation
6. Rainy, tropical forest of the Amazon
7. A white metal used to harden steel
8. The body of lawmakers of Canada
9. Land south of the United States, where Spanish, French, or Portuguese is spoken
10. A way of treating rubber with sulfur so that it will not melt in hot weather or become stiff in cold weather
11. The sap of the tree used to make rubber
12. A person of mixed ancestry, usually Spanish or Portuguese and Indian
13. Tropical storm with strong winds
14. Grassy plain in South America
15. A Spanish person born in the Americas

Finding the Facts

1. What two islands that are part of our country lie in the Atlantic Ocean?
2. What did the United States make Puerto Rico in 1952?
3. What and where are Midway, Wake, Guam, and American Samoa?
4. What three countries are our northern neighbors?
5. What two European groups claimed land in Canada?
6. In what ways do the people of Canada make a living?
7. What country is our nearest Latin-American neighbor?
8. What is the land between Mexico and South America called?
9. What is the chain of islands stretching in a curve from Florida to northern South America called?
10. What canal joined the Atlantic Ocean and the Pacific Ocean?
11. What mountains in South America stretch along the Pacific Ocean?
12. What is the second longest river in the world?
13. Name three persons who led the fight for freedom in South America. Which countries did each person help free?
14. How was Bolivia formed?
15. How did Paraguay become independent?

16. Which South American country once belonged to Portugal?
17. What kind of government does Colombia have?
18. What kind of government is most common in South America today?
19. What is Colombia's most important money crop?
20. What is the most valuable product and export of Venezuela?
21. Which two South American countries rank among the top six in the world in the production of bauxite?
22. What are Ecuador's chief products?
23. What are Peru's chief minerals?
24. What are two important minerals of Bolivia?
25. What is Chile's most important export?
26. What are Argentina's chief seaports?
27. Why does Uruguay have few factories?
28. What is another name for "Paraguayan tea"?
29. What is raised in the Amazon Valley?
30. Where is Brazil's coffee land? What makes Brazil's climate good for coffee growing?
31. What are Brazil's chief cities?
32. What makes transportation difficult in many places of Latin America?
33. What steps are Latin-American nations taking today to develop themselves?

Learning from Maps

1. Use the map of Canada on page 459 to answer these questions: Which province has the most highland? Which has the most lowland? Which provinces and territories share the Laurentian Upland?
2. Use the scale of miles on the map of Canada on page 459 to find the distance: (a) from the city of Quebec to Vancouver; (b) from Montreal to Toronto; (c) from Winnipeg to Edmonton.
3. On the map of Mexico, Central America, and the West Indies, on page 476, locate and name the nations bordering the United States. Which countries of Central America are farthest north? Which is farthest south? Which faces only the Pacific? Which is the largest island of the West Indies?
4. Study the products map of Central America and the Caribbean countries on page 487. Which countries grow corn? Which countries grow bananas? Which countries have silver?
5. Turn to the map of South America on page 492. Locate and name the countries. Which two countries lie farthest north? What parallel of latitude is close to this northern border? Which country extends farthest south? Which country is the largest?
6. On the same map find the answers to these questions: What ocean borders South America on the east? On the west? Compare the eastern coastline with the western. Which has more and better harbors? Why? Which coastline has more mountains? Which two countries have no coastline?
7. Study the map of products of South America on page 496. Which countries have oil? Which countries have bauxite? Which country has emeralds?

Using Study Skills

1. **Time Line:** The following events are not listed in the right order. Copy the statements in the right order and place them on a time line. Check in your book for the dates.

   a. Luis Muñoz Marín elected first governor of Puerto Rico
   b. Ponce de León founds San Juan
   c. Battle of Midway marks turning point of World War II in the Pacific
   d. United States sets up naval base at Pago Pago on Samoa Islands
   e. French Quebec founded by Champlain
   f. French made an official language in Canada, equal to English
   g. Father Hidalgo organizes movement to free Mexico
   h. Panama becomes independent republic
   i. United States stops buying Cuba's sugar
   j. Brazil's capital moved to Brasília.

2. **Chart:** Look at the chart comparing Canada and the United States on page 460. Which country is larger in area? Which country is larger in population? What is the highest point in Canada? In the United States? Which of these two points is higher? Which country has the lowest point? What is the largest province in Canada? What is the largest state in the United States? Which is the larger, the province or the state? Which is smaller, Prince Edward Island or Rhode Island?

3. **Graph:** What does the pictograph on this page show? What does each figure equal? Which country had the largest population in 1982? Which country had the smallest population in 1982? About how many people lived in Mexico in 1982? Was that more or less than the number of people who lived in Canada? Which country had more people, Mexico or Brazil? About how many more people lived in Canada than in Cuba in 1982? About how many fewer people lived in Brazil than in the United States in 1982?

Population of Selected American Countries	1982 population size rounded to nearest 10 million
United States	🯅🯅🯅🯅🯅🯅🯅🯅🯅🯅🯅🯅🯅🯅🯅🯅🯅🯅🯅🯅🯅🯅🯅
Canada	🯅🯅🯅
Mexico	🯅🯅🯅🯅🯅🯅🯅
Brazil	🯅🯅🯅🯅🯅🯅🯅🯅🯅🯅🯅🯅
Cuba	🯅 Each figure equals 10 million people.

4. **Diagram:** Look at the diagram showing how wood is made into paper on page 465. What is the first thing that happens to the logs in the mill? How are chips made into pulp?

Thinking it Through

1. Each numbered event was the cause of a lettered event. Match the events.
   (1) After our war with Spain in 1898, Spain gave up some of its colonies.
   (2) The United States wanted to be able to get from the Atlantic Ocean to the Pacific quickly.
   (3) San Martín drove the Spanish out of Argentina.
   (4) In 1535 a French explorer discovered and explored the St. Lawrence River.
   (5) Spain ruled its colonies with a firm hand.
   (a) The Panama Canal was built.
   (b) France claimed land in North America.
   (c) Puerto Rico, Wake, and Guam became United States possessions.
   (d) South Americans began to fight for freedom.
   (e) Argentina gained its independence.
2. Canada and the United States are close neighbors. What might happen if they did not continue to work together?
3. The wars for independence in the South American colonies were fought for many of the same reasons as the American Revolution. What were some of them?

Projects

1. The Explorers' Committee might write to one of the airlines to find the time required to fly from: New York to the Virgin Islands; Chicago to Guam; your home town to Puerto Rico.
2. Bring in samples or pictures of products from United States possessions. Make name cards for each of the possessions. Then arrange them for display.
3. Choose a committee to plan a bulletin board about Canada. Bring in pictures from newspapers and magazines, travel folders, and post cards.
4. Plan a cruise to Central America in which you stop at a principal port of each country bordering the coast. You might write to your nearest travel agency and ask for booklets which will give ideas of places to be visited.

   Use the maps in your book or wall maps in your classroom to find about how far it is from one port to the next. List something of interest to be found in or near each place you plan to stop.
5. With the help of your teacher or parents, prepare a menu for a meal typical of a Latin American nation.
6. The Reading Committee might like to find stories about the building of the Panama Canal, the way of life of the American Indians of the Amazon Valley, or how Patagonia ("Land of the Big Feet") got its name.

510

Learning About Maps and Globes

Maps and globes are special tools. They help us to understand our earth and the people, places, and things on it. Maps and globes are useful tools only if we know how to use them. The lessons in this section will help you improve your skills in using maps and globes. These map and globe skills will help you to better understand the world around you.

Words to Learn

You will meet these words in this unit. As you read, you will learn what they mean and how to pronounce them. The Word List will help you.

contour line
density
elevation
grid
legend
meridians of longitude
parallels of latitude
peninsula

plain
plateau
population
prime meridian
profile
projection
relief
site

1 Latitude and Longitude

How do pilots flying around the world say exactly where they are? They use the geographer's "zip code." You can learn to use it, too. You start by learning about some imaginary lines.

Look at the globe on the right. Lines called *parallels* (par'ə lelz) *of latitude* run east and west. They never meet. Like train tracks, they are always the same distance apart. Parallels of latitude are measured in degrees north and south of the equator. From the equator to each of the poles, there are 90 degrees.

North of the equator, parallels of latitude have the letter "N" in their "zip code." "N" stands for "north." South of the equator, latitudes are given the initial "S." Degrees are shown by the symbol " °." For example, on the map below, the first parallel shown north of the equator is at 20 degrees. It is labeled "20° N."

Parallels of Latitude

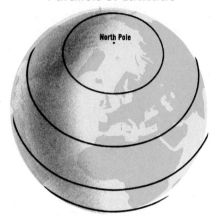

The airplanes on the maps below are flying along parallels of latitude. Are they going east and west or north and south? Find the plane flying at 40 degrees south.

Parallels of Latitude

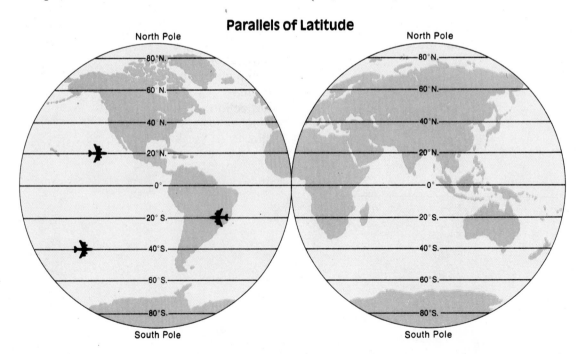

Meridians of Longitude

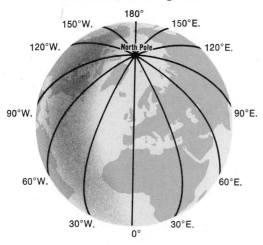

Look at the globe above. Lines called *meridians* (mə rid'ē ənz) *of longitude* connect the North and South poles. These lines, unlike parallels of latitude, eventually meet. They come together at the poles. Like the parallels, however, meridians have numbers. Those numbers measure degrees east and west. We begin counting degrees of longitude at an imaginary starting line. It runs through Greenwich, England. That line is called the *prime meridian* (prīm mə rid'ē ən). East of the prime meridian, all meridians have the letter "E" in their "zip code." It stands for "east." West of the prime meridian, all meridians are given the initial "W." For example, look at the globe. The prime meridian is at 0 degrees. The next meridian of longitude shown to the east is labeled "30° E." That is the short way of saying the line is 30 degrees east of the prime meridian.

Look at the planes on the maps below. They are flying along meridians of longitude. Are they flying east and west or north and south? Find the plane flying at 60 degrees east. Which continent will it cross? Now find the plane flying at 100 degrees west. Which continent has it already crossed?

Where is the "middle" of the United States in degrees of longitude?

Meridians of Longitude

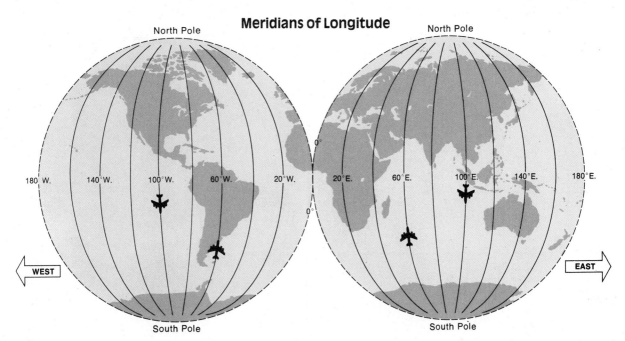

2 Making a Map from the Globe

Only a globe can show the true shape of the earth. That is because a globe and the earth are both round. But it is not always practical to carry a globe around. So people use maps instead. The way a mapmaker shows the round earth on a flat surface is called a *projection* (prə jek′shən). You can see four different projections on these two pages. But there are many more.

No one can make a map projection without some distortion. You can understand the problem by doing a simple experiment. Remove the peel from an orange in one big piece. Now try to lay the peel flat on a table. The only way to do it is to stretch it or tear it.

Mapmakers are faced with the same problem when they draw maps. They solve it by stretching or dividing parts of the globe. The maps shown here, for example, are fairly accurate pictures of the earth. Some regions, however, are quite distorted. Regions near the center of each map are quite accurate.

No projection is perfect. Therefore, different projections are used to show different things. Look at the map of the Western Hemisphere, below. A hemisphere, you remember, is a half of the earth. The Western Hemisphere is the half of the earth on which we live. On this projection, the equator is in the center of the map. Therefore, the shapes of places near the equator are fairly accurate. But places far from the center are not shown in their true shapes.

Now look at the map of the Northern Hemisphere, or polar map. Pilots may use this projection when flying over the North Pole. What is shown in the center of this map? Where is the equator? What parallels of latitude are shown on this map?

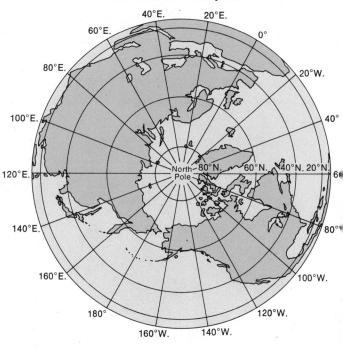

Western Hemisphere

Northern Hemisphere

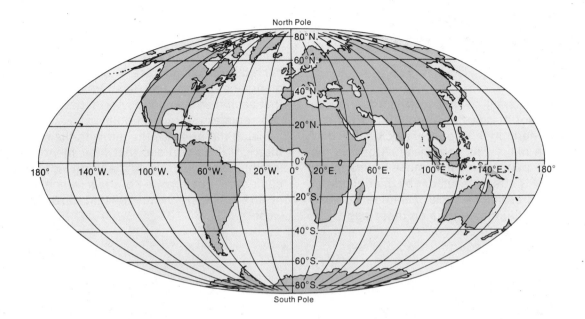

North Pole

80°N.
60°N.
40°N.
20°N.
0°
20°S.
40°S.
60°S.
80°S.

180°   140°W.   100°W.   60°W.   20°W. 0° 20°E.   60°E.   100°E.   140°E.   180°

South Pole

Look at the map above. It has been stretched to show all of the earth's land and water areas. It is a useful projection for showing the whole world at a glance. Again, areas close to the center of this map have accurate shapes. But all around the outer edge there is great distortion. Compare this projection with a globe. Which continents are shown closest to their true shapes? Which continents do you think are most distorted?

Below is yet another projection. Remember the orange peel? If you had pressed it flat it would have looked much like this map. This projection is useful for showing truer shapes of land areas. But the oceans have been broken, or interrupted. Would this map be a useful one for sailors? What has happened to Antarctica?

What kind of map could be drawn to show Antarctica best? Remember that Antarctica is around a pole, the South Pole.

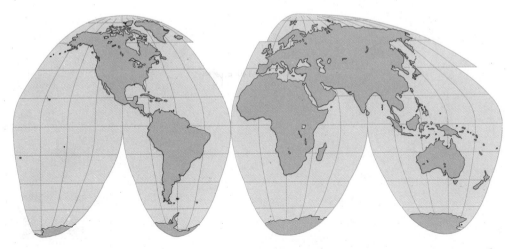

3 How Maps Show Directions and Locations

Imagine one small town located somewhere in the wide world. How can you find it? How can you tell where on the globe it is located? A *grid* (grid) can make your job easier. A grid is the crisscross pattern on a map made by imaginary lines. The pattern is made by meridians of longitude crossing parallels of latitude. You can see different kinds of grids on these pages.

A map grid can help you find directions as well as locations. If the meridians on a map are curved, you cannot use a compass rose. All meridians meet at the North Pole. This means that each meridian points north. Each meridian can serve as a direction pointer.

Match the grids on the left with the maps on the right. You can see that their meridians of longitude all point toward the North Pole. Where could you put arrows to show which way is north? Where are the arrows that show east and west?

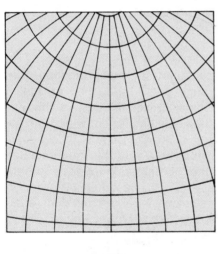

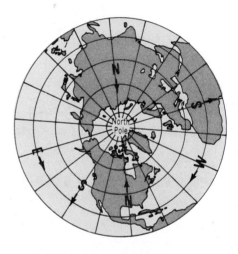

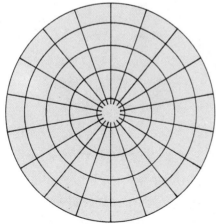

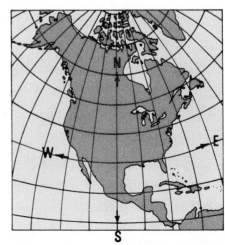

Look at the grid on the right. All of its lines are straight. The meridians of longitude appear to be parallel to each other. On a globe, however, these lines are not parallel. They meet at the North and South poles. See how distorted this map is. Land and water areas near the poles look larger than they are on a globe.

Why would anyone want a map as distorted as this? The map is useful because all directions can be shown throughout the map with one compass rose. Therefore, one compass rose shows north for every place on the map. This projection is sometimes called "the sailor's map." All lines of latitude cross all lines of longitude at right angles. Therefore, sailors can draw a straight line from where they are to where they are going. This line will show direction. Then with a compass, they can set their course.

A grid is also useful for pinpointing exactly where a place is located. Suppose you know both the degrees of latitude and the degrees of longitude of a place. You can then explain exactly where in the world that place is located.

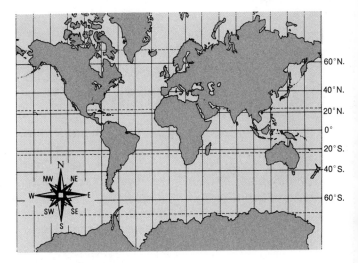

You learned that degrees of latitude and longitude are like a global zip code. The zip code helps you find and describe a location quickly.

On the map below, which letter is located at 30 degrees north latitude and 60 degrees west longitude? Which letter is located at 30 degrees south latitude and 40 degrees east longitude? Now give the locations in degrees for the two remaining letters.

Latitude and Longitude

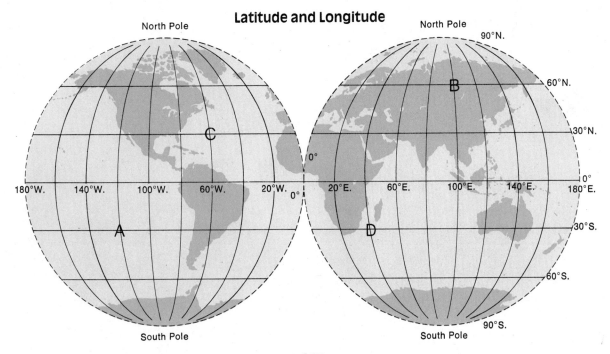

4 Using Different Kinds of Population Maps

Every 10 years, the government counts the number of people in our country. At that time, important population facts are recorded. The total number of people who live in a country is a *population* (pop'yə lā'shən).

Information about population can be shown in many ways. Graphs and tables are often used. But a special map helps people see this information at a glance. Two kinds of population maps are shown on these pages. The map below is a population dot map. A dot map shows *density* (den'sə tē), or thickness. Each dot stands for 10,000 people. In places where many people live, the dots are close together. In places where few people live, the dots are far apart. The same facts are shown differently on the large map to the right. In this case, a computer has been given population figures. It has used these figures to produce this map. You can see that the map works somewhat like a graph.

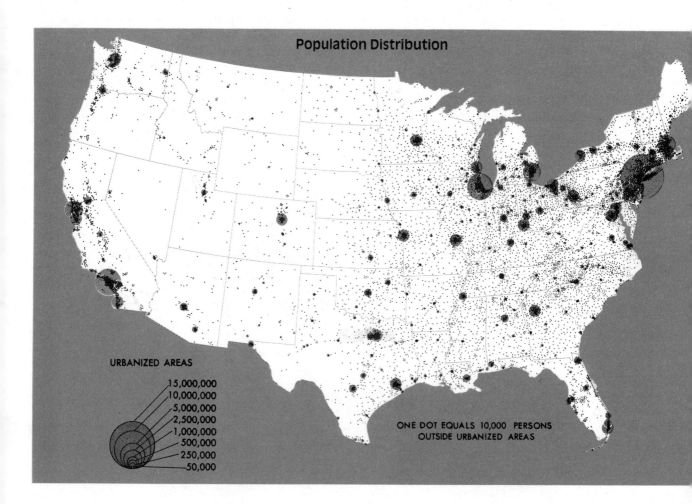

Population Distribution

URBANIZED AREAS

15,000,000
10,000,000
5,000,000
2,500,000
1,000,000
500,000
250,000
50,000

ONE DOT EQUALS 10,000 PERSONS
OUTSIDE URBANIZED AREAS

Compare the computer map with the population map in the text on page 219. How do the maps show population density in different ways? Which map shows the shape of the country more accurately? Which map, in your opinion, shows more about population density?

Identify the major population centers on the computer map. Turn to the map of the United States on pages A-4–A-5. You can also use the dot map to help you. Which cities are shown by the three tallest "needles"? Identify other large cities in Texas, Michigan, and Pennsylvania. You can use both maps to guess where the population center of our country is located. To understand a population center, imagine a population dot map placed on top of a pin. Each

dot shows where one of the more than 220 million Americans lives. The point where the map balances on the pin will be the population center.

The population center of the United States is always changing because people move. Early in our history, people lived mainly along the eastern coast of our country. More people lived in the New England region than in the southern coastal states.

As pioneers moved west, so did the population center. During some periods, great numbers of people moved. Use the two maps on these pages to make a guess where the population center is now located.

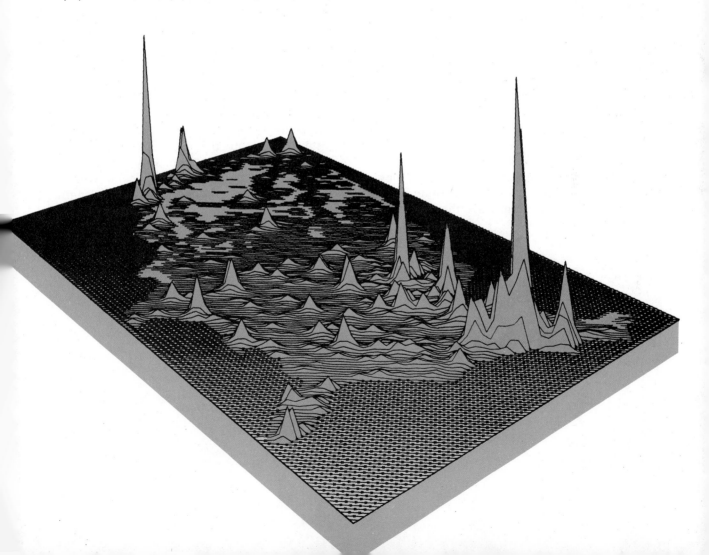

5 Understanding Contour Lines

All land surfaces are measured straight up from the level of the sea. This height above sea level is called *elevation* (el'ə vā'shən). Say that a mountain's elevation is 6,000 feet (1,800 m). That means the top of the mountain is 6,000 feet (1,800 m) higher than sea level.

Map makers have several ways of showing elevation. One way is by drawing a map with *contour* (kon'toor) *lines.* Contour means shape. A contour line connects points on a land surface that have the same elevation.

Below is a diagram of two mountains. Imagine that you can slice them into four layers. The whole surface of each layer has the same elevation. Now imagine you can take each layer out of the mountains and trace its outline on paper.

You can see that the contour lines of the map follow the same shape as the mountain. Notice that parts A, B, and C all have the same elevation. You can tell their height is the same. They are all located along the same contour line. Name two other points that have the same elevation. How can you tell their height is the same?

Another way to show height is with color. Look at the second contour map. Shades of blue have been used to show different elevations. What is the height of the land colored dark blue? Is it higher or lower than the light blue part?

The drawing on the right, above, is an elevation *profile* (prō'fīl). A profile is a side view. The mountains appear to be sliced in half to show their height. The artist has drawn and colored them to show areas above and below sea level. What is in the area below sea level?

The maps on the right show contour lines in two different regions of the United States. In the map at the left, the contour lines are drawn far apart. They show almost flat or gently rolling farmland in Iowa. In such areas, the highways and city streets can follow a rectangular pattern.

In the map on the right, contour lines are drawn close together. They show the steep, mountainous country of West Virginia. The tops of the mountains are shown by the shortest lines. Notice the ribbon-shaped roads, railroads, and towns. Why are they shaped differently from roads and towns in Iowa?

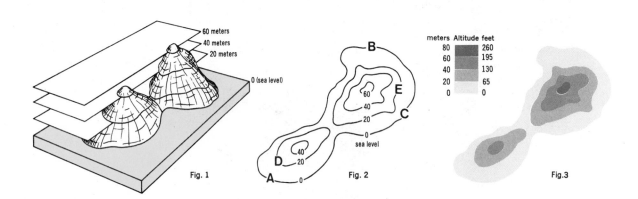

Fig. 1

Fig. 2

meters	Altitude	feet
80		260
60		195
40		130
20		65
0		0

Fig.3

ELEVATION

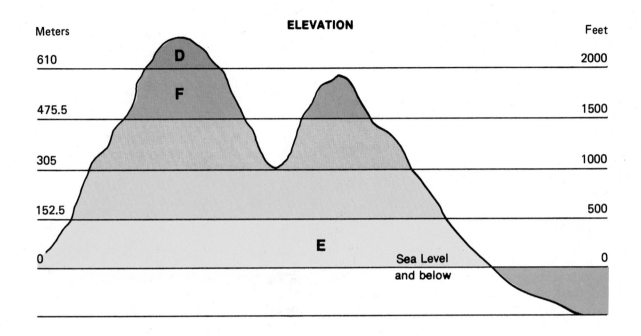

Meters		Feet
610	D	2000
475.5	F	1500
305		1000
152.5		500
0	E	0
	Sea Level and below	

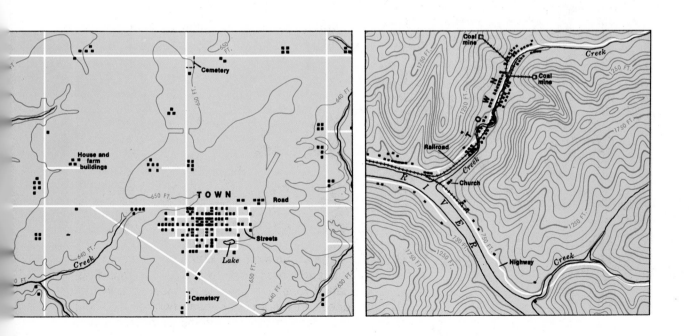

6 How Maps Show the Surface of the Earth

The earth's surface is uneven. It has four main landforms. Mountains are the highest of these landforms. Hills are lower than mountains, but have sloping sides, too.

Plains (plānz) are the earth's flatlands. *Plateaus* (pla tōz'), with flat land but steep sides, are usually found at high elevations. Plains are often closer to sea level.

How does a map maker show these different landforms? One way is by using color. On the map below, landforms shown by colors are listed in the *legend* (lej'ənd), or key. Is Las Vegas on a plain, a hill, a plateau, or a mountain? Near what landform is Butte (byoot)?

The mapmaker can draw little pictures of the landforms. Which ones do you see on this map?

The mapmaker can add color to the relief map. Color and shading together show the elevation of areas. Is Santa Fe on a plain or a plateau?

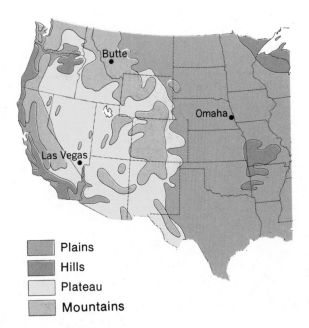

	Plains
	Hills
	Plateau
	Mountains

The mapmaker can shade in areas to show the land's high and low places. This shading is called *relief* (ri lēf'). Relief maps show differences in height. Is Kansas (written KANS. on the map) in the mountains or on the plains?

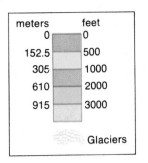

meters		feet
0		0
152.5		500
305		1000
610		2000
915		3000

Glaciers

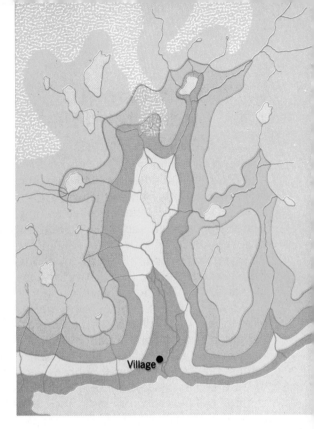

Village

A map maker can show relief with contour lines. You have already learned that contour maps show elevation. But they also tell us about the earth's natural shape. As you have read, contour means shape.

Contour lines that are close together show steep, hilly land. Contour lines that are far apart show nearly flat or gently rolling land.

The photograph below shows part of the area drawn on the contour map. Is the lake higher or lower than the village? Which contour lines show the steep mountain sides? Look at the lines that show the mountain tops. Do you think these mountain tops are pointed or fairly flat?

7 Using Maps to Understand History: Cattle Drives

American cattle drives, cowhands, and cow towns are famous all over the world. Yet few of us realize that the cattle drives lasted only a few years. They started about 1865, soon after the Civil War. By 1887, they were over.

During that period, millions of longhorn cattle were herded overland from Texas to Kansas and Missouri. The longhorns were a tough, hardy breed of cattle that had come north from Mexico. On cattle drives, the cattle grazed on the grass of the open range.

In towns such as Sedalia, Missouri, and Dodge City, Kansas, the longhorns were fattened and then loaded onto railroad cars and shipped to Chicago. From there, they were sent to growing eastern cities. Millions of immigrants, new arrivals from Europe, had increased the demand for beef.

The long "rivers" of cattle were led by hardworking cowhands. These people, some of them teenagers, stopped stampedes of nervous cattle. They rounded up strays. They outwitted cattle rustlers. They slept under the stars and ate their meals beside a chuck wagon.

The chuck wagon was the kitchen of the cattle drive. But it was also a compass. Before going to sleep, the cook pointed the wagon's hitching pole toward the North Star. The next morning, it showed the cowhands the way to go.

The map shows the four main cattle trails. Use the map scale to figure some distances. Suppose you were a cowhand driving cattle from near San Antonio, Texas, to Sedalia, Missouri, over the Sedalia Trail. About how many miles (kilometers) would you have to go? Most cattle drives covered about 10 miles (16 kilometers) a day. How many days would your trip take?

Suppose you were driving cattle from San Antonio, Texas, to Dodge City, Kansas, over the Western Trail. How many days would your trip take?

Long distances, floods, and dry runs of two and three days without water were but a few of the hardships of the trail. For a few years, however, nothing stopped the cattle drives. Ranchers made quick fortunes. Cowhands got $100 for their many weeks of trouble.

Railroads were built into the cattle country. These railroads could quickly move cattle to market. Look at the map showing the western railroads. Why would cities like Kansas City, St. Louis, and Chicago become important meat packing centers?

As farmers moved west, they fenced in their lands. They did not want the herds damaging their crops. The railroads continued to move further and further west, too. As farmers and railroads moved west, the easternmost cattle drives ended. Ranchers used the westernmost trails. Which cattle trail would be the last one used? By 1887, the days of the cattle drives had passed into history, Rails, not trails, became the key to western trade with the East.

Transcontinental Railroads in the 1880s

---- Modern state boundaries

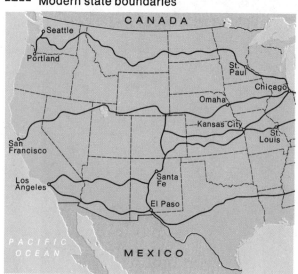

524

Cattle Trails of the West
about 1870

——— Railroads

▬▬ Trails

MONT.
TERR.

WYOMING

TERRITORY

DAKOTA

TERRITORY

NEBRASKA

MINNESOTA

WISCONSIN

IOWA

ILL.

Chicago

Cheyenne

COLORADO

TERRITORY

Ellsworth

KANSAS

Dodge City

Abilene

Newton

Sedalia

MISSOURI

NEW MEXICO

TERRITORY

GOODNIGHT-LOVING TRAIL

WESTERN TRAIL

CHISHOLM TRAIL

SEDALIA TRAIL

INDIAN

TERRITORY

ARKANSAS

T E X A S

LOUISIANA

MISS.

San
Antonio

GULF OF
MEXICO

Kilometers   390

Miles   245

WASH.

ORE.

IDAHO

MONT.

WYO.

N.D.

S.D.

MINN.

WIS.

MICH.

MICH.

VT.

ME.

N.Y.

N.H.

MASS.

R.I.
CONN.

NEV.

UTAH

COLO.

NEB.

IOWA

ILL.

IND.

OHIO

PA.

N.J.

DEL.
MD.

CALIF.

W.
VA.

VA.

KY.

KAN.

MO.

ARIZ.

N.M.

OKLA.

ARK.

TENN.

N.C.

MISS.

ALA.

GA.

S.C.

TEXAS

LA.

FLA.

Using Maps to Compare the Location of Cities

8

What if you were a settler in a new land? How would you decide where to build a town? What things would you look for in a *site* (sīt)? A site is the place where something is located. Every site has special land and water features. The sites of Boston, New York City, and Philadelphia are shown on the facing page.

The early settlers from Europe had to choose sites for their towns. They had arrived in a wilderness. Among the things the settlers looked for were the following:

- fresh water sources
- safe harbors for ships
- land that could be defended easily
- rivers for transportation routes
- fertile countryside on which to grow crops

The map on this page shows the location of three early cities: Boston, New York City, and Philadelphia. These cities are near the ocean and several rivers. Thus, they could serve as "hinges," linking the inland areas with Europe. Goods and people could pass back and forth through their ports. A port is a passageway or opening.

Boston and Philadelphia were once larger than New York. All these cities grew at different rates. This came about because of their location in relation to the rest of the country.

Look at the map below. The mountains are shown. New York City could send goods north, first up the Hudson River, and then west through the mountains. It was harder for Philadelphia to trade with inland areas of the country. Boston, too, was blocked off by mountains. Each city's growth was influenced by its location. If you lived near the western end of Lake Ontario, which of the cities would be easiest for you to travel to by road and water?

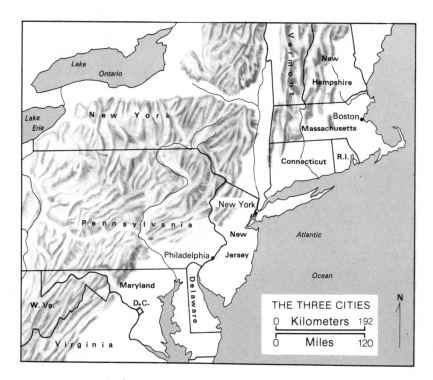

THE THREE CITIES
| 0 | Kilometers | 192 |
| 0 | Miles | 120 |

N

The Three Cities

Boston was first settled on a small *peninsula* (pə nin'sə lə). A peninsula is land surrounded by water on three sides. The site had a good source of fresh water. Its deep harbor protected ships from the open seas. Nearby islands and peninsulas kept out the Atlantic's stormy waves. Forts could be built on these places. The narrow neck of the peninsula could also easily be defended. The town was built at the far western end of Massachusetts Bay. Later this location helped link Boston to many inland communities.

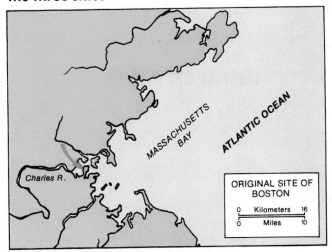

Dutch settlers bought Manhattan Island from the Delaware Indians in 1626. Today, it is the biggest and busiest port city in our country. The map shows some reasons for picking this site in the first place. Look at the land and water features. Why is New York Harbor a safe port for ships? Why did the settlers think Manhattan could be defended easily against attack?

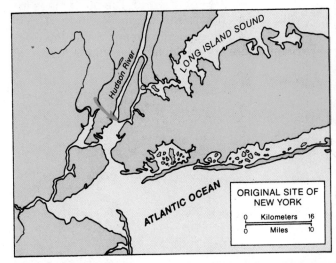

Philadelphia was founded by William Penn. He did not try to find land that could be defended easily. He believed Philadelphia would be a city of peace. He laid down three other rules for choosing a site, however. (1) The site should be on high, dry land. Such land was considered healthier than low, swampy land. (2) The surrounding countryside should be fertile. (3) The site should have deep water nearby where ships could dock. Philadelphia, unlike Boston and New York City, was not on the coast. What river gave it a port and a route to the sea?

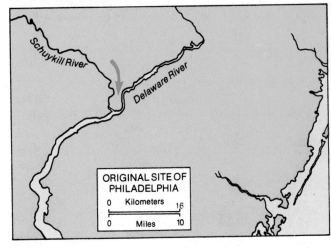

9 Using an Atlas

Use the table of contents to find the atlas section in your book. The atlas in your book is a special reference (ref'ər əns). A reference is something you use to get information. Your atlas can be a valuable aid if you know how to use it.

It is important to know what maps are in your atlas. The title of each map tells you what part of the world the map shows. One map in your atlas shows the entire world. The other maps in your atlas show parts of the Western Hemisphere. Why do you think maps of the Eastern Hemisphere are not included in your atlas?

Map A

In addition to knowing what part of the world a map shows, you need to know what kind of map it is. Maps can be grouped according to the kind of information they show. Some of the maps commonly found in atlases are political maps, physical maps, and special-purpose maps. Your atlas has examples of all three kinds of maps.

Often you want to find a city, a state, or a country on a map. The best map to use to find these places is a political map. Political maps show the location of cities and tell you what cities are capitals. They show the boundaries between political divisions such as countries, states, counties, and provinces. Some political maps use different colors to make it easier to tell different countries, states, or other political divisions apart.

Map A on this page is a political map. It shows part of one of your atlas maps. Give the title of the map and its page number. What political divisions are shown on this map? Which city, Buenos Aires or La Plata, is the capital of Argentina?

Map B on the next page is a physical map of the same area shown in **Map A. Map B** also shows just part of one of the maps in your atlas. What is the title of the atlas map and on what page is it found? What do the different colors on **Map B** represent?

Physical maps help you to picture what the earth's surface looks like. Colors and shading often are used, as they are on **Map B,** to show landforms. Physical maps also show and label many other natural features such as mountains, rivers, lakes, deserts, and glaciers. How high is Mount Aconcagua?

Now compare **Map A** and **Map B.** You will see that **Map A,** which is a political map, shows many physical features. **Map B,** which is a physical map, includes many political features. Al-

528

Map B

What kinds of climate are found within the area of **Map C?** What kind of climate do the pampas of Argentina have? What is the climate just west of the Andes near the Tropic of Capricorn?

Now use your atlas to answer these questions. What map or maps would you use to name the countries of North America? What states border Florida? What kind of climate does most of Canada have?

All the maps in the atlas in your book show latitude and longitude. Use your atlas to answer these questions about latitude and longitude. Give the approximate latitude and longitude of Sucre, Bolivia. What city in South America is situated at about the same longitude as Miami, Florida? Give the longitude of these cities.

Map C

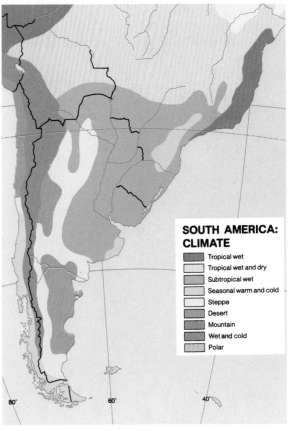

SOUTH AMERICA: CLIMATE

- Tropical wet
- Tropical wet and dry
- Subtropical wet
- Seasonal warm and cold
- Steppe
- Desert
- Mountain
- Wet and cold
- Polar

most all political maps show some physical features, and almost all physical maps show some political features. Some maps showing both political and physical features are called physical-political maps.

Special-purpose maps include road maps, rainfall maps, population maps, weather maps, climate maps, and vegetation maps. **Map C** on this page shows part of one of the special-purpose maps in your atlas. Find the map in your atlas.

Map C shows the same area as **Map A** and **Map B.** Notice that international boundaries are shown on **Map C,** but that the countries are not labeled. However, you can refer to **Map A** or **Map B** to find the names of the countries or parts of countries shown on **Map C.**

REFERENCE
SECTION

Physical Features of the United States

Reread pages 4 through 15. Then refer to the map on pages 6–7 to complete the exercise that follows. Number a paper from **1** through **20**. After each number, write the name of the feature shown on the map below.

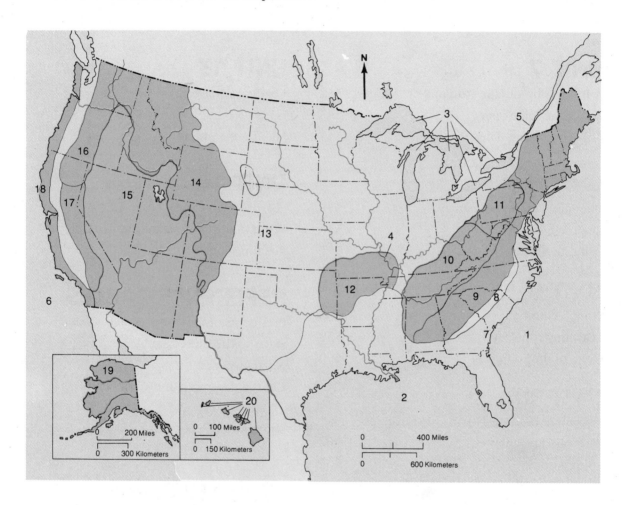

Reviewing the Text

Reread pages 4–15. Then number a paper from **1** through **13**. After each number, write the word or words in parentheses that correctly complete each statement.

1. (Climate, weather) is the (climate, weather) that an area has over a long period of time.

2. The amount of precipitation tells you how (hot or cold, wet or dry) an area is.

3. The length of the seasons (is, is not) important in describing the climate of a region.

4. Parts of the earth near the equator are in the (low, high) latitudes.

5. Lines of latitude run (north and south, east and west).

6. Places in the (low, high) latitudes generally have a warmer climate than places in the (low, high) latitudes.

7. Most of the United States is in the (low, middle, high) latitudes.

8. Ocean currents (do, do not) influence climate.

9. In places where the winter is long, the growing season is (shorter, longer) than it is in places where the winter is short.

10. In the United States, the region west of the Mississippi River receives (less, more) precipitation than the region east of the Mississippi.

11. The United States can grow (only a few, many different) crops because it has (only a few, many different) kinds of climates.

12. Natural resources are things that are (made by people, found in nature).

13. The United States is (poor, rich) in natural resources.

Reading a Graph

To follow page 21

Refer to the graph below to answer the questions that follow. Number a paper from 1 through **8**. After each number, write the answer to the question.

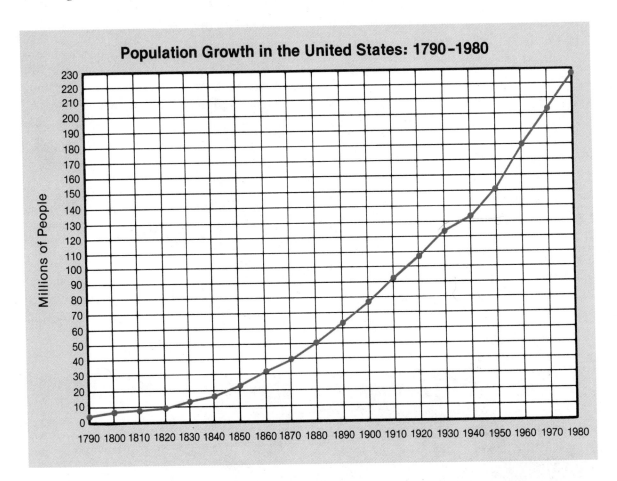

Population Growth in the United States: 1790–1980

Millions of People

1790 1800 1810 1820 1830 1840 1850 1860 1870 1880 1890 1900 1910 1920 1930 1940 1950 1960 1970 1980

1. What kind of graph—circle, bar, or line—is the graph above?

2. What does the graph show? How many years does the graph cover?

3. About how many people lived in the United States in 1790? In 1980?

4. About how many times more people lived in the United States in 1870 than in 1790?

5. What happened to the population between 1870 and 1880?

6. During which ten-year period—1930 to 1940 or 1940 to 1950—was there a greater increase in population?

7. During what ten-year period was the population half of what it was in 1980?

8. About how much did the population increase between 1950 and 1980?

Can You Match These?

Each word or phrase below goes with one of the groups of early American people listed in the box. Number a paper from 1 through 24. After each number, write the name of the group that goes with the word or phrase.

Pacific Northwest Indians	Eastern Woodlands Indians	Maya
Southwest Indians	Eskimos	Aztecs
Plains Indians	Polynesians	Incas

1. igloos

2. Hawaii

3. terraces

4. wigwams

5. Cuzco

6. potlatches

7. caribou

8. good road system

9. longhouses

10. Tenochtitlán

11. buffalo

12. totem poles

13. tepees

14. written language

15. cliff dwellings

16. irrigation

17. cloth of pounded bark

18. Andes Mountains

19. calendar

20. "slash-and-burn" farming

21. canoes of tree trunks

22. Alaska

23. Kingdom of the Sun

24. adobe

ENRICHMENT

Using a Route Map

To follow page 48

The map below shows the route Columbus took through the Caribbean Sea on his first voyage to the New World in 1492 and 1493. Refer to the map to answer the questions that follow. Number a paper from 1 through 9. After each number, write the answer to the question.

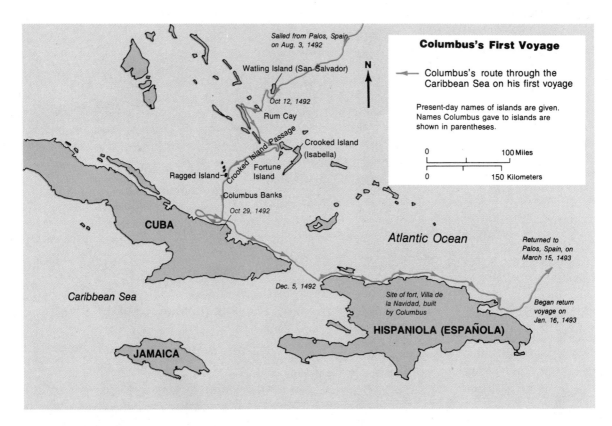

1. How is Columbus' route shown on the map? How do you know the direction in which he traveled?

2. What name did Columbus give to the first island on which he landed?

3. Did Columbus visit Crooked Island before or after he visited Rum Cay?

4. When did Columbus arrive on the coast of Cuba?

5. About how far did Columbus sail to go from Cuba to Hispaniola?

6. In what general direction did Columbus sail as he traveled along the coast of Hispaniola?

7. How many days did Columbus' first voyage last? (Count from the day he left Palos to the day he returned.)

8. Which part of Columbus' voyage took longer, the outward trip or the return trip?

9. On what island did Columbus build a fort?

536

A biography is the story of a person's life. The short biography below tells about John Cabot, whom you have read about in this unit. When you have finished reading the biography, number a paper from 1 through 8. After each number, write the word or words in parentheses that correctly complete each statement.

John Cabot

John Cabot's Italian name was Giovanni Caboto. He was born in Genoa, Italy, probably in 1451. Later his family moved to Venice, where Cabot became a merchant. On one of his trading voyages, he visited Mecca, in what is now Saudi Arabia. Mecca was a great trade center where products from Europe and Asia were bought and sold. But the overland journey to obtain spices and other goods from the East was long and slow. Like Columbus, Cabot believed that the earth was a globe and that Asia could be more easily reached by sailing west across the Atlantic Ocean.

Cabot tried to get Spain or Portugal to back an ocean voyage to Cathay (China). But Spain had already sent Columbus, and Portugal had plans for a voyage to Asia around the southern tip of Africa. Cabot then went to England. There he obtained the backing of a group of merchants and of the English king, Henry VII. The merchants provided Cabot with a ship. King Henry gave him a royal charter, granting him the right to claim for England any new lands that he found.

Cabot sailed from Bristol late in May, 1497 on a small ship named the *Matthew*. On June 24, he landed somewhere on the coast of North America—probably Newfoundland or Cape Breton Island, in what is now Canada. Cabot was sure he had reached the northeast coast of Asia, and he sailed back to England to report his find.

Encouraged by the news, Henry VII gave Cabot a small fleet and sent him on another voyage in 1498. It is believed that Cabot first sailed back to Newfoundland and then went south as far as the Chesapeake Bay before storms wrecked most of his ships. For many years it was believed that Cabot survived this voyage and died in England the following year. But because of more recent evidence, historians now believe that Cabot perished when his ship went down in a storm.

1. John Cabot was an (Italian, Englishman).

2. Cabot was probably born in (1451, 1497)

3. Cabot's voyages to North America were made for (England, Spain).

4. Cabot thought he could easily reach Asia by sailing (east, west).

5. Cabot landed on the coast of North America in (1451, 1497).

6. Cabot probably landed in what is now (Chesapeake Bay, Canada).

7. Cabot believed he had reached (Mecca, Asia).

8. Cabot made (two, three) voyages to North America.

ENRICHMENT

A chart is a useful way to show information. On a piece of paper, copy the chart that has been started for you below and complete it. You may need to reread pages 55 through 64. When you have completed the chart, number a paper from 1 through 6. After the numbers, write the answers to the questions that follow.

Early European Settlements in North America				
Name of Settlement	Country Making Settlement	Date of Settlement	Present-day State or Country	Leader (if any)
St. Augustine	Spain	1565	Florida	
San Diego				
Quebec				
Montreal				
New Amsterdam				
Fort Christina				
Roanoke Island				
Jamestown				
Plymouth				

1. What is the name of the oldest settlement in North America? Where is it?

2. In what year was Roanoke Island settled? By what country?

3. What settlement made by Sweden is listed on the chart? With what other early settlement was its leader associated?

4. What leader was responsible for the founding of two early French settlements? In what country are they?

5. What early Dutch settlement is included on the chart? When was it founded?

6. Was Jamestown founded before or after Plymouth? How many years before or after?

Number a paper from **1** through **15**. After each number, write the letter of the description in **Column II** that goes with the name in **Column I**.

Column I

1. Samuel Adams

2. Cecil Calvert

3. Thomas Gage

4. Patrick Henry

5. Anne Hutchinson

6. Thomas Jefferson

7. James Oglethorpe

8. Thomas Paine

9. William Penn

10. Paul Revere

11. Peter Stuyvesant

12. George Washington

13. Roger Williams

14. John Winthrop

15. James Wolfe

Column II

a. English Catholic who started the colony of Maryland

b. Patriot who warned the colonists of the British march to Lexington and Concord

c. Colonist who said, "Give me liberty or give me death!"

d. British general who captured Quebec in the French and Indian War

e. Puritan minister who founded the settlement of Providence

f. English Quaker who received a charter to the lands west of the Delaware River

g. Puritan leader who helped found Boston

h. Dutch governor who surrendered New Amsterdam to the English

i. Colonist who left Massachusetts Bay to start the settlement of Portsmouth

j. Commander of the American forces during the Revolution

k. Main author of the Declaration of Independence

l. Author of *Common Sense*, which urged colonists to cut their ties with Britain

m. A Boston leader of the Sons of Liberty who set up committees of correspondence

n. British general who sent troops to Lexington and Concord

o. Founder of colony for debtors in Georgia

ENRICHMENT

The events listed below are not in the order in which they happened. Write the events in the correct order. After you have finished, copy and complete the time line that has been started for you. Remember that there may be more than one event for the same date.

1. First Continental Congress meets
2. Boston Massacre takes place
3. British Parliament passes the Stamp Act
4. British Parliament passes the Townshend Acts
5. French and Indian War ends
6. Boston Tea Party takes place
7. Continental Congress adopts the Declaration of Independence
8. British Parliament passes the Tea Act
9. Battles of Lexington and Concord occur
10. British Parliament passes the Sugar Act
11. Second Continental Congress meets
12. Battle of Bunker Hill takes place

1763 1764 1765 1767 1770 1773 1774 1775 1776

This illustration shows British troops marching through the town of Concord, Massachusetts.

Read the paragraphs below. Then number a paper from **1** through **6**. After the numbers, write the answers to the questions that follow.

Patrick Henry (1736–1799) was a Virginian who was a famous patriot as well as a famous orator (ôr′ə tər). An orator is a skilled public speaker. Patrick Henry often spoke in the cause of freedom and liberty.

After becoming a lawyer, Henry was elected to the Virginia House of Burgesses in 1764. He soon became a leader in the fight against the British government. As revolutionary fever grew, the colonial governor of Virginia twice dissolved the House of Burgesses or delayed its meeting. The members of this assembly met in 1774 at the first Virginia convention and again in 1775 at the second Virginia convention. It was at the second convention, held at St. John's Church in Richmond, that Patrick Henry delivered his famous "Give Me Liberty" speech on March 23, 1775. The last part of the speech is given below.

Patrick Henry's "Give Me Liberty" Speech

Gentlemen may cry peace, peace. But there is no peace. The war is actually begun! The next gale that sweeps from the north will bring to our ears the clash of resounding arms! Our brethren [brothers] are already in the field! Why stand we here idle? What is it that gentlemen wish? What would they have? Is life so dear, or peace so sweet, as to be purchased at the price of chains and slavery? Forbid it. Almighty God! I know not what course others may take; but as for me, give me liberty or give me death!

1. When was Patrick Henry born? When did he die? What did he do after becoming a lawyer?

2. What is an orator?

3. When was Patrick Henry's "Give Me Liberty" speech delivered?

4. To what group of people did Henry deliver his famous speech? Where was it delivered?

5. Henry predicted that "the next gale that sweeps from the north will bring to our ears the clash of resounding arms." In less than a month after Henry's speech, important battles did take place in a northern colony. What were these battles?

6. How do you think Patrick Henry's speech affected his listeners?

ENRICHMENT

Reading a Battle Map

To follow page 96

The map below will help you better understand the Battle of Yorktown. Refer to the map as you reread pages 94–95. Then number a paper from **1** through **8**. After the numbers, write the answers to the questions that follow.

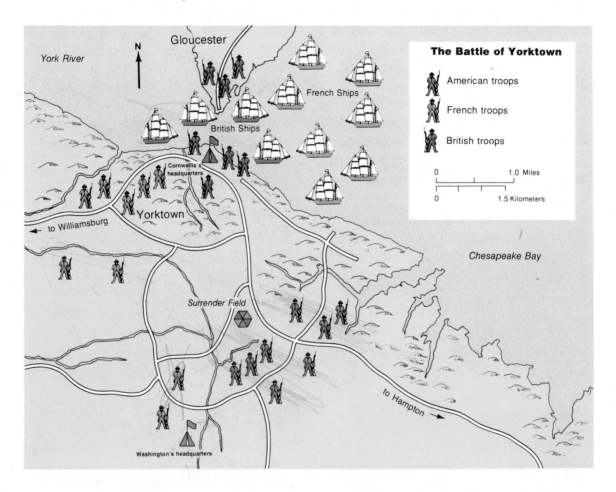

1. In what state is Yorktown?
2. Who led the British forces at the Battle of Yorktown? Who led the American forces?
3. Why were the British unable to escape by land?
4. In what direction from Yorktown were the French troops? Where were the American troops?
5. What bodies of water lie to the north of Yorktown?
6. Why were the British unable to escape by boat?
7. Who won the Battle of Yorktown?
8. Describe where the surrender took place.

Carefully read each statement below. Then number a paper from **1** through **10**. If the statement is true, write **True** after the number. If it is false, write **False** after it. Then give the reason for each answer in a complete sentence.

This money used by the colonies looks different from the money we use today.

1. The first plan of government in the United States was the Declaration of Independence.

2. The Declaration of Independence was adopted after the Articles of Confederation became the law of the land.

3. Under the Articles of Confederation, each state had a voice in Congress.

4. Under the Articles of Confederation, Congress had no power to tax the states.

5. America's debt after the Revolutionary War hurt American trade and business with other countries.

6. Much of the money printed by Congress during the Revolution was worthless after the war.

7. Trade among the states went smoothly after the war.

8. Shays' Rebellion was a revolt of unpaid war veterans.

9. George Washington felt that the Articles of Confederation were not working well.

10. Congress called a meeting to try to solve the problems of the Articles of Confederation.

ENRICHMENT

A flow chart is a special kind of chart that shows the steps in a process. Study the flow chart below, then number a paper from **1** through **6**. After the numbers, write the answers to the questions that follow.

How a Bill Becomes a Law

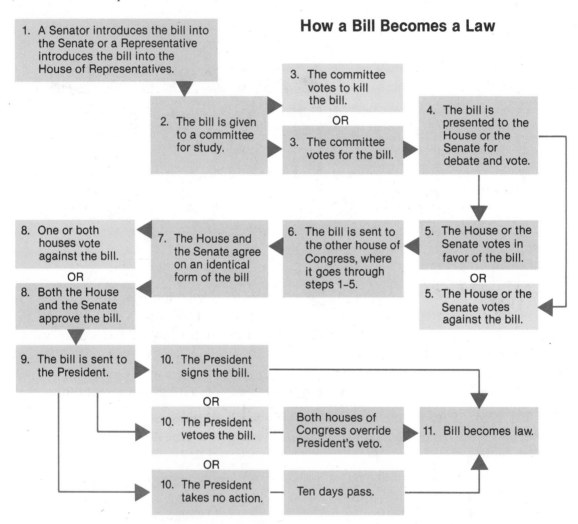

1. What does this chart show?
2. Where can a bill be introduced and by whom?
3. What happens to a bill if it is approved by the house in which it originated? What happens if that house votes against it?
4. What happens to a bill after it is approved by both the House and the Senate?
5. What three actions can the President take on a bill?
6. Can a bill become a law if the President takes no action on it? Explain.

Reviewing the Text

Number a paper from **1** through **20**. After each number, write the word or words that belong in the blank. Choose the words from the list that appears in the box below. You may wish to reread pages 113–118.

Cabinet	Virginia	Washington, D.C.	Constitutional Convention
Congress	Henry Knox	Martha Custis	
Mount Vernon	Capitol	Potomac River	Thomas Jefferson
Philadelphia	Pierre L'Enfant	Benjamin Banneker	Maryland
Alexander Hamilton	French and Indian War	Revolutionary War	President
New York City			

George Washington was born in ___1___ in 1732. After inheriting the plantation that was known as ___2___, he married ___3___. Washington fought in both the ___4___ and and the ___5___. Later he served as president of the ___6___. He was then elected the first ___7___ of the United States.

Soon after Washington became President, it became clear that he would need help in his job. ___8___ therefore formed three executive departments. One was the State Department. Washington named ___9___ as the first Secretary of State. The second department set up was the Department of the Treasury. ___10___ served as the first Secretary of the Treasury. The Department of War was established to take care of the nation's defense. The first Secretary of War was ___11___. Other executive offices also were created. Their officers came to be known as the President's ___12___.

When Washington took office, the temporary capital of the United States was ___13___. The country needed a permanent capital and, in 1790, George Washington chose a site on the ___14___. Land for the new capital city was given by the states of Virginia and ___15___. The new city's designer was a Frenchman named ___16___. When he left the job in 1791, work on the capital continued under the direction of ___17___. The building at the center of the capital is the ___18___, the place where Congress meets. The streets spread out from this building like the spokes of a wheel. In 1800, the government moved from the temporary capital of ___19___ to its permanent home—now known as ___20___.

ENRICHMENT

Number a paper from 1 through 16. After each number, write the name of the person that completes each of the following statements. Choose the name from the list that appears in the box below. You will need to use some names more than once.

Daniel Boone	Meriwether Lewis	Oliver Hazard Perry
Tecumseh	William Clark	Francis Scott Key
William Henry Harrison	Charbonneau	Andrew Jackson
Thomas Jefferson	Sacajawea	
Napoleon	James Madison	

1. _____asked Congress to declare war against Great Britain in 1812.

2. _____sold the Louisiana Territory to the United States for 15 million dollars in 1803.

3. _____wrote the poem that later became our national anthem.

4. _____led settlers west through the Cumberland Gap in 1775.

5. _____was a Shoshone Indian who served as a guide for the Lewis and Clark expedition.

6. _____helped to found the University of Virginia, the nation's first state university.

7. _____fled from the White House when the British captured Washington, D.C., in 1814.

8. _____defeated the British fleet in a battle on Lake Erie in 1813.

9. _____was defeated by United States troops at Tippecanoe Creek, Indiana, in 1811.

10. _____bought the Louisiana Territory for the United States.

11. _____successfully defended the city of New Orleans against the British in 1815.

12. _____was a French-Canadian fur trader who acted as a guide for Lewis and Clark.

13. _____was leader of the American forces that defeated the Indians at Tippecanoe Creek, Indiana.

14. _____was the American President who sent an expedition to explore the Louisiana Territory.

15. _____was a former army officer chosen as one of the leaders of the expedition to explore the Louisiana Territory.

16. _____served as President Jefferson's secretary and later was chosen as one of the leaders sent to explore the Louisiana Territory.

The map below shows some of the early trails to the west used by settlers during the 1840s to the 1860s. Study the map and the map key to answer the questions that follow. Number a paper from **1** through **8**. After each number, write the answer to the question.

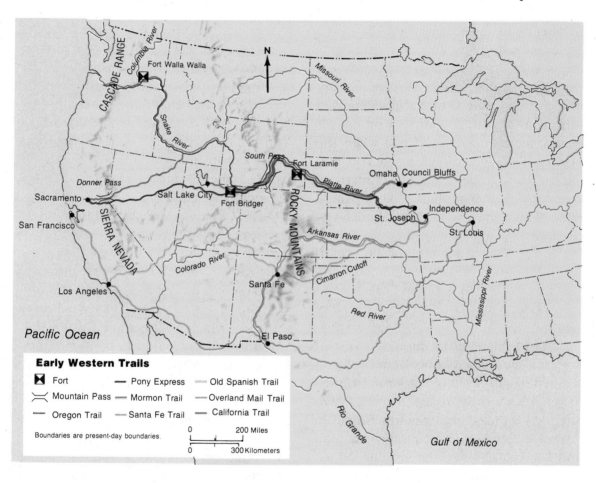

Early Western Trails

- Fort
- Mountain Pass
- Oregon Trail
- Pony Express
- Mormon Trail
- Santa Fe Trail
- Old Spanish Trail
- Overland Mail Trail
- California Trail

Boundaries are present-day boundaries.

0   200 Miles

0   300 Kilometers

1. What trail started at St. Louis?
2. What trail linked St. Joseph with Sacramento?
3. Name the three forts located along the Oregon Trail.
4. What trail connected the Oregon Trail with Sacramento? What mountains did this trail cross? Through what pass did it go?

5. Name three trails that used the South Pass through the Rocky Mountains.
6. What short cut could travelers use going from Independence to Santa Fe?
7. About how far was it between Santa Fe and El Paso by the Overland Mail Trail?
8. What river did the Oregon Trail follow from Fort Walla Walla to its western end?

ENRICHMENT

Read the short biography below. Then number a paper from 1 through 6. After the numbers, write the answers to the questions that follow.

Elizabeth Cady Stanton

Elizabeth Cady Stanton (1815–1902) was a leader in the early movement to gain rights for women in the United States. As the daughter of a judge, she became aware early in life of the many laws that discriminated (dis crim'ə'na'tid) against women, or treated them unfairly. In 1840, when she married Henry Stanton, she insisted on leaving the word "obey" out of her marriage ceremony. The Stantons settled in Seneca Falls, New York, where they raised seven children.

Elizabeth Stanton and her husband worked for the abolition of slavery. Elizabeth Stanton also worked to get New York State to pass a law giving married women property rights.

In 1848, Elizabeth Stanton was one of several women who called the first women's rights convention in the United States. Several hundred women and men attended the meeting, which was held in Seneca Falls in July 1848. Elizabeth Stanton and Lucretia Mott led the meeting. When her turn to speak came, Mrs. Stanton called for several reforms. She wanted married women to have the right to own and sell property. She also wanted women to have the right to the custody, or the care and keeping, of their children. But her most daring proposal called for women's suffrage (suf' rij). Suffrage is the right to vote. After much debate, the convention voted to support Elizabeth Stanton's proposals. Today, women have all these rights.

Below is part of Elizabeth Cady Stanton's Seneca Falls speech:

> Resolved, That all laws which prevent woman from occupying such a station in society as her conscience shall dictate, or which place her in a position inferior to that of man, are contrary to the great precept [laws] of nature, and therefore, of no force of authority.

For the next 40 years, Elizabeth Cady Stanton continued to work for equality for women. She lectured, wrote, and edited the feminist magazine *The Revolution*.

1. Who was Elizabeth Cady Stanton? When was she born? In what year did she marry Henry Stanton?

2. What two movements did Elizabeth Stanton work for?

3. Where was the first women's rights convention in the United States held? Who were the leaders of the meeting?

4. Name two of the rights for women that Elizabeth Stanton called for at the Seneca Falls meeting.

5. Explain in your own words what Elizabeth Stanton meant in the part of her speech quoted above.

6. Do you think you would like to have known Elizabeth Stanton? Explain.

Number a paper from **1** through **14**. After each number, write the word or words in parentheses that correctly complete each statement.

1. In the middle 1800s, the United States was deeply divided over the issue of (war, slavery).

2. The United States (was, was not) the only nation that practiced slavery in the 1800s.

3. One of the most famous slave rebellions was led by (Nat Turner, Harriet Tubman) in Virginia in 1831.

4. The Underground Railroad worked to help (slaves travel to freedom, owners get back their runaway slaves).

5. By 1819, Mississippi and (Louisiana, Missouri) had entered the Union as slave states.

6. In 1820, the number of free states (equaled, did not equal) the number of slave states.

7. The Missouri Compromise allowed Missouri to enter the Union as a (free, slave) state.

8. During the 1830s, William Lloyd Garrison began to publish a paper called the (*Abolitionist, Liberator*).

9. Isabella Baumfree was a freed slave who became famous under the name (Harriet Tubman, Sojourner Truth).

10. (Frederick Douglass, Henry Clay) was known as "the Great Compromiser."

11. In 1850, Congress decided to (allow, abolish) the slave trade in Washington, D.C.

12. Under the Fugitive Slave Law, the government helped to (return, free) runaway slaves.

13. Most Southerners (approved, disapproved) of *Uncle Tom's Cabin.*

14. The (North, South) was in favor of protective tariffs.

Frederick Douglass was the subject of a popular song in the 1850s.

Illustrations such as photographs or drawings are often used to provide additional information about what we read. Captions are phrases or sentences that explain illustrations.

Reread the section "Death of Abraham Lincoln" on page 173 and study the illustration and caption below. Then number a paper from 1 through 7. After the numbers, write the answers to the questions that follow.

President Lincoln was assassinated in his private box at Ford's Theater, in Washington, D.C., on April 14. An *assassination* (ə sas′ə nā′shən) is the murder of an important person, especially for political reasons.

1. Is the illustration above a photograph or a drawing?

2. Explain in your own words what the illustration shows.

3. Where and when did the event illustrated take place?

4. Who is the man holding the gun in the illustration? At whom is the gun pointed?

5. Do you think this illustration shows exactly how the President was killed? Explain.

6. What kind of illustration would show exactly what happened?

7. If there were no caption, would you be able to tell whether the illustration shows a present-day scene or something in the past? Explain.

Using a Time Line

To follow **page 184**

The events listed below are not in the order in which they happened. Write the events in the correct order. After you have finished, copy and complete the time line that has been started for you. Remember that there may be more than one event for the same date.

Congress passes the Homestead Act

Hawaii becomes a territory of the United States

The Civil War ends

Gold discovered at Pikes Peak

The United States buys Alaska

The Comstock Lode discovered in Nevada

The Battle of Little Bighorn fought

Queen Liliuokalani comes to the throne in Hawaii

The first transcontinental railroad completed

| 1859 | 1862 | 1865 | 1867 | 1869 | 1876 | 1891 | 1900 |

These men paused in their search for gold in order to have their picture taken.

551

ENRICHMENT

A Biography of Jane Addams

Read the short biography below, then number a paper from **1** through **7**. After each number, write the letter of the answer that correctly completes each statement.

Jane Addams

Jane Addams (1860–1935) was the founder of Hull House, one of America's first settlement houses. She also crusaded for world peace and for the right of women to vote.

Jane Addams was born in Cedarville, Illinois, on September 6, 1860. Her family was a large and wealthy one with a tradition of public service. Jane wanted to be a doctor, but she was not well enough for the hard study of medical school. To improve her health, her family sent her to Europe.

While traveling, Jane wondered what she could do to help people. Remembering the Chicago slums she had seen as a child, she thought of starting a settlement house to provide education and recreation for the poor. Jane traveled to London to study the famous English settlement house, Toynbee Hall. When she returned to Chicago in 1889, Jane and her friend Ellen Gates Starr rented an old house that had once belonged to the Hull family. This became Hull House.

Between 1870 and 1900 millions of immigrants came to the United States. Many found life very hard in the new country. Jane Addams welcomed them warmly to Hull House. Some came to play games. Some listened to poetry readings or took classes in painting, music, or acting. Others studied English and citizenship. A day nursery cared for children whose mothers worked. Hull House became a center of the community.

Shortly after opening Hull House, Jane Addams began working for laws that would end child labor, so that children could go to school. She was angry because women could not vote, so she campaigned for woman suffrage. Jane Addams' fame spread, and when her book *Twenty Years at Hull House* was published in 1910, she won nationwide recognition for her work.

1. Hull House was a_____.
   a. medical school
   b. voting place
   c. settlement house

2. Hull House is in_____.
   a. Cedarville, Illinois
   b. Chicago, Illinois
   c. London, England

3. _____helped Jane Addams in founding Hull House.
   a. Susan B. Anthony
   b. Arnold Toynbee
   c. Ellen Gates Starr

4. Hull House was founded in_____.
   a. 1860 b. 1870 c. 1889

5. Hull House did *not* provide_____.
   a. classes in English
   b. rooms for immigrants
   c. a day nursery for children

6. Jane Addams' book, _____, won her nationwide fame.
   a. *Hull House*
   b. *My Life at Hull House*
   c. *Twenty Years at Hull House*

7. Jane Addams died in_____.
   a. 1860 b. 1889 c. 1935

A dictionary is an alphabetical list of words and their meanings. It provides the spelling, pronunciation, part of speech, and meaning for each word given. Sometimes a dictionary tells where a word comes from.

Refer to the sample dictionary entry below to answer the questions that follow. Number a paper from 1 through 8. After each number, write the correct answer.

> **muck • rake** (muk′rāk′) *v.* To search for and expose corruption, scandal, or the like, especially in politics. *n.* a rake used for gathering and spreading muck. From *muckraker,* used in 1906 by Theodore Roosevelt in reference to the "man with a Muck-rake" in John Bunyan's *Pilgrim's Progress.*

1. The word muckrake has
   a. one syllable
   b. two syllables
   c. three syllables

2. The correct pronunciation of muckrake is
   a. muk rāk′
   b. muk′rāk′
   c. muk′rak′

3. The word muckrake is
   a. only a verb
   b. only a noun
   c. both a verb and a noun

4. How many meanings are given for muckrake?
   a. one
   b. two
   c. three

5. The word muckrake is related to the word muckraker. Who first used the term muckraker? When was it used?

6. Muckrake is a compound word, that is, it is made up of two words written together. What two words make up muckrake? How could you find out more about the meaning of muckrake?

7. The word muck probably means
   a. mud and filth
   b. a tool
   c. a search

8. A person likely to be a muckraker would be a
   a. doctor
   b. pilot
   c. reporter

ENRICHMENT

Can You Match These?

To follow page 213

Number a paper from **1** through **18**. After each number, write the letter of the name in **Column II** that goes with the item in **Column I**. Some names are used more than once.

Column I	Column II
1. Rough Riders	a. Henry Ford
2. steel mills	b. Thomas Edison
3. Nineteenth Amendment	c. Charles A. Lindbergh
4. Standard Oil	d. John F. Kennedy
5. radio	e. Jane Addams
6. Hull House	f. John D. Rockefeller
7. telephone	g. Orville and Wilbur Wright
8. Model T	h. Gugliemo Marconi
9. Peace Corps	i. Theodore Roosevelt
10. phonograph	j. Walter Reed
11. League of Nations	k. Alexander Graham Bell
12. yellow fever	l. Franklin D. Roosevelt
13. Panama Canal	m. Susan B. Anthony
14. Kitty Hawk	n. Andrew Carnegie
15. electric light bulb	o. Woodrow Wilson
16. New Deal	
17. *Spirit of St. Louis*	
18. motion pictures	

The Saint Lawrence Seaway

The map below shows the Saint Lawrence Seaway. The diagram shows how a lock works. Study the map and diagram to answer the questions that follow. Number a paper from 1 through 8. After each number, write the answer to the question.

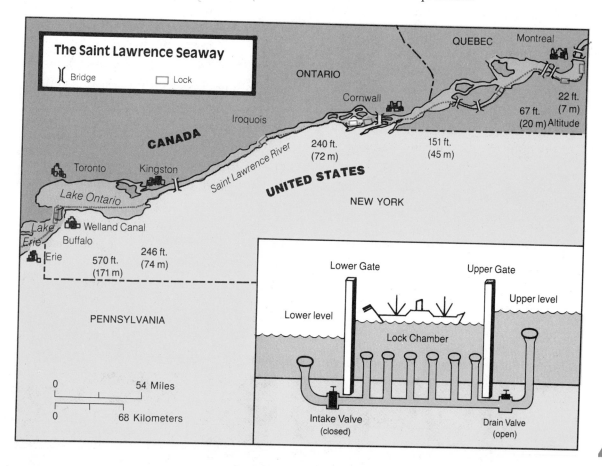

1. What two countries are served by the Saint Lawrence Seaway?

2. What body of water shown on the map is at the westernmost end of the Seaway?

3. About how far would a ship travel along the Seaway going from Kingston to Cornwall?

4. How many locks are shown on the map? How many bridges are shown?

5. Is the Seaway higher at its western end or at its eastern end?

6. What is the difference in altitude between the eastern and western ends of the part of the Seaway shown above?

7. Does the diagram show the water level in the lock chamber being raised or lowered?

8. Is the ship in the diagram traveling to the right or to the left?

ENRICHMENT

555

Reviewing the Text

Number a paper from 1 through 14. After each number, write the word or words in parentheses that correctly complete each statement.

1. Connecticut is one of the (New England, Middle Atlantic) states.

2. The (Piedmont, Appalachian Highland) lies between the Atlantic Coastal Plain and the (Piedmont, Appalachian Highland).

3. (Waterways, Railroads) have always been the cheapest means of transportation in the United States.

4. The (Saint Lawrence Seaway, Erie Canal) was built to connect the Great Lakes with the Hudson River.

5. (Peter Cooper, Robert Fulton) introduced the locomotive to the United States.

6. The Nineteenth Amendment gave (blacks, women) the right to vote.

7. (Farming, Manufacturing) is the leading industry of New England.

8. One of the leading states in quarrying stone is (New Jersey, Vermont).

9. Fishing close to the coast is called (inshore, deep-sea) fishing.

10. The largest city in New England is (New York, Boston).

11. (Anthracite, Bituminous) coal is scarcer and more expensive than other kinds of coal.

12. (Steel, Iron) is made from (steel, iron).

13. The Declaration of Independence was signed in (Philadelphia, New York).

14. One of the great steelmaking centers of the United States is the city of (Harrisburg, Pittsburgh).

Quarrying stone and manufacturing steel are two important industries in the United States.

Using an Index

An index is a list of subjects discussed in a book, showing the page or pages where each subject is found. An index appears at the back of a book. Each subject listed in an index is called an entry. Main entries are general subjects. They are printed in heavy, or **boldface**, type. Subentries are specific topics under general subjects. They are indented and printed in lightface type. Main entries are listed in alphabetical order. Subentries are listed in alphabetical order under main entries. The number or numbers following an entry tell the page or pages on which information on that subject can be found. Sometimes an index gives information about illustrations. This information is often printed in slanted, or *italic*, type. Study the sample entries from an index page shown to the right. This sample will help you understand how an index is useful in finding information readily and easily.

Use the index in your book to answer the questions that follow. Number a paper from 1 through 6. After each number, write the answer to the question.

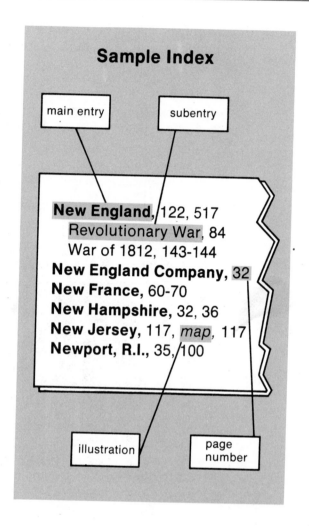

Sample Index

main entry

subentry

New England, 122, 517
   Revolutionary War, 84
   War of 1812, 143-144
New England Company, 32
New France, 60-70
New Hampshire, 32, 36
New Jersey, 117, *map,* 117
Newport, R.I., 35, 100

illustration

page number

1. You can find the index in your book by referring to the table of contents. On what page does the index in your book begin?

2. On what pages is there general information about the Middle Atlantic states?

3. What subentries are listed under the main entry *Northeastern states?*

4. Where would you look if you wanted to find information about New York City? Philadelphia?

5. Is there a main entry for *Manufacturing in New England?* Is there a subentry for this topic? On what pages is there information on this subject?

6. Suppose you wanted to find information on the geography of the Northeastern states. Where would you look? Is there information in your book on the geography of the Northeastern states? If so, on what page or pages?

ENRICHMENT

Using a Graph

Study the graph from page 274 of your book that appears below. Then number a paper from **1** through **8**. After the numbers, write the answers to the questions that follow.

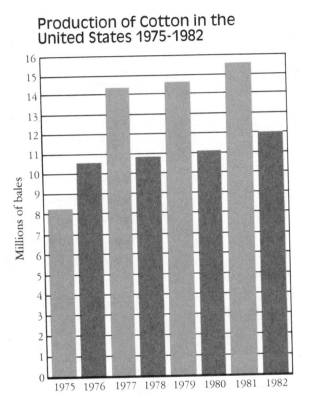

Production of Cotton in the United States 1975-1982

Millions of bales

1975 1976 1977 1978 1979 1980 1981 1982

1. What kind of graph—circle, line, or bar—is the graph above?

2. What does this graph show?

3. In which of the years shown was the most cotton produced in the United States? How many bales were produced in this year?

4. In what two years shown was cotton production most nearly the same?

5. How many more bales of cotton were produced in 1982 than in 1975?

6. In which of the years shown were the fewest bales of cotton produced? How many bales were produced in this year?

7. How many more bales of cotton were produced in the year of greatest production than were produced in the year of least production?

8. Look on page 273 to find out how much a bale of cotton weighs. If 2,000 pounds equals one ton, how many tons of cotton were produced in 1982?

Learning from Maps

To follow page 277

Study the map below to answer the questions that follow. Number a paper from
1 through 7. After each number, write the answer to the question.

**Products of the
Southeastern States**

1. What information does the map above
   provide?

2. The map uses different symbols to
   show products that are important
   throughout the Southeastern states.
   Each symbol is identified at some point
   on the map. What symbol is used to
   show furniture? What product do logs
   represent?

3. In what four states is oil an important
   product?

4. If you study the map, you will see that
   the production of textiles seems to be
   related to a certain natural feature.
   Explain.

5. In what states is iron ore an important
   product?

6. Name five products that are important
   in both North Carolina and South
   Carolina.

7. Does Florida produce more manufactured goods or more farm products?

ENRICHMENT

Listed below are some of the important cities of the Southeast. Number a paper from 1 through 12. After each number, write the name of the state in which the city is located. Then write the letter of the phrase that describes the city.

1. Birmingham

2. Charlotte

3. Baltimore

4. Norfolk

5. Jackson

6. Annapolis

7. Charleston

8. Louisville

9. Memphis

10. Mobile

11. High Point

12. Miami

a. World's largest market for cotton and hardwood

b. Headquarters for many oil companies

c. Site of largest naval base in the United States

d. Railroad center also noted for the production of chemicals

e. Largest city in the Southeast

f. Chief manufacturing center of the southern Appalachian region

g. Has one of the finest harbors on the Gulf of Mexico

h. Famous tourist city also noted for clothing production

i. Center of group of towns specializing in textiles and knitted goods

j. Important furniture manufacturing city also known for textiles

k. Home of United States Naval Academy

l. Market city also noted for tobacco products, furniture, paint, and bricks

Reread pages 299-311, then number a paper from **1** through **21**. After each number, write **True** if the statement is true. Write **False** if the statement is false. If the statement is false, give the reason for your answer in a complete sentence.

1. The Northwest Territory became part of the United States after the Civil War.

2. Congress made a plan to divide the Northwest Territory into smaller areas that could become states.

3. Congress sold large tracts of land in the Northwest Territory to land companies, which, in turn, sold the land to settlers.

4. The Indians gave up their lands in the Northwest Territory without a struggle.

5. The Ohio River served as a great highway for settlers moving into the Northwest Territory.

6. In the years after 1787 most people traveled west either by flatboat or by covered wagon.

7. By the early 1800s, only a few hundred settlers had moved into the Northwest Territory.

8. The first settlement in Ohio was Cleveland.

9. The United States bought the Louisiana Territory from Spain.

10. The size of the United States was doubled by the Louisiana Purchase.

11. President Jefferson sent Lewis and Clark on an expedition to explore the Louisiana Territory.

12. Ohio, Illinois, and Indiana were new states made from the Louisiana Territory.

13. Under the Missouri Compromise, Missouri was admitted to the Union as a free state.

14. The problem of slavery in the new states created from the Louisiana Territory led to the Civil War.

15. Forests covered most of the lands west of the Mississippi River.

16. Inventions such as the McCormick reaper and the steel plow made farming easier on the prairies.

17. The Homestead Act encouraged settlers to move west.

18. The Battle of Little Bighorn showed Americans that the Sioux could easily be defeated.

19. The National Road was not important in the settlement of the North Central states because it was never extended west of Wheeling, West Virginia.

20. Travel and transportation by water and rail were important to the development of the North Central states.

21. The invention of the *Clermont* proved the importance of electricity.

ENRICHMENT

Writing Captions

To follow page 337

Captions are words, phrases, or sentences that help explain pictures and other illustrations. Most of the illustrations in your book have captions. Number a paper from **1** through **6**. After the numbers, write captions for each of the illustrations below. Write two or three sentences for each caption. For help, review pages 296–337.

1.

2.

3.

4.

5.

6.

A chart is a useful way to show information. Study the chart below to answer the questions that follow. Number a paper from 1 through 7. After each number, write the answer to the question.

The North Central States				
State	Capital	Area (sq. mi.)	Population	Nickname
Illinois	Springfield	56,400	11,448,000	Prairie State
Indiana	Indianapolis	36,291	5,471,000	Hoosier State
Iowa	Des Moines	56,290	2,905,000	Hawkeye State
Kansas	Topeka	82,264	2,408,000	Sunflower State
Michigan	Lansing	58,216	9,109,000	Wolverine State
Minnesota	St. Paul	84,068	4,133,000	Gopher State
Missouri	Jefferson City	69,686	4,951,000	Show-me State
Nebraska	Lincoln	77,227	1,586,000	Cornhusker State
North Dakota	Bismarck	70,665	670,000	Sioux State Flickertail State
Ohio	Columbus	41,222	10,791,000	Buckeye State
South Dakota	Pierre	77,047	691,000	Sunshine State Coyote State
Wisconsin	Madison	56,154	4,765,000	Badger State

1. What is the title of the chart above?
2. What kinds of information does the chart give?
3. What is the largest state on the chart? What is the smallest state?
4. Which state shown on the chart has the largest population? Which has the smallest?
5. Which two states shown are most nearly the same size? Which two states have most nearly the same population?
6. About how many times larger than Ohio is Kansas? About how many people does Indiana have in comparison with Ohio?
7. What is the nickname of Indiana?

ENRICHMENT

Study the graph below to answer the questions that follow. Number a paper from 1 through 6. After each number, write the letter of the correct answer.

Leading Cotton Producing States

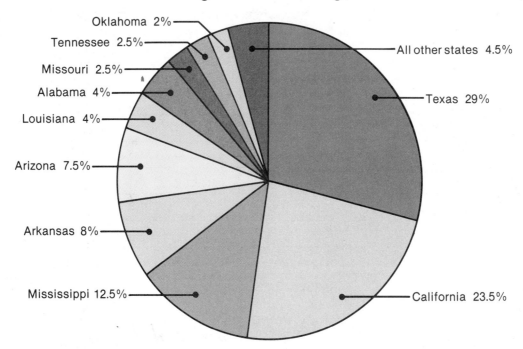

1. The graph above is a _____ graph.
   a. circle
   b. line
   c. bar

2. The graph shows _____ of cotton produced in different states.
   a. tons
   b. bales
   c. percentages

3. Texas and California together produce _____ of the cotton in the United States.
   a. less than half
   b. exactly half
   c. more than half

4. Mississippi produces about _____ as much cotton as California.
   a. one fourth
   b. one half
   c. three fourths

5. Alabama and Louisiana together produce about as much cotton as _____.
   a. Arkansas
   b. Texas
   c. Mississippi

6. Of the states shown, _____ produces the least cotton.
   a. Tennessee
   b. Missouri
   c. Oklahoma

A City Map

Refer to the map and map key below to answer the questions that follow. Number a paper from **1** through **10**. After each number, write the answer to the question.

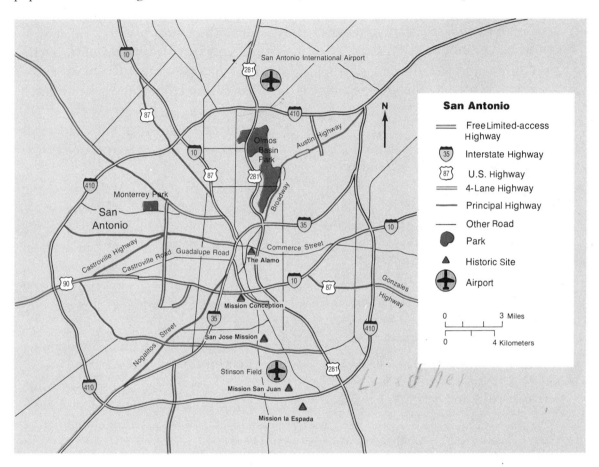

1. What city does the map above show?

2. What road makes a ring, or circle, around the city?

3. From the center of the city, in what two general directions does Interstate Highway 10 lead? In what general direction does Interstate Highway 35 lead?

4. Give the location of the Alamo by naming the streets that pass near it.

5. How many airports are shown on the map?

6. In what direction from Monterrey Park is Olmos Basin Park?

7. How many missions in addition to the Alamo are shown on the map?

8. About how far is San Antonio International Airport from the Alamo?

9. What main highway is a good route from the Alamo to San Antonio International Airport?

10. What is another name used for U.S. Highway 87?

ENRICHMENT

Do You Know These Facts?

To follow page 369

Number a paper from 1 through 19. After the numbers, write the word or words that complete the statements below.

1. The South Central states are Arkansas, Louisiana, Oklahoma, and _____.

2. Two important tributaries of the Mississippi River that flow through the South Central states are the _____ and the _____.

3. The explorer _____ claimed the whole Mississippi Valley for France.

4. The city of _____ was founded by Jean de Bienville in 1718. It later became the capital of the Louisiana Territory.

5. The three countries to which the Louisiana Territory belonged at different times were _____, Spain, and the United States.

6. _____ led American settlers to Texas, even though the land was still part of Mexico.

7. Between 1836 and 1845, Texas was a _____.

8. At the Battle of the Alamo, Mexican troops under the leadership of _____ defeated the Americans defending the mission.

9. _____ flags have flown over Texas during its history.

10. There was a great rush to claim land in _____ when the United States government opened it to settlers in 1889.

11. The leading crop of the South Central states is _____.

12. About one fourth of the cane sugar grown in the United States comes from _____.

13. The state of _____ has more cattle, sheep, and goats than any other state.

14. _____, a mineral buried deep in the earth, is found in large amounts in Texas, Louisiana, and Oklahoma.

15. Large deposits of _____, the mineral from which aluminum is made, are found in _____.

16. _____ is the chief trading and shipping center for the lower Mississippi Valley.

17. _____ was the capital of Texas while the area was under Spanish and Mexican rule; today _____ is the capital of Texas.

18. The capital and largest city of Oklahoma is _____.

19. _____ are used to pump oil that is buried deep within the ground.

Learning from Maps

The map below shows Grand Canyon National Park and the area surrounding it. Refer to the map and the map key to answer the questions that follow. Number a paper from 1 through 10. After each number, write the answer to the question.

1. In what state is Grand Canyon National Park?

2. What is the name of the river that flows through the Grand Canyon?

3. About how long is Grand Canyon Natonal Park from east to west?

4. What road leads from Jacob Lake across the Kaibab Plateau to North Rim?

5. Only one bridge crosses the Colorado River in Grand Canyon National Park. What kind of bridge is it? Do you think it is a foot bridge or an automobile bridge? Explain.

6. What are the names of the two Indian reservations to the south of Grand Canyon National Park? What is the name of the reservation east of the park?

7. In what direction is Point Sublime from Steamboat Mountain? Which of these peaks is higher?

8. In what town is Park Headquarters?

9. What is the name of the canyon east and north of the Grand Canyon?

10. Compare the map on this page with the map on page 377. In which general direction does the Colorado River flow through the Grand Canyon?

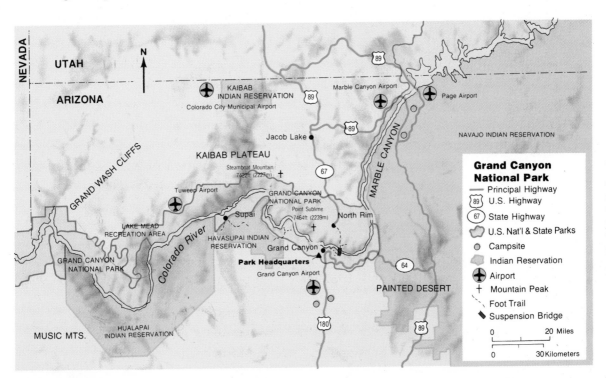

Learning from Graphs

To follow page 396

Refer to the graph below to answer the questions that follow. Number a paper from 1 through 6. After each number, write the letter of the correct answer.

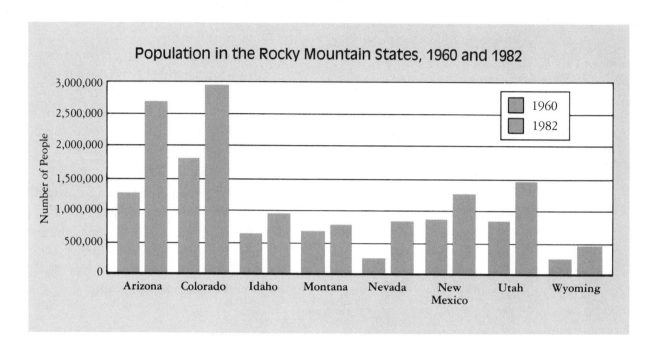

1. The graph above is a _____ graph.
   a. circle
   b. line
   c. bar

2. Of the three states with the smallest populations in 1960, _____ grew the most by 1982.
   a. Idaho
   b. Nevada
   c. Wyoming

3. The state that increased the most in population between 1960 and 1982 was _____.
   a. Arizona
   b. Colorado
   c. Utah

4. The state with the largest population in both 1960 and 1982 was _____.
   a. Arizona
   b. Colorado
   c. New Mexico

5. The population of _____ more than doubled between 1960 and 1982.
   a. Arizona
   b. Colorado
   c. Nevada

6. The two states that increased the least in population between 1960 and 1982 were _____.
   a. Idaho and Montana
   b. Montana and New Mexico
   c. Montana and Wyoming

Writing a Paragraph

To follow page 397

Use each of the numbered groups of words below to write a paragraph of three or four sentences. Before you begin, think what the main idea of each paragraph will be. Remember that each sentence in the paragraph should be related to the main idea. Number each paragraph.

1.

| Rocky Mountain states | plains | |
| mountains | plateaus | rivers |

2.

| Pueblo Indians | Navahos | |
| Apaches | missions | Spaniards |

3.

| Salt Lake City | Brigham Young | |
| Mormons | grasshoppers | sea gulls |

4.

| gold | silver | uranium |
| copper | petroleum | coal |

5.

| national park | Colorado | |
| Utah | Wyoming | Arizona |

ENRICHMENT

Study the diagram below to answer the questions that follow. Number a paper from 1 through 9. After each number, write the answer to the question.

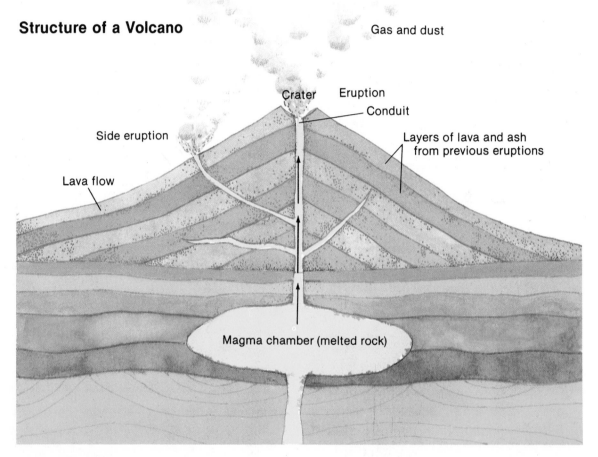

Structure of a Volcano

Gas and dust

Crater   Eruption

Conduit

Side eruption

Layers of lava and ash from previous eruptions

Lava flow

Magma chamber (melted rock)

1. What does the diagram above show?

2. What is magma?

3. Through what part of the volcano does the magma rise to the surface?

4. What is the saucer-shaped opening at the top of the volcano called?

5. When a volcano erupts, liquid rock called lava may pour out onto the earth's surface. What happens to the lava?

6. What materials besides lava may result from an eruption?

7. In the diagram shown above, what are the different materials that make up the volcanic mountain?

8. Would you describe the structure of the volcanic mountain as layered or unlayered?

9. Explain how the mountain will change if the volcano erupts again.

Is It True?

Number a paper from 1 through 12. After each number, write **True** if the statement is true. Write **False** if the statement is false. Then give the reason for your answer in a complete sentence.

1. The Pacific states are California, Nevada, Oregon, Washington, Alaska, and Hawaii.

2. All the Pacific states border the ocean.

3. The highest mountain in the United States is in the Pacific states.

4. None of the Pacific states lies in either the high latitudes or the low latitudes.

5. In the 1800s, the United States government sent Captain John Sutter to explore the Far West.

6. The first transcontinental railway was completed before the first telegraph line linked California with the East.

7. The forty-niners used three main routes to reach California.

8. Building the first transcontinental railroad was an easy job.

9. Captain Robert Gray gave the United States its claim to the region that is now Washington and Oregon.

10. The Oregon Trail was a relatively short trail that crossed Oregon.

11. For many years, the United States and Great Britain shared the Oregon Country.

12. The Nez Percé Indians lost much of their land in Oregon.

Railroad workers such as these helped bring the east and the west together.

ENRICHMENT

An outline tells the main ideas, or topics, about a subject. Outlines are useful in helping to review what you have read. The outline below, which covers pages 434–443 in your book, has been started for you. Copy the outline on a sheet of paper and fill in the missing topic headings.

Living and Working in Alaska and Hawaii
  I. Alaska
    A. Farming in Alaska
      1.
      2. Tanana River
    B.
      1. Lumbering
      2.
        a.
        b. Other minerals
    C. Alaska's fishing industry
    D.
    E.
    F. Cities in Alaska
      1.
      2.
      3.
      4.
  II. Hawaii
    A. Farming in Hawaii
      1.
      2.
    B.
    C.
    D. Cities in Hawaii
      1.
      2.

Alaska

Hawaii

Learning from Maps

Refer to the map below to answer the questions that follow. Number a paper from 1 through 10. After each number, write the word or words in parentheses that correctly complete each statement.

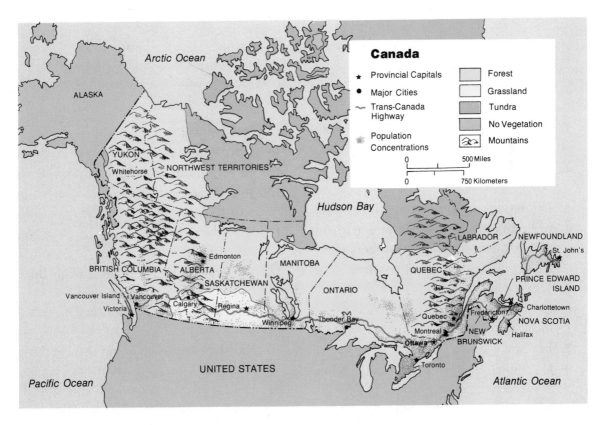

1. (Eight, Nine) of Canada's provinces or territories border the United States.

2. Most of Canada's population is concentrated in the (south, north).

3. (Forest, Tundra) covers most of the Northwest Territories.

4. Mountainous areas are found in the (eastern and western, northern and southern) parts of Canada.

5. Areas of no vegetation are found in Canada's (Atlantic provinces, Arctic islands).

6. The Trans-Canada Highway runs (north and south, east and west).

7. The end points of the Trans-Canada Highway are (Victoria and Charlottetown, Vancouver Island and St. John's).

8. Most of Canada's grasslands are in (Alberta and Saskatchewan, Saskatchewan and Manitoba).

9. Forests, grasslands, and tundra all are found in (British Columbia, Alberta).

10. Calgary is a (provincial capital, major city).

Which South American Country Is It?

To follow page 506

Reread pages 491–506 and refer to the map on page 492 to answer the questions that follow. Number a paper from **1** through **25**. After each number, write the name of the country or countries that each phrase describes.

Argentina	Bolivia	Brazil	Chile
Colombia	Ecuador	French Guiana	Paraguay
Peru	Suriname	Uruguay	Venezuela

1. The Andes Mountains extend through these countries

2. The only part of South America that is not independent

3. The largest country in South America

4. Rank among the top six countries in the world in the export of bauxite

5. Its neighbors are Brazil, Bolivia, and Argentina

6. Ranks second in the production of oil in South America

7. Its capital city is Lima

8. Has more factories than any other South American country

9. Produces more tin than any other country in North America or South America

10. The equator passes through it

11. Ranks fifth in the world in the production of oil

12. Produces more than half of the world's iodine

13. Has two capitals

14. One of its important products is guano

15. Covers about half of the Amazon Basin

16. Has the richest copper mines in the world

17. Was formed from parts of Peru and Argentina

18. Declared its independence from Brazil in 1825

19. The largest city in South America is found here

20. Has the longest coast on the Pacific of all South American countries

21. Produces one fourth of the world's meat and one fifth of its wheat

22. Lake Maracaibo is found here

23. Lake Titicaca is found here

24. Produces about three fourths of the world's coffee

25. Montevideo is this country's capital and largest city

Read the paragraphs below, then number a paper from **1** through **8**. After each number, write the word that belongs in the blank.

When the Spaniards came to South America, to the land south of Brazil, they saw Indians there wearing silver bracelets and silver necklaces. They supposed there must be much silver in the land, so they named the country "Silver Land," which in their language is Argentina. Argentina, as it turned out, really had very little silver, but we call it Silver Land just the same.

Although Argentina has little silver, the people there have quite a lot of money. They do not get the money out of the ground from silver mines. They make it by selling wheat and meat. It would have been more fitting if they had called Argentina "Wheat Land" or "Meat Land" instead of "Silver Land," but not nearly so pretty. In Argentina there are enormous farms that produce wheat and corn. There are also enormous fields called *pampas* where cattle and sheep are raised. The men who look after these cattle and sheep are called "*gauchos*." Gauchos wear *ponchos*. A poncho is a kind of square blanket with a hole in the center through which the gaucho puts his head. He uses it as a coat by day and as a blanket by night. A gaucho always carries a big knife, which he uses as a sword, as a hatchet, or as a table knife. His *lariat* is a rope with weights on the ends.

1. The paragraphs above are about the country of _____.

2. The name *Argentina* means "Silver Land" in _____.

3. Much of Argentina's wealth comes from _____ and _____.

4. _____ are fields where cattle and sheep are raised.

5. The men who look after the cattle and sheep are called _____.

6. A _____ is a kind of square blanket worn as a piece of clothing.

7. A rope used by a gaucho is called a _____.

8. The photograph shows a _____ riding a horse and carrying a _____.

ENRICHMENT

PRESIDENTS
of the United States

George Washington
(1732–1799)
Years in Office: 1789–1797
Residence: Virginia
Vice-President: John Adams

John Adams
(1735–1826)
Years in Office: 1797–1801
Residence: Massachusetts
Vice-President: Thomas Jefferson

Thomas Jefferson (1743–1826)
Years in Office: 1801–1809
Residence: Virginia
Vice-Presidents: Aaron Burr
George Clinton

James Madison
(1751–1836)
Years in Office: 1809–1817
Residence: Virginia
Vice-Presidents: George Clinton
Elbridge Gerry

James Monroe
(1758–1831)
Years in Office: 1817–1825
Residence: Virginia
Vice-President: Daniel D. Tompkins

John Quincy Adams (1767–1848)
Years in Office: 1825–1829
Residence: Massachusetts
Vice-President: John C. Calhoun

Andrew Jackson
(1767–1845)
Years in Office: 1829–1837
Residence: Tennessee
Vice-Presidents: John C. Calhoun
Martin Van Buren

Martin Van Buren
(1782–1862)
Years in Office: 1837–1841
Residence: New York
Vice-President: Richard M. Johnson

William Henry Harrison
(1773–1841)
Years in Office: 1841–1841
Residence: Ohio
Vice-President: John Tyler*

John Tyler
(1790–1862)
Years in Office: 1841–1845
Residence: Virginia

James K. Polk
(1795–1849)
Years in Office: 1845–1849
Residence: Tennessee
Vice-President: George M. Dallas

Andrew Johnson
(1808–1875)
Years in Office: 1865–1869
Residence: Tennessee

Zachary Taylor
(1784–1850)
Years in Office: 1849–1850
Residence: Louisiana
Vice-President: Millard Fillmore*

Ulysses S. Grant
(1822–1885)
Years in Office: 1869–1877
Residence: Illinois
Vice-Presidents: Schuyler Colfax
Henry Wilson

Millard Fillmore
(1800–1874)
Years in Office: 1850–1853
Residence: New York

Rutherford B. Hayes
(1822–1893)
Years in Office: 1877–1881
Residence: Ohio
Vice-President: Wm. A. Wheeler

Franklin Pierce
(1804–1869)
Years in Office: 1853–1857
Residence: New Hampshire
Vice-President: William R. King

James A. Garfield
(1831–1881)
Years on Office: 1881–1881
Residence: Ohio
Vice-President: Chester A. Arthur*

James Buchanan
(1791–1868)
Years in Office: 1857–1861
Residence: Pennsylvania
Vice-President: J. C. Breckinridge

Chester A. Arthur
(1830–1886)
Years in Office: 1881–1885
Residence: New York

Abraham Lincoln (1809–1865)
Years in Office: 1861–1865
Residence: Illinois
Vice-Presidents: Hannibal Hamlin
Andrew Johnson*

Grover Cleveland
(1837–1908)
Years in Office: 1885–1889
1893–1897†
Residence: New York
Vice-Presidents: Thos. A. Hendricks
Adlai E. Stevenson

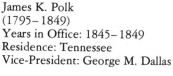

Benjamin Harrison
(1833–1901)
Years in Office: 1889–1893
Residence: Indiana
Vice-President: Levi P. Morton

William McKinley
(1843–1901)
Years in Office: 1897–1901
Residence: Ohio
Vice-Presidents: Garret A. Hobart
　　　　　　　Theodore Roosevelt*

Theodore Roosevelt
(1858–1919)
Years in Office: 1901–1909
Residence: New York
Vice-President: Charles W. Fairbanks

William Howard Taft
(1857–1930)
Years in Office: 1909–1913
Residence: Ohio
Vice-President: James S. Sherman

Woodrow Wilson
(1856–1924)
Years in Office: 1913–1921
Residence: New Jersey
Vice-President: Thomas R. Marshall

Warren G. Harding
(1865–1923)
Years in Office: 1921–1923
Residence: Ohio
Vice-President: Calvin Coolidge*

Calvin Coolidge
(1872–1933)
Years in Office: 1923–1929
Residence: Massachusetts
Vice-President: Charles G. Dawes

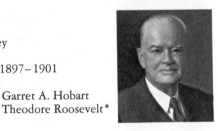

Herbert Hoover
(1874–1964)
Years in Office: 1929–1933
Residence: California
Vice-President: Charles Curtis

Franklin D. Roosevelt
(1882–1945)
Years in Office: 1933–1945
Residence: New York
Vice-Presidents: John Nance Garner
　　　　　　　Henry A. Wallace
　　　　　　　Harry S. Truman*

Harry S. Truman
(1884–1972)
Years in Office: 1945–1953
Residence: Missouri
Vice-President: Alben Barkley

Dwight D. Eisenhower
(1890–1969)
Years in Office: 1953–1961
Residence: New York
Vice-President: Richard M. Nixon

John F. Kennedy
(1917–1963)
Years in Office: 1961–1963
Residence: Massachusetts
Vice-President: Lyndon B. Johnson*

Lyndon B. Johnson
(1908–1973)
Years in Office: 1963–1969
Residence: Texas
Vice-President: Hubert Humphrey

Jimmy Carter
(1924–   )
Years in Office: 1977–1981
Residence: Georgia
Vice-President: Walter F. Mondale

Richard M. Nixon
(1913–   )
Years in Office: 1969–1974
Residence: California
Vice-Presidents: Spiro Agnew
                Gerald R. Ford**

Ronald Reagan
(1911–   )
Years in Office: 1981–
Residence: California
Vice-President: George Bush

Gerald R. Ford
(1913–   )
Years in Office: 1974–1977
Residence: Michigan
Vice-President: Nelson Rockefeller

†Cleveland was elected for a second term after Benjamin Harrison.
*Succeeded from the vice-presidency on the death of the President.
**Succeeded from the vice-presidency on the resignation of the President.

ALABAMA
Capital: Montgomery
Population: 3,943,000
Area (sq. mi.): 51,609
    (sq. km): 133,667
State Flower: Camellia

ALASKA
Capital: Juneau
Population: 438,000
Area (sq. mi.): 586,412
    (sq. km): 1,518,800
State Flower: Forget-me-not

ARIZONA
Capital: Phoenix
Population: 2,860,000
Area (sq. mi.): 113,909
    (sq. km): 295,023
State Flower: Saguaro cactus

ARKANSAS
Capital: Little Rock
Population: 2,291,000
Area (sq. mi.): 53,104
    (sq. km): 137,539
State Flower: Apple blossom

CALIFORNIA
Capital: Sacramento
Population: 24,724,000
Area (sq. mi.): 158,693
    (sq. km): 411,013
State Flower: Golden poppy

COLORADO
Capital: Denver
Population: 3,045,000
Area (sq. mi.): 104,247
    (sq. km): 269,998
State Flower: Rocky Mountain
           columbine

CONNECTICUT
Capital: Hartford
Population: 3,153,000
Area (sq. mi.): 5,009
    (sq. km): 12,973
State Flower: Mountain laurel

DELAWARE
Capital: Dover
Population: 602,000
Area (sq. mi.): 2,057
    (sq. km): 5,328
State Flower: Peach blossom

FLORIDA
Capital: Tallahassee
Population: 10,416,000
Area (sq. mi.): 58,560
    (sq. km): 151,670
State Flower: Orange blossom

GEORGIA
Capital: Atlanta
Population: 5,639,000
Area (sq. mi.): 58,876
    (sq. km): 152,488
State Flower: Cherokee rose

HAWAII
Capital: Honolulu
Population: 994,000
Area (sq. mi.): 6,450
    (sq. km): 16,705
State Flower: Hibiscus

IDAHO
Capital: Boise
Population: 965,000
Area (sq. mi.): 83,557
    (sq. km): 216,412
State Flower: Mock orange

ILLINOIS
Capital: Springfield
Population: 11,448,000
Area (sq. mi.): 56,400
    (sq. km): 146,075
State Flower: Violet

INDIANA
Capital: Indianapolis
Population: 5,471,000
Area (sq. mi.): 36,291
    (sq. km): 93,993
State Flower: Peony

IOWA
Capital: Des Moines
Population: 2,905,000
Area (sq. mi.): 56,290
    (sq. km): 145,790
State Flower: Wild rose

KANSAS
Capital: Topeka
Population: 2,408,000
Area (sq. mi.): 82,264
    (sq. km): 213,063
State Flower: Sunflower

KENTUCKY
Capital: Frankfort
Population: 3,667,000
Area (sq. mi.): 40,395
    (sq. km): 104,623
State Flower: Goldenrod

LOUISIANA
Capital: Baton Rouge
Population: 4,362,000
Area (sq. mi.): 48,523
    (sq. km): 125,674
State Flower: Magnolia

MAINE
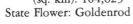
Capital: Augusta
Population: 1,133,000
Area (sq. mi.): 33,215
    (sq. km): 86,026
State Flower: White pine
    cone and tassel

MARYLAND
Capital: Annapolis
Population: 4,265,000
Area (sq. mi.): 10,577
    (sq. km): 27,394
State Flower: Black-eyed Susan

MASSACHUSETTS
Capital: Boston
Population: 5,781,000
Area (sq. mi.): 8,257
    (sq. km): 21,386
State Flower: Mayflower

MICHIGAN
Capital: Lansing
Population: 9,109,000
Area (sq. mi.): 58,216
    (sq. km): 150,779
State Flower: Apple blossom

MINNESOTA
Capital: St. Paul
Population: 4,133,000
Area (sq. mi.): 84,068
    (sq. km): 217,735
State Flower: Ladyslipper

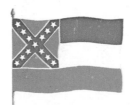

MISSISSIPPI
Capital: Jackson
Population: 2,551,000
Area (sq. mi.): 47,716
    (sq. km): 123,584
State Flower: Magnolia

MISSOURI
Capital: Jefferson City
Population: 4,951,000
Area (sq. mi.): 69,686
    (sq. km): 180,486
State Flower: Hawthorn

MONTANA
Capital: Helena
Population: 801,000
Area (sq. mi.): 147,138
    (sq. km): 381,086
State Flower: Bitterroot

NEBRASKA
Capital: Lincoln
Population: 1,586,000
Area (sq. mi.): 77,227
    (sq. km): 200,017
State Flower: Goldenrod

NEVADA
Capital: Carson City
Population: 881,000
Area (sq. mi.): 110,540
    (sq. km): 286,297
State Flower: Sagebrush

NEW HAMPSHIRE
Capital: Concord
Population: 951,000
Area (sq. mi.): 9,304
    (sq. km): 24,097
State Flower: Purple lilac

NEW JERSEY
Capital: Trenton
Population: 7,438,000
Area (sq. mi.): 7,836
    (sq. km): 20,295
State Flower: Violet

NEW MEXICO
Capital: Santa Fe
Population: 1,359,000
Area (sq. mi.): 121,666
    (sq. km): 315,113
State Flower: Yucca

NEW YORK
Capital: Albany
Population: 17,659,000
Area (sq. mi.): 49,576
    (sq. km): 128,401
State Flower: Rose

NORTH CAROLINA
Capital: Raleigh
Population: 6,019,000
Area (sq. mi.): 52,586
    (sq. km): 136,197
State Flower: Dogwood

NORTH DAKOTA
Capital: Bismarck
Population: 670,000
Area (sq. mi.): 70,665
    (sq. km): 183,022
State Flower: Wild prairie rose

OHIO
Capital: Columbus
Population: 10,791,000
Area (sq. mi.): 41,222
    (sq. km): 106,764
State Flower: Scarlet carnation

OKLAHOMA
Capital: Oklahoma City
Population: 3,177,000
Area (sq. mi.): 69,919
    (sq. km): 181,089
State Flower: Mistletoe

OREGON
Capital: Salem
Population: 2,649,000
Area (sq. mi.): 96,981
    (sq. km): 251,180
State Flower: Oregon grape

PENNSYLVANIA
Capital: Harrisburg
Population: 11,865,000
Area (sq. mi.): 45,333
    (sq. km): 117,412
State Flower: Mountain laurel

RHODE ISLAND
Capital: Providence
Population: 958,000
Area (sq. mi.): 1,214
    (sq. km): 3,144
State Flower: Violet

SOUTH CAROLINA
Capital: Columbia
Population: 3,203,000
Area (sq. mi.): 31,055
    (sq. km): 80,432
State Flower: Yellow jessamine

SOUTH DAKOTA
Capital: Pierre
Population: 691,000
Area (sq. mi.): 77,047
    (sq. km): 199,551
State Flower: Pasqueflower

TENNESSEE
Capital: Nashville
Population: 4,651,000
Area (sq. mi.): 42,244
    (sq. km): 109,411
State Flower: Iris

TEXAS
Capital: Austin
Population: 15,280,000
Area (sq. mi.): 267,338
    (sq. km): 692,402
State Flower: Bluebonnet

UTAH
Capital: Salt Lake City
Population: 1,554,000
Area (sq. mi.): 84,916
    (sq. km): 219,931
State Flower: Sego lily

VERMONT
Capital: Montpelier
Population: 516,000
Area (sq. mi.): 9,609
    (sq. km): 24,887
State Flower: Red clover

VIRGINIA
Capital: Richmond
Population: 5,491,000
Area (sq. mi.): 40,817
    (sq. km): 105,716
State Flower: Dogwood

WASHINGTON
Capital: Olympia
Population: 4,245,000
Area (sq. mi.): 68,192
    (sq. km): 176,616
State Flower: Rhododendron

WEST VIRGINIA
Capital: Charleston
Population: 1,948,000
Area (sq. mi.): 24,282
    (sq. km): 62,628
State Flower: Rhododendron

WISCONSIN
Capital: Madison
Population: 4,765,000
Area (sq. mi.): 56,154
    (sq. km): 145,438
State Flower: Wood violet

WYOMING
Capital: Cheyenne
Population: 502,000
Area (sq. mi.): 97,914
    (sq. km): 253,596
State Flower: Indian paintbrush

UNITED STATES OF AMERICA: *Area,* 3,615,122 (sq. mi.), 9,363,123 (sq. km); *Population,* 234,315,000
Capital: Washington, D.C.; *Area,* 69 (sq. mi.), 176 (sq. km); *Population,* 623,000

North America

Country	Capital	Area Sq. Mi.	Sq. Km	Population	Products
Canada	Ottawa	3,851,809	9,976,139	24,885,900	industry, dairy products, lumber, minerals, fish, cattle, furs
Greenland	Nuuk	840,000	2,175,600	51,000	fish, sheep
Iceland	Reykjavik	39,768	103,000	232,000	potatoes, hay, sheep cattle, fish

Central American and Caribbean Countries

Country	Capital	Area Sq. Mi.	Sq. Km	Population	Independent	Products
Bahamas	Nassau	4,404	13,935	260,000	1973	Tomatoes, lumber, fruit
Barbados	Bridgetown	166	431	300,000	1966	Sugar, molasses, rum, cotton
Belize	Belmopan	8,867	22,965	148,300	1981	Sugarcane, citrus fruits, corn
Costa Rica	San José	19,695	50,700	2,300,000	1821	Bananas, coffee, cacao
Cuba	Havana	44,208	114,524	9,800,000	1898	Tobacco, sugar, nickel
Domínica	Roseau	300	777	82,000	1967	Bananas, oil, cacao
Dominican Republic	Santo Domingo	19,332	48,734	5,700,000	1844	Sugar, coffee, cacao
El Salvador	San Salvador	12,792	21,393	5,000,000	1821	Coffee, cotton, corn
Guadeloupe	Basse-Terre	687	1,779	314,800	(French)	Sugarcane, bananas, rum
Guatemala	Guatemala City	50,647	108,889	7,700,000	1821	Coffee, bananas, cotton
Haiti	Port-au-Prince	10,700	27,750	6,100,000	1804	Sisal, coffee, sugar
Honduras	Tegucigalpa	59,160	112,088	4,000,000	1821	Bananas, coffee, lumber
Jamaica	Kingston	4,411	10,962	2,200,000	1962	Sugar, rum, bananas, coffee
Martinique	Fort-de-France	431	1,116	307,700	(French)	Sugar, bananas, rum
Netherlands Antilles	Willemstad	817	2,124	256,000	(Dutch)	Oil
Mexico	Mexico City	758,450	1,972,547	71,300,000	1810	Cotton, petroleum, coffee, lead
Nicaragua	Managua	57,145	130,000	2,600,000	1821	Coffee, cotton, corn
Panama	Panama City	29,127	75,650	1,900,000	1903	Bananas, abacá, cacao
Trinidad and Tobago	Port-of-Spain	1,980	5,128	1,100,000	1962	Asphalt, oil, bananas, cacao

South America

Country	Capital	Area Sq. Mi.	Sq. Km	Population	Independent	Products
Argentina	Buenos Aires	1,073,700	2,776,889	28,438,000	1816	Meats, wheat, wool, hides
Bolivia	La Paz; Sucre	416,040	1,098,581	5,600,000	1825	Tin, tungsten, lead, zinc
Brazil	Brasília	3,288,045	8,511,965	127,700,000	1822	Coffee, cotton, cacao, iron
Chile	Santiago	286,396	756,945	11,500,000	1810	Copper, nitrates, wheat
Colombia	Bogotá	439,553	1,138,914	25,600,000	1819	Coffee, petroleum, cattle
Ecuador	Quito	104,506	283,561	8,500,000	1822	Bananas, cacao, coffee
French Guiana	Cayenne	91,000	34,750	66,800	(French)	Rice, timber, rum
Guyana	Georgetown	83,000	215,000	900,000	1966	Bauxite, sugar, timber, rice
Paraguay	Asunción	157,047	406,572	3,300,000	1811	Lumber, tannin, livestock
Peru	Lima	482,258	1,285,216	18,600,000	1821	Cotton, sugar, lead, copper
Suriname	Paramaribo	55,400	163,265	420,000	1975	Bauxite, rice, coffee, lumber
Uruguay	Montevideo	72,173	177,508	2,934,942	1825	Wool, meat, hides
Venezuela	Caracas	352,150	912,050	18,700,000	1821	Petroleum, iron ore, coffee

Word List

a bad   i it   oo wood   u cup   ə *stands for*
ā cake   ī ice   o͞o food   ur turn   a *as in* ago
ä father   j joke   oi oil   yo͞o music   e *as in* taken
b bat   k kit   ou out   v very   i *as in* pencil
ch chin   l lid   p pail   w wet   o *as in* lemon
d dog   m man   r ride   wh white   u *as in* helpful
e pet   n not   s sit   y yes
ē me   ng sing   sh ship   z zoo
f five   o hot   t tall   zh treasure
g game   ō open   th thin
h hit   ô off   <u>th</u> that

A

abolish (ə bol′ish): to do away with

abolition movement (ab′ə lish′ən mo͞ov′mənt): movement against slavery

adobe (ə dō′bē): brick made of sun-dried clay

alliance (ə lī′əns): an agreement of friendship between nations

altitude (al′tə to͞od′): the height of land above sea level

amendment (ə mend′mənt): a law that is added to the Constitution

anthracite (an′thrə sīt′): hard coal

aqueduct (ak′wə duct′): a pipe or channel that carries water over long distances

archeologist (är′kē ol′ə jist): a scientist who digs up the remains of ancient cultures and then studies the tools and other artifacts that are found

Articles of Confederation (kən fed′ə rā′shən): plan of government that united the states into a confederation, or union

artifacts (är′tə faktz′): human-made remains of ancient cultures

asbestos (as bes′təs): a mineral that will not burn

assembly (ə sem′blē): a group of leaders who made laws for a colony

assembly line (ə sem′blē līn): a method of manufacturing in which each worker is responsible for adding a particular part to the product as it moves by on a belt

B

balsam (bôl′səm): the sap of a tree used in making medicine and perfume

basin (bā′sin): low region surrounded by higher lands

bauxite (bôk′sīt): the ore from which aluminum is made

Bill of Rights: the first ten amendments to the Constitution

bituminious (bī to͞o′mə nəs): soft coal

blockade (blo kād′): the closing of an area to prevent people or supplies from going into or out of it

boll (bōl): small seed pod of the cotton plant

boycott: (boi′kot): to refuse to buy, sell, or use any goods as a protest

bran (bran): the darker, outer coat of a wheat seed

C

Cabinet (kab′ə nit): a group of persons, chosen by the President, to help with the duties of the executive branch

canal (kə nal′): a waterway built to connect two bodies of water

cannery (kan′ər ē): a factory where food is prepared and canned

capitol (kap′it əl): the building in which lawmakers of a state or country meet

carpetbagger (kär′pit bag′ər): a Northerner who moved to the South after the Civil War

cash crop: a crop that is raised mainly to make money

census (sen′səs): an official count of the people in a country

charter (chär′tər): a paper granting certain rights, such as permission to make settlements

citizen (sit′ə zən): a person who is a member of a country and who is protected by its laws

citrus (sit′rəs) **fruit:** type of fruit such as oranges, lemons, and grapefruit

civil (siv′əl) **rights:** the right of all citizens to be treated equally under the law

civilization (siv′ə li zā′shən): culture that has a high level of development

climate (klī′mit): the kind of weather a place has

coke (kōk): coal from which gas has been removed

Cold War: unfriendliness after World War II between the United States and its allies on one side and the Soviet Union and its allies on the other side

colony (kol′ə nē): settlement that lies far away from the country that governs it

combine (kom′bīn): a machine that cuts grain and separates kernel from straw

commonwealth (kom′ən welth′): a group of people making up a nation or state

communism (kom′yə niz′əm): a system of government under which all property and goods are controlled by the government

compromise (kom′prə mīz′): the settlement of a disagreement by having each side give up some part of its claims

concentration camp (kon′sən trā′shən kamp): prison camp

Confederacy (kən fed′ər ə sē): the nation formed by the states that seceded from the Union

confederation (kən fed′ə rā′shən): a plan for union of states or provinces

conservation (kon′sər vā′shən): the wise use of natural resources

constitution (kon′stə tōo′shən): a group of written laws governing a nation or a state

Continental (kon′tə nent′əl) **Divide:** a ridge in the Rockies that separates the rivers flowing east from the rivers flowing west

contour (kon′toor) **line:** a line on a map connecting points of equal elevation

convention (kən ven′shən): a meeting held for a common purpose

conveyor (kən vā′ər): a moving belt which carries loads from one place to another

cotton belt: area in the South where cotton grows well

Creole (krē′ōl): a Spanish or French person born in the West Indies or Latin America

crop rotation (krop rō tā′shən): a way of building up the soil by planting different crops on the same land every 2 or 3 years

cultivator (kul′tə vā′tər): a machine used to loosen the soil and uproot weeds

culture (kul′chər): the way of life of a people

current (kur′ənt): a stream of water flowing through the ocean

D

dam (dam): a wall or bank built across a river to stop the flow of water

dehydration (dē′hī drā′shən): the removal, or taking out, of water by a special process

delegate (del′ə gāt′): representative

delta (del′tə): land built up by mud and sand brought down by a slow river

democracy (di mok′rə sē): government by the people

density (den′sə tē): term used to describe how closely together people live in an area

depression (di presh′ən): a time when there is little business and much unemployment

derrick (der′ik): the framework built to support the machinery needed to drill an oil well

dictator (dik′tā′tər): a ruler who completely controls

discrimination (dis krim′ə nā′shən): unfair treatment

disk harrow (disk har′ō): a machine with sharp, curved blades, used to break up lumps of earth

drill (dril): a tool used to bore holes into the earth

dry farming: a way of conserving moisture in dry areas by growing only one crop every 2 years on the same plot of ground

E

earthquake (urth′ kwāk′): a movement of a part of the earth's surface caused by a shift of rock or other disturbance

ejido (ə he′dō): land turned over to a farming village by the government of Mexico

elect (i lekt′): to vote for a person for an office

electronics (i lek tron′iks): a special branch of electricity used in industry

elevation (el'ə vā'shən): height above the earth's surface or above sea level

empire (em'pīr): group of lands and people under the control of one country

estuary (es'chōō er'ē): an arm of the ocean which extends into the land

executive branch (eg zek'yə tiv branch): branch of government that carries out the laws that Congress makes

expedition (eks'pə dish'ən): an exploring party

export (eks'pôrt'): a good or product that is shipped out of a country

extinct (eks tingkt'): no longer in existence

F

fault (fôlt): a break in a rock mass

federal system (fed'ər əl sis'təm): system in which the governing powers are divided between the national government and state governments

feed lot: a pen where cattle are fed special feed to fatten them for market

fleece (flēs): the thick wool of a sheep

flood (flud) **plain**: lowland that is often covered by water when rivers overflow their banks

flowing (flō'ing) **well**: an oil well which produces oil in a steady stream without being pumped

fortyniner (fôr'tē nī'nər): a person who went to California to seek gold

frontier (frun tēr'): area that lies at the edge of a settled region

G

gap (gap): a narrow valley in mountains

gaucho (gou'chō): a cowhand of the pampas

geyser (gī'zər): a spring which throws hot water and steam high into the air

glaciers (glā' shərz): huge sheets of ice that move very slowly over the land or down a valley

great circle route (rōōt): most direct and shortest route between two places on the globe

grid (grid): a crisscross pattern on a map made by imaginary lines

growing season (sē'zən): the time of year when crops can be grown outdoors

gusher (gush'ər): an oil well from which the oil shoots high into the air

H

hacienda (hä'sē en'də): a large plantation

helium (hē'lē əm): a very light gas which does not burn or explode

Hispano (his pan'ō): a Spanish-speaking person

historian (his tôr'ē ən): a person who studies the past

hogan (hō'gän): a dome-shaped Indian house built of poles, tree bark, and mud

holocaust (hol'ə kôst'): the destruction of a people

homestead (hōm'sted'): piece of public land granted to a settler under the Homestead Act

House of Representatives (rep'ri zen'tə tivz): the part of Congress that has the most members

hurricane (hur'ə kān'): a tropical storm with strong winds

I

immigrant (im'ə grənt): person who moves from one land to settle in another country

import (im'pôrt): a good or product brought in from other countries

impressment (im pres'mənt): seizing of sailors

inaugurate (in ô'gyə rāt'): to put into office

indentured (in den'chərd) **servant**: a person who works a certain length of time for the person who has paid the cost of his or her passage to America

independence (in'di pen'dəns): freedom from the control of another country

indigo (in'di gō'): a plant from which a blue dye is made

industry (in'dəs trē): a word that refers to manufacturing and other businesses

inlet (in'let'): a narrow strip of water which reaches far inland

interior (in tēr'ē ər): an area which lies inland, away from the border and the coast

---

a bad, ā cake, ä father; e pet, ē me; i it, ī ice; o hot, ō open, ô off; oo wood; ōō food, oi oil, ou out; u cup, ur turn, yōō music; ə ago, taken, pencil, lemon, helpful

---

international (in'tər nash'ən əl): belonging to, or having to do with, two or more nations

irrigation (ir'ə gā'shən): bringing water to dry land through pipes or sprinklers

J

judicial branch (jōō dish'əl branch): branch of government that explains the meaning of laws

L

latex (lā'teks): the sap of the tree used to make rubber

Latin (lat'in) **America:** land south of the United States, where Spanish, French, or Portuguese is spoken

latitude (lat'ə tōōd): the distance north or south of the equator

lava (lä'və): hot melted rock

legend (lej'ənd): an explanation of the symbols on a chart or map

legislative branch (lej'is lā'tiv branch): branch of government which makes laws

legume (leg'yōōm): a vegetable, such as peas or beans, that grows in pods

levee (lev'ē): a bank of earth built along a river to keep it from overflowing its banks and flooding the land

lignite (lig'nīt): brown coal

linseed (lin'sēd') **oil:** a product made from crushed flaxseed

llano (lä'nō): a grassy plain in South America

locomotive (lō'kə mō'tiv): an engine which can move on its own power

longitude (lon'jə tōōd'): distance east or west of the prime meridian

Loyalist (loi'ə list): colonist who was against the Revolutionary War

M

merchant marine (mur'chənt mə rēn'): the ships which carry on the trade of a nation

meridian of longitude (mə rid'ē ən uv lon'jə tōōd'): imaginary line on a map or globe measuring distance in degrees east or west of the prime meridian

mestizo (mes tē'zō): a person of mixed ancestry, usually Spanish or Portuguese and Indian

militia (mi lish'ə): group of colonists who served as soldiers when they were needed

missile (mis'əl): weapon designed to be thrown or fired toward a target

mission (mish'ən): a church settlement built by Spaniards in the Americas

mohair (mō'her'): cloth made from goat hair

muckraker (muk'rāk'ər): newspaper or magazine writer who criticized big business

N

natural resource (nach'ər əl rē'sôrs): material found in nature that is useful or necessary for human life

naturalized citizen (nach'ər ə līzd sit'ə zən): a person born in one country who becomes a citizen of another country

naval (nā'vəl) **stores:** turpentine, tar, and resin made from the gum of the pine tree

navigator (nav'i gā tər): a person who guides a ship

neutral (nōō'trəl): not taking the part of either side in a conflict

nomad (nō'mad): a wandering hunter

O

oil shale (shāl): a type of rock that may be a source of energy

open-pit mining: mining done on the surface of the earth

oral (or'əl) **history:** interviews in which people talk about their past

P

pampa (pam'pə): a treeless plain in South America

parallel of latitude (par'ə lel' uv lat'ə tōōd): imaginary line on a map or globe measuring distance in degrees north or south of the equator

parliament (pär'lə mənt): an assembly that makes the laws of a country

pasteurize (pas'chə rīz): to kill germs in milk by means of heat

Patriot (pā'trē ət): colonist who believed in independence

peninsula (pə nin'sə lə): a body of land surrounded almost entirely by water

phosphate (fos′fāt): a mineral needed for growth by plants and animals

pioneer (pī′ə nēr′): a person who does something first, preparing the way for others to follow

pitchblende (pich′blend′): mineral from which uranium is obtained

plain (plān): an area of level or nearly level land

plantation (plan tā′shən): a large farm on which one crop is raised

plateau (pla tō′): an area of flat land raised above the surrounding land

pollution (pə lōō′shən): act of making the environment dirty

population (pop′yə lā′shun): the total number of people living in an area

potlatch (pot′läch): special feast of the Pacific Northwest Indians

prairie (prer′ē): a grassy plain

precipitation (pri sip′ə tā′shən): any form of water that falls to earth, such as rain, hail, or snow

prime meridian (prīm mə rid′ē ən): the meridian from which longitude east and west is measured

processing (pros′es ing): preparing food for marketing

profile (prō′fīl): a side view

projection (prə jek′shən): a way of showing the round earth on a flat surface

province (prov′ins): a division of Canada somewhat like a state in our country

pueblo (pweb′lō): an Indian village consisting of stone or clay houses and joined in groups

Q

quarry (kwôr′ē): an open pit from which stone is cut

R

ratify (rat′ə fī′): to approve officially

raw (rô) **sugar**: the brown crystals that form when the juice of sugarcane is boiled and allowed to cool

rayon (rā′on): a cloth that looks and feels like silk

reaper (rē′pər): a machine for cutting grain

refinery (ri fī′nər ē): a building in which raw materials are changed into finished products

reforms (ri fôrmz′): changes to make things better

relief (ri lēf′): shading, color, or lines used on a map to show the land's surfaces

repealed (ri pēld′): cancelled

representative (rep′ri zen′tə tiv): a person who acts for a group

republic (ri pub′lik): a nation in which the people govern through their chosen representatives

reservation (rez′ər vā′shən): an area set aside by the government for the use of American Indians

reservoir (rez′ər vwär′): a place like a lake, formed behind a dam, where water is stored

ridge (rij): a long and narrow chain of hills or mountains

S

saga (sä′gə): an old Viking story

scalawag (skal′ə wag′): any white Southerner who worked closely with Northern officials during Reconstruction

secede (si sēd′): to withdraw from an organization

seed drill: a machine used to plant wheat or other small grains

segregation (seg′rə gā′shən): the separation of blacks from whites

selva (sel′və): a rainy, tropical forest of the Amazon

Senate (sen′it): the part of Congress made up of two members from each state

shaft (shaft) **mining**: a way of mining coal through a deep hole

sharecropping (sher′ krop′ing): system in which a person works on another's farm and shares crops with the landowner

shearing (sher′ing): cutting off the wool of sheep

site (sīt): the position or location of a town or building

slag (slag): what is left after iron is smelted

---

a bad, ā cake, ä father; e pet, ē me; i it, ī ice; o hot, ō open, ô off; oo wood; ōō food, oi oil, ou out; u cup, ur turn, yōō music; ə ago, taken, pencil, lemon, helpful

---

slave (slāv): person who is the property of another person

slave state: a state that allowed slaves to be used

slum (slum): an old area that is falling apart

smelt (smelt): to separate metal from ore by heating the ore

sod (sod): the part of the soil containing grass and its roots

soil erosion (i rō′zhen): the washing away of soil by heavy rains or floods

sound (sound): a body of water like a large bay, extending into the land

soybean (soi′bēn): a kind of legume first brought to this country from China

spawning (spôn′ing) **place:** a fresh-water nesting place where salmon lay their eggs

spinning jenny (jen′ē): an early machine which could spin many threads at a time

sterilize (ster′ə līz′): to kill germs

stocks (stokz): shares of ownership in a company

strike (strīk): to stop working until employers meet workers' demands

strip mining: a way of mining coal when it is close to the earth's surface

subtropical (sub trop′i kəl) **land:** land that lies near the tropics

suburb (sub′urb): a community close to, or on the outer edge of, a city

suffrage (suf′rij): the right to vote

sulfur (sul′fər): a yellow mineral

Supreme Court (sə prēm′ kôrt): the highest court in the United States

surplus (sur′plus′) **product:** that which is left when needs are satisfied

T

taconite (tak′ə nīt): a hard rock containing iron

tariff (tar′if): a tax on goods brought into a country

tax (taks): money that must be paid by people to support the government

technology (tek nol′ə jē): the use of knowledge and skills to build useful machines

temperate region (tem′pər it rē′jən): a place in the middle latitudes

tenant (ten′ənt) **farmer:** a person who pays rent for farmland either with crops or money

tenement (ten′ə mənt): narrow, uncared for apartment building

territory (ter′ə tôr′ē): a settled area, not yet a state, governed by Congress

textile (teks′tīl): woven cloth

threshing (thresh′ing) **machine:** a machine that separates kernels of grain from stalks

toll (tōl): a sum of money paid for use of a road

totem pole (tō′təm pōl): a tall Indian pole carved with people and animals

tourist (toor′ist): a person who travels for pleasure

trade (trād) **wind:** a steady wind that blows toward the equator

transcontinental (trans′kon tə nent′əl): across the continent

treaty (trē′tē): an agreement between groups of people or nations

tributary (trib′yə ter′ē): a river that flows into a larger river

trust (trust): form of big business in which several companies join together to control an industry

tundra (tun′drə): a large treeless plain

tung (tung) **oil:** oil made from the nuts of a tree brought from China

tungsten (tung′stin): a metal used to harden steel

turnpike (turn′pīk): a road that has a toll gate

V

vegetation (vej′ə tā′shən): the plant life in a region

veto (vē′to): refuse to approve a bill

Viking (vī′king): one of the seafaring people, often from Norway, who were among the first Europeans to find North America

volcano (vol kā′nō): an opening in the earth's surface through which steam, ashes, and lava flow

vulcanize (vul′kə nīz′): to treat rubber with sulfur so that it will not melt or become stiff

---

a bad, ā cake, ä father; e pet, m̄e; i it, ī ice; o hot, ō open, ô off; oo wood; o͞o food, oi oil, ou out; u cup, ur turn, y͞oo music; ə ago, taken, pencil, lemon, helpful

---

590

Index

For pronunciations see guide on page 585.

California, 404–434; ceded by Mexico, 138; cities in, 430–433; climate in, 408; farming in, 275, 424–426; fishing in, 428; geography of, 404–406; gold in, 139–140, 385, 410–412, 429; Indians of, 35; lumbering in, 427; manufacturing in, 426; mining in, 429; national parks in, 429; settlement of, 139–140, 410

Callao (kä yä'ō), Peru, 502

Calvert, Cecil, 79, 81

Calvert, George (Lord Baltimore), 79

Canada, 17, 317, 376, 418; and the Alaskan Highway, 437; Atlantic provinces, 464–465; British Columbia, 470–472; farming in, 464; and fugitive slaves, 158; geography of, 458–460; history of, 460–463; Indians in, 460, 463; prairie provinces, 470; Quebec and Ontario provinces, 466–469; and the Revolutionary War, 91; and the St. Lawrence Seaway, 311; and the War of 1812, 131–132

Canadian Pacific Railway, 462

Canadian Rockies, 458–459

canals, 142–143, 229, 310–311, 328

Caracas (kə rä'kəs), Venezuela, 497

Carolinas, 262, 265; settlement of, 60, 79. See also North Carolina; South Carolina

carpetbaggers, 176

Carson, Kit, 381, 397, 410

Carson City, Nevada, 397

Cartagena (kär'tə jē'nə), Columbia, 495

Carter, Jimmy, 213

Carteret, George, 74

Cartier, Jacques (kär tē ā', zhäk), 53, 461

Carver, George Washington, 266–267, 274, 276

Cascade Range, 9, 404–405, 408, 458

Casper, Wyoming, 397

Castro, Fidel (käs'trō, fē del'), 489

cattle drives, 180–181, 524–525

Central America, 482–487; farming in, 484–487; geography of, 482–483; history of, 483–484; Indians of, 38–40

Central Pacific Railroad, 180, 413–414

Cerro de Pasco (ser'ro dä päs'kō), 501

Chaco (chä'kō), 491

Champlain (sham plān'), Samuel de, 53, 57, 461

Charbonneau (shär bə nō'), 128, 415

Charles I, King of England, 79

Charles II, King of England, 74, 79

Charleston, South Carolina, 79, 287

Charleston, West Virginia, 287

Charlotte (shär'lət), North Carolina, 287

Charlotte Amalie (shär'lət a mäl'ə), Virgin Islands, 455–456

Chattanooga (chat'ə noo'gə), 287

checks and balances, 110

Cherokee (cher'ə kē) Indians, 126, 265

Cheyenne, Wyoming, 397

Cheyenne (shī'en') Indians, 36

Chicago, Illinois, 195, 296, 332–333

Chief Justice, 110

children: on the frontier, 125; and World War II, 209

Chile (chil'ē), 491, 494–495, 501

China, 17, 212, 417–418

Chinese immigrants, 179, 195, 413

Chippewas (chip'ə wäz), 301

Church of England, 61, 70

cities: in Alaska, 437–438; in Canada, 465; and immigration, 148, 195–197; on maps, 526–527; in Mexico, 481; in the Middle Atlantic states, 252–254; in New England, 241–243; in the North Central states, 330–337; in the Northeastern states, 232; in the Pacific Coast states, 430–434; in the Rocky Mountain states, 394–397; in South America, 499–505; in the South Central states, 364–369; in the Southeastern states, 283–290. See also individual cities

citrus fruit, 275–276, 357, 424–427

civil rights movement, 216–217, 352

Civil War, 163–176; causes of, 163–164, 266, 306

Clark, George Rogers, 93, 299, 304

Clark, William, 128, 304–305, 415–416

Clay, Henry, 159, 161

Clemens, Samuel, 385–386

Clermont (klar'mont), 142, 310

Cleveland, Moses, 300, 336

Cleveland, Ohio, 196, 336

climate, 11–15, 318, 396; and altitude, 13; in Canada, 460; and cotton, 271–272; in the Great Plains, 181; and latitude, 12; in the North Central states, 298; and oceans, 13; in the Pacific states, 35, 408–409; in the Rocky Mountain states, 376, 378; in the South Central states, 346; and sugarcane, 357

Clinton, DeWitt, 142, 229

clipper ships, 247, 417–418

coal, 14; in Alaska, 435; in Canada, 464–465; in the Middle Atlantic states, 244–247; in the North Central states, 325–327; in the Rocky Mountain states, 391; in South America, 501; in the Southeastern states, 281

coastlines, 10

Cochise (kō chēz'), 381

coffee, 439, 441, 485, 489, 495, 499, 501–503

coke, 249

Cold War, 212–213

Colombia (kə lum'bē ə), 200, 484, 491, 494–495

colonial period, 55–64, 70–90, 228, 262

Colorado, 376–397; cities in, 394–396; farming in, 317, 389; gold in, 180; settlement of, 385–386

Colorado Plateau, 376–389

Colorado River, 376, 379, 389, 391, 397, 424

Colorado Springs, Colorado, 396

Columbia Plateau, 404, 434

Columbia River, 408, 414, 426, 432

Columbus, Christopher, 44–47, 349, 450, 487

Columbus, Ohio, 332

combines, 315, 317, 357

Common Sense, 89

communications, 141, 146, 412–414

communism, 211–212

Compromise of 1850, 161

computers, 220

Comstock Lode, 180, 385–386

concentration camps, 210

Concord, battle of, 87–88

Concord, New Hampshire, 243

Confederate States of America, 164

Congress: establishment of, 109–111; and the Northwest Territory, 299–300; and Reconstruction, 175–176

Connecticut, 226–228, 235–243; cities of, 243; farming in, 238; settlement of, 72, 228

conservation, 219–220

Constitution (ship), 131

Constitutional Convention, 106–112, 118

Constitution of the United States, 106–112, 283; amendments to, 111–112, 175–176, 205, 232–233, 251. See also Bill of Rights

Continental Congress, 87–89, 102

Continental Divide, 376

contour lines, 520–521, 523

Cook, James, 414, 421

Cooper, Peter, 142–143, 229

copper, 248, 326, 389, 391, 435, 467, 470, 501

corn, 149; in Central America, 485; in New England, 238; in the North Central states, 313–315, 319; as pioneers' best crop, 302–303

corn belt, 313–315

Cornwallis, Charles, 93–94

Coronado, Francisco Vasquez de (kôr'ə nä'dō), 51, 379

Cortés, Hernando (kôr tes', er nän'dō), 50–51

Costa Rica (kōs'tə rē'kə), 482–487

cotton: in America, 388; and the Civil War, 169; in Peru, 501; in the South Central states, 356; in the Southeastern states, 264–266, 271–274

cotton belt, 266, 271–272

cotton gin, 148, 266

covered wagons, 301–302, 384, 416

cowhands, 180–181, 524; modern, 359

cranberries, 238, 252

Crazy Horse, 182

Creek Indians, 126, 265

Creoles, 494

crop rotation, 272

Cuba (kyoo'bə), 50, 198–201, 213; history of, 488–489; immigrants from, 218, 489; missile crisis, 489; peoples of, 482

cultures, 20–21

Cumberland Gap, 124, 262–263

Acknowledgments (continued)

© William Garnett: 10

© Joel Gordon: 220

© Grant Heilman Photography: 8

Historical Pictures Service: Chicago: 72

The Huntington Library: 52, 117 top, 144

The Image Bank: © William A. Allard, 359; © Ernest Braun, 429; © Gerald Brimacombe, 329; © Bill Carter, 334; © Arthur d'Arazien, 357; © Peter Frey, 504; © Larry Dale Gordon, 458; © Geoffrey Gove, 251 top left, 468; © Eddie Hironaka, 430; © Ted Horowitz, 431 left; © Don Klumpp, 472; © Harvey Lloyd, 393 top right; © Richard & Mary Magruder, 469 bottom; © Nick Nicholson, 453, 454; © Robert Phillips, 333; © Jeff Smith, 236; © Alvis Upitis, 225; © Luis Villota, 469 top right, 478

Imperial War Museum, London: 215 bottom left

© International Harvester: 307

Iowa State University, Photo Service: 379

Courtesy Jamestown-Yorktown Foundation: Ingham Foster Collection, 61

© F. Jellanger Widere A-S, Oslo, Norway: 523

© Jones and Laughlin: 249

© Normal Kaschub: 117 bottom right

Courtesy Kennedy Galleries, Inc., New York: 156

© Justin Kerr: 38

© Ruth & Louis Kirk: 24 top, 25 top left

Church Archives, Church of Jesus Christ of Latter-Day Saints: 385 left

Library of Congress: 86, 144-145 center, 172, 174, 199

Magnum Photos: © Bob Adelman, 217

The Mansell Collection: 59

© Steve McCutcheon: 438

The Metropolitan Museum of Art: Harris Brisbane Dick Fund, 173

© Lawrence Migdale: 431 right

Monkmeyer Press Photo: © Paul Conklin, 218; © Mike Kagan, 289 bottom; © Rhoda Sidney, 19

Munson-Williams-Proctor Institute, Utica, New York: 145 top left

Courtesy Museum of the City of New York: The Harry T. Peters Collection, 108

NASA: 189, 366

National Gallery of Art, Washington, D.C.: *The Washington Family*, by Edward Savage, Andrew W. Mellon Collection, 1940, 118; *Salute to General Washington In New York Harbor*, by L.M. Cooke, Gift of Edgar William and Bernice Chrysler

Garbisch, 1953, 113; *Susanna Truax*, by Gansevoort Limner, Gift of Edgar William and Bernice Chrysler Garbisch, 1980, 77 top left

National Gallery of Canada, Ottawa: 83

National Portrait Gallery, Smithsonian Institution, Washington, D.C.: 160

Courtesy of The New York Historical Society, New York City: 76 top, 78, 102, 129, 130, 144-145 bottom, 145 bottom right, 157, 161, 164, 167, 168

The New York Public Library: Astor, Lenox & Tilden Foundations, Prints Division, 167 center left, 385 right, 550; The I.N. Phelps Stokes Collection, Prints Division, 77 bottom, 132, 167 bottom, 310

PFI: © C.E. Rotkin, 245, 275

Photo Researchers, Inc.: © Jules Bucher, 500 bottom left; © Victor Englebert, 279; © Jack Fields, 457; © Farrell Grehan, 63 top left; © Tom Hollyman, 452 bottom; © Russ Kinne, 327; © George Leavens, 5; © Porterfield-Chickering, 556; © Lily Solmssen, 241; © Southern Living, 354 top; © Lisl Steiner, 575

© Photri: 250, 251 top right, 252, 431 bottom, 469 top left, 480 center, 485, 500 bottom right, © Lani, 494

The Oakland Museum: History Department, 414

Courtesy Oklahoma Historical Society: *Run of 1893, Opening of the Cherokee Strip*, photographer E.R. Mosteller, 353

Old Sturbridge Village: Photograph by Henry E. Peach, 76 bottom

Courtesy Oregon Department of Transportation, Salem: 417

Organization of American States: 506

© C. Ostman: 500 top

Abbey Aldrich Rockefeller Folk Art Center, Williamsburg, Virginia: 75

© Joseph Schuyler: 2

Shostal Associates: © Arthur d'Arazien, 280; © N. Manewal, 498 right; © J. McGibbeny, 381; © J. Peacock, 435

Smith College, Northampton, Mass.: The Sophia Smith Collection, Women's History Archive, 158

© Bob & Ira Spring: 9, 428

Tom Stack & Associates: 395 top; © Stewart M. Green, 386; © R. Wick, 317

Courtesy Standard Oil Co.: 484

Starwood: © Lelia G. Hendren, 116 top

Stock Boston: 240; © Frederik D. Bodin, 243; © Michael Collier, 62 bottom; © Gabor Demjen, 466; © Owen Franken, 463, 493, 502; © Raoul Hackel, 235; © Ellis Herwig, 449, 483; © Peter Menzel, 452 top, 480 bottom; © J. Rawle, 282; © John Running, 259, 375; © Cary S. Wolinsky, 251 bottom, 480 top

State Historical Society of Wisconsin: McCormick Collection, 149

State Street Bank & Trust Co., Corporate Art Collection, Boston: 140.

Swarthmore College: Swarthmore Peace Collection, 197

Sygma: © Michael Evans, 579 bottom right

Taurus Photos: 367 top; © K. Collidge, 393 bottom left; © Eric Kroll, 286; © L.L.T. Rhodes, 349 left; © Katherine S. Thomas, 378; © Ronald R. Thomas, 393 center; © R. Thompson, 393 bottom right, 395 bottom; © Reggie Tucker, 388; © Fred West, 313

Union League Club, New York City: Photograph by Bruce C. Jones, 123

UPI/The Bettmann Archive: 365, 451

U.S. Government Office of Media Services: 215 bottom right

Courtesy U.S. Capitol Historical Society: National Geographic photographer George F. Mobley, 90

© Courtesy U.S. House of Representatives: 352

U.S. Naval Academy Museum: 41

The Valentine Museum, Richmond, Virginia: 167 top right

Virginia Historical Society: Photograph by Ronald H. Jennings, 89

George Washington University Gallery of Art: 124

© R. Weiss: 382

West Light: © Bob Waterman, 155

White House Historical Association: Photographs by National Geographic Society, 576, 577, 578, 579 left

Woodfin Camp & Associates: © Keith Garrett, 260; © George Hall, 253, 404, 442 top; © David Alan Harvey, 264; © George Herban, 409; © Sylvia Johnson, 424; © Loren McIntyre, 498 left; © Sepp Seitz, 237; © Al Stephenson, 288 bottom, 289 top; © William S. Weems, 283; © Roger Werth, 405

© Jack Zehrt: 116 bottom, 117 bottom left